Psychology in Learning and Instruction

Patricia A. Alexander

University of Maryland

PEARSON

Merrill
Prentice Hall

Upper Saddle River, New Jersey
Columbus, Ohio

Library of Congress Cataloging-in-Publication Data

Alexander, Patricia A.
  Psychology in learning & instruction / Patricia A. Alexander.
    p. cm.
  Includes bibliographical references and index.
  ISBN 0-13-974874-1
    1. Learning, Psychology of. 2. Teaching—Psychological aspects. I. Title:
  Psychology in learning and instruction. II. Title.

LB1060.A454 2006
370.15′23—dc22

2004043179

Vice President and Executive Publisher: Jeffery W. Johnston
Publisher: Kevin M. Davis
Editorial Assistant: Sarah Kenoyer
Production Editor: Mary Harlan
Production Coordinator: Jolynn Feller, Carlisle Publishers Services
Design Coordinator: Diane C. Lorenzo
Photo Coordinator: Valerie Schultz, Monica Merkel, Lori Whitley

Text Design and Illustrations: Carlisle Publishers Services
Cover Design: Jason Moore
Cover Image: Corbis
Production Manager: Laura Messerly
Director of Marketing: Ann Castel Davis
Marketing Manager: Autumn Purdy
Marketing Coordinator: Brian Mounts

This book was set in New Caledonia by Carlisle Communications, Ltd. It was printed and bound by Courier Kendallville, Inc. The cover was printed by the Lehigh Press, Inc.

Photo Credits: *(t) = top; (c) = center; (b) = bottom; (l) = left; (r) = right.* Patricia A. Alexander: pp. 40, 41, 42, 52; American Montessori Society: p. 59; AP Wide World Photos: pp. 19(tr), 50; Jerry Bauer, courtesy of Harvard Graduate School of Education: p. 55; © Bettman/Corbis: p. 170; Robert Brons/Getty Images Inc.–Stone Allstock: p. 24; Lori Brunner: p. 299(r); Steve Castillo: p. 209; C Squared Studios/Getty Images, Inc.–Photodisc: p. 323; Corbis/Bettmann: pp. 17, 18, 116(t), 129, 193; E. Crews/The Image Works: p. 30; © Dorling Kindersley: p. 211; Kenneth Eward/Photo Researchers, Inc.: p. 13; EyeWire Collection/Getty Images, Inc.–Photodisc: p. 295; Dr. Robert Friedland/Science Photo Library/Photo Researchers, Inc.: p. 26; Jay Gardner/Basic Books, Inc.: p. 185; Joe Gawlowicz: p. 203(l); Bill Gerace: p. 69; Mike Good © Dorling Kindersley: p. 30; Frank Greenaway © Dorling Kindersley: p. 239; Jeff Greenberg/PhotoEdit: p. 120; Paul Harris © Dorling Kindersley: p. 1; Harvard University/Harvard University News Office: p. 54; Eric Hausman: p. 328; Hubble Heritage Team (AURA/STScl/NASA): p. 63; Courtesy of International Business Machines Corporation (unauthorized use not permitted): p. 268; Photo by Jonas: p. 306; Library of Congress: p. 49; Felicia Martinez/PhotoEdit, courtesy of Robert Solso: p. 19(l); Gunter Marx © Dorling Kindersley: p. 36; Jason McCawley/Photolibrary.com: p. 190; Paul Miller: p. 286(r); Denise Muth: p. 165; National Library of Medicine: p. 17; Norman Rockwell Family Agency © 1964/The Norman Rockwell Entities: p. 130; Chuck Painter/Stanford University News Service: pp. 187, 305; Photo Lennart Nilsson/Albert Bonniers Forlag AB: p. 24; Phototake/Carolina Biological Supply Company: p. 24; Laurence Pordes © Dorling Kindersley, courtesy of the British Library: p. 89; Mark Richards/PhotoEdit: p. 146; P. Saada/Eurelios/Science Photo Library/Photo Researchers, Inc.: 28; Gregory Sams/Photo Researchers, Inc.: p. 109; Science Photo Library/Photo Researchers, Inc.: p. 19(b); Susan Vogel: p. 91; Matthew Ward © Dorling Kindersley: p. 167; Warren Anatomical Museum, Countway Library of Medicine, Harvard Medical School: p. 24; Steven J. Waskow: p. 228; Provided by subject: pp. 85, 102, 105, 116(b), 132, 139, 151, 155, 163(both), 184, 197, 199, 200, 203(r), 206, 214, 218, 220(both), 227, 231, 235, 242, 246(both), 250, 252, 253, 280, 281, 286(l), 287, 288, 291, 299(l), 302, 308, 343, 346, 348.

Pearson Prentice Hall™ is a trademark of Pearson Education, Inc.
Pearson® is a registered trademark of Pearson plc
Prentice Hall® is a registered trademark of Pearson Education, Inc.
Merrill® is a registered trademark of Pearson Education, Inc.

Pearson Education Ltd.
Pearson Education Singapore Pte. Ltd.
Pearson Education—Canada, Ltd.
Pearson Education—Japan

Pearson Education Australia Pty. Limited
Pearson Education North Asia Ltd.
Pearson Educación de Mexico, S.A. de C.V.
Pearson Education Malaysia Pte. Ltd.

10 9 8 7 6 5 4 3 2 1
ISBN: 0-13-974874-1

To my mother and father, Rosie and William Mullins, who above all others have shown me unconditional love and support;

To my son and daughter-in-law, John Alexander and P. Karen Murphy, who give purpose to my life;

To my granddaughters, Lauren Renee and Paige Skylar Alexander, who bring beauty and innocence into this world.

Educator Learning Center: An Invaluable Online Resource

Merrill Education and the Association for Supervision and Curriculum Development (ASCD) invite you to take advantage of a new online resource, one that provides access to the top research and proven strategies associated with ASCD and Merrill—the Educator Learning Center. At www. educatorlearningcenter.com, you will find resources that will enhance your students' understanding of course topics and of current educational issues, in addition to being invaluable for further research.

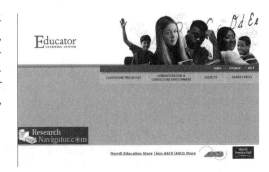

How the Educator Learning Center Will Help Your Students Become Better Teachers

With the combined resources of Merrill Education and ASCD, you and your students will find a wealth of tools and materials to better prepare them for the classroom.

Research

- More than 600 articles from the ASCD journal *Educational Leadership* discuss everyday issues faced by practicing teachers.
- A direct link on the site to Research Navigator™ gives students access to many of the leading education journals, as well as extensive content detailing the research process.
- Excerpts from Merrill Education texts give your students insights on important topics of instructional methods, diverse populations, assessment, classroom management, technology, and refining classroom practice.

Classroom Practice

- Hundreds of lesson plans and teaching strategies are categorized by content area and age range.
- Case studies and classroom video footage provide virtual field experience for student reflection.
- Computer simulations and other electronic tools keep your students abreast of today's classrooms and current technologies.

Look into the Value of Educator Learning Center Yourself

A four-month subscription to Educator Learning Center is $25 but is **FREE** when packaged with any Merrill Education text. In order for your students to have access to this site, you must use this special value-pack ISBN number **WHEN** placing your textbook order with the bookstore: 0-13-172289-1. Your students will then receive a copy of the text packaged with a free ASCD pincode. To preview the value of this website to you and your students, please go to **www.educatorlearningcenter.com** and click on "Demo."

Acknowledgments

A book of this scope never arises solely from the head of its author but is born of the contributions of many. Clearly, the debt I owe to my former and current graduate students and friends within the educational psychology community is immeasurable. Among those in my educational family whose ideas and efforts are mirrored in the pages of this volume are P. Karen Murphy, Joanne Sanders-Reio, Helenrose Fives, Michelle Buehl, Thomas Reio, Michelle Riconscente, Liliana Maggioni, Emily Fox, C. Stephen White, Jonna Kulikowich, Tamara Jetton, Mary Tallent-Runnels, and Kevin Meuwissen. I wish to offer a special acknowledgment to the late Bradford Woods, a member of my academic family who will be sorely missed but not forgotten.

There are also my colleagues at the University of Maryland, who have always been generous with their insights and guidance, including Allan Wigfield, who read and commented on earlier versions of the development chapters. Further, the research of Kathryn Wentzel, John Guthrie, James Byrnes, Roger Azevedo, Stephen Graham, Karen Harris, Marilyn Chambliss, and Bruce VanSledright has greatly enriched the content of each chapter.

Although too numerous to mention, there are many within the broader educational research community whose theories and research have helped me forge responses to the guiding questions that frame the chapters. Among those individuals, I especially acknowledge my late dear friend, Paul Pintrich, who was always there with critical comments and creative recommendations and who will remain an inspiration to me and so many others in this field.

This project would never have been realized without the support and wisdom of my editor and friend, Kevin Davis.

There are few who can coax and persuade like Kevin, who would accept nothing from me but the very best I could give. I would also like to thank Mary Benis, who improved upon my thoughts and words while editing this volume, and Barbara Lyons, who worked hard to make this book a success. There was also Mary Harlan, who was thorough and diligent in her management of production at Merrill/Prentice Hall, and Jolynn Feller, who coordinated production at Carlisle Publishers Services.

The reviewers of this volume also deserve my gratitude for identifying the strengths and weaknesses of earlier chapter drafts: Jerry Carlson, University of California, Riverside; Jerrell C. Cassady, Purdue University; Paul J. Gerber, Virginia Commonwealth University; Barbara Greene, University of Oklahoma; Gary Phye, Iowa State University; Paul Pintrich, University of Michigan; Cathy A. Pohan, San Diego State University; Charles Jeffrey Sandoz, University of Southwestern Louisiana; John R. Surber, University of Wisconsin, Milwaukee; James VanHaneghan, University of South Alabama; Enedina Garcia Vazquez, New Mexico State University; Allan Wigfield, University of Maryland; and David Yun Dai, University of Albany, State University of New York.

Finally, there are the thousands of students and teachers I have taught over the past decades. The questions that frame these chapters are theirs—questions that deserve to be explored and addressed within the educational community. I firmly believe that the answers to these fundamental questions will contribute to the optimal instruction and learning of students of all ages and all backgrounds.

Discover the Companion Website Accompanying This Book

The Prentice Hall Companion Website: A Virtual Learning Environment

Technology is a constantly growing and changing aspect of our field that is creating a need for content and resources. To address this emerging need, Prentice Hall has developed an online learning environment for students and professors alike—Companion Websites—to support our textbooks.

In creating a Companion Website, our goal is to build on and enhance what the textbook already offers. For this reason, the content for each user-friendly website is organized by chapter and provides the professor and student with a variety of meaningful resources.

For the Professor—

Every Companion Website integrates **Syllabus Manager**™, an online syllabus creation and management utility.

- **Syllabus Manager**™ provides you, the instructor, with an easy, step-by-step process to create and revise syllabi, with direct links into Companion Website and other online content without having to learn HTML.
- Students may logon to your syllabus during any study session. All they need to know is the web address for the Companion Website and the password you've assigned to your syllabus.
- After you have created a syllabus using **Syllabus Manager**™, students may enter the syllabus for their course section from any point in the Companion Website.
- Clicking on a date, the student is shown the list of activities for the assignment. The activities for each assignment are linked directly to actual content, saving time for students.
- Adding assignments consists of clicking on the desired due date, then filling in the details of the assignment—name of the assignment, instructions, and whether it is a one-time or repeating assignment.

- In addition, links to other activities can be created easily. If the activity is online, a URL can be entered in the space provided, and it will be linked automatically in the final syllabus.
- Your completed syllabus is hosted on our servers, allowing convenient updates from any computer on the Internet. Changes you make to your syllabus are immediately available to your students at their next logon.

For the Student—

Common Companion Website features for students include:

- **Chapter Objectives**—Outline key concepts from the text.
- **Interactive Self-Quizzes**—Complete with hints and automatic grading that provide immediate feedback for students. After students submit their answers for the interactive self-quizzes, the Companion Website **Results Reporter** computes a percentage grade, provides a graphic representation of how many questions were answered correctly and incorrectly, and gives a question-by-question analysis of the quiz. Students are given the option to send their quiz to up to four email addresses (professor, teaching assistant, study partner, etc.).
- **Web Destinations**—Links to www sites that relate to chapter content.
- **Message Board**—Virtual bulletin board to post or respond to questions or comments from a national audience.

To take advantage of the many available resources, please visit the *Psychology in Learning and Instruction* Companion Website at

www.prenhall.com/alexander

Brief Contents

Contents

Chapter 1

Building the Context

GUIDING QUESTIONS

- What role can psychology play in everyday educational practice?
- What areas of psychological theory and research have the most to say about learning and instruction?
- How does the sociohistorical context affect learning and instruction?

IN THEIR OWN WORDS ....

*P*ATRICK WELSH *is a respected high-school English teacher in Alexandria, Virginia, and a regular contributor to the* Washington Post.

Tuesday will mark a merciful end to the disorienting hot air of my summer. I'm not talking about the weather. I'm talking about my exposure to the theories, reforms, initiatives and spin of education experts and bureaucrats—both in Alexandria where I have been teaching for the past 30 years and from think tanks and centers of higher learning across the country. What I heard and read over the past three months had so little to do with kids or classrooms that I felt as if I had been launched into space. Soon, though, I'll be on solid ground again as the real world of education rushes back to me in the form of some 120 seniors. . . .

Last week's hot air was by far the most oppressive. The "in-service" days that teachers must undergo the week before school starts usually seem dull and irrelevant, but this year the Alexandria school system outdid itself. For two days teachers attended workshops on Standards Based Education (SBE), the new panacea for public schools, which in essence claims we can raise student achievement if we understand what is "absolutely essential for all students to know and be able to do."

The underlying fallacy is that any single concept can save the world. Every good teacher has to pick and choose from many ideas, knowing that each class is different, that methods that work with one group of kids won't necessarily work with another.

Whatever the moralists and reformers say, and however hard I find it to tell the difference between "essential learnings" and "performance indicators," I do know a few things about teaching. I know a few things about turning on students, whose heads are full of Lauryn Hill and Dave Matthews, to poetry of John Donne, A. E. Houseman and Adrienne Rich. And I know something about how to get kids to write more clearly and gracefully. But most important, I know that being a teacher is an opportunity to touch lives, and affect the future. That's my "benchmark"—and it's the benchmark of most teachers I know, who can't wait for that first bell to ring in the new year on Tuesday morning.

Note: From "Our teachers' ed: Another week of hot air" by P. Walsh, *Washington Post*, Sept. 5, 1999. Copyright 1999 by *Washington Post*, Reprinted with permission.

What Role Can Psychology Play in Everyday Educational Practice?

Throughout this text you will be introduced to real people with real educational questions and concerns. Patrick Walsh is one of those real people. His words tell an important story and raise critical questions. They tell of a gifted teacher's frustration with the endless flood of educational reforms that appear year after year and his wish to replace empty rhetoric with meaningful concepts that will work for different students, varied contexts, and diverse tasks. Patrick's commentary also leaves us questioning what kinds of concepts, theories, or principles might really contribute to improved learning and teaching.

Patrick Walsh is rightly concerned that easy fixes or cure-alls do little to help teachers and students cope with the diversity and complexity inherent in the educational enterprise. What educators need is well-tested, practical information that is directly relevant to schools and to the teachers and the students who populate them. And teachers must be able to "pick and choose" among the countless ideas and techniques to which they are introduced.

The Union of Psychology and Pedagogy

Fortunately, not all professional development activities, in-services, and workshops are as empty and meaningless as the one Patrick Walsh describes. In fact, there is a wealth of practical, well-tested information coming from the field of educational psychology that can aid both students in their efforts to become better educated and better prepared to thrive and teachers as they guide students on their journeys toward competence.

This book is devoted to the exploration of psychological concepts, theories, and principles that can answer important and fundamental questions about learning and instruction. Several of those guiding questions are presented at the outset of each chapter and frame the discussion that follows. Like the excerpts that introduce each chapter, these questions come from real teachers and students trying to understand how psychology and education can come together to enhance learning for all students. The responses to those questions are based on the research literature in educational psychology and related disciplines. Thus, this book is not only problem based in its approach, but also evidence based.

Patrick Walsh is not the first person to see teaching as an opportunity to "touch lives and affect the future." William James, considered by many to be the father of American psychology, said much the same thing in his *Talks to Teachers* over a century ago. *Talks to Teachers* was actually a series of seminars James presented to practicing teachers at the closing of the 19th century (James, 1899/1979), in which he shared some fundamental principles of psychology and delivered one of the first psychology classes for teacher educators.

> The teachers of this country, one may say, have its future in their hands. The earnestness which they at present show in striving to enlighten and strengthen themselves is an index of the nation's probabilities of advance in all ideal directions. (James, 1899/1979, p. 21)

James clearly understood the power of education for the individual learner and the nation. He also recognized that psychology was a critical resource for committed educators, even though he cautioned them against seeing psychology as a panacea for educational concerns. Foreshadowing the present-day field of educational psychology, James proclaimed that **psychology,** the science of thought and behavior, and **pedagogy,** the science of teaching, were unquestionably intertwined and equally important foundations of effective educational practice. He believed strongly that teachers need to understand the workings of their students' minds if they are to succeed in educating.

However, because James realized that the times were demanding for teachers, he worried about overburdening them with yet another set of guidelines or principles that they would feel compelled to adopt. What was particularly troublesome for him was the potential for these psychological guidelines or principles to be treated as abstract notions, removed from teachers' everyday educational responsibilities.

> Our teachers are overworked already. Everyone who adds a jot or tittle of unnecessary weight to their burden is a foe of education. (James, 1899/1979, p. 27)

It is fascinating to reflect on James's words now. More than 100 years may have passed, but much of James's message in his *Talks to Teachers* still rings true. Teachers remain concerned professionals who seek new knowledge and insights that might improve the learning of their students (Berliner & Biddle, 1995; Hawley & Jackson, 1995). In addition, psychology continues to be an invaluable source of fundamental knowledge for teachers, inherently intertwined with effective pedagogical practice (Peterson, Dickson, & Clark, 1990). Even though our psychological knowledge has expanded greatly over the past century, most of the topics James addressed in *Talks to Teachers*—including interest, perception, and memory—can readily be found in the pages of modern psychology textbooks.

Nonetheless, those engaged in educational policy and practice still inadequately tap the potential richness of psychology (L. M. Anderson et al., 1995), and this intrinsic union of psychology and pedagogy is not always recognized or respected by practitioners or the general public (Spielberger, 1998). Those of us who conduct the research or espouse the theories are sometimes to blame, because we do not always communicate our understandings to those outside our professional circles (L. M. Anderson et al., 1995; Salomon, 1995). Sometimes we do not know exactly how our realizations or insights translate into everyday practice, which is the heart of Patrick Walsh's criticism of those who populate "think tanks and centers of higher learning." But the fact remains that there is much to be gained by wedding educational psychology to everyday educational practice, a union that is as complex and dynamic as it is fruitful (Alexander, 2001; Berliner, 1993).

The Changing Faces of Psychology and Teaching

Psychology has not been dormant for 100 years but has undergone dramatic transformation. The psychology of James's day has become increasingly more specialized. In fact, the American Psychological Association (APA), the main professional organization for psychologists, now boasts a membership of over 84,000 affiliated with 52 recognized divisions that are aligned with 42 specific forms of psychology, including developmental, school, clinical, experimental, organizational, and community psychology (Evans, Sexton, & Cadwallader, 1992). Although several of these psychological fields are invested in learning and instruction, it is educational psychology that most directly represents the integration of psychology and pedagogy that James envisioned. Educational psychology is dedicated to learning across the life span in all its formal and informal manifestations.

Teaching, too, has witnessed its share of transformation in the past century. If James believed that teachers of the 1890s were taxed to their limits, what would he think of the teaching profession in the 21st century? What James understood as demanding and burdensome times may be seen as far quieter and simpler, devoid of freeways, television, standardized testing, e-mail, cellular phones, and nuclear bombs, to say nothing of virtual reality. Such changes have made psychology even more relevant to today's teachers. The dynamic and complex nature of today's classrooms clearly enhances the value of knowing the psychological basics of learning and instruction and understanding how to put those fundamentals to effective use (Anderson et al., 1995).

Whether the year is 1906 or 2006, the challenges of teaching can be better met when those responsible for guiding the learning and development of others come to that educational environment with a deep understanding of learners and the learning process. If educators are to be successful in fostering students' growth and development, they must possess certain strengths:

- a fundamental sense of how learning unfolds
- an extensive repertoire of instructional techniques and approaches based on sound evidence
- the capacity to stimulate thought, spark engagement, and address diversity
- the competence to analyze, create, or choose tasks, texts, and tests that are appropriate for learners and for instructional goals

The Ad Hoc Committee on the Teaching of Educational Psychology, created by Division 15 (Educational Psychology) or the APA, came to a similar conclusion (Anderson et al., 1995). They endorsed what they termed a *contemporary psychological perspective* for practicing teachers. Teachers with such a perspective think about how the social and instructional contexts of the classroom affect and are affected by individual students' knowledge, strategic processing, development, motivations, sociocultural backgrounds, and the like. The committee also held that the concepts, principles, and theories of educational psychology can effectively serve as the root of that contemporary psychological perspective.

> A teacher who holds a contemporary psychological perspective is able and disposed to consider how learners' knowledge, motivation, and development contribute to the meanings they make, the actions they take, and what and how they learn in classrooms. A teacher who holds a contemporary psychological perspective thinks about how the social and instructional contexts of the classroom (e.g., subject-matter instruction and assessment, classroom management systems) affect and are affected by individual students' knowledge, learning, motivation, and development. A psychological perspective provides a teacher with a way to "get hold of" a complex situation and think about its problems and possibilities in light of views of human learning. (Anderson, Blumenfeld, Pintrich, Clark, Marx, Peterson, 1995, p. 145)

Within just the past several decades, untold studies have been conducted, and thousands of volumes have been written about learning and human development, the linchpins of educational psychology. The collective wisdom in those millions of pages can help educators in:

- recognizing the systematic changes learners are undergoing, as well as marked deviations from typical development
- finding a window into learners' thoughts and motivations
- identifying and stimulating reasoning and strategic thinking among students
- evaluating, constructing, and interpreting tasks and tests that are integral parts of formal learning
- appreciating and addressing the tremendous diversity found in all educational communities

Without question, theory and research in educational psychology have much to contribute to learning and instruction in this new century.

What Areas of Psychological Theory and Research Have the Most to Say About Learning and Instruction?

In fostering this contemporary psychological perspective within current educational practice, it is important not to recreate the problems that marked past associations between psychology and pedagogy. The notion that effective educational practice moves in only one direction, from psychological theory and research to meaningful practice, is precisely what James warned against a century ago—a warning more recently echoed by others in the educational community (Peterson et al., 1990; Schön, 1983). Effective practice comes from the marriage of theoretical and practical knowledge, in what Korthagen and Kessels (1999) call a "realistic approach" to the study of psychology in education.

The hallmarks of a realistic approach are the questions, problems, and issues that teachers and learners face. In effect, it begins with naturalistic and realistic situations to which existing psychological research and theory can contribute and dismisses disembodied psychological knowledge. In this way the knowledge, beliefs, and experiences of teachers and students become the guides for discussion of psychological concepts, principles, or theories. For this reason each chapter of this text begins with several basic questions about learning and instruction and about psychology's role in those processes. In addition, this volume is titled *Psychology* in *Learning and Instruction* to avoid the common but misleading phrase, "psychology *for* learning and teaching," which privileges only one of the essential components of effective education.

In order to achieve a meaningful integration of psychology and pedagogy, we must confront one significant problem from the outset: The body of psychological concepts, principles, and theories is vast and ever expanding. Even when the discussion begins with commonplace educational questions, problems, and issues, the knowledge that can be brought to bear is unmanageable and too fragmented to serve the needs of students and teachers. To help narrow the field, we can turn to the groundbreaking work of the APA's Presidential Task Force on Psychology in Education (APA Board of Educational Affairs, 1995), completed in conjunction with the Mid-Continent Regional Educational Laboratory.

In 1990 Charles D. Spielberger, then APA president, commissioned a task force composed of renowned educational theorists and researchers. Like William James before him, Spielberger believed that the accumulated knowledge base in psychology should prove invaluable to educators, yet its collective wisdom had exerted only limited influence in educational reform and everyday instructional practice (Spielberger, 1998).

Therefore, the mission of the task force was to distill the massive body of psychological research literature into core, evidence-based principles that could effectively guide educational reform and practice. After several years of concerted effort, the task force produced its final report.

> Our immediate goal in offering these learner-centered psychological principles is to provide a framework that can contribute to current educational reform and school redesign efforts. Through dialogue with concerned groups of educators, researchers, and policy makers, these

learner-centered principles can evolve further to contribute not only to a new design for America's schools, but also to a society committed to lifelong learning, healthy human development, and productivity. In developing these principles, psychology—together with other disciplines—can contribute to the betterment of America's schools and the enhancement of the nation's vital human resources. (APA Board of Educational Affairs, 1995, Preamble.)

The 14 learner-centered psychological principles displayed in Figure 1–1 are the focus of that report (Lambert & McCombs, 1998). Each principle stands for volumes of studies that span generations, and each represents the best thinking of task force members and their constituent communities of practice.

The principles identify four areas of psychological research important to educational reform: cognitive and metacognitive factors, motivational and affective factors, developmental and social factors, and individual differences. Within these areas particular issues are specified, such as the nature of the learning process, the effects of motivation on effort, social influences on learning, and standards and assessment. For each critical issue the task force offers a principle for effective practice.

Principles are broad, encompassing statements that put complex ideas into simple language. As such, principles are not prescriptive; they cannot tell teachers what to do for any particular student on any given day—nor should they. Instead, principles are most useful as general guides, important reminders about the nature, goals, and processes of learning and teaching.

In 1993 Alexander and Murphy (1998b) were asked to analyze the initial draft of the principles in light of existing psychological research. To perform such an extensive review and analysis, they first distilled the specific principles into five global statements (see Figure 1–2). They then proceeded to identify bodies of work relevant to those general areas. Those same five areas—development and individual differences, the knowledge base, strategic processing and executive functioning, motivation and affect, and situation or context—along with a section on assessment, which Alexander and Murphy described as an essential addition to the initial draft, are the organizing structure for this text. The task force did use their analysis when completing its final

---

Cognitive and Metacognitive Factors

- *Nature of the learning process.* The learning of complex subject matter is most effective when it is an intentional process of constructing meaning from information and experience.
- *Goals of the learning process.* The successful learner, over time and with support and instructional guidance, can create meaningful, coherent representations of knowledge.
- *Construction of knowledge.* The successful learner can link new information with existing knowledge in meaningful ways.
- *Strategic thinking.* The successful learner can create and use a repertoire of thinking and reasoning strategies to achieve complex learning goals.
- *Thinking about thinking.* Higher order strategies for selecting and monitoring mental operations facilitate creative and critical thinking.
- *Context of learning.* Learning is influenced by environmental factors, including culture, technology, and instructional practices.

Motivational and Affective Factors

- *Motivational and emotional influences on learning.* What and how much is learned is influenced by the learner's motivation. Motivation to learn, in turn, is influenced by the individual's emotional state, beliefs, interests, and goals, and habits of thinking.
- *Intrinsic motivation to learn.* The learner's creativity, higher order thinking, and natural curiosity all contribute to motivation to learn. Intrinsic motivation is stimulated by tasks the learner perceives to be of optimal novelty and difficulty, relevant to personal interests, and providing personal choice and control.
- *Effects of motivation on effort.* Acquisition of complex knowledge and skills requires extended learner effort and guided practice. Without learners' motivation to learn, the willingness to exert this effort is unlikely without coercion.

Developmental and Social Factors

- *Developmental influences on learning.* As individuals develop, there are different opportunities and constraints for learning. Learning is most effective when differential development within and across physical, intellectual, emotional, and social domains is taken into account.
- *Social influences on learning.* Learning is influenced by social interactions, interpersonal relations, and communication with others.

Individual Differences

- *Individual differences in learning.* Learners have different strategies, approaches, and capabilities for learning that are a function of prior experience and heredity.
- *Learning and diversity.* Learning is most effective when differences in learners' linguistic, cognitive, and social backgrounds are taken into account.
- *Standards and assessment.* Setting appropriately high and challenging standards and assessing the learner as well as learning process—including diagnostic, process, and outcome assessment—are integral parts of the learning process.

■ **Figure 1–1** **The learner-centered psychological principles.**

Note: From *Learner-Centered Psychological Principles: A Framework for School Reform and Redesign* by Learner-Centered Principles Work Group of the APA Board of Educational Affairs, 1997, Washington, DC: APA. Copyright 1997 by APA. Reprinted with permission.

Development and Individual Differences

- Learning, although ultimately a unique adventure for all, progresses through various common stages of development influenced by both inherited and experiential/environmental factors.

The Knowledge Base

- One's existing knowledge serves as the foundation of all future learning by guiding organization and representations, by serving as a basis of association with new information, and by coloring and filtering all new experiences.

Strategic Processing and Executive Functioning

- The ability to reflect on and regulate one's thoughts and behaviors is essential to learning and development.

Motivation and Affect

- Motivational or affective factors, such as intrinsic motivation, attributions for learning, and personal goals, along with the motivational characteristics of learning tasks, play a significant role in the learning process.

Situation or Context

- Learning is as much a socially shared understanding as it is an individually constructed enterprise.

■ **Figure 1–2   Five general statements related to the learner-centered psychological principles.**

Note: From "The Research Base for APA's Learner-Centered Principles" by P. A. Alexander and P. K. Murphy in N. M. Lambert and B. L. McCombs (Eds.) *How students learn: Reforming schools through learner-centered education* (pp. 26–60), 1998, Washington, DC: APA.

version of the principles; for example, the general areas they targeted are now closely mirrored in the headings used to organize the final 14 principles, and their suggestion to address assessment more explicitly contributed to the formation of a new principle that appears in the final document.

The extensive work of all those associated with APA's learned-centered principles (1997) helps to answer the fundamental question that began this discussion: What role can psychology play in everyday educational practice? The answer is that psychology has an essential and integral role to play in all facets of learning and instruction—from the knowledge that students construct to the creativity that teachers exhibit, and from the reasoning teachers display to the differences students manifest.

How Does the Sociohistorical Context Affect Learning and Instruction?

Even as teachers are absorbed in the thoughts and actions of the moment, they still have a foothold in the past and an eye toward the future. They want to understand what has come before in educational practice and what they can expect in the

years to come. They want to understand where their thoughts, beliefs, and experiences fit in the overall educational fabric.

From a broad, sociohistorical perspective, we can observe the powerful trends in education and in society that have taken shape over the centuries and can recognize the tremendous influence they have had on learning and teaching in the past and in the present. We can also begin to appreciate the power they will exert in the years to come. Another advantage of this viewpoint is that it puts any subsequent discussion of particular psychological concepts, principles, and theories in a wholly different framework, which is often overlooked in the professional literature and in everyday practice. This macroscopic perspective helps to identify an entire set of realistic problems, issues, and questions that transcend individual teachers, classrooms, or schools and cross multiple realms of research. These are problems, issues, and questions that must be understood and addressed if any real progress in learning and instruction is to be made (Alexander & Knight, 1993; Alexander, Murphy, & Woods, 1996).

At various locations on this planet, there are fascinating images (e.g., the crop circles of England) and topographical patterns (e.g., the Grand Canyon) that cannot be seen unless one is hundreds of feet above them. In a similar way, many actions and events relevant to learning and instruction take on a discernible and meaningful pattern when one assumes a more macroscopic perspective. Unfortunately, few have witnessed these educational patterns because of the demands of the moment (Woods & Murphy, 2002).

Within the course of a single day, teachers must make hundreds of instructional decisions. Many times those decisions are fairly routine, such as selecting the next student to respond to a question, picking an example to illustrate a certain point, or choosing which questions to include on a homework assignment. At other times, however, those decisions are demanding and consequential—for example, determining whether to request special testing for a particular child or arranging students into work groups for an upcoming project. Cumulatively, these continuous, everyday demands succeed in keeping teachers focused on the here and now without the opportunity to contemplate learning and teaching from a broader, more sociohistorical standpoint. Nonetheless, the choices that teachers make are unquestionably tied to the time, place, and culture of the schooling.

Based on a review of the literature in teaching and teacher education, Alexander and Knight (1993) identified three trends that have shaped the instructional landscape in the past and that promise to do so in the decades to come. Those three trajectories, depicted in Figure 1–3, are incremental, stationary, and iterative trends.

Incremental Trends

Incremental trends are those forces in society that have undergone dramatic change over the centuries. Their existence has unquestionably altered our world and, therefore,

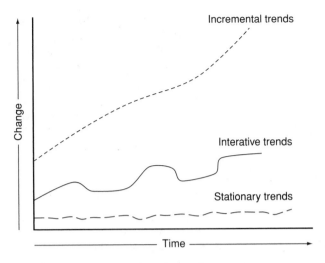

■ Figure 1–3 Educational trends.

Note: From "Of squalls and fathoms: Navigating the seas of educational innovation" by P. A. Alexander, P. K. Murphy, and B. S. Woods, 1996, *Educational Researcher, 25*(3), pp. 31–36, 39. Copyright 1996 by *Educational Researcher.* Reprinted with permission.

Where is the life we have lost in living?
Where is the wisdom we have lost in knowledge?
Where is the knowledge we have lost in information?

T. S. Eliot, "The Rock"

the nature of learning and instruction. Three such incremental forces that have left their indelible marks on the educational experience are information, media, and population.

Information

Educational researchers and practitioners find it important to draw a distinction between *information* and *knowledge* (R. C. Anderson, 1977). As used here, **information** refers to the universe of facts, concepts, or images found in the external environment and, thus, available to be taught or learned. Information comes from innumerable sources, such as television, magazines, signs, the Internet, and human conversation. **Knowledge,** on the other hand, represents what an individual or group culls or constructs personally from that universe of information.

For instance, you may pass the same road sign every day on your way to work, but until you pay attention to that sign or contemplate its message, it remains only information; it does not achieve the status of knowledge. Similarly, the untold theories, hypotheses, and research findings about human learning and development that have been written about and discussed throughout human history constitute information about these domains. The portion of that informational universe that I have internalized or applied in my own teaching and research signifies my knowledge of human learning and development. Some individuals carry this distinction even further. They discriminate between *knowledge* and *wisdom,* reserving the latter for discernment or scholarly knowledge. This text will focus only on *information* and *knowledge* and will leave wisdom for the sages.

Folklore has it that information doubles every 5 years or so. As diSessa (1989) noted, this statement may be impossible to verify but is nonetheless intuitively logical and appealing. Some may even see 5 years as a rather conservative estimate in light of modern technological advancements that put information literally and instantaneously at our fingertips. Whatever the actual rate of information growth, there is undoubtedly much more that could be taught in today's classroom and, reciprocally, much more that could be learned than there was just a year ago. This unbridled spawning of information presents several real concerns for teachers and their students.

Keeping Up to Date

Competent teachers are knowledgeable in their subject areas (Shulman & Quinlan, 1996), but this burgeoning of information means that they must be even more vigilant if they are going to stay reasonably current in their fields, especially in relatively new domains (e.g., instructional technology) or those more susceptible to new discoveries (e.g., astronomy). In certain cases this new information transforms the way a field is conceptualized or portrayed. For instance, after the launch of the Hubble telescope, each new image transmitted back to Earth from the far reaches of space held the potential to reshape astronomical understandings and alter long-held conceptions.

This challenge of being up-to-date is not restricted to teachers or astronomers. Most of us have experienced the phenomenon of learning some new procedure or concept, only to have to dismantle or relearn it when its flaws or weaknesses were subsequently discovered (Guzzetti & Hynd, 1998). And who has not encountered confusing, outdated, or misleading information in school textbooks or professional literature (Beck, McKeown, & Gromoll, 1989; McKeown, Beck, Sinatra, & Loxterman, 1992)? It seems that as soon as a book is published, certain information in it is already inaccurate or passé. It is virtually impossible to keep our personal knowledge bases completely current and accurate.

Deciding on Classroom Content

Imagine for a moment that you have been put in charge of determining the program of study for an entire school; whatever you decide will become the focus of learning and teaching in that school. How do you decide what in this vast universe of information will become the focus of the school experience? How will you decide on the critical content areas or topics? What information will you include, and what will you exclude?

Every year educators are faced with similarly overwhelming tasks. For each classroom, school, school district, or even nation, some person or group is debating what small portion of the universe of information should become part of classroom discourse (Hirsch, 1996). Even for experts the task of encapsulating an entire field is no simple matter. Remember that it took a collection of renowned experts years to articulate 14 guiding principles from the domain of psychology that pertain to school reform or redesign. Moreover, the increased reservoir of information in every field makes such curricular decisions more difficult with each passing year.

Inevitably, the content of schooling becomes highly selective, and socioculturalists, multiculturalists, and historians remind us that there is great power in deciding *whose* histories and *which* perspectives become the subject matter of schooling (Banks, 1993; Giroux & McLaren, 1986). Peter McLaren (1998), a critical pedagogist, conceptualizes the content of schooling as sociopolitical oppression.

> The political space that education occupies today continues to de-emphasize the struggle for teacher and student empowerment; furthermore, it generally serves to reproduce the technocratic, corporate, and capitalist ideologies that characterize dominant societies. It is, in fact, reasonable to argue that education programs are designed to create individuals who operate in the interest of the state, whose social function is primarily to sustain and legitimate the status quo social order. (p. 1)

Mentioning Versus Teaching

As more and more information finds its way into school curricula and teachers continue to be saddled with noninstructional responsibilities, there is great temptation to replace teaching with mentioning. **Mentioning** is a concept Durkin (1978–1979) introduced more than 2 decades ago to signal teachers' rather superficial treatment of important concepts and skills. Mentioning stands in contrast to effective instruction, wherein teachers allow sufficient exploration and discussion of ideas to ensure that students learn. As Durkin observed reading instruction in upper elementary classrooms, she painstakingly categorized and catalogued the various forms of instruction she witnessed in an attempt to determine how much actual teaching of reading comprehension was occurring. To the shock of the reading community, she reported that less than 5% of the instructional time involved the explicit teaching of reading comprehension. Ten years later, Alexander (1983) attempted to replicate Durkin's study and found virtually the same pattern of teaching versus mentioning.

When Jetton and Alexander (1998) surveyed more than 300 teachers about the types of reading approaches and the amount of discussion they used in their classrooms, the teachers frequently blamed a lack of time for their failure to implement the types of techniques and discussions they believed would facilitate deeper learning. In effect, many of these teachers were aware that they were mentioning, but they did not see how to deal with all the required content in any other way.

Among the consequences of mentioning is that students may have an illusion of knowing, just as teachers have an illusion of teaching (Alexander & Knight, 1993). In other words, just as teachers may not always realize that they are devoting inadequate time and attention to important content, many students may be operating under the illusion that they have a clear or deep understanding of subject matter when, in actuality, that understanding is fragmented or shallow. This issue is revisited in the discussion of knowledge (chapter 4) and strategic learning/strategic teaching (chapter 7).

Experiencing Informational Numbness

Many of today's learners seem to suffer from what can be called **informational numbness**. This hypothetical condition is a natural outgrowth of the constant bombardment of information that members of postindustrial societies experience on an almost-unceasing basis. It is almost impossible to calculate how much information students encounter in a single day from television, radio, computers, and the print media, to say nothing of direct human contact. Perhaps as a survival mechanism, or perhaps as a consequence of physical desensitization, these learners appear to wrap themselves in a virtual *informational force field*, which only particularly powerful or personally relevant information manages to penetrate, making the critical transformation from information to knowledge. Finding ways to break through this informational force field—to get and hold students' attention in the classroom—becomes increasingly more challenging yet imperative for teachers (Alexander & Jetton, 1996; Mitchell, 1993).

Media

The primary medium for learning and teaching has shifted once over the centuries and is currently shifting again. Socrates, thanks to the writings of his pupil Plato, has come to symbolize effective teaching. As a teacher, Socrates relied on verbal interaction—especially, enticing stories and effective questioning—to convey matters of principle to his students. Because there were no textbooks, blackboards, overheads, or PowerPoint, the sharing of ideas between students and teachers was rooted in an oral tradition. Most often, teachers would explain or describe ideas they believed to be of value, and students would recite back those ideas or verbally demonstrate their understanding of what they had learned.

The oral tradition remained the principal medium for learning and teaching until the 15th century, when Johannes Gutenberg's press and the economical production of paper started putting more and more ideas in print and in the hands of broader segments of the population. The printed word in the form of books, newspapers, and the like still dominates the educational landscape and serves as the key means by which ideas deemed important are made relatively permanent and accessible to learners (Alexander & Kulikowich, 1994; Yore, 1991). This long dominance of traditional print media and the linear processing that goes along with it is being challenged by new media—hypermedia, to be exact, the computer-based media. Twenty years ago, few individuals could have imagined the impact hypermedia technology would have on our everyday lives. In just a decade the number of homes in postindustrial countries that have computers and online access has increased 40-fold. Before long, computer online access will become a standard feature of homes and offices as well as classrooms (Garner, Zhao, & Gillingham, 2000; Gillingham, Young, & Kulikowich, 1994). Even now, to find information on pandas, check the show times for a particular movie, schedule a flight, or locate the capital city of Nebraska, many Americans under 30 are more likely to turn on their computers than open a book. Major television networks and leading newspapers have realized the power of this new medium. In fact, the number of visits to some online news shows, like MSNBC, already exceeds the number of individuals who actually watch the parent television program. However, this computerization of society does have consequences for learning and teaching.

The Generational Gap

In most aspects of learning and instruction, it is the older one who is also wiser. That is to say, it generally falls to the older generation to guide or facilitate the learning and development of the next. But that typical developmental pattern is violated when it comes to hypermedia; it is relatively common to see students teaching peers or their teachers about new technologies.

Teachers do not need to be the sole authorities in classrooms (Alvermann & Hayes, 1989; Garner & Gillingham, 1998), and both students and teachers profit from shared learning and shared teaching (Palincsar & Brown, 1984). However, far too many of today's teachers remain less knowledgeable and frequently less comfortable with technology than those they instruct (Hawkins, 1996; Reinking, McKenna, Labbo, & Kieffer, 1998). Consequently, the opportunities that turn students' familiarity with hypermedia into an instructional asset can be missed (Kamil, Intrator, & Kim, 2000) when the nonlinear, audiovisual tendencies or proclivities of students are met with the linear, more traditional print approach of their teachers (Alexander, Kulikowich, & Jetton, 1994). On the other hand, some researchers argue that computers in the classroom are underused, oversold (Cuban, 2001), and certainly understudied (Murphy, 2001a).

Quality, Accuracy, and Appropriateness

Thousands of individuals log onto the Internet each day and cruise the information superhighway. That superhighway provides access to more information than could be physically held by any humanly created structure and does so in a matter of seconds. However, serious questions must be asked about the quality, accuracy and appropriateness of what is read, seen, or heard online (Bruce & Bruce, 2000). There is little control over what finds its way onto the information superhighway and who can freely access that content (Alexander & Kulikowich, 2002). Pornographic or hatemongering sites do exist, and educators need to be concerned about any information that finds its way into the learning environment. There is also the issue of how accurate some online content is or how distorted its message (Alexander & Kulikowich, 2002). Anyone can be an online source of information.

Similar questions can be raised about television, movies, popular recordings, and print media. For instance, Afflerbach and VanSledright (2001) found that elementary students have distorted notions about historical figures and events, such as Pocahontas or the Vietnam War, because of their treatment in popular movies and books. VanSledright (2002) calls this the Disney effect. Because teachers or parents cannot always be present to monitor their students' or children's media consumption, teachers can help students approach this vast storehouse of information as intelligent consumers, both in and out of the classroom.

Hyperspace

When Alexander, Kulikowich, and Jetton (1994) reviewed the research on linear and nonlinear text processing, they realized that hypermedia is not equally effective for all learners. As with more traditional forms of print media, there are significant differences between those who are capable of cruising the information superhighway and those who get lost, break down, or never get on. Those differences include ease of access, knowledge of the topic, familiarity with technology, and personal interest.

Access may be the first step in using this newest form of media to improve learning, but it is only the beginning. Plenty of students spend hours online playing games or chatting with others (Garner et al., 2000), which may not translate into deeper or more enduring learning (Alexander & Wade, 2000). It takes guidance and meaningful incorporation into the classroom culture to turn this technological tool into a mechanism for greater learning and better teaching.

Population

Various factors beyond a simple mathematical progression have contributed to the burgeoning **population.** For one, the life expectancy of those residing in postindustrial countries has almost doubled in the past century as a result of the many miracles of medical science and improved living conditions in these economically advanced countries (Storandt & VandenBos, 1989). Some predict that children born early in the 21st century can expect to live to be 120 if the rate of longevity continues unabated. This swelling of the Earth's population has significant implications for learning and instruction, in terms of both the numbers to be taught and the diversity within this population on every dimension of human development (Ackerman, Kyllonen, & Roberts, 1999).

More Individuals to Educate

Every year teachers start the school year with more and more students, fewer and fewer materials, and less and less space. Many schools could not manage at all without portable or makeshift buildings. Cafeterias and auditoriums have been converted into classrooms, and teacher resource or conference rooms have given way to more essential instructional purposes (Alexander & Knight, 1993). Many brand new schools built a few years ago to accommodate the growing student population are already above capacity.

Although the research on the teacher-student ratio is somewhat ambiguous, it is clear that overcrowded conditions do not forward the educational goals of anyone—not teachers, administrators, students, or parents (Finn, 1998). However, discussion of optimal class size falls by the wayside when districts are faced with an influx of students and a concomitant shortage of qualified teachers. In some regions emergency teacher certification becomes a necessary evil, and the teacher substitute may be any person—with or without a college diploma—willing to take on the responsibility of a room full of students.

Greater Diversity

One of the fascinating ramifications of this increased number of students is a qualitative change as well. Specifically, as numbers go up in classrooms, so does variability. This phenomenon is referred to as the *fan-spread effect* in statistical analysis, because it has the physical appearance of the type of fan women used to hold on formal occasions (Bryk & Weisberg, 1977). In a classroom of 20 third graders, for example, it is possible to find a child who cannot read a complete sentence fluently or with understanding, as well as a child who reads well above grade level. When that number jumps, say to 27, that possibility jumps as well, resulting in an even wider span of reading abilities than was likely before.

The paradox, of course, is that a teacher with 27 students, rather than 20, is potentially less able to address this broader spectrum of individual differences. In addition, this variability is not restricted to cognitive differences, such as reading proficiency, mathematics skills, or memory capacity. The widening range of student diversity is seen in all aspects of human variability, including socioemotional, physical, and cultural factors (Alexander & Murphy, 1999a). Figure 1–4 summarizes the consequences of these trends.

Stationary Trends

The influence of incremental trends on learning and teaching is exacerbated by the existence of two **stationary trends,** whose transformation has been so minimal or so gradual that it almost seems that no change has occurred. These two trends are mental hardware and mental software (Alexander & Knight, 1993). **Mental hardware** refers to the physical-chemical centerpiece of human thinking and behaving—the brain. Mental hardware is included under stationary trends to demonstrate that the fundamental

Information
- Struggle for teachers to remain up-to-date in subject matter areas
- Difficulty in determining what information should be valued in schools
- Tendency for teachers to *mention* rather than *teach*
- Increasing numbness from continuous onslaught of information

Media
- Technological gap between teachers and students
- Little regulation of quality and accuracy of information presented online
- Loss of some students in hyperspace

Population
- More students to be educated
- Concomitant increase in human variability

■ **Figure 1–4   Consequences of incremental trends.**

structure and capacity of the human brain has not been dramatically altered across the centuries. In fact, to the untrained eye, the brain of someone alive during the time of Socrates would look remarkably like that of a person of similar age and size born in this century (Pinker, 1997).

Like the physiochemical structure of our brains, the basic mental processes, or **mental software,** that underlie human thought and action have also remained surprisingly consistent (Alexander, Murphy, & Woods, 1996). Many of the ways in which humans reason and solve problems have not been radically altered even as the surrounding world has changed.

For instance, the techniques that many memory experts use to recall vast amounts of information, like the method of loci, have been around since the time of Socrates and Plato (Goetz, Alexander, & Ash, 1992). Used by ancient orators, the method of loci involves putting in a particular order the names or images of information to be remembered. Each item in that ordered list is then mentally placed in consecutive spots in some familiar locale, like the rooms in one's home or the streets in one's neighborhood. This memory technique could be great for remembering lots of things, like a grocery list (e.g., bananas–front hall; milk–living room; cereal–hallway). The problem comes with more lengthy lists or with nonlinear tasks, like a navigation path on the Web. Such traditional memory aids may simply not be up to contemporary learning tasks, which can be rather chaotic, nonlinear, or expansive (Alexander, Kulikowich, & Jetton, 1994).

Limitations of Human Memory

Figure 1–3 shows the widening gap between incremental and stationary trends, which underlies many of the problems encountered in schools and classrooms (Alexander, Murphy, & Woods, 1996). More of the same does not seem to be the answer: Even if the memories of all students could be improved by 20% or 30%, which would be quite an accomplishment, their minds still could not keep pace with the production of new information (diSessa, 1989). The limits of human memory, in the face of the informational demands each mind encounters, are all too evident (Goetz, Alexander, & Ash, 1992). It is becoming increasingly apparent that teachers must help students work smarter, rather than merely asking them to work harder. Students must rethink the role of the individual mind in learning and development if they are to confront the challenges that incremental trends pose (Salomon, Globerson, & Guterman, 1989).

Inevitable Variability

Some say that education is the great equalizer. However, individual differences are human inevitabilities (Ackerman, Kyllonen, & Roberts, 1999). In fact, Stanovich (1986) argues that wonderful teaching may simply exacerbate the differences that already exist in a classroom. He refers to this possibility as the *Matthew effect*. Stanovich suggests that education is an experience, a learning opportunity, to which individuals come with varied interests, goals, abilities, and motivations. Students draw differently from that experience based on their individual differences. Thus, the same lesson produces different outcomes. Those with more knowledge and more interest in the lesson content and with an orientation to learn from the experience will gain more than those who start with fewer of these characteristics (Alexander & Murphy, 1999a). Thus, the rich get richer, educationally speaking.

Iterative Trends

Perhaps the mounting disparity, or tension, between incremental and stationary trends contributes to the formation of recurring forces in the history of education (Alexander, Murphy, & Woods, 1996). Like strong undertows that lurk beneath relatively calm waters, **iterative trends** are those movements or events that continually reappear on the educational landscape (Alexander & Knight, 1993). Their labels are typically different and their configurations slightly changed, but they are educational movements that seem to reoccur with frightening regularity. When Patrick Walsh in the opening excerpt of this chapter railed against the latest academic mandates within his district, he was voicing his disdain for iterative trends in student assessment.

Iterative trends owe their existence, in part, to the push and pull between educational expectations and aspirations and the realities of everyday practice. There is an almost desperate need to do something to address the less-than-optimal state of learning and teaching, which leads educational reformers to revert to variations of familiar practices of programs. Alexander, Murphy, and Woods (1996) call this "doing what we know." The result is often the reincarnation of theories and movements that can be traced to generations and even centuries past (Cuban, 1993).

In the field of literacy, for example, there is a recurring conflict between whole-word or whole-language approaches and more phonics-based approaches (Hiebert & Raphael,

1996). Two of those cycles have occurred in just the past 50 years. In addition in the course of educational history, there have been numerous iterations of the debate over group versus individual, discovery versus directed, or teacher-centered versus student-centered practices. In fact, educators have gone "back to the basics" so many times that they should probably know the way by heart at this point.

What is so fascinating about the attempts to forcibly move education in one direction or another is that theory and research, along with the common sense derived from everyday practice, have repeatedly shown that learning and achievement are never completely one-sided (Alexander, Murphy, & Woods, 1996). Effective learning and teaching are both a group and an individual experience. The process is sometimes a matter of discovery, sometimes directed, and it shifts purposefully and meaningfully from teacher to student and from student to student. Effective practice is not extreme but is rather a question of when, where, and for whom different variants of educational practice should be implemented. Figure 1–5 summarizes the effects of both stationary and iterative trends.

Contribution of Educational Psychology

The powerful theories and well-conducted research found in educational psychology can be excellent guides through the complex and perilous territory of educational practice. The remainder of this text explores concepts, theories, and principles in educational psychology that should prove useful in coping with the various conditions and concerns arising from the interplay of incremental, stationary, and iterative trends. For instance, in response to the growing diversity in classrooms and the difficulties that arise in recognizing, appreciating, and adapting to such diversity, the chapters on development (chapters 2 and 3) consider what the notions of typical and maximal performance mean in relation to students' thinking, motivations, and sociocultural backgrounds.

The influence of living in an information age comes to the forefront in the section on knowledge (chapters 4 and 5). Those chapters explore what it means to know something and consider various principles for effective teaching. They also ask how knowledge and knowing change for different subjects, such as history or mathematics. To confront the gap between information and knowledge, these chapters focus on the perplexing problem of transfer. Research on transfer can

---

Stationary Effects
- Reliance on traditional processes for nontraditional tasks
- An overloading of human memory
- Potential exacerbation of individual differences

Iterative Effects
- Recycling of educational remedies
- Tendency to seek simple solutions to complex problems

■ **Figure 1–5 Consequences of stationary and iterative trends.**

explain why students repeatedly fail to use what they know in alternative situations and contexts where that knowledge would prove invaluable. Such understanding can aid in the orchestration of learning environments that promote flexible and effective use of existing knowledge and skills.

A discussion of misconceptions and persuasion in chapter 6 tackles another sticky issue: How is it that we form erroneous or naive ideas that remain highly resistant to change even in the face of powerful evidence? And what can teachers do to challenge students' erroneous, misleading, and sometimes damaging concepts or attitudes, so that students can progress in their learning and achievement? The chapter examines how aspects of the learning task, instructional materials, and characteristics of the learners themselves, all contribute to the formation or deconstruction of naive conceptions.

The chapters on strategic processing (chapter 7) and problem solving (chapter 8) bring additional theory and research to bear on educational trends. This section distinguishes between skillful and strategic behavior and ponders the role each plays in learning and development. It also inspects the kinds of problems and tasks individuals face both in and out of school, so that the elements of those problems and tasks can be teased apart. The text shows that certain problem configurations are more commonplace in particular subject-matter areas and explores learner profiles in relation to problem solving.

This section also discusses a range of strategies that can be applied to the given array of problems. Some of those strategies have a general and broad use, whereas others are closely linked to certain subjects or particular tasks. Some of the strategies are rather traditional, such as those employed by the ancients to retain their cultural legacy. Others are novel or less prototypical and seem particularly relevant for living and learning in this informational and technological age— for example, identifying and navigating nonlinear sources.

The areas of motivation and affect are examined in chapters 9 and 10, which look closely at learners' self-perceptions, interests, and desires and the contributions these make to successes and failures in school. This section addresses questions that trouble many teachers:

- What can be done with students who have lost all belief in their ability to succeed?
- Is a decline in motivation an inherent part of the educational process?
- Do external rewards help or hinder students' learning and development?

This discussion explores ways to break through the informational force field, uncovering techniques that make the content of instruction truly relevant and valuable to students without merely dressing it up or sugarcoating it.

The issue of diversity arises again in the investigation of theory and research on situation and context (chapters 11 and 12). Those chapters touch on the role of human and nonhuman resources in creating an effective learning environment, recognizing how such resources can alter the course of learning and instruction (chapter 11). One goal of this segment is to contemplate techniques, such as cooperative or shared learning, that build positively on the cognitive, motivational, and sociocultural diversity in the classroom community. Several of these techniques also make good use of hypermedia (chapter 12) and extend the learning experience beyond the confines of a single classroom (Scardamalia, Bereiter, McLean, Swallow, & Woodruff, 1989). Through the application of technology, teachers can turn to others who possess specialized knowledge and skills—one way to stay up-to-date in this information age (Cognition and Technology Group at Vanderbilt 1996).

The final section of the book targets the area of assessment, investigating testing practices in terms of large-scale, high-stakes assessment (chapter 13), as well as teacher-made measures (chapter 14). Because testing weighs so heavily among teachers' concerns and exerts great influence on what is taught, these chapters examine what constitutes valid assessment practices, determining what teachers can do to cope with the demands of district and statewide testing, as well as what they can do to construct better tests for their own classrooms.

The future of learning and instruction—for all its challenges and controversies—remains exciting and promising, especially for those with the passion and the drive to meet those challenges and controversies head on. The theories and research of educational psychology—interpreted and shaped by practical, everyday knowledge and experience—can assist in that venture.

■ Summary Reflections

What role can psychology play in everyday educational practice?

- The relation between psychology and pedagogy must be mutual and reciprocal, with teachers holding to a contemporary psychological perspective.
- The relation between psychology and pedagogy must be grounded in realistic situations.

What areas of psychological theory and research have the most to say about learning and teaching?

- The 14 learner-centered psychological principles describe critical tenets for integrating psychology and pedagogy.
- Research support falls into six areas: development and individual differences, knowledge, strategic processing, motivation and affect, situation or context, and assessment.

How does the sociohistorical context affect learning and teaching?

- Three interrelated educational trends—incremental, stationary, and iterative—influence teachers and students.
- The goal of this text is to reunite psychology and pedagogy to enhance learning and development for all.

Chapter 2

Exploring Development and Its Biological Bases

GUIDING QUESTIONS

- What is development?
- What are the defining themes in human development?
- What are the biological bases of development?

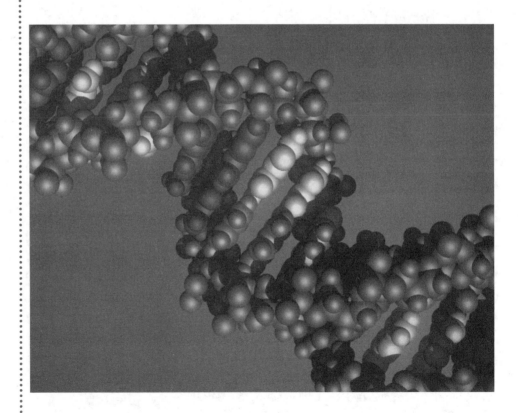

IN THEIR OWN WORDS ....

Every day is a lesson in development for Pam Bechtel, who has been teaching health and physical education to high-school students in the rural Midwest for 19 years. Her students face many of the same physical, mental, and social/emotional challenges that confront all adolescents. *

Want to learn about human development? Just watch this group of 14- and 15-year-olds play a co-ed game of basketball. Todd has the ball at the moment. Sporting a 5 o'clock shadow at 10 o'clock in the morning, he maneuvers his muscular 6-foot frame easily down the court. Sally and several other freshman girls keep their eyes glued to his every move, and not because they are into the game. Todd passes the ball to Kevin, who has far more "heart" than athletic skill. In fact, Kevin is one of the smallest students in the class. He probably doesn't weigh more than 80 pounds, but his small size has never dampened his enthusiasm. He has a quick mind and a great sense of humor. It is easy to see why he is so popular with his classmates.

As Kevin goes for the pass from Todd, Victoria (Stretch to her classmates) picks off the ball. Victoria is even taller than Todd and extremely coordinated. She is also the most aggressive student in the class and rarely passes to teammates. She and I have had several "talks" about her temper and her aggressiveness. Victoria's competitive drive may be a reflection of her father's attitudes. He was a star athlete in basketball and track and field. He is convinced his daughter will follow in his footsteps, and maybe even go pro. The family lives and breathes sports.

When Victoria goes in for a layup, she accidentally—or not so accidentally—runs into Sally. Two boys rush to Sally's aid. Is their eagerness related to the fact that Sally is quite developed physically? Sally could easily be mistaken for a senior. She wears clothes that accentuate her assets and more makeup than a Kabuki actor. It is hard to get her involved in any of the games—she complains about the damage they do to her hair, nails, and makeup. Sally's physical maturity is not my only concern. She brags about being sexually active, and

her boyfriend is a 17-year-old dropout who already has one child to support. I have tried to talk frankly about this with Sally and her parents, who claim they cannot control their daughter anymore. It is a painful thing to watch children follow paths that can only lead them into misery and trouble.

After Victoria runs into Sally, Betsy makes a side comment to Victoria about easing off Sally. Betsy has no patience with Victoria's aggressiveness, any more than she can stomach the way Sally panders to the boys in class. That's Betsy—she operates with a razor-sharp sense of right and wrong. Her world has no room for moral grays. Physically, Betsy is also another interesting case. With her haircut, style of dress, and boyish physique, she could almost pass for one of the guys. Everybody knows Betsy would rather be hunting or fishing with her grandfather, whom she adores, than doing anything else. She is just like her mother, Louise, who has been my close friend since elementary school. She looks like her, too. Louise was the last of our group to go through puberty, but when she did, she left the rest of us in the dust. If the same thing happens to Betsy, Sally will have some major competition for the boys' attention—although not the kind of attention Betsy is likely to relish.

It is fascinating to teach adolescents: so much is changing for them so quickly. They are leaving childhood behind, but they have a long way to go before they are ready to accept the demands of being an adult. Developmental No-Man's Land, that is how I see adolescence. As their teacher, I see hints of what sorts of adults my students are becoming, for better or worse, and I sometimes catch glimpses of what they ideally could be. You do what you can to help them find the best parts of themselves, and to question those behaviors and attitudes that are less positive or dangerous. And I try to assure them that the anxiety and uncertainty that they are now experiencing will eventually pass. If only I could make them believe it!

*In this and all subsequent opening vignettes, all names except that of the featured teacher are fictitious.

What Is Development?

Human development is about change. The science of **human development,** one of the oldest and most fertile branches of psychology (Gesell & Ilg, 1946; Hall, 1904), is an attempt to understand the transformations that humans undergo from conception until death. Thus, developmental psychology is a vast discipline. The field of human development often categorizes the types of changes humans experience into three major domains:

- **Neurological and physical development**—how our brains and bodies change over time both in their form

and in their functioning. Neurological development involves the changes that occur in the brain and the central nervous system (Berninger & Richards, 2002), whereas physical development encompasses change in the body and the way the body moves (i.e., motor development; J. M. Tanner, 1990). Physical development is the aspect of human development that absorbs Pam Bechtel daily. Her students are focusing on physical development when they wonder about such questions as, Am I destined to be short like my parents and grandparents? Why do some people mature physically faster than others do? Together, neurological and physical development form the biological bases for all forms of human development.

- **Cognitive development**—how our minds and mental processes change over time. Cognitive development is concerned with questions like, Are we born with the ability to understand and use language, or is this a learned ability? Can we expect 8-year-olds to grasp abstract and complex issues?
- **Social and emotional development**—how our concepts of ourselves, our relationships with and understandings of others, and our emotions develop. The social/emotional domain encompasses the social, emotional, and moral dimensions of human existence (Erikson, 1963). Complex questions relate to social/emotional development: How and why do friendships form? Do we control our emotions, or do they control us? Are we equipped with a moral compass, or are right and wrong culturally determined?

Despite the division of the field into these three broad domains, it is important to remember that neurological/physical, cognitive, and social/emotional development do not operate independently. Each developmental domain affects and influences the other (Berk, 1999). Further, although the terms *development* and *maturation* are often used interchangeably in everyday conversation, they have distinct meanings to those who study development. Specifically, *development* encompasses all systematic changes that occur in humans, regardless of their source, whereas **maturation** refers to those systematic transformations that are rooted in our biology or genetics. Consequently, even though we can talk about moral development, there is some question about the degree to which the patterns of change result from maturation or from social and cultural influences.

The field of human development can help us understand the neurological/physical, cognitive, and social/emotional changes that we all experience as human beings. And understanding these changes is central to effective teaching. An effective educator needs to understand such things as what students can and cannot comprehend, what interests and motivates them, how they reason, and what they know or believe they know about the subject at hand.

The field of human development provides educators with information that is fundamental to understanding students. For example, human development offers a detailed picture of what physical, cognitive, and emotional traits are typical for individuals at a particular period of development. It also helps teachers understand what range of variations might typically be seen among individuals at a particular age. Without such information teachers can follow a preset curriculum that they have been handed, but they cannot ascertain whether that curriculum is appropriate for their students. Without such information teachers can apply instructional methods, but they cannot understand the probable efficacy of those methods with their students or the ways in which those methods could or should be adapted to better meet the special needs of students.

> **Learner-Centered Psychological Principle 10**
> *Developmental influence on learning.* As individuals develop, they encounter different opportunities and experience different constraints for learning. Learning is most effective when differential development within and across physical, intellectual, emotional, and social domains is taken into account.
>
> Learner Centered Principles Work Group of the APA Board of Educational Affairs, 1997

What Are the Defining Themes in Human Development?

The multitude of questions posed about human change across the centuries reflect one of three overarching themes of human development:

- **Source**—What are the roots or determiners of human change?
- **Continuity**—Does change unfold in a continuous manner, or does it occur in distinct steps or stages?
- **Stability**—Are the neurological/physical, cognitive, and social/emotional characteristics that differentiate individuals stable, or can they be modified?

These three themes pertain to all forms of change and, thus, serve as foundations for the science of development (Byrnes, 2001).

Source

Source involves the forces that dictate or stimulate human transformation. As already mentioned, maturation assumes that our biology or genetics remains a powerful source of human development. Overall, sources of change can be *endogenous,* or within us, such as our genetic makeup. Or they can be *exogenous,* or outside us, such as our home environment. The nature-versus-nurture controversy is central to this developmental theme. In other words, are we who we are because it is in our natures to be so, or did we become who we are because of the nurturing we have experienced? Predominant theories of development recognize both endogenous and exogenous influences on human change (Plomin, 1990). What distinguishes those theories is the relative weight placed on nature and nurture, giving rise to four developmental perspectives: biological determinism, environmental shaping, active adaptation, and cultural contextualism (see Table 2–1). Moreover, each of these perspectives gives rise to varied expectations for educators and for educational practice.

Table 2–1   Sources of development: Four perspectives.

Perspective	Leading Theorist/ Researcher	Nature/ Nurture Position	Educational Implications
Biological Determinism	Sigmund Freud (1856–1939), father of psychoanalysis	Emphasizes the neurological and physiological conditions underlying mental and emotional development; believes that environment or experiences can trigger but not cause mental distress	Education should allow students to maximize strengths and compensate for their needs; it should identify students' innate strengths and needs; it might advocate differentiated programs of study.
Environmental Shaping	John B. Watson (1878–1958), father of behaviorism	Sees development as shaped by the specific associations forged between environmental factors (stimuli) and resulting reactions (responses); sees differences in development as differences in conditioning	Education is about conditioning; it should punish and reinforce students' responses systematically to ensure desired outcomes; students' futures depend on environmental shaping.
Active Adaptation	Jean Piaget (1896–1980)	Believes that individuals play an active role in their development; sees individuals' mental maturity as critical in determining what is learned from the environment or experience	Education entails providing students with age- and ability-appropriate experiences that stimulate adaptation; it should ascertain learners' levels of cognitive maturity.
Cultural Contextualism	Lev Vygotsky (1896–1934)	Considers development to be a social and cultural experience; cannot think of the developing mind as separate from the sociocultural context	Education is an extension of the sociocultural environment; it should use social resources in the learning environment; tasks and assessment should consider group processing.

Learner-Centered Psychological Principle 12

Individual differences in learning. Learners have different strategies, approaches, and capabilities for learning that are a function of prior experience and heredity.

Learner Centered Principles Work Group of the APA Board of Educational Affairs, 1997

Biological Determinism

Biological determinism holds that physical, cognitive, and social/emotional makeup is largely locked away in genetic codes (Gesell, 1940). Aspects of our biological natures establish how we look, think, behave, and feel now and in the years to come (Plomin, 1986). There may be some room for change within that existing framework, but individuals cannot radically alter their basic biological or neurochemical structures, no matter how hard they try.

Kevin, the diminutive student in Pam Bechtel's class, can exercise, eat well, and subject himself to stretching regimens. However, if he is genetically programmed to be short, then his efforts will not make him tall. Similarly, if Kevin is cognitively endowed with the capacity to process numerical data with incredible speed and accuracy, he will retain this innate ability regardless of instruction. Whether he makes use of that ability is another issue. Biological determinism also pertains to the social/emotional aspects of life. As dis-

cussed in Chapters 9 and 10, some theorists see basic drives, such as the need for food, shelter, or security, as the source of human motives and actions (N. E. Miller, 1948).

Data from studies of identical twins separated at birth offer some support for biological determinism (Bouchard, 1984; Bouchard & McGue, 1981). These studies document remarkable similarities in mental and social/emotional functioning even when the life experiences of the twins differed markedly (Pinker, 2002). In the case of Oscar Stohr and Jack Yufe (Begley, 1979), Oscar was reared as a Catholic in Czechoslovakia, but his twin brother, Jack, was taken to the Caribbean and reared as a Jew. Yet when these twins were reunited after decades, Oscar and Jack demonstrated notable similarities that could not be attributed to their upbringing. Not only did they manifest the same quirky behaviors (e.g., sneezing to scare others) and habits (e.g., flushing the toilet before and after use), but they also scored very similarly on a battery of personality and aptitude measures.

Although they cannot be considered conclusive evidence, data on identical and fraternal twins and on adopted siblings consistently suggest that nature has a great deal to do with development (Loehlin, 1992; Scarr, Weinberg, & Waldman, 1993). Collectively, these studies suggest that critical aspects of physical structure, mental processing, and social/emotional profiles may come as standard equipment when we enter the world (Pinker, 1997).

Based on his work in psychotherapy and psychoanalysis, Sigmund Freud (1856–1939) serves as an excellent model for biological determinism. Most people associate Freud with his work on the unconscious and his techniques for

Sigmund Freud

John B. Watson

bringing buried memories to the surface of awareness (1938/1973). However, Freud (1905/1953) believed that all psychological conditions can be traced to strengths or weaknesses in individuals' neurology (i.e., brain structure) and physiology (i.e., physical makeup).

Although he tempered his views later in life, Freud did not waver in his belief that mental well-being could never be divorced from a person's brain or physical functioning (Freud, 1925). As a biological determinist, he held that every mental condition had identifiable causes beyond human control. Environmental events may trigger mental illness, for instance, but the sources of such conditions remain endogenous.

Attention to the biological bases of development waned in popularity during the latter half of the 20th century but has enjoyed a renaissance (Pressley & McCormick, 1995), much of which can be credited to expanding research on the structure and functioning of the brain. Thanks to sophisticated equipment and procedures, such as magnetic resonance imaging (MRI), the ability to explore the human brain and study its functioning has reached new heights. These developments have also led to the formation of new fields of study, such as neuropsychology and psychopharmacology (Pinker, 1997), which explore the relation between psychology and biological forces.

Environmental Shaping

Although some individuals believe in the power of nature, others focus on the power of nurture in development (Skinner, 1953). These individuals represent the **environmental shaping** perspective; they see life experiences and the nature of one's surroundings as the principal catalysts of human change. Further, they posit that development unfolds through such experiences, as opposed to being hardwired in the human genome (Reese & Overton, 1970). Those holding to this developmental orientation would take the findings of the twin studies to task, arguing that even if genetics does account for as much as 70% of development, the remaining 30% could mean the difference between a

Mozart and a mediocre musician, a Michelangelo and an artistic amateur (Plomin, 1990).

Perhaps no one offers a clearer model of environmental shaping than John B. Watson (1878–1958). The father of behaviorism, Watson carried beliefs in the power of environment to the extreme. He thought that psychology needed to be purged of concepts like *consciousness* or *mind* (Watson, 1913). To him such ideas get in the way of sound psychological research. What really matters is behaviors—externally manifested and measurable actions—and the confluence of environmental conditions (stimuli) that produce them (Watson, 1930).

> Give me a dozen healthy infants, well-formed, and my own specified world to bring them up in and I'll guarantee to take any one at random and train him to become any type of specialist I might select—doctor, lawyer, merchant-chief, and, yes, even beggar-man and thief, regardless of his talents, penchants, tendencies, abilities, vocations, and race of his ancestors. (Watson, 1924, p. 104)

If educators want to mold human development, they cannot rely on the serendipitous occurrence of life events. Instead, they need to understand how an individual (or animal, for that matter) comes to associate particular stimuli with particular reactions. Then, educators must use such knowledge to condition desired outcomes. For example, a child smiles at the sight of her favorite blanket but screams at the sight of a dog because she associates the former with feelings of love and comfort and the latter with harsh and threatening sounds. Systematically pairing particular behaviors with either pleasant or unpleasant outcomes (e.g., good grades with hugs and bad grades with restrictions) can increase or decrease their likelihood (Skinner, 1953). Thus, Watson believed that developmental outcomes could be effectively orchestrated through environmental manipulation. Creating the right set of environmental conditions, in effect, produces the desired outcome.

Watson's version of environmental shaping leaves little room for the influences of temperament and propensities that others allowed. Watson saw children and youth as rather passive receptors of environmental and experiential influences, a position out of favor with current educational researchers and practitioners.

Active Adaptation

Other developmentalists are more dualistic in their orientation toward human change; they acknowledge both nature and nurture to some degree. Some dualists conceive of development in passive terms, with individuals at the relative mercy of both exogenous and endogenous forces. Others see humans as having the power to influence their own developmental courses. From the vantage point of **active adaptation,** humans are active players in the change process (Byrnes, 2001).

No one is a more respected model of this orientation than Jean Piaget. A biologist by training, Piaget (1896–1980) dramatically altered the course of developmental research in the 20th century in several ways. First, Piaget (1932, 1952) endowed the science of development with a comprehensive theory that it had sorely lacked—a theory that pertains to cognitive, linguistic, and social/emotional change. Before Piaget developmentalists were absorbed in describing, rather than explaining, human behavior and establishing developmental norms (Gesell, 1940; Hall, 1904).

Second, Piaget (1955) believed in the reciprocity of endogenous and exogenous forces. As he saw it, biological/genetic nature affects the way individuals respond to their environments. Conversely, their environments and experiences can directly influence their basic neurophysiology. For example, another student in Pam Bechtel's class—we'll call her Brigid—has always been very physically coordinated. Not long after she could walk, she was rolling and tumbling in the yard. This experience, combined with her small stature, gave her an edge in gymnastics. But these neurophysiological conditions afforded Brigid only certain possibilities (Burtt, 1939). In addition, Brigid studied with

Jean Piaget

some of the best gymnastic coaches in the region. She devoted hours to enhancing whatever edge her biological and genetic makeup afforded her. These environmental factors—lessons, excellent coaches, hours of practice—increased her coordination and sharpened her physical skills. Brigid's very strict diet and her intensive training regimen also delayed the onset of puberty. While her 16-year-old peers were developing breasts and more womanly shapes, Brigid retained her girlish shape and small stature. Clearly, her actions had directly affected her physiology.

Third, Piaget argued that the value of rich environments and stimulating experiences depends directly on the individuals' ability and willingness to adapt their current thinking and behavior to the new information conveyed in those external events (Piaget, 1952). That is, what individuals can perceive and grasp from any experience rests on their motivation and level of mental maturity.

Cultural Contextualism

An alternative new orientation toward development has gained favor in recent years. **Cultural contextualism** puts great weight on environmental factors and offers a view of human change not anticipated in the preexisting developmental literature (M. Cole, Gay, Glick, & Sharp, 1971). At the core of this orientation is the belief that human development cannot be thought of solely in terms of the individual mind or individual change. Instead, development is a socially motivated and socially experienced process (Bronfenbrenner, 1989; Luria, 1981).

Nor can development be divorced from the time and place in which it occurs (M. Cole, 1996). In many ways development reflects the values and experiences of the culture in which an individual lives. Thus, to provide for her students' physical and motor development, Pam Bechtel must keep in mind that these adolescents are growing up on farms in the rural Midwest early in the 21st century, in a rather conservative and homogeneous community where family histories can be public knowledge and personal legacies exist.

Among researchers and theorists who have contributed significantly to the cultural-contextual perspective (e.g., Bronfenbrenner, 1989; Rogoff, 2000), Lev Vygotsky (1896–1934) is at the vanguard. A Russian physician, Vygotsky was a contemporary of Piaget and, like Piaget, was a dualist fascinated with children's language and thought (Vygotsky, 1962). Also like Piaget, Vygotsky dedicated himself to the systematic study of the emergence and progression of language and thought.

However, Vygotsky and others holding to a cultural-contextual perspective place much greater weight on the social context than is true for other nature-nurture orientations. Vygotsky (1978) argued that children's abilities are not stable during any particular developmental period. Instead, abilities shift with the social context and the assistance provided by more capable and knowledgeable individuals. For example, Victoria's athletic performance can vary greatly depending on the others with or against whom she plays. In addition, her abilities are certainly enhanced by the quality of the coaching she receives, which is true for students' mental and linguistic performance as well (Perkins, 1992).

Lev Vygotsky

Continuity

Regardless of the degree to which educational researchers or practitioners attribute human development to endogenous or exogenous factors, they are still faced with questions about the path of that change, or **continuity.** To some like Watson and Vygotsky, development unfolds gradually and continuously (i.e., **continuous**). To others like Freud and Piaget, development is marked by distinct steps and discrete stages (i.e., **discontinuous**). Those who study development and those who guide the development of others tend to fall on one side of this issue or the other. That is, they conceive of change in terms of either *evolution* (i.e., continuous) or *revolution* (i.e., discontinuous).

Issues of the continuity of development do not warrant the same level of attention paid to questions of nature or nurture but are no less important. Indeed, educators should be aware that there are certain advantages and disadvantages associated with evolutionary or revolutionary orientations toward human change, and those advantages and disadvantages influence a range of educational functions, including the description and prediction of student characteristics and behavior, as well as efforts to explain their cause.

For example, teachers who accept stage theories of cognitive development may have a clearer sense of what to expect with regard to their students' reasoning ability or language facility than those for whom development is rather continuous. On the other hand, the expectations that typically accompany stage theories may lead teachers to withhold potentially valuable experiences from their students under the belief that such experiences would be beyond their mental capabilities (Case, 1985, 1992). Thus, stage theories function as a double-edged sword for practicing teachers.

Stability

Unlike the issues of source and continuity, which are based on the universal nature of development, **stability** deals with

human differences (Byrnes, 2001). It looks at the physical, cognitive, and social/emotional characteristics that differentiate individuals and asks whether those differences are significant (M. Cole & Cole, 2001). Further, stability explores whether such differences are modifiable. In other words, can the trajectory of individuals' development be changed once it has been set in motion by their heredity or the environment (Berk, 1999)?

The Roots of Human Differences

Dolly, the infamous cloned sheep, set off a scientific and ethical debate.

One of the great paradoxes of development is that all humans are alike in certain physical, mental, and social ways; yet all humans are unique. No two individuals are exactly the same—even if they are genetic clones. To many educational researchers, the differences among humans are as fascinating and as inevitable as their remarkable similarities (Ackerman, Kyllonen, & Roberts, 1999). Whereas some researchers have dedicated themselves to understanding the similarities among humans, others have devoted themselves to unraveling the mysteries of human diversity (Carroll, 1993; Cronbach & Snow, 1977; E. Hunt, 1999). The science of individual differences first took root at the end of the 19th century and remains an active and highly controversial field of study (Snow, 1989).

Sir Francis Galton

More than any other individual, Sir Francis Galton (1822–1911) turned fascination with human uniqueness into the science of individual differences. A cousin of Charles Darwin, Galton applied Darwin's evolutionary principles to the human species (1869/1979, 1883). As a result, he set psychology and education on a path still followed today—a course hailed by some and condemned by others (Seldin, 1999). Galton's explorations of human differences began when he noticed that many of the students achieving honors at Cambridge University were the sons or brothers of previous winners (1874/1970). This made him wonder whether the factors underlying human intelligence, which he called *eminence,* were part of one's genetic makeup. He decided to put this hypothesis to the test. After collecting lineage data on prominent individuals, Galton concluded that eminence was hundreds of times more likely in the families of successful individuals than in the general population, thus giving credence to his belief that a predisposition to intelligence was inherited, passed down from one generation to the next like skin or eye color.

The Bell Curve

To help him make sense of his thousands of measurements, Galton borrowed an idea from the Belgian astronomer

Adolphe Quételet (E. Hunt, 1993), who had been studying errors in astronomic observations. When Quételet began plotting those errors, they formed a bell-shaped distribution, like the one pictured in Figure 2–1. In effect, what Quételet determined was that calculation errors were often relatively similar in magnitude; most were only a few points from the expected number. Also, he noted that the greater the magnitude of the error, the rarer its occurrence, and that errors were just as likely to be below as above the expected number. These patterns in observation errors were what gave Quételet's distribution its rather curious shape.

When Galton began studying his volumes of human data, he hypothesized that this same bell-shaped pattern should fit his observations (1869/1979, 1883). After all, he reasoned, most adults are of relatively similar height or weight, and those who are quite short or tall or skinny or fat are fairly uncommon. Once Galton began plotting the data, his assumptions about the shape of the distribution were repeatedly upheld (1888). Not only did the thousands of measurements on height and weight follow this curious pattern, but so did his data on people's reaction time and their visual and auditory acuity. Galton thus became convinced that this bell-shaped pattern applied to any sensorimotor characteristic (1869/1979).

As a way to give this bell-shaped curve greater specificity, Galton carved it into various segments with specific percentages of observations allotted to each, as seen in Figure 2–1. The average, or mean, of his measurements was the centerpoint of the distribution, with equal numbers of segments and observations on either side of that mean. Over time, Galton became increasingly convinced that this same bell-shaped pattern was not only descriptive of human sensorimotor data, but also of any mental or cognitive measurements (1869/1979, 1883).

This concept of the bell-shaped curve, or **normal distribution,** still remains foundational for theory and research on human differences (Herrnstein & Murray, 1994; Horn, 1985). It is generally accepted that any measured characteristics—from verbal ability to memory—will conform to this normal distribution. Thus, notions of normality and exceptionality have been built around this bell-shaped distribution (Ackerman, Sternberg, & Glaser, 1989). Specifically, **normality** is associated with the middle of the distribution, the area of greatest concentration, where more than two thirds (68.3%) of individuals fall. Deviations from these more typical levels become increasingly rare toward the edges or fringes of the curve (Neisser, 1998). In fact, only 4.2% of observations are found in the more extreme segments of the distribution, making such differences especially significant or profound. Thus, **exceptionality** is associated with outlying areas in this normal distribution.

What Are the Biological Bases of Development?

Underlying the three themes of development, especially the theme of source, are questions about the biological bases of human change. Even those who situate the catalysts for development completely outside the individual must argue against the power of human biology (Pinker, 2002). The role of biology cannot be ignored in the debate over nature and nurture. The biological bases of human development en-

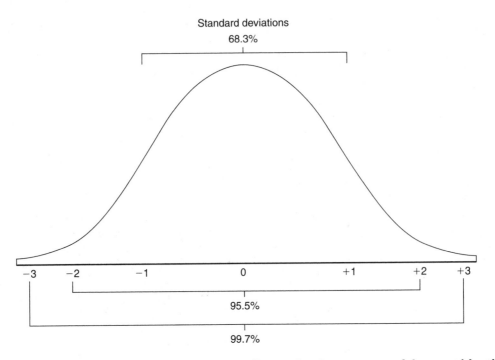

■ **FIGURE 2–1   The shape of a normal distribution. The bell curve has become one of the most identifiable and influential shapes in the study of development and individual differences.**

compass a number of elements, including the structure and function of the brain and neurological system, physiological changes, and motor development.

Neurological Development

For educational researchers the relation between mind and brain remains a complex puzzle. There are those like Virginia Berninger and Todd Richards who argue that "the mind is the brain at work" (2002, p. 3). Others in the field consider the mind to be more ethereal, removed from the physical entity we call the brain (Pinker, 2002). Between these two extremes is the acknowledgment that the workings of the human mind are inextricably linked to the structure and function of the brain and other components of the neurological system. To survey your current knowledge of those topics, you should complete the Thought Experiment: A Little Brain Teaser, which follows, and keep those questions in mind throughout this section.

Knowledge about the brain and its development has grown by leaps and bounds in the past quarter century. New technologies such as MRI and computer-assisted tomography (CT or CAT scan) have opened up the black box of the human brain for study in ways never before dreamed possible. For several centuries knowledge of the structure and functions of the brain came almost exclusively from studies of the diseased and the deceased. This approach allowed the medical community to identify the overall macrostructure of the brain (e.g., hemispheres and folds) and to relate certain injuries and diseases to particular anomalies in that structure. But such analyses could not show the healthy brain at work, capture the workings of mi-

> ### Learner-Centered Psychological Principle 13
> *Learning and diversity.* Learning is most effective when differences in learners' linguistic, cultural, and social backgrounds are taken into account.
>
> Learner Centered Principles Work Group of the APA Board of Educational Affairs, 1997

crostructures (e.g., brain cells) central to mental performance, or link everyday activities to specific brain functions. With the new imaging technologies and an ability to explore the workings of the brain almost from the moment of conception, a great deal is now known about neurological development.

The Prenatal Period

Although the 1990s are called the decade of brain research and new technologies have made it possible to probe deeply into the structure and working of the brain, educators often have limited exposure to the brain and its development during their professional preparation (Berninger & Richards, 2002). Consequently, the burgeoning literature in fields like neuroscience, neurophysiology, and neuropsychology remains disassociated from educational practice, even though teachers' mission is to educate the minds of students.

It is important to remember that the literature on the relations between the brain and learning is very much in its

---

Thought Experiment ....

A Little Brain Teaser

Directions: Below are several questions about the brain and neurological system intended to assess what you already know about these topics. Even if you are not sure of the answer, offer your best guess.

1. What is the average size of the adult brain?
   a. 1 pound
   b. 2 pounds
   c. 3 pounds
   d. 4 pounds
   e. 5 pounds
2. Which of the following pairs of adjectives best describes the brain of a healthy, functioning individual?
   a. gray and solid
   b. pink and solid
   c. gray and gelatinous
   d. pink and gelatinous
3. Neurons share a common structure that includes which of the following? List all that apply.
   a. axon
   b. convolutions
   c. neurotransmitters

   d. dendrites
   e. cell body
4. Much of what we know about the brain has been learned in the past 25 years. True or false?
5. All the neurons we will have as adults are already formed before birth or soon thereafter. True or false?
6. Particular areas of the brain are dedicated solely to the performance of specific tasks, such as reading, seeing, or hearing. True or false?
7. It is possible for an infant to suffer serious trauma to sections of the brain and still live a relatively normal life. True or false?
8. There is a correspondence between brain development and students' physical, motor, cognitive, and social/emotional development. True or false?

(Answers at the end of the chapter)

infancy. Many of the recommendations or interpretations that arise in that literature are based on **correlation research;** that is, research that shows that some aspect of human performance or condition co-occurs with particular features or activities within the brain. Nonetheless, there is much to know about how the brain develops and how that process corresponds to physical, motor, and cognitive development (H. T. Epstein, 2001).

The rate and complexity of brain development are truly amazing. The human brain begins to take shape at the moment of conception, and in no more than 19 days after fertilization, a neural tube takes shape. That tube, which forms through the process of **neuralation,** will become the brain and spinal cord (see Figure 2–2). By Day 25 that neural tube closes and forms three distinct sections: the hindbrain, midbrain, and forebrain. The hindbrain, which is attached to the spinal cord, is responsible for many basic biological functions, including breathing and the beating of the heart, along with certain voluntary responses like walking. The midbrain, which is involved in some bodily movements (e.g., startle reflex), has the primary function of connecting the hindbrain to the forebrain. The forebrain, the largest region in the adult brain, encompasses the cortex, cerebral hemispheres, and limbic system. In this region higher order mental functions such as memory and reasoning appear to be centered.

In addition to the formation of the neural tube, many components of the neurological system make their appearance in the first weeks following conception. For example, the spinal cord begins to take shape by Day 40; and the cerebral hemisphere, a key area of the brain, becomes more pro-

nounced within 50 days of fertilization. The rudimentary brain areas observed on Day 25 are more pronounced by Day 100. For instance, the folds and contours that are known as **cerebral convolutions,** and associated with the mature adult brain, are evident by Week 24 of the prenatal period.

Two characteristic neurological processes that occur during prenatal development are cell proliferation and cell migration (Eliot, 1999). **Cell proliferation** refers to the extremely rapid creation of neuron and glial cells. **Neurons** are nerve cells, the building blocks of the neurological system. **Glial cells** have the primary function of providing nourishment and support to the neurological system. Between the 5th and 20th weeks of gestation, thousands of brain cells form every second. In fact, it is estimated that about a half million neurons grow every minute during this period until neuron development peaks in the 4th month of gestation. By birth or soon thereafter, the production of neuron cells is complete. Interestingly, even as billions of neuron cells are being created during this period of rapid growth, millions of cells are dying; the brain manufactures many more neurons than it ever plans on using. Such overproduction is another remarkable feature of neurological development (Pressley & McCormick, 1995).

What is as amazing as their proliferation is the fact that neurons undergo **cell migration.** How cells migrate remains one of the great mysteries of the brain; however, neurons, much like migratory animals, seem genetically compelled to travel to specific destinations within the neurological system once they have been created. Glial cells also play a role in that migration; in fact, glial cells seem to function like neurological tracks along which the neurons

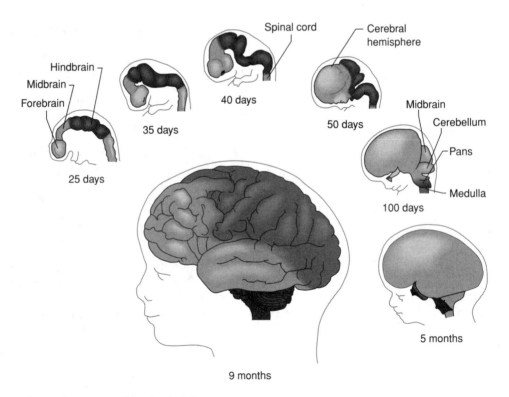

■ **FIGURE 2–2   The early stages of brain development.**

NEURON

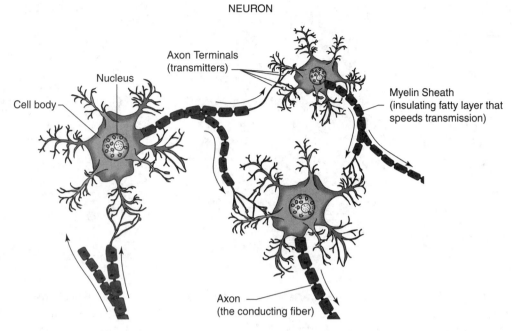

Cell body

Nucleus

Axon Terminals
(transmitters)

Myelin Sheath
(insulating fatty layer that
speeds transmission)

Axon
(the conducting fiber)

■ **FIGURE 2–3   Neuron structure.**

travel. Upon their arrival at their final destinations, neurons take on particular and varied functions (Berninger & Richards, 2002; Pressley & McCormick, 1995).

Although neurons vary in location, configuration, and function, they share a typical structure, depicted in Figure 2–3. That structure includes the cell body, dendrites, an axon, and a myelin sheath. The **cell body** houses the nucleus, or cell control center, with dendrites and the axon branching from the cell body. The nucleus produces substances needed for cell processing and maintenance, along with chemicals required for the transmission of impulses from one neuron to another. Those transmissions are the means by which thoughts and actions are carried throughout the neurological system. Dendrites and axons, which are critical to impulse transmission, begin to form once the neuron has completed its migration. Each neuron has one **axon** that carries impulses away from the cell body toward other neurons and a number of **dendrites** that direct impulses toward the cell body.

The spaces that exist between neurons are called **synapses.** Those spaces are filled with **neurotransmitters,** chemicals that allow impulses to be carried between neurons. A waxy substance called **myelin,** made up of glial cells, surrounds the cell in a **myelin sheath,** which enhances the synaptic connections. Like insulation this sheath increases the speed and efficiency of electrochemical impulses and, thus, brain functioning. The buildup of myelin around the cell membrane is termed **myelination.**

Postnatal Maturation

The astonishing rate of cell growth and specialization in the human brain is most pronounced in the last 3 months of the prenatal period, extending into the first 2 years of life. This phase of brain development is called the **brain growth spurt** period (Eliot, 1999). Even though humans have acquired all their neuron cells by birth or soon thereafter, brain development is far from complete. In fact, at birth the brain has achieved only about 25% of its adult size (which is approximately 3 lbs.); by age 2 that percentage has jumped to 75%.

The thrust of brain development during the first year of life is attributable to changes in both the microstructure (e.g., neurons, dendrites, and synapses) and the macrostructure (e.g., cortex and cerebellum; Barnes, 1986). Even though neurons cease to grow in number by birth, they continue to grow in weight and size. Much of the increase before the first birthday results from an increase in the waxy myelin sheath around the axons, improving the transmittal capacity of those cells. This myelin sheath is referred to as the **white matter** of the brain. **Gray matter,** by comparison, refers to protein growth within the neuron cell body. The dendrites also continue to grow and branch, as evidenced in the changes seen in Figure 2–4a and b. In fact, more than 80% of dendrite branching occurs after birth. In addition, the number of synapses expands, along with a corresponding increase in the volume of neurotransmitters within the synaptic spaces.

After birth the neurons begin to cluster, as seen in Figure 2–4c; forming neural forests (Barnes, 1986). These clusters add to neural efficiency and to the complexity of mental functions. Through the process of **pruning,** neural connections that are redundant or underused are eliminated, allowing the neurochemical energy to be consolidated in areas of higher activity. This pruning is particularly evident from preadolescence through the early years of adolescence (Conel, 1939–1963).

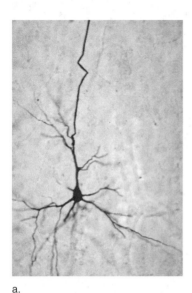 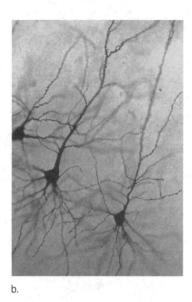 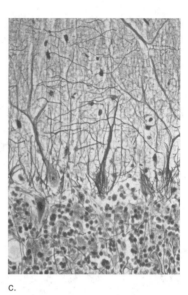

a.   b.   c.

■ **FIGURE 2–4   Changes in the body and interconnections of neurons: (a) By birth, neuron production ceases; (b) the branching between neurons and cell mylineation continues to develop; (c) as development progresses, neuron clusters or forests form, increasing the efficiency of neurological functioning.**

Beyond the changes in the microstructure, there are important transformations in the macrostructure of the brain during the first years of life (see Figure 2–5). At birth the midbrain, brain stem, and spinal cord are the most developed areas of the neurological system. In fact, the spinal cord and brain stem are almost fully myelinated by birth. These portions of the "lower" brain are involved in regulating infants' sleeping and waking states and simple biological functions such as breathing and digestion (Eliot, 1999). Soon after birth the midbrain undergoes myelination, followed by the cerebellum, which is fully myelinated by age 2. This pattern of development continues as the thalamus and other regions increase in their myelination soon after birth. The remaining regions of the brain—including the cortex and the hippocampus, which are involved in reasoning, memory, and other higher order processes—are among the last to become fully myelinated (Luria, 1980). These regions of the brain are also involved in the control of emotions, which might explain why infants and young children are emotionally expressive long before they learn how to regulate those emotions. The development of white matter extends into adolescence or early adulthood for the higher order cortical regions.

The specialization that occurs for components of the microstructure also applies to the macrostructure of the brain (Berninger & Richards, 2002). At the broadest level, that specialization takes the form of lateralization. **Lateralization** refers to the particular functions associated with the right and left sides, or hemispheres, of the cerebrum (see Figure 2–5), which are connected by the corpus callosum. Through the corpus callosum these left and right sides of the brain communicate.

Although there are other conduits for communication, cross-hemisphere interaction via the corpus callosum is essential for normal brain functioning, as evidenced by split-brain studies, in which the performance of patients suffering trauma to one side of the brain has been investigated (Springer & Deutsch, 1985). Perhaps no clinical case is more famous than that of railroad worker Phineas Gage. Gage had the misfortune to end up with a 13.5-pound, 3-foot-7-inch tamping iron driven through his skull when an explosive charge went off prematurely. To the amazement of his fellow workers and the medical community, Gage sur-

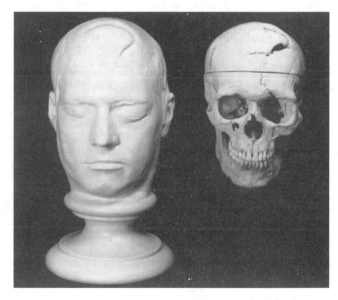

Phineas Gage is perhaps the best known case study in brain lateralization.

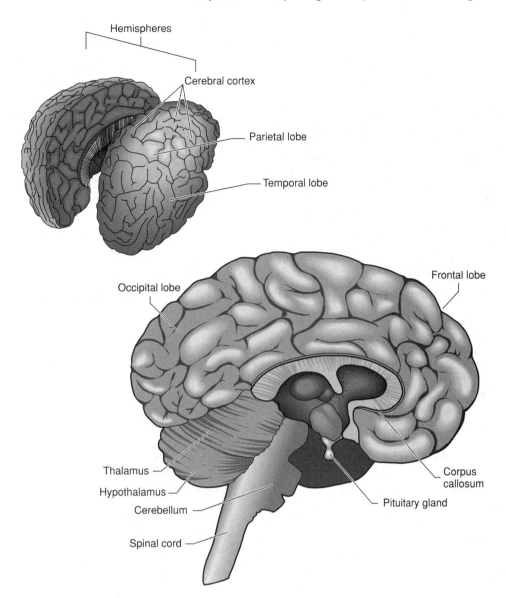

■ FIGURE 2–5   Areas of the mature brain.

vived this horrific accident. However, his personality and social behaviors were dramatically altered. The once hard-working and socially engaging individual became rude and lazy. He also lived the rest of his life under the microscope, providing the medical and psychological research communities with a unique opportunity to study brain lateralization and specialization.

Particular sections within the topography of the brain have been linked to certain cognitive functions (see Figure 2–6). Two of the best known are the Broca and Wernicke areas, both of which are involved in linguistic ability (Pinker, 2002). In the mid-1800s Broca, a neurologist, realized that the folds and convolutions he observed in patients were not random but followed discernible patterns. He also determined that patients with damage to one particular area in the left frontal lobe

could understand spoken language but were no longer able to speak fluently. This region became known as the Broca's area.

Another neurologist, Wernicke, made a comparable discovery about a region of the left temporal lobe. Wernicke found that patients with damage to this area could produce language but could not comprehend what others said. Wernicke's area, as it is called, and the Broca's area are connected deep within the cerebral cortex, contributing to the ability to produce and receive verbal language with understanding.

Each hemisphere of the cerebrum is divided into five lobes with specialized functions, including those displayed in Figure 2–6. These functions have been mapped by correlating damage to certain regions with a loss of specific abilities or dramatic changes in personality, as in the case of

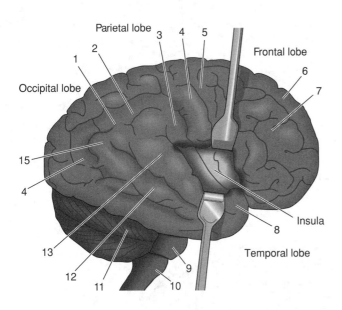

Parietal lobe

Frontal lobe

Occipital lobe

Insula

Temporal lobe

1. Reading
2. Somatic association area
3. Speech (Wernicke's area)
4. Primary sensor area
5. Primary motor area
6. Frontal association area
7. Speech (Broca's area)
8. Olfaction
9. Pons
10. Medulla oblongata
11. Cerebellum
12. Auditory association area
13. Hearing
14. Vision
15. Visual association area

■ **FIGURE 2–6   Mapping of brain functions.**

Phineas Gage. In addition, brain mappings have been performed by tracking the flow of blood to various regions during the performance of certain mental tasks, like reading or mathematical calculations.

This notion of brain specialization is linked to another important feature of brain development that carries into the postnatal period—plasticity (Barnes, 1986). **Plasticity** is the way in which the brain adapts or adjusts in response to experiences. Although some measure of plasticity is always present in the neurological system, the brain is most plastic prior to and soon after birth (Eliot, 1999). There have even been rare cases in which infants who have had a substantial portion of one hemisphere removed are able to function relatively normally in later life (Pinker, 2002). The adaptability of the brain is also seen in individuals who have lost the use of a sense or a limb. For example, those who have lost sight neurologically develop their ability to read through other senses.

Plasticity comes with both advantages and disadvantages (Sigelman & Shaffer, 1995). On the plus side, the neural

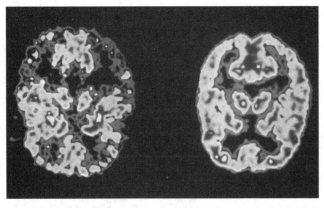

During brain activity particular regions show evidence of increased blood flow.

pathways are highly sensitive to the stimulation provided by experiences. Those connections that are triggered by the environment become reinforced or strengthened, whereas those that are not stimulated disappear. In addition, a high level of plasticity permits neurons loosely committed to certain functions to assume other neural duties when difficulties such as trauma or disease arise (Pinker, 2002).

On the down side, there are clearly limits to the brain's ability to readjust; the brain is not completely malleable. As Pinker (2002) puts it, the brain is not "silly putty" that can take on any shape or function. Further, plasticity calls attention to how fragile the brain is, especially the brain of a fetus or a young child (Eliot, 1999). Poor nutrition, a lack of positive stimulation, or negative experiences can all have long-term and far-reaching effects on a developing child.

Neurological Development and Schooling

The ideas regarding the brain and its role in human learning and development that have crossed the threshold into educational practice are often oversimplified and unsupported claims that have little in common with research findings (Berninger & Corine, 1998). What, then, can teachers take into the classroom to guide the day-to-day learning and development of their students? The burgeoning literature on neurology—still in its infancy—provides an answer.

Although Much of Brain Development Occurs In Utero or Soon After Birth, the Years of Schooling Are Associated with Significant Changes in the Neurological System   Teachers from pre-K through college enter their students' lives at a time when myelination of critical regions of the brain is occurring (Eliot, 1999), contributing to more effective and efficient mental functioning. Even the most ardent believer in the biological bases of human development must acknowledge the roles played by experience and stimulation of the neurological system (Pinker, 1997). In addition, because the interconnections among neurons either strengthen or fade in response to experiences during the school years (Pressley & McCormick, 1995), educators need to create learning environments that provide adequate practice of fundamental mental processes and that stimulate higher level thinking.

Because of the Complexity and Interconnectivity of the Brain, Stimulation of the Neurological System by Multiple Modalities Seems Advisable Berninger and Richards (2002), authors of *Brain Literacy for Educators and Psychologists*, offer recommendations for forging a learning environment that is conducive to the maturing brain. They discuss the importance of using multiple modes of representation (e.g., visual or verbal) and varied coding systems (e.g., numeric or linguistic) when designing instructional materials and approaches, especially for students for whom existing pedagogical processes have not worked effectively. As these researchers note, the brain is a complex organ that receives and stores information in many modalities and also incorporates redundancy into information processing. Thus, it makes sense for teachers to appeal to those characteristics by presenting relevant subject matter in multiple modalities, drawing on the neurological versatility and redundancy that already exists.

For All of Its Potential and Sophistication, the Brain Remains a Fragile, Living Organ That Needs Care and Attention The brain of a mature adult is a pinkish, rather gelatinous, and quite vulnerable organ. According to Satinover (2001), "The brain is not really a single organ but a vertical stack of them, the newer ones above the older in evolutionary order, with the latest spread out on top" (p. 9). But whether it is one organ or several, the brain is a living entity that can be damaged by trauma, disease, or a lack of proper nutrition. Given the importance of the brain to a rich and fulfilling life, everyone should take whatever steps are necessary to ensure the health of this organ and the neurological system. Teachers can help their students understand the effects of poor nutrition on subsequent development, as well as the havoc that drugs, alcohol, and other substances can wreak on the neurological system.

Transformations in the Microstructure and the Macrostructure of the Brain Have Correlates in Phases of Physical, Motor, Cognitive, and Linguistic Development Models of motor development, stages of cognitive development, theories of moral reasoning—all these topics of subsequent discussion—have parallels to the changes unfolding in brain development (H. Epstein, 2001). Not only are mind and brain intertwined, but so are neurological development and other forms of human development. What remains open to question is whether those developmental parallels are purely coincidental or whether their co-occurrence suggests an underlying cause-and-effect relation,

with neurological development contributing to the onset of physical, motor, cognitive, and social/emotional changes.

Against the background of this discussion of the nature and structure of the brain, you should revisit the questions posed earlier in this chapter in the Thought Experiment: A Little Brain Teaser. See how much you have learned about the brain and its development.

Physical Development

Physical development represents the "growth and aging of the body, including changes in physiological functioning of the body's organs and in motor abilities" (Sigelman & Shaffer, 1995, p. 533). There are two periods in the course of human development when the body undergoes particularly rapid physical transformation: the first during the first several years of life and the second during adolescence (Seifert, Hoffnung, & Hoffnung, 1997). By the time students enter adolescence, they are twice the weight they were in childhood and more than a foot taller (J. M. Tanner, 1991).

The Patterns of Physical Maturation

The average newborn weighs about 7.5 pounds and is around 20 inches long—a fraction of adult stature. Remarkably, by the time children reach 2 years of age, they have already gained around 20% of their adult height and weight. Along with the magnitude of this change, there are specific directions in which this physical maturation moves from conception through childhood.

Cephalocaudal Development

Cephalocaudal development means that physical change from infancy through adolescence moves downward, from head (*cephalic*) to tail (*caudal*), as seen in Figure 2–7. In this depiction the ratio of the head to the body is much greater for the fetuses and the infant than for the adolescent and the adult. An understanding of brain development corroborates this pattern, with much of maturation during the prenatal and infancy periods focused on the neurological system. It is not surprising, therefore, that at birth the head accounts for about 25% of the body length. Later in children's maturation, the trunk and then the legs evidence the fastest growth. By the time individuals reach adulthood, the head accounts for only 12% of body length, whereas the legs constitute about 50% of adult stature.

Proximodistal Development

At the same time that this head-to-tail development is occurring, the human body is growing from the center outward, a process known as **proximodistal development.** Inside the womb of a growing fetus, the organs and chest take shape before the arms, hands, and fingers form (Seifert et al., 1997). This pattern of development explains the soft and pliable nature of the bones in young children's

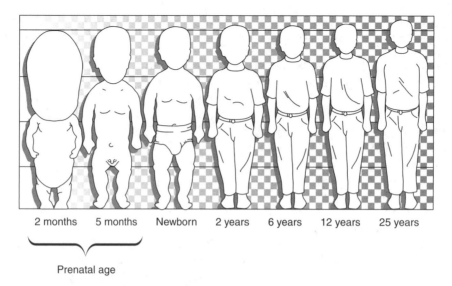

2 months   5 months   Newborn   2 years   6 years   12 years   25 years

Prenatal age

■ **FIGURE 2–7   Depiction of cephalocaudal development.**

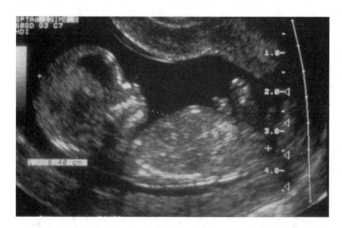

Within the womb the head of the fetus is predominant, and the organs and chest form before the extremities.

extremities, one reason that they cannot immediately stand or walk after birth, unlike other species. Only after the bones have hardened through ossification and have become proportionally larger do children have the strength and balance needed for motor control.

Secular Trend

One other pattern in physical development illustrates the interrelation between maturation and environmental conditions (Sigelman & Shaffer, 1995): A shift has occurred in the rate of human development across generations. In other words, while the directional patterns of physical development have remained consistent across the centuries, the time required for those transformations and their magnitude have changed. Because of its historical nature, this pattern is called a **secular trend** (Meece, 2002), much like the trends discussed in Chapter 1.

Basically, humans growing up in industrial and postindustrial societies are taller and heavier than their ancestors and are reaching puberty and full stature sooner. Historical displays of clothing and furnishings from the 1700s and 1800s make such generational changes readily apparent. Today's individuals stand 2 inches to 3 inches taller on average than those living in the 1700s. The weight and girth of the average citizen has also expanded (Seifert et al., 1997). In fact, efforts are underway to change the size of seats in public places, such as movie theaters and airplanes, to accommodate a physically expanding population.

Factors Affecting Puberty   Today's children are achieving puberty much sooner than their predecessors. In the late 1800s, menarche, or the onset of menstruation, occurred around 16 years of age. By the early 1900s, the average age of menarche was just over 14, whereas today menarche usually occurs around 12 years of age. Overall, puberty now begins between 11 and 16 years of age for males and between 8 and 11 years of age for females (Gallahue & Ozmun, 1998; Schickedanz, Schickedanz, Forsyth, & Forsyth, 2001).

Both biological and environmental factors seem to underline this more rapid onset of puberty. Biologically, genes play a significant role in the onset of puberty. The hypothalamus is genetically programmed to trigger production of hormones in the endocrine system. During childhood the levels of male (e.g., testosterone) and female (e.g., progesterone) hormones are relatively comparable. The onset of puberty brings a significant rise in gender-specific hormones for males and females (Sigelman & Shaffer, 1995).

Environmental factors, including better nutrition and health care, have also helped to accelerate the onset of puberty. Countries relatively free from malnutrition and growth-retarding diseases have populations that reach puberty sooner than do those in countries plagued by such undesirable conditions. Even within relatively affluent countries like the United

States, the effects of poverty on physical maturation are still evidenced. For instance, malnourished adolescents in the United States reach puberty later than those who are well fed (Meece, 2002).

In addition, the increased weight of the population is an important factor in the changing rates of puberty, especially for females. A certain ratio of body fat to muscle tissue is required before females' bodies respond to the hormones that trigger menarche (Frisch, 1991). For that reason girls who have more body fat and are less physically active may experience the onset of puberty before girls who are lean or are physically engaged. Thus, young girls highly involved in gymnastics or other athletic endeavors may remain physically immature longer than their peers. Even adult women who are aggressively involved in sports, such as marathon running, may not experience regular menstrual cycles (Frisch, Wyshak, & Vincent, 1980).

Obesity   The rate of weight gain within industrial and postindustrial societies, especially the United States, has become a cause for concern among health professionals (American Academy of Pediatrics, 2003). **Obesity** is a condition that exists when a person's body weight exceeds the norm for that individual's age, sex, and height by more than 20% (AAP, 2003). Obesity is becoming an increasing problem for all demographic groups, including young children.

The rate at which obesity has afflicted children and adolescents in the United States is astonishing, increasing from 17.6% of 6- to 12-year-olds in the 1960s to 29% in the 1990s. This exceptional rate of change is evidence that the problem of obesity cannot be laid solely or even largely at the feet of genetics (Schickedanz et al., 2001). Instead, multiple conditions are contributing to this unhealthy trend among children and youth; for example, a lack of vigorous and routine exercise and poor nutritional habits. The AAP (2003) found that this problem is even greater for girls, minorities, and those living in poverty.

The prevalence of childhood overweight and obesity is increasing at an alarming rate in the United States as well as in other developed and developing countries. Prevalence among children and adolescents has doubled in the past 2 decades in the United States. Currently, 15.3% of 6- to 11-year-olds and 15.5% of 12- to 19-year-olds are at or above the 95th percentile for [Body Mass Index] on standard growth charts based on reference data from the 1970s, with even higher rates among subpopulations of minority and economically disadvantaged children (Ogden, Flegal, Carroll, & Johnson, 2002; United States Department of Health and Human Services, 2001). Recent data from the Centers for Disease Control and Prevention also indicate that children younger than 5 years across all ethnic groups have had significant increases in the prevalence of overweight and obesity (Mel, Scanlon, Grummer-Strawn, Freedman, Yip, & Trowbridge, 1998; Ogden, Troiano, Breifel, Kuczmarski, Flegal, & Johnson, 1997). (American Academy of Pediatrics, 2003, pp. 424–425)

Motor Development

As the physical body is growing and maturing, individuals also experience motor development. **Motor development** is "the change in motor behavior over the lifespan and the processes that underlie that change" (Clark, 1994, p. 245). Motor development actually entails two related phenomena: motor control and motor learning. **Motor control** pertains to the interconnections between the physical body and the neurological system (Gabbard, 2004); motor control represents the body and the brain working in sync (Connolly & Forssberg, 1997). **Motor learning** refers to the noticeable improvements in movements that arise from the interaction between maturation and life experiences (Clark & Metcalfe, 2002). The motor learning that individuals achieve, especially in the later phases of development, reflects their repeated participation in select physical activities.

Leading researchers in motor development agree that there is a discernible sequence to motor development, even though there is some variability in the specific periods identified (Connolly & Forssberg, 1997; Gallahue & Donnelly, 2003). In general, that sequence begins with simple reflexes and progresses to increasingly more sophisticated and specialized movements until later adulthood. Six critical periods of motor development are identified in the research of Jane Clark and colleagues (Clark, 1994; Clark & Whitall, 1989): reflexive, preadapted, fundamental, context-specific, skillful, and compensation. Clark and Metcalfe (2002) refer to this continuous life-span sequence as a mountain of motor development, which is depicted in Figure 2–8. Although there are relative ages attached to each of these periods, such ages are only rough approximations. The demonstration of particular motor abilities (e.g., walking) or biological changes (e.g., onset of puberty) more accurately demark each phase of motor development.

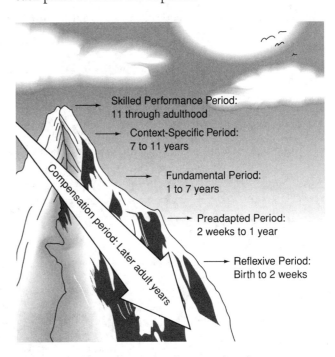

Skilled Performance Period:
11 through adulthood

Context-Specific Period:
7 to 11 years

Fundamental Period:
1 to 7 years

Preadapted Period:
2 weeks to 1 year

Reflexive Period:
Birth to 2 weeks

Compensation period: Later adult years

■ **FIGURE 2–8   Mountain of motor development.**

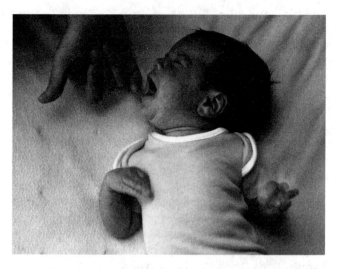

In rooting, a survival reflex, newborns instinctively turn their faces in the direction of a touch.

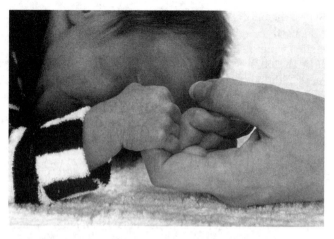

When an object comes into contact with infants' palms, they involuntarily curl their fingers around the object. This primitive reflex is called the Palmar grasp.

Reflexive Period

The reflexive period is all about a newborn's initial response to the new world outside the womb. For the first few weeks after birth, motor development is reflexive, or spontaneous in nature, as the newborn experiences an environment less physically constrained than the one occupied during gestation. **Reflexes** are automatic, or involuntary, reactions to specific stimuli that appear to be genetically hardwired. **Spontaneous actions** are common, simple actions, like waving or thrashing, that do not appear to be connected to any specific stimuli (Clark, 1994).

Variations in reflexes first take shape during the reflexive period (J. M. Tanner, 1990). For instance, certain reflexes stay for a lifetime (e.g., blinking or knee jerking), whereas others fade away in infancy or early childhood (e.g., sucking or rooting). Some reflexes appear to be central to human survival, such as those associated with breathing, blinking, or sucking. Such responses are aptly termed *survival reflexes* (Haywood, 1993). In contrast, some reflexes seem to be remnants of an evolutionary past with little direct role in contemporary human survival. These *primitive reflexes*, like the Palmar grasp, tend to disappear in the first months of life as the cortical areas of the brain continue to be myelinated (H. T. Epstein, 2001).

Preadapted Period

The second critical period of motor development, which extends throughout the first year of life, is the preadapted period. During this time infants learn how to perform rudimentary bodily movements within the constraints of their neurophysiological capacity. These rudimentary movements, displayed in Figure 2–9, include sitting up, crawling, creeping,

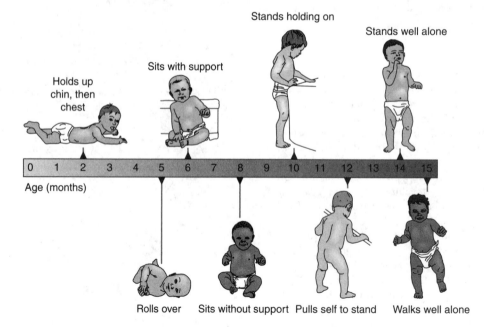

■ FIGURE 2–9   The appearance of rudimentary movements: motor development milestones.

standing, and walking. These movements are common to all healthy, normally developing children (J. M. Tanner, 1990).

According to Clark (1994), infants have three core motor problems to solve in order to master the rudimentary movements of this phase: locomotion, manipulation, and posture. Specifically, infants must acquire the ability to move through the environment (locomotion). In addition, they must be able to pick up and use objects in the environment (manipulation). However, before infants can tackle locomotion and manipulation, they must be able to position or orient their bodies in certain ways and to maintain those orientations (posture). The problems of locomotion, manipulation, and posture are directly linked to cephalocaudal and proximodistal development, as discussed earlier. In effect, changes in the head-to-body ratio and the continued maturation of the extremities and the skeletal system allow infants and young children to move, stand upright, grasp, and maintain equilibrium (Haywood, 1993). The preadapted period concludes when infants achieve the ability to walk and feed themselves without help.

Fundamental Period

Once rudimentary movements are mastered, young children have more command of their environment and are able to expand their repertoire of motor skills (J. Keogh & Sugden, 1985). At this point children enter the fundamental period of motor development, which typically extends through early childhood and allows for the strengthening of certain rudimentary movements and the introduction of new motor abilities. Thus, children who learned to stand and walk during the rudimentary period become more assured in their ability. In addition, they acquire the ability to run, skip, hop, and even dance around the room. They also learn how to feed and dress themselves more effectively and to use implements like scissors or crayons (Haywood, 1993). The skills acquired during this period have been described as the building blocks of later skilled motor performance (Clark, 1994).

The abilities to skip or to color a picture represent different levels of motor skill development. Specifically, activities such as standing, walking, running, or skipping are referred to as *gross motor skills* because they involve the control of large muscles of the body to move the arms, legs, or head. *Fine motor skills* pertain to the movement and regulation of small muscles of the body, such as those required to grasp and hold objects with the fingers. These fine motor skills are important to schooling in which activities such as holding a pencil, writing letters, or manipulating the pages of a book are routine practices.

Context-Specific Period

The context-specific period follows the fundamental period and often concludes at the onset of adolescence when target skills are attained. Clark and Metcalfe (2002) describe this phase as a transition between the acquisition of fundamental motor skills and highly skilled performance. Throughout the context-specific period, fundamental movements undergo continued refinement dependent on the biological and environmental constraints that individuals face. The degree or rate of refinement will correspond to the neurological and physiological development being experienced (H. T. Epstein, 2001).

However, some degree of motor control and learning will also be directly related to opportunities for physical activity. Thus, the context-specific period, unlike preceding phases, is not universal. Rather, the achievement of this and subsequent phases of motor development will depend in part on the level of involvement in particular physical activities (e.g., running or throwing), which in turn will be linked to specific physical propensities, abilities, talents, motivations, and experiential opportunities (J. Keogh & Sugden, 1985).

Often the particular movements learned during this phase develop as a result of involvement in sports. For example, young people might begin to play soccer and acquire the ability to pass a ball to another player by kicking it with their feet or butting it with their heads. Other youngsters playing baseball learn how to hold and swing a bat and to catch a line drive. Engagement in any athletic activity typically entails learning new motor skills that extend beyond fundamental movements. Running may be a part of many sports—including soccer, baseball, gymnastics, and track—but each task may require the participant to run differently or to use other parts of the body while engaged in running.

Engagement in specific physical activities during the context-specific period has more benefits than the simple acquisition of particular motor skills. It can also affect preadolescents' and young adolescents' physiological and neurological development (Dyer, 1977). In other words, the effects of routine participation in certain physical activities help shape the body, especially as youths begin to undergo their second significant growth spurt (J. M. Tanner, 1991). Such activity is apt to increase body and muscle mass in certain areas, while reducing the likelihood of obesity, which plagues so many sedentary teens (AAP, 2003).

In addition, during late childhood and early adolescence, the myelination of the cortical areas associated with higher order functions occurs (Luria, 1980). Thus, regular engagement in physical activities that call upon students to reason and problem solve could potentially stimulate those areas of neural development. There may even be social benefits to regular physical engagement; for instance, the need to work with others sharing a similar goal can provide avenues for social development (Wentzel, 1999).

Skillful Period

Another level of refinement that typically occurs with the onset of adolescence and progresses into the adult years is called the skillful period. "When a movement is performed efficiently, consistently and with adaptive versatility," it is considered skillful (Clark, 1994, p. 242). As with the prior phase, this period of motor development is context specific. It is also selective because not all individuals will reach this point in their motor development; years of continued and effective practice are required, along with a certain level of physical and neurological potential. Thus, this period has also been described as the peak performance period because it reflects the achievement of high competence or expertise in select arenas of activity (Haywood, 1993).

Although any number of individuals can participate in specific sports, a more restricted number will reach peak status. The continued involvement, general health, physical stamina, and motivation required to maintain growth and development in athletic endeavors are tremendous. When those factors are combined with the need for specific talents or well-honed skills, it is understandable that few reach and maintain an elite level of motor development (Clark & Metcalfe, 2002).

Compensation Period

From the reflexive period through the skillful period, motor control and motor learning are continually improving and becoming more refined and specialized. However, with age, trauma, or disease, the physical and neurological processes at the root of motor development show decline. During the compensation period, the biological and environmental constraints on motor performance increase, requiring individuals to adapt compensatory behaviors. For example, an elderly individual with hip problems may come to rely on a cane or a walker for improved mobility.

Although the compensation period is typically associated with older adulthood, it can occur at any time as a result of illness, trauma, or genetic disorder. Typical constraints associated with this period include a loss of stamina, strength, agility, and cardiovascular health, all of which underlie locomotion, manipulation, and posture. Even the quickness of mental processing and sensory abilities integral to motor learning become constrained. When these conditions arise, individuals enter the compensation period, which continues through the remainder of the life span. Characteristically, individuals must work ever harder to counter the biological and neurological constraints that are expanding.

Like the reflexive, preadapted, and fundamental periods, the compensation period will be experienced by all individuals. However, the onset or rate of compensation is highly variable, particularly given the increased life span of those living in industrial and postindustrial societies, as discussed in Chapter 1 (Haywood, 1993). Factors affecting the onset or severity of motor decline include the level of physical wellness individuals have achieved, their genetic predisposition to physical or mental disabilities, and the environmental conditions under which they have lived. In light of the importance of continued motor activity to a healthy and rewarding life, individuals are encouraged to explore alternative means of physical behavior when existing avenues are no longer accessible (Clark & Metcalfe, 2002).

Physical Development and Schooling

In the opening scenario, it may be evident why Pam Bechtel, a health and physical education teacher, is concerned with her students' physical development. However, the nurturance of physical development is the responsibility of all teachers, because students' bodies and minds are interconnected (Pinker, 2002). The growth and maturation of one of these realms of

> *Our growing softness, our increasing lack of physical fitness, is a menace to our security.*
>
> John F. Kennedy

human development affects the growth and maturation of the other. Several principles for optimal teaching and learning pertain directly to students' physical and motor development.

Wellness Should Be Promoted as Part of the School Culture   Concern for optimal physical development is not restricted to the hours students spend in health and physical education classes but must be part of the entire school culture—a culture committed to physical and mental wellness. **Wellness** means more than the prevention or correction of problems, such as the problem of obesity among school-age populations (AAP, 2003). A school culture devoted to wellness guarantees a healthy and safe learning environment for students—a drug-free, violence-free, and chemical-free (e.g., asbestos or lead) zone (National Center for Chronic Disease Prevention and Health Promotion, 2003). Such a school employs faculty and staff who are knowledgeable about and able to address students' nutritional and physical needs. It also ensures that all students face their academic studies well fed (Actions for Healthy Kids, 2003). Such a concern includes the food served by or made accessible through the schools. These components and others are central to creating healthy schools that nurture the whole student and create healthy habits that can stimulate positive physical development across the life span.

The Body and Mind Should Work Together Within the Learning Environment   Early-childhood teachers have long appreciated the importance of physical and motor activities as part of the learning process (C. S. White & Coleman, 2000). From gross-motor (e.g., large-block center) to fine-motor (e.g., cutting and pasting) activities, these early-childhood teachers understand that little children's bodies should naturally be involved in their learning. As these children progress through the educational system, however, this appreciation for mind/body relations can easily get lost in the focus on subjects such as reading and mathematics. Bringing movement into the classroom does not mean requiring jumping jacks in reading or sit-ups in history; there can be reasonable opportunities for physical engagement outside physical education classes. For instance, because it is difficult for preadolescents and adolescents to sit for hours on end, these students should have sufficient time to stand and move during transitions between lesson components or between classes. There should also be occasions before, during, or after school to enhance the context-specific abilities that are taking shape. Even the physical arrangement of a room and the movement it affords should be given consideration by teachers at all levels of schooling. Are the desks or chairs comfortable, accommodating the size and shape of students? Are the materials in the room accessible, arranged to be conducive to safety and mobility?

Teachers Should Be Role Models of Physical Wellness
Perhaps the most important guideline for teachers concerned with their students' physical development is to see themselves as wellness role models (Santrock, 2001). Just as

teachers should model desired behaviors or strategies in reading, mathematics, or other academic areas, they should try to exemplify the healthy lifestyle they want to see in their students. James Santrock (2001) offers a self-assessment for educators to gauge whether they are serving as positive role models with regard to overall physical and mental wellness. That self-assessment is presented in the Thought Experiment: A Wellness Self-Assessment, which follows. You may want to see how you measure up.

Thought Experiment ....

A Wellness Self-Assessment

Directions: Use the following brief assessment to evaluate your health in four areas: exercise/fitness, eating habits, alcohol/drug use and cigarette smoking, and stress control.

A=almost always   S=sometimes   N=almost never   A   S   N

Exercise/Fitness

1. I maintain a desired weight and avoid being overweight or underweight.

2. I do vigorous exercise (such as running, swimming, walking briskly) for 15 to 30 minutes at least 3 times a week.

3. I do exercises that improve my muscle tone (e.g., yoga, calisthenics, lifting weights) for 15 to 30 minutes at least 3 times a week.

4. I use part of my leisure time to participate in individual, family, or team activities that increase my fitness level (e.g., gardening, bowling, golf, baseball).

Eating Habits

5. I eat a variety of foods each day, such as fruits and vegetables, whole-grain breads and cereals, lean meats, dairy products, peas and beans, and nuts and seeds.

6. I limit the amount of fat, saturated fat, and cholesterol I eat.

7. I limit the amount of salt I eat.

8. I avoid eating too much sugar, especially frequent candy snacks or soft drinks.

Alcohol/Drugs, Smoking

9. I avoid drinking alcoholic beverages or drink no more than one or two drinks a day.

10. I avoid using alcohol or other drugs as a way of handling stressful situations or problems in my life.

11. I avoid smoking cigarettes or using other nicotine substances.

Stress Control

12. I have a job or do other work that I enjoy.

13. I find it easy to relax and express my feelings freely.

14. I have good resources, such as close friends or relatives, whom I call on in times of stress.

15. I participate in group activities (e.g., church or community organizations) or hobbies that I enjoy.

Scoring and Interpretation

Give yourself 3 points for each item you answered A (almost always), 2 points for each S (sometimes), and 1 point for each N (almost never) answer. If you scored 40–45, your physical and mental health should be excellent; you will be a good wellness role model for your students. If you scored 35–39, your physical and mental health should be good, and you are likely to be a good health role model for your students; however, there are some areas you can improve. If you scored 30–34, your physical and mental health need some work; there are too many aspects of your physical and mental health that you practice only some of the time or do not practice at all. Work on improving these habits to be a good health role model for students. If you scored below 30, you likely will be a poor health role model for students. Give some serious thought to getting yourself in better physical and mental shape; your students will benefit from your efforts. Regardless of your total score, examine the pattern of your scores. For example, you might have excellent physical health habits and weak mental health habits. Or you might fall down just in one area of physical health, such as exercise/fitness. Everyone has room to improve.

Note: From *Educational Psychology* (p. 45) by J. W. Santrock, 2001, Boston: McGraw Hill. Copyright 2001 by McGraw Hill. Adapted with permission.

• •

■ Summary Reflections

What is development? What are the defining themes in human development?

■ Three central themes about human change remain constant: source, continuity, and stability.

■ Four orientations address the source, or cause, of physical, cognitive, and social/emotional changes.
  • To biological determinists, such as Freud, changes reflect neurological and physiological natures.
  • The environmental shaping perspective, represented by Watson, focuses on the environment.
  • For Piaget development reflects how humans actively adapt to their environments through their mental processing—both nature and nurture.
  • Cultural contextualists like Vygotsky emphasize the broader sociocultural context—social interactions and social addresses.

■ Continuity considers the character, or landscape, of developmental change.
  • Human development may unfold gradually, that is, continuous.
  • It may occur in dramatic leaps and bounds, that is, discontinuous.

■ Stability deals with the degree to which physical, cognitive, and social/emotional characteristics differentiate individuals.
  • Those characteristics may be modifiable or indicative of exceptionality.
  • Galton is considered the father of individual difference research.

What are the biological bases of development?

■ The brain forms the centerpiece of the neurological system and is strongly linked to physical, cognitive, and social/emotional development.

  • Much critical brain development unfolds during the prenatal period.
  • The macrostructure (e.g., cerebral cortex) and microstructure (e.g., neurons) develop rapidly.
  • Neurons have common structures—a cell body, dendrites, an axon, and a myelin sheath.

■ Brain development involves the increase in white matter and gray matter.
  • The systematic buildup of white matter through myelination corresponds to increased mental capabilities.
  • It is important to provide learning activities that are mentally stimulating and that present information through multiple modalities.

■ Physical development follows three important directions.
  • Two directions are genetically triggered: the body grows from head to tail (cephalocaudal) and from the inside out (proximodistal).
  • The third pattern (secular trend) results from the interaction of maturation and the environment.

■ Motor development entails both motor control and motor learning.
  • During the reflexive period (0–2 weeks) and the preadapted period (2 weeks to 1 year) infants learn to master the environment outside the womb.
  • In the fundamental (1–7 years) and the context-specific periods (7–11 years), children acquire more sophisticated and particularized movements and skills.
  • The skillful period (11–adult) is about honing abilities to the level of expertise.
  • During the compensation period, declines in motor abilities are addressed through compensatory actions.

■ Answer Key to Thought Experiment: A Little Brain Teaser

1. c

The average adult brain weighs about 3 lbs.

2. d

The healthy functioning brain is rather pink and gelatinous.

3. a, d, and e

The key elements include the axon, dendrites, and cell body. Neurotransmitters are chemicals found within the synapses, and convolutions are the folds of the cerebral cortex.

4. True

The decade of the 1990s, in particular, produced many new findings about the brain.

5. True

Although neurons change in size and weight well into adolescence, their number does not increase after birth or soon thereafter.

6. False

There is a great deal of redundancy in brain activities, even though areas of the brain are more involved in certain activities than others.

7. True

Because of the plasticity of the fetal or infant brain, a loss of function due to trauma to certain areas can sometimes be compensated for by other brain regions that take on new or expanded functions.

8. True

The course of brain development is correlated to changes in physical, motor, cognitive, and social/emotional abilities.

Chapter 3

Understanding Cognitive and Social/Emotional Development

GUIDING QUESTIONS

- How does the mind change with age and experience?
- What are the patterns in the way students grow socially, emotionally, and morally?
- What developmental principles should guide instruction for early-childhood, middle-school, and high-school students?

IN THEIR OWN WORDS

As a middle-school teacher in a rural Virginia county, I directed an alternative reading and mathematics program for fourth- to sixth-grade students with an array of special needs.

To others at Stony Ridge Middle School, we were affectionately known as "Mom's Zoo." I guess to the outside world we must have truly looked like an odd collection of humanity. All of the students who came to the "family"—that's what we called ourselves—needed more attention than my fellow teachers at Stony Ridge could give them in their classrooms.

Each of my 16 students was a case study in exceptionality. For instance, there was Sam, a fifth grader who could only read or write at a kindergarten level, and Jackie, a sixth grader who scored below the second-grade level in reading and mathematics. At the other end of the spectrum, there was Carole, who blew the top off every achievement, intelligence, and aptitude test the district gave her, and Bart, who could perform complex mathematics before the age of 4.

The students were socially and morally different as well. For example, both Randy and Steve, two of my sixth graders, had already been institutionalized. Randy had been in the state institution for severely emotionally disturbed children for over a year. Because he injured one of his caretakers, he was removed from that facility and returned to Stony Ridge. Steve had done time in juvenile facilities for petty crimes like shoplifting and vandalism.

That is where I came in. Because of my success in teaching some of the "tougher" cases, my interest in exceptionalities, and my willingness to experiment with alternative approaches, the school administrators turned to me. They gave me the opportunity to create an alternative program for those students not adequately served by the standard curriculum—the gifted and the challenged. The administration's request of me was simple: "Do what you can to meet the individual needs of these special students in reading and mathematics." Needless to say, my colleagues at Stony Ridge thought I had holes in my head. Who would ever put these extremes together in one classroom? What kind of educational program could I create for such a conglomeration? But from the beginning I was excited about working with these fringe children—those on the edges of cognitive and social/emotional normality.

There were noticeable successes and disappointments. After 2 years Sam was reading at a fourth-grade level, and Steve had apparently turned his life around. Bart went to Harvard after his sophomore year of high school, and Carole was the valedictorian of her university class and later Virginia's teacher of the year. However, Randy and his family dropped out of sight after 1 year, and I heard some years later that he ended up in the state penitentiary.

When I think back on this program, which was the most rewarding and exciting experience of my educational career, I have tried to understand why it worked so well. One reason was that we believed we were responsible for each other's successes and setbacks. That meant we would use whatever abilities or energies we had to help one another. Sam's achievements were also Bart's, and Randy's problems were also Carole's. We believed that we were much more than a collection of statistical outliers struggling alone in an educational context. We were truly a family learning together.

In retrospect, I realize that some of that success must have been beginner's luck. I had had some preparation in development, but that was sketchy. I know now that I would have been far better prepared for this challenge if I had been better versed in cognitive and social/emotional development. Not only would I have been better equipped to determine the specific strengths and needs of those wonderful students, but I also would have been better able to outline instructional approaches well suited to them. A small part of me wishes I could go back to that time and those students with the understanding of cognitive and social/emotional development I have today.

How Does the Mind Change with Age and Experience?

Cognitive development involves the systematic changes in the mental processes that underlie all learning and performance, including perception, reasoning, problem solving, and verbal facility. Much of what is known about cognitive development can be traced to the writings of one individual, Jean Piaget, who was introduced in Chapter 2 and who is rightly considered the father of cognitive development (Byrnes, 2001).

Piagetian Theory

Jean Piaget (1896–1980) was one of those remarkable minds that come along only rarely in human history. Even as a child, Piaget was clearly endowed with an unusual capacity to engage in systematic investigation and to build upon direct, detailed observations. While other children were playing with toys and enjoying their childhood, Piaget was already immersed in the scientific study of animals and fossils. Before he was 10, Piaget wrote a book about the birds that were found around his home in Neuchâtel, Switzerland. At 10 he prepared a report on the albino sparrow that was published in a respected scientific journal. It was perhaps inevitable that Piaget would turn his extensive knowledge of biology and his keen powers of observation to the study of the developing minds of his own children—observations that formed the basis for the first comprehensive theory of cognitive development.

As a young man, Piaget went to Paris to work with Théodore Simon and Alfred Binet to develop a standardized measure of intelligence for the French government. During his work in Simon's lab, Piaget became fascinated with the answers children gave to certain questions. What intrigued him was the similarities in the incorrect answers the children produced. Piaget considered those similarities to be nonrandom and hypothesized that such responses were evidence that young children's mental processing was qualitatively different from that of older children or adults. He devoted the rest of his professional life to testing that hypothesis and expanding it into a comprehensive theory of mental development.

Piaget's theory and research remain an enduring legacy for several reasons. First, the general descriptions that Piaget offered about the developing mind have an intuitive appeal and continue to resonate with everyday experiences. He was able to offer a reasonable explanation for what many others have witnessed in the words and behaviors of children and youth. Second, part of Piaget's genius as a developmental researcher was evidenced in his skill at devising deceptively simple tasks that effectively uncovered information about children's mental processing. Variants of these tasks are still used in developmental research (Byrnes, 2001). In one of his classic tasks, Piaget would show an infant a small toy and then, once the infant's attention was secured, cover the toy with his ever-present beret. What Piaget discovered was that babies younger than 9 months of age seem to promptly forget about the toy once it is covered—out of sight, out of mind. But around 9 months of age, children begin to realize that the toy is still there—just hidden from view. Such consistent responses to this and other tasks became the basis for Piaget's (1952) stage theory of cognitive development.

Further, as explained in Chapter 2, the perspective that Piaget forwarded on cognitive development gave individuals a direct and significant role in their own mental growth. Piaget argued that learning is not simply determined by heredity (endogenous) or dictated by life experiences (exogenous). Rather, Piaget (1952) held that new understandings result from the active and creative processing of information in the environment by the individual mind, which operates under the constraints of its mental maturation and life opportunities. Because of the unique construction of understandings produced through this active processing, Piaget's perspective on cognitive development has been labeled **cognitive constructivism** (D.C. Phillips, 1995).

> *Children have real understanding only of that which they invent themselves, and each time that we try to teach them something too quickly, we keep them from reinventing it themselves.*
>
> Jean Piaget

Key Concepts

Several concepts are central to Piaget's constructivist perspective on development: equilibration, assimilation, and accommodation. Piaget had long been fascinated with the question of where knowledge comes from, a question we will explore more fully in Chapter 4. He found that philosophical notions about the nature of knowledge did not help to unravel the mystery about how the ideas in people's minds take root and change over the course of their lifetimes. Piaget believed that the answer to that complex mystery lay in the marriage of human biology and philosophy and the field he dubbed *genetic epistemology*.

Fundamentally, Piaget saw development as a process of continuous adaptation. That is, the inner world of the mind adapts to the incongruous information or events it encounters in the external world. Piaget believed that it is human nature for individuals to strive for balance, or stasis, but he also recognized that development demanded inevitable transformations in existing understandings. Individuals must change if they are to develop. For Piaget the reconciliation of these two seemingly contradictory states—stasis and change—occurred through the process of **equilibration,** the means by which individuals incorporate new or disparate knowledge and experiences into their existing knowledge structures.

Piaget also believed that there were three essential states in this process: equilibrium, disequilibrium, and more stable equilibrium (Siegler, 1998). According to Piaget, people start in a state of *equilibrium*, or balance. Then, as new experiences arise and new information is encountered that do not replicate or reinforce existing understandings, they find themselves in a state of *disequilibrium*. They are confronting information or perceptions that do not jive with what they have known or understood about that world. For that disequilibrium to be resolved, they must find a way to reconcile the situation—to bring the internal and external worlds into realignment. That resolution can come in the form of assimilation or accommodation.

When **assimilation** occurs, the new information or experiences are absorbed by existing knowledge structures, or **schemes.** In effect, existing frames of reference are flexible enough to assimilate the new information. Perhaps that assimilation occurs because the incoming information can be shaped or transformed to fit with current understandings or because the understandings that preexisted were sufficiently vague to accept this varied experience. Recently, my granddaughter Lauren, who had just turned 3, was in child care and was learning about family relationships. On the way home from school that day, Lauren wanted to call her GaGa, the name she had given me. Once on the phone, she proudly announced: "GaGa, you are my grandma!" Lauren's scheme for GaGa had just acquired a new and seemingly important piece of information: her GaGa was also her grandma. This assimilation may have occurred because Lauren's prior understanding of the term *grandmother* had no association with her own family members or because her concept of *GaGa* was fluid enough to accept this new revelation. Whatever the reason, *GaGa* and *grandma* became linked in her mind.

Unlike the behaviorists (e.g., Watson and Skinner), who hold that individuals engage in tasks to obtain external rewards or to avoid punishments, Piaget believed that individuals want to make use of their new understandings, sometimes on a repeated basis, because of the pleasure that such learning brings. In other words, mental insights are pleasures in and of themselves. Lauren's parents did not need to prompt her to call me with her new realization. She was too excited to keep it to herself. And for weeks afterward, I was reminded that I am her grandma and she is my granddaughter. Piaget called this tendency to use new understandings *functional assimilation*.

Sometimes the process of adaptation is not as simple as the grandma example. In such cases existing schemes must be tweaked or modified if the new and conflicting information is to become part of one's internal mental world. This process is called **accommodation.** The changes in my conception of Santa Claus over the years are clear instances of accommodation. Like many young children who hear about Santa, I first envisioned him as a fat, jolly man with a white beard and a red suit. If anyone had asked me at the tender age of 5 where Santa lived, I probably would have proclaimed the North Pole. At some point, in later elementary school, I came to the realization that the idea of Santa Claus was much more abstract and cultural in nature. Thus, the very core of my prior understanding had to be altered if I was going to understand Santa in this new way. This is the nature of accommodation. For Piaget these processes of assimilation and accommodation work in tandem to permit continued cognitive development, which he believed unfolded in specific stages.

Developmental Stages

Chapter 2 described two distinct views about the continuity of change. Some see human change as a process of continuous transformation, whereas others believe that change occurs through more dramatic steps or stages. As a biologist Piaget was well aware of those two perspectives. When it came to human development, however, Piaget believed strongly in discontinuous change, arguing that critical mental transformations were necessary before higher forms of mental reasoning and problem solving could be realized. He described those critical transformations as four distinct cognitive stages: sensorimotor, preoperations, concrete operations, and formal operations (see Table 3–1).

Sensorimotor

At birth, children are transported into a new and strange world. Their initial efforts are aimed at survival and at familiarizing themselves with that new world. Thus, the body itself and the senses become the young children's primary tools of cognitive development, and growth comes through direct physical connection with the external world. Given the primary role of the senses in the first months after birth, Piaget referred to this initial period of cognitive development as the **sensorimotor stage.**

During this period infants are absorbed in meeting their immediate physical and emotional needs (Piaget, 1926/1930b), and they cry to have caregivers acknowledge and attend to those needs. Because infants can deal only in the immediate and the concrete, the here-and-now (Piaget, 1952), they immediately stop paying attention when an intriguing object is covered or hidden from view. Spanning the time roughly between birth and 2 years of age, the sensorimotor stage is a period of rapid mental change. Consequently, Piaget thought of the sensorimotor stage as embracing a number of substages (Siegler, 1998; Sigelman & Shaffer, 1995).

Table 3–1	Piaget's stages of cognitive development.	
Stage	**Approximate Ages**	**Mental Processing**
Sensorimotor	Birth to 1.5–2.0 years	Infants rely on their senses to connect with the world; they enter this stage with only innate reflexes and later begin to use their minds to solve sensorimotor problems; they always think in the here-and-now and in terms of their own physical and emotional needs and comforts.
Preoperations	2–7 years	Children think in terms of symbols or mental representations, as reflected in their language processing; they engage in pretend play; they are still highly egocentric and thus unable to think from others' perspectives; they problem solve in only one direction and can be easily fooled by physical perceptions, such as those pertaining to mass or length.
Concrete Operations	7–11 years	Children's reasoning becomes logical and increasingly more symbolic; they solve practical problems with concrete referents; they are able to sort and classify objects and think categorically; they think forward or backward through a problem or situation.
Formal Operations	11 years or older	Those in this stage are able to think and problem solve abstractly; they can deal with the hypothetical and consider long-range consequences; they can weigh problems from multiple perspectives.

Substage 1: Reflex Modification (Birth to 1 Month)

As explained in Chapter 2, newborns must rely on their inborn reflexes to respond to the new world outside the womb. Piaget considered reflexes, like sucking or grasping, to be the first tools of the developing mind. For example, babies suck as an innate response, but just weeks after birth, they show evidence of modifying their inborn reflexes to adapt to their particular environments. Thus, a newborn begins to suck differently on a mother's finger than on the mother's nipple. Piaget saw this adaptation as a form of cognitive accommodation.

Substage 2: Primary Circular Reactions (1 to 4 Months)

Before long, infants begin to notice that certain actions bring either wanted or unwanted outcomes (Kaye & Marcus, 1981). For instance, they start to realize that food is not forthcoming when they suck on a finger. Actions that have favorable outcomes are repeated again and again—that is, **circular reactions**—whereas those that prove unsatisfying cease. Piaget believed that the execution of repetitive behaviors was a key to continued development because these circular reactions permit individuals to associate a certain action with a particular outcome and the effects that action engenders (Siegler, 1998).

Throughout the entire sensorimotor stage, Piaget identified three shifts in these circular actions. Between the ages of 1 and 4 months, as infants gain increasing motor control over their bodies and their reflexes, they seek to replicate bodily actions that bring them pleasure. This lowest form of repetition is termed a *primary circular behavior*. For example, when my granddaughter Paige discovered the pleasure of sticking her hand or any part of it in her mouth, she tried to reproduce the hand-to-mouth movement, even though her control of that movement was still largely trial and error in those first few months after birth.

Substage 3: Secondary Circular Reactions (4 to 8 Months)

Later, infants' goal-directed repetitions extend beyond their bodies to objects within their environment—*secondary circular reactions* according to Piaget. For example, when Paige was a few months old and was flailing her arms in her infant's seat, she accidentally hit an attached toy. That act produced a squeaking sound that both startled and pleased her, and in hopes of reproducing the sound, she started squirming and flailing her arms again. Before long she had refined her movements to produce the pleasing noise with greater regularity—a secondary circular reaction.

Substage 4: Coordination of Secondary Schemes (8 to 12 Months)

As young children begin to approach their first birthdays, they take yet another step in their cognitive development. Specifically, these young minds show the ability to string together two or more secondary circular reactions in the performance of a routine. For example, Paige is fascinated with the large clip-on earrings I wear. When she was younger and those earrings were in sight and in reach, she would use her grasping skills to get hold of them. By the

Infants repeat actions that result in pleasurable feelings.

time she was 9 months old, she was much more purposeful and skillful in her actions. Even if I turned my head so that the earrings were no longer within reach, she grabbed and turned my face to a more favorable position so that she could employ her grasping abilities.

Stage 5: Tertiary Circular Reactions (12 to 18 Months)

Over the course of their early development, infants become even more active in their exploration of their world. They do more than simply repeat the same actions over and over again; they become experimenters, trying out variations of the actions they have previously initiated. For example, when my granddaughter Lauren was younger, she had a boat she played with in the bath tub. She happily discovered that the boat would fill with water, which she could then pour out in the tub or on the floor. Not content with this one action-reaction, Lauren began to experiment with other toys in the tub to see how many could serve as water dispensers. And as with other circular actions, Lauren repeated these activities over and over again, manifesting *tertiary circular reactions*.

Substage 6: Beginnings of Representational Thought (18 to 24 Months)

The final substage in the sensorimotor period is a transitional period that prepares children for the cognitive demands of the next stage. Paige can help explain this transitional period of cognitive development. Now, when she sees me, she starts searching for my earrings, even if they are not visible. She grabs my face, moves my hair—whatever it takes to unearth the prize—and thereby illustrates that she has some lasting memory or mental representation of the target objects and actions. This enduring knowledge of objects not directly visible in the environment is known as **object permanence.** The consistent ability to form and act upon mental representations is critical to young children's transition to the preoperational stage.

Preoperations

Several transformations co-occur as infants become toddlers—transformations that help propel them into the next stage of cognitive development. First, as discussed in Chapter 2, their brains continue to myelinate in areas associated with linguistic production and reception and with thinking and reasoning. Young children are also maturing in physical stature and in their motor skills. Together these conditions give toddlers an increased ability to physically navigate their environments. In addition, they are acquiring the ability to express their wants and needs to others around them; they begin to realize that the things they see and do can be represented in words or images. A broom becomes a horse during imaginary play, and the sound *mama* not only evokes some response, but also signifies a particular person. Young children at this stage are beginning to think symbolically, as indicated by their language, problem solving, and imaginative play (Piaget, 1955). With this transformation, which generally occurs around age 2, young children move into a new realm of development—**preoperational thinking.**

There are several defining attributes of the preoperational mind, which exists roughly between the ages of 2 and 7. Even though many mental processes are still beyond the capabilities of preoperational children, they make tremendous cognitive advancements during this formative stage. Central to the preoperational stage is the fact that toddlers become able to use symbols and signs in their thoughts and actions. When children use objects in their environment to represent something analogous, like a broom for a horse or a doll for a baby, they are using **symbols** (Siegel, 1998). On the other hand, when children use a word or another object that has no physical resemblance to the target as its representative, they are using **signs.** When Lauren began to realize that the word *mama* was a verbal marker for her mother or that her GaGa was also her grandmother, she was demonstrating a grasp of linguistic signs. The effective application of both symbols and signs is characteristic of symbolic thinking—one of the critical attributes of preoperational thought.

Over the course of the preoperational stage, young children become more skilled at engaging in conventional rather than idiosyncratic communication. For children to move effectively through the world around them, they must come to rely on words that have meaning to others. Lauren's personal term for me, GaGa, is a case of idiosyncratic communication. In order to broaden her sphere of communication, however, she needed to acquire a more conventional way to identify me to others outside the immediate family. Thus, *GaGa* translated into *grandmother* in conventional speech.

Another cognitive achievement of the preoperational stage has to do with young children's conception of time. Prior to the preoperational period, the infant was trapped in the here and now, there was no past and no future. With the ability to form mental representations that endure beyond the moment, the preoperational mind becomes free to move forward or backward in time. Although temporal processing remains quite limited during this stage, toddlers have a newly discovered means to explore their world and their place within it.

The limitations in the thinking and reasoning of preoperational children are associated with the processes of egocentrism, conservation, centration, and reversibility. To Piaget idiosyncratic speech was evidence of **egocentrism,** or the tendency to view the world through one's own knowledge and experiences without regard to other perspectives. Although the word *egocentrism* is often a pejorative term when applied to more mature individuals, in applying it to children's cognitive development, Piaget wanted to demonstrate that those in preoperations, for whom the sphere of existence is understandably limited, must first make sense of the world through their own personal experiences. Recently Lauren has been grappling with the idea of night and day. When she goes to bed, she talks about the sun going to sleep. When she wakes up in the morning, she announces that it is time to get up because the sun is awake. In Lauren's mind night and day are dictated by when the sun goes to sleep and wakes up—just as she goes to sleep and wakes up. Thus, her sense of the world mirrors her own life experiences—the epitome of egocentric thinking. Even though people never completely set aside this tendency to be egocentric, the subsequent stages of cognitive development are much less influenced by this self-orientation.

Another cognitive tendency exhibited by preoperational thinkers pertains to the principle of conservation, which is illustrated by an often-repeated experiment. Young children watching a set amount of liquid being poured from a short, wide beaker into one that is tall and slender believe that the amount of liquid has changed. This consistent response to a classic Piagetian task demonstrates young children's failure to understand that particular properties of an object (e.g., mass, volume) remain the same even when surface features (e.g., container or shape) change—a principle known as **conservation.** To put this principle to the test, try your hand at the classic Piagetian task in Part 1 of the Thought Experiment: Taking Piaget's Theory to Task, which follows.

One of the reasons that preoperational children perform in the manner that they do on these classic tasks is that they seem able to attend to only one attribute or feature of a problem at a time. This process is termed **centration.** In effect, preoperational children center on the size of the containers but not the overall quantity or volume of the liquid.

A preoperational child fails to realize that the amount of liquid remains constant when it is poured from one container into another of a different size or shape.

Thought Experiment ....

Taking Piaget's Theory to Task

Part 1: The traditional approach.   Below is a traditional Piagetian task dealing with *conservation of number*. Try out this task on a child (or children) between the ages of 2 and 5.

Directions: Find a few simple objects like buttons or pennies that are consistent in size, shape, and color. First, arrange them in the way illustrated in A. Ask the child whether each row has the same number of objects. Then rearrange the objects to match the pattern in B. Again ask the child whether the number of objects in the two rows is the same. If Piaget's predictions hold, the child should see the number of objects as the same for the first set but different for the second.

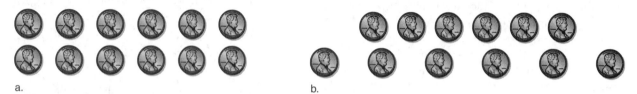

a.   b.

Part 2: An alternative approach.   Below is a twist on Piaget's traditional conservation of number task. Use objects that young children would find very appealing (e.g., M&Ms®, pennies, or grapes).

Directions: As in the traditional task, you will be arranging a number of objects in two rows. For this experiment, however, you are going to vary the arrangement and the directions. Specifically, you are going to have a greater number of objects (e.g., M&Ms®) in the more tightly clustered row and fewer objects in the row that is spread farther apart, as shown below. Tell the children that they can *have* the M&Ms® (or pennies) in either row. Then let them pick the row they want. If the predictions of Piaget still hold, the children will still be drawn to the spread-out row with fewer objects. But if the predictions of neo-Piagetians are correct, the children will select the more clustered row that actually does contain more of the treasured objects.

....

Another intriguing pattern in preoperational thinking has to do with reasoning patterns. Even though preoperational children exhibit the ability to think symbolically, they do not yet have the mental ability to manipulate those representations. For example, these young minds can represent an event or sequence only in the order in which they experienced it (Piaget, 1952). They are generally unable to play back the sequence of an event or problem in reverse order. In Piagetian terms these children cannot exhibit **reversibility.** For example, Lauren likes to try her hand at storytelling. One of her favorites at the moment is "The Three Little Pigs." In her rendering, Lauren mentions the main players and their key actions in the standard sequence (e.g., building houses of straw, sticks, and then bricks). However, if I were to ask her to describe those events in the reverse order, even with aid of props like hand puppets, she would find the task mentally overwhelming. Her mental world moves in one direction only.

Concrete Operations

Logical reasoning marks the shift into the **concrete operational stage.** According to Piaget, children around the age of 7 achieve the ability to engage in coordinated mental actions, or **operations.** These operations give children

the capacity to formulate dynamic rather than static mental representations; that is, concepts and ideas can be more flexibly and efficiently manipulated. Concrete operational children begin to overcome the cognitive limitations that characterize preoperational thinking, as evidenced in their problem-solving behaviors and their language use.

Even with props, preoperational children cannot reverse a sequence of events easily or successfully.

Concrete operational thinkers can consider multiple aspects or features of a situation or problem simultaneously—an ability called **decentration.** Thus, if asked to select the block that would come next in a sequence, concrete operational thinkers can attend to both shape and color.

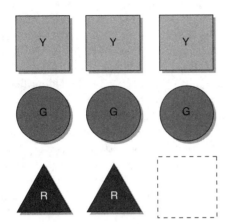

These young children can also readily attend to size, shape, and color when confronting simple problems of geometric analogy using colored blocks (White & Alexander, 1986). To select the correct block in the following problem, the children had to attend to those three attributes simultaneously.

However, as is indicative of concrete operational thinking, these children needed the help of blocks with familiar attributes to work through the problem.

Other advancements at this stage of development include the ability to see events or experiences from multiple vantage points and from multiple directions as in reversibility (Inhelder & Piaget, 1958, 1964). In addition, these children can now understand that core properties of an object (e.g., mass) remain the same even when surface features (e.g., containers) are altered—the principle of conservation. When Lauren finally achieves concrete operational thought, she should be able to tell the story of "The Three Little Pigs" from the perspective of the wolf and even outline the key events in reverse order.

Concrete operational thinkers also begin to see the patterns and relations in the world around them. These patterns allow them to sort and classify objects in their environment (e.g., table, chair, sofa = furniture). Indeed, **classification,** or the systematic grouping of objects and ideas, is an important aspect of the concepts forming during this period of cognitive development (Inhelder & Piaget, 1964). With the problem presented in Figure 3–1, for example, if children in the preoperational stage were asked whether there were more teddy bears or more toys, they would likely respond that there were more teddy bears. They have not yet learned the rule of **class inclusion,** whereby some categories (e.g., teddy bears or toy trains) are subsumed in other more inclusive categories (e.g., toys). Children who have reached the concrete operational stage of mental development, by comparison, would recognize that *toy* is a category that subsumes both teddy bears and toy trains. Therefore, their answer to the question would be more toys.

All of these newly acquired cognitive operations make the world more predictable for children at this stage and give them the capacity to solve practical, everyday problems. However, their problem solving still requires concrete referents that permit them to stay focused on the problem at hand. For that reason manipulatives, like blocks or counting sticks, are often used in early-childhood classrooms. They make the acquisition of mathematical concepts, such as quantity, or the performance of simple mathematical problems, such as simple addition or subtraction, easier for young children (White & Coleman, 2000).

One final transformation that is evidenced within the concrete operational stage pertains to young children's use of language. Beyond the fact that children during this period are continuing to develop richer vocabularies that reflect their growing conceptual sophistication, they are far

Question: Are there more teddy bears or more toys?

■ FIGURE 3–1   A case of class inclusion.

more able to use language in meaningful social exchanges. This change can be seen in the movement away from ego-centric speech or collective monologues into more interactive conversations. In a room full of 3- or 4-year-olds, one is apt to hear a great deal of talking; these children even seem to be engaged in conversations with one another. However, much of the conversation really consists of parallel talk. When children reach the concrete operational stage, they have the ability to take someone else's perspective and actually share ideas verbally with others. They can listen, consider others' points or perspectives, and respond accordingly.

Formal Operations

By the time children approach the end of the concrete operational period, they have made tremendous cognitive advancements. They can think logically, provided there are concrete referents; they can consider multiple attributes in problem solving; and they can weigh others' perspectives. Despite these impressive mental transformations, significant limitations remain. Most notable is the inability to think beyond concrete, specific experiences to more abstract concepts. Only those who achieve **formal operations,** usually at age 11 or older, manifest this ability and the reasoning capability that accompanies it (Inhelder & Piaget, 1964; Piaget, 1930a). It is important to recognize that not all individuals, regardless of age, make the shift from concrete to formal operations. Innate problems, trauma, or extremely limited life experiences can inhibit such cognitive advancement.

Meece (2002) describes four mental operations that are central to this stage: propositional logic, scientific reasoning, combinational reasoning, and probability/proportional reasoning. **Propositional logic,** which has its roots in formal logic, pertains to the ability to judge the internal consistency of arguments, even if the individual statements conflict with everyday experiences. Consider the following if/then statements:

> If birds live in the ground,
> And a gronker lives in a tree,
> Then a gronker is not a bird.

Those still in concrete operations would not be able to accept that birds live in the ground and therefore, would judge this syllogism to be false. However, a person who has attained formal operations and is capable of propositional logic would realize that the syllogism as presented is internally consistent. A gronker, whatever that might be, would not fit the given characteristics of birds. The ability to track the logic of arguments, whether conveyed orally or in print, is essential for higher level thinking and problem solving. The processing of certain mathematical or analogic statements also depends on propositional reasoning:

$$\text{If } x = 7, \text{ then } 2x + 4 = \underline{\hspace{2cm}}$$

arm : body :: branch : _____

Children or adolescents who achieve formal operations are also capable of **scientific** or **hypothetico-deductive reasoning,** which means they can generate and test hypotheses or predictions. Scientific reasoning can be thought of as evidence-based reasoning; it is the systematic and careful testing of a tentative explanation for a given situation (i.e., hypothesis). Those who engage in educational research rely on their capacity for hypothesis generation and testing. Indeed, many of the domains of study considered in Chapter 5, including science and history, rest on students' investigative skills.

Inhelder and Piaget (1958) also identified **combinatorial reasoning,** or the process of conceptualizing how various substances could be combined and understanding the potential consequences of their blending. The ability to combine materials in some systematic way is at the root of combinatorial reasoning. For example, if individuals are presented with a number of differently colored chips (e.g., 5 green, 4 red, and 3 blue) and are asked to determine how many different combinations of four chips could be produced, prior to reaching formal operations, they would not have the mental facility to deal systematically with this task. There might be some trial-and-error attempts at responding, but no formal logic would be applied.

Finally, in order to deal with the complexity of problems that occur in the world, those who achieve formal operations must also be able to engage in probability and proportional reasoning. **Probability reasoning** involves calculating the likelihood of a given event, based on the existing conditions. In order to make a reasoned judgment about the probability of some occurrence, individuals must be able to determine how often such an event occurs and how likely they are to experience good fortune or bad luck. This kind of calculation often involves **proportional reasoning,** which entails determining the relation of one component to another component or to the whole, often expressed as a ratio (e.g., 1:20,000).

As an example, individuals might be presented with a bag containing 6 yellow chips, 4 red chips, and 2 blue chips and be asked to figure out the likelihood (i.e., probability) of drawing a blue chip from the bag. A reasonable answer would require both probability and proportional reasoning; respondents would have 2 chances out of 12 (the total number of chips in the bag) or approximately a 17% chance to snag a blue chip.

Unfortunately, individuals frequently set aside proportional logic in the course of their everyday decision making (Paulos, 1988, 1998). Adults buy up lottery tickets even though their chances of winning may be 1:1,000,000,000. At the same time, Americans refuse to quit smoking even though the scientific evidence suggests that approximately 90% of lung cancer deaths in the United States are caused by cigarette smoking (National Cancer Institute, 2003).

> *We think in generalities, but we live in details.*
>
> Alfred North Whitehead

Rethinking Piagetian Theory

Like any major theory, Piaget's theory of cognitive development has been questioned and scrutinized since it became part of the educational literature. Despite subsequent disagreements or alternative perspectives, there is broad agreement that Piaget was correct in his contention that the thinking of children and adults is qualitatively different. Further, there is recognition that Piaget captured some significant and enduring patterns in the mental processing of children and youth. In addition, there is general acknowledgment of Piaget's unparalleled contributions to the field of cognitive development and the undeniable influence of his theory and research on educational research and practice. Nonetheless, several serious concerns have been raised about Piaget's theory, and alternative viewpoints have been presented.

Perceived Limitations

Since Piaget first framed his stage view of cognitive development, persistent concerns have been raised regarding the suitability of the tasks used to identify the key attributes of each developmental stage, the validity of the established stages, the generalizability of documented patterns, and the universality of the theory.

Task Suitability

Critics of Piagetian theory have questioned the suitability of Piaget's classic tasks for multiple reasons related to their language, object familiarity, and motivational quality (Bidell & Fischer, 1992; Gelman & Baillargeon, 1983). Some argue that the language used to coax thinking from young children is abstract, complex, and not particularly kid friendly. Thus, when children are asked by an adult whether containers have the same amount of liquid, children may not be certain what the adult is really asking. As a result, the children may provide what they think is the desired response, leading to an underestimation of their cognitive capabilities (Bidell & Fischer, 1992; Gelman, 1969).

Researchers also question whether more familiar objects and more motivational contexts would promote better performance from young children. For example, Rochelle Gelman's research (Gelman & Gallistel, 1978; Gelman, Meck, & Merkin, 1986) suggested that recasting traditional Piagetian tasks, using simpler language and more familiar objects framed in more motivational contexts, would allow young children to demonstrate their cognitive capabilities better. As a case in point, Gelman (1972) recast the classic conservation task as a game involving plates and mice. Specifically, Gelman placed two toy mice on one plate and three on another. She then asked children as young as three which plate was the "winner." Children were readily able to pick the winner (i.e., the plate with the larger number of mice). Gelman then modified the basic task by altering the number or spatial arrangement of the mice. Still the children were able to pick the winner, as long as the number of mice did not get too big for the children to count.

Part 2 of the Thought Experiment: Taking Piaget's Theory to Task provides another modification of Piaget's conservation task. Try out this second task with some 2- to 5-year-olds to see whether you find evidence of more logical thought in preoperational minds.

Stage Validity

Perhaps the most salient feature of Piaget's theory is its stages. Yet some believe that the case for a stage theory has not been adequately made. In fact, they counter the notion of a stage theory by demonstrating the "trainability" of a number of the cognitive processes that Piaget places at the heart of his stage designations. For example, he assumed that those in the preoperational stage have not mastered the process of conservation essential for logical reasoning. But researchers have found that young children can be trained to process conservation tasks with a high level of accuracy (Alexander, White, & Daugherty, 1997). If these central processes are truly indicative of a particular stage of mental development, they should not be susceptible to training, according to these researchers.

In addition, researchers have raised specific questions about the validity of the final stage of cognitive development—formal operations. What concerns some researchers is the large number of youth and adults who do not manifest the mental processes indicative of this stage. For example, only about half of college students consistently demonstrate formal operations using Piagetian tasks, and many adults continue to struggle with scientific reasoning (Neimark, 1975).

For other researchers the thinking and reasoning of older adults was not well captured by the various mental operations that Piaget identified. Some argued for developmental theories that better accommodate the extensive life experiences of adults or consider the neurological and physical changes that occur in later adulthood (Labouvie-Vief, 1992). It could well be that other factors, such as prior experience and continuing formal education or professional development, play a more significant role in the continued cognitive development of adults than Piagetian theory acknowledges (Ackerman, 2003; Fischer, 1980).

Generalizability

The assumption underlying Piaget's stage theory is that it is generalizable, that is, its stage designations apply to all mental activities in which a person engages. For instance, it should not matter whether young children are counting teddy bears or buttons or whether middle-school students are working on a mathematics or a history problem. Individuals' demonstration of concrete or formal operations (or the lack thereof) should be consistently displayed; the stage of performance should not be contingent on contextual variables.

In reality, the performance of children and youth suggests that people may not be uniformly logical or illogical. For example, when individuals are working in areas of personal interest or high familiarity, they may be more likely to demonstrate higher levels of reasoning (Kuhn, 1992). It may also be the case that individuals' ability to solve mathematical problems may not be comparable to their ability to reason in history, biology, or some other complex domain. Consequently, more researchers are arguing for a domain-specific rather than a domain-general pattern for cognitive development (Alexander, 2003a, 2003b; Flavell, Miller, & Miller, 1993). Chapter 8 explores this issue more deeply.

Counterevidence to generalizability has actually been documented for classic Piagetian tasks. For instance, researchers have determined that children's understanding of conservation of number, mass, and liquid does not develop at the same time (Siegler, 1998). Instead, children's grasp of conservation of number appears to emerge earlier than that of mass (Elkind, 1961). Conservation of weight seems to develop even later (Katz & Beilin, 1976). This kind of variability weakens any case for generalizability.

Universality

When Piaget framed his theory of cognitive development, he presented it as a universal theory applicable to any culture into which children are born. However, researchers who are more culturally contextual in their orientation (see Chapter 2) believe that culture has a more significant place in cognitive development (M. Cole, Gay, Glick, & Sharp, 1971) and could work against the universal display of stage-related processes. In fact, Cole and Cole (2001) identify four specific ways that culture can result in unevenness in children's patterns of cognitive development.

Occurrence and Nonoccurrence of Particular Activities   Cole and Cole (2001) make the case that children cannot learn something that they have not had the opportunity to experience. Imagine the confusion of a child who grows up in a desert area where water is scarce trying to reason through Piaget's conservation of liquids task. On the other hand, even children as young as 3 or 4 living among desert tribes can probably track and hunt animals with a skill well beyond the abilities of adults in postindustrial societies. Judging these children on the basis of activities that are not part of their cultural experience would likely result in a gross underestimation of their mental abilities.

Frequency of Basic Activities   The frequency of activities within a culture also matters. As the research on expertise makes clear, repeated practice contributes to improved performance (Chi, Glaser, & Farr, 1988). Thus, it is not surprising that children growing up in environments where particular activities are routinely practiced show a greater propensity toward those activities than do children living in other environments. For example, Carraher, Carraher, and Schlieman (1985) found that the computational abilities of Brazilian children selling goods on the street were quite sophisticated, even though they were unable to demonstrate those abilities on the types of school tasks to which American students are routinely exposed. Because selling goods and calculating costs were critical to the existence of these 9- to 15-year-olds, they became highly skilled in these particular processes. However, these mental operations did not necessarily generalize to other types of logical reasoning or even to other mathematical tasks.

Interrelatedness of Activities   Cole and Cole (2001) also describe the effect of culture on the learning of associated enterprises. They use the culturally valued activity of making pottery as a case in point. If making pottery is a valued cultural activity, then it is more likely that participants will more readily acquire the cognitive skills that are tied to that activity, such as molding clay, firing and glazing pots, or selling wares. As Cole and Cole aptly state, it is one thing to mold clay in kindergarten class and quite another to mold clay as part of a family's livelihood.

Apprenticing Experiences   When an activity is valued within a cultural community, more opportunities are apt to exist for children to learn that activity in collaboration with experienced adults or masters. In effect, these children begin to apprentice under the watchful and caring eye of a parent or other community member (Rogoff, 1990). This guidance allows the children to learn the target cognitive activity in a way they would not if they were left to their own devices. Rogoff (1990) refers to this culturally rich form of modeling as a *cognitive apprenticeship*.

Social Interactions

These four aspects of cultural influence on students' acquisition of cognitive processes lead to one of the strongest criticisms leveled at Piagetian theory: The nature of cognitive development as outlined by Piaget attends in a limited manner to the effect of social interactions on the performance of mental operations by children and youth (Resnick, Levine, & Teasley, 1991). In other words, Piaget's theory gives little consideration to the direct and meaningful influence that others exert on children's thinking and reasoning, even though children and adults rarely engage in mental processing in isolation, without the support or guidance of others in their environment (Lave, 1988). Indeed, it is considered a sign of intelligence to ask for clarification or seek assistance when confronted with an ambiguous or highly demanding task (Newman & Goldin, 1990). And none of us are the same reasoners when we work in isolation that we are when we are free to work with the support and guidance of others (Perkins, 1993).

Vygotsky's Perspective on Cognitive Development

One of the most interesting contrasts to Piaget's theory of cognitive development comes in the writings of Lev Vygotsky, who was introduced in Chapter 2. Although Vygotsky never produced a theory as comprehensive as Piaget's he succeeded in illuminating some of the apparent limitations in Piaget's thinking, especially in regard to social and cultural factors. Vygotsky's counterpoints to Piagetian theory and other prevailing notions of human learning and development have become some of the most influential in contemporary thought.

Vygotsky's writings have had significant impact in the United States and Western Europe only in the past few decades, even though he was a contemporary of Piaget and wrote during the 1920s and 1930s. However, Vygotsky's work fell into disfavor within his native Russia with the rise of Stalin, making it difficult for translations to find their way into the educational literature in the United States and Western Europe. In addition, Vygotsky died in his 30s from tuberculosis, leaving one of his most famous works, *Thought and Language,* not fully revised (Kozulin, 1999).

Within *Thought and Language* Vygotsky (1934/1986) discussed his differences with Piaget on the issues of children's thinking and language development. That volume and other available writings from Vygotsky and colleagues (e.g., Luria, 1976) clarify the differences between Vygotsky's and Piaget's views of cognitive and linguistic development. Those differences are summarized in Table 3–2.

Perhaps the most significant difference, as discussed in Chapter 2, was Vygotsky's protrayal of a relatively seamless growth in mental processing, conceptual understanding, and linguistic ability (Beilin, 1992). Whereas Piaget (1952) conceptualized development in terms of invariant stages, Vygotsky conceptualized development as a continuous process shaped and stimulated by the sociocultural context. With the classic task of hiding a toy under a hat, Piaget found that infants who had not reached the sensorimotor stage and, thus, had not achieved the ability to retain memory of a nonvisible object operated on the out-of-sight, out-of-mind principle. Vygotsky (1934/1986) argued that infants begin to realize that a toy is still present even when covered by a hat, not because they acquire some new mental operations but because repeated social interactions stimulate such a response. The fact that children appear more capable in more supportive contexts argued against stages of development, according to Vygotsky (1978).

Piaget does not see a child as a part of the social whole. Social factors are shown as an external force that enters the child's mind and dislodges the forms of thinking inherent in the child's intelligence. (Vygotsky 1934/1986, p. 45)

Vygotsky and Piaget also differed on the direction of development. Specifically, Piaget (1955) believed that children's minds mature and then influence their social interactions. Vygotsky (1962, 1987) argued that social interactions trigger cognitive and linguistic development. In other words, the direction of development for Vygotsky was *socialization to internalization,* in contrast to the *internalization to socialization* articulated in Piaget's theory.

In addition, Vygotsky gave greater weight to social context in a child's development than Piaget did. Vygotsky (1978) argued that children's abilities are not stable during any particular developmental period, as Piaget (1952) suggested. Instead, abilities shift with the social context and the assistance provided by more capable and knowledgeable individuals. Thus, students' abilities are either enhanced or inhibited by the quality of the academic support they receive within the classroom (Perkins, 1992).

Vygotsky and Piaget also perceived the relations between language and thought differently. For Piaget (1955) children's use of language is a powerful indicator of their mental maturity. For Vygotsky (1962) the very act of putting thoughts into words fundamentally enriches the understanding of those ideas.

The Neo-Piagetian View

When researchers and theorists found themselves questioning Piaget's views of cognitive development, they were faced with two varied paths. They could either pose dramatic alternatives to Piaget's theory, like Vygotsky's sociocultural perspective, or they could attempt to reconcile their specific concerns without abandoning the theory altogether. This latter path was taken by **neo-Piagetians,**

Table 3–2	Contrasting the theoretical stances of Piaget and Vygotsky.	
Characteristic	**Piagetian Theory**	**Vygotskian Theory**
Developmental Continuity	Development occurs in a series of distinct and invariant stages.	Development unfolds in a continuous process devoid of set stages.
Direction of Development	Development begins with a maturation of the mind; the mind can then be stimulated and expanded through social interactions and the adaptations such interactions foster.	Development is formed through human contacts and the verbal interactions they stimulate; the understanding derived from these interactions then becomes internalized.
Role of Others	How children function depends largely on their level of mental maturity.	How children function varies greatly with the sociocultural context and the human resources present.
Relationship of Thought and Language	The language patterns of children are indicative of their mental maturity and related thinking processes.	Putting thoughts into words changes those thoughts, leading to deeper and richer conceptualizations.

researchers who sought to expand or clarify dimensions of Piagetian theory while retaining most of his basic assumptions about mental growth (Fischer & Farrar, 1988). Some of the neo-Piagetians focused on the number or character of the specific stages (Labouvie-Vief, 1992). Others wanted to reconcile the seeming variability that resulted when Piagetian principles were applied to specific children, tasks, or domains (Fischer & Grannott, 1995; Flavell, 1985).

Perhaps the best known of the neo-Piagetian theories was articulated by Robbie Case (1985, 1992; Case & Griffin, 1990). Two aspects of Case's theory of intellectual development stand out as particularly noteworthy: the nature of his stages and the conceptual structures underlying those stages. Like Piaget, Case depicted cognitive development as unfolding in four unique stages. However, at the heart of Case's stages are the forms of mental representations that guide the thinking and performance at each stage and the outcomes those representations engender. Each stage is marked by increasingly more sophisticated mental representations that are stimulated, in part, by the development of memory and strategic processing. For example, in the *sensorimotor control structures stage* (birth to 1½), the representations infants and children form are based on direct sensory information. Similarly, the actions those representations trigger are sensory, in the manner of physical or motor reactions. For instance, when my granddaughter Paige is handed the telephone, she typically squeals with glee because she enjoys hearing the sounds that come from it and likes pushing the buttons. She understands the way a telephone sounds, feels, or looks.

As Paige matures cognitively and reaches the *relational control structures stage* (1½ to 5 years), she will form an internal mental image of concepts that will allow her to generate other internal representations. In effect, she will have internalized some of the essential attributes of a telephone, and that mental representation will allow her to draw pictures of telephones or engage in role-playing using a pretend telephone—actions that are not dependent on direct physical contact with the object being represented. At this stage young children's thinking remains rather two-dimensional, or bipolar; things are perceived as good or bad, large or small, telephone or not telephone.

Later, when Paige is within the *dimensional control structures stage* (5 to 11 years), she will operate on more complex and abstract representations of concepts, which will allow her to make comparisons between concepts on multiple dimensions and to transform those dimensions in relatively simple ways. This internal representation can also evaluate the nature of objects she encounters in her environment. For example, Paige will be able to understand how communicating by cellular phone is different from using a pay phone or how talking to someone in person is different from talking to them on the phone. Therefore, in time Paige will be able to judge the "telephoneness" of particular objects.

Finally, by the time Paige reaches the *abstract control structures stage* (11 to 18½ years), her mental representations will be extremely complex and highly abstract. A telephone will be more than a physical, sensory object that can be touched or heard. It will be an object that can be compared and contrasted along two or more dimensions. At this point a telephone will be an idea that will likely be part of mental structures linked with everything from inventions to human communications to personal relations.

The mental representations that frame Case's four-stage theory also relate to central conceptual structures, which are another of his significant contributions (Case & Griffin, 1990; Case & Okamoto, 1996). **Central conceptual structures** are networks of concepts and conceptual relations that allow children and youth to perform a range of related tasks to which those structures pertain. In particular, Case believes that Piaget's focus on specific mental operations was too small a unit of analysis and, thus, not reflective of human information processing. Instead, Case theorizes that there are mental components (i.e., central conceptual structures) that are broader and more integrated than mental operations. And these components are more explanatory of individuals' abilities to grasp and then perform a range of spatial, numeric, and linguistic tasks.

What Are the Patterns in the Way Students Grow Socially, Emotionally, and Morally?

Because of the importance of various facets of social research, an entire chapter is devoted to the topic of socially shared learning and teaching (see Chapter 11). This chapter concentrates instead on several theories and models that have been central to the investigation of social and moral development.

Two Perspectives on Social Development

Social development refers to the patterns that emerge in human contacts: how individuals interact with others with whom they interact and for what purposes. One of the defining stage theories of psychosocial development was framed by Erik Erikson. A more contemporary perspective on social relations was articulated by Urie Bronfenbrenner. These two varied perspectives differ in the role that society and culture play in the change process.

Erikson's Theory of Psychosocial Development

What Piaget's stage theory did for cognitive development, Erik Erikson's (1963, 1980) theory did for psychosocial development. Erikson (1902–1994), a follower of Freud, expanded on Freud's perceptions of the psychosexual stages in human growth. Erikson believed that people's responses to critical but typical life events transformed their self-perceptions and their ability to interact posi-

Table 3–3 Erikson's stages of psychosocial development.

Underlying Conflict	Associated Ages/ Periods	Related Behaviors
Trust Versus Mistrust	Birth–1 year	Infants either form trusting and loving relationships with caregivers or develop a general mistrust of others and the world around them.
Autonomy Versus Shame and Doubt	1–3 years	Young children must gain some control over their minds and bodies, for example, through walking, feeding or dressing themselves, or using the bathroom. If they succeed with the guidance and support of others, they sense autonomy. If not, they can experience persistent shame and self-doubt.
Initiative Versus Guilt	3–6 years	Children explore their independence and emerging roles through make-believe and self-initiated tasks. If caregivers are too controlling and do not encourage this self-initiative, or if parental expectations for control are too high, children can experience guilt or frustration.
Industry Versus Inferiority	6–11 years	With the onset of formal education, children confront a variety of new tasks. If they succeed at these tasks through their own efforts or by cooperating with peers, children develop a sense of competence and industry. If not, they can internalize feelings of inferiority.
Identity Versus Identity Confusion	Adolescence	Adolescents begin to question their future place in society. Questions about personal identity and personal values, career roles, and avocations absorb them. If they are able to answer some of these questions, their sense of self begins to take shape. If not, they become confused as to who they are and who they will become.
Intimacy Versus Isolation	Young adulthood	Close relationships and intimacy are essential for young adults. If these bonds can be forged and a commitment made to others, then intimacy is achieved. Without such intimacy, the individual must confront feelings of isolation and loneliness.
Generativity Versus Stagnation	Middle adulthood	Later in adulthood, when individuals look back on their lives, they need to feel that they have been of value to others and have contributed to society through their efforts. Positive self-evaluations promote feelings of generativity, whereas negative judgments produce a sense of stagnation.
Ego Integrity Versus Despair	Old age	In the final stages of life, it is critical that individuals view themselves and their lives as good or satisfying, leaving them content. If they are full of regrets or dissatisfaction, these older adults face despair instead of ego integrity.

tively with others. Specifically, Erikson (1968) focused his theory around eight significant life events, or conflicts, and humans' responses to them. The resulting eight stages are summarized in Table 3–3.

Trust Versus Mistrust

The biological bases of development showed how completely dependent infants are on others for their survival. Infants' ability to form trusting relations with their primary caregivers is the basis for the first stage of psychosocial development, **trust versus mistrust** (Erikson, 1963). When infants succeed at forging loving and trusting relations with their caregivers, the result is trust. If they are thwarted in those attempts, they may face a life marked by mistrust of others.

Autonomy Versus Shame and Doubt

With maturation infants begin to gain some mastery over their bodies and their surroundings, as when they struggle to walk, feed themselves, or use the bathroom (Erikson, 1968). Erikson labeled this stage **autonomy versus shame and doubt.** When their efforts prove rewarding, toddlers

(1 to 3 years) feel a sense of autonomy. If they cannot do as they wish or fail to meet the expectations of others, they can experience shame and self-doubt.

Erik Erikson

Initiative Versus Guilt

During the preschool years, the social world of many children expands beyond their home and primary caretakers (Erikson, 1980). These preschoolers (3 to 6 years) are concerned about whether they can gain some control over their immediate surroundings. Those that succeed in these initial forays gain a sense of initiative; those who do not succeed may experience guilt. Thus, Erikson referred to this stage as **initiative versus guilt.** An important factor in determining whether children experience initiative or guilt is the control exerted by caregivers. If caregivers are too controlling and do not encourage self-initiative or if parental expectations for control are too high, children are more likely to experience guilt or frustration than initiative (Erikson, 1968).

Industry Versus Inferiority

Throughout the initial years of schooling, children continually confront new information and new tasks. In many ways children's sense of self is greatly affected by the effort they put forth to accomplish those various tasks and the competence they feel as a result. Erikson's stage of **industry versus inferiority** focuses on this reality. Specifically, when students work hard and achieve at a satisfactory level, they can experience a sense of industry. Those who cannot keep pace or do not meet the task goals may well feel inferior (Erikson, 1963).

Identity Versus Identity Confusion

Adolescents are dealing with remarkable biological and hormonal changes. Concurrently they are struggling with their social and sexual identities and their emerging adult roles. These are the defining themes of Erikson's **identity versus identity confusion** stage. Those who have a clear sense of who they are and what they want to become develop a positive sense of identity in this stage. In contrast, the adolescents who do not find their place in the social milieu or who remain unsure about their future contributions will struggle with identity confusion.

Intimacy Versus Isolation

As students move from high school into college or the workplace, they are weighing issues of intimacy (Erikson, 1963, 1968). Deep and lasting relationships will be at the core of their lives for years to come. Without them these young adults face isolation and loneliness. Undergraduate students readily recognize themselves in this stage, with so much of their energy directed outside the classroom to the formation of personal relationships that may last throughout their lives.

Generativity Versus Stagnation

The final two stages of Erikson's theory become increasingly more self-reflective, as befits a mature life (Erikson, 1963). Thus, during middle adulthood the psychosocial issue revolves around **generativity versus stagnation.** That is, those in middle age struggle with the question of whether they have contributed to others' lives or to society in a positive way. Those contributions can be through younger generations or through work-related accomplishments. Those who feel that such contributions exist experience generativity, whereas those who do not sense stagnation.

Ego Integrity Versus Despair

During old age the **ego integrity versus despair** stage, individuals spend time looking back over their lives. These reflections often focus on whether their lives have been satisfying, positive, and worthwhile. When older adults feel that they have lived a good and rewarding life and have been true to their values and goals, they sense ego integrity. However, if older adults' lives are marked with regrets and unfulfilled dreams or if they focus on what could have been or should have been, they experience despair.

Despite the intuitive appeal of Erikson's theory and the readily identifiable conflicts he identified, there have been serious criticisms of his work, especially with his lack of attention to the sociocultural influences that are ever present in individuals' lives. In effect, Erikson saw specific psychosocial conflicts as universal across all cultures. In addition, he also did not consider the nature of the social supports or inhibitors that individuals encounter as they develop socially.

Bronfenbrenner's Ecological Perspective: A Sociocultural Alternative

Bronfenbrenner's view of social relations is an extension of the cultural-contextual orientation to human development discussed in Chapter 2. Several aspects of Bronfenbrenner's perspective stand in sharp contrast to Erikson's theory. For example, Erikson conceptualized change as involving appropriate or inappropriate responses to the life crises that happen to us. But for Bronfenbrenner human development is a dynamic, ecological system in which an individual is inextricably and actively situated (M. Cole & Cole, 2001). In fact, individuals come with their own social addresses, which consist of the many subsystems in which they simultaneously participate. Such social addresses include home, school, neighborhood, and, of course, classroom.

Bronfenbrenner's ecological approach is thus all about the person in his or her environment, with that environment being "any event or condition outside the organism that is presumed to influence, or be influenced by, the person's development" (1979, p. 359). The relation between the person and the social environment is reciprocal; that is, individuals are not only changed by those interactive environmental systems, but they also change the systems to which they belong. Bronfenbrenner's (1989) approach entails

Urie Bronfenbrenner

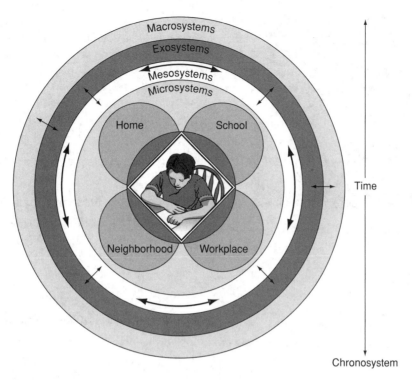

■ FIGURE 3–2   An ecological perspective on human development.

Note: From *Child Development in the Social Context* (p. 648) by C. B. Kopp and B. Krakow, 1982, Reading, MA: Addison-Wesley. Copyright 1982 by Addison-Wesley. Adapted with permission.

five nested and highly interrelated social systems (see Figure 3–2) on a continuum from specific and local to general and pervasive: microsystem, mesosystem, exosystem, macrosystem, and chronosystem.

At the most personal level is the **microsystem,** the setting in which individuals live and the face-to-face interactions with others who are part of that system. Families, classroom environments, and neighborhoods are all aspects of this microsystem, as are activities, roles within social units, and interpersonal relations.

However, these critical social groups are not isolated from one another; there are natural linkages that occur between two or more of the social settings in which individuals participate, and those linkages form the **mesosystem.** For example, there are potentially powerful relations between home and neighborhood and between home and school. Bronfenbrenner argues that the positive associations among these key social systems are needed to foster individuals' development.

Other important social forces influence students regularly, even if students do not interact with them directly. The local school board, medical organizations, and social services in the region fall within the broader ecological context of the **exosystem.** At the broadest level, diffuse but pervasive sociocultural systems invisibly but powerfully mold development. The **macrosystem** includes such pervasive forces as cultural beliefs, social customs, and economic values.

Bronfenbrenner understands that changes also occur over time in the microsystem, mesosystem, exosystem, and macrosystem and in the relations among these systems. One of the most obvious changes is the increasing complexity in the interactions between the individual and these environmental systems. The **chronosystem** captures the systemic changes that come to pass over time.

Emotional Development

It takes many years, experiences, and efforts to recognize, understand, and regulate our emotions (S. B. Eysenck, Pearson, Easting, & Allsopp, 1985; J. D. Mayer & Salovey, 1993). **Emotions** are subjective responses to life experiences; they can be pleasant or unpleasant, intense or fleeting, moderate or severe. Within months after birth, infants are capable of displaying various emotions physically and vocally; they can show happiness, sadness, or discontentment in the faces and sounds they make. However, young children still have not acquired an understanding of the emotions they feel or an ability to regulate those feelings (Meece, 2002).

Even as early as 12 months of age, young children demonstrate an ability to read the emotions of others. For example, a stern look from a parent can stop a child from reaching for an object; a warm smile can encourage a toddler to take another step or two. Eventually, young children's ability to read the emotions of others progresses to empathy. Thus, as children acquire the cognitive ability to assume the perspective of others, they also begin to demonstrate the ability to react to the emotions of others. This is **empathy** (Piaget, 1932). For example, a 3-year-old who sees her younger sister in distress may offer a comforting hug, or she may laugh gleefully along with a playmate who is expressing delight. Throughout the preschool years, children's range of emotions expands,

The faces and sounds that infants make convey emotions.

along with their awareness of the possible sources of those emotions (Meece, 2002). Along with happiness and sadness, emotions like guilt, pride, or shame become part of children's emotional repertoires. Such feelings, which anticipate the reactions of others, likely contribute to the increased regulation of emotions that begins during the preschool years.

Continued development of the range and regulation of emotions is characteristic of late adolescence and adulthood. As individuals mature emotionally, they learn how to read others and social situations more effectively. They also respond to others and to situations with suitable emotions at reasonable levels (Goleman, 1995). However, not all individuals reach this level of emotional maturity or display the same degree of emotional intelligence. Even within the bounds of normal emotional development, there is great variability (S. B. Eysenck et al., 1985), as suggested by the literature in emotional intelligence (Goleman, 1995).

Emotional intelligence, a phrase recently made popular by Goleman (1995), refers to individuals' ability to assess a particular social situation and to use information to guide their emotional response. The roots of emotional intelligence reach well back into the psychological literature on social intelligence, which Thorndike (1920) defined as "the ability to understand and manage men and women, boys and girls—to act wisely in human relations" (p. 228). Emotional intelligence has been described as a form of social intelligence that "involves the ability to monitor one's own and others' emotions, to discriminate among them, and to use the information to guide one's thinking and actions" (J. D. Mayer & Salovey, 1993, p. 433). Salovey and Mayer (1990) categorized emotional intelligence in five domains: self-awareness, managing emotions, motivating oneself, empathy, and handling relationships.

Self-awareness entails self-observation and the realization that an emotional reaction is occurring. Managing emotions means understanding the sources of one's feelings, addressing those sources when possible, and handling feelings effectively and in socially appropriate ways. Motivating oneself involves channeling emotions in order to accomplish a particular goal; channeling may require postponing self-gratification and setting aside unproductive emotions. As discussed earlier, empathy is a sensitivity and responsiveness to the positive or negative emotional manifestations of others. And finally, Salovey and Mayer (1990) describe handling relationships as social competence or as managing others' emotions.

Despite the intuitive appeal of Goleman's conception of emotional intelligence and the resulting domains described by Salovey and Mayer (1990), the research on this dimension is still very much in its infancy. Much more needs to be learned about emotional intelligence before Goleman's assumptions and these five domains can be supported or rejected with empirical evidence.

Two Perspectives on Moral Reasoning

Contrasting perspectives are nothing new in developmental literature. An examination of moral reasoning begins with the groundbreaking theory of Lawrence Kohlberg. Then, as a counterpoint to that theory, the research of Carol Gilligan places gender at the center of the debate on moral reasoning.

Kohlberg's Theory of Moral Reasoning

By far the most well-known and widely researched theory of moral reasoning is that articulated by Lawrence Kohlberg (1984). **Moral reasoning** deals with the thinking, feeling, and rationalization that occur in the face of social and moral dilemmas and the choice of a course of action. Kohlberg (1976, 1981) believes that moral reasoning follows a specific and unwavering pattern of development, moving from preconventional to conventional and then to postconventional judgments. He made this determination after posing a series of social/moral problems to young males and categorizing their responses. One moral problem that Kohlberg used in his research was the Heinz dilemma, which questions one's willingness to steal to save a loved one. After analyzing and categorizing the decisions respondents made and the explanations they provided, Kohlberg (1975, 1984) determined that moral reasoning falls into three distinct levels, each consisting of two associated stages (see Table 3–4).

HEINZ DILEMMA

In Europe, a woman was near death from cancer. One drug might save her, a form of radium that a druggist in the same town had recently discovered. The druggist was charging $2,000, ten times what the drug cost him to make. The sick woman's husband, Heinz, went to everyone he knew to borrow the money, but he could get together only about half of what it cost. He told the druggist that his wife was dying and asked him to sell it cheaper or let him pay later. But the druggist said no. The husband got desperate and broke into the man's store to steal the drug for his wife. Should the husband have done that? Why?

L. Kohlberg, 1969, p. 379

Table 3–4 Comparing Kohlberg's and Gilligan's stages of moral development.

	Kohlberg's Theory of Moral Reasoning		Gilligan's Stage Theory	
Level	**Level**	**Stage**	**Level**	**Level**
I. Preconventional morality (3–9 years)	Emphasis on avoiding punishments and gaining rewards	**1. Heteronomous (punishment-obedience)** — Children learn which actions/responses result in rewards and which ones instigate punishment. Their efforts center on obeying those individuals with the power to dispense such rewards and punishments.	**I. Orientation to individual survival**	The self is the only matter of concern, and the actions of the self are constrained by a lack of power. Right is determined individualistically.
		2. Instrumental — Actions that serve children's needs are judged as good, whereas those that result in unwanted outcomes are seen as bad. The measure of evaluation is self-satisfaction.	**Transition: selfishness to responsibility** Females begin to question the selfishness of judgments and consider their responsibilities to others.	
II. Conventional morality (9–20 years)	Focus on social/cultural rules of conduct	**3. Good boy–good girl morality (golden rule period)** — Children internalize simple and conventional moral codes shaped by the sociocultural environment (e.g., "Good boys don't curse"). Actions are then judged as right or wrong.	**II. Goodness as self-sacrifice**	One's responsibility to others and consensual judgments are critical. The collective view determines what is right.
		4. Authority and social order (maintaining morality) — Individuals understand the existence of a moral code that maintains order in society (e.g., driving laws). This code is set by authorities and must be obeyed in order to maintain social order.	**Transition: goodness to truth** The morality of actions is ascertained by the goodness or care they convey rather than in their appearance to others.	
III. Postconventional morality (20–adulthood)	Accent on broad moral principles	**5. Social contract** — Individuals must consider the principles underlying rules and regulations. Therefore, no rules should be blindly followed.	**III. Morality of nonviolence**	Care becomes a universal obligation, and the principle of nonviolence governs all morality.
		6. Universal ethical principle — Individuals seek to live by abstract, universal principles of morality, justice, and equality that cannot always be captured by rules and regulations dictating moral or social behavior.		

Preconventional Morality

Young children operating at the lowest level of moral reasoning, **preconventional morality** (3–9 years), think only in terms of their needs or well-being (Kohlberg, 1976). These children have not yet achieved the ability to think in terms of social conventions or mores. What drives moral decisions in Stage 1 of Level I (**heteronomous or punishment/ obedience**) is the punishments or rewards children anticipate for their actions (Kohlberg, 1984). Thus, they would likely respond to the Heinz dilemma by saying that Heinz should not take the drug because he would go to jail (i.e., be punished).

When children reach Stage 2, **instrumental morality,** they still operate from an egocentric position (Kohlberg, 1969). Judgments about what is right or just are predicated on what will serve them and their needs best. Thus, children at this stage would likely decide that Heinz should not steal the drug because he may need it himself at some point in the future. The self-serving nature of this judgment is quite transparent.

Conventional Morality

Moral reasoning at Level II of Kohlberg's (1975, 1984) theory, **conventional morality** (9–20 years), revolves around established rules or conventions of social and moral conduct. Stage 3 of this level, **good boy–good girl morality,** has been described as the golden rule period (Kohlberg, 1984). Children believe that they must follow without question the rules established by those in authority; that is what good boys and good girls do. They also believe that those who treat others right are treated fairly in return. A child at this stage would say that Heinz should not take the drug because good people do not steal.

Individuals who reach Stage 4, **authority and social order,** believe that the rules and regulations put into place by authorities are necessary for the welfare of society. Those who would violate such conventions risk social disorder. Thus, Stage 4 reasoners accept existing social codes without hesitation. With respect to the Heinz dilemma, those at this stage would oppose his taking the drug. They would likely argue that laws against stealing must be obeyed or individuals would feel free to take things at will, resulting in social chaos.

Postconventional Morality

Those who attain Level III, **postconventional morality** (20 years or more), no longer strictly adhere to existing rules of social or moral conduct. They can consider a moral dilemma from the perspective of underlying principles of social justice and common good. This level of reasoning does not usually appear before late adolescence or early adulthood. Regrettably, many individuals never demonstrate the ability to reason morally at this level (Kohlberg, 1984).

Reasoning within Stage 5 of this level, **social contract,** considers rules from the perspective of the common good (Kohlberg, 1969, 1981). When rules violate this social contract, they should be modified and maybe even disobeyed. An individual analyzing the Heinz problem from this orientation might allow for the theft of the drug on the grounds that a life might be saved. For the rare few who achieve Stage 6, **universal ethical principle,** moral reasoning arises from principles of justice, right, and equality that apply to all. These universal principles take precedence over the legal or social rules that others create. An individual who lives by these principles might argue that any law that puts profits above the sanctity of life is inherently unjust (Kohlberg, 1975). Consequently, it would be just for Heinz to risk his own freedom to save the life of another. Kohlberg considered Martin Luther King, Jr.'s "Letter from a Birmingham Jail" an excellent illustration of the universal ethical principle of moral reasoning.

> One may well ask, "How can you advocate breaking some laws and obeying others?" The answer lies in the fact that one has not only a legal but a moral responsibility to obey just laws. One has a moral responsibility to disobey unjust laws, though one must do so openly, lovingly and with a willingness to accept the penalty. An individual who breaks a law that conscience tells him is unjust, and accepts the penalty to arouse the conscience of the community, is expressing in reality the highest respect for law. An unjust law is a human law not rooted in eternal law and natural law. A law that uplifts human personality is just; one which degrades human personality is unjust. (Kohlberg, 1981, pp. 318–319)

Gilligan's Counterpoint to Kohlberg's Theory

Although Kohlberg's theory has held up rather well under hundreds of studies and it does consider both cognitive and social aspects of moral decisions (Gibbs, 1979; Gibbs &

Lawrence Kohlberg

Schnell, 1985), it has come under significant criticism. Much of that criticism revolves around the narrow sample Kohlberg used to establish his stages and moral norms (Gilligan, 1982). In his original study, Kohlberg relied on the decisions and justifications of 20 young males from the Chicago area, whom he followed for many years. But moral reasoning may look very different from the perspective of females or those from non-American, nonurban, or non-White cultures (Williams & Bybee, 1994).

Carol Gilligan (1977, 1993), for one, took Kohlberg to task on the issue of gender bias. She argued that the use of a male standard devalues the concern for others that females exhibit in their reasoning. Consequently, women are more apt to be judged as developmentally inferior, plateauing at Kohlberg's Stage 3 (1976). As a counterpoint to Kohberg's theory, Gilligan examined the moral reasoning of females from various walks of life. Her resulting stage theory, called the **morality of care,** differs from Kohlberg's in several ways (see Table 3–4).

First, Gilligan (1982) believes that the moral ideal that Kohlberg espoused was that of a self-sufficient, independent individual governed by abstract principles of right or justice. From her extensive interviews, Gilligan concluded that women operate from the vantage point of consensus building and the social collective. For that reason Gilligan (1977) cast the development of moral reasoning in terms of an expanding concern for others' well-being. Thus, in Level I, **orientation to individual survival,** females are entirely self-absorbed. In Level II, **goodness as self-sacrifice,** women frame their decisions around principles of consensus building and social participation (Gilligan, 1993). Finally, in Level III, **morality of nonviolence,** care for others becomes a universal obligation. Because of this overriding caring, the principle of nonviolent behavior toward others comes to govern all moral decisions: First do no harm.

A second distinction between Gilligan's and Kohlberg's theories has to do with periods of transition. Specifically, Gilligan included two important periods of transition in her theory. During the first transition, from **selfishness to responsibility,** females sense some discomfort with their entirely egocentric view of morality. The selfish orientation of level I begins to give way, in some measure, to a growing

Carol Gilligan

sense of responsibility to others. The second transition, from **goodness to truth,** is marked by a struggle to reconcile one's responsibility to oneself and one's responsibility to others (Gilligan, 1982). The willingness to act in a manner that would appear unkind or irresponsible on the surface in order to follow beliefs about nonviolence initially disrupts and confuses the individual.

The tenets and the components of Gilligan's theory have not been widely investigated (Pratt, Golding, Hunter, & Norris, 1988; L. J. Walker, 1989). Therefore, they must be treated as intriguing concepts that raise relevant questions about the standards for moral reasoning that Kohlberg proposed. Nonetheless, Gilligan was right to criticize Kohlberg's narrow and potentially biased sampling of moral decision making (Williams & Bybee, 1994). Kohlberg's methodology may have masked critical differences in the reasoning of those who do not share the sociocultural address of his young male respondents. To better understand this concern about the sociocultural bases for moral judgments, explore the questions raised in the Thought Experiment: Cultural Differences in Moral Thinking.

Thought Experiment ....

Cultural Differences in Moral Thinking

Is each of the following acts wrong? If so, how serious a violation is it?

1. A young woman is beaten black and blue by her husband after going to a movie without his permission, despite having been warned not to do that again.
2. A brother and a sister decide to get married and have children.
3. The day after his father died, the oldest son in a family gets a haircut and eats chicken.

These are three of 39 acts presented by Richard Shweder, Manoamohan Mahapatra, and Joan Miller (1990, pp. 165–166) to children aged 5 to 13 and adults in India and the United States. Hindu children and adults rated the son's having a haircut and eating chicken after his father's death as among the most morally offensive of the 39 acts they rated, and the husband's beating of his disobedient wife was not considered wrong at all. American children and adults, of course, viewed beating one's wife as far more serious than breaking seemingly arbitrary rules about appropriate mourning behavior. Although Indians and Americans could agree that a few acts, like brother/sister incest, were serious moral violations, they did not agree on much else.

Indian children and adults viewed the Hindu ban against behavior disrespectful of one's dead father as a universal moral rule; they thought it would be best if everyone in the world followed it, and they strongly disagreed that it would be acceptable to change the rule if most people in the society wanted to change it. For similar reasons, they believed that it is a serious moral offense for a widow to eat fish or wear bright-colored clothes or for a woman to cook food for her family or touch her children during her menstrual period. To orthodox Hindus, rules against such behavior are required by natural law; they are not arbitrary social conventions created by members of society. Hindus also regard it as morally necessary for a man to beat his disobedient wife in order to uphold his obligations as the head of the family.

In their study Schweder et al. (1990) found that universalistic moral thinking—the tendency to view rules of behavior as universally valid and unalterable—increases with age among Hindu children in India but decreases with age in the United States. This finding suggests that the course of moral development is different in different societies.

Note: Adapted from *Life-Span Human Development* (2nd ed., p. 348) by C. K. Sigelman and D. R. Shaffer, 1995, Pacific Grove, CA: Brooks/Cole.

What Developmental Principles Should Guide Instruction for Early-Childhood, Middle-School, and High-School Students?

The richness of the developmental literature provides teachers with suggestions for orchestrating learning environments that complement the developmental profiles of their students. Teachers can furnish young children with stimulating and inviting experiences that feed their inherent curiosity and desire to learn. Likewise, teachers can encourage middle-school children to look more deeply at the world around them and help those learners hone the tools they will require for independence and self-determination. Further, teachers can help adolescents map their futures by identifying their unique abilities and interests and by encouraging these learners to make reasoned and thoughtful choices. All of this, however, requires teachers to recognize the milestones of student development and to take advantage of the information and guidance those milestones afford (see Table 3–5).

Early-Childhood Education: A Period of Exploration

For many young children, the first years in school are an exciting time of personal exploration (White & Coleman, 2000). Indeed, the confluence of physical maturation, improved motor skills, increased cognitive abilities, and expanding social horizons sets the stage for a promising period of learning (Cowan, 1995; Ginsburg & Opper, 1988; Whitehurst & Lonigan, 1998). More than any other period of schooling, the early childhood years set the foundation for subsequent learning. Rousseau

(1762/1911) and others (U. S. Department of Health and Human Services, 1994) would describe this as the most critical period in children's formal learning.

Characteristics of Early-Childhood Students

By the time young children first experience formal learning, they have typically developed enough trust in caregivers and gained sufficient control of their own bodies to venture out from the security of their familiar home environments (Erikson, 1963). The ability to think symbolically allows these young minds to participate in linguistic and mathematical tasks that would have been beyond their abilities earlier (Piaget, 1955).

Of course, the essential learning tools of these young students remain their senses, so they learn best when they are both mentally and physically engaged (K. H. Rubin, Fein, & Vandenberg, 1983). Improved coordination of their fine and gross motor abilities also supports these children's physical and mental engagement (Roberton, 1984; J. M. Tanner, 1990). They are now able to manipulate small implements like pencils, crayons, or scissors (fine motor); and they are able to jump, skip, and run in a coordinated manner (gross motor).

Because of these increased physical and cognitive abilities, the world of print opens up to these young children. Untold avenues for exploration come with the ability to read (Adams, Treiman, & Pressley, 1998; Juel, 1988). Similarly, because these young children can now make sense of numeric symbols, they can perform simple mathematical tasks, such as counting, adding, and subtracting (English, 1997). When these newly formed abilities combine with their increasing attention spans, improved memories, and the ability to distinguish the real from the imagined, these young children are primed for academic exploration (Astington, 1993; Wellman & Gelman, 1998).

Table 3–5 Developmental milestones.			
	Physical	**Cognitive**	**Social/Emotional**
Early Childhood (5–7 years)	Increases in height and weight proceeding at a slow pace until adolescence Body proportions becoming more similar to those of adults Increasing fine motor abilities such as those needed for drawing and writing Gross motor processes like those used in skipping, jumping, or dancing becoming more coordinated Increases in physical speed and endurance	Symbolic thinking enhanced, allowing for linguistic and mathematical learning Concept formation aided by the ability to think categorically Improved attention and memory Ability to solve simple problems with concrete aids, such as adding or subtracting with toy counters Expanding vocabulary and use of more complex language structures Grasp of distinctions between real/pretend Exploration of social relations through play	Exploration of independence and emerging role through make-believe and self-initiated tasks Expanding social relations New tasks and shared experiences promoting feelings of industry and desire for success Egocentrism in moral reasoning with concern for rewards/ punishments or self-satisfaction
Middle School (9–11 years)	Increased coordination in gross and fine motor processes Faster reaction times Initial pursuit of domain-specific motor tasks such as those used in organized sports or specialized physical activities (e.g., dancing) Initiation of growth spurt and onset of puberty in some females Reaching 70% to 90% of adult height	Improvement in logical thought Increased ability to use multiple problem-solving strategies at once Base of background knowledge expanded Increased ability to self-monitor and self-regulate Ability to modify language to fit audience and to learn through verbal exchanges Evidence of emerging formal operational thought	Increased need for industry with more diverse and complex tasks Increased demand for social interaction and cooperation Moral reasoning at the conventional level, with actions shaped by compliance with moral codes Actions judged as right or wrong
Secondary School (14–18 years)	Physical growth spurt and puberty likely ongoing in males but concluded in females Increased muscle mass in males Increased fat cells in females Heightened pursuit of domain-specific motor and physical activities Greater concern for appearance Rise in sexual drives	Ability to think and solve problems of an abstract/ hypothetical nature Ability to consider long-range consequences Ability to weigh problems from multiple perspectives Complex language patterns Ability to see relationships among seemingly diverse concepts Ability to be novel or creative in thinking Capability of self-regulation	Expanding sphere of social influences Questions about the future arising Sense of self taking shape Issues of intimacy arising Moral reasoning still based on compliance with conventional codes Abstract principles of justice and fairness operating in a few

Most children in kindergarten and first grade exhibit an honest excitement about learning and an enthusiasm for exploration (Paris & Cunningham, 1996). Because children at this age are still quite self-centered and limited in their abilities to interact socially, the early childhood years are also periods of social experimentation (Munuchin & Shapiro, 1983). Children in kindergarten and first grade must learn how to function within a large social unit, they must learn how to meet their own needs in a socially appropriate way. These young children must also learn how to follow simple social conventions necessary for maintaining order in a classroom (Kohlberg, 1976).

Effective Learning Environments for Early-Childhood Students

To promote optimal learning, teachers need to create learning environments that complement young children's physical, cognitive, and social/emotional characteristics (Bredekamp, 1987). Effective early-childhood environments should have the attributes summarized in Table 3–6.

● **Ensure safety and security.** Because young children are widening their social circles and moving beyond familiar and comfortable territory (Munuchin & Shapiro, 1983), the classroom must be a warm and

Table 3–6   Attributes of effective learning environments.

Academic Level	Environmental Characteristics	Illustrative Case
Early Childhood	Ensure safety and security Create symbolic richness Encourage physical and cognitive engagement Expose children to enticing and varied experiences Operate on simple and clear rules for social interaction Support exploration and choice Use play as an opportunity for learning and self-expression	Sister Collette's kindergarten class is lively and inviting. Samples of children's work are everywhere in the room, which is divided into several learning areas. At this time three children are playing at the home center, making a pretend dinner for their make-believe family. Four children are sitting at the center table with Sister Collette, who is working on their letters and sounds. A parent volunteer, Mrs. O'Brien, is at the art center with several children who are making valentine cards for their parents. Marcus and two classmates are busy building a spaceship in the big blocks area of the room, while Milly and her best friends, Sasha and Kensha, are playing a counting game in the back corner with the teacher's aide.
Middle School	Afford opportunities for extended exploration of topics and domains Focus problem solving around personally relevant problems Provide opportunities for specialized physical activities Encourage cooperative and shared learning activities Encourage students to consider issues from multiple perspectives Require support for decisions and opinions Stimulate strategic thinking and self-evaluation	Christopher Sperl has been a fourth-grade teacher for 5 years. Christopher thinks it is important for students to explore important topics deeply, so he ties aspects of the curriculum—such as mathematics, history, and science—together in thematic units. These thematic units stress hands-on problem solving. Right now, students are hard at work on the ecology unit. Some are looking up information on endangered species on the computer, while others are working on interview questions they are going to ask select community leaders. Christopher and the students discuss some of the projects they can pursue and also decide together how some of those projects will be evaluated.
Secondary School	Encourage the pursuit of individual interests Expose students to varied career fields Promote individualization, creativity, and self-determination Involve students in decision making Build on social interactions and peer relations Introduce complex, abstract problems and content Support students' social involvement and activism Allow time for specialized physical and motor activities	Pam Bechtel's health class keeps students invested and engaged. Pam does not shy away from controversial and sensitive topics, like drug use and teen pregnancy. Nor does she believe in lecturing to these students. Instead, she allows them to consider various sides of the issues, requiring that they justify and support their positions with solid evidence. The students also must weigh the long-term effects of certain positive and negative behaviors. Pam encourages her students to participate in socially valued activities. This past Thanksgiving, for instance, her class served meals at a homeless shelter. Some students volunteer as tutors for students with special learning needs. Much of the work in health class is done in groups, and students help determine their project grades.

welcoming place. Young children must be able to put aside fears for their immediate well-being if they are going to see the learning environment as a place to explore and discover (White & Coleman, 2000).

- **Create symbolic richness.** Young children's newly acquired ability to think symbolically remains fragile. Therefore, teachers must encourage meaningful symbolic thinking by filling the environment with meaningful and enticing symbolic representations (Juel, 1988). The alphabet, common words/phrases, books, magazines, calendars, numbers, devices for

weighing and measuring, and simple clocks are just a few of the materials that could be part of a learning environment rich in symbols (Morrow, 1997). Teachers should refer to such materials often and promote students' interaction with them (Geary, 1994).

- **Encourage physical and cognitive engagement.** Given that children still rely heavily on their senses to understand their world, the early-childhood environment should be a place where mind and body are partners in learning (K. N. Rubin et al., 1983). Effective early-childhood rooms should be filled with manipulative, hands-on objects and materials that can be stacked, counted, sorted, and compiled (Paris & Cunningham, 1996). For example, children can say *three* while counting three buttons and then writing down the numeral 3.

Maria Montessori, an Italian physician, was one of the most influential early childhood educators of the past century.

• **Expose children to enticing and varied experiences.** The famous early-childhood educator Maria Montessori (1964) understood the importance of enticing and varied experiences for developing young minds. Her ideas are still alive in effective early-childhood classrooms today (Cuffaro, 1991; Kostelnik, 1992). Like Montessori effective teachers bring the world to these young children, stimulating their senses and their minds. Children might watch eggs hatch in a makeshift hatchery, look at leaves through magnifying glasses, or guess which objects will float or sink in a basin of water. The classroom becomes a place of exploring the world and learning from that exploration.

• **Operate on simple and clear rules for social interaction.** Because young children are still quite self-centered and not socially facile, they need guidance on how to interact with peers (Damon, 1983). Thus, effective early childhood classrooms operate around a few simple and clearly explained rules (e.g., treat others with respect, share). Children also need to be aware of the rewards and punishments that result from complying with or disobeying these community rules (Kohlberg, 1975). Since they are preconventional reasoners, these rewards and punishments shape their social behavior.

• **Support exploration and choice.** Although young students need a predictable framework in which to learn and thrive, they still benefit from occasional exploration and choice (Paris & Cunningham, 1996). Some free play or open choice time is commonly scheduled in early-childhood classrooms. During this time children can select which activities they will pursue and with whom. To maintain order, however, some teachers control the number of children who can play in any learning area (e.g., art center) at once. Teachers may also encourage certain students to try new activities, instead of staying with one or two favorites (White & Coleman, 2000).

• **Use play as an opportunity for learning and self-expression.** To young children play is a wonderful arena for learning (K. H. Rubin et al., 1983). Through play, children use their minds in imaginative and creative ways. They not only problem solve during play, but they also interact socially and physically with others (Pellegrini, 1988). In their play they try on different personas and act out particular roles. Effective early-childhood teachers learn much about young children's development by watching and listening to them during play.

Middle School: A Period of Expansion

Whereas early-childhood education builds a solid foundation for development, the middle-school years are about expansion. During those preadolescent years—when children's physical, cognitive, and social/emotional capabilities continue to grow and improve—education broadens and deepens their existing structures and abilities.

Characteristics of Middle-School Students

Preadolescent students have passed some developmental hurdles. Their bodies have become stronger and more proportioned, and their movements faster and more coordinated. In fact, most have reached 70% to 90% of their adult height. Toward the conclusion of this preadolescent period, some females experience growth spurts and the onset of puberty (J. M. Tanner, 1990). Also, during this period many children find satisfaction in some form of specialized physical activity like basketball, soccer, or gymnastics (Seifert et al., 1997).

In addition, middle-school students are able to see the world without the egocentric blinders that constrain everything younger children do and say (Damon & Hart, 1988). Middle schoolers are also faced with more diverse, subject-specific, and complex tasks than younger students (Erikson, 1980), resulting in a greater need for personal industry and an increased chance for academic frustration. Student motivation often declines during the middle-school years (Wigfield, Eccles, & Pintrich, 1996), although these children's background knowledge and conceptual understanding expands (Sigelman & Shaffer, 1995).

A few preadolescent students may show evidence of emerging formal operational thought, but most are concrete operational thinkers (Inhelder & Piaget, 1958). Thus, they can think logically and use multiple strategies simultaneously, making them better equipped to solve or reason through an array of academic problems. When problems are personally relevant and include concrete referents, these children's mental abilities are even more efficient and effective (Alexander, Pate, Kulikowich, Farrell, & Wright, 1989). Preadolescents can also display an emerging ability to self-monitor and self-regulate their performance (Flavell, Miller, & Miller, 1993).

Interactions with others become more important during middle school (Wentzel, 1999a, 1999b) and are helped by preadolescents' ability to modify their language to fit their audience (W. Deutsch & Pechmann, 1982). They can also listen and react to the ideas of others, thereby gaining from social exchanges. However, as conventional moral reasoners, they still tend to see the world in terms of right or wrong, black or white, as defined by established moral and behavioral codes (Kohlberg, 1981).

Effective Learning Environments for Preadolescent Students

In light of the physical, cognitive, and social/emotional milestones associated with the middle-school years, what should teachers do to orchestrate meaningful learning environments?

- **Afford opportunities for extended exploration of topics and domains.** As noted, early childhood is about initial forays into learning. By comparison, middle schoolers deepen their understandings of particular topics or academic subjects (Alexander, 1997b). Thus, good teachers at this level promote academic exploration by allowing time and resources to investigate intriguing problems, such as endangered species. And integrated units of study that bring together several content areas (e.g., history, mathematics, and reading) allow for a richer and more principled pursuit of knowledge and skills (Harris & Alexander, 1998).

- **Focus problem solving around personally relevant problems.** When middle-school teachers choose tasks and activities to reinforce students' understanding, they would be wise to target problems that this age group sees as personally relevant (Bransford, Brown, & Cocking, 1999). Such problems permit students to use their expanding base of background knowledge, give them the concrete focal point they need to think logically, and potentially raise their interest or motivation. In some cases students can help choose the problems they investigate, adding to their sense of ownership and the personal relevance of the task (Wigfield et al., 1996).

- **Provide opportunities for specialized physical activities.** Cognitive pursuits are not the only areas that become more specialized during this period; physical and motor activities do as well (Seifert et al., 1997). The physical developments that preadolescent students experience, combined with their increasing social abilities, make the middle-school period an opportune time to encourage students' interests in organized or specialized physical activities, from baseball to ballet. Research suggests that involving students early in such regular physical activities puts them on the path to lifelong wellness (S. N. Walker, Sechrist, & Pender, 1987).

- **Encourage cooperative and shared learning activities.** Because of their enhanced ability to communicate with others, preadolescent students profit from group learning experiences (Berk, 1999). Therefore, middle-school classrooms often make greater use of cooperative and collaborative activities. One benefit of these group learning approaches is that teachers do not always need to be the instructional guides (Webb & Palincsar, 1996); students at this age can learn from one another. Thus, cooperative and shared learning activities should be common tools in teachers' pedagogical repertoires.

- **Encourage students to consider issues from multiple perspectives.** Although these students still think in a rather linear and concrete way, they can weigh evidence from multiple perspectives (Piaget, 1955). Thus, middle school is an excellent time to explore multiple sources and even opposing sides of a topic. In fact, planning lessons as cases of persuasion, where two sides of a problem are juxtaposed, can enhance understanding, increase interest, and foster the exploration of unquestioned ideas (Fives & Alexander, 2001).

  As one example, instead of learning about Galileo and his scientific discoveries as a collection of dry facts, a group of fifth graders considered the effect that Galileo's findings had on prevailing beliefs about the world, the universe, and religion (Fives & Alexander, 2001). They looked at this question through the eyes of both Galileo and selected religious and political leaders of the time. They also learned how Galileo suffered as a result of his scientific discovery. When science learning is cast as persuasion, fifth graders become more invested in learning about important scientific discoveries and are less apt to consider science a sterile and uncontroversial subject.

- **Require support for decisions and opinions.** Effective middle-school teachers realize that learning is enhanced when students must support and justify their decisions and opinions. Chambliss (with Murphy, 2002), for instance, has worked extensively with this age group and found that their thinking, discussion, and writing improves when they are taught the skills of argumentation and explanation. She teaches her students how to identify a writer's or a speaker's argument and then to judge whether that point has been well supported. Further, she helps students learn how to frame their own arguments or premises and to include evidence that justifies such statements. Beyond augmenting students' thinking abilities, these activities can provide a base for later formal operational thought (Inhelder & Piaget, 1958).

- **Stimulate strategic thinking and self-evaluation.** Just as preadolescent students need guidance in learning how to ponder issues from multiple perspectives or how to frame and support an opinion, they need to be encouraged in their strategic processing (Pressley & McCormick, 1995). Strategies are procedures or techniques that aid performance or circumvent problems (Alexander, Graham, & Harris, 1998). Because of their importance to optimal learning and development, an entire chapter is devoted to them (Chapter 7).

  Teachers must recognize that strategic learning can be promoted by explicitly introducing various strategies to students and encouraging them to fit those procedures to the tasks at hand (Paris, Wasik, & Turner, 1991). For example, what steps can teachers suggest to enable students to distinguish more important from less important information in what they read or hear?

Concern for strategic thinking, including the ability to judge the quality of one's own work, needs to be evident in middle-school classrooms. And students need to be encouraged to expand their strategic repertoire, so that they have the right mental tools for the specific problems they encounter (Paris et al., 1991).

High School: A Period of Experimentation

Most adolescents define their identities (e.g., Who am I?) and consider the person they are becoming (e.g., Who will I be?) during the high-school years. In high school immediate and pressing needs clash with concerns for the future. Thus, adolescence is, in many ways, a time for physical, cognitive, and social/emotional experimentation under the watchful and caring gaze of knowledgeable adults.

Characteristics of Secondary-School Students

Adolescence is a period of physical, cognitive, and social/emotional transformation and upheaval (Sigelman & Shaffer, 1995). Teenage males are often in the throes of growth spurts and puberty, whereas females, who have likely completed this transformation, are confronting their heightened feelings of sexuality (J. M. Tanner, 1991). As bodies mature, muscle mass increases among males and fat cells among females. Concern for appearance and attractiveness is evident in this period, particularly among females (Pesa, 1999). In addition, increasing numbers of adolescents confront issues of intimacy and become sexually active. In fact, about 50% of females between 15 and 19 have had sexual intercourse (Zuckerman, 1999).

Adolescence also brings significant cognitive changes. Some high-school students move into formal operational thought, while their peers remain concrete and linear in their thinking (Piaget, 1930b). Those in formal operations can solve complex, abstract, and hypothetical problems. In addition, they can consider the long-range consequences of actions, weigh multiple perspectives simultaneously, and ponder future possibilities.

Other factors aid these students in reasoning and analysis. They are capable of using complex language in oral and written communication, and they can apply their linguistic skills in their expanding social circles (Piaget, 1955). In addition, adolescents can grasp relations among seemingly diverse concepts (i.e., analogical reasoning) and can devise their own novel or creative solutions to problems (Piaget, Montangero, & Billeter, 1977). Even though moral reasoning for most adolescents is still based on compliance with conventional codes, a few teenagers may differentiate right and wrong on the basis of abstract principles, such as justice and fairness (Kohlberg, 1981).

Effective Learning Environments for Adolescent Students

The physical, cognitive, and social/emotional characteristics of adolescents can lead to several recommendations for creating environments that foster their learning.

- **Encourage the pursuit of individual interests.** Experimentation involves pursuing individual or personal interests (Alexander, 1997a). By the time students reach high school, they should have curricular and extracurricular activities and topics in which they are personally invested. Effective teachers learn how to discover these personal interests and weave them into classroom tasks and discourse (Alexander & Jetton, 2000). Finding opportunities to combine students' individual interests with instructional goals can maintain students' engagement in the content and the learning process. It can also highlight the value of subject matter that might otherwise be treated with indifference. Personal interest can maintain students' pursuit of knowledge, even when problems are highly challenging (Alexander, 1997b).
- **Expose students to varied career fields.** As stated, secondary students are not just absorbed in the present, but are also concerned about the future. One critical question about the future pertains to career options (Ginzberg, 1972). In a few years, these students will be entering the world of work and are more likely to make wise decisions about their futures if they are exposed to various careers. However, that exposure must be more than a superficial, romanticized, and dramatized treatment of well-known occupations (e.g., doctor, lawyer, teacher, nurse). If students are making career decisions based on what they see on television, in movies, or in magazines, they will not understand what jobs are available and what they require (Ginzberg, 1972). Unfortunately, many high schools do an inadequate job of assisting students in this school-to-work transition, leaving students with fuzzy notions and unrealistic expectations (Grotevant, Cooper, & Kramer, 1986).
- **Promote individualization and creative processing.** One of the advantages of formal operations is that students can think and act independently and creatively (Piaget et al., 1977). Adolescents are able to devise their own approaches to problem solving and make reasoned choices. Effective learning environments for these students encourage them to do just that. Rather than merely asking them to execute problems in the exact way they are taught, teachers should encourage high-school students to formulate their own tasks or solution strategies (Pressley & McCormick, 1995). And teachers should give these students latitude in determining how such tasks or problems will be addressed and evaluated.
- **Involve students in decision making.** Teachers who work effectively with adolescents respect and appreciate these students and their abilities (Wigfield et al., 1996). Such respect and appreciation is evident when teachers give students a voice in curricular decisions. In fact, teachers can solicit students' ideas and opinions on all facets of learning, including the criteria by which assignments or projects are evaluated. This involvement promotes students' development of self-regulation and self-monitoring abilities

(Zimmerman, 1990). In addition, teachers should give students the chance to judge their own work on the basis of those criteria and then compare their judgments to those of the teacher. Through such activities students learn that their thoughts and views matter, and they gain skill in self-evaluation.

- **Build on social interactions and peer relations.** Social interactions and peer relations are unquestionably a large part of adolescent life (Erikson, 1980). Effective learning environments at the secondary level include group activities, class discussions, and peer learning that can tap into this social dynamic (Webb & Palincsar, 1996). Students can then learn from their classmates, not just from their teacher. Further, such arrangements can prove useful when students are at varying cognitive and moral stages of reasoning. The ideas of concrete operational thinkers can be intermingled with those of students who reason at a more sophisticated and abstract level.
- **Introduce complex, abstract problems and content.** The expanding minds of adolescent students make high school an excellent time to focus on problems and subject matter that are complex and abstract (Inhelder & Piaget, 1958). Although subjects such as algebra, physics, chemistry, political science, or philosophy are within the cognitive reach of some middle-school students, it is not until high school that many are ready for such demanding content. Effective learning environments include ample content and problem-solving tasks that require students to use their newly found capabilities to think abstractly (Piaget, 1930a).
- **Support students' social involvement and activism.** Whether students are at the conventional or postconventional level of moral reasoning, they should be encouraged to think beyond their own personal needs and wants (Gilligan, 1977). Encouraging students to consider larger social, cultural, and political issues can support these students' moral development (Kohlberg, 1975). Including discussions of broad and contentious social, cultural, and political issues in the curriculum can foster this learning process. However, it is also important to consider social and cultural differences when such issues are discussed (Shweder et al., 1990).

■ Summary Reflections

How does the mind change with age and experience?

- ■ Jean Piaget, who is credited with founding the field of cognitive development, identified four distinct stages and multiple substages.
  - During the sensorimotor stage, infants negotiate the world through direct sensory means.
  - In the preoperational stage, young children begin to show evidence of some rudimentary mental processes.
  - In the concrete operational stage, children engage in fundamental mental operations but are still grounded in the concrete, the everyday.
  - With formal operations individuals manifest complex and abstract reasoning and problem solving.
- ■ There are definite limits to Piaget's theory of cognitive development: task suitability, stage validity, generalizability, and universality.
- ■ Two alternatives to Piaget's views are well known.
  - Vygotsky's sociocultural perspective differs markedly along four dimensions, including the continuity and direction of development.
  - Robbie Case's theory, a neo-Piagetian approach, also identifies four stages but focuses on the mental representations that characterize them.

What are the patterns in the way students grow socially, emotionally, and morally?

- ■ Two perspectives on social development were presented.
  - Erik Erikson identified eight personal crises, or challenges, that unfold across the life span and focused on individuals' ability to confront those crises successfully.
  - Bronfenbrenner saw psychosocial development as shaped by the reciprocal relations that individuals form with others who populate their social systems, from the most personal and intimate (microsystem) to the most diffuse and pervasive (macrosystem).
- ■ Emotional development involves the range of emotions individuals express, their understanding of the sources for such feelings, and their ability to express themselves in socially appropriate ways and to reasonable degrees.
- ■ Two contrasting theories about moral reasoning were discussed.
  - Kohlberg framed the dialogue around the stages of reasoning that arise in the resolution of moral dilemmas.
  - Gilligan reshaped the dialogue by nesting it within a feminist orientation.

What developmental principles should guide instruction for early-childhood, middle-school, and high-school students?

- ■ Developmental milestones mark the course of development that students follow and help teachers serve as more informed guides.
- ■ These milestones vary by academic level.
  - Early childhood is a period of exploration, a time when young children first venture into the world of formal learning.
  - Middle school is a period of expansion, when students build on the foundation of knowledge and skills established during early childhood.
  - High school involves experimentation as students deal with physical, cognitive, and social/emotional changes and look to their futures as contributing members of society.

Chapter **4**

The Nature of Knowledge and the Process of Knowing

GUIDING QUESTIONS

- What is knowledge?

- What kinds of knowledge should be part of the educational experience?

- What principles of knowledge promote effective educational practice?

IN THEIR OWN WORDS

HELENROSE FIVES *has been a mathematics/ science and history teacher in a Catholic school for 6 years and the lead teacher for Grades 7 and 8 for 3 years. Located in the heart of a major metropolitan area, her school serves a predominantly minority population.*

It was the last period of the day. The 36 students in the seventh and eighth grade classes had been assembled to listen to a guest speaker on drug use and abuse. As the seventh grade homeroom teacher, I was ready to sit back and let someone else be in charge of my students' learning for the next 40 minutes. The speaker was a vibrant, middle-aged, African American man who brought visions of a drill sergeant to mind. In his booming voice, he attempted to generate responses from my students, who were being their normal adolescent selves at the close of a Friday, refusing to do much in the way of participating. Still, this man had something about him, and you knew the students would be drawn into his message eventually.

As a means of engagement, the speaker asked my students to name the members of the Supreme Court. Suddenly, there was a great deal of shifting in the seats and downcast eyes everywhere—my own included. As the history teacher, I had never covered this topic in my class. The gentleman then asked the students, "Can you name *just one*?" He certainly had the "wait time" strategy down to a science, but the students were looking anywhere but at him.

Then, out of the corner of my eye, I saw a hand go up. This couldn't be, I thought to myself. Gloria is going to answer this question? Gloria had not passed one history test all year. But there she was, looking at her classmates with an expression that could only mean, "How can you all be so dumb? Anybody can answer this question." Ready to be impressed, the other students and I perked up. Gloria cleared her throat and began, "Judge Judy, Judge Joe Brown, Judge Mathis, Judge Hatchett . . . " At this point the room erupted in laughter, and the speaker shot me a look that said, "What kind of school is this anyway?" If there had been a hole . . . well, you get the idea. Anyway, the speaker started to explain the difference between the Supreme Court and Court TV. Then he moved on to a question about alternative names for marijuana. Every hand in the room shot up, followed by an outpouring of colorful terms and expressions.

That incident caused me to question everything I had been doing throughout the year. How could these 36 students come up with a seemingly endless list of terms for marijuana but not produce the name of a single Supreme Court justice? How could Gloria confuse that litany of TV judges with the justices of the Supreme Court? And why was I so frustrated and perplexed by this one incident?

On the one hand, I have to question how important the names of Supreme Court justices are to these students anyway. How many voting adults could answer the same question? Where should this information rank in our list of things to know? It was and still is easy for me to justify my students' lack of knowledge in this situation. I was also annoyed that my students were once again seen as lacking some valued information. I don't think my students lack knowledge or ability. Rather, the knowledge they have and use is just not valued outside their community.

Living in the Farm [the housing project] and walking down the Avenue [its main street] to and from school, these students need to know 101 words for marijuana. They hear those expressions routinely. These words are part of daily conversation and their common knowledge. Without this kind of knowledge they could not survive. But I don't want their knowledge and abilities to be confined to that world immediately outside this school, either. I want more for them than that.

I did find some positive points in that episode, too. For one, 35 of the 36 students were aware that they didn't know the members of the Supreme Court, and they sure knew that Gloria's list of judges was way off the mark. That showed me that they had some understanding of the Supreme Court and the judicial system. What was also encouraging is that the first question out of my seventh graders' mouths when we got back to homeroom was "Who *are* the members of the Supreme Court, Ms. Fives?" The speaker's question suddenly became a source of intrigue for my students and the seed for a class project we designed together. By the end of that project, my students probably knew more about the Supreme Court than most adults in this country. If only the guest speaker would ask my students that same question today.

What Is Knowledge?

In *Democracy and Education* John Dewey (1916/1944) took a philosophical look at many issues that underlie Helenrose's reflections in the opening segment. What role should schools play in the lives of students? Where does knowledge fit in the educational process?

As civilization advances, the gap between the capacities of the young and the concerns of adults widens. Learning by direct sharing in the pursuits of grown-ups becomes increasingly difficult except in the case of the less advanced occupations. Much of what adults do is so remote in space and in meaning that playful imitation is less and less adequate to reproduce its spirit. Ability to share effectively in adult activities thus depends upon a prior training given with this end in view. Intentional agencies—schools—and explicit material—studies—are devised. The task of teaching certain things is delegated to a special group of persons.

Without formal education, it is not possible to transmit all the resources and achievements of a complex society. It also opens a way to a kind of experience which would not be accessible to the young, if they were left to pick up their training in informal associations with others, since books and the symbols of knowledge are mastered. (Dewey, 1944, pp. 7–8)

As Dewey saw it, schools are fundamentally sociopolitical institutions that perform numerous functions for society. Schools are a mechanism for society's self-preservation; they communicate its sociocultural heritage from one generation to the next. Schools also contribute to the formation of an informed citizenry and promote the optimal development of all. Moreover, schools are the means for enculturating society's young into the social mainstream and the conduits for experiences and training not afforded by everyday life.

Teachers like Helenrose carry these societal expectations heavily on their professional shoulders, as evidenced by her reaction to her students' limited knowledge of the Supreme Court. Teachers recognize that they have a responsibility to guide learners in their academic development. Reflective teachers realize that knowledge helps them fulfill many of education's roles—serving as a cultural archivist, contributing to self-fulfilled persons, developing an informed citizenry (Schön, 1983).

Reflective teachers also recognize that they cannot be the sole source of students' knowledge. The task of educating students is much too extended and far too complex for any teacher to fulfill alone. And the universe of academic content is far too vast. Educators must thoughtfully and wisely select from this universe, considering school curricula and professional standards but ultimately determining on their own which ideas and experiences merit time and attention in their classrooms. Reflective teachers continually wrestle with the question of which specific concepts and practices will most benefit their students, not just here and now, but also for years to come (Schön, 1983, 1988). Teachers must also decide on the best ways to bring this chosen content to life and give it meaning for their students.

Although knowledge is a centerpiece of formal education (Lambert & McCombs, 1998), educators rarely have the luxury of exploring the nature of knowledge (Murphy, 2003). Such a pursuit may seem too removed from everyday practice, too abstract or esoteric to warrant consideration when there are 15, 20, or more students to educate. However, questions about knowledge and knowing are foundational to learning and teaching. How students conceptualize knowledge and knowing directly influences their educational aims, approaches to learning, academic success, and personal investment in inquiry (Pajares, 1992; Schommer, 1990). Likewise, teachers' conceptions of knowledge and knowing are mirrored in their instructional goals, their pedagogical decisions, and their assessment practices (Garner & Alexander, 1999). Two teachers handed the same set of instructional materials will convey those materials differently if their views on knowledge and knowing differ.

Conceptualizing Knowledge and the Process of Knowing

Concepts of knowledge and knowing have many iterations and interpretations (Reynolds, Sinatra, & Jetton, 1996). In fact, every student and teacher has constructed a personal theory of knowledge and knowing, however unvoiced or untested that theory might be (Chinn, 1998). Those with a background in education or psychology have likely been introduced to formal theories of learning and development—such as behaviorism, information processing, or constructivism—which have undergone years of analysis and empirical testing. These theories try to explain how students become educated or enculturated. Through the study of such formal theories, individuals acquire a vocabulary of relevant terms and concepts that allow them to share their understandings or experiences with others. Thus, learning theories serve as frameworks for pedagogical and curricular decision making, helping teachers specify what content and techniques should be part of the educational experience.

Formal learning theories represent diverse orientations to knowledge and knowing, although the differences are often subtle and not readily identified. One reason the distinctions may be hard to see is that learning theories are often treated as dichotomous or are studied in isolation (Bredo, 1996). Thus, students of psychology or education are exposed to behaviorism as the conditioning of human actions, seemingly divorced from thinking or reasoning. This theoretical orientation is then contrasted to cognitive perspectives, divorced from human actions. It is not evident where knowledge and knowing sit within these broad views of learning or what similarities, if any, exist in their explanations about how knowledge takes shape.

However, knowledge and knowing cannot be cast in simple or dichotomous terms. What separates different views is the emphasis placed on the universe *within* and *without* the human mind and the degree to which the focus is on one (i.e., the individual mind) or many (i.e., groups, society, or culture). Therefore, this discussion will contrast several theories according to their more individual or more social orientation toward knowledge and knowing. They will be positioned on a continuum based on how their adherents describe the process by which knowledge takes form (i.e., Is knowledge individually acquired or socially constructed?) and where knowledge is presumed to reside (i.e., Is knowledge in the mind or in the environment?). These two guiding questions are central to the philosophical study of knowledge, which is termed **epistemology.**

Before beginning this analysis of formal theories, take a few minutes to reflect on your own beliefs about knowledge and knowing. The Thought Experiment: Plotting Your Personal Theory of Knowledge will assist you in your self-examination.

Thought Experiment ....

Plotting Your Personal Theory of Knowledge

Directions: Below is a line on which you can plot your personal beliefs about knowledge. At one extreme, knowledge and knowing are viewed as entirely individually oriented. At the other, knowledge and knowing are viewed as completely socially oriented. To place your views about knowledge and knowing on this continuum, consider the following two questions.

Where does knowledge come from?

   Do you believe that knowledge takes shape in the mind? Or is knowledge formed within the environment or during human interactions? Those on the individually oriented side of the continuum emphasize the mind as the creator of knowledge. From this perspective what we call knowledge ultimately takes root in the mind of each individual, whether in an extremely rich and inviting environment or one that is austere (Reynolds, 1992). By comparison, those on the socially oriented side perceive of knowledge as the product of the environment or social interactions. According to the socially oriented perspective, all knowledge is seeded and continually fed by social and cultural interchanges. Without the sociocultural collective, in essence, there would be no means or need to know (Sfard, 1998).

Where does knowledge reside?

   Do you, like those at the more individually oriented end of the continuum, believe that knowledge exists in some form within the human mind? Or do you believe that knowledge exists out in the world to be found or discovered through life experiences or through human interactions?

As you place your *X* on the continuum below, weigh your responses to these two questions. If you believe that knowledge is entirely the creation of the individual mind *and* resides there, then you are at the extreme end of individually oriented. If, on the other hand, you believe that knowledge already exists within the world or takes shape only during the process of human interaction *and* if you believe that knowledge remains part of that external world, then your beliefs are strongly socially oriented.

Perhaps you have more interactive beliefs about knowledge and knowing. For example, you may believe that the individual mind is a key to the formation of knowledge and that knowledge exists in some measure within that mind, *but* you may also see the environment and sociocultural forces as powerfully shaping that knowledge. Or maybe you believe that human interaction with the environment and people who are part of that environment are the source of knowledge *but* you believe that knowledge comes to reside in one's mind. In those cases your beliefs would fall somewhere between the two extremes. Your specific location on the knowledge continuum depends on the degree to which your beliefs weigh more on the side of the individual or on society and the environment.

Individually _ Socially
Oriented   Oriented

....

Viewing Knowledge from Different Theoretical Frameworks

These same two questions of where knowledge comes from and where it resides can be asked of several current theories of learning, which are collectively displayed on an individual-to-social continuum in Figure 4–1. It is not essential that you identify with any one of those theories, but it is important to understand how you perceive knowledge and how you act on that perception in your learning or teaching.

   Three caveats should be shared about the discussion that follows. First, to make the distinctions between theories more apparent, the boundaries that exist between them have been sharpened. In reality, the delineations and interpretations of these theories in the educational literature are often more vague and fuzzy than portrayed here. Second, the placement of each theory is only an approximation. Adherents of these theoretical perspectives rarely achieve consensus when it comes to questions about knowledge and

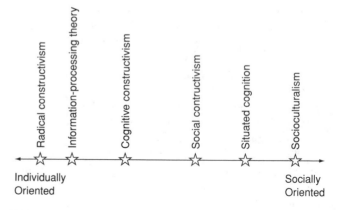

■ **FIGURE 4–1   Learning theories on a continuum of individual-to-social orientation.**

knowing. And finally, formal theories, like personal theories, are not set in stone; they are fluid and dynamic.

Behaviorism

Many textbooks on learning theory or educational psychology begin with a discussion of behaviorism, which was the dominant theory of human learning in the first half of the 20th century. Behaviorists like Watson (1924) and Thorndike (1924) set out to eliminate from the study of human learning the brand of "mentalism" advocated by William James (1890), John Dewey (1902/1956), and others. This strict form of behaviorism sought a purely scientific investigation of human learning that relied strictly on the observable. It was, in effect, the study of human actions devoid of the interference of human thought or reasoning (Bredo, 1996). Any consideration of the black box of the human mind was absent in behavioral treatments of teaching and learning, for learning was a matter of conditioning behavior, not enhancing thinking or knowledge (Watson, 1924).

To behaviorists the goal of learning was reshaping human action, which could be achieved by tapping into natural stimulus-response (SR) pairings that already exist to form a new SR pattern (i.e., **classical conditioning**). This was the crux of Pavlov's much-described experiment, in which he linked the sound of a bell to the presentation of food that naturally elicited salivation in dogs. Eventually, the bell alone triggered the salivation, demonstrating that the dog had been conditioned, or had learned. Behaviorists like B. F. Skinner (1968) proved that even voluntary human actions could be conditioned through the systematic and effective use of reinforcers and punishments (i.e., **operant conditioning**). For instance, undergraduates in many classrooms spontaneously raise their hands when they want to speak, regardless of whether a professor has requested or required that behavior. They do it because they have been systematically reinforced for raising their hands throughout their educational careers.

Because behaviorists adhering strictly to the tenets of Pavlov, Skinner, and Watson are interested solely in observable human behaviors, they talk about learning but not about knowledge or knowing. They would judge learning, in the form of new SR patterns, to be environmentally triggered (Reynolds et al., 1996). Behaviorism would leave concepts of knowledge to those who follow more cognitive and sociocultural paths toward learning and development. Consequently, behaviorism is not plotted on the knowledge continuum.

Information-Processing Theory

Individually Oriented ⟶ Socially Oriented

The **information-processing (IP) theory** is one of the older theoretical perspectives on human learning and one that sparked several of the alternative viewpoints on the continuum. IP theory tries to explain how individuals take in information from the environment and transform it into

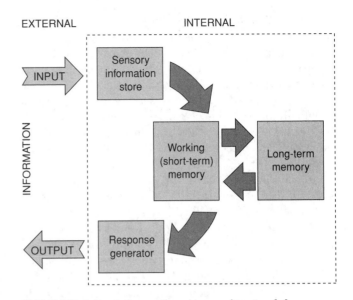

EXTERNAL   INTERNAL

INPUT → Sensory information store → Working (short-term) memory ⇄ Long-term memory → Response generator → OUTPUT

INFORMATION

■ **FIGURE 4–2   Information-processing model.**

Note: From *Essentials of Learning for Instruction* by R. M. Gagné, 1974, Hinsdale, IL: Dryden Press. Copyright 1974 by Dryden Press. Adapted with permission.

knowledge stored in the mind. A simple model depicting this transformation is displayed in Figure 4–2.

To IP theorists knowledge is formed as individuals take in, or input, information from their environments (Newell & Simon, 1972; Simon, 1989). Depending on the attributes of the individual (e.g., prior knowledge, memory capacity, attentional patterns, or strategic capabilities) and the relevance or salience of the information, certain messages from the environment are input, processed, stored as knowledge, and subsequently output as behavior. As terms like *input, stored,* and *output* suggest, the roots of IP go back to efforts to create intelligent or thinking machines—machines that could mimic basic human actions. This field of research is aptly called *artificial intelligence* (Simon, 1978).

The primary task of the individual, according to IP theory, is to move information effectively and efficiently from the external environment into the primary store of human knowledge, **long-term memory (LTM).** Information that reaches LTM has, in effect, found its way to the hard drive of the mind, where it can be repeatedly accessed and updated and where it will serve to direct subsequent information encounters, transmissions, and actions. To achieve this goal, however, information from the environment must pass through a series of mental stores (Broadbent, 1938), each of which has a unique role to play in transforming environmental messages into individual knowledge.

Because information encountered in the environment is vast, continuous, and multisensory, only a small portion survives the perilous journey to LTM. The **sensory information store (SIS)** gathers together the impulses and images picked up by the senses and fuses them into an impression that can be mentally grasped. SIS is also referred to as the **sensory register.** Even though the capacity of SIS is expansive, the life span of the sensations and impressions it formulates is brief. That means that students sitting in a classroom hearing or reading about and discussing the Supreme Court will be able to attend to only a small measure of the information in the learning environment. Of course, students and their teachers can take steps to increase the amount of sensory information that eventually makes it into memory. For example, students can record information they hear during class lectures or discussion, and teachers can revisit important information or display it through various media.

To survive the journey to LTM, sensations and impressions in SIS must enter the realm of consciousness to be contemplated and analyzed. This function occurs in **working memory (WM),** also called **short-term memory (STM).** In many ways WM is the gateway to LTM. Unlike SIS the capacity of WM is notoriously limited (G. A. Miller, 1956). We have all experienced the constraints of WM when we have struggled to keep a list of names or numbers in mind, only to suffer the loss of that information when some added tidbit entered our environment and our awareness. Information can stay in WM as long as we ponder it or turn it over in our minds, as when we try to remember a set of numbers by saying them over and over in our heads. Thus, to keep information about the Supreme Court alive, students might find it useful to rehearse what they have read or heard or put that content into their own words. They might also find it useful to ask themselves questions as they read.

From an IP perspective, Helenrose's students might actually have heard the names of the Supreme Court justices on television or radio. However, that exposure was insufficient to ensure that the information survived the journey from WM to LTM. There could simply have been too few occasions when information about the Supreme Court came into direct contact with these student's minds. The more exposure these students had to this information, the more likely they would have been to retain it. It is also possible that the information on the Supreme Court was buried in an information flow and, therefore, lacked the potency or uniqueness necessary to catch these students' attention and interest.

According to IP theory, once information reaches LTM, it becomes knowledge and can presumably reside in memory indefinitely (R. M. Gagné, 1977). However, before knowledge can be put to use, it must find its way out of LTM and back into WM, where it can be reconsidered. Then it must reach the **response generator,** where the brain converts conscious thoughts into behaviors, or outputs. These outputs are externalized through one or more sense organs; for example, a student might *talk* about Supreme Court judges or *diagram* the place of the Court within the branches of government.

Based on this model, what would information-processing theorists advise Helenrose? They would be concerned about the students' inability to produce the name of even one Supreme Court judge, especially if those students had been exposed to that information. IP theorists would focus their energies on the individual student's knowledge base and the efficiency or effectiveness of his or her mental functioning. Because knowledge, to an information-processing theorist, not only arises in the individual mind but also resides there, this theory is positioned at the individually oriented end of the knowledge continuum (see Figure 4–1).

IP theory distinguishes between information and knowledge and draws attention to those thoughts, feelings, and impressions that remain locked away from public view in the black box of students' minds—something behaviorism does not do (Goetz, Alexander, & Ash, 1992). Teachers who hold to an information-processing view see merit in providing their students with specific techniques for processing information more efficiently and effectively, like summarizing or outlining. IP teachers also focus on the organization and coherence of information during instruction, and they prime students' existing knowledge so that information can move more quickly to LTM (Goetz et al., 1992).

Cognitive Constructivism

Individually - - - - - - - - - - - - - - - - ☆ - - - - - - - - - - - - - - - - Socially
Oriented   Oriented

Despite its initial popularity, several aspects of IP theory did not sit well with many educational theorists, researchers, and practitioners. Their dissatisfaction helped to spark alternative perspectives on learning with varied views of knowledge and knowing. For instance, some argued that IP theory left the impression that information is simply plucked, fully formed, from the environment. According to these critics, insufficient emphasis was placed on individuals' ability to formulate, or *construct,* knowledge and on the importance of society and culture in learning and teaching. Also, because of IP's linear and one-directional flow, little was made of the possibility of simultaneous and continuous influence of existing knowledge on the formation of new understandings. Finally, many found the exactness or finality of the stored information, as described in IP, to be unacceptable (D. C. Phillips, 1995).

In framing alternatives to IP, theorists sought to give more power to individuals or groups in the formulation of knowledge and to treat knowledge as more variable and far less certain. The result was several schools of **constructivism** that share one fundamental characteristic. They hold that knowledge is created, or constructed, by individuals or groups and not simply acquired (Byrnes, 1996). In these alternative frameworks, knowledge or knowing cannot exist without human construction.

Beyond this common principle, the schools of constructivism differ markedly. **Cognitive constructivism,** like IP theory, portrays knowledge as being individually formed, and both cognitive constructivism and IP represent knowledge as an individual possession (Sfard, 1998). Whether knowledge results from the linear processing of information or is constructed from experiences, it remains personal or idiosyncratic. In addition, both IP and cognitive constructivism see the knowledge in LTM as pivotal to learning and development (Reynolds et al., 1996). However, whereas IP theorists concentrate on the mental process by which information is transformed into knowledge, cognitive constructivists emphasize the manner in which human minds grow or develop biologically *and* socially. Because of this subtle distinction and its attention to the idiosyncratic character of knowledge, cognitive constructivism moves closer to the socially oriented side of the knowledge continuum (see Figure 4–1).

In forming their developmental orientation to knowledge, cognitive constructivists draw heavily on the writings and theories of Jean Piaget, one of the most influential psychologists of all time (Byrnes, 1996), who was mentioned in chapters 2 and 3. Trained as a biologist, Piaget was invested in understanding how the mind (and the knowledge it constructs) changes with age and experience, that is, how thinking develops. In Piaget's (1955) well-known theory of cognitive development, humans pass through distinct stages of mental maturation, with certain mental constraints and capabilities marking each stage and each stage signifying an increasing level of mental sophistication reflected in more complex constructions of knowledge.

As for Helenrose's situation, cognitive constructivists would likely weigh these seventh and eighth graders' potential to appreciate the intricacies of the American judicial system, of which the Supreme Court is just one piece. They would consider her students' inability to respond in relation to their level of mental reasoning and the suitability of prior exposures to the concept of the Supreme Court. In other words, Helenrose's students may have failed to retain the information on the Supreme Court because that information was not cast in a learning activity appropriate for their mental development.

Not all cognitive constructivists see mental development as occurring in stages (Case, 1985; Siegler, 1991). However, most accept that the level of mental maturation has a great deal to do with the information individuals can grab from their environments. Mental maturity also affects the constructions or interpretations people make and the knowledge that ultimately becomes part of their mental histories. For a 4-year-old, who relies on direct physical contact to get information and generally thinks only in terms of immediate needs, the idea of a Supreme Court is probably beyond his mental capabilities, regardless of the number of times the concept is presented. By comparison those who have matured cognitively can deal with difficult and abstract concepts, such as the American judicial system. They can also engage in complex reasoning (e.g., "What do I really need to know about the Supreme Court anyway?") and can consider issues from multiple perspectives (e.g., "Is the judicial system of the United States equally just for the poor and the rich?").

Teachers who give credence to the cognitive-constructivist perspective are careful to select materials and experiences that are developmentally appropriate for their students (Siegler, 1991). They understand that 4-year-olds do not see the world or process information in the same way that 14-year-olds or 40-year-olds do. Therefore, these teachers' expectations for their students vary greatly, as do the instructional tasks and educational experiences they incorporate into their classrooms. From this perspective Helenrose should ask herself not only what her students can grasp about the American judicial system, but also what they would benefit from knowing about this concept at this point in their development. Teachers who tend toward a cognitive-constructivist viewpoint are also sensitive to the signs their students convey about their cognitive functioning, and these teachers create learning activities that complement and strengthen their students' existing mental abilities.

Radical Constructivism

Individually Oriented ☆--- Socially Oriented

Individuality is taken to an even higher level by **radical constructivists.** In fact, a radical constructivist would probably not have been concerned about Gloria's announcement that Judge Joe Brown and Judge Judy were members of the Supreme Court. Rather, these theorists would explore the students' ideas about judges without attention to the correctness of the initial responses. They would appreciate and build on whatever interpretations or constructions the students have made—constructions as unique as fingerprints.

As exemplified by the writings of von Glasersfeld (1991), radical constructivism is the educational equivalent of existentialism in philosophy (Woods & Murphy, 2002). In existentialism life and reality are truly individual creations; reality and purpose are meaningless beyond the individual's perception of them. Much the same can be said about radical constructivism. For these theorists there is no reality or truth in the world that we must struggle to attain and internalize as knowledge. The very concept of an objective reality or truth is an educational illusion. The only reality is what the individual mind can conjure.

Many who have espoused a radical-constructivist outlook come from the fields of mathematics and science, where there is a tendency to treat information as right or wrong, black or white. In these domains many problems presented to students are algorithmic in nature. In other words, students solve these typical problems by applying linear processes that result in an accepted outcome.

Ernst von Glasersfeld's writing sparked extensive debate about the idiosyncrasies of knowledge.

As the seventh- and eighth-grade science teacher in her school, Helenrose is expected to cover the topic of gravity. Most of us would acknowledge the existence of gravity, and we would say that we know about and believe in the existence of gravity as a force in the universe that keeps our feet firmly set on the planet. However, according to radical constructivists, Helenrose should resist any tendency to treat gravity as scientific fact or truth in her teaching, because no one can know about gravity in any unbiased or objective way (von Glasersfeld, 1991). The only reality of gravity exists in each person's mind, and its only truth is what each person constructs. Instead of judging her students' constructions of gravity against an accepted standard, Helenrose should employ whatever human or physical resources exist in her classroom to enrich her students' personal understandings of this concept, whatever those understandings might be.

An example from mathematics may clarify this perspective further. A first grader presented with the problem 2 + 2 = X might offer the solution 5. Radical constructivists believe that such a first grader should be free to apply an alternative logic, even to a problem like 2 + 2. A teacher should not respond as if there is one correct reality that this child must internalize. Instead, the task is to try to understand the idiosyncratic logic that the child is using to construct the response and provide opportunities for questioning and exploring so as to enrich the student's personal construction (Steffe & D'Ambrosio, 1995). Radical constructivism is placed in an extreme position on the continuum because of this subjective orientation toward knowledge. Nonetheless, radical constructivism does remind us how often educators treat school content as truths that their students are to accept and memorize.

Social Constructivism

Individually Oriented ------------------------☆------------- Socially Oriented

In contrast to IP theory, cognitive constructivism, and radical constructivism, three knowledge frameworks are increasingly more socially oriented in their views of knowledge. The first of these is **social constructivism.** During the 1930s, when Piaget's work was gaining popularity, it drew the attention of a young Russian scholar, Lev Vygotsky (1934/1986), and his colleagues, including Luria (1976) and Bakhtin (1981). As discussed in chapter 3, Vygotsky recognized the insightfulness of Piaget's theories but argued that Piaget overlooked the force that society and culture exert on human learning and development. Vygotsky's writings illustrated how thinking and learning are dependent on social interactions and reflective of cultural values.

From birth an infant begins to interpret the world through the words and actions of others. The verbal play that occurs between parents and babies illustrates that influential social interaction; for example, "What's that? Is my little girl hungry? Are you telling Mommy that you're hungry?" As the child matures, so does the nature of the interactions; the exchanges become more extensive and expand beyond the child's immediate physical or social/emotional needs. In addition, the child may become more directive in these interactions, often initiating or shifting the direction of such exchanges. With in-

creasing age and experience, children have more knowledge, more ideas, and stronger views to contribute. Thus, the level of adult-student interactions in Helenrose's classroom would be appreciably different from that of a first-grade classroom.

Because the individual mind does not develop in a vacuum but is always part of a social and cultural milieu, social constructivists do not divorce the mind from society. Even in the most formal of learning environments, there is a continuous dependence on human-to-human interactions; for instance, a teacher clarifies an idea for a student, or a classroom discussion takes place. In the opening scenario, the speaker's questioning and later the classroom discussion and ensuing project led Helenrose's students to a richer understanding of the Supreme Court. Social constructivists stress the direct and undeniable effect of such social and cultural factors on knowledge construction. Because people see the world differently as a result of sociocultural forces, their construction of ideas will differ also.

What is sometimes overlooked in discussions of Vygotsky's (1978, 1934/1986) writings is the premium he placed on the presence of a more informed or more capable other in the learning environment. Vygotsky's concept of the **zone of proximal development** was intended to capture this gap between what any person can accomplish mentally when working alone and what can be accomplished with the support or guidance of a more knowledgeable or capable other (M. Cole & Engeström, 1993).

Even though social constructivists, following in the footsteps of Vygotsky and others (Bakhtin, 1981; Luria, 1976), see society and culture as essential for learning, they still allow for individual cognition, as well as an individualistic character to knowledge. In other words, although heavily influenced socially and culturally, knowledge remains a uniquely personal construction. Thus, social constructivists talk in terms of mental structures and cognitive development, but their interests lie more in understanding how the sociocultural context contributes to the learning and development of the individual and how the nature of human-to-human interchanges shapes what one comes to know.

Situated Cognition

Individually Oriented --☆----- Socially Oriented

Situated cognition, also known as *situativity theory* and *situated action* (Greeno & the Middle School Mathematics Through Application Project Group, 1998), stands apart from the other perspectives discussed here in two ways: (a) its focus on physical and human resources in the environment and (b) its concern for the immediate context and process of knowing rather than the product of knowledge. The term *situated* reminds educators that all knowledge exists *in situ*, that is, situated in a particular time and place. Situated cognitivists would not be very interested in what Helenrose's students knew before or after the assembly on drug use. What would capture their attention would be the confluence of human and nonhuman resources in that assembly room that stimulated the exchanges between the students and adults.

Several factors help to explain this unique orientation. First, many who helped frame this relatively new theory of human learning came from the fields of artificial intelligence and educational technology (Clancey, 1993). These theorists shifted from an interest in developing intelligent machines to promoting the intelligent use of those machines. Their background in technology prompted situated cognitivists to talk about the physical as well as the human resources provided by the environment (Gillingham et al., 1994). Within this framework there is as much interest in human-machine interactions as there is in human-to-human interchanges. In some ways the computer can take on the role of the knowledgeable, capable "other" that Vygotsky envisioned. Situated cognitivists do not overlook the social aspects of learning, but their sense of collaboration and social learning often involves shared problem solving that includes technology (Cognition and Technology Group at Vanderbilt [CTGV], 1996).

Citing the research of J. J. Gibson (1966), situated cognitivists talk about how the environment, with all of its resources, "affords" human thinking. Gibson, a maverick in psychological circles, rejected much of the perception research of his day. Instead, he hypothesized that human perceptions are direct, automatic, and continuous, as humans move through the environment noticing subtle shifts in light and texture. The need to contemplate or interpret what was perceived did not play into Gibson's radical notions of perception, which certainly set him apart from most perceptual psychologists.

Situated cognitivists have carried Gibson's work into the classroom. **Affordances** are potential resources available to those who can recognize and take advantage of them. According to this theoretical view, Helenrose should not be concerned about her students' knowledge of the Supreme Court. Rather, Helenrose should be worried about her students' perceptiveness. Maybe these students have not learned how to see all the rich information their environments afford them, or maybe they function in an environment that limits their perceptions. In either case the relation between learner and environment may not be working to these students' advantage.

Even though the mention of person-environment interactions is reminiscent of IP theory, there are some significant differences. In situated cognition the interplay between person and environment has nothing to do with the individual mind or the storage of knowledge in LTM, as it does in IP theory. For situated cognitivists the moment of interplay between individuals and the environment is the crux of knowing (Greeno & MSMAPG, 1998).

Many who adhere to this perspective do not even like to use the word *knowledge* since it suggests the existence of a durable, individual memory store. When knowledge is mentioned, it is most often understood as the individual's ability to read the existing environment, both human and physical, and use that understanding to guide thoughts and actions (Greeno & MSMAPG, 1998). In situated cognition, knowledge is strongly bound to the context at hand, ensuring its temporal character and distancing it from frameworks that focus on individual stores of knowledge. In fact, this school of thought has undergone a series of name changes (i.e., from *situated cognition* to *situativity*) in an attempt to highlight its concern for the process of thinking and knowing and to erase the image of an individual mental store.

This framework has significant implications for learning and instruction. Within a situated-cognitive framework, Helenrose would be especially concerned with orchestrating learning environments rich with resources that could afford students' thinking and problem solving. Her assessment of what her students "know" would focus on shared problem-solving tasks, often involving technology. Consequently, if the target of instruction was the Supreme Court, Helenrose might pose a problem to the class: "Explore the way the Supreme Court influences your everyday lives." Among the resources she might provide her students would be Websites rich with information about the Supreme Court, along with online access to legal experts willing to answer students' questions. Of course, some traditional resource materials like textbooks and videos might also be available. As a gauge of their learning, Helenrose might have the students engage in discussion or create a hypermedia presentation about the Supreme Court's influence in their lives.

Socioculturalism

Individually .... ☆ Socially
Oriented   Oriented

The rise of constructivism in the 1970s can be attributed in part to the growing popularity of writings by Vygotsky (1978) and his Russian associates. During that same period, educational researchers became aware of the literature in social and cultural anthropology, particularly the writings of Lave (1988), Rogoff (with Gauvain, 1986), and M. Cole (with Engeström, 1993). Like the works of Vygotsky, these writings voice concerns with the mechanistic tone of cognition, as mirrored in IP and artificial intelligence research. However, this work raised awareness of social and cultural forces to a new level and contributed to the theoretical framework called **socioculturalism.** To socioculturalists, portraying human thinking and learning as mechanistic, devoid of emotions and goals and deprived of social contact, is to miss the very essence of humanness. The roots of learning and development exist in human sociocultural interactions and the way groups, not individuals, construct understandings.

Specifically, socioculturalists argue that individualistic interpretations of learning and development are misleading.

Such views do not pay adequate homage to the social collective that directly or indirectly determines what any one individual can come to know. To socioculturalists what one person knows is not important, but rather what knowledge is shared as members of particular social or cultural groups (Bronfenbrenner, 1979). What a student like Gloria knows about the justices of the Supreme Court, for instance, is of little consequence except as it reflects her sociocultural heritage. From this vantage point, what becomes meaningful is determining how concepts like justice differ for cultural, ethnic, or gender groups.

Like situated cognitivists socioculturalists are more interested in the process of knowing than in any residual outcome, except when knowledge is portrayed as the lore, traditions, or heritage of societies or cultures (Bronfenbrenner, 1979). The socioculturalists may have even stronger reactions to the word *knowledge* than do adherents of situated cognition, because the term carries with it images of individual acquisition and possession, rather than shared social or cultural understandings (Sfard, 1998).

Thus, a socioculturalist would be invested in the ideas and interpretations that students from a local housing project developed about legal or social justice and the ways these concepts are carried out in their social context. Socioculturalists would also be intrigued by the way Helenrose's students went about negotiating meaning about the Supreme Court and the judicial system through social interaction. In addition, these theorists would consider how objects in the environment, as cultural artifacts, contributed to this unfolding process (Rogoff, 1990). Further, they might study why these urban children's conceptions of the American legal system differ from those of children raised in rural areas. As a rule, socioculturalists are not as enamored with technology as situated cognitivists are but see computers as cultural tools that help a group engage in a valued task.

For socioculturalists schools are fundamentally conduits of cultural knowledge. In the past, anthropologists like Margaret Mead (1988) studied specific cultural enclaves or groups, like the Samoan people. In more recent times, however, social and cultural anthropologists have found interesting groups to study right in their own backyards. Classrooms and schools—with their particular customs, mores, and values—have become fertile ground for sociocultural study. Collectively, their perspectives on schools and classrooms as cultural contexts and on knowledge as meaning negotiated within those contexts place socioculturalists at the social endpoint on the knowledge continuum (Figure 4–1).

What Kinds of Knowledge Should Be Part of the Educational Experience?

Before the 1960s the cadre of terms available to discuss the particular stages and forms of knowledge involved in effective teaching and learning would have been relatively small.

The concept of knowledge had most often been treated as a single, unified entity in the educational literature (Alexander, 1998a). That unitary treatment of knowledge changed dramatically in the latter part of the 20th century, as a result of IP theory and the burgeoning interest in the inner workings of the human mind and the relationship between humans and computers (Schank, 1984). Especially in the 1970s and 1980s, it was difficult to pick up an education book or article that did not refer to some specific form of knowledge. For that reason Alexander, Schallert, and Hare (1991) took on the task of organizing the plethora of knowledge terms into some coherent framework. The outcome was a glossary of commonly used knowledge terms, some of which are used throughout this text.

Prior Knowledge

The matriarch of the lexical family of *knowledge* is the global term *prior*, or *background, knowledge*. Because no two people have had the same life experiences and do not perceive, interpret, or remember the same event in the same way, personal mental histories are as unique as fingerprints. However, the life experiences people have in common with others can be strong bonds and powerful catalysts for subsequent communication and learning (Bronfenbrenner, 1979). Because the majority of Helenrose's students come from the same inner-city housing project and walk down the same city streets, they could potentially relate to the assembly on drug abuse in ways that students from other backgrounds would not. In fact, the school authorities probably chose to have that assembly because they understood how these students' lives and their knowledge have been dramatically influenced by the drug culture.

Prior knowledge encompasses all that a person knows or believes, whether positive or negative, accurate or inaccurate, real or imagined, verifiable or nonverifiable (Alexander, 1998a; Alexander et al., 1991). Prior knowledge is a word that stands in lieu of individuals' mental histories, that is, their "personal stock of information, skills, experiences, beliefs, and memories." (Alexander, Schallert, & Hare, 1991, p. 317). Every sound, smell, taste, or sight that is encountered has a chance of imprinting itself on a person's thoughts. It may well be one sign of cognitive maturity that the boundaries between positive and negative, accurate and inaccurate, real and imagined, and verifiable and nonverifiable become somewhat sharper. However, these boundaries are never completely delineated in thoughts and memories, regardless of mental maturation.

The extensive body of cognitive research of the 1970s, 1980s, and 1990s made clear that prior knowledge is continually at work, influencing how people see and interact with the world around them, whether they are conscience of that influence or not (Alexander & Murphy, 1998b). Thus, no meaningful discussion of learning and teaching can take place without acknowledging the power of prior knowledge. No one can effectively teach individuals without linking to the thoughts, feelings, perceptions, interests, and beliefs that are part of their mental histories (Alexander, 2000).

Unlike the blank slate, or *tabula rasa*, that Locke (1699/1938) envisioned, people carry their mental histories with them. This prior knowledge becomes, in effect, the filter through which all that is subsequently seen, heard, or felt comes to be understood or construed. Thus, prior knowledge is a significant factor in many aspects of human learning and development:

- The degree to which individuals understand and remember what they see or hear (Alvermann, Smith, & Readence, 1985; R. C. Anderson, Reynolds, Schallert, & Goetz, 1977)
- The interpretations they make or mental constructions they form (R. Anderson, Pichert, Goetz, Schallert, Stevens, & Trollip, 1976; CTGV, 1996)
- The judgments people make about what is relevant, accurate, or important (Alexander, Jetton, Kulikowich, & Woehler, 1994; Chinn & Brewer, 1993)
- The ways individuals allocate time and attention to particular information or tasks (Reynolds & Shirey, 1988; Wade, 1992)
- The determination that something is interesting, credible or persuasive (Dole & Sinatra, 1998; Murphy, 1998; Petty & Cacioppo, 1986)
- Individuals' willingness or desire to behave strategically and the nature of the strategies they use (Alexander, Graham, & Harris, 1998; Alexander & Judy, 1988)
- The goals and self-judgments people make, including beliefs about their likely success and their self-worth (Eccles, Wigfield, & Schiefele, 1998; Pintrich & Schunk, 1996)
- Learners' continued academic development (Alexander, 1997b; Stanovich, 1986)

Clearly, prior knowledge is an impressive force in the learning environment. Helenrose may want to unearth what her students already know and consider how their personal mental histories are likely to enhance or impede their subsequent growth and development. She may also want to ascertain what educational experiences would argument her students' current understandings and counterbalance perceptions that seem nonproductive or potentially detrimental.

Prior knowledge can exist in three states: declarative, procedural, and conditional (Alexander et al., 1991). Just as matter exists in at least three states—solid, liquid, and gas—so knowledge can undergo similar transformations, even while retaining its basic elements. Each state of knowledge has its own character and role in learning and teaching, yet anything that is known well is known declaratively, procedurally, *and* conditionally.

Declarative Knowledge

At times knowledge can take the form of specific labels, facts, definitions, explanations, or descriptions—what Gilbert Ryle (1949) called **declarative knowledge,** or the *thats* of knowledge, because it completes the statement, "I know that . . . " This state of knowledge has long been a mainstay of the school experience. Textbooks, including this one, and curriculum documents are often filled with such factual information. Without declarative knowledge there would be no way to describe or explain the world around us or communicate those understandings to others. Knowing about the Supreme Court, its role in the American political system, and the names of Supreme Court judges—these are examples of declarative knowledge.

These particular pieces of factual knowledge may exist as separate or fragmented elements in memory, or they can be part of integrated systems of ideas (Byrnes, 1996). Students new to a topic have minimal declarative knowledge to draw on, and even this knowledge is often loosely configured in memory (Alexander, 1997b). The declarative knowledge of competent learners, by comparison, is more central to the topic, more extensive, and more interconnected. In other words, competent students have more principled declarative knowledge (Gelman & Greeno, 1989).

Representation

Researchers coming from an IP or artificial intelligence background have devoted themselves to understanding how knowledge in various forms is likely stored in memory (J. R. Anderson, 1983; Minsky, 1975). One theory in particular has proven influential in capturing the organization of declarative knowledge in human memory—schema theory (R. C. Anderson, 1977). Perhaps the most prevalent theory of knowledge structures in the latter half of the 20th century, schema theory was influenced both by research in artificial intelligence and by the philosophical and theoretical writings of Kant (1787/1963), Wulf (1922/1938), Bartlett (1932), and Piaget (1926). At its simplest, a **schema** is an interconnected body of conceptual knowledge, a general framework of related ideas stored in LTM (Rumelhart, 1980). Schemata (the plural of *schema*) serve as the prototypes against which the world and its information can be judged. These schemata are **instantiated,** or particularized, when one or more of their specific elements are activated by conditions in the environment (R. C. Anderson, 1977).

A simplistic schema for the concept of the Supreme Court is displayed in Figure 4–3. Helenrose's students

---

Learner-Centered Psychological Principle 2
Goals of the learning process. The successful learner, over time and with support and instructional guidance, can create meaningful, coherent representations of knowledge.

APA Board of Educational Affairs, 1997.

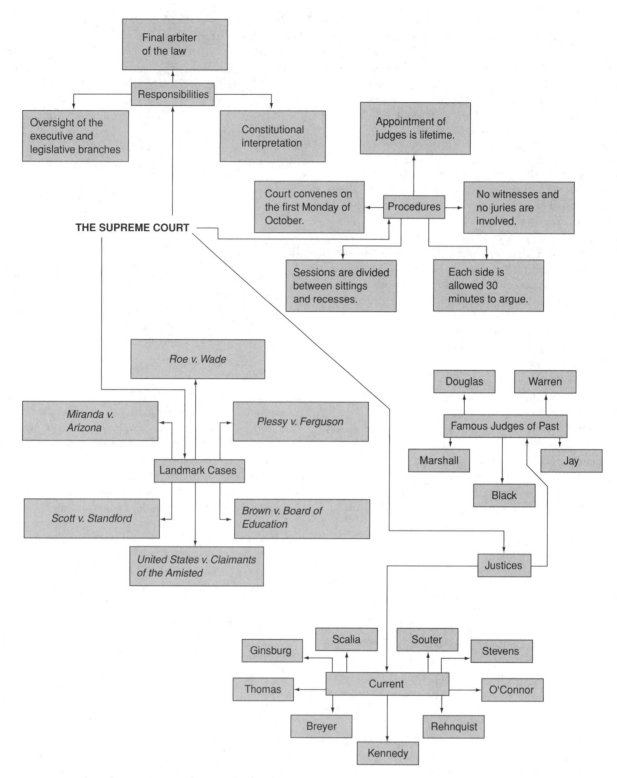

■ FIGURE 4–3   A model schema for the Supreme Court.

could have had such a mental representation after completing their group project. At that point if a guest speaker had asked them to name a justice of the Court, this base of knowledge would have been instantiated. The recollection of one judge's name might have activated the names of other justices and have carried these students mentally to related ideas, such as key cases or court procedures. The more elements students have in their schemata and the more linkages they have within and across concepts, the closer they may come to achieving principled understanding.

Certain IP researchers concentrate on the representation of declarative knowledge units that are much smaller than schemata (J.R. Anderson, 1990; R.C. Anderson et al., 1976).

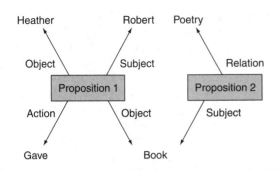

A representation of the sentence "Robert gave a book of poetry to Heather" as a network of two propositions

■ **FIGURE 4–4   A propositional network.**

These researchers see memory as a network of information composed of **propositions,** or small, interconnected units of semantic information—such as subjects, actions, and objects—composed of links and nodes (J. R. Anderson, 1990). Proposition networks have been helpful in explaining how individuals make sense of language. Figure 4–4 shows how a simple sentence about Robert and Heather and a book of poetry would be configured as propositions. The sentence "Robert gave a book of poetry to Heather" does not actually exist as a unique unit in memory, but as separate elements tied together through a process called *spreading activation* (E. D. Gagné, Yechovich, & Yechovich, 1993). The result is a new construction or interpretation.

Another way declarative knowledge can be represented is in terms of mental images (Paivio, 1971; Sadoski, Kealy, Goetz, & Paivio, 1997). Unlike schemata or propositions, these images are not language-based representations but are graphic or pictorial ones, also called *iconic memories.* They enable you to visualize your bedroom or conjure up your mother's face. Certain events or episodes can also be captured in memory as a series of images. Like a mental movie, minds can play back these events, termed *episodic memories,* in surprisingly rich detail (Martindale, 1991). For instance, if you were asked to describe your home, you might see the front door in your mind, walk through that door into the living room and kitchen, maybe even visualizing the color of the sofa or the pictures on the wall.

The more significant or dramatic an event, the greater the likelihood it will be embedded in the mind. For example, most people can tell where they were and what they were doing when they heard about President John F. Kennedy's assassination, the Challenger disaster, or the tragic events of 9/11. Called **flashbulb memories** (R. Brown & Kulik, 1977) because of their startling nature, these particular images are not only the most emotionally laden and vivid of mental recollections, they are also among the most enduring (D. C. Rubin & Kozin, 1984). These occurrences remind us that a single image or episode can encompass a wealth of declarative knowledge.

Learning

Teachers expect to see a transformation in conceptual knowledge as students move toward competence in a subject-matter domain. Their concepts should become richer and more cohesive in structure if learning is occurring. Some of those concepts may actually be restructured. For example, through formal instruction and everyday experiences, a personal understanding of the Supreme Court and myriad related concepts expands or shifts. At times the new information fits easily within existing knowledge structures, allowing those structures to grow from within. Learning about another historical Court case or a tradition of the Court, for instance, might add a dimension to an existing Supreme Court schema. This process, called **accretion** by schema theorists (Rumelhart, 1980), corresponds to Piaget's (1926) notion of **assimilation.** Everyday learning takes this form of quiet accretion, or assimilation, and can go virtually unnoticed.

At some point in learning, however, new pieces of related information are encountered, or an experience conflicts or clashes with prior notions. When this happens, existing knowledge structures cannot simply subsume the new information or insights. Instead, those structures must be moderately or radically transformed; that is, existing concepts must be **tuned,** or **restructured** (Rumelhart, 1980). Such transformations parallel Piaget's concept of accommodation (1926). For example, thinking that the Supreme Court is beyond political influence and then realizing that it can be swayed by the opinions and desires of presidents and political parties that helped put the justices into power would require a reformulation of the original concept of the Supreme Court. The result would be a dramatically different mental structure (Vosniadou & Brewer, 1987).

What is interesting about the fine tuning or the radical restructuring of concepts is that preconceptions, that is, existing notions, can be highly resistant to confusing or conflicting information (Chinn & Brewer, 1993). Often, inconsistent or unpleasant information is simply overlooked or ignored. At other times individuals temporarily acknowledge such conflicting information but then revert to their more firmly established conceptions (Guzzetti & Hynd, 1998). The highly resistant nature of many student ideas, even in the face of powerful evidence, has long been an enigma to practitioners and researchers alike. Chapter 6 looks more intensely at conceptual change and persuasion and weighs the factors that facilitate or inhibit significant changes in students' thoughts and beliefs.

By means of a simple experiment involving an ambiguous passage, Bransford and Johnson (1973) illustrated the way existing conceptual knowledge guides thoughts and interpretations. Preconceptions direct attention and aid comprehension, but they also blind individuals to information that does not fit easily and simply into what they already know. Put this idea to the test by reading the passage in the Thought Experiment: Now You See It, Now You Don't.

Thought Experiment ....

Now You See It, Now You Don't!

Directions: Read the following passage **only once.**

The view was breathtaking. From the window one could see the crowd below. Everything looked extremely small from such a distance, but the colorful costumes could still be seen. Everyone seemed to be moving in one direction in an orderly fashion, and there seemed to be little children as well as adults. The landing was gentle, and luckily the atmosphere was such that no special suits had to be worn. At first there was a great deal of activity. Later, when the speeches started, the crowd quieted down. The man with the television camera took many shots of the setting and the crowd. Everyone was very friendly and seemed glad when the music started.

Now turn quickly to the questions at the very end of the chapter.

Note: From *Human Cognition: Learning, Understanding, and Remembering* (p. 151) by G. D. Bransford, 1979, Belmont, CA: Wadsworth.

....

Any deviations between your recollections and the actual text show how past experiences and expectations impose themselves on the recall of written information. Readers who focused on the parade were apt to miss the gentle landing; those who paid attention to the space aspect of the passage may have overlooked the colorful costumes. Existing knowledge can help, or it can hinder what we perceive.

Assessment

Many standardized or large-scale tests that have become benchmarks of school achievement are chock full of declarative knowledge tidbits, partly because declarative knowledge is relatively easy to assess. However, there is much debate among educational researchers and practitioners about the value of this practice (R. L. Linn, 1995). In fact, schools have been strongly criticized for spending inordinate amounts of time on declarative knowledge at the expense of other states of knowledge or the very process of knowing. Who has not been required to commit to memory long lists of events, dates, formulas, people, or places, like the state capitals, the multiplication tables, or the periodic table? Perhaps cultural values, rather than the educational system, are to blame for this fascination with declarative knowledge. Indeed, Americans seem to revere those who pluck seemingly obscure pieces of knowledge from memory at lightning speed.

Declarative knowledge itself is not the villain. This knowledge forms the building blocks of conceptual understanding, and tests of declarative knowledge allow educators to efficiently gauge students' breadth of knowledge about academic topics and domains. The problem is in the

overwhelming preference this one state of knowledge is given over procedural and conditional knowledge. Educators seem to presume that the acquisition of declarative knowledge will somehow result in the development of other states and forms of knowledge, but this is not necessarily the case (Paris, Lipson, & Wixson, 1983). Nor does the essential nature of declarative knowledge mean that learning must always begin with declarative knowledge and then move to alternative states and forms. It is quite possible to start with a more holistic procedure and use its performance to instigate the acquisition of the more factual elements (CTGV, 1990).

Procedural Knowledge

Mental history does not always manifest itself as factual information or as understandings that can be easily labeled or defined. Ryle (1949) categorized **procedural knowledge** as the *hows* of understanding, and he considered this proceduralization of knowledge to be critical to efficient and effective functioning.

> Theorists have been so preoccupied with the task of investigating the nature, the source, and the credentials of the theories that we adopt that they have for the most part ignored the question of what it is for someone to know how to perform tasks. In ordinary life, on the contrary, as well as in the special business of teaching, we are much more concerned with people's [competencies] than with their cognitive repertoires, with the operations than with the truth that they learn. Indeed even when we are concerned with their intellectual excellences and deficiencies, we are interested less in the stocks of truths that they acquire and retain than in their capacities to find out truths for themselves and their ability to organize and exploit them, when discovered. Often we deplore a person's ignorance of some fact only because we deplore the stupidity of which his ignorance is a consequence. (G. Ryle, 1949, p. 28)

When a person is first in the throes of acquiring some new procedure, its individual components or its declarative elements are more evident. For example, before any law student would ever consider trying a case in front of any court (much less the Supreme Court), he or she would work to acquire a great deal of relevant declarative knowledge—from appropriate terminology to awareness of legal precedents. Over time, however, with continued exposure and practice, these separate elements would begin to combine and fuse into action-related sequences, referred to as **productions.** With even more practice, these actions would become almost second nature, or *automatic*, to the lawyer, and once automaticized, they would be executed with little mental effort or conscious energy.

College students certainly experience the effects of knowledge proceduralization in their everyday lives. For instance, you are probably reading and comprehending this sentence fluidly and effortlessly. You do not have to pause to sound out each word, call up its definition, or contemplate what the strings of words mean. It all seems to occur instantaneously because your reading skills have become highly proceduralized, as has so much of what defines mature learners. Of course, as discussed in the chapters on strategic process and problem solving, this automaticity does not occur for all learners (Alexander, Graham, & Harris, 1998).

Representation

Whereas Ryle (1949) looked at procedural knowledge from a more philosophical perspective, John Anderson (1983) studied its nature and structure. His research resulted in the ACT and ACT-R models of human memory. In these models the ability to perform any procedure can be represented as a series of actions, or productions, regulated by certain conditions or circumstances known as **production rules.** Certain conditions elicit certain responses. Figure 4–5 shows the productions and rule structures involved in writing a check, expressed as a series of if-then statements.

Still others have described human memory as consisting of conceptual prototypes that guide human thought and action, much as a script directs an actor's words and movements. These mental prototypes have been called **scripts, frames,** or **plans** (Minsky, 1975; Schank & Abelson, 1977). A simplistic example of a script that might be followed in trying a case is shown in Figure 4–6. It shows the specific actions that take place in a jury trial, each of which stands for much declarative and conditional knowledge.

These simple production and script examples illustrate that performance of any act encompasses quite a bit of declarative (and conditional) knowledge. Consequently, many educators—including Dewey (1916/1944), Bruner (with Goodnow & Austin, 1956), and Bransford (with Brown & Cocking, 1999)—argue for the presence of more procedural learning in classrooms. Especially those educators more interested in the process of *knowing* than the by-product of *knowledge* stress a variety of instructional techniques that

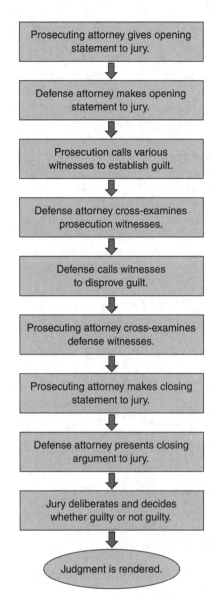

■ **FIGURE 4–6   Simple script for a jury trial.**

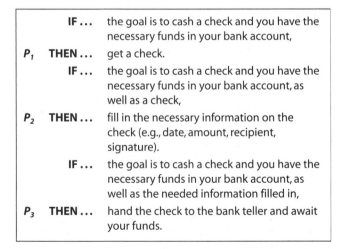

■ **FIGURE 4–5   Three simple productions in the act of cashing a check.**

emphasize procedures and actions, including activity-based or problem-based learning and hands-on science and mathematics (A. L. Brown & Campione, 1990; Greeno & MSMAPG, 1998).

Learning

What signifies learning from a procedural perspective? Generally speaking, students display more efficient and effective performance of key procedures as they become better educated in a field. In other words, their procedures or scripts become more automatic, more elaborate, and more efficient; they develop what William James (1890) described as positive "habits of the mind." The catalyst for such automaticity is continued practice or performance of those actions in rich contexts.

It is not always possible to put individuals in the actual situations that would allow for repeated performance of rather complex procedures. For example, fighter pilots and astronauts cannot afford to hone their procedures in real-life situations, the cost in human and nonhuman resources would be too great, and the risks too high. Similarly, it would not be conceivable for Helenrose's students to demonstrate their understanding of the judicial system by arguing a case in a real courtroom. However, technological advances have allowed for rather sophisticated simulations of problem-solving or decision-making contexts (de Jong & van Joolingen, 1998; Reimann & Schult, 1996). Through such simulations learners at all stages of academic development can engage in meaningful practice that extends and reinforces their procedural and declarative knowledge.

Assessment

Measuring procedural knowledge is not as simple as gauging declarative understanding. However, the growing interest in alternative states and forms of knowledge and the rising popularity of theories stressing process over product have sparked the search for alternative forms of evaluation. The development of performance-based assessments, holistic scoring rubrics, and student portfolios are three examples of these emerging tools for measuring the *hows* of knowledge, along with the *thats* (Baxter, Elder, & Glaser, 1996; Wittrock & Baker, 1991). Chapter 14 devotes attention to alternative assessments.

Conditional Knowledge

Research in problem solving and strategic learning has created awareness of a third state of knowledge—one that has garnered even less attention in educational practice than procedural knowledge. This third state deals with understanding *when, where,* and *for what reason* knowledge should be brought into play. Newell and Simon (1972) christened this particular state **conditional knowledge** because it pertains to the conditions of knowledge use. These conditions vary from those specified in production rules in that they are not generally fixed. Instead, they are far more fluid and are determined by factors in the immediate environment. Thus, it falls more to individuals to read situations and bring their declarative and procedural knowledge to bear in whatever fashion is most suitable.

By the conclusion of the Supreme Court project in Helenrose's classroom, her seventh graders could readily have responded to questions like those they missed during the initial assembly (i.e., with declarative knowledge). They could also have conducted a mock trial following the script outlined in Figure 4–6 (i.e., with procedural knowledge). If Helenrose had confronted some significant disruptive behavior later in the school year, the class might have decided to use their acquired knowledge of the law and legal procedures to conduct a judicial review of their accused peers. They would then have seen how their understanding of the judicial system could have value in a current situation. They would have been displaying conditional knowledge in the form of transferred knowledge (Alexander & Murphy, 1999b).

Representation

Because it is relatively new as a knowledge concept and because it deals with flexible and situated performance, there are no distinct representations in memory for conditional knowledge. It is perhaps best to think of conditional knowledge as attached to the various representations of declarative and procedural knowledge. Conditional understanding comes into play when learners' thoughtful perception of a situation leads them to activate relevant conceptual knowledge that would be useful but atypical for that situation. For instance, a student in Helenrose's class, preparing for the mock trial, might remember ideas he acquired when he took part in a debate in fifth grade. By seeing the correspondence between a mock trial and a debate that student would be evidencing conditional understanding in the form of analogical thought (Alexander & Murphy, 1999b). Thus, conditional knowledge could be represented within schemata or propositional networks as new associations or links that bring together seemingly unrelated elements.

From a procedural standpoint, the triggers of conditional knowledge might take the form of secondary production rules that can be flexibly invoked when a learner senses the need. For example, the specific procedures attorneys follow must be altered by the conditions that emerge in the courtroom. Although every defendant has the right to speak (i.e., a production rule), a defense lawyer who judges the prosecution's case to be weak and sympathy for the defendant high might decide not to call the defendant to the stand. This secondary rule for calling or not calling a client to the stand is one of a multitude of secondary and more flexible rules that result in a particular performance. By adapting a script to fit the characteristics of the case at hand, this attorney would be demonstrating conditional knowledge.

Conditional knowledge can also entail greater cognitive flexibility when one instantiates conceptual knowledge. For example, a central and salient attribute of the schema for *car* may be an understanding that cars must have wheels. However, a car show might feature a jet car that moves completely on air currents. Willingness to accept this object as a car will depend on the ability to mentally position this vehicle at some future time and place. Conditional knowledge pertains to understanding which aspects of knowledge are more or less appropriate for a given time and place. In other words, it is not just a question of whether knowledge *should* be applied, but *how* and *when* that knowledge would be best used.

Learning

Learners who become increasingly knowledgeable in a given area are able to display flexibility even as their actions become more automatic. The key to this apparent paradox may lie in the fact that enhanced automaticity does not completely eliminate thought or reasoning. An awareness of what one is doing lies very near the surface of consciousness, ready to be called into action at a moment's notice. In addition, when individuals are more practiced at what they are doing, they have more cognitive energy to allocate to related thoughts and actions, thus increasing the likelihood that they will perceive conditions that deepen their thoughts or enrich their actions.

The act of driving a car can readily illustrate this concept. Practiced drivers do not need to ponder the particulars of operating their vehicles. Even when driving to work during rush hour on a congested freeway, they do not have to think about the basics of steering, maintaining speed, or keeping a safe distance. Those actions operate on automatic pilot for the most part. However, with the slightest deviation from typical conditions, such as when brake lights flash, experienced drivers rapidly stop the automatic pilot and almost instantaneously decide on a course of action. In this case automaticity and flexibility are working hand in hand.

The more teachers help students understand the conditional or contextual dimensions that may exist in the performance of academic tasks, the more likely students are to use what they know more flexibly. Along with the *whats*, therefore, educators must provide ample occasions for meaningful application of knowledge under varying conditions. Moreover, educators should discuss possible variations in knowledge use and should serve as models of such flexibility and conditionality for their students. Under these circumstances students are apt to have deeper and richer understandings of whatever concepts are being taught.

Assessment

Conditionality is difficult to measure. At the very least, it requires some gauge of learners' personalizations or variations of established routines and some evidence that those variations contribute to improved outcomes. This assessment might be accomplished by presenting students with more novel or creative tasks once their declarative and procedural knowledge begins to take hold. Of course, students should not be encouraged to do something different just for the sake of creativity or flexibility, unless it serves some meaningful goal or positive end. However, because learners must be cognizant of the conditions under which an action or modification in that action is warranted, conditional knowledge would appear to be a natural arena for self-evaluation. It also may involve declarative knowledge as learners attempt to justify or rationalize whatever variations they make.

Interaction of Knowledge and Learning

Explicit Versus Tacit Knowledge

In many ways the structure of human knowledge is like an iceberg. The tip of the knowledge formation, regardless of its impressive nature, only hints at the massive structure hidden from view. The component of knowledge that surfaces in the realm of consciousness is referred to as **explicit knowledge** (Prawat, 1989). When the guest speaker asked Helenrose's students to name a justice of the Supreme Court, he was asking them to make their knowledge explicit.

Prawat describes explicit knowledge as analyzed, because individuals can bring it into their immediate thoughts, turn it over in their heads, put language to it, and even share it with others (Prawat, 1989). **Tacit knowledge,** by comparison, is that portion of our knowledge base that lies outside our direct awareness (Schön, 1983). Sometimes when individuals act on intuition or some sixth sense, they are operating from this tacit base of knowledge.

Explicit knowledge is the primary focus of classroom learning. Teachers and students are continually engaged in the process of raising understandings to a conscious level, framing thoughts in language, examining and evaluating what rises to the surface, and communicating such thoughts to others. Those students who engage in such processes with ease are those who are judged as smarter or more capable students. Whether students' understandings are declarative, procedural, or conditional in form, they must become part of the classroom discourse to be heard and considered.

There are reasons that some knowledge exists tacitly in people's minds. Some knowledge can be so complex or so infused in people's thoughts that they simply cannot mentally grab hold of it. There are also times when thoughts or mental pictures exist, but not in a form that can be readily analyzed or communicated. In addition, knowledge may exist in an unanalyzed state simply because there has been no occasion to reflect on it.

Learner-Centered Psychological Principle 1
Nature of the learning process. The learning of complex subject matter is most effective when it is an intentional process of constructing meaning from information and experience.

APA Board of Educational Affairs, 1997.

It is important to remember that even though tacit knowledge is unavailable for analysis or is seemingly impossible to communicate, it can be highly influential. Cultural, moral, and spiritual principles may be so much a part of an individual's being that they are difficult to isolate and even more difficult to explain simply and clearly to others. Nonetheless, these tacit understandings serve as the filter through which other information and experiences are colored and shaped (Alexander et al., 1991). In essence, tacit knowledge guides personal thoughts and actions just as the mass beneath the water directs the movement of the iceberg.

It is also important to remember that captivating or thought-provoking activities or exchanges, like the drug assembly, can be a catalyst for human reflection—an opportunity to ponder questions or issues that might otherwise remain unexplored and unanalyzed. One of the goals of teaching should be to give students opportunities in which tacit understandings can be put into some concrete form. Through effective teaching, students can acquire the language or the cognitive tools needed to give voice to previously unanalyzed or unconscious knowledge, to give such concepts the concreteness that allows for comparison and contrast. Of course, some knowledge is simply too complex or too diffused to be fully or adequately analyzed, and that portion of tacit knowledge may remain buried forever in the sea of unconsciousness.

Unschooled Versus Schooled Knowledge

All that individuals know does not result from formal learning experiences. The flood of information that Helenrose's students rattled off about marijuana certainly did not come from health class or some academic text. So how do 12- and 13-year-olds reconcile the lessons of the streets with the lessons of the classroom? How do they come to know drugs as societal evils when they see people prosper financially from their sale or when family members whom they love are users or dealers? Where does the hype of drugs end and the reality of the concept begin? All of these experiences and interpretations become mixed together in these students' thoughts and cannot be readily or completely distinguishable.

Thus, even though the idea of learning conjures up thoughts of schooling and formal education, learning takes place everywhere. Indeed, everyday life and the people and experiences that are part of that life are potent teachers. The term **unschooled,** or **informal, knowledge** marks those understandings acquired as a result of out-of-school experiences (Alexander, 1998b; Gardner, 1991). Vygotsky (1934/1986) referred to these less formalized understandings as **spontaneous concepts.** Because individuals do not typically set out to learn from such everyday experiences, unschooled knowledge is often associated with unintended or **incidental learning** (E. D. Gagné et al., 1983). From dressing oneself to engaging in appropriate social conversation, from cooking a meal to learning how to parent—where would anyone be without unschooled knowledge?

Other knowledge that we acquire comes from more structured educational experiences. As Dewey (1916/1944) explained, schools are seen by many as conduits for the type of understandings that do not arise easily, if at all, from everyday lives. For instance, most people are unlikely to pick up the formulas for determining the area of circle or a triangle simply as a consequence of their everyday living. Formal education is often focused on what Vygotsky calls **scientific concepts,** or ideas that are abstracted or generalized from routine human interactions (1934/1986). The outcome of such purposeful or *intentional learning* is referred to as **schooled,** or **formal, knowledge** (Gardner, 1991).

Although schools are not the only places that formal knowledge is acquired, they are perhaps the most common (Alexander, 1998b). In schools the information and skills targeted for formal instruction are commonly organized around traditional disciplines or academic domains, such as biology, history, or American literature. According to Vygotsky (1934/1986), the character and the source of unschooled and schooled knowledge are distinct, and these distinctions affect what and how students learn. First of all, unschooled knowledge may be more tacit than schooled

knowledge and, thus, less accessible for reflection, perhaps because people are not often called on to explain their thoughts and actions in out-of-school environments as they are routinely required to do during formal instruction (Gardner, 1991).

In addition, because unschooled knowledge is rather nebulous, often diffuse, and sometimes indescribable, it can be more resistant to change than formally acquired knowledge. Because it is difficult to pinpoint the specific nature of informal ideas, it is challenging to target those notions in teaching. In other words, unless teachers can make some determination about the thinking or reasoning underlying students' actions, it will be difficult to orchestrate the kind of learning experiences that will promote understanding. Evidence of this phenomenon exists in the research on persuasion, which explores the reasons individuals accept or reject ideas presented to them (Petty & Cacioppo, 1986).

Further, when understandings informally acquired conflict with ideas more formally obtained, it is often unschooled knowledge that wins, whereas schooled knowledge is forgotten or disregarded (Gardner, 1991). The literature in mathematics and science is replete with studies supporting this trend, especially in fields like physics, where everyday experiences seemingly conflict with the concepts formally taught (Chinn & Brewer, 1993; Guzzetti, & Hynd, 1998). The principle of falling objects is a case in point. It states that two objects dropped in a vacuum will fall at the same rate, regardless of their mass (e.g., a feather versus a steel ball). First-year physics students commonly memorize and regurgitate this concept as part of their studies, yet these same students often act as if they have never heard of this principle when confronted with this problem outside school. One simple explanation is that students do not carry their schooled knowledge into life outside the classroom; they seem to have separate compartments in their memories for schooled and unschooled knowledge. Another explanation is that students do not hold schooled knowledge in the same regard as their everyday understandings.

Thus, students' formal knowledge often exists as **inert knowledge** (Whitehead, 1929/1967). According to Whitehead, inert knowledge is that which does not guide actions or color perceptions in any meaningful way. It simply lies dormant and unused in the mind, unconnected to any awareness of reality and experience. Knowledge about the judicial system may have made its way into the minds of Helenrose's students but soon became buried beneath more relevant or frequently used knowledge so that it was rendered virtually impotent.

The fact that so much schooled knowledge lies fallow or becomes stagnant is not inevitable, however. By ensuring that students have multiple occasions to explore relevant ideas, not only declaratively but also procedurally and conditionally, teachers can prevent knowledge from becoming inert. The more educators understand about the interplay of schooled and unschooled knowledge, the more effectively they can build on the strengths of everyday cognition and break down the invisible barriers that exist between formal and informal learning experiences (Alexander & Murphy, 1999b). Thus, Helenrose should confront the inconsistencies that exist for her students, even as she presents them with the lessons about human justice that she deems valuable. She can show them where and how these schooled lessons fit within their world outside the classroom, thus narrowing the distance between schooled and unschooled knowledge and helping to keep schooled knowledge alive in these students' thinking.

What Principles of Knowledge Promote Effective Educational Practice?

If the goal of psychology *in* learning and instruction is to become a reality, then there needs to be pedagogical value to these theories and concepts of knowledge and knowing. Several fundamental principles arise from this psychological work and should be evident in effective instructional practice. These principles are pertinent regardless of teachers' theoretical orientations or the age and background of their students.

Knowledge Is Idiosyncratic

What is a teacher like Helenrose to do when faced with the reality of 25 different mental histories in a single classroom? How can such human variability be given more than lip service in today's dynamic and demanding classrooms?

Anticipate and Embrace Diversity in What Students Say and Do One of the first principles of effective teaching is to expect differences in what students say and do. Just because students read or hear the same words, teachers cannot assume that they internalize or interpret that information similarly. Teachers must not behave as if knowledge is black or white, right or wrong, simply plucked fully formed from the world. What students encounter in classrooms and elsewhere are just the seeds of what they eventually may come to know, and teachers need to plant and nurture those seeds of knowledge. When teachers are surprised by what they hear or see from their students, they are being reminded that teachers' understandings are not necessarily those of their students.

Effective teachers should try to anticipate what unique answers might emerge from the minds of their students, instead of relying on their students to guess what is in their teachers' minds. As Socrates did with Plato, teachers should let ideas emerge and take shape through dialogue and discourse. To illustrate the idiosyncratic nature of knowledge, try a simple experiment. Look at the pictures in the Thought Experiment: Is This Your Cup of Tea? Mark any of the objects that represent a cup. Then ask an acquaintance or two to do the same. What this simple activity reveals is that even a commonplace object like a cup will be perceived differently as a result of each individual's unique history and the idiosyncratic knowledge born of that history.

Thought Experiment ....

Is This Your Cup of Tea?

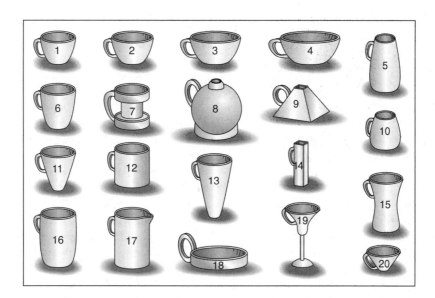

Directions: Put an X through any of the above figures that fit the description of a cup. Ask an acquaintance or two to do the same. Then see whether you can determine why you arrived at such similar or dissimilar interpretations of such a common notion.

Look for Patterns and Explanations in Students' Correct and Incorrect Responses   Radical constructivism teaches a critical lesson about effective teaching. Errors are rich sources of information about what students are thinking or doing and should not be ignored or dismissed (Steffe & D'Ambrosio, 1995). Errors can be more enlightening than correct responses, because they reveal something about the respondents' thinking and can stimulate exploration and discussion. Even though Gloria's answer was offbeat, her response was a key to how she conceptualized the legal system and how she perceived courtroom proceedings. If the response had not occurred in such a public forum, Helenrose could have probed Gloria's answer—not to ridicule her or dismiss her answer as wrong, but to draw out her thinking.

As Alexander and colleagues conducted research on the development of students' subject-matter knowledge (Alexander et al., 1989), they discovered the wisdom of exploring seemingly erroneous answers. In one study in which they investigated elementary, high-school, and college students' knowledge of human biology and human immunology, they found that errors were not random, thoughtless productions. Instead, there was an identifiable, systematic nature to what students thought, even when their answers were not completely accurate.

The researchers uncovered these patterns by producing multiple-choice tests with very specific levels of distracters (i.e., wrong answers). At the sixth-grade level, for example, those distracters came from human biology, science, and a nonscientific domain. In this example, an increasingly more discriminating distracter was used for the high-school and college students.

> Carpals are:
> 1. the small bones of the wrist. (correct, human biology)
> 2. the muscles of the foot. (incorrect, human biology)
> 3. types of fish found in streams. (incorrect, science)
> 4. groups of people who travel to work together. (incorrect, nonscience) (Alexander, Pate, Kulikowich, Farrell, & N. L. Wright, 1989, p. 288)

The researchers determined that a significant number of students displayed nonrandom error patterns, with more than half of their errors occurring in one of the three error categories. For example, although some sixth graders had the tendency to choose a human biology distracter, others were drawn to the nonscience distracters. However, the sophistication of students' errors improved with age and exposure to the field. When the results were tallied, 100% of the undergraduates had identifiable error patterns and were more likely to resist the science distracters in favor of the distracters from either human biology/immunology or general biology. Other researchers working in mathematics and reading have long argued the merits of viewing errors as important clues to students' knowledge and mental processing (J. S. Brown & Burton, 1978; Goodman & Burke, 1972).

Knowledge Begets Knowledge

One of the most powerful notions to emerge from the decades of research on knowledge is Stanovich's (1986) concept of the Matthew Effect, named for its literary allusion to Matthew 25:29: "For unto every one that hath shall be given, and he shall have abundance; but from him that hath not shall be taken away even that which he hath." What Stanovich proposed is that students who are cognitively or motivationally richer get richer by building on the resources they already possess. Conversely, those who begin their academic journeys with limited cognitive and motivational resources face the prospect of falling further and further behind their more privileged classmates.

> **Learner-Centered Psychological Principle 3**
> *Construction of knowledge.* The successful learner can link new information with existing knowledge in meaningful ways.
>
> APA Board of Educational Affairs, 1997.

This reality must be faced head-on in the educational system. Teachers must not stand by and simply watch as the gap widens between the haves and the have nots. Even though inherent differences among individuals will never be erased, teachers must not unintentionally contribute to the problem by overlooking what students do know or by presenting them with educational tasks that are ill suited to their abilities or needs. Knowing is an effortful enterprise, but one that is worthy of pursuit.

Bring Students' Understandings to the Foreground   In planning lessons or organizing activities, effective teachers are always predicting what their students are likely to know about the subject at hand. And when content is expected to be novel or complex for students, effective teachers take the time to establish or reinforce foundational or background information. They also guide students through academic rough spots, a process founded on the work of Vygotsky and known as scaffolding (Palincsar & Brown, 1984). But good teachers do not simply let students' knowledge serve as a backdrop for instruction; instead, they find suitable ways for their students to display or share their knowledge.

A variety of well-researched pedagogical techniques can be used to bring students' current understandings to the surface and emphasize them in instruction. Ogle (1986), for instance, devised K-W-L, which is illustrated in Table 4–1. In this procedure students begin by sharing what they already know (K) about a given topic. Next, they share in discussion and in writing questions they would like to have answered in their subsequent study of the topic (W). Finally, after a period of study and exploration, often entailing both individual and group work, students discuss

Table 4–1 Sample K-W-L chart for the Supreme Court.

K (Know)	W (Want to Know)	L (Learned)
Branch of the government	Who is on the Supreme Court?	
Highest court	How many justices are there?	
Made up of judges	Are there juries?	
Part of the judicial branch	How do you get on the Court?	
9 or 12 judges	What kinds of cases do they try?	
	How long is somebody on the Court?	
	Are there any minority judges?	

what they have learned (L) by providing answers to the student-generated questions. In a later version of this teaching technique, the K-W-L Plus (Carr & Ogle, 1987), students organize and summarize their knowledge of the topic by developing a concept map, which might be similar in appearance to the sample schema provided in Figure 4–3. This process can be highly effective in uncovering and enriching students' knowledge.

K-W-L and similar techniques can help teachers turn over some instructional control to students (Ogle, 1986). Such approaches encourage students to assume the role of problem posers or question generators. Thus, students' curiosity about a topic and their appraisals of their own knowledge base are made public. More important, students see that they can make valid contributions to the learning environment and need not rely on others to assign those instructional duties.

Analyze the Tasks Involved in Assignments Many cognitive psychologists like Robert Gagné (1977) have discussed the importance of task analysis in learning and instruction. **Task analysis** is the systematic analysis of the component processes involved in performing a specific activity. For example, in their attempts to mimic human thinking and performance, IP theorists like John Anderson (1983) elaborately determined each step involved in performing common academic tasks, such as solving the problem $614 + 438 + 683 =$ _____. The productions involved in this task are shown in Figure 4–7.

Flower and Hayes (1981) performed a procedural analysis of writing that became the foundation for training and research on written composition for many years (see Figure 4–8). Unlike the very particularized and linear representation in Figure 4–7, this analysis is a more general and recursive

Directions: Start at the top of the graphic, and follow the productions in the sequence indicated by the arrows, moving from left to right through the three columns.

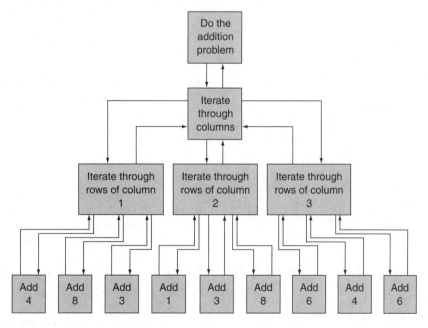

■ **FIGURE 4–7** **A representation of the solution to an addition problem ($614 + 438 + 683 =$ _____).**

Note: From *The Architecture of Cognition* by J. R. Anderson, 1983, Cambridge, MA: Harvard University Press. Copyright 1983 by Harvard University Press. Adapted with permission.

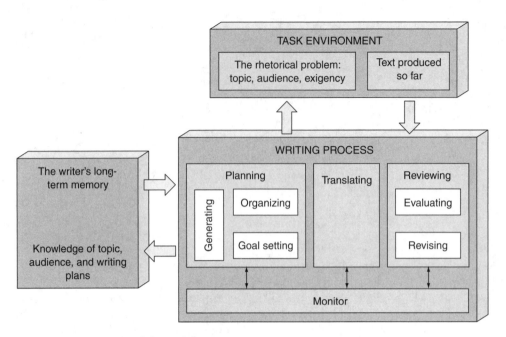

■ FIGURE 4–8   Procedural analysis of the writing process.

Note: From "A Cognitive Process Theory of Writing" by L. Flower and J. R. Hayes, 1981, *College Composition and Communication, 32*, p. 370. Copyright 1981 by *College Composition and Communication.* Adapted with permission.

representation of the writing process, whether students are producing a paragraph or an entire composition.

Because teachers are mature learners, they sometimes forget what they are requiring their students to know or do to complete an assignment or perform an activity. Task analysis is a reminder of those demands and can help educators understand where students' thinking or processing may go awry. Certainly, teachers cannot engage in detailed or microscopic analysis of all instructional tasks, but they do need some means of evaluating those tasks.

Recognizing this need, researchers participating in the Teachers as Research Partners (TARP) Project for improving science education devised a simple rubric with which teachers can gauge their curriculum (Stuessy, Alexander, Kulm, & McBride, 1992). This rubric involves asking two questions about each lesson: How *novel* is this content likely to be for my students? and How *cognitively demanding* is the task I am asking students to perform? Participating teachers were shown how to evaluate these two dimensions (i.e., novelty and complexity) across four aspects of their lessons: the subject-matter content, the instructional support or scaffolding, the outcome expected, and the cognitive strategies required. A multiyear analysis showed that teachers trained in using the rubric were more instructionally effective than untrained teachers, as documented by independent classroom observations. Moreover, their students acquired more scientific understanding than the comparison students, as determined by achievement tests. All in all, it seems that educators who reflect on the content and processing demands of their instructional lessons improve their teaching and benefit their students.

Knowledge Is Never Context Free

Human learning and development never take place in a vacuum but unfold in a specific time and place. Therefore, all knowledge is colored and shaped by the sociocultural contexts in which it is acquired (Alexander & Murphy, 1998b). Frisby (1998) explains that both intentional and incidental learning occur in many nested contexts. Classrooms, typically the most immediate context of formal knowledge, are nested in schools, which exert their own influence on student learning. Schools, in turn, are nested in communities, and so the progression goes. Each of these embedded contexts contributes in a particular way to human learning and development (Bronfenbrenner, 1979). Consequently, any serious school reform requires a coordinated effort among these interrelated levels of educational influence, making enduring and effective change problematic and unwieldy (Senge, 1990).

Learner-Centered Psychological Principle 11
Social influences on learning. Learning is influenced by social interactions, interpersonal relations, and communication with others.

APA Board of Educational Affairs, 1997.

Ensure That the Classroom Environment Supports Student Learning One of the lessons learned from situated cognitivists is that students learn better when they are in an environment that affords them the resources for active and meaningful engagement (Greeno & MSMAPG, 1998). Such resources are both human (e.g., teacher, students, parents) and nonhuman (e.g., books, computers). In addition, effective learning environments attend not only to students' cognitive needs, but also to their social and motivational development.

To address these social and motivational dimensions in learning environments, Woolfolk (1998) built on work done by J. L. Epstein (1989) on effective family structures but conceptualized them in terms of the classroom context. Specifically, Epstein used the acronym TARGET to identify six characteristics of home environments that predict motivation among children: task, autonomy/authority, recognition, grouping, evaluation, and time. In terms of classrooms, task refers to the design of the learning activities and assignments; autonomy/authority represents the extent to which students assume leadership for or control over their learning; recognition means the formal and informal use of rewards or incentives; grouping involves organizing students into individual, small, or large groups; evaluation entails the assessment or monitoring of student learning; and time signifies the appropriateness of the workload for the time allotted. To these Woolfolk added the dimension of teacher expectations, which encompasses teachers' beliefs about their students and their academic abilities.

Woolfolk (1998) then outlined various pedagogical strategies that teachers can use to address each of these seven dimensions within the classroom context. For the task dimension, for example, she suggests that teachers begin lessons by relating the content to students' everyday lives and personal interests. For grouping, Woolfolk discusses the value of using variable grouping patterns in the classroom. For time she recommends that teachers allow students to work at their own pace and be more flexible in their scheduling for tasks and courses.

Further, because knowledge is acquired in many forms and through multiple media, teachers should present central concepts through multiple modalities. For example, Helenrose is more likely to reach her students if she uses an array of tools and methods to convey information about the Supreme Court. Whereas some of her students may respond to a classroom discussion, others may understand better when they explore the topic through hypermedia. Still other students may grasp key concepts better when they are physically and concretely involved in the learning, as through roles in a mock trial. Teachers who use a variety of methods have a greater chance of maintaining their students' interest and attention.

Initiate Learning by Anchoring It to Meaningful and Thought-Provoking Experiences Through an approach called **anchored instruction,** John Bransford and his colleagues at Vanderbilt (CTGV, 1997) set out to counter the inert knowledge they saw arising from traditional methods of content delivery. They did so by anchoring the curriculum to stimulating experiences intended to provoke students' thinking and learning. For CTGV (1990) anchored instruction took the form of videodiscs that posed complex problems for students to explore over an extended period of time.

John Bransford, known for his Jasper Series, has a long history of shaping understanding about knowledge and knowing.

Initiating activities have long been seen as effective tools for sparking interest and introducing a lesson (Gagné, 1977). However, the particular anchors that CTGV devised were not set aside, as many initiating activities are. Instead, those *macrocontexts* were intended for prolonged use and were woven throughout the learning. They allowed teachers not only to grab their students' attention, but also to hold it (Mitchell, 1993). Another advantage of anchored instruction is its shared structure. In this case students collaborated around the problems posed in the videodiscs. Anchored instruction represents learning environments that "permit sustained exploration by students and teachers and enable them to understand the kinds of problems and opportunities that experts in various areas encounter and the knowledge that these experts use as tools" (CTGV, 1990, p. 3).

Using the latest in hypermedia technology, CTGV (1996) anchors are also a rich source of visual/spatial information for teachers and students. One of the early macrocontexts allowed fifth graders to explore the movie *Young Sherlock* as a means of improving their literacy skills and social studies knowledge. The research group later created the Jasper series, which depicts the adventures of one Jasper Woodbury and focuses on the development of students' mathematical, scientific, and historical knowledge. Both of these approaches have been successful in promoting students' learning in these content areas (CTGV, 1990, 1996).

The concepts behind anchored instruction are not new to education; Dewey (1913) argued for experience-based and problem-based learning like that reflected in the work of CTGV. And instructional anchors can come in many forms, as long as they provoke students' thinking and allow for extended exploration of knowledge under a variety of instructional arrangements.

Knowledge Reflects Experiences In and Out of School

Efforts to institutionalize learning or constrain it in a rigid manner can result in students viewing knowledge and knowing as a job, as routine labor rather than as a personal pursuit (Bereiter & Scardamalia, 1989). Knowledge seeking occurs in and out of classrooms, as the power of unschooled knowledge makes clear (Gardner, 1991). Therefore, effective teachers must use the ubiquitous nature of knowledge and knowing to their advantage by fostering bidirectional, seamless learning between the classroom and the world outside.

Extend the Learning Environment Beyond the Walls of the Classroom   The world is a powerful teacher and a boundless source of educational experiences. A multitude of real-world experiences can demonstrate, reinforce, or extend any concept one wishes to teach. Textbooks can help to capture some of the world outside the classroom, but their descriptions, illustrations, and explanations are abstract and one-dimensional. Effective teachers need to think beyond the formal curriculum, the textbooks, and the instructional routines and take advantage of the resources in the world at large.

The lack of real-world contexts for learning is all too commonplace, as the research of Guthrie and his colleagues has shown (1996). As part of his Concept-Oriented Reading Instruction (CORI) Project, Guthrie tries to have teachers see the real world as a valuable source of scientific knowledge that can be brought into the classroom. For example, while learning about amphibians and reptiles, the middle-school students in the project study and care for frogs. The research on CORI has shown this hands-on approach to be an important component in the project's success, especially when coupled with reading and writing activities (Guthrie et al., 1996).

However, it is sometimes difficult for teachers to see beyond the confines of their classrooms. I observed a science teacher who was covering the process of photosynthesis by having his students read the relevant section of their textbook and then answer related questions orally and in writing. What was particularly noteworthy was that this teacher's room was filled with plant life and the windows of his classroom looked out onto a nature center. Yet that teacher never thought to use those plentiful resources to make photosynthesis come to life for his students.

Unfortunately, the world and its experiences are not equally accessible to all students. Many of the students in Helenrose's classroom have never ventured beyond their inner-city neighborhood and have little idea what life is like across town, much less across the oceans. However, technology makes it feasible to reach outside the classroom, the neighborhood, or the culture to enrich knowledge and the process of knowing. By using hypermedia, for example, Bereiter and Scardamalia (1989) linked students in classrooms around the globe. Their Computer-Supported Intentional Learning Environment (CSILE) Project had students in distant classrooms engaged in the study of a hypothetical culture. Not only did these students acquire knowledge about remote cultures, but they also developed relationships with the students in the distant classrooms who collaborated with them on this complex task.

Look for Learning Opportunities in the Experiences and Interests of the Students   The content of instruction need not arise from the teacher or the established curriculum. The lives and interests of students are natural conduits for meaningful educational experiences. James (1992) put it well when he said that the way to get the attention of

students is to dovetail the lesson to the ideas they already find interesting.

> From all these facts there emerges a very simple abstract programme for the teacher to follow in keeping the attention of the child: Begin with the line of his native interests, and offer him objects that have some immediate connection with these. (James, 1890, p. 768)

For example, when Helenrose decides to teach gravity in her science class, she would be wise to find out how the concept of gravity connects with her students' existing interests and experiences. Perhaps she could use basketball free throws during recess to illustrate how gravity influences the trajectory of the ball. In addition, teachers need to be alert to teachable moments; sometimes events just happen that become wonderful triggers for teaching and learning. Gloria's unexpected answer to the guest speaker's question about the Supreme Court proved to be just such a trigger for Helenrose and her students. Because Helenrose valued her students' interest in the topic and was flexible enough to alter the course of her planned instruction, she and her students became much more informed about the American judicial system.

Knowledge Is Socially and Culturally Constructed

Embrace the Spectrum of Sociocultural Backgrounds, Not Just Those That Are Mainstream   As Bronfenbrenner (1979) points out, individuals are members of many cultures, and those memberships affect what and how they think and learn. Some of Helenrose's students, for example, are not only members of her classroom community and the local neighborhood, but also members of the African American culture, as well as participants in the culture of poverty. Given this myriad of cultural identities, educators cannot teach culture as though it were merely some set of historical names and facts. To see just how much sociocultural histories come into play in teaching and learning, read each of the sentences in the Thought Experiment: Cups and Culture, and try to image the events being described.

Thought Experiment ....

Cups and Culture

Directions: For each of the sentences below, try to form a mental image of what is being described.

> Great Aunt Estelle was pouring a *cup* of tea and serving scones to her guests during high tea.
>
> Sylvia sat drinking a *cup* of cappuccino at the local coffeehouse, while listening to the young poet recite his latest dirge.
>
> The baby laughed as he threw his drinking *cup* on the floor.
>
> The soccer team held up the winner's *cup* in triumph, as the fans screamed wildly.

How would students from diverse sociocultural backgrounds have performed on this task? Could they have seen the object in Great Aunt Estelle's hand as a dainty cup of china, complete with matching saucer? Could they have conjured up the image of a wide-mouth vessel for the cappuccino? Could they have appreciated the not-so-subtle differences between infants' drinking cups and a sports trophy? In other words, would their sociocultural histories have helped or hindered them in understanding the subtleties reflected in those sentences?

Helenrose related well to her students because she acknowledged her students' cultural heritages in her curriculum. She made their backgrounds a centerpiece of the class activity, for example, tracing the Supreme Court's record with regard to slavery and civil rights. The students' cultural perspectives also contributed to a less-than-favorable view of American justice, which was not dismissed but was acknowledged and discussed.

> *Culture is activity of thought, and receptiveness to beauty and humane feeling. Scraps of information have nothing to do with it.*
>
> A. N. Whitehead, 1929/1967, p. 1.

Show Students That the Pursuit of Knowledge Is Unending and Pleasurable   As Bandura's (1986) research in social learning demonstrated, individual's actions can significantly affect those who look up to those individuals. Other people in a student's environment become models for how that student speaks, dresses, and acts. In schools teachers become models of learning for their students, even when they do not intend to. Teachers who manifest an inquisitive nature and who demonstrate a value for knowledge and for knowing can foster similar attitudes and approaches in their students. In contrast, teachers who are simple purveyors of declarative knowledge and who lack enthusiasm for their subjects develop more passive and unmotivated students.

Teachers should demonstrate that knowledge is not always certain or simple to acquire and that effort to discover meaning is a worthwhile undertaking rather than an indicator of some intellectual weakness (Buehl, Alexander, & Murphy, 2002; Schommer, 1990). Such views about knowledge have been linked to higher student motivation and achievement. Consequently, if Helenrose wants her students to be active knowledge seekers, she should manifest her own interest in knowing and become an active and willing participant in the learning process. For those who place a premium on the construction of knowledge and the process of knowing, such modeling within the learning environment may actually be more important than any single fact or skill students ultimately acquire.

Teachers' pursuit of knowledge also serves an important pedagogical function. The literature is quite clear that teachers' subject-matter knowledge is linked to their instructional effectiveness and, thus, to their students' achievement (Shulman & Quinlan, 1996). However, every academic field, from history to physics, remains in formation. Accordingly, every lesson or instructional unit can become another opportunity for teachers to construct new understandings about their domains—instead of a routine presentation of well-worn content.

■ Summary Reflections

What is knowledge?

- Varied beliefs about the nature of knowledge and knowing affect what is taught and what is learned in schools.
- Six learning theories differ in how knowledge takes shape and where it ultimately resides.
- Cognitive constructivism, information processing, and radical constructivism place increasingly more emphasis on the individual mind in the formation and retention of knowledge.
- Increasingly more attention to social and cultural forces is manifest in social constructivism, situated cognition, and socioculturalism, along with greater interest in the process rather then the product of knowing.
- Theoretical differences carry over into curricular goals and pedagogical decisions.
  - IP teachers devote time and energy to improving their students' ability to take in information from the environment and store it in memory.
  - Cognitive constructivists take pains to determine the level of their students' mental maturity and provide comparable educational materials and experiences.
  - Radical constructivists are invested in understanding students' idiosyncratic views of the world and individual approaches to problem solving.
  - For situated cognitivists and socioculturalists, the environment and social context become paramount—learning environments with adequate resources and ample opportunities for social interaction.
  - Concern for technology is more indicative of situated cognitivists than socioculturalists.
  - Social constructivists try to pair students with more knowledgeable and capable others who can stimulate their thinking and scaffold their learning.

What kinds of knowledge should be part of the educational experience?

- Prior knowledge, the matriarch of knowledge terms, encompasses three fundamental states—declarative, procedural, and conditional knowledge.

- Explicit knowledge includes that part of prior knowledge that is within the realm of consciousness and can be communicated to others.
- Tacit knowledge is unvoiced and often buried knowledge that is not directly shared with others but continues to shape thoughts and actions subtly.
- Schooled knowledge typically derives from formal educational experiences, whereas unschooled knowledge comes from everyday encounters.

What principles of knowledge promote effective educational practice?

- Students' knowledge is as unique as their fingerprints.
  - Teachers must expect differences in students' construction, interpretation, and communication of their understandings.
  - Teachers must recognize the patterns in students' thinking and appreciate the logic behind their shared understandings.
- Existing knowledge shapes what students come to learn—for better or for worse.
  - Teachers must uncover what students know or believe and build on that foundation.
  - Teachers need to look thoughtfully at the activities they incorporate into the curriculum and compare the demands of the tasks to the knowledge and experiences of each student.
- Knowledge is never divorced from its sociocultural context.
  - Effective teachers create rich and stimulating learning environments that support knowledge construction.

- Teachers should formulate extensive and meaningful experiences to which instructional tasks and social interactions can be appropriately anchored.
- Knowledge guides perceptions of and interactions with the world.
  - Educators should break down the barriers between in-school and out-of-school learning.
  - Teachers should use students' own lives and experiences as the basis for instructional experiences.
- Knowledge is a sociocultural construct.
  - Teachers should present ideas and concepts from a multicultural perspective so that every student's life and experiences are represented and appreciated.
  - Teachers must be models of knowledge seeking for their students, manifesting the pleasure of knowledge pursuit.

....

■ Thought Experiment Questions: Now You See It, Now You Don't!

Directions: Answer the following questions based only on what you remember. Do not look back!

1. What was the theme of this passage?

2. Write down as much as you can remember from the passage. Include as many details as possible.

3. When you have finished, compare your recollections to the original passage. List the ideas or details you overlooked *and* those you added or changed.

Chapter 5

Learning and Teaching in Academic Domains

GUIDING QUESTIONS

- What is an academic domain?
- What do academic domains have in common?
- How do differences in academic domains affect learning and instruction?

IN THEIR OWN WORDS ....

As a veteran educator, PRICILLA MURPHY has done it all in the past 20 years—high-school mathematics teacher, high-school assistant principal, middle-school principal, and now central administrator. Whatever her specific role, however, mathematics has never been far from Pricilla's professional identity.

Given that I have dedicated so much of my professional life to the teaching of mathematics, you may be surprised to learn that mathematics was *not* my favorite subject in high school. In fact, I was not very successful in my math classes, with a B in Algebra I, C in geometry, and D in Algebra II. I just could not see what relevance any of those courses had to my life. As a native-born Texan, I had never seen a snow-plow and certainly saw no reason for solving problems related to it or to planes, trains, or boats. So I just did what I could to get through and get by.

Ten years after graduating from high school, and after the birth of my three daughters, I decided to enter the academic realm again. But to be honest, I was not sure my brain would function at a college level. So I selected Introductory Finite Mathematics as one of my first three classes. I was sure mathematics would be my downfall, and I wanted to get the agony over as quickly as possible.

That mathematics class was a phenomenal experience—one that changed my life. The professor, Dr. Schatz, spent the first two sessions of the class assisting each of us in the analysis of the first problem. We took the question apart and put it back together. Understanding the problem was the primary focus of the class; the answer was only secondary to our thinking and reasoning. Each class was a unique problem-analysis opportunity. Dr. Schatz explored different approaches for solving the problems and encouraged us to develop individual strategies. He would give us the answer just to make sure a correct strategy was reinforced.

The following semester, I enrolled in Introductory Calculus. I used the analysis techniques from my first course to solve the problems. Three years later with many advanced mathematics courses under my belt, I earned a degree and teaching certification in mathematics.

I went on to teach high-school mathematics for 9 years—from Introductory Algebra to Calculus, from remedial learners to gifted and talented students. Whatever the course or the presumed competency level, I used the Schatz approach to assist my students in mastering mathematics concepts. We also focused on problems relevant to their life experiences. I abandoned snowplow problems and used student names and personal experiences to discuss the analysis process. Answers became the means for thinking mathematically and not the ends. I thoroughly enjoyed watching my students discover some of the same beauty in mathematics I found years before in Dr. Schatz's finite mathematics course.

Several years later, I assumed the principalship of a large middle school. I found that the teachers lacked confidence in their ability to teach even basic mathematics concepts to their students. I heard all kinds of excuses. "I was never very good in math." "I can barely balance my checkbook." "I just can't do it." However, with the help of some excellent mathematics teachers, who volunteered to tutor their fellow teachers, we instituted a "Mathematics Across the Curriculum" approach. After the initial trepidation, teachers began to enjoy the challenge of infusing mathematics into other subject matter. Teachers' confidence grew and our students were happily doing mathematics as part of their social studies or science projects. Some time later, one teacher who had been a reluctant participant in our little mathematical experiment came by my office. She confessed that she now believed that our schoolwide approach to mathematics had been a real learning activity for both teachers and students. I cannot tell you what that one vote of confidence meant to me then and now.

What Is an Academic Domain?

For better or for worse, schooling throughout the world is conceived and organized around particular fields of study, such as reading or mathematics. Whether students are from the Netherlands, Singapore, Argentina, or South Africa, their educational experiences revolve around such school subjects as writing, science, and history. These recognized and institutionalized educational fields, or subjects, are termed **academic domains** (Alexander, 1997b). This orientation of learning-by-subject has a tremendous effect on teachers and on the students they guide. For example, teachers are typically trained or certified to teach designated subjects, like mathematics or reading, especially in the middle and upper grades. In addition, many teachers hold very strong views about the nature of academic do-

mains and organize their instruction accordingly (Lampert, 1990; Lemke, 1990). Further, publishing and testing companies invest millions of dollars in the development of subject-matter materials that shape school curricula.

Students are not immune to the influence of academic domains either. Children as young as 6 talk about school in terms of these academic domains (Buehl & Alexander, 2000). They conceive of schooling as doing math or reading or working in their social studies book. Even at this young age, students have already begun to judge themselves and others as good or bad in particular subjects. Pricilla Murphy's personal account serves as a reminder of what lasting effects these self-judgments can have on students and teachers. Because of their strong presence in learning and instruction, it is important to explore the characteristics of these formalized and institutionalized domains of study.

Although academic domains are trademarks of formal education in modern society, they have been in existence throughout recorded history (Durant, 1954–1975). For example, education in ancient China focused on reading and interpreting the writings of Confucius. In ancient Athens boys born to privilege studied writing, music, and gymnastics and later apprenticed under independent teachers who instructed them in oratory, science, philosophy, and history. Centuries later, during the Reformation, there was a movement to create compulsory education. One outcome was the advancement of the *gymnasium*, or secondary school, with its emphasis on Greek and Latin, along with logic, rhetoric, psychology, ethics, and theology. Current conceptions of schools still bear some resemblance to the early models of compulsory education.

In recent history various educational historians, philosophers, and researchers have pondered the question of what constitutes an academic domain and what it means to *know* any given subject (Phenix, 1964; Schwab, 1964). Educators have also debated whether academic domains exist in nature, to be discovered or uncovered by humankind, or whether all domains are merely human contrivances devised by societies to make their existences more palatable or to organize education into manageable units (Bereiter, 1994). Whether domains are real or contrived, they can be distinguished from one another in the broader world. Historians conceive of their mission differently from the way mathematicians do (VanSledright, 2002), and the tools scientists use vary from those of writers (Rutherford & Ahlgren, 1990). Moreover, these actual or perceived differences among domains influence how they are taught in school settings.

Most educational historians, philosophers, and researchers agree that domains are formalized bodies of knowledge (Alexander, 1998c). Thus, the declarative, procedural, and conditional knowledge that constitutes a domain cannot be acquired simply from everyday life but must be derived through systematic instruction. Domains inevitably involve some level of abstraction, especially for those who become competent in them (Popper, 1972). In addition, the concepts, principles, and theories that constitute domains must achieve social acceptability and, therefore, must withstand the continuous scrutiny and testing of recognized domain experts (Shulman & Quinlan, 1996).

Reasons to Study Domains of Knowledge

Scholarly debates about domains may seem of limited merit to students who must complete tonight's mathematics homework or pass tomorrow's history test. Also, the debates may not seem helpful to teachers who are required to operate in an educational community where learning is framed in terms of specified courses and curriculum mandates. But these dialogues and debates do matter in very real ways to teachers and students alike. Over time, the perspectives of the research community shape trends in instruction and assessment, which alter how teachers teach and students learn.

Whether they are rooted in nature or are sociocultural creations, academic domains serve as the arenas of the educational experience and the platform for school achievement.

There are still other reasons for focusing on learning and teaching in academic domains. For one, the decades of research devoted to formulating general laws of human learning and development have not proven particularly fruitful (Shulman & Quinlan, 1996). Learning may simply be too complex and too dynamic to be cast in such a definitive manner. What we do know is that learning varies with the context, and subject matter is a major factor in the educational context, a point voiced repeatedly in the psychological literature of the past decade (Alexander & Murphy, 1998b).

Lee Shulman is one of the leaders in the movement toward domain specificity in psychological studies.

This trend toward greater domain specificity in the educational psychology literature touches all aspects of human learning, including the work in development, motivation, and strategic processing. Rather than talk about whether students are globally bright or motivated, the research community is now more apt to talk about the domains in which students perform better or worse or in which students are more or less motivated (Harter, 1992). Rather than label students as strategic or nonstrategic, researchers are more likely to consider the tasks and fields in which students manifest strategic differences (Pressley, Goodchild, Fleet, Zajchowski, & Evans, 1989). Also, instead of trying to define teacher effectiveness divorced from content, researchers are engaged in studies of pedagogy within specific fields (Ball, 1993; Wineburg, 1991b).

As Shulman and Quinlan (1996) note, educational psychology has had an on-again/off-again relationship with subject-matter domains. Domains were the defining force in educational psychology for the first 2 decades of the 20th century. Dewey (1897/1972) was among the first to *psychologize* subject matter, thereby initiating an effort to connect domains to psychological processes and to submit subject matter to careful philosophical and empirical study. This interest in subject-matter areas faded from the research scene, however, when educational psychologists became invested in the search for general theories, principles, and concepts of human learning and development, a trend that continued until the 1990s.

More recent educational research has clearly witnessed a renaissance of domain-specific inquiry. Leading researchers who helped usher in the decades of information-processing research, including John Bransford (with Johnson, 1973) and Ann Brown (with DeLoache, 1978), turned their attention to studies of learning in mathematics, science, and history. And many others have joined their ranks. Leinhardt (1989), Ball (1993), and Lampert (1990), for instance, have looked deeply at the nature of mathematics learning and teaching, whereas Wineburg (1991a) and VanSledright (2002) delved similarly into the domain of history. In science diSessa (1993) has investigated what it means to learn and teach physics, Ben-Zvi (with Eylon, & Silberstein, 1987) and colleagues concentrated on chemistry, and M.C. Linn (1992) focused on physical science, especially in conjunction with computer technology.

Motivational researchers, as well, have become more domain specific in their theories and models. For example, research on attributions, self-regulation, interest, self-efficacy, and goal theory now looks at learners in relation to specific instructional domains or related tasks (Pintrich & Schunk, 2001). And the work of Bandura (1977), Schunk (1991), and Zimmerman (1989) is concerned with the ways in which learners judge and regulate their performance in academic domains. In addition, expectancy-value researchers, including Wigfield and Eccles (1989), ask how well students expect to do in subject-matter areas and how important the students perceive those subjects to be. Alexander and colleagues (Alexander, Jetton, & Kulikowich, 1995; Alexander & Murphy, 1998a) have examined the interest that students report for domains like biology, statistics, and physics and the ways in which these interests relate to their performance.

Initial Caveats

As these emerging lines of inquiry suggest, there is perhaps no better time to ask what educational psychology has to say about learning and teaching in academic domains. However, certain parameters need to be established for that discussion here. First, domains are highly complex and fluid, and many colleagues have devoted their professional careers to studying the intricacies of learning and teaching in such fields as reading (Alvermann & Hayes, 1989), writing (Harris & Graham, 1996), history (Seixas, 1996), mathematics (Greeno & MSMAPG, 1998), and science (M.R. Matthews, 1994). This chapter can touch on only a few of the attributes and issues that these experts have extensively researched and cannot capture the subtleties that exist.

Second, academic domains frequently involve a number of interrelated or associated fields, each with its own defining qualities, vocabulary, problems, and inherent issues. In science, for instance, there are fields as varied as chemistry, biology, astronomy, and genetics. However, this discussion will deal with the overarching, or root, domain. Third, the focus here is on academic domains as they are presently configured and taught in schools, not as they should be taught. For example, when it comes to mathematics,

schooled problems will be discussed for which students typically solve for the right answer—the kind of snowplow problems that Pricilla Murphy spoke about in the opening scenario. Even though this type of work runs counter to current conceptions of effective mathematical learning and teaching (Lemke, 1990), it nonetheless remains common practice. With each academic domain, gaps between actual and desired practice take the form of instructional issues, and every domain has instructional issues that require attention if optimal learning is to occur.

What Do Academic Domains Have in Common?

Perhaps the most important shared dimension of academic domains is that they all arose from practical needs. In order to survive and thrive, humankind required some means to communicate beyond the grunt or the gesture (i.e., reading and writing). There was also a need to record the customs and traditions of a people for posterity and to frame particular events in a certain perspective (i.e., history). Survival also demanded that societies discern the patterns in nature around which their lives revolved; for example, planting cycles and the movements of the tides (i.e., science). Similarly, there was a need to count, weigh, and measure commodities with some consistency (i.e., mathematics).

> In the opinion of Herbert Spencer, that supreme expert in the collection of evidence post judicium, science, like letters, began with the priests, originated in astronomic observations, governing religious festivals, and was preserved in the temples and transmitted across the generations as part of the clerical heritage. We cannot say, for here again beginnings elude us, and we may only surmise. Perhaps science, like civilization in general, began with agriculture; geometry, as its name indicates, was the measurement of soil; and the calculation of crops and seasons, necessitating the observation of the stars and construction of a calendar, may have generated astronomy. Navigation advanced astronomy, trade developed mathematics, and the industrial arts laid the bases of physics and chemistry.
>
> Counting was probably one of the earliest forms of speech, and in many tribes it still presents a relieving simplicity. The Tasmanians counted up to two: "Parmery, calabawa, cardia"—i.e., "one, two, plenty.". . . Damara natives would not exchange two sheep for four sticks, but willingly exchanged, twice in succession, one sheep for two sticks. Counting was by the fingers; hence the decimal system. Toes added to fingers created the idea of twenty or a score. . . The measurement of time by movements of the heavenly bodies was probably the beginning of astronomy; the very word *measure*, like the word *month* (and perhaps the word *man*—the measurer), goes back apparently to the root denoting the moon. (Durant, 1954, pp. 78–79)

Regrettably, much of the pragmatic value of domains has been lost to many students. Domains have become abstracted, disembodied courses of study, rather than meaningful assemblages of knowledge and skills that serve societal needs. Part of the task for teachers is to help their students rediscover the practical value of school subjects, discovering that the domains, like mathematics, are more than academic trials that all students must endure.

Modes of Encryption

All academic domains, as broadly conceived involve **encryption**, the codification or representation of the concepts and procedures in symbolic form (Goldin, 1992; Kulikowich, O'Connell, Rezendes, & Archambault, 2000). For some fields the primary mode of encryption is linguistic (e.g., reading, writing, and history). For others it may be numeric or graphic (e.g., science). As a domain, mathematics is particularly demanding in this respect, because students must navigate multiple modes of encryption (i.e., numeric, linguistic, graphic, and formulaic).

As part of its encryption, an academic field also has its own lexicon or vocabulary that students must come to understand if they are to perform competently (Lampert & Blunk, 1998). For instance, students must be conversant with the concepts of primary and secondary sources in history, just as they must grasp the meaning of terms like *theory* or *hypothesis* in science. Similarly, until children comprehend simple ideas like more or less, bigger or smaller, and longer or shorter, they are unlikely to do well at mathematical tasks based on those concepts. Students who do not become fluent in the language of an academic domain or who do not grasp the meaning of its central concepts will never achieve competence in it.

Thus, teachers should familiarize students with the codes and concepts of domains and should orchestrate learning environments where meaningful dialogue around domain concepts is commonly practiced (Lemke, 1990). Moreover, students should have opportunities to translate thoughts from one mode of encryption into alternative symbolic forms (Goldin, 1992).

Typical Tasks

Each domain also has tasks or problems associated with the educational experience, these are referred to as schooled tasks or problems (Stewart, 1987). Where would reading be without story time or science without experimentation? Although these typical school problems change across grade levels and over time, they bestow an identifiable flavor on formal learning in each field. Part of this flavor comes from the national and local curriculum materials that frame the educational experience in schools. Elementary-school students throughout the United States encounter problems like $45 - 21 = \_\_\_$, or $20 \div 5 = \_\_\_$, while geometry students tackle problems involving proofs. In language arts, students discuss a story they just read about a ravenous caterpillar, or they write their own sagas, which they share with classmates. Sample tasks like these can be easily identified with their related

domains, validating their status as schooled (Bereiter, 1994).

For certain academic domains, such as mathematics and science, mainstream problems are more well structured or well defined, whereas for other domains, such as reading and history, tasks are typically more ill structured or ill defined (Alexander, 1998c). Fredericksen (1984) describes well-structured tasks as those for which there are typically agreed-upon answers and rather accepted means of getting to those answers. Ill-structured problems, by comparison, can have a wide range of acceptable outcomes and as many means of reaching those ends as there are students in the class.

Underlying Processes

Just as there are certain tasks and problems that typify academic domains, there are also fundamental processes that mark individuals as members of these academic communities. For instance, historical thinking requires a conception of time and causality and demands the ability to build interpretations across multiple documents. Experts in science must be acute at observing and chronicling and must be able to formulate hypotheses from emerging data or test the hypotheses articulated by others. A rather ill-structured domain, writing also has its fundamental processes: the ability to conceive of a topic and to translate thoughts into words that are meaningful and appropriate to the intended audience.

Whatever the domain, teachers must infuse its underlying processes into the classroom culture. This concern for process was at the heart of Professor Schatz's finite mathematics class and became the foundation of Pricilla Murphy's approach to teaching mathematics. According to the research in cognition, teachers should make these processes clear and explicit to students, rather than leaving them buried in the day-to-day transactions that occur. This approach requires teachers to be well informed in these domains (Alexander, 1997b; Shulman & Quinlan, 1996), capable of modeling these processes with a variety of domain tasks and explaining them in understandable ways.

Instructional Issues

Domains bring certain problems or issues into the classroom. Sometimes these issues represent a conflict between teachers' beliefs about effective practice and the practices supported by empirical research (Pajares, 1992). In the domain of reading, for example, a significant number of teachers shy away from any explicit instruction in letter-sound correspondence and comprehension strategies, despite evidence that such knowledge is essential for learning to read and reading to learn, respectively (Stanovich, 1986). A similar dilemma arises in the domain of writing, where some popular instructional programs are not well substantiated by the research (Adams, 1990; Hillocks, 1984).

At other times the issues reflect significant discrepancies between the actual practice of the domain and the academic version to which students are exposed. For instance, there are marked differences between the thinking and reasoning scientists engage in and the stress placed on memorizing scientific facts in elementary schools. Similarly, in mathematics there is undue weight put on doing arithmetic computations in classrooms and inadequate emphasis on understanding the reasoning that underlies such computations.

Still other issues have more to do with real or perceived complexities in the domain itself. In the domain of history, for example, problems arise when schooled ideas, central to the domain, run counter to the information fictionalized in popular media like movies and videos. Thus, students trying to build historical understanding find it difficult to set aside the misleading and fictitious content they encounter out of school. Similarly, science students formulate naive or erroneous conceptions from what they see or hear in the world around them, in part because they are not taught how to conduct systematic observations or to formulate reasonable explanations. The influence of naive or erroneous conceptions on students' learning is given extensive treatment in chapter 6.

By understanding the issues that are prototypical of academic domains, educators can take whatever steps are necessary to ameliorate these problems. However, as long as educators must represent complex and demanding fields of study in intellectually honest ways to young and developing minds (Metsala, 1999), there will be instructional issues that need to be addressed. How educators avail themselves of the psychological research in formulating responses to these issues is critical.

How Do Differences in Academic Domains Affect Learning and Instruction?

Although academic domains share particular dimensions, they also have important differences. It is impossible here to explore the full array of domains that are part of formal education across the life span. Instead, this discussion will center on five general fields—reading, writing, history, mathematics, and science. These are traditional domains that generally form the foundation of the educational experience, especially in the early years. In addition, there is a solid base of research on the processing that underlines learning in these domains (Alexander, 1998c). And there is evidence that children and adults have varied perceptions of these domains and of their competencies and motivations relative to them (Harter, 1992).

Reading

Reading involves deciphering a written message and constructing meaning from the linguistic clues the message provides.

Learning to Read

Learning to read, which is the thrust of early reading instruction, entails breaking the linguistic code (i.e., **decoding**) and achieving fluency or automaticity in converting these encryptions into meaning (i.e., **encoding**). In alphabetic languages such as English, code-breaking encompasses underlying processes that must be effectively executed if students are to construct meaning from any segment of text (e.g., letters, words, or sentences). The initial forays into the world of print can be complex and precarious.

Sound-Letter Relationships

Although most students eventually become fair to good readers, approximately 25% of the school population struggles to make sense of text and falls into the category of poor or remedial readers (Adams, 1990). Even after decades of investigation, researchers are still trying to pinpoint the psychological processes that undergird reading. Such knowledge could be used to facilitate language development in young minds.

As stated, learning to read involves associating written symbols with sound units and with the interpretations these associations evoke in the reader. The association between language symbol and sound is referred to as **graphophonemics**. **Graphemes** are the letter patterns that are common to a particular language, such as *th, eigh*, or *m* in English. The word *bench*, for example, consists of four letter patterns, *b-e-n-ch*. **Phonemes** are the smallest units of sound into which language can be broken. The word *mat*, for instance, contains three phonemes—/m/, /a/, and /t/. Standard English consists of about 40 common phonemes (Mayer, 1998). Thus, graphophonemics is the process of putting letter patterns and sound units together. Before children can read efficiently, they must be able to access and manipulate those common speech sounds and do so rapidly (i.e., fluently) and almost effortlessly (i.e., automatically).

It is not surprising that many students who have difficulties learning to read manifest problems in **phonemic** or **phonological awareness,** the sensitivity to the sounds that comprise a given language. Phonological awareness can be diagnosed by giving individuals several tasks (Metsala & Ehri, 1998):

1. to identify the number of sounds in the words they hear (e.g., dash = 3; paper = 4)
2. to pronounce actual words (e.g., *grief*) or pseudowords (e.g., *plenk*) accurately
3. to tell what words would result when given sounds are blended together (e.g., /d/ + /a/ + /t/)
4. to produce the sound that results when particular letters are added (e.g., /s/ + *pine*=spine) or deleted (e.g., *space* − /s/ =pace).

The psychological research has consistently demonstrated the potency of phonological awareness on later reading achievement, over and above other critical variables (Stanovich, 1990).

The Structure and Meaning of Language

Learning to read also demands an understanding of the grammatical structure of language (i.e., **syntax**), along with the meaning of its linguistic units (i.e., **semantics**). The importance of both syntactic and semantic knowledge is evident in the following two sentences:

> They fed her the animal crackers.
> They fed her animal the crackers.

These sentences contain exactly the same words, but the roles they play (i.e., their parts of speech) differ, as does the overall meaning that is subsequently conveyed. Without syntactic and semantic knowledge, the different messages in these sentences stay locked away.

Comprehension, along with the idea of knowledge construction explored in Chapter 4, denotes this process of meaning making. Comprehension and constructivist theorists hold that meaning making relies heavily on the prior knowledge readers bring to any text. Thus, even when readers can decode a text accurately and fluently, they may fail to draw meaning from it if the message lies outside their realm of experience. You can test this assumption by reading the text in the Thought Experiment: Confronting the Complexity of Text.

Thought Experiment ···

Confronting the Complexity of Text

Directions: Read the following paragraphs *one time* and then see whether you can answer the questions that follow.

Ising Model

In formulating techniques to deal with complexity and chaos we have relied on mathematical models. Here I shall mention a physical model that is proving to be quite helpful in a number of areas where cooperative phenomena are involved. Specifically, I am speaking about the Ising model of ferromagnetism that is empirical in character. This describes macroscopic magnetism on a microscopic level. The atoms of magnetic objects constitute minute magnets called *spins*. The macroscopic magnetism is due to the alignment of the spins. When a ferromagnetic object is heated, it loses its magnetism because the spins point in random directions and their magnetic moments cancel out one another. When the ferromagnetic object is cooled, it regains its magnetism because the spins get realigned.

The *Ising phenomenon* is useful in complex systems analysis because it involves directionality and cooperative behavior among the subsystems. Furthermore, the phenomenon is a manifestation of phase transitions. Refreshing applications about the behavior of schools of fish, firefly flashing, and human imitation such as switching soap brands have been discussed by Callen and Shapero.

A. B. Cambel, 1993, pp. 207–208

1. What was the key idea of this text?
2. For what courses would you read a passage such as this?
3. How would you briefly explain the Ising model?
4. What does the word *spin* mean in this context?

···

Prior knowledge is represented in part by the extensiveness of the reader's written and oral **vocabulary,** the corpus of words that hold meaning for them (McKeown & Curtis, 1987). Vocabulary measures have long been used as predictors of reading achievement; their predictive ability seems to rest on several factors (Metsala, 1997). First, students with rich written or oral vocabularies have likely made the link between letter and sound that is a threshold for learning to read. Second, learners with extensive vocabularies have probably been raised in print-rich environments where oral and written communication is commonplace (Nagy & Scott, 2000). Children who are raised in such print-rich, literacy-oriented homes and communities come to school with advantages in the domains of reading and writing.

Moreover, children learn written language not only by decoding but also by analogy. That is, children often use some familiar word in their written vocabulary (e.g., *dance*) to help them pronounce words that are unfamiliar (e.g., *prance*; Goswami, 2000). And finally, rich vocabularies contribute to fluency in reading, which is important because it lessens the cognitive load and allows readers to focus on meaning instead of on linguistic cues (Stanovich, 1990).

Instructional Issue: Changing Thrusts in Learning to Read

The study of reading became a recognized field of research only in the 19th century. Even though the principal elements of reading acquisition have been in place for decades, their relative importance in reading research and in instructional practice has shifted periodically. Predominant in these shifts is the emphasis placed on the linguistic symbols themselves (i.e., code emphasis) or on the understandings constructed from those linguistic cues (i.e., meaning emphasis). Among the volumes that are markers of the code-versus-meaning shift in emphasis are such classics as *Learning to Read: The Great Debate* by Jean Chall (1983), *Why Johnny Can't Read* by Rudolph Flesch (1955), and Marilyn Adams's (1990) *Beginning to Read: Thinking and Learning About Print.* Overall, the psychological research supports a balanced reading program that acknowledges the predictive role of phonological awareness in reading achievement, but not at the expense of meaningful engagement with print (Alexander & Jetton, 2000).

The educational psychology research also supports efforts to intervene with those students who initially demonstrate weaknesses in phonological awareness or in any of the other underlying processes upon which reading ability seems predicated, such as syntactic and semantic knowledge (Hiebert & Taylor, 1994). Questions do remain about the long-term effects of remedial reading programs, especially when such programs are of limited duration, do not begin during the preschool years, or are of limited scope. On the other hand, reading programs like the Early Literacy Project (Englert, Raphael, & Mariage, 1994) incorporate components found to promote reading development in children who are at risk, such as early intervention, one-on-one or small-group instruction, and attention to both code and meaning.

Beyond the debate over code versus meaning, there have been important changes in the way that learning to read is conceptualized. Those changes are reflected in how reading is perceived, not only in early childhood or elementary-school classrooms, but also in homes and communities (Hiebert & Taylor, 1994). These significant changes in perception are summarized in Table 5–1 as comparisons between reading readiness and emergent literacy (Bruning, Schraw, & Ronning, 1999).

Gone are the days when educators operated under the assumption that reading instruction should begin at a threshold age. Gone also are the beliefs that learning to read

begins only when children set foot in a preschool or first-grade classroom. To the contrary, educators now realize that literacy begins at birth and takes place in the home and community as much as in the classroom. They also recognize that all forms of literacy—reading, writing, speaking, and listening—are interconnected in life and should, therefore, be interconnected in instruction. Thus, rediscovering the practical or functional nature of reading becomes important to learning. Students should not see reading as abstracted from everyday life but as central to it. And development in reading should be seen as a lifelong endeavor, which does not cease once a child learns to break the linguistic code.

Reading to Learn

In many ways learning to make sense of the symbols on a page is just a first step in a lifelong process (Alexander, 1997a), a process of **reading to learn.** Of all the domains, perhaps none has more importance to continued learning in other fields than reading. The printed word remains the avenue by which individuals acquire a wealth of knowledge about everything from philosophy to physics. Even in those domains where the primary mode of encryption is numeric, like mathematics, descriptions of procedures or schooled problems often entail reading (Rehder, 1999). As Pricilla Murphy can attest, word problems in mathematics still represent challenges for teachers and students alike, even if they are not about snowplows (Mayer & Hegarty, 1996). Thus, reading has been described as a threshold domain.

Just as there are fundamental processes underlying the ability to read, there are also processes associated with reading to learn that distinguish more or less successful students. Garner and Alexander (1991) have described these as the skill, will, and thrill of reading. The skill portion in reading to learn encompasses

- sensitivity to the various structures of text

Table 5–1	Comparison of reading readiness and emergent literacy views.	
	Reading Readiness	**Emergent Literacy**
Focus	Reading as a critical skill in literacy	Broad literacy development, including reading, listening, and speaking
Prototypical View of Reading	Reading as a hierarchy of skills	Reading as a functional activity
Function of Language Activity	Preparation for reading	Multifaceted language development experience, including all forms of language
Focus in Learning to Read	Formal instruction in reading	Engagement with literate adult, adult modeling self-exploration peer interaction, formal instruction in reading, writing, speaking, and listening
Sequencing of Instruction	Read first, write later	Simultaneous use of all language forms—writing, reading, speaking, and listening
Nature of Curriculum	Sequenced reading instruction and hierarchical array of reading skills	Variable language sources, language-based activities that include reading

Note: From *Cognitive Psychology and Instruction* (3rd ed., p. 249) by R. H. Bruning, G. J. Schraw, and R. R. Ronning, 1999, Columbus, OH: Merrill. Copyright 1999 by Merrill. Reprinted with permission.

- a repertoire of text-processing strategies that corresponds to those genres and structures
- an ability to monitor and self-evaluate one's own performance

The will and thrill dimensions of reading to learn pertain to the motivation and personal investment that are required of those who seek knowledge through the printed word (Wigfield & Guthrie, 1997). Successful readers are those who have a goal of mastery or understanding and who are willing to expend the mental energy required to achieve it. They also exhibit a passion for reading. This approach is in sharp contrast to that of many students who engage in reading only to get the task finished or whose work ethic is far from optimal. These motivational dimensions of reading to learn are covered in detail in chapters 9 and 10.

Text Structures

When ideas are inscribed in language, we refer to them as **text** (Alexander & Jetton, 2000). Definitions of text have changed in recent years. Whereas text once referred primarily to formally written language, like the ideas on this page, it now encompasses composed, more formal oral language, such as a teacher's lecture or a politician's speech. Such oral text can thus be distinguished from **talk,** which is essentially conversational, uncomposed communication. Whether they are written or oral, texts typically assume three forms—narrative, expository, and mixed.

Narrative Texts **Narrative texts** are essentially stories that have a recognizable structure, called a **story schema** or **grammar,** which consists of common elements (Graesser, Golding, & Long, 1991). These elements include characters, a setting, a plot, conflict, and resolution. The power of a story schema, or grammar, has long been evident in the research literature. Students who are already aware of these narrative structures perform better in reading tasks because this schema gives rise to reader expectations and predictions (R.C. Anderson, 1977). Similarly, knowledge of story schema is a valuable writing tool because it allows writers to communicate in a form that is comfortable to their readers. Despite its pervasiveness in all forms of storytelling, many younger or less able readers are unaware of this underlying structure. For this reason Graesser and colleagues (1991) maintain that it is important to give young readers explicit training in story schema, or grammar.

Expository Texts Expository text also has recognizable structures that can facilitate learning. **Exposition** is text written more to inform than to entertain. Many of the books or written materials that students read as part of their courses fit into this category. The research suggests that exposition can be more challenging to students than narration (Alexander & Kulikowich, 1994; Goldman, 1997). One reason is that exposition does not have just one typical schema, like narration, but various structures that can even shift from paragraph to paragraph. Typical expository structures include description cause/effect, chronology, comparison/contrast, and problem/resolution. An example of each of these forms is presented in Table 5–2. Students appear even less aware of the common structures in exposition than in narration, even though this knowledge translates into better performance (Goldman, 1997).

Another factor that affects students' learning from exposition is information density. Writers of exposition, especially of texts written for classroom use, sometimes appear to pack each sentence, paragraph, or page of exposition with names, dates, and concepts, allowing little opportunity to elaborate on that factual information (Alexander & Kulikowich, 1994). This problem is compounded by the fact that students are asked to learn about topics for which they have limited background knowledge (Beck, McKeown, & Gromoll, 1989). In addition, each chapter or lesson may cover some new topic or theme with few linkages to the topics or themes already presented. Further, many of the texts read in academic courses were written by content experts rather than gifted writers. Consequently, the quality of their writing can sometimes be questioned (T. H. Anderson & Armbruster, 1984a, 1984b).

Table 5–2   Examples of expository text structures.

Structure	Example
Description	The best-known American species is the blue jay. This bright blue bird with crested head lives from eastern North America west to Kansas.
Cause/Effect	Lightning heats the air, which rushes into the wall of cooler air. When the hot and cold air collide, thunder is heard.
Chronology	Jay was born in New York City and was graduated from King's College (now Columbia University) in 1764. He studied law and was admitted to the bar in 1768.
Comparison/Contrast	The jays form a subfamily in the larger family which includes ravens, crows, and magpies. They are smaller than crows and usually more colorful.
Problem/Resolution	Lightning usually strikes the highest object on the ground. To avoid danger, anyone caught in a lightning storm should lie down or stay low to the ground.

Note: Based on *World Book Encyclopedia.*

Mixed Texts   Like exposition, mixed texts pose special challenges to students. As the name implies, **mixed text** possesses characteristics of both narration and exposition (Alexander & Jetton, 1996). In terms of purpose, mixed texts seem written not just to inform but also to entertain, and their structures correspond to both narration and exposition. Biography is one of the most common examples of mixed text.

A historical novel and this chapter can both illustrate attributes of mixed text. Michener's (1985) *Texas* uses actual events and characters as the backdrop for the story it tells. The reader encounters not only the elements of story grammar discussed earlier, but also paragraphs that describe a structure (e.g., the Alamo), present famous people (e.g., Santa Ana and Travis), or chronicle events (e.g., the battle at Goliad). The expository elements are there to forward the fictional story. This chapter is also an example of mixed text, but in this instance, the expository qualities of the text are predominant, and the story elements, like the opening scenarios, are incorporated to enhance the academic content.

Many of the texts encountered in everyday life, including the morning newspaper or a multimedia Website, fall somewhere between pure narration and pure exposition. One problem with mixed text is recognizing where the informational content begins and the story ends. This is particularly problematic for students who have a limited background in a topic (e.g., Texas history) or who are less familiar with this text form (e.g., historical fiction).

Strategic Text Processing and Self-Monitoring

Because of the demands of reading to learn, students must be able to employ a range of procedures that aid them in understanding and remembering. Procedures that are consciously and effortfully used to promote understanding are called **strategies** (see chapter 7). The procedures that are often required to make sense of text are general cognitive and metacognitive strategies. **Cognitive strategies** include procedures like rereading and paraphrasing, which involve reflective mental activity (Pressley, 1995). **Metacognitive strategies** involve the monitoring of such cognitive efforts (Garner, 1987).

For example, as you are reading this chapter, you may realize that you are not quite sure about the difference between narrative and expository texts (i.e., a metacognitive judgment). Thus, you might read the pertinent paragraphs again and then see whether you can describe the characteristics of these two genres in your own words (i.e., cognitive strategies). You might then reflect on your performance and determine that you now understand what distinguishes these two forms (i.e., metacognitive processing).

Instructional Issue: The Role of Strategy Instruction

According to Pressley (Harris & Pressley, 1991; Pressley, 1995), most effective readers use multiple cognitive strategies simultaneously when trying to learn from text. He suggests that four strategies in particular—predicting, questioning, clarifying, and summarizing—are useful when reading to learn. However, whatever strategies students elect to use, the research data are consistent: Better learners have a range of strategies on which they can draw, and they use these strategies purposefully and flexibly. Further, better students are good at determining how well they are achieving their academic goals and whether additional cognitive effort is warranted.

Even in light of such compelling evidence, however, few students are provided with any explicit instruction in how to maximize their strategic efforts (Rosenshine, 1997). Indeed, since its heyday in the 1980s, strategy research has become relatively scarce in the reading literature. Consequently, many students have only fragmented and even misleading knowledge about the various cognitive and metacognitive procedures that would facilitate their text-based learning (Alexander & Jetton, 2000; Garner, 1987).

Several reasons explain this waning popularity of strategy instruction. First, the idea of explicit strategy instruction conflicts with certain philosophical orientations in reading and learning in general (Rosenshine, 1997). As discussed in chapter 4, radical constructivists and socioculturalists would see the explicit treatment of strategic knowledge as unnatural or inauthentic. Second, the routine problems that students encounter in classrooms may lull them into a false sense of understanding—an illusion of knowing. Strategic processing is less likely under these habitual circumstances (Alexander, Graham, & Harris, 1998). Moreover, most of the strategies used in text-based learning are more heuristic than algorithmic in nature (McKeachie, 1996). In other words, there are no guarantees that their use will translate into better outcomes.

Strategy researchers must shoulder some of the blame for the waning popularity of strategy instruction, as well. Working within an information-processing theoretical framework, these researchers of the 1970s and 1980s often taught strategies as an inflexible set of procedures that were to be unquestionably applied to any reading task. For instance, the components of SQ3R, a common procedure for studying, were to be religiously followed for all text-based learning tasks, regardless of the learner's goal, the complexity of the text, or the parameters of the task. This approach converted potentially useful strategies into habits that might prove nonfacilitative—a case of teaching strategies nonstrategically (Alexander, Graham, & Harris, 1998).

The nature of teacher preparation also impacts the level of strategy instruction going on in today's classrooms. Specifically, many teachers have never been explicitly trained in text-based strategies. Thus, they may lack the specific knowledge they need to model and explain such strategies to their students (Rosenshine, 1997).

Writing

Like reading, writing is a language-based field centered on human communication. In contrast to reading, in which the problem is unraveling whatever mystery lies in some given message, writing is a production task (Bazerman, 1995). Writers of all ages set out to communicate to some known or unknown audience for some specific purpose—whether that writer is a second grader answering homework questions or a textbook writer attempting to explain the field of educational psychology.

Characteristics of Effective Writing

Effective writing entails assessing the context of the communication, conceptualizing the potential message, and producing and evaluating the written product. Contextual issues include determining the purpose for writing (e.g., to entertain or to inform). In addition, before good writers put pen to paper or fingers to keyboards, they consider their readership. For whom are they writing? What is the audience apt to know about the topic, and what voice or level of linguistic complexity would be most suitable? T. H. Anderson and Armbruster (1984b) refer to this component as **audience appropriateness.** Effective writers must also consider the interests, expectations, and beliefs the audience may bring to the text.

Conceptualizing the Text

Chapter 4 introduced Hayes and Flower's (1986) model of writing (see Figure 4–8), which identified the processes of generating, organizing, and goal setting. As writers conceptualize or plan their written messages, they must pull relevant knowledge from long-term memory (i.e., *generating*) and devise some suitable structure for that knowledge (i.e., *organizing*). Further, in choosing a suitable organization, writers must consider both the *macrostructure* (i.e., the net-work of main ideas) and the *microstructure* (i.e., the supporting details) of their written message. And writers must establish criteria for executing their planned structure (i.e., *goal setting*). Kellogg (1994) adds a fourth process to this conceptualizing phase, *information collection*. Just as I have done many times in preparing this chapter, writers seek out additional information to incorporate into their texts because their existing knowledge may be insufficient to complete the task.

Transforming Thoughts into Words

Once writers begin to convert their ideas into words on the page, they move into what Kellogg (1994) calls *translation* and Hayes (1996) refers to as the *text interpretation* phase. Throughout this phase good writers remain sensitive to the quality of emerging text (i.e., *reviewing* and *evaluating*). The ability of writers to establish and maintain their purpose or aim is known as *unity,* or *focus* (Beason, 1993). They must also consider the *cohesiveness* of the resulting text, which is the linkage that forms between words, sentences, and paragraphs (Kintsch & van Dijk, 1978).

One step that an experienced writer takes to assist readers, who must merge thoughts across text segments, is to provide them with signaling (Meyer, 1975). *Signals* are words (e.g., *first, next,* or *because*) or phrases (e.g., *most important, by comparison,* or *on the other hand*) that tell readers how textual units fit together or how important these ideas are to the message. Because signaling helps the reader connect ideas across sentences, it can contribute to textual coherence. Thus, texts that are more coherent or considerate make it easier for readers to draw inferences or construct viable interpretations (T.H. Anderson & Armbruster, 1984b).

Read the text in the Thought Experiment: Making Text More Considerate and see what can be done to improve that paragraph.

Thought Experiment ....

Making Text More Considerate

Directions: Below is a brief descriptive text about foxes. As you read it, notice how the author treated each sentence as a completely separate idea, making it harder for the reader to move easily through this text.

Foxes
A fox is an animal. It belongs to the same family as dogs and wolves. The fur of foxes is valuable. Foxes look like dogs. The ears of a fox are larger than those of a dog. Foxes are furrier than dogs. The nose of a fox is longer and more pointed than the nose of a dog. There are many kinds of foxes. There are silver foxes. There are blue foxes, which are also called arctic foxes. There are platinum foxes. The fur of these foxes is very valuable. Foxes live in many countries in the northern hemisphere. Some people chase foxes as a sport. This is called a fox hunt.

Now make this text more considerate. Before you begin, think about ways to reorganize and combine the ideas included so that they flow more smoothly. Add signals to help a reader fit this information together.

As the text takes shape, good writers are careful to provide sufficient explanation, depth, and proof, often in the form of primary or secondary sources, which may include anecdotes, quotations, observations, and philosophical principles (Rafoth, 1988). Writers must consider how much detail to include and how information can be summarized—decisions that are highly dependent on the knowledge of the audience.

Effective writers are also concerned with the stylistic expression of their messages, evident in the clarity, variation, and uniqueness of words, phrases, and clauses. Stylistic expression should be appropriate for the desired aim or purpose of the text (Bazerman, 1995). Texts that are more expository in nature may include fewer emotionally charged words, whereas texts written to change views on some controversial topic (e.g., drug use) may appeal to the readers' emotions. In such cases the perceived accuracy of the writer's ideas is an important consideration. Additional stylistic considerations include decisions about whether a word is commonly known, how concrete or abstract the language should be, and what variety of sentence types and patterns would be appropriate (Beason, 1993). Surface features of the text, such as conventional structures and standard spellings, also play a role in text quality (Elbow, 1981).

Reviewing and Revising

Once the translation from thought into words has occurred, the task is far from over for effective writers who engage in review and revision (Byrnes, 1996). In fact, expert writers frequently make significant changes in the overall structure of their writings. Younger or less effective writers, on the other hand, spend little time in review or revision, as pointed out in the data from the National Assessment of Educational Progress (Applebee, Langer, Mullis, & Jenkins, 1990). In fact, 40% of the 9-year-olds tested and 22% of the 13-year-olds made no revisions in the texts they produced for that assessment, even though time was set aside specifically for that purpose. When revisions are made by younger or less effective writers, most focus on the surface elements of the text, such as grammar or mechanics (Beason, 1993). This pattern may relate to their inability or their lack of interest in identifying and correcting any problems or weaknesses.

Instructional Issue: Effective Writing Instruction

In *Reading as Communication* May (1990) discusses the developmental patterns he witnessed in young children's unconstrained writing (see Table 5–3). Children move from a featural stage, where they seem to play with linguistic symbols in print, to a semiphonetic stage, where they manifest some awareness of sound-letter relationships in writing. At some point children attempt to represent in their written productions each of the sounds they hear in spoken words, which May calls the phonetic stage of writing. With continued exposure to print and opportunities to write, children begin to follow most of the accepted conventions in personal writings,

although more complex rule productions (e.g., vowel generalizations) still present them with difficulties. This phase constitutes the transitional stage of writing. Finally, children achieve the stage of conventional writing, where they produce text that follows conventional rules of grammar and spelling.

In keeping with the philosophy of emergent literacy, some educators operate under the assumption that children will progress through the stages May describes without any explicit instruction in writing conventions, such as standard spelling (Hillocks, 1984). In fact, there is concern among meaning-emphasis teachers that any attempt to correct young children's explorations in written language will stifle their development. But at what age or under what conditions should children be expected to achieve conventionality in their writings? When and how should teachers point out to young writers that there is a more appropriate or acceptable way to translate their thoughts into words?

Within the educational literature, there are various instructional programs that give writing a central role in literacy education—for example, Cognitive Strategy Instruction in Writing (CSIW; Englert, Raphael, Anderson, Anthony, & Stevens, 1991) and Self-Regulated Strategy Development (SRSD; Harris & Graham, 1996). What is surprising, however, is that some popular instructional programs in use in schools seem to ignore the educational literature on best practice, whereas other programs based on empirical research, like CSIW or SRSD, must fight for broad-based acceptance. In an extensive analysis of writing programs, Hillocks (1984) found that certain popular programs had studiously avoided the research on effective writing practices, which support a more balanced mode of instruction. Others have voiced similar concerns (Harris & Graham, 1996).

One reason (though obviously not true of all teachers nor in all classrooms) is that the whole language and the process approach often place such an emphasis on the student's natural development of writing abilities within authentic contexts that many students—including those who struggle with writing within these classrooms—do not get instruction in writing and self-regulation strategies that is as explicit as they need. While for some students a mini-lesson, student-teacher conferences, or brief modeling may suffice to help them come to their own methods of writing, this is not the case for many students, especially students with writing problems.

Also, as students reach the upper elementary, middle, and secondary grade levels, the demand for writing performance increases. The number of writing genres in which students need expertise also increases. These students often require more explicit instruction and even greater support or scaffolding than that offered in many whole language or process writing classrooms. (p.x)

History

As long as there has been a need for humans to remember and relate events in their lives or to keep records of objects or people important to them, there has been history. Back in

Table 5–3 Developmental stages in young writers.

Writing Stage	Examples
Featural	J N R E T C T N E 4-7-88
Semiphonetic	I WNT mj K a s r m a Nd L Vrr N r N r
Phonetic	4-4-88 I LoUkd For Maie ES dr B a s g d.
Transitional	I went up to the uper playgrownd evryone was there! becuse it was a miksed up day!
Conventional	My Mom is in the kitchen.

Note: From *Reading as Communication: An Interactive Approach* (pp. 76–79) by F. May, 1990, Columbus, OH: Merrill. Copyright 1990 by Merrill. Adapted with permission.

3600 BC, Sumerian scribes carved official documents, property records, and shipping logs on clay tablets. Those tablets also became tools for preserving religious ceremonies, sacred rites, and legends. Now, much of what is known about that ancient civilization is due to the painstaking manner in which these events and ideas were documented for the future (Durant, 1954–1975). Whether inscribed on clay, stone, paper, or online, documents like the Sumerians' tablets become the basis for historical thinking and reasoning. By studying records or stories, historians seek to unearth the distant or recent past, not just to speculate on what was but also to grasp what is and what will be. This is the conclusion drawn by Leinhardt, Stainton, and Virji (1994) from their studies of expert and novice historians.

> History is a process of constructing, reconstructing, and interpreting past events, ideas, and institutions from surviving or inferential evidence to understand and make meaningful who and what we are today. The process involves dialogues with alternative voices from the past itself, with recorders of the past, and with present interpreters. The process also involves coherent, powerful narratives that describe and interpret the events, as well as skillful analyses of quantitative and qualitative information from a theoretical perspective. (p. 88)

Dimensions of Historical Thinking

Despite its noble roots and its laudable goals, the domain of history has had a rather rocky relationship with psychology (Bell, 1917; Wineburg, 1996). As the field of educational psychology was taking shape at the turn of the 20th century, there was an interest in historical thinking and reasoning. However, these interests were often more philosophical than empirical or educational.

Exceptions to the trend included the early research of Judd (1915) and Bell and McCollum (1917). Judd's (1915) *Psychology of High-School Subjects,* for instance, addressed some of the same cognitive processes related to historical thinking that are treated here—chronological thinking, analysis of documents, causal reasoning, and preexisting beliefs. Bell and McCollum (1917) explored the question of what constitutes historical thinking and determined that being able to compile a "straightforward and probable" account from the mass of documents that exist is of the greatest significance. The ability to respond to factual questions, by comparison, was judged the least essential quality of historical thinking.

Emerging Literature

Like other early cognitive studies of human learning, initial forays into historical thought ran afoul of behaviorism and almost vanished from the American research scene until quite recently. The current trend toward domain-specific explorations of teaching and learning (Alexander & Murphy, 1998b; Shulman & Quinlan, 1996) has helped fuel a resur-

gence of interest in history. The growing body of research on learning history has afforded insights into this domain and the processes that foster historical thinking. Specifically, the emerging literature has

- portrayed how individuals of varying ages and differing levels of expertise conceptualize history (Leinhardt et al., 1994)
- analyzed the quality and effects of history texts used in schools (Afflerbach & VanSledright, 2001; Beck, McKeown, Sinatra, & Loxterman, 1991)
- illustrated how more or less experienced students or experts engage in history-related tasks, such as navigating through documents (VanSledright & Frankes, 1998)
- examined teachers' epistemological views of history (Greene, 1994; Wade, Thompson, & Watkins, 1994)
- described how history is taught and assessed in classrooms (Brophy & VanSledright, 1997; Spoehr & Spoehr, 1994).

However, limited research has been done on what actually works pedagogically in classrooms (VanSledright, 2002). For instance, history is still subsumed within the composite field of social studies in most elementary-school classrooms. Thus, young children's development of historical thinking and understanding is intertwined with exposure to geography, civics, and sociology. What effects this meshing of multiple domains has on children's perception of historical knowledge or the place history holds in their world views is only beginning to be questioned and investigated.

Moreover, while psychological research in history is expanding, it has not yet achieved the prominence of that found in other domains. In fact, a number of the leading vol-

Gaea Leinhardt is among the scholars examining expert/novice differences in domains such as history and mathematics.

umes on subject-matter knowledge either overlook the field of history completely or nest the research on history learning and teaching under the amalgamated topic of social studies (e.g., Bruning et al., 1999; Byrnes, 2001; Mayer, 1998). The knowledge and skills central to historical thinking and understanding—including students' ability to search documents, judge the merits of evidence, and identify or compose arguments—are too significant to be overlooked or treated lightly.

Putting Historical Facts in Perspective

One of the most important lessons to be learned about historical thinking, a lesson that harkens back to the early work of Bell and McCollum (1917), pertains to the appropriate place of facts in the study of history. Although historians see facts as essential to making sense of the past, they do not hold them in the same esteem as they appear to be held by students and teachers (Wineburg, 1991b). According to Spoehr and Spoehr (1994), the role of facts in history is analogous to the place the alphabet plays in the domain of reading. Facts are essentially starting points for historical thinking, but they are not the centerpiece of this domain and clearly not the endpoint.

> Focusing exclusively on facts is what makes history study so deadly dull for so many students in so many schools; students get the idea that history is just one damn thing after another, and that their job is to memorize as many facts as possible, preferably in chronological order. (p. 71)

The problem is that much of history education is precisely about factual information—memorizing laundry lists of names and dates, which in isolation cannot provide any deep understanding of the past (Brophy & VanSledright, 1997). School curricula and achievement measures commonly ask students to identify key sociopolitical events or persons and to put correct dates or recognized periods with named events or persons. Perhaps it is not surprising that many students fail to savor the value or beauty of history when they are fed a diet consisting solely of historical facts (Spoehr & Spoehr, 1994). Even the idea of historical "facts" does not sit well with many contemporary history researchers; all things are open to interpretation and should not be treated as unquestionable truths (VanSledright, 1996, 1998).

Teachers who understand that history is not merely the memorization of decontextualized facts may still hold a view of history that is not as intricate or grounded as that of historians. Leinhardt et al. (1994) constructed semantic maps based on lessons taught by two experienced history teachers, Sterling and Peterbene, and contrasted those with historian Mallon's semantic maps. As these maps suggest (see Figure 5–1), the history teachers' and historian's conceptions varied not only in the ideas mentioned but

also in the emphasis on the ideas and the connections among them. The semantic maps of the two teachers, for example, reflected their differing professional orientations. Sterling (see Figure 5–1a) conceptualized history as a multilayered discipline, whereas Peterbene (see Figure 5–1b) saw history more as a human experience. The map of historian Mallon (see Figure 5–1c) emphasized causal connections and sociocultural issues and changes, as well as linkages between history and other domains, including literature and social and political sciences—ideas unmentioned by the teachers.

Critical Processes

If not facts, then what processes underlie the history domain? The research literature identifies several key components of effective performance in history: (a) understanding time and causality, (b) locating and evaluating evidence, (c) making reasonable interpretations, and (d) formulating explanations.

Conceptions of Time and Causality

Two of the most fundamental cognitive abilities that underlie historical thinking are understanding time and understanding cause/effect. In essence, unless students possess some ability in these two areas, they cannot engage in historical thinking. Fortunately for most elementary teachers, children typically acquire some rudimentary conception of time before they begin school (Byrnes, 1996). For example, by the age of 2, children make verbal distinctions between *now* and *not now,* and preschoolers are typically able to create simple narratives in which they relate a very limited sequence of events.

However, as the research of Friedman (1990) makes clear, young children lack an understanding of time that embraces longer spans and some conventional standards. For instance, preschoolers may have difficulties with events that extend beyond a 24-hour period and that do not actually pertain to their own everyday lives. Between the ages of 8 and 12, children's temporal abilities markedly expand to the point where they can deal with time spans of weeks, months, and even years. They also come to understand societal conventions such as time zones.

Because the chronology of historical events poses difficulties to many students in the early elementary grades, some educators have chosen to rely on the *expanding communities* orientation, which has long been a part of early-childhood education (Brophy & VanSledright, 1997). This approach is one in which children's historical sense is initially built around their notions of self and their immediate family. From there the historical concepts are successively expanded to discussions of community, state, country, and then regions of the world. Although a widely accepted practice in early-childhood education, this approach has its critics among history researchers who argue that this approach

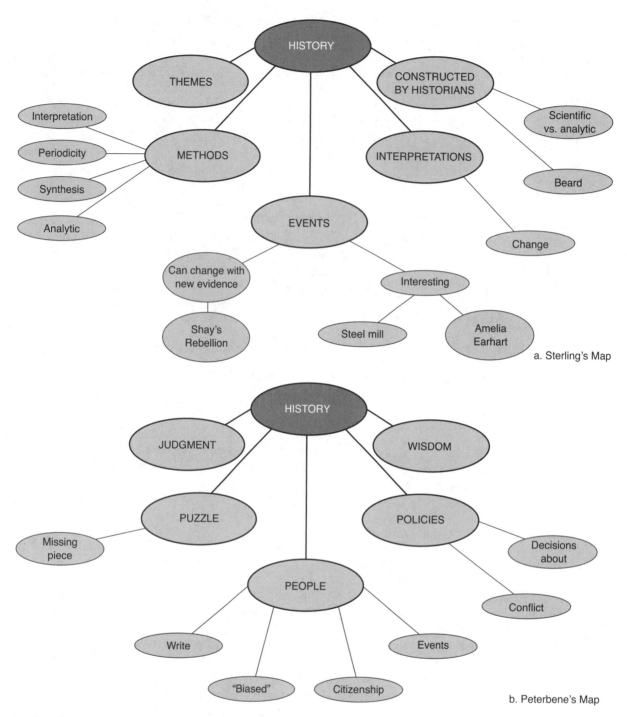

■ Figure 5–1   Semantic maps of a history lesson ("What Is History?").

Note: From "A Sense of History" by G. Leinhardt, C. Stainton, and S.M. Virji, 1994, *Educational Psychologist, 29*(2), pp. 84–86. Copyright 1994 by *Educational Psychologist.* Reprinted with permission.

can actually make it more difficult for children to see the themes and structures that underlie human history. These individuals also contend that children are able to deal with longer spans and more complex notions of time if there is sufficient guidance and practice in the classroom (Levstik & Barton, 1996).

Historical thinking is not merely about *when* events occurred, but also *why,* a part of historical understanding that

rests on the ability to master the idea of cause and effect (Byrnes, 1996). Very young children are known to manifest a level of causal reasoning. For example, a 2-year-old understands that putting a hand on a hot stove can have painful consequences. However, the level of causal reasoning required in historical analysis is far more complicated; it often demands weighing multiple causes and outcomes and frequently requires learners to put themselves in the positions

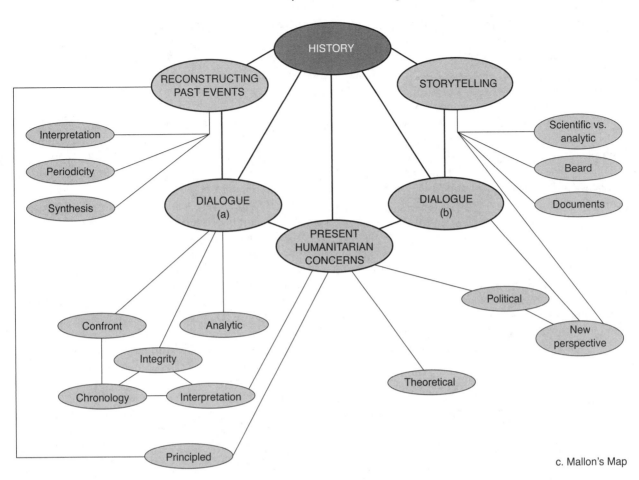

■ **Figure 5–1** *Continued.*

Note: From "A Sense of History" by G. Leinhardt, C. Stainton, and S.M. Virji, 1994, *Educational Psychologist, 29*(2), pp. 84–86. Copyright 1994 by *Educational Psychologist*. Reprinted with permission.

Bruce VanSledright's research has contributed to current views on history teaching.

of others. Moreover, a cause in history can be far removed in time and space from the effect that it produces.

Because of the challenge causal reasoning presents, teachers need to anticipate varying levels of sophistication in this ability in the elementary grades. They should also be prepared to guide and support students in their causal reasoning, moving them very gradually into more complex cause-and-effect problems. Teachers should begin with relatively simple and more relevant situations for which students likely have adequate personal experience.

Document Search

As Bell and McCollum (1917) noted more than 80 years ago, sifting through the "confused tangle" of written documentation is perhaps the most essential key to achieving historical understanding. The documents that provide historians with the evidence they require include both primary and secondary sources. **Primary sources** are firsthand accounts or records, such as letters, diaries, autobiographies, court records, or business ledgers. **Secondary sources** involve an analysis or interpretation of the past by others. History textbooks, biographies, or scholarly treatises fit into this category.

Based on his studies of how historians examine primary and secondary source materials, Wineburg (1991a) identified three strategies they use in their documentary searches: corroboration, contextualization, and sourcing. Through **corroboration** historians compare the events or details presented in one source with those offered in other accounts before accepting them as probable or valid. For instance, to establish England's perspective on its American colonies, the historian seeks converging evidence from both British and colonial sources.

Contextualization involves situating some particular event or account in the sociopolitical context in which it occurred. In judging the British response to the growing independence of its New World colonies, for example, historians might consider the Empire's reliance on cheap imports or the added pressures it was facing internally (e.g., in India) and externally (e.g., with France). Finally, before formulating hypotheses or incorporating evidence, historians engage in **sourcing;** they consider who provided the information and what motives or beliefs may have shaded their perceptions. It is one thing to read an unflattering account of King George from an American rebel like Thomas Payne; it is quite another to find a damaging description of George's mental stability in the personal diaries of a trusted member of the court.

Although historians typically engage in these general search strategies, especially sourcing, and rarely rely on any one source when forming an interpretation, students rarely use multiple or primary sources in history learning but rely instead on school texts or rather pedestrian outlets (e.g., encyclopedias) as their historical authorities (VanSledright, 2002). Further, even when multiple, primary sources are used, students infrequently consider the context of that material and often lack the text-processing strategies they need to make sense of what they find.

One of the problems in relying on school texts as the foundation for history learning is evident in McKeown and Beck's (1990) research. Time and time again, these researchers have shown how the treatment of key concepts in history books (e.g., taxation without representation) is so superficial or misleading that students achieve no deep or clear understanding of the concept, even with repeated exposures. In addition, the structures of these textbooks may be highly inconsiderate of the reader or even incoherent. In fact, some researchers have found it necessary to write their own instructional materials. Chambliss (1995), for instance, set out to provide elementary students with explicit instruction in understanding and composing arguments and explanations in social studies. However, she found that the quality of writing in the existing school materials was inadequate for teaching students about historical arguments, leading her to create her own texts.

The problems in drawing evidence from documentary materials are not solely attributable to the materials but also relate to the text-processing abilities of the readers. In a telling study, Afflerbach and VanSledright (2001) revealed how demanding and frustrating the act of reading even quality historical texts can be for students. The authors worked with 7 fifth graders as these children tried to make sense of texts dealing with the early American colonial period. One chapter in an innovative history book dealt with the hardships faced by Jamestown colonists during the winter of 1609 (Hakim, 1993). The chapter was a mixed text and included some primary source material—excerpts from the governor's diary, as well as a poem attributed to Stephen Vincent Benet.

From think-aloud protocols and interviews, the researchers concluded that the use of multiple and primary sources posed formidable challenges for all but the most talented readers. In fact, the researchers determined that such embedded segments are extraordinarily demanding and can inhibit the construction of meaning because they distract, confuse, or confound less able readers. This finding may have been due in part to the archaic vocabulary and complex syntax used in the primary source material but also reflected the fifth graders' limited skill at *intertextual referencing.* The students were not prepared to compare, contrast, or combine information across texts, such as the diary and the textbook descriptions. Until these processes of engaging

multiple sources and encountering primary source materials become more commonplace in American classrooms, the situation that Afflerbach and VanSledright (2001) describe seems unlikely to change.

Interpretation

Historical thinking is about interpretation—formulating an opinion about some aspect of the past. But these opinions or interpretations can be just a "purely subjective exercise" (Spoehr & Spoehr, 1994, p. 72). For historians interpretations are only as good as the evidence on which they are founded. Even commonly accepted facts are open to interpretation and must therefore be carefully examined.

In constructing evidence-based interpretations, individuals must not only consider the broader context in which critical events unfolded, but must also evaluate their own positions. **Positionality** is a term VanSledright (1998) coined to represent the interpreter's local and present position—the physical, social, and psychological place from which the interpretation arises. Seixas (1996) would relate this concept to the notion of temporal bearings. For school-aged individuals positionality comes from a multitude of nonschool sources, including books, television, and conversations with friends and families. According to VanSledright (1998), teachers are in the best position to understand the temporal bearings of their students and judge the potential effects positionality can have on their historical interpretations. He believes that effective teachers of history should employ various pedagogical strategies to unearth students' current positions (VanSledright 1998, 2002):

- posing relevant questions, such as how or why students see an event or individual as significant
- listening to students and the arguments or elaborations they make
- placing students' temporal bearings in the forefront of historical discussion
- teaching students how to reason logically, emphatically, and imaginatively with documentary evidence

Explanation

Not only must students search texts for relevant evidence and make reasoned interpretations, but they must also communicate those interpretations to others in an appropriate manner. This task is called **explanation.** The appropriateness of students' explanations is judged by whether they have provided sufficient or suitable support for their contentions. Students are also expected to cast their views in a fitting rhetorical frame—narrative, expository, or mixed. In other words, students may structure their explanations by telling a story that captures their views (i.e., narrative) or by formally arguing their stance or chronicling events (i.e., exposition). They may also combine both narrative and expository components (i.e., mixed).

Leinhardt and her colleagues (1994) took a close look at students' historical explanations and found that they often made reference to four phenomena: events, structures, themes, and metasystems. Events—like wars, political movements, or assassinations—are actions of peoples or societies. Given the focus on facts in history, the presence of such events in students' explanations is not surprising. Structures, by comparison, are long-standing organizations with social features, such as systems of government or class divisions. Themes are the explanatory principles—a sort of cultural lore—that arise over time for events or structures that are central to some people's past (e.g., the causes of the Civil War). Metasystems are the cognitive and metacognitive tools students use to achieve understanding, including analysis, synthesis, and the process of interpretation discussed earlier.

Developing effective historical explanation is often difficult for students because they do not know what constitutes suitable evidence and they have not mastered the various rhetorical frames required to put forward their explanations. For instance, few students know how to state an argument clearly or effectively or how to follow that argument with substantiating evidence (e.g., events or themes). Chambliss (1995) has found that students can improve in this dimension of historical thinking if they are presented with well-crafted models and explicit instruction on the nature of text-based argumentation and explanation. However, too few teachers receive adequate preparation in explanation or in the rhetorical frames common to explanation. Therefore, they are less likely to serve as effective models for their students.

To assist students in reaching competence in the rhetorical forms of history, Greene (1994) recommends a *writing-to-learn* approach. In his view teachers should incorporate both informal and structured writing in history instruction so that students not only recognize the forms of argument and explanation in the writings of others, but gain confidence in producing these forms as well. As Greene sees it, "Different kinds of writing can encourage different intellectual activities" (1994, p. 95).

Instructional Issue: History Education and the Disney Effect

As children construct their historical knowledge, they draw on information that exists everywhere in their environment, regardless of whether that information comes from reliable sources or whether that information is accurate. Because the domain of history is essentially one of telling stories of the past, the potential intrusion of nonschooled and highly misleading information is particularly acute. This situation has been well documented in Afflerbach and VanSledright's (2001) research on what middle-school students internalize during their history instruction. As fifth graders shared their thoughts on reading about the settling of Jamestown, the researchers discovered a remarkable intrusion of nonschooled information about key events and figures, such as John Smith and Pocahontas. Many of these intrusions came from mass media, most notably the Disney movie *Pocahontas*. Consequently, VanSledright (2002) calls this phenomenon the "Disney effect."

Students are influenced by the information from a variety of sources, including television, movies, the internet, maga-

zines and newspapers. They have yet to examine the assumptions that what seems "from the past" (e.g., Disney's *Pocahontas*) and appears convincingly authoritative is thus true and real. As a result, students like those in our study might be expected to accept the first version of the past they encounter, such as a film or video, and use it as a reference point to judge what they study in school. (Afflerbach & VanSledright, 2001, p. 704)

Even if effect of such nonauthoritarian sources is as pervasive and insidious as Afflerbach and VanSledright (2001) describe, there is no consensus about the actions teachers or parents should take to prevent its occurrence. Actually, one might question whether this effect *can* be prevented and whether it is restricted to young minds. Adults who encounter some mix of fact and fantasy in popular media—such as historical fiction, movies, or docudramas (e.g., Stone's *Nixon*)—may be just as hard pressed to know where historical accuracy stops and creative license begins.

Mathematics

Mathematics as a field of study was already well entrenched by the time the Egyptians designed and constructed their famous pyramids around 3000 BC. During this same period, the Egyptians' need to monitor the fluctuations of the Nile and measure the land inundated by that sacred river became the foundation for the field of geometry. By 2000 BC the Babylonians' focus on commerce heightened interest in numeration and resulted in the creation of a rather sophisticated computational system. Human need has never been far from the heart of mathematical thinking. Further evidence of the practical side of mathematics exists in the measurements societies devised—measurements for which human body parts became the standard. Thus, along with the length of feet becoming a foot, the spread of the hand became the span, the length of the last joint of the king's thumb was defined as an inch, and the distance from the fingertips to the elbow served as the cubit.

Mathematics is best understood as an *agglomerative* domain, which means its subdomains share a core of knowledge and principles orchestrated around dimensions of quantity and space (Barrows, 1998). Some of the traditional offshoots of mathematics familiar to American students reflect an emphasis on these two fundamental properties, for example, arithmetic (quantity) and geometry (space). However, as students move through school, this common core and the resulting linkages among the branches of mathematics often get lost. Thus, students not only lose the sense of continuity in mathematics but also disassociate the schooled knowledge from the world outside the classroom.

Characteristics of Mathematical Thinking

In his recent book, *What Counts: How Every Brain Is Hardwired for Math*, Brian Butterworth (1999), a cognitive neuropsychologist, provides support for the contention that humans have an innate sense of number. Based on his extensive work with clinical cases of dyscalculia, that is, the inability to comprehend or process numbers effectively, Butterworth builds a convincing case that even infants can sense number, up to 3 or 4. Further, he reports that the same region of the brain (i.e., the left parietal lobe) is associated with both number sense and movements of the fingers and hands, which helps to explain why young children and some adults use their fingers to help them count.

Although there is evidence that certain fundamentals of mathematical thinking emerge without the aid of formal schooling, most individuals would not progress far in their mathematical thinking and reasoning without specific guidance. As Geary (1995) argues, natural selection may have given humans a mathematical jump start, but we are not neurologically or biologically configured to deal easily with base-10 systems, the processes of borrowing and carrying, or fractions, radicals, and exponents. Without effort and effective teaching, such mathematical abilities may not develop adequately, if at all.

A longitudinal study English and Alexander (1997) conducted brought this point home. As they followed a group of young American and Australian children from preschool through second grade, these researchers witnessed how much time teachers on both sides of the globe devote to mathematical concepts. They also saw how important this guidance and exposure was to these children's mathematical reasoning, including their number sense, understanding of space and dimension, and patterning abilities.

Much of what occurs in public education in the name of mathematics focuses on mathematical problem solving. In fact, elementary students see mathematics as something they *do*, rather than as a way to think and reason. This situation is clearly echoed in Pricilla Murphy's accounts of her early mathematical preparation. Nothing is wrong with mathematical problem solving, or *doing* mathematics, but some researchers have shown that elementary-school mathematics rarely progresses beyond simple arithmetic computation and rarely engages students verbally or motivationally (Lampert, 1990). To fully understand the nature of mathematical thinking, we need to look at the rudiments that allow mathematical problem solving to unfold—quantification, patterning, abstraction and generalization, and representation and translation.

Quantification

Before students can engage in mathematical thinking, they must acquire a sense of quantity, amount, or number—that is, **quantification.** Counting is one of the most primitive forms of human communication and remains essential to everyday survival. Empirical evidence supports Butterworth's argument that we are all hardwired for number to some degree. Infants as young as 4 or 5 months of age display arithmetic expectations when confronted with simple addition or subtraction tasks involving controlled presenta-

tions of Mickey Mouse dolls (Wynn, 1992) or Ernie and Elmo dolls (T.J. Simon, Hespos, & Rochat, 1995).

The cognitive literature reports various techniques that have been used to test infants' sense of quantification and supports the notion that even infants manifest some sensitivity to number or quantity, seemingly from birth. For example, 1-week-old babies physically respond when an image containing two items changes to one with three items or vice versa (Pinker, 1997). Similarly, Canfield and Smith (1993) studied eye fixations in 5-month-olds as certain pictures were flashed two or three times on the right side of a screen and then appeared on the left. Canfield and Smith found that these infants generally fixed their vision on the right side of the screen and then moved their gaze to the left at the appropriate time, in anticipation of the picture.

By the time children approach school age, they have a noticeably more developed sense of quantity, as demonstrated by their ability to establish the number, or cardinal, value of objects. Almost every preschool child tested in a longitudinal study, for example, could readily count to 10 although, as Byrnes (1996) clarifies, such counting does not establish what these young children comprehend about 10-ness. In part to learn what preschoolers do comprehend about 10-ness, Gelman and Gallistel (1978) investigated whether preschoolers understand five fundamental principles of cardinality.

> **One-one principle**—Each object in counting has one and only one number name.
> **Stable-order principle**—The number names assigned to objects have a consistent order: 1 always precedes 2, which comes before 3, and so on.
> **Cardinal principle**—In counting, the final number named indicates the total quantity.
> **Order-irrelevance principle**—Regardless of how a group of objects is presented, its total remains the same.
> **Abstraction principle**—The principles of counting remain invariant regardless of what is counted.

In general, Gelman and Gallistel (1978) found that even 3-year-olds display some understanding of these principles, and by 4 or 5 most children show these mathematical abilities when presented with age-appropriate tasks.

Interestingly, although the youngest child appears equipped to deal with quite small sets of numbers, even well-educated adults struggle to grasp quantity when the set of numbers is extremely large or extremely small. Paulos (1988) terms this frustrating human condition *innumeracy*, whereas Hofstadter (1995) calls it *number numbness*.

> Innumerate people characteristically have a strong tendency to personalize—to be misled by their own experiences or by the media's focus on individuals and drama. (Paulos, 1988, p. 6)

Once numbers reach beyond the millions or into the realm of nanoseconds, most otherwise competent brains cease to cope. Thus, in many ways the power of phenomena is lost to individual minds when those phenomena are cast in the thousands rather than personalized in the ones. Consider, for example, how people respond with deep emotion when a reporter tells a story about a child with a rare disorder struggling for life. But these same people are virtually numb when told that the death toll from a pandemic like AIDS approaches 50 million.

One technique used to make complex numbers more comprehensible is analogy and metaphor (K.C. Cole, 1998). Speaking before the United Nations in January 2000, Vice President Al Gore tried to make the impact of the AIDS crisis in sub-Saharan Africa more concrete by telling his audience that 11,000 Africans die of AIDS every day and that more people will die of AIDS in the first decade of the new millennium than in all of the wars of the 20th century combined. Mathematicians, too, make use of analogies and metaphor. In *The Universe and the Teacup* K.C. Cole (1998) provides some captivating examples of such analogic thought. For example, she notes that Sir James Jeans, a noted physicist who wanted to illustrate the extraordinary heat characteristic of nuclear fusion, wrote that a mere pinhead heated to the temperatures found at the center of the sun would emit "enough heat to kill anyone who ventured within a thousand miles of it" (p. 20). Cole also tells of a Berkeley professor who draws a line at one end of a blackboard to represent zero and another line at the opposite end to represent a trillion. The professor then asks his students to estimate where a mark signifying a billion would fall. Most students place their marks about one third of the way between the two lines, even though the mark should actually fall very near the zero point. Such exercises clearly help make the inconceivable more conceivable.

Patterning

In recent history mathematicians have come to greater consensus on what the nature of mathematics entails; in effect, they see mathematics as the science of patterns (Devlin, 1994). Those patterns may be in number, shape, motion, or even human behavior, and they may be quite simple—like the block designs created by first graders—or highly complex—like the fractals discovered by Benoit Mandelbrot. If they are to achieve competence in mathematics, individuals must be able to discern and eventually represent patterns.

The other processes discussed here could not exist without the ability to perceive regularities in nature or to conceive of such patterns in the abstract. However, what is called patterning in this discussion others have labeled learning by analogy or analogical reasoning (Dreyfus & Eisenberg, 1996). Those researching analogical reasoning among young children have found that preschoolers and kindergartners can be trained to recognize and produce rather sophisticated geometric patterns. This finding contradicts Piaget's (1952) estimation that analogical reasoning is beyond the cognitive capabilities of those younger than 11 or 12. There is also evidence that the ability to perform analogical reasoning tasks is highly correlated with perform-

Patterns are everywhere in nature, as this fractal shows.

ance on mathematical thinking measures—further evidence for the fundamental nature of patterning (Devlin, 1994). Not surprisingly, increasing attention is being given to patterning as part of elementary-school mathematics (National Council of Teachers of Mathematics, 1989).

Advancements in the tools of mathematics, especially the computer, have allowed mathematicians to discern patterns in even the most jumbled arrays, such as weather patterns or fissures in rocks. Complex patterning is also behind the newer fields of fractal geometry and chaos theory. Mathematicians continue to ponder whether nature is inherently patterned and whether these patterns can be mathematically represented (Barrows, 1998).

Abstraction and Generalization

Many mathematical operations, including addition and subtraction, arise from actual physical experiences, such as counting sheep or marking off a plot of land. Nevertheless, to exist as a domain, mathematics must extend beyond the immediate physical world, and its concepts and procedures must apply to more than the sheep being counted or land being measured. Even though the words *abstraction* and *generalization* are often used rather interchangeably in everyday discourse, they convey different but related concepts to mathematicians (Davis, Hersh, & Marchisotto, 1995).

Abstraction denotes processes in which marks or symbols come to represent more than their explicit physical nature, either through extraction or idealization. **Extraction** corresponds to Gelman and Gallistel's (1978) explanation of the abstraction principle, such as when a 2-year-old realizes that the rules for counting M&Ms® are not true just for M&Ms®. In effect, a one-to-one correspondence is established between each M&M® and a corresponding number that does not exist in a 2-year-old's physical environment. The Thought Experiment, Extracting a Solution helps illustrate this process.

Thought Experiment ....

Extracting a Solution

Directions: Carefully examine Figure A and Figure B. See whether you can find some way in which these two figures are completely identical. (Hint: You may want to think of Figure A as a maze.)

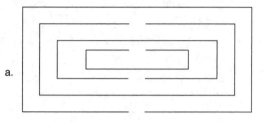
a.

b.

(Answers at the end of the chapter)

Note: From *The Mathematical Experience* (2nd ed., p. 146) by P.J. Davis, R. Hersh, and E.A. Marchisotto, 1995, Boston: Birkhauser. Copyright 1995 by Birkhauser. Reprinted with permission.

....

Idealization occurs when physical objects in the environment are internalized as perfect mathematical forms (Davis et al., 1995). For example, if you use a compass to draw a circle on a piece of paper and then look at the circle with a magnifying glass, you will find that it is full of imperfections caused by flaws in the paper, irregularities in the pencil lead, and so on. Still, it will probably be easy to accept that shape as a circle and move on from there because perfect circles, rectangles, lines, and other mathematical forms do not exist anywhere in the real world—only in abstraction (K.C. Cole, 1998). The widespread use of notational systems for representing mathematical concepts is another occasion of abstraction. Thus, the commutative law of multiplication can be linguistically written:

The result of multiplication is the same, regardless of the order in which the terms are multiplied.

It can also be symbolically depicted:

$$ab = ba$$

Just as important as abstraction in mathematical thinking is the related process of **generalization,** which involves consolidating information into a more parsimonious, yet more encompassing, statement. In the following example, the consolidation captures the separate elements into a neater, but stronger, product.

Initial statements: If a number ends in 0, it is divisible by 2.
If a number ends in 2, it is divisible by 2.
If a number ends in 4, it is divisible by 2.

Consolidation: If a number ends in an even digit, it is divisible by 2. (Davis et al., 1995, p. 151)

Without generalization there would be no means for mathematicians to cope with the infinite amount of information in the physical world or in the realm of the abstract.

Without generalization there would be no rules, principles, or theorems around which the domain of mathematics could exist.

Representation and Translation

Mathematics demands that individuals function fluently in multiple modes of representation. **Representation** is the process by which individuals form an internal, mental model of the information before them or an external depiction of that internal model (Dreyfus & Eisenberg, 1996). These representations, which express some portion of the information encountered, can be formal or informal, visual or verbal. **Translation,** which Butterworth (1999) calls *transcoding,* refers to the ability to convey that internal or external model in some alternative format, as when thoughts are symbolically represented in words, pictures, or numbers.

Although numbers are the primary mode of encryption in mathematics, these numbers must be communicated and translated through other modalities, including words. Learning the symbols of mathematics is, in essence, acquiring another language (Alexander & Kulikowich, 1994), and many students struggle with this numeric scheme or suffer when numeric and linguistic representations are intertwined, as in word problems (Mayer, 1998).

Goldin (1992) depicted this same concept in a more graphic and complex manner in Figure 5–2. Specifically, Goldin conceptualizes school mathematics as involving five systems of representation, which involve various modes of encryption: imagistic, affective, verbal/syntactic, formal notational, and executive/heuristic. In the imagistic system, students must use their senses to perceive the structure or pattern of the mathematical concept. This perception may, in turn, cause them to contemplate or represent what they sense in words (verbal/syntactic system) or symbols (formal notational system). As they move back and forth in their minds, describing, perceiving, or formulating, students must also monitor and plan what actions they will take (executive/heuristic system). All the while, of course, affective

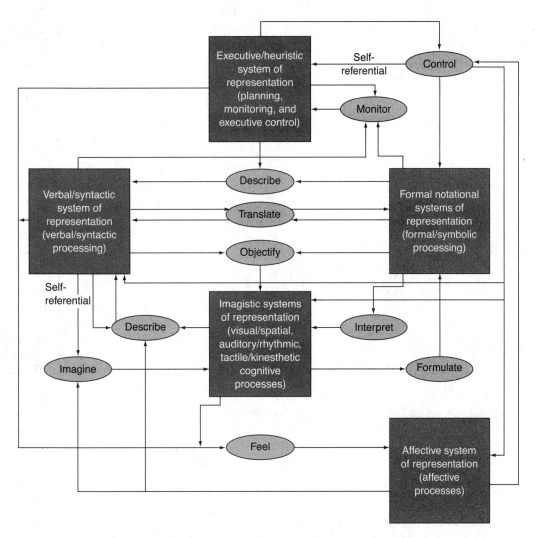

■ Figure 5–2   Representational systems in mathematical thinking.

Note: From "Toward an Assessment Framework for School Mathematics" by G. A. Goldin in R. Lesh and S. J. Lamon (Eds.), *Assessments of Authentic Performance in Elementary Mathematics* (p. 84), 1992, Washington, DC: American Association for the Advancement of Science. Copyright 1992 by the American Association for the Advancement of Science. Reprinted with permission.

or motivational reactions are at work (affective system), as when students weigh their interest or sense of competence in the task.

One reason that mathematics presents such a formidable field to some students is that they are not taught how to navigate these various representational systems. Even within the realm of formal notational systems, students may not be comfortable with the interpretations, descriptions, or translations that must occur, not just numerically, but also graphically and formulaically. Some students do not easily or fluidly grasp how a set of numbers can be represented by a formula.

X	Y
1	2
2	4
3	6
4	8
5	10

$y = 2x$

And it can be depicted graphically:

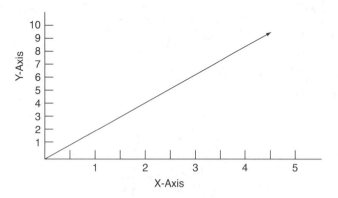

Similarly, they cannot see that the relationship between these sets of numbers can be stated linguistically:

> For every unit increase in X, there is a corresponding increase of 2 units in Y.

To become competent in mathematics, learners must become fluent in all of these forms of encryption and must be able to move readily from one form to another. Although mathematicians can readily think numerically, graphically, formulaically, or linguistically about structures and patterns in nature, most individuals must translate one mode into another with effort (Kulikowich et al., 2000). And most must also be taught how to perform these translations, even how to read the mathematical symbols.

What further complicates these processes of representation and translation is that many of the texts used by mathematics students do not integrate well the numeric and graphic representations with the linguistic content (Kulikowich et al., 2000). These inconsiderate texts apparently overlook the fact that students are not equally competent in all modes of encryption. For instance, students may have difficulty processing problems that include relational statements, especially ones like the following:

> Kevin read 6 more books last year than Holly. Kevin read 18 books. How many books did Holly read?

Students see the word *more* and presume that the answer is going to be greater than 18.

Hegarty, Mayer, and Monk (1995) describe examples like this one as *inconsistent versions* of word problems, because the language can be misleading to those who process the words superficially or erroneously. A *consistent version* of the problem would be one in which the language cues and the mathematical procedures complement each other:

> Kevin read 6 more books last year than Holly. Holly read 18 books. How many books did Kevin read?

Not even college students are exempt from relational translation problems. In fact, Mayer (1982) found that college students frequently falter when working relational problems in algebra. Their errors can sometimes be attributed to careless reading or to a misunderstanding of what is being asked. For students with reading problems, the linguistic aspects of representation and translation can be especially troublesome,

as witnessed by the difficulty word problems pose. Evidence also suggests that limited dialogue and the ritualistic practice of mathematics problems exacerbate students' difficulties in moving across representation systems (Lampert, 1998).

The good news is that providing learners with training in representation and translation can significantly improve their performance. Lewis (1989), for instance, found marked improvement in college students' solutions of relational problems after only two 30-minute training sessions. In this training Lewis taught students how to represent relational problems, like the consistent version of the book problem, on a number line.

$$\text{HOLLY} \xrightarrow{\text{more}} \text{KEVIN}$$
$$18$$

Other researchers have also determined that training in problem representation and translation can result in significantly improved mathematical thinking. Several of these researchers focus on the multiple representation systems that Goldin (1992) outlines in his model (Figure 5–2). Kulikowich and colleagues (2000) make representation and translation key components in classes in statistics and measurement. In these courses they target linguistic, spatial/graphic, numeric, and formulaic representations, and they work with students to ensure that they can communicate statistical concepts in various forms. Kulikowich et al. have seen the cognitive benefits of this instruction for their undergraduate and graduate students and have found that the students feel more confident of their statistical ability and less anxious about the content when trained in these representational systems.

Instructional Issue: Doing Mathematics Rather Than Thinking Mathematically

Because of the way schools treat mathematics, students come to equate this domain with arithmetic computation—solving school problems to get the right answer (Lampert, 1990). A centerpiece of mathematical thinking does involve problem solving, but not the overly simplistic and highly contrived forms of problem *doing* that masquerade for problem solving in many schools. Students taught mathematics in this ritualistic manner have little opportunity to discover the beauty of mathematics that Pricilla Murphy came to see or the pleasure she still feels in exploring the world mathematically (Dreyfus & Eisenberg, 1996). It is easy to understand why movements like radical constructivism, described in chapter 4, have gained such a following among mathematics educators.

Paradoxically, even though American schools devote inordinate amounts of time to doing mathematics, students continue to perform below expectations on tests of mathematical achievement. One reason is that much of the problem solving that occurs in schools is decontextualized. In other words, a problem like $12 + 8 = ?$ does not carry much meaning for young or inexperienced problem solvers, whereas simply giving those numbers some concrete or personal referent could quickly increase young students' per-

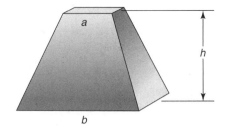

Here's a hint to help you devise a plan:

If you cannot solve the proposed problem, look around for an appropriate related problem. For example, do you know how to find the volume of a pyramid? If so, you know that the procedure for computing the volume of a pyramid is to multiply the area of the base times the height and divide the result by 3.

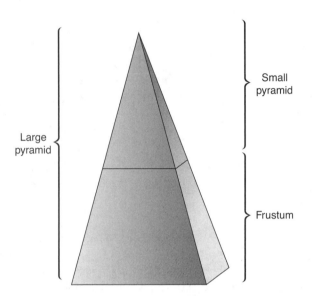

Here's a flash of insight provoked by the related problem:

To find the volume of the frustrum, subtract the volume of the big pyramid from the volume of the small pyramid.

Here's how to develop the plan based on the procedure for a related problem:

The volume of the big pyramid is $b^2(h+x)/3$ and the volume of the small pyramid is $a^2(x)/3$ where b is the base of the big pyramid, a is the base of the small pyramid, x is the height of the small pyramid, and $(h+x)$ is the height of the big pyramid.

■ **Figure 5–3   Putting Polya's problem identification guidelines to the test.**

Note: From *The Promise of Educational Psychology: Learning in the Content Areas* (p. 182) by R. E. Mayer, 1998, Adopted from Polya (1945, 1965) Upper Saddle River, NJ: Merrill/Prentice Hall. Copyright 1999 by Prentice Hall, Inc. Reprinted with permission.

formance (Ross, McCormick, & Krisak, 1986). This push to contextualize or anchor mathematical thinking is behind the effective Jasper series, developed by Bransford, Zech, Schwartz, Barron, Vye, and the CTGV (1996). In a 12-videodisc series, the adventures of Jasper Woodbury become the anchoring point for studies of complex mathematical problems, such as distance = rate × time. Middle-school students become familiar with the central character, Jasper, and are afforded rich details for problems.

Thus, although problem solving is an essential component of mathematical learning, it should be approached in an engaging manner and should promote analysis, reflection, and creativity among students. Model programs in mathematical problem solving, including the work at Vanderbilt, owe much to the work of George Polya (1945) and his classic volume, *How to Solve It*, which contains valuable guidelines for developing mathematical problem solving ability. In addition to the processes of representation and translation, Polya stresses the importance of problem identification, solution planning, and problem monitoring.

Problem identification entails a careful analysis of the given problem and a search for a more familiar problem that

is similar in its underlying structure. As seen in Figure 5–3, a student who cannot figure out how to solve for the area of a frustum may know how to solve for the area of a pyramid. Using that familiar knowledge, the student can then subtract the area of the smaller pyramid from that of the larger pyramid, leaving the area of the frustrum. This example shows that analogical reasoning, discussed earlier, is a key to problem identification; it allows students to see a relevant pattern across two seemingly unrelated structures.

It is also important that students acquire knowledge of the underlying structures of mathematical problems so that they are not distracted by the surface features of a problem, like the words or the numbers. Every problem that talks about trains leaving Chicago is not a case of *distance = rate × time* any more than every word problem using *more* is automatically an addition problem. Just as texts have discernible structures, so, too, do the mathematical problems that students typically encounter in schools. In fact, Riley and colleagues (Riley & Greeno, 1988; Riley, Greeno, & Heller, 1983) believe that individuals operate mathematically by invoking representative problem frameworks from their memories. These mental representations include both **problem**

CHANGE

Jonna has 3 snowplows. Murphy gives her 2 more snowplows. How many snowplows does Jonna have now?

COMBINE

Jonna has 3 snowplows. Murphy has 2 snowplows. How many snowplows do the two girls have all together?

COMPARE

Jonna has 3 snowplows. Murphy has 2 snowplows. How many more snowplows does Jonna have than Murphy?

■ **Figure 5–4   Common problem schemata for arithmetic problems.**

schemata (i.e., prototypical problem models) and **solution schemata** (i.e., frameworks for how to solve such problems). Three common problem schemata are the change, combine, and compare formats illustrated in Figure 5–4.

There is ample evidence that good problem solvers spend much more time than poor problem solvers do thinking about what they are going to do before they ever begin their computations (Schoenfeld, 1985). Good, self-questioning problem solvers follow the general guidelines that Polya (1945) outlined. For instance, once good problem solvers have identified the underlying structure of a problem or have found a reasonable model to follow, they consider the strategies that would best serve them in obtaining a solution.

Effective programs in problem solving encourage students to value this planning time and also teach them the benefits of monitoring their performance as they work through problems. Schoenfeld (1985), in particular, has illustrated the power of planning and monitoring during problem solving. In his research Schoenfeld found that even college students in advanced mathematics classes show a tendency to rush to a solution when presented with a problem—a tendency that contributes to errors in their performance. The students operate under the misconception that jumping into the problem saves time. In fact, failing to adequately analyze a problem costs students valuable time, something they may realize when they find that they have calculated themselves into a dead end.

In addition, the relatively good mathematics students in Schoenfeld's (1985, 1988) research did not always effectively monitor what they were doing. For example, they did not repeatedly check to see whether their emerging solutions seemed reasonable in terms of the given information or whether glitches in their computations might send them in the wrong direction. The problems caused by inadequate planning and monitoring are even more likely for younger and less experienced students, but here again, the good news is that students can be taught how to plan and monitor more effectively (Schoenfeld, 1985). The more such reflective practice is part of the learning environment and the more students are encouraged to share their thinking with others, the greater the gains in mathematical learning (Lampert, 1990).

Science

We live in a world that bears witness to the contributions of science—from medicine to space exploration and from genetic engineering to weather forecasting. Broadly defined, **science** is the domain devoted to understanding the physical, psychological, biological, and social universe in which we live (Rutherford & Ahlgren, 1990). Science could not exist as a field without the presumption that patterns in nature are there to be uncovered or discovered by our senses and our minds.

> *There are no valid reasons—intellectual, social, or economic—why the United States cannot transform its schools to make scientific literacy possible for all students. What is required is national commitment, determination, and a willingness to work together toward common goals.*
>
> Rutherford & Ahlgren, 1990, p. 214.

Far too many individuals never acquire the fundamentals of scientific literacy, much less sense the aesthetics of this domain (M.Matthews, 1994). Studies reveal that large segments of the population not only lack an understanding of basic scientific concepts and methods, but also operate under illogical or irrational notions. However, any educational reform in the domain of science demands an understanding of what constitutes scientific literacy. Among the varying definitions (Glynn, Yeany, & Britton, 1991; Lemke, 1990), there is some consensus that scientific literacy entails not only knowledge *of* science but also knowledge *about* science. According to Michael Matthews (1994), students who are scientifically literate should be able to do the following:

1. Understand fundamental concepts, laws, principles, and facts in the basic sciences
2. Appreciate the variety of scientific methodologies, attitudes, and dispositions and appropriately utilize them
3. Connect scientific theory to everyday life and recognize chemical, physical, and biological processes in the world
4. Recognize the manifold ways that science and its related technology interact with the economics, culture, and politics of society
5. Understand parts of the history of science and the ways in which it has shaped and been shaped by cultural, moral, and religious forces (pp. 32–33)

Like mathematics, science encompasses an array of subdomains (e.g., chemistry, biology, and physics), each with its own unique characteristics. However, whereas reading was described as a threshold domain and mathematics as an agglomerative domain, science is an integrated domain because competence in science rests on knowledge from several fields. Specifically, science is inextricably linked to the domains of history, philosophy, and mathematics no scientific phenomenon can be divorced from its historical and philosophical roots (Alexander, 1997a). For example, if students merely memorize facts about Galileo—such as his heliocentric, or sun-centered, theories—they come away with a limited and misleading scientific understanding. They fail to realize how Galileo's scientific finding that the earth traveled around the sun conflicted at that point in history with humanity's need to see itself as the center of the universe. Thus, students would overlook the threats such a theory posed to prevailing religious beliefs, and they would have no conception of the price Galileo paid for remaining firm in his scientific convictions.

Such interconnections between science and the domains of mathematics, history, and philosophy have been reinforced by Project 2061 (American Association for the Advancement of Science, 1993). The goal of Project 2061 is to ensure scientific literacy for all Americans by 2061, the year Halley's comet returns. The researchers, teachers, and administrators participating in the project collaborated to produce *Benchmarks for Science Literacy*, a guide to orchestrating effective science experiences for school-aged learners. The framework for *Benchmarks* speaks directly to the "union of science, mathematics, and technology" (AAAS, 1993, p. 3) and explains how history, philosophy, and science support each other.

Characteristics of Scientific Reasoning

Because science is essentially about formulating hypotheses, theories, and laws from data, it demands a grasp of many of the dimensions of mathematical thinking already discussed: quantification, patterning, abstraction, generalization, representation, translation, and problem solving. To these core abilities must be added observing and chronicling, inquiring and discovering, and formulating and testing hypotheses.

Observing and Chronicling

At their core, scientists are explorers in search of understanding, and the most important tools that they use in these explorations are their perceptions and their reasoning abilities. Scientific thinking begins with careful observation of the world around us and the gathering of pertinent data systematically and accurately from those observations (Dunbar, 1996). Thus, scientists must view the world with a critical and probing eye (i.e., **observing**), and they must document what they see for subsequent analysis (i.e., **chronicling**). From that point scientific thinking becomes a process of validating those observations and the explanations that arise from them through mathematical representation and computation. Even the most sophisticated scientific apparatus, like the Hubble telescope, exists to augment scientists' senses—providing access to phenomena too small to see with the naked eye, too large to hold in the visual field, or too far away to observe at all (Devlin, 1994).

The power of observation and chronicling was evident in Galileo's reflections while he formulated his theory of pendulum motion. In his personal notes of 1632, Galileo acknowledged his debt to the "marvellous property of the pendulum, which is that it makes all vibrations, large or small, in equal times" (Drake, 1978, p. 399). Combining his keen observations with mathematical analysis and experimentation, Galileo laid the groundwork for the refutation of Aristotelian physics and the development of the science of motion. But how was Galileo able to see the pattern in pendulum motions that others had failed to see?

Although humans are by nature curious creatures, predisposed to conjecture or speculation, the level of observation and the quality of data required by scientific reasoning do not necessarily come easily or naturally (Kuhn, Amsel, & O'Loughlin, 1988). Such processes must be learned and reinforced. One reason we must work at observation and data collection has to do with human perception. Cognitive research has repeatedly demonstrated that humans see with a biased eye (Glynn et al., 1991), frequently seeing what is hoped for or expected, missing critical information, and overlooking essential evidence. Pinker (1997), director of MIT's Center for Cognitive Neuroscience, explains that humans are generally so-so scientists because our brains were meant for survival in the physical world rather than for objective truth. "Conflicts of interest are inherent to the human condition . . . and we are apt to want *our version* of the truth, rather than the truth itself, to prevail" (p. 305).

These misperceptions and conflicts of interest inherent in human thinking help to explain why individuals form naive and resistant theories. Cognitive research in the domain of science has focused on these incomplete and often misleading views of the world, which some term *misconceptions* (M.C. Linn, Songer, & Eylon, 1996). An entire segment of chapter 6 is devoted to this topic because of the threat misconceptions or naive theories pose to subsequent learning, not just in science but in all academic domains.

Despite their importance rigorous scientific observation and experimentation are not always practical or necessary (Wollman & Lawson, 1977). If a meatloaf prepared for dinner turns out poorly, the cook is not apt to conduct systematic scientific observations and controlled experimentation to determine the exact nature of the problem (Dunbar, 1993). That approach could require many days and many pounds of meat. Most people would make a reasonable guess at the problem (e.g., oven too hot or too much garlic) and store that notion away until the next meatloaf.

Nonetheless, humans are much too content with their overall lack of logical or scientific response and are simply not held accountable for their scientific illiteracy (Paulos, 1988). People tend to believe the advertisements that they have won 10 million but fail to see any merit in buckling up their seatbelts. They simply disregard the improbability of winning the millions but discount the strong likelihood of suffering serious damage if not buckled up. In defense of humankind, a lack of specific knowledge about everyday phenomena does not always interfere with the quality of life. People can know virtually nothing about how a microwave works yet manage to reheat the leftover meatloaf. Their cluelessness poses no problem, unless that piece of technology fails. However, it is precisely the everyday or the familiar that science educators see as the starting point for scientific literacy.

> Students need to have many and varied opportunities for collecting, sorting and cataloguing; observing, notetaking and sketching; interviewing, polling and surveying; and using hand lenses, microscopes, thermometers, cameras, and other common instruments. They should dissect; measure, count, graph, and compute; cultivate; and systematically observe the social behavior of humans and other animals. Among these activities, none is more important than measurement, in that figuring out what to measure, what instruments to use, how to check the correctness of measurements, and how to configure and make sense out of the result are at the heart of much of science and engineering. (Rutherford & Ahlgren, 1990, p. 188)

This excerpt from *Science for All Americans* reminds educators that those opportunities for students to sharpen their observational skills must come hand in hand with guidance in recording or documenting what they see. Just as in mathematics, students must be taught how to represent phenomena in multiple forms—linguistically, graphically, and numerically. One glimpse at a page from Leonardo da Vinci's notebook makes evident the power of chronicling and representing (see Figure 5–5).

Inquiring and Discovering

It is difficult to think about observation and chronicling as aspects of scientific literacy in the absence of an inquiring mind or a desire to discover the whys or hows of objects or events. Indeed, the overarching goal of this approach to teaching science is to engage students *in* science rather than simply have them learn *about* it (M.R. Matthews, 1994). One of the best known advocates of inquiry or discovery approaches to science is Jerome Bruner (with Goodnow, & Austin, 1956).

Modern discovery approaches owe much to Bruner's generative theory of learning, popularized in his 1961 article "The Act of Discovery." The tenets of this theory include the premise that students learn best when they use what they already know as the basis for subsequent learning. Bruner also held that immersing students in exploring the structures around them, let-

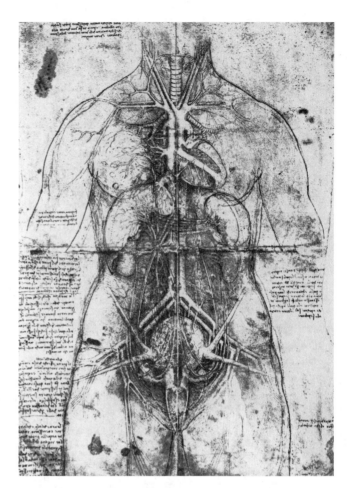

■ **Figure 5–5   The value of chronicling: taking a page from Leonardo da Vinci.**

Jerome Bruner's writings on discovery learning have been highly influential.

ting them deduce important relations and principles instead of merely telling them what educators believe students need to know, results in richer, more meaningful learning. Indeed, cognitive research supports the argument that active engagement in science learning is vastly superior to the simple memorization of science facts (Glynn et al., 1991).

Contemporary researchers who employ modified versions of discovery or inquiry approaches report learning and motivational benefits to participating students. One of these contemporary programs is the Concept-Oriented Reading Instruction (CORI) Program conceived by Guthrie, Van Meter, and colleagues (1996). In this project science learning is propelled by hands-on exploration of familiar objects like frogs, birds, or ponds. The children work in groups to answer a puzzling question posed by their teacher; for example, "How are deserts and ponds similar?" Students are also encouraged to search for relevant information or evidence and to keep careful records of what they find or observe.

Despite the general appeal and widespread acceptance of these approaches, the documented results have not always been encouraging. In his critique of two decades of science curricula, for example, Welch (1979) concluded that inquiry approaches seldom achieved the outcomes expected. Reasons for the disappointing results included poor teacher preparation, flaws in students' and teachers' beliefs about science, and a failure to ground the discovery experience in effective conceptual and strategy instruction. Even Bruner (1974) distanced himself from the various manifestations of discovery learning that appeared. "Discovery was being treated by some educators as if it were valuable in and of itself, no matter what it was a discovery of or in whose service" (p. 15).

As more successful research programs have established, inquiry and discovery approaches should not set students loose without adequate preparation or scaffolding (Alexander, 1997a). If discovery learning is to result in greater learning, students must have the requisite background knowledge, key processes and strategies must be modeled and discussed, and instructional guidance and feedback must be continuously available in the learning environment (Carey, Evans, Honda, Jay, & Unger, 1989). A study by A.J. Reynolds and Walberg (1991) substantiated the influence of students' background knowledge and exposure to science matters. Of course, other factors, including the amount of time students engage in scientific learning, also matter.

Formulating and Testing Hypotheses

One recurring theme is that scientific literacy is unlikely to emerge without systematic and appropriate instruction. Nowhere is this generalization more evident than in the research on hypothesis formation and hypothesis testing. **Hypotheses** are fundamentally predictions or explanations about how things occur or relate (Carey et al., 1989). Whether individuals devise their own explanation for some data (i.e., **hypothesis formation** or **generation**) or set out to ascertain the validity of an existing explanation (i.e., **hypothesis testing**), a healthy degree of skepticism, a logical mind, and a suspension of judgment are requisite (M.R. Matthews, 1994).

All of the elements of scientific literacy that M.R. Matthews (1994) identifies require an ability to formulate a reasonable explanation for patterns observed or discovered, yet many children and adults are less than stellar at this process. Part of the problem is that people tend to engage in hypothesis *confirmation* rather than *disconfirmation*. In other words, they look for evidence to validate their predictions rather than disprove them, and this confirmation bias makes it hard for them to abandon their biases and prejudices. A classic experiment by Wason (1966) brings this tendency to light in the Thought Experiment: Confirmation.

Thought Experiment ....

Confirmation: The Four-Card Task

Directions: Below are cards with letters on one side and numbers on the other. Given the stated rule, which of the four cards shown here would you definitely turn over in order to see whether the rule is true?

Rule: If a card has an *A* on one side, it has a 9 on the other side

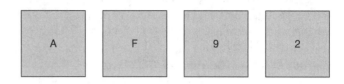

Note: from *Reasoning* by P. Wason in B.M. Foss (Ed.), *New Horizons in Psychology*, 1966, London: Penguin. Copyright 1966 by Penguin. Adapted with permission.

If you were like many of the individuals Wason tested, you would have turned over only the *A* card, or maybe the *A* and 9 cards. In that case you were trying only to confirm rather than disconfirm the stated rule. Under the principles of formal logic, you should have turned over the *A* card and the 2 card because the rule states that all *A* cards have a 9 on the other side, not that all 9 cards have an *A* on the other side. You should also turn over the 2 card because the appearance of an *A* would disconfirm the rule. Wason found that even individuals trained in formal logic chose incorrectly in this experiment.

More recent evidence indicates that students, particularly those in the United States, do not exhibit the kind of formal scientific thinking that hypothesis testing or hypothesis formation requires (Dunbar, 1993). For example, Karplus and colleagues (1979) found that more than one third of the eighth graders presented with proportional reasoning problems or problems involving experimental controls failed to employ formal thinking but instead relied heavily on simple intuition or some other less sophisticated approach.

Another tendency seen among students is rushing to judgment. With only one or two factors or conditions occurring together, students tend to form causal inferences (Kuhn et al., 1988). For example, a dear friend of mine happened to wear the same pair of socks on two occasions when she beat a particular opponent at tennis. My friend now wears those same "lucky" socks every time she plays this individual, as if they will help her win. Given humankind's tendency to confirm rather than disconfirm hypotheses, my friend is fast to persist in her quirky behavior, even in the face of a loss or two, as long as there is a periodic win while she is wearing those particular socks.

The good news in all of this is that students can significantly improve their scientific thinking and formulate and test hypotheses more effectively after appropriate instruction (Wollman & Lawson, 1978). Such instruction includes guidance from teachers in how to form and test predictions, present contradictory evidence or rival explanations, control and manipulate particular factors or conditions, and check and recheck results (Rutherford & Ahlgren, 1990). Through effective instruction students can recognize that experimentation is not about producing a desired outcome but about putting ideas and beliefs about the world to the test—questioning, not confirming, what is initially held to be true (Carey et al., 1989).

Instructional Issue: Learning to "Talk" Science

Many science educators believe that the only way to achieve the level of literacy articulated in documents like *Benchmarks* is to alter the underlying epistemological beliefs of students (Schauble, 1990) and teachers (von Glasersfeld, 1991). How these changes are to be achieved, however, is a debated issue. Some individuals, like Michael Matthews, believe that a deeper understanding of history, mathematics, and philosophy would "puncture the perceived arrogance and authority of science" (1994, p. 9) and promote the three Rs of science literacy—reason, realism, and rationality. Others, like von Glasersfeld (1991), seek to shake up students' and teachers' epistemological leanings for another purpose. Their goal seems to be to stress the fallibility of science and the sociopolitical shadings of all scientific knowledge. Notions of rationality or accuracy have less of a place in this orientation.

These two camps come together in their agreement that attitudes toward science must change and that teachers and students must become more verbally engaged in the study of science. Science is not a domain for passivity or for simple memorization or regurgitation of scientific concepts, principles, or theories (M.C. Linn et al., 1996). This view of science is represented in the writings of J. Lemke, who proclaims that "learning science means learning to *talk* science" (1990, p. 1). Assuming a science-as-fallible perspective, Lemke offers guidelines for replacing limited views of science with more appropriate perceptions. Thus, science as a "simple description of the way the world is" becomes science as a "social activity, an effort to make sense of the world" (1990, pp. 130–131). Lemke also suggests that teachers acknowledge and work to resolve conflicts of interest between the curriculum and students' values.

Although suggestions for talking science are worth consideration, it is important to remember what the research of Shulman (with Quinlan, 1996), Berliner (1987), and others (Alexander & Jetton, 1996) has substantiated. Those who would guide the science learning of others cannot effectively engage their students in productive talk if they themselves are not scientifically literate, that is, if they do not exhibit the qualities of observing, chronicling, inquiring, discovering, hypothesis formulating, and hypothesis testing that they wish to stimulate in students. Talk can unearth and enrich these processes, but talk alone cannot ensure their acquisition.

■ Summary Reflections

What is an academic domain?

- Academic domains are recognized fields of study and the knowledge and experience central to those fields.
- The past several decades have witnessed a resurgence of interest in the nature of and differences in academic domains.

What do academic domains have in common?

- Every academic domain is encrypted, or symbolically represented, in a recognizable manner—whether numeric, linguistic, graphic, or formulaic.
- Academic domains are associated with typical tasks or activities.
  - For some domains those tasks are well structured with readily identifiable solutions and strategies.
  - Other academic domains have ill-structured tasks with many acceptable outcomes and many pathways to derive those outcomes.
- All domains are represented by fundamental processes, determined by the common tasks and the modes of encryption.
- Each domain comes with its own set of instructional issues that must be effectively addressed if optimal learning is to result.

How do differences in academic domains affect learning and teaching?

- The distinctions among common academic domains influence the manner in which they are taught and learned.
- Teachers and students benefit from recognizing and responding to the variations among subjects such as reading, writing, history, mathematics, and science.
- The mode of encryption, typical school tasks, underlying processes, and instructional issues shape the five basic academic domains.

■ Solution to Thought Experiment: Extracting a Solution

As the letters show, the path that would be transversed in both figures is basically identical. (From the outside O go to the door at A. The door at A leads to two halls, B and C, both of which leads to the door D. The door D leads to two halls, E and F, both of which lead to the door G. The door G leads to two halls, H and I, both of which lead to the door J. The door J leads to the innermost chamber S.)

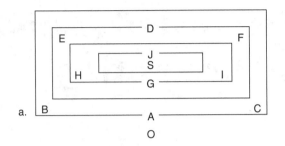

Note: From *The Mathematical Experience* (2nd ed., p. 147) by P.J. Davis, R. Hersh, and E.A. Marchisotto, 1995, Boston: Birkhauser. Copyright 1995 by Birkhauser. Adapted with permission.

Chapter 6

Changing Knowledge and Beliefs and Promoting Transfer

GUIDING QUESTIONS

■ Why is it sometimes difficult to alter students' naive conceptions?

■ How can students' knowledge and beliefs be changed?

■ What can be done to promote the transfer of knowledge?

IN THEIR OWN WORDS

LeeAnn Delli has been teaching young children since 1992. A trained school psychologist, she presently teaches 17 energetic and inquisitive second graders at an elementary school in suburban Columbus, Ohio.

One of my goals this year was to help my students explore the way scientists group animals. Animals fascinate children this age. So this was a great opportunity for the class to learn more about animals and to practice classification skills, too.

To begin this unit, I asked the children to show me how they thought scientists classified animals. I let them use whatever mode of expression they wanted. Some drew pictures; others wrote stories or made concept maps. As they started sharing their depictions, I realized that Millie had very simplistic notions about animal classifications. When she proudly displayed her marvelous pictures, it was apparent that she had sorted the animals by color. In one group she had placed polar bears, a Persian cat, and white doves. In another she had included a green turtle, a lizard, a parrot, and a snake. Although Millie's groupings were among the most naive, many other children also had unsophisticated ideas about animal characteristics. Some distinguished domestic animals from wild animals. Some sorted animals according to their habitat, whether land, sea, or air. Others classified animals according to their appendages—legs, fins, or wings—or even according to size.

Rather than just telling the children what characteristics scientists actually use, I decided to make this a *real* exploration. We began by searching magazines for pictures of all kinds of animals that we could sort later. We then read a book about a little boy who was pondering the same question we were. Entitled *How Do Scientists Classify Animals?*, the book explains the differences between vertebrates and invertebrates. After reading the book and discussing this mode of classification, the children tried to sort their animal pictures into these two classes. Some students, like Sam, understood the difference between vertebrates and invertebrates right away. Others, like Millie, continued to focus on simple surface characteristics like the animals' color or size.

We extended our exploration. We watched a video that told the children even more about many of the animals in their pictures. It also gave us another chance to talk about the concepts of vertebrates and invertebrates. And we didn't stop there. As a next step, the children became mini-scientists. They observed and recorded information about their family pets or the animals in school habitats like our classroom pond. We took field trips to the county park conservatory and the zoo. At each stage we discussed our findings in terms of the distinctions between vertebrates and invertebrates.

To finish this unit, I again asked the children to represent their understanding of how scientists classify animals. When her turn came to share, Millie presented her classmates with another series of wonderful drawings. This time, however, she had sorted her animals not by color, but according to the houses she saw at the zoo—reptiles, mammals, birds, and so on. Although she never talked about vertebrates and invertebrates during her presentation, she had clearly come a long way from believing that animals are classified simply by color.

Why Is It Sometimes Difficult to Alter Students' Naive Conceptions?

LeeAnn's story of her second graders' experience exploring animal classifications illustrates that the path to knowledge development is not simple or straightforward (Petty & Cacioppo, 1986). Within the classroom setting, students like Millie do not necessarily correct erroneous ideas or beliefs merely because they encounter new information. They may, in fact, ignore new information or try to make it fit their pre-existing notions (Chinn & Brewer, 1993; Kardash & Scholes, 1995; Vosniadou & Brewer, 1992).

Indeed, reshaping Millie's mistaken notions was not a task that her teacher could fully accomplish, although she noted with satisfaction that Millie had come a long way by the end of the unit when she was able to sort her animals according to the houses they lived in at the zoo.

This chapter begins by exploring the nature of **misconceptions,** erroneous ideas also known as naive theories or naive conceptions, which constitute serious obstacles to understanding (Champagne, Gunstone, & Klopfer, 1985; Pines & West, 1983). It also discusses the process of conceptual change as defined and analyzed by educational practitioners and researchers (Limón & Mason, 2002; Mayer, 2002; Sinatra & Pintrich, 2003; Vosniadou, 1994, 2003). Changing students' powerful underlying misconceptions is one of the most frustrating and perplexing challenges faced by teachers (Dole & Sinatra, 1998; Hatano & Inagaki, 2003).

As LeeAnn tried to change the children's misconceptions about animal classification, she was also working to facilitate **transfer,** the use of knowledge and skills acquired under one set of conditions in alternative conditions (De Corte, 1999; McKeough, Lupart, & Marini, 1995). She encouraged her students to apply their own groupings of animals to what they were learning about animal classification through their reading, discussion, and hands-on activities. Some, like Sam, were able to apply this knowledge readily in differing contexts; others had difficulty seeing its broader applicability. Knowledge that is transportable and adaptable to varied contexts is knowledge that has power and greater value

(Dewey 1916/1944). Promoting transfer is therefore one of a teacher's most essential tasks.

The Power of Life over Schooled Knowledge

Can you think of any instances in your own experience when you may have harbored ideas or beliefs that were resistant to change? Do you think any concepts you mastered in school may still incorporate basic misconceptions? You can check yourself on this possibility by completing the Thought Experiment: Exposing Our Personal Theories, which asks you to clarify concepts you have probably encountered in school on multiple occasions.

Thought Experiment ....

Exposing Our Personal Theories

Directions: Offer your best explanation of the following scientific and historical concepts.

1. Explain what causes the seasons of the year on this planet. You can share your thoughts pictorially or verbally.

2. What does the phrase "taxation without representation" mean, and why was this idea important in United States history?

3. How do plants obtain their food?

....

Let's consider your response to the first question. In the opening scenes of the video, *Private Universe*, new graduates from Harvard University answer a similar question about why our planet experiences seasons of the year. One after another, these bright and well-educated individuals confidently explain that the seasons result from the earth's changing distance from the sun. In summer, they state, the orbit of the earth brings it closer to the sun, making it warmer, whereas in winter the earth moves farther away from the sun, producing colder weather. To their science teacher's astonishment, high-school students in Cambridge, Massachusetts, expressed similar ideas and even drew sketches like the one in Figure 6–1 to prove their point.

How does your own response to Question 1 compare? The students' explanations seem to make sense, and they coincide with images you may remember from your science textbooks, right? In fact, the topic, seasons of the year, does appear in every standard science curriculum, not just in elementary school and high school, but also in college

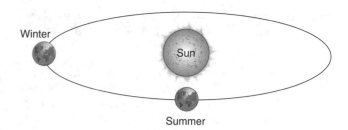

■ FIGURE 6–1   A common but misleading depiction of seasonal change.

courses. However, the fact that seasons actually result from the tilting of the earth relative to the sun's rays and have nothing to do with how close the earth is to the sun seems to have been untaught, mistaught, or merely unlearned by large segments of the population.

Teachers are not alone in their surprise and dismay about what students think they know. Educational researchers have long been perplexed by the remarkable durability of incorrect intellectual concepts such as the students' explanation for the seasons (De Corte, 1999; Vosniadou, 2002). We all live with ill-formed or misformed conceptions or beliefs of one kind or another in every domain, from science to history, and from mathematics to economics (Alexander, 1998c; Mayer, 2002). One study revealed that teachers assumed students understood the concept of taxation without representation after repeated exposure, yet students could offer only cursory and fragmented explanations of this important idea (Beck & McKeown, 1989). Did you understand that this phrase reflected the American colonists' feelings that it was unfair for them to pay taxes to the English crown when they were given no direct or effective voice in governance?

Research literature provides many such cases in which students display underdeveloped or malformed concepts, like the notion that heavier objects fall faster in a vacuum than lighter ones (Vosniadou, 1994) or that AIDS can be transmitted through casual human contact (Kardash & Scholes, 1995; Slusher & Anderson, 1996). There is also ample evidence that students manifest unexpectedly inappropriate interpretations or misunderstandings long thought to have been displaced by convincing information, persuasive instruction, or mental maturation (Pines & West, 1983). In other words, students like the high-school science students in Cambridge, Massachusetts, seem to "get it" when they are studying a topic, but when their ideas are challenged or probed, they display unexpected flaws or gaps in comprehension.

Even people with training in science and mathematics sometimes give explanations or justifications for phenomena that directly contradict scientific evidence and teaching but are seemingly reaffirmed by everyday experiences (Roth, 1990). In Question 3, for instance, when people are asked how plants obtain food, most explain that the roots carry food from the soil to the leaves. In school, however, students learn about the process of photosynthesis and are explicitly told that through this process plants produce food in their leaves. Even if you remembered the term *photosynthesis* and could offer a cursory definition of this process, have you abandoned completely the naive theory that food is in the soil or that roots transport that food to the plant? For many life has conspired to overwhelm this schooled knowledge (Chinn, 1999; Roth, 1990).

The Nature of Conceptual Change

Erroneous or unsophisticated views of the world that color learning can be broken down primarily by reforming the mental concepts on which they are based (Chi & Roscoe, 2002; Vosniadou & Brewer, 1992). LeeAnn was attempting to bring about such conceptual change, or conceptual learning, when she tried to expand her students' grasp of animal classifications by helping them explore the concepts of vertebrates and invertebrates. Reading a book together, looking at a related video and discussing it, hands-on study of family pets, and guided observation of animals at a local zoo—these multiple modes enabled most of the children to shed their simplistic notions about animal classifications. For LeeAnn's second graders, conceptual change meant acquiring a more sophisticated understanding of animal classifications.

To educators holding a cognitive perspective, learning is about changing the way a person thinks, reasons, believes, and processes information, in part by expanding or altering the individual's existing knowledge base (Murphy & Alexander, 2004; Sinatra & Pintrich, 2003). One significant dimension of that knowledge base is conceptual knowledge. **Concepts,** as discussed, are the labels we apply to webs of ideas linked by shared characteristics, relations, or essential attributes (Pines & West, 1983). For example, the pictorial representation of the Supreme Court in Figure 4–3 can be thought of as a simplified illustration of that concept.

In the broadest sense, the terms **conceptual change** and **conceptual learning** pertain to all modifications of conceptual knowledge structures (Carey, 1985; Rumelhart & Norman, 1981), whether that change happens easily, as it did for Sam, or with great difficulty, as in Millie's case. Although certain concepts seem highly resistant to change or seemingly immune to educational intervention—like students' notions about the seasons—most conceptual learning occurs without fanfare or intense effort. Thus, conceptual change encompasses not only dramatic shifts in knowledge but also everyday developments in human understanding (Rumelhart, 1980). In this regard, research literature on conceptual change may appear misleading, because it stresses dramatic or hard-to-achieve understandings rather than simple learning.

Although most research has focused on science and mathematics, conceptual change occurs in all academic domains (Chinn, 1999; Limón, 2002). However, because science and mathematics typically encompass well-structured problems with agreed-upon answers, it is probably easier to uncover students' naive or ill-formed concepts in these domains (Alexander, 1998c). It is easier to pin down students' erroneous grasp of the rule for multiplying fractions, for example, than it is to clarify students' misconceptions about historical people or events. In addition, the intrusions that everyday perceptions and encounters make into scientific and mathematical domains may be more readily understood (Vosniadou, 1994). For instance, it is not hard to perceive the difficulty of grasping the principle of falling bodies—the notion that weight has no effect on bodies as they fall in a vacuum—when heavy objects are often seen plummeting to the ground, whereas feathers float ever so slowly.

For still other reasons the conceptual change literature is greatly intertwined with the domains of science and mathematics. For a long time, those within the science and mathematics communities have been aware that the general populace does not necessarily see the world as they do (diSessa, 2002). Moreover, the distinctions between novices and experts in these domains may be more readily apparent than they are in other fields, such as history or reading (Chi, Glaser, & Farr, 1988). As a result, cognitive researchers in the 1970s and 1980s tried to delineate the differences between novices and experts in specific fields like physics and chess (Champagne et al., 1985; Chi et al., 1988), endeavoring to understand the less sophisticated notions in these fields that seemed to be barriers to the attainment of expertise. The resulting body of research, especially the studies dealing with the well-structured domains of science and mathematics, is what we refer to as the conceptual change literature.

During this same period, researchers in social psychology also began to investigate the apparent immutability of peoples' thoughts and perceptions (Dole & Sinatra, 1998). However, their focus was not on well-formed intellectual conceptions, like the seasons of the year or photosynthesis, but on the constancy of people's attitudes or beliefs about certain topics in the face of compelling, contrary evidence. My mother, for example, has been smoking since she was 15. Cancer warnings, deteriorating health, admonitions from doctors, and pleas from family members have had no real effect on her smoking behavior. She remains convinced that she will be fine and that all the concern is unwarranted. Social psychologists would look deeply at my mother's beliefs and attitudes toward smoking.

Because social psychologists were more interested in bringing about a change of attitude with regard to an issue, rather than transforming novices into experts, the label *persuasion* was applied to their work. Nonetheless, the research in conceptual change and persuasion shares common ground in its focus on changing how people understand and respond to the world around them (Chinn, 1999).

Levels of Conceptual Change

The processes required to make simple adjustments to conceptual knowledge are different from those needed to reshape understandings drastically. D. E. Rumelhart (1980), one of the early information-processing researchers, identified three mechanisms of conceptual change that result in differing levels of mental transformation: accretion, tuning, and restructuring.

Accretion

Accretion is the simplest and subtlest form of change and perhaps the most common. It involves an elaboration or enrichment of existing knowledge structures through experience or the acquisition of relevant information (Rumelhart, 1980). In fact, Vosniadou (1994) refers to this simplest form of conceptual change as enrichment. The idea of what it means to be alive can help illustrate this mechanism of change. An examination of ideas that children and adults hold about *alive* versus *not alive* is a classic focus in the development literature (Piaget, 1926/1930b). In fact, Piaget used the guiding question What does it mean to be alive? as a basis for defining stages of conceptual understanding that reflect growing sophistication in reasoning. Once children responded to Piaget's initial question, he probed further by asking whether particular animals, plants, or objects were alive and why. Others, most notably Susan Carey (1985), have used similar questions and probes to test Piaget's judgments about young children's conceptual development. She wanted to find out whether the children's answers were evidence of the dramatic mental shift required of stage theories or were reflective of a gradual change process.

Lauren is a typical 3-year-old who seems to equate being alive with things in her environment, especially humans (e.g., her mom, dad, and grandma) and familiar animals (e.g., her dog Portia and the squirrels in the backyard), that move or behave in certain ways (e.g., run, walk, or make sounds). Over several months' time, Lauren's concept of *alive* has developed through accretion. She has painlessly extended her understanding by incorporating new people (e.g., her babysitter, the new neighbor), animals (e.g., a raccoon, a bear), and behaviors (e.g., Portia's breathing and having babies) into her existing knowledge categories.

Because accretion generally entails the incorporation of new information into existing conceptual frameworks, it corresponds closely to Piaget's (1926/1930b) notion of assimilation. As much of the literature on conceptual change has focused on troublesome notions and dramatic transformations, the process of accretion has often been downplayed in the literature. However, accretion remains a basic, albeit unheralded, mechanism for conceptual growth and development (Limón Luque, 2003).

Weak Restructuring

Sometimes existing conceptual structures cannot accept contradictory information or respond to a novel or anomalous experience (Rumelhart. 1980). More is involved than merely accumulating new facts, experiences, or relations, for people to learn or grow conceptually, existing mental frameworks must be reshaped or adjusted in some manner—a case of **weak restructuring.** Piaget's (1926/1930b) idea of *accommodation* captures this process of conceptual adaptation, whereby minor modifications to knowledge structures occur that require some shifting or reordering of categories or related attributes.

Tuning is the term that Rumelhart (1980) applied to nonradical adjustments, or tweakings, of knowledge struc-

tures. Carey (1985) and others (Vosniadou & Brewer, 1992) talk about this level of change as weak restructuring. Tuning, or weak restructuring, often involves modifying the parameters or attributes of a concept. For example, as Lauren gets older, she is beginning to realize that the word *alive* can have more than one interpretation. When asked whether her great-grandfather is alive, Lauren says no because she knows that he is dead. She also responds that Barney is not alive because he is make-believe. And even though physiological movement or action remains central to her concept, Lauren recognizes that someone can be immobile and still be alive (e.g., a person in the hospital). Further, she realizes that some objects that move (e.g., her bicycle) are not alive because they do not move by their own power. Thus, her concept of *alive* is taking on new and more sophisticated dimensions.

As these examples suggest, ideas in a conceptual framework may get shuffled around or clarified while the core concepts—the theoretical underpinnings that link them together—generally remain intact. In several years Lauren may even accept that humans and other creatures like dogs and squirrels are not completely separate categories but, in fact, all fall within the broader category of living things. Such an outcome, which is a case of generalization, would still constitute weak restructuring (Limón Luque, 2003; Vosniadou & Brewer, 1992). What is important about this idea is that children's conceptual framework can change significantly without their need to move into a new stage of mental processing.

Radical Restructuring

When the extension or elaboration of knowledge structures no longer suffices and when virtually new concepts arise from existing ones, the result is profound reconstructions—changes that reflect an alteration in fundamental world views (Vosniadou, 1994). This form of conceptual change is called **radical restructuring** (Vosniadou & Brewer, 1992). According to Carey (1985), radical restructuring must be accompanied by theory or belief change that impacts all the components of a concept. Carey would argue that Lauren was experiencing radical restructuring if she abandoned her root concept of *alive* being some form of physiological condition (e.g., moving, running, breathing) and adopted a biological conception of life, one that may or may not entail physical actions.

Vosniadou (1994, 2003) would concur with this assessment and sees radical restructuring as requiring a shift in an individual's perception of reality, that is, an ontological shift. In her studies of astronomical knowledge, for instance, Vosniadou has recognized that radical restructuring requires young children to abandon one belief system (e.g., a flat earth theory) in favor of another (e.g., a spherical earth theory). Until that occurs, students can memorize new facts about the earth and can even produce reasonable answers to school questions but will still retain their naive conceptions. Thus, until students see new information or evidence as inconsistent with their prevailing views of the world, no fundamental or permanent transformation will take place in their conceptual understanding. Without that transformation students will have achieved only a fragile restructuring in their understanding, which will not hold its shape when instruction abates or when everyday experiences begin to intrude (Alexander & Murphy, 1999b).

Even those who are experts in fields of study are not immune to conceptual resistance or radical restructuring. In fact, the most dramatic form of conceptual restructuring seems to occur in this special population (Alexander, 1997b; Perkins & Simmons, 1988). Precisely because the knowledge of experts is so extensive and highly interrelated, a misconception can potentially infect much of what they know. Thus, when experts hold to erroneous notions that undergird much of what they understand and perceive, changing those core conceptions will likely unravel much of what they believe to be true about their fields. In these cases nothing short of a paradigmatic shift will permit them to restructure their conceptions, as when the study of mechanics shifted from Aristotelian to Galilean and then Newtonian conceptualizations (Alexander, 1997a).

A special label, Gordian misconceptions, has been given to the misconceptions held by experts in a field of study (Perkins & Simmons, 1988). Gordian misconceptions are named after the fabled Gordian knot. Legend has it that Alexander the Great, when faced with Gordius's challenge to unravel an unfathomably complex knot, did not attempt to untie it, as others had done with disastrous results. Instead, this wise leader merely took his sword and cut through the knot. Similarly, when experts face powerful and irrefutable evidence that alters their fundamental knowledge and beliefs about reality, they have little choice but to undergo a radical ontological transformation (M. R. Matthews, 1994). However, such intense, radical restructuring is quite rare and likely to be of minimal concern to school-aged learners who are still building their knowledge in academic domains.

Sources of Conceptual Resistance

In a review of the literature, Chinn and Brewer (1993) studied people's reactions to evidence that did not match their scientific beliefs or theories (i.e., anomalous data). The reviewers determined that the reasons people gave for resisting contradictory information fell into four categories as summarized in Table 6–1. Others (Limón & Mason, 2002; Sinatra & Pintrich, 2003) would also include motivational and sociocultural forces that can impede conceptual change.

Characteristics of Existing Knowledge

Some ideas are so deeply entrenched that they are hard to question or confront. In other cases notions are so inter-

Category	Factor	Explanation
Table 6–1	**Factors that prompt resistance to contradictory information.**	
Characteristics of existing knowledge	Entrenchment of prior knowledge	The more deeply embedded ideas are in the knowledge base, the harder they are to change.
	Ontological beliefs	Because these are persuasive beliefs about the world that influence thoughts and responses in many areas, they are extremely resistant to change.
	Epistemological commitment	Younger or less sophisticated learners tend to operate from rather commonsense notions, whereas scientists hold to rather rigorous standards of scientific evidence.
	Background scientific knowledge	The background knowledge that individuals accept as scientifically valid can lead them to accept or reject evidence.
Characteristics of the new theory	Availability of a plausible alternative theory	Inconsistent data are more easily ignored or rejected when they are not part of some alternative theory or conception.
	Quality of the alternative theory	A quality theory is one that tends to be accurate, consistent, broad in scope, simple, and fruitful.
Quality of the anomalous data	Credibility	In science, credibility of the data reflects the source, the methods of data collection and analysis, and the replication of outcomes.
	Ambiguity	If data are easily open to reinterpretation, they are easier to ignore or reject.
	Multiple data	When multiple sets of data or studies point to the same conclusions or outcomes, the contradictory data become more convincing.
Manner of processing	Deep processing	Seriously reflecting on data and weighing that data more deeply are more likely to result in conceptual change.

Note: From "The Role of Anomalous Data in Knowledge Acquisition: A Theoretical Framework and Implications for Science Instruction" by C. A. Chinn and W. F. Brewer, 1993, *Review of Educational Research, 63*, p. 15. Copyright 1993 by *Review of Educational Research*. Adapted with permission.

twined with a view of the world that they infiltrate and govern many other ideas (Pines & West, 1983). And confronting any one erroneous idea that is part of a world view without considering the underlying issue is unlikely to bring about any significant conceptual change. For example, until Millie confronted her belief that animals of different colors could not have other *underlying* characteristics in common, she could not begin to classify animals more scientifically. To do so would have violated her basic view of the world.

Chinn and Brewer (1993) found that when people have primitive beliefs about scientific concepts, it is hard to get them to see the merits of contradictory evidence. The 3-year-old who sees Barney, the purple dinosaur, dancing and singing on television and associates movement with being alive would be unlikely to consider the idea that Barney is an imaginary creature. Unsophisticated beliefs do not support pursuit of more complex explanations for what is seen or heard (Carey, 1985).

An individual with more limited scientific exposure is also more likely to resist powerful evidence that conflicts with current understandings. Less scientific thinkers do not know how to formulate hypotheses and test them systematically. Like Millie, they believe that if something looks or feels right intuitively, it should be accepted as fact, plain and simple.

Characteristics of the New Theory

Resistance is not always linked to an individual's existing knowledge base; perhaps the alternative theory under consideration is weak. Chinn and Brewer (1993) found that anomalous data are sometimes simply seen as a random occurrence and not really as part of any compelling theory. For example, even if a young child is shown a Barney doll that does not move or breathe, she may not give up her notion that Barney is alive. This one bit of evidence may not be sufficient to replace her existing theory.

Conversely, evidence is more powerful if there is no room for alternative interpretations. Experts certainly benefit from weighing alternative theories or explanations, but the very existence of rival explanations can dampen the power of any one theory for those who are novices in an area (Alexander, 1997b). For instance, the fact that educators can argue over whether development occurs continuously or discontinuously may be intriguing, but it also makes it more difficult to accept one viewpoint or the other with strong conviction.

In addition, a new theory may be too specialized or too complex for individuals to grasp. For example, it would do little good to explain the concept of *alive* to Lauren on the basis of molecular functions. Such evidence may be accurate, but it falls outside the mental reach of such a young child (Piaget, 1952).

Quality of the Data or Evidence Provided

Chinn and Brewer (1993) established that evidence is more compelling if it comes from a credible source. Second, it would appear that clear and definitive data are more convincing to students than data that are ambiguous or iffy. And third, if the goal is to change students' minds, it helps to present the same evidence from multiple sources. Adults, too, are more apt to be convinced if they hear the same message from several credible sources (Murphy & Alexander, 2002b).

The Manner in Which Information Is Processed

Chinn and Brewer (1993) also realized that resistance may result from the manner in which an individual thinks through the information. If the processing of the information is superficial, the information is unlikely to penetrate, and the person will cling to preexisting ideas. In contrast, if the individual ponders the data critically and deeply, there is a far greater possibility of conceptual change.

Learner Goals and Motivations

Gale Sinatra and Paul Pintrich (2003) have added a new dimension to the study of conceptual change. Specifically, they have explored the notion of **intentional conceptual change,** which they characterize as "goal-directed and conscious initiation and regulation of cognitive, metacognitive, and motivational processes to bring about a change in knowledge" (p. 6). Behind this provocative idea is the recognition that sometimes conceptual change does not just *happen* to individuals; sometimes they *seek* change. If you are reading this text because you have decided to improve your knowledge of educational psychology, Sinatra and Pintrich would view you as an intentional learner, and the transformations that occur in your knowledge base would represent intentional conceptual change.

Simply stated, individuals who seek conceptual change, who are open to the opportunity, and who are reflective about their level of understanding are more likely to experience conceptual change. Thus, learners' goals, intentions, and regulatory actions would seemingly contribute to change even under less conscious or purposeful learning conditions; their goals and motivations help create a disposition toward conceptual change. Unfortunately, without this intent to change their current thinking or even an awareness of their current level of understanding, students may be content with their existing knowledge base, oblivious to any need to alter present conceptions.

The Sociocultural Context

Historically, studies of conceptual change have focused on the structure and processes of the individual mind in relation to a particular concept or network of concepts. However, contemporary researchers have a heightened sensitivity to the place of sociocultural factors in the change process (Ferrari & Elik, 2003). Because learning is a social process, conceptual learning must be equally social in character. Thus, culture plays a role in deciding which concepts become entrenched and closed to deep exploration and which are considered less central and open to question. Within some cultural communities, for instance, it would be difficult to explore concepts such as evolution, the origin of the universe, or genetic manipulation, regardless of the compelling evidence (Southerland & Sinatra, 2003).

The sociocultural environment of the classroom also figures in conceptual change (Gorodetsky & Keiny, 2002). The degree to which students' understandings are brought to the surface, valued, and discussed helps determine how aware students are of their relevant conceptions. In addition, interactions among peers can serve as catalysts to change in a way that didactic teaching may not (Hennessey, 2003). Through social discourse students may gather pertinent data and be exposed to alternative perspectives on issues. They may also recognize that ideas deserve to be reflected upon and analyzed rather than simply memorized (Ferrari & Elik, 2003). However, as discussed in Chapter 11, many teachers have not learned how to marshal the power of the sociocultural environment with techniques that promote the social exchange of ideas. Students in such classrooms have little opportunity to make their thoughts public or to examine personal understandings in the light of others' knowledge and beliefs.

How Can Students' Knowledge and Beliefs Be Changed?

Researchers offer teachers valuable recommendations for confronting potential sources of resistance. Teachers' efforts also serve to highlight certain limitations within the conceptual change literature of the early 1990s. For instance, learners' interests and goals were given relatively little weight in theories of conceptual change of that era (Sinatra & Pintrich, 2003). In addition, the focus of attention was very narrow, emphasizing problems in the domains of science and mathematics with agreed-upon solutions (Limón Luque, 2003). Contemporary research, however, has recognized the importance not only of knowledge changes, but also of changes in the beliefs with which that knowledge is deeply intertwined (Vosniadou, 2002). Such research has led to the articulation of new models of change and guidelines for

teachers hoping to stimulate change in their students (Dole & Sinatra, 1998; Murphy & Alexander, in press).

Confronting Potential Sources of Resistance

Chinn and Brewer (1993) believe that conceptual change is likely if teachers take specific instructional aim at the four potential sources of resistance that they uncovered. In other words, conceptual learning is more likely if teachers seek to (a) influence students' prior knowledge, (b) present students with a viable alternative model, (c) offer convincing evidence, and (d) prompt deep processing of relevant information (see Table 6–2).

Influencing Prior Knowledge

If students' knowledge is the source of their conceptual resistance, teachers must focus directly on that knowledge. First, teachers can try to bring students' current understandings to the surface rather than allowing them to stay buried or entrenched. When LeeAnn had her students express their understandings of animal classifications at the start of the lesson, she was attempting to bring their buried concepts to the surface—to make them public. The students' drawings, stories, and concept maps provided her the information on which she and they could subsequently build.

Sometimes teachers need to explore students' world views if they want related concepts to change. A primary-grade teacher, for instance, might find it worthwhile to do a lesson on real and make-believe, in which the children could explore questions about real life and fantasy that would encompass many pertinent concepts—including whether Barney is alive or not. Within such broad lessons, educators can introduce children to the grays of concepts—helping them see that ideas are not simply right or wrong, black or white (Afflerbach & VanSledright, 2001). This approach can help students understand that questions like what it means to be alive can have multiple interpretations

Table 6–2	Techniques for promoting changes in students' conceptualizations.
Target	**Strategy**
Influencing prior knowledge	Reduce the entrenchment of students' prior notions
	Help students construct appropriate ontological categories
	Foster appropriate epistemological commitments
	Help students construct needed background knowledge
Introducing alternative theories	Introduce an intelligible alternative
	Make sure that the alternative theory is plausible
	Make sure that the alternative theory is compelling
Introducing the anomalous data	Make the anomalous data credible
	Avoid ambiguous data
Influencing processing strategies	Use multiple lines of data when necessary
	Encourage deep processing

Note: From "The Role of Anomalous Data in Knowledge Acquisition: A Theoretical Framework and Implications for Science Instruction" by C. A. Chinn and W. F. Brewer, 1993, *Review of Educational Research, 63,* p. 31. Copyright 1993 by *Review of Educational Research*. Adapted with permission.

that are defensible. In other words, Barney is alive if they are referring to the person behind the funny costume, but not alive if they mean the purple dinosaur itself.

In addition, teachers can promote accretion and fine tuning (Rumelhart & Norman, 1981); they can help students enrich their conceptual knowledge by exposing them to meaningful and inviting experiences. From these, students can develop more sophisticated conceptions, sometimes without the need for conceptual restructuring. LeeAnn was particularly effective at immersing her students in experiences that could enrich their concepts about animals and their scientific classifications (Vosniadou & Brewer, 1992). Showing the children pictures, taking them to the zoo, watching a video, and reading the book *How Do Scientists Classify Animals?* were just a few of those concept-building experiences.

Introducing New Theories

When teachers want to replace students' naive or inaccurate theories with more viable alternatives, they need to consider several factors. They must make sure that the alternative theory is intelligible, plausible, and compelling. First, they must ask themselves whether the theory they are offering will be comprehensible (i.e., intelligible) to their students. What students cannot comprehend they are unlikely to accept. Second, the alternative theory should seem reasonable or plausible to students, based on their life experiences. And finally, the new theory needs to be sufficiently detailed and illustrated to prove convincing or compelling. Just mentioning a theory and assuming that it will be understood and accepted is pedagogically risky and highly ineffective (Guzzetti & Hynd, 1998).

Introducing the Anomalous Data

Sometimes the evidence or data themselves contribute to conceptual intractability. Under those circumstances, if teachers want the evidence to penetrate and contribute to a new conceptualization, they must support their explanations with data that students find credible and unambiguous. In addition, teachers need to support their contentions in multiple ways with evidence from multiple sources. As LeeAnn recognized, conceptual change is more likely in young minds if learning is multisensory, that is, if the students hear, see, and physically engage an idea (Piaget, 1952). Moreover, regardless of age, students are more likely to experience conceptual change when anomalous data are confronted on multiple occasions. Without multiple exposures students' emerging concepts remain fragile and are easily disassembled by more intuitively comfortable—but misleading—interpretations (Hynd, Alvermann, & Qian, 1997).

Influencing Deep Processing

Finally, if teachers want to stimulate conceptual change in their students, they would be well advised to model the mental tools their students require for deep processing. As discussed in chapter 7, those tools, called strategies or reasoning processes (Weinstein & Mayer, 1986), allow students to look beyond the surface of a problem.

Strategies help students to probe, question, reflect, and summarize (Garner, 1990). They allow them to consider evidence and to weigh its credibility (Alexander, Graham, & Harris, 1998). And strategies assist students in synthesizing information from multiple sources to form a tentative theory or explanation (Pressley et al., 1989). LeeAnn's technique of sorting and classifying animals into different groups was a rudimentary strategy intended to spark children's thinking and, thus, their conceptual learning. The more mental tools students have available to them, the greater their chances of breaking the hold misconceptions have on their conceptual development (Perkins & Simmons, 1988).

Shortcomings of Early Conceptual-Change Research

The research of Chinn and Brewer (1993) and others (Champagne, Klopfer, & Gunstone, 1982) took critical steps toward clarifying why certain naive scientific conceptions remain intractable even in the face of contradictory evidence. Early researchers also gave teachers useful suggestions, like those of Chinn and Brewer (1993), for stimulating conceptual change. However, this foundational research simply did not go far enough to meet the needs of teachers and students; three major shortcomings became evident.

Limited Attention to Students' Cognitive Maturity

At the beginning of their animal study, LeeAnn's second graders provided abundant examples of malformed or unsophisticated notions. They offered many different ideas regarding animal classification, but none came close to grasping the characteristics scientists actually use. According to Piaget's (1952) theories, the naiveté of the children's thinking was a reflection of their stage of cognitive development. Because the children had not yet achieved formal operations, they could not be expected to understand the more abstract concept of vertebrates and invertebrates used by scientists to classify animals.

Like Piaget others have viewed conceptual change in terms of cognitive development, although often in a less strict or stagelike manner (Carey, 1985; Roth, 1990). These non-Piagetian developmentalists, too, stress the association between mental maturity and cognitive change, although their focus is on the continuous rather than the discontinuous nature of human growth. These theorists and researchers also consider changes in individuals' thinking in terms of cognitive development, emphasizing again that changes in understanding are, to some extent, linked to cognitive maturation.

Developmental issues have not always been given their rightful due in the research on conceptual change. Until recently, there was only limited discussion regarding the critical level or stage of mental maturity that must precede significant conceptual restructuring, particularly of the radical sort (Vosniadou, 1994). The theoretical and practical implications are, however, of the utmost importance. When LeeAnn assessed the difficulties of Millie and others in grasping the concept of vertebrates and invertebrates, she undoubtedly considered whether they were cognitively ready for the task.

Underestimation of Motivational and Emotional Factors

As mentioned earlier, the foundational work on conceptual change paid limited heed to students' motivations. Early change researchers seemed to discount the idea that such factors as students' goals and interests are as important to conceptual change as their mental processing of evidence. Change was conceived as a "coldly cognitive" experience (Pintrich, Marx, & Boyle, 1993). Recent researchers, on the other hand, have worked to infuse findings from motivation into discussions of change (Dole & Sinatra, 1998; Sinatra & Pintrich, 2003). From this emerging perspective, one might conclude that some of the students in LeeAnn's class may not have seen the personal value of learning about vertebrates and invertebrates. Thus, at least initially they may have been unwilling to look deeply at the evidence or exert the mental energy required to change their existing conceptions.

Pintrich and colleagues (1993) are not alone in their thinking (Guthrie, McGough et al., 1996) nor are they the first. In fact, Aristotle's *Rhetoric*, which remains a classic work in the persuasion literature, speaks to this very issue. Provoking changes in knowledge and beliefs, Aristotle said, requires not only gaining the confidence of the listener by establishing the speaker's character and forwarding a logical argument, but also tapping into the emotions and attitude of the listener. Touching the learner's mind and heart can provoke a change that is deep and enduring (Guzzetti & Hynd, 1998).

In addition, some individuals have personality traits that make them more open to change than others (Alexander & Murphy, 1998a; Sá, West, & Stanovich, 1999). Some people seem stubborn, hard headed, or argumentative, whereas others seem open-minded or perceptive. Those who are more closed-minded may seek out or attend to only infor-

> *Even if our speaker had the most accurate scientific information, still there are persons whom he could not readily persuade with scientific arguments. True instruction, by the method of logic, is here impossible.*
>
> L. Cooper, 1932, p. 6.

mation that bolsters their own views, ignoring any counterarguments or confusing evidence. Open-minded people, in contrast, may actually enjoy considering perspectives other than their own (Sá et al., 1999).

Vague Notions About What Makes a Message Compelling or Persuasive

Chinn and Brewer (1993) showed that the quality of the theory or evidence presented has a great deal to do with changing students' minds. However, until recently the literature on conceptual change was vague about the characteristics of compelling information. A clearer picture of mind-changing messages began to take shape when researchers interested in conceptual change became aware of the related research on persuasion (Kardash & Scholes, 1995; Petty & Cacioppo, 1986).

Persuasion is the process of stimulating or compelling individuals to alter their personal beliefs, even long-held beliefs (Murphy, 1998). To understand this process, persuasion researchers have intensively studied the characteristics of messages that provoke readers or listeners to reflect on their beliefs. The characteristics uncovered, such as the credibility of the author, can be directly applied by teachers who want to change students' resistant or naive beliefs about academic subjects. Later, this discussion explores the characteristics of persuasive text.

The Merits of Combining Research on Conceptual Change and Persuasion

The research on persuasion is an important complement to the ongoing research on conceptual change because it further enhances teachers' ability to bring about a profound change in students' knowledge and beliefs. The merger of these two literatures opens new vistas onto the realm of change, contributes to new classroom practices, and prompts teachers and students to question their own educational beliefs (Chinn, 1999; L. Mason, 2002).

Focus of Change

Conceptual change and persuasion look at change through different lenses and for varied purposes. The work on conceptual change, as conducted by cognitive researchers, concerns shifts in students' academic knowledge. Do students possess accurate factual or procedural knowledge relative to

Aristotle

academic domains and problems? Persuasion research, principally the dominion of social psychologists, focuses on individuals' attitudes or beliefs. Do individuals espouse reasonable or socially acceptable beliefs or attitudes about a range of personal or social issues, such as those pertaining to human relations or political systems? By combining these two fields, teachers are better equipped to promote change in students' knowledge and beliefs.

Domains/Problems of Interest

Conceptual-change and persuasion researchers also investigate varying, complementary domains and problems. For instance, most of the problems explored in the conceptual-change literature come from science or mathematics, fields in which problems often have accepted right answers solved by step-by-step procedures. By contrast, persuasion researchers typically consider more ill-structured domains (e.g., history or sociology) and controversial problems (e.g., abortion, drug use, or segregation), which are rarely investigated by conceptual-change researchers (Chinn, 1999; Hynd, 2001b). The marriage of these two fields prepares teachers to promote changes in a wide range of subject-matter areas and deal with problems that are both well structured and more open ended.

Paths to Change

Also complementary are the paths these two literatures advocate for stimulating transformations in knowledge or beliefs. As noted about Chinn and Brewer's review, conceptual-change researchers rely heavily on the rational processing of evidence. Persuasion, by comparison, cannot depend solely on the rational to provoke belief changes; the motivational or emotional paths to belief change are as critical as the mental processing of convincing data (Dole & Sinatra, 1998). Through the merger of these two fields of study, the motivational and emotional dimensions of change are given the attention sometimes overlooked in the conceptual-change literature.

Key Findings

The work of conceptual-change researchers like Chinn and Brewer (1993) and Vosniadou (1994) helped to pinpoint the nature of resistant concepts in science and mathematics. This body of work also identified procedures for breaking down that resistance. The persuasion literature also explored resistant beliefs and attitudes and produced models for altering seemingly intractable perspectives. Central to those models were insights into the characteristics of compelling messages (Alvermann, 2001; Slusher & Anderson, 1996). For example, researchers studying the quality of persuasive messages have determined that texts carefully crafted to anticipate and confront readers' naive theories can be quite effective at altering conceptions (Alexander, Murphy, Buehl, & Sperl, 1998). Because of their confrontational style, such texts are called **refutational;** they take aim at readers' emotions and their logical reasoning (Hynd et al., 1997).

One form of refutational text that has proven particularly effective at changing students' misleading notions is **two-sided refutation** (Guzzetti & Hynd, 1998). These texts are crafted to present both sides of an issue, but also to dismantle arguments on one side. For example, the book LeeAnn chose to model scientific classification might have first described the way nonscientists sort and classify animals and might than have discussed why such approaches seem sensible. However, if the author went on to argue for an alternative classification scheme, systematically pointing out the weaknesses or flaws of other less scientific schemes, that book would have been framed as two-sided refutation.

Professional writers often use two-sided refutation to craft persuasion arguments. A good example of such a text is the magazine article featured in the Thought Experiment: Weighing Two Sides of an Issue, which takes on the issue of school integration. See whether you can recognize the author's position on integration and the pro and con arguments he includes. Pay close attention to the way he dismantles the arguments that do not fit with his particular viewpoint.

Thought Experiment ························

Weighing Two Sides of an Issue

Why We Need to Raise Hell
It's not only white racists who shun poor black kids. So do wealthy blacks

Before we gave up on integration, we should have tried it. Instead, for the past 40 years, we played a shell game with desegregation in which blacks chased after whites who would not stand still long enough to be integrated with. The result: public schools so separate and vastly unequal that Plessy v. Ferguson, *not* Brown v. Board, *might as well be the law of the land.*

This sorry situation is, to be sure, mostly the fault of whites who pay lip service to equal rights but cut and run as

Norman Rockwell's 1963 painting, *The Problem We All Live With*.

soon as enough blacks move into their neighborhood. But many privileged African Americans are no more committed to public school integration than their white counterparts if it means sending their children to class with poor black kids. The main obstacle to integration is not race but class.

In fact, there is a good deal of integration going on among those who can afford it. Consider the small number of schools, both public and private, where something approaching stable integration exists. What most have in common is an affluent clientele and a determination to maintain a diverse student body. The well-educated black parents who can afford to send their kids to private school—or to live in one of the expensive areas with a good public system—are accustomed to dealing with whites as equals. Their well-scrubbed, well-dressed, well-mannered offspring blend right in with the well-scrubbed, well-mannered white children and pose no perceived threat.

Moreover, these "safe" black children are always in a very distinct minority. There are enough of them for blacks to feel they are not just tokens but not so many that whites feel uneasy. The poor kids who attend such schools are charity cases, gifted children carefully selected to make sure they fit in.

It amounts to a cynical bargain. White parents congratulate themselves for doing the racial right thing at no real cost to themselves. Affluent blacks get the assurance that their children will learn to get along in the white world in which they will someday compete and the status that goes with sending them to a prestigious school. Most poor black children, meanwhile, are stuck in decrepit ghetto classrooms.

What is truly dismaying about all this is the degree to which privileged African Americans—including myself—have acquiesced to the process. Just like many whites, a lot of us walked away from the fight for school integration once we made sure our own progeny would receive its undeniable benefits by enrolling them in high-priced private academies. This hypocritical approach reflects the desire to seek the best for one's own and frustration with recalcitrant whites. But it also undercuts our ability to prevail on whites to support public school integration. Why should they do what we are unwilling to do ourselves?

In cities such as Washington, it is not uncommon for black school administrators and teachers to enroll their children in private or suburban schools. If the city schools are not good enough for their offspring, they are not good enough for Chelsea Clinton or anyone else. By mismanaging the schools, the black professionals who run them have betrayed the best of the African-American tradition, which values education above all else, and have given whites who never believed in integration an easy excuse for abandoning it.

Herewith a radical proposal for breaking the impasse: revive the civil rights movement, which went into limbo long before some of its most important goals were accomplished, and aim it not only at racist whites but also at complacent middle-class blacks. All of us need a jolting reminder that integration's real purpose was not to produce Norman Rockwellish racial brotherhood. It was a strategy to ensure that black children, especially poor ones, would receive the same quality of in-struction, textbooks and facilities that white children do. The genteel race mixing that goes on among the elite is no substitute for a determined national effort to include poor nonwhite children in America's bounty—and if it takes a new round of sit-ins to put the issue back on the national agenda, so be it.

Such a campaign would be disruptive and strongly opposed, but then so was the battle to desegregate lunch counters. America has never made progress on racial issues unless there was enough agitation to force society to take action. Just as it did in Plessy v. Ferguson, *the Supreme Court is again defending the racial status quo—and it always will in the absence of intense political pressure.*

Black economist Glenn C. Loury makes a powerful case for the rediscovery of black racial honor. He believes progress toward racial equality depends on acknowledging and rectifying the dysfunctional behaviors in the black community. This is usually taken to mean the underclass must clean up its act before it can move into the mainstream. But there are dysfunctional behaviors outside the ghetto that could also stand re-examination: the white notion that the country has already done enough to secure racial equity, and black middle-class complicity in the deterioration of inner-city schools. In both cases, honor depends on rediscovering our commitment to treating all children fairly. If it takes new turmoil to bring that about, that is a price we should be willing to pay.

Guiding Questions:

What is the author's primary message about integration and racism?

What are the pro and con arguments that the author sets up about American integration?

How does the author dismantle the arguments in support of past and current integration efforts?

• •

An Alternative Model of Change

The merger of the conceptual-change and persuasion literatures has expanded and deepened educators' understanding of the change process, making it more likely that profound and lasting changes in knowledge and beliefs will result. Several researchers who have merged the findings of the conceptual-change and persuasion literatures have forged new models of knowledge and belief change (e.g., Dole & Sinatra, 1998). Such models are important because they point the way to effective educational interventions. P. Karen Murphy offers one of those alternative change models (see Figure 6–2).

This change model has been tested multiple times (Alexander, Murphy, Buehl & Sperl, 1998; Murphy, 1998; Murphy & Alexander, 2004), using texts covering an array of subjects, including AIDS, human development, V-chip

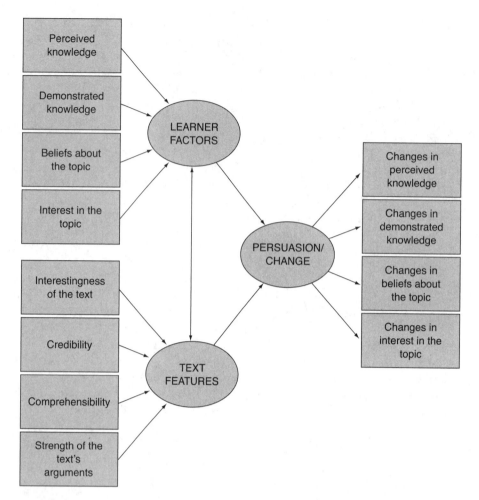

■ FIGURE 6–2   General models of learner factors and textual features affecting persuasion.

Note: From *Toward a Multifaceted Model of Persuasion: Exploring Textual and Learner Interactions* by P. K. Murphy, 1998, unpublished doctoral dissertation, University of Maryland, College Park. Adapted with permission.

P. Karen Murphy

technology, school integration, same-sex marriages, and doctor-assisted suicide. These texts have come from everyday sources such as newspaper editorials and magazine articles, like the article shown in the Thought Experiment on persuasion.

As depicted in Figure 6–2, this alternative view of the change process addresses several of the shortcomings of the earlier change research and incorporates other noteworthy features. First, rather than just listing the factors that influence change, like prior knowledge or compelling evidence, Murphy's (1998) model illustrates how those factors come together. For example, the learner factors and text factors both individually and collectively spark persuasion. Second, like Chinn and Brewer (1993), Murphy portrays students' preexisting knowledge and beliefs as important. However, in this model both perceived knowledge and demonstrated knowledge, as well as beliefs about and interest in the topic, are important agents of change. **Perceived knowledge** is what individuals think they know about some topic. Prior to introducing students to Jack White's article in the persuasion Thought Experiment, a teacher might first use a probe like the following:

Indicate how much you know about school integration by placing an X at the appropriate point on the line.

| | | | | | | | | | | |

Relatively   A Great
Nothing   Deal

Demonstrated knowledge, by comparison, is what individuals show they know about that topic. For example, that same teacher might ask students to share what they know about concepts like separate but equal, *Brown v. Board of Education*, or *Plessy v. Ferguson* to gauge their demonstrated knowledge about integration efforts. Teachers who possess data about their students' perceived and demonstrated knowledge are better able to orchestrate their lessons to bring about change in that base of knowledge.

To uncover students' beliefs, this model might pose open-ended questions to students before any topic is introduced. This approach lets teachers understand students' initial positions and also serves as a means of monitoring shifts in beliefs after instruction. Before beginning a unit on segregation/integration, for example, students might be asked to respond to a statement like the following:

Americans have never really given integration a chance to work.

| | | | | | | | | | | |

Strongly   Strongly
Disagree   Agree

Students' interest in a topic can be similarly measured by uncovering how much the topic matters to them. For instance, before exploring the subject of segregation, a history teacher might want to know whether students are interested in that topic. Have they read anything on the subject? Have they had any discussions about it? Have they been active in any social or political groups connected to the topic? Answers to such questions would give clues to students' deep-seated or personal interests in the topic. According to the research, students with some level of personal interest are more likely to engage deeply in the learning process and therefore experience change (Alexander, Jetton, & Kulikowich, 1995).

Murphy (1998) also found that a number of text characteristics are important to the change process. Specifically, oral or written texts judged as more interesting, credible, comprehensible, or strong in argumentation are more apt to provoke change in students than texts rated lower on those characteristics. For example, after reading or hearing a message like that in the persuasion Thought Experiment, students might be asked to answer questions like those in Figure 6–3. Their ratings would be predictive of their level of change.

A unique feature of Murphy's alternative model is its broad definition of change. In the conceptual-change literature, evidence of change was limited to modifications in students' factual and procedural knowledge. However, in this alternative model persuasion or change occurs when instruction produces shifts in students' perceived and demon-

---

Article Reactions

DIRECTIONS: Below is a list of statements about the article you have just read. Place an X on the line following each statement to indicate the degree to which you agree with the statement.

1. The author presented a balanced perspective on the issue.

| | | | | | | | | | | |

Strongly   Strongly
Disagree   Agree

2. I found the author to be credible.

| | | | | | | | | | | |

Strongly   Strongly
Disagree   Agree

3. The arguments presented in the article were persuasive.

| | | | | | | | | | | |

Strongly   Strongly
Disagree   Agree

4. The article was easy to understand.

| | | | | | | | | | | |

Strongly   Strongly
Disagree   Agree

5. I was moved emotionally by the article.

| | | | | | | | | | | |

Strongly   Strongly
Disagree   Agree

6. The article was very interesting.

| | | | | | | | | | | |

Strongly   Strongly
Disagree   Agree

■ **FIGURE 6–3   Assessment of text features.**

strated knowledge or their beliefs about or interest in the topic under consideration.

This alternative model has at least three implications for bringing about deep and enduring changes in students. First, the model and related research point out the critical importance of gaining access to students' underlying knowledge and beliefs, the nature of which cannot be assumed. Simple measures, like those illustrated in this discussion, can be used to achieve that access with relative ease. Second, the model makes it clear that change is more likely to occur when teachers attack naive theories or beliefs from multiple directions. Teachers should not depend solely on a presentation of new information or a discussion of beliefs to bring about desired change in students but should attend to as many factors as possible in the confines of the lesson. Finally, the model demonstrates that the characteristics of the learner and the attributes of the message interact to bring about changes in knowledge or beliefs. Therefore, teachers must consider that interaction when devising lessons.

Guidelines for Promoting Profound and Enduring Changes in Knowledge and Beliefs

Alexander and colleagues have built on this alternative model to frame an approach to teaching that promotes deeper and more reflective processing of information in classrooms (Alexander, Fives, Buehl, & Mulhern, 2002; Fives & Alexander, 2001; Fives, Alexander, & Buehl, 2001). This approach takes into consideration not only the three implications just discussed but also other insights that come from the integrated literatures on conceptual change and persuasion (e.g., Alvermann, 2001; Dole & Sinatra, 1998; Guzzetti & Hynd, 1998; Pintrich et al., 1993). This approach is called *Teaching for Persuasion* (Fives & Alexander, 2001), and its guidelines are discussed later here.

Take Time to Find Out What Students Understand, Believe, or Care About, and Incorporate That Information into Instruction Teachers should not become complacent in their instruction and assume that they have a clear picture of their students' existing base of knowledge, their relevant beliefs, or their interests (Dienes & Barry, 1997). It is wise to take some time to unearth such critical information before introducing new topics or concepts. Then, during instruction teachers should acknowledge students' understandings and perspectives in positive and nonjudgmental ways.

For instance, LeeAnn Delli let her students play with their own approaches to classify and categorize animals at the outset of her lesson on vertebrates and invertebrates. This approach gave her insights into the children's mental processing. LeeAnn could also have referred to the children's particular perspectives when the opportunity arose during instruction. For example, she might have mentioned that a particular student put animals together that lived in the jungle and in the desert, just like the habitats the students saw at the zoo.

Ensure That High-Quality Oral and Written Texts Are Used in Classrooms The messages that students read or hear do have a direct effect on what they come to understand (Chambliss, 1995; Hynd, 2001a, 2001b). Consequently, teachers should strive for the inclusion of high-quality texts in their classrooms. High-quality texts, whether delivered orally or in writing, not only frame arguments and evidence clearly and appropriately, but also consider alternative theories and multiple perspectives on issues or concepts (Chambliss & Garner, 1996; Hynd et al., 1997).

Given the questionable quality of many subject-matter texts, teachers must be prepared to supplement and extend existing texts when the need arises. Of course, teachers themselves must be capable of viewing even well-structured domains or topics in varied ways and anticipating the more naive conceptions that students may hold. For instance, a high-school science teacher dealing with the topic of the seasons could point out that pictures in the science textbook may be misleading and may leave the impression that the earth is significantly closer to or farther from the sun at certain times in its orbit. Thus, that teacher can dislodge students' interpretations of this picture as reaffirming their nearer/farther explanation for the seasons.

Establish the Value or Importance of What Is Being Taught Motivational factors play an important role in changing students' knowledge and beliefs (Linnenbrink & Pintrich, 2002; Sinatra, 2002). By helping students recognize the merits of particular topics or tasks, teachers are more likely to stimulate students' interest or enhance the value assigned to those topics or tasks. For example much is gained if teachers show students how a particular topic or task relates to them personally and to their everyday lives (Dewey, 1916/1944). For this reason the instructional units in the successful CORI program (Guthrie, Van Meter et al., 1998) start out with captivating hands-on activities, to generate interest and help set the stage for the conceptual learning that follows.

Stress the Idea That Teachers Are Just One Source of Credible Information Students are not apt to engage in deep processing or reflection on any topic if they assume that their only task is to figure out what the teacher thinks is correct (Petty & Cacioppo, 1986). Nor are they apt to manifest critical and reflective thinking if they risk ridicule or reprimand any time they pose an alternative explanation or frame a counterargument. Creating an open and risk-free environment demands that teachers remove themselves as the one true authority.

This approach does not require teachers to avoid any evaluative comments or shy away from presenting prevailing views. Students need to see their teachers as credible and informed (Hynd, 2001b), but teachers must not be too quick to provide the correct or expected response to a problem. Instead, they should encourage students to arrive at their own conclusions and outcomes (Guzzetti & Hynd, 1998). To shift the role of authority and give students the opportunity for greater self-determination, teachers should allow some activities in the classroom to be student-led or student-directed (Ryan & Deci, 2000b). LeeAnn, for example, could have allowed students to select among possible activities or experiences for their unit on animal classifications. Should they watch the video about animals, read a book about animal classifications, or look up some information on the computer? Permitting her students to make this curricular determination would increase their feeling of involvement in the unit while exposing them to multiple sources of credible information.

Teach Students How to Frame Sound Arguments and Provide Support for Their Assertions   The skills of argumentation and persuasion do not come naturally or easily (Toulmin, 1958), as Aristotle emphasized in his *Rhetoric* (Cooper, 1932). In the realm of conceptual change, individuals must be able to offer convincing evidence or compelling examples to support their positions (Toulmin, 1958). Even though some adults have difficulty in this regard, research shows that students as young as 9 or 10 can be taught how to recognize weak and strong arguments in text and to develop sound arguments of their own (Chambliss, 1995; VanSledright, 1996).

The models of persuasion that teachers provide students, both orally and in writing, are one step in this learning process. Those models can help students see the difference between weak and strong arguments and can illustrate how certain features, like the picture accompanying the article in the persuasion Thought Experiment, can make arguments more persuasive. LeeAnn might prompt her young students to support their own approaches to classification or evaluate the strengths of others' classification systems. Students would thus come to see that simply producing an answer or solution is not sufficient. They need to explore the reasoning and the assumptions reflected in the answer (M. C. Linn, Songer, & Eylon, 1996).

Evaluate Not Only the Answers That Students Produce, But Also Their Processes of Analysis and Argumentation   Teachers should establish the importance of thinking critically by assessing students on the basis of not only their responses, but also their analysis or alternative perspectives (Campione, Shapiro, & Brown, 1995; Garner, 1990). Teachers may say that they care about students' views or value students' willingness to become deeply engaged in a topic, but unless teachers evaluate process as well as product students are unlikely to alter their perception of learning.

Students often do what is required to get a good grade in a class (Schellings & van Hout-Wolters, 1995) even if that means suppressing their own beliefs or understandings in favor of the position espoused by the classroom authority, particularly their teacher or their textbook (Alexander, Jetton, Kulikowich, & Woehler, 1994; Schellings, van Hout-Wolters, & Vermunt, 1996). When Alexander and colleagues (1994) interviewed students in science classes, some of the brightest commented that they occasionally give answers that they know are wrong but that are the answers their teachers expect. To those students, getting the grade or the teacher's recognition is more important than being right in a scientific sense.

Model Ways to Judge the Credibility or Positionality of Sources   Students in today's world are inundated with information, much of which is questionable or comes from highly suspect sources (Bereiter, 2002). If students are not to be susceptible to the "noise" that surrounds them, they must have the tools to evaluate the sources of such information (M. C. Linn et al., 1996). This need is particularly important in this era when anyone can contribute to information on the World Wide Web (Landow, 1992), and the resulting texts can easily find their way into children's conceptual framework.

Teachers can serve as effective models of the ability to judge the credibility of sources (Wineburg, 1991b). They can provide students with criteria for judging sources (VanSledright, 1996), and they can also explain that certain sources might be associated with particular stances or positions (Alexander & Jetton, 2003). Moreover, they can model the importance of cross-validation or cross-referencing as a means to establish credibility. Because the information that students encounter both in and out of school can have potent effects on their understandings and their beliefs (Afflerbach & VanSledright, 2001), at the very least teachers can help students become more sensitive to the persuasive features of sources that may not be reliable.

What Can Be Done to Promote the Transfer of Knowledge?

The goals of education extend beyond the creation and enrichment of knowledge and beliefs, they concern the utility and transportability of knowledge—that is, **transfer,** or the ability to use what is learned in one situation in a novel situation (De Corte, 1999; Marini & Genereux, 1995). If educators succeed at changing students' minds but fail at helping students see the usefulness of their learning in new and varied contexts, the educational mission remains incomplete. However, this fundamental goal is hard to accomplish.

When LeeAnn was introducing her students to the way scientists group animals, one of her goals was to help them understand the underlying basis for scientific classification. Rather than simply telling them what characteristics scientists use and expecting them to memorize the information, she encouraged her students to conduct their own exploration and discover the answer themselves. This approach resembles that advocated by Gestalt psychologists, who rejected behaviorist notions of learning. The German psychologists who were part of the Gestalt movement of the early 20th century believed that the behaviorist orientation to learning, which stressed environmental shaping and conditioning, overlooked the power of human problem solving (Duncker, 1945). They believed that the key to problem solving was not rote memorization of relevant information, but rather understanding of the underlying structure of problems or tasks. Once this underlying structure is grasped, individuals can apply their knowledge more broadly and fluidly in other contexts. Take a moment to explore this distinction in problem solving by completing the Thought Experiment: Trying Your Hand at a Puzzling Task.

Thought Experiment ....

Trying Your Hand at a Puzzling Task

Directions: Here are three different parallelograms. Explain how to determine the area of each.

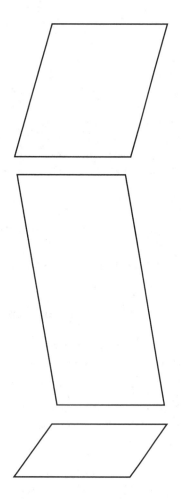

(Answer at the end of the chapter)

Note: From *Productive Thinking* by M. Wertheimer, 1959, New York: Harper & Row. Copyright 1959 by Harper & Row. Adapted with permission.

• •

This puzzle activity is actually a version of a classic problem devised in the 1940s by M. Wertheimer, a leading Gestalt psychologist. He used such problems to illustrate what he referred to as the difference between reproductive and productive thinking (Wertheimer, 1945/1959). **Reproductive thinking** means echoing or mimicking thoughts or procedures presented by others. **Productive thinking,** on the other hand, involves constructing new interpretations or devising new insights from available information. With this activity students who are reproductive thinkers try to recall the formula that they were taught for finding the area of parallelograms, revert to some sort of trial-and-error method until they hit upon a workable solution, or just quit. In contrast, productive thinkers try to understand the basic forms that are presented and explore how their knowledge of related objects, such as rectangles, can assist them in deriving a solution.

Were you a reproductive or a productive thinker in solving the Thought Experiment?

If you solved the puzzling task by applying your knowledge of how to find the area of a rectangle to determine the dimensions of those parallelograms, you reshaped and redefined the problem to conform to what you knew and could do. You were thereby engaging in transfer (McKeough et al., 1995; Salomon & Perkins, 1989). Productive thinkers transfer; nonproductive thinkers fail to use the knowledge they possess in a less familiar situation (Wertheimer, 1945/1959) and thus fail to transfer.

The Nature of Transfer

Gestalt psychologists argued vehemently that methods relying on rote memorization or meaningless drill and practice were detrimental to deeper learning (Duncker, 1945). They saw such approaches as restricting individuals' abilities to perceive situations in alternative ways. They also believed such methods limited individuals' examination of underlying problem structures and related principles, the very approaches that promote transfer. These concerns, voiced more than 50 years ago, are still being raised today (Marini & Genereu, 1995). Educational practitioners and researchers continue to see rote and mindless instruction as hindrances to optimal learning (Alexander & Murphy, 1999b).

Rote instruction, however, is just one factor contributing to the failure to transfer that is so often observed—and deplored—by educational practitioners and researchers (Griffin, Case, & Capodilupo, 1995). The issue of transfer remains one of the most troubling to practitioners and researchers alike (McKeough et al., 1995). Even in classrooms where teachers stress understanding over memorization and principled knowledge over piecemeal information, students are not immune to the failure-to-transfer malady.

Marilyn Chambliss (personal communication, 2000) shares a real experience from her classroom-based research. She talks about her efforts to teach fourth and fifth graders about argument structures in social studies and science texts, with the goal of having the students able to use such structures in their own writing. She vividly describes the wonderful results from her students as they worked in groups with a particular science text. As she moved from group to group and also analyzed the transcripts, Chambliss saw ample evidence that the students comprehended what the authors were trying to say and could see the strengths and weaknesses of their written arguments. In addition, these student groups produced solid paragraphs when requested to cast their own positions in writing.

Later, however, when Chambliss asked the students to engage in those same processes on their own, using texts similar in structure but different in topic, only a few appeared to have learned the procedures they previously had demonstrated so clearly. Chambliss also found that the student groups that performed so effectively with science texts experienced many more problems when the task shifted to social studies. Thus, the students' solid performance in group settings did not transfer to their individual performance or to an alternative domain. This experience emphasizes that transfer is a complex and multifaceted phenomenon.

Extraordinary Versus Everyday Transfer

Although few in the educational community would claim that students manifest effective transfer consistently, there is great debate about how well or how often transfer occurs. At one extreme some claim that occurrences of transfer are "rarer than volcanic eruptions and large earthquakes" and as difficult to predict (Detterman, 1993, p. 2). And no age group or population is excluded from this harsh judgment. Detterman goes on to state that "if you want people to learn something, teach it to them" (1993, p. 21). In other words, teachers should not count on any form of transfer occurring in their students but should teach them exactly what they want the students to know.

At the other extreme, some researchers see evidence of transfer everywhere "There are vast areas in which transfer is not a problem at all and where it is so straightforward that no one bothers to do research on it" (Bereiter, 1995, p. 26). Transfer thus perceived pertains to the learning of fundamental processes, such as reading or writing skills, and to the application of conceptual learning across contexts, such as using the knowledge of motion in physical education as well as in physics. For example, most learners acquire the ability to read and comprehend innumerable texts that they were never specifically taught to read. According to Bereiter

(1995), there are fundamental processes acquired in almost every domain that are regularly and almost effortlessly transported across tasks and across contexts.

One way to reconcile these two opposing perspectives is to think of transfer as assuming multiple forms (Campione et al., 1995). This is the approach that Debra Gentner and A. B. Markman (1997) take, distinguishing between *extraordinary* and *everyday* transfer. Detterman (1993) would, in their judgment, hold to the extraordinary view; that is, he sees transfer as involving significant insights that others would judge as highly creative or transforming. Galileo's observations of pendulum motions as the trigger to his science of motion or Franklin's fascination with lightning as a catalyst to his principles of electricity would represent this form of transfer. Gentner and Markman (1997) likened this extraordinary form of transfer to comets—riveting, brilliant, and rare flashes of perspicacity that streak through an individual's mind.

In contrast, the much more numerous, mundane, highly predictable, and less dramatic occasions of transfer—the kind Bereiter (1995) describes—often go unnoticed. These cases of everyday transfer, according to Gentner and Markman (1997), are like planets that move about the heavens in predictable and regular fashion. Thus, a 5-year-old, who learns to count to 10 with attribute blocks spontaneously counts to 10 when handed teddy-bear counters that look nothing like the initial set of blocks. Society may not judge this act as a remarkable or earth-shattering event, but it is an important step in this 5-year-old's learning, transferring understanding of the counting principle to a new situation.

How can both these extraordinary and everyday forms of learning warrant the label *transfer*? As Gentner and Markman (1997) note, both comets and planets are regulated by similar fundamental principles despite their diverse looks or actions, and both are astronomical phenomena. Likewise, both Franklin's discoveries about electricity and the 5-year-old's realization about counting deal with the underlying principle that knowledge acquired under one set of circumstances can be used in another that appears dissimilar. In other words, both illustrate productive rather than reproductive thinking, and productive thinking is transfer.

Positive Versus Negative Transfer

What individuals know (or think they know) about the world can sometimes blind them to learning opportunities (Murphy, 1998). People may be tempted to search for the familiar in novel situations or for reconfirmation of existing beliefs. In so doing, they can miss other more salient characteristics that might send them in a different mental direction. To make this point, try your hand at another classic task in the Thought Experiment: Putting Your Knowledge to the Test.

> *The argument against transfer becomes more believable when one realizes that universities are full of people who are attempting to make one significant transfer. They are called professors.*

D. K. Detterman, 1993, p. 2.

Thought Experiment ···

Putting Your Knowledge to the Test

Directions: You have been given only the objects pictured here to work with—a candle, a box of thumbtacks, and a book of matches. Your task is to devise some means of mounting that candle vertically to a nearby wall so that it can serve as a source of light. Good luck!

Note: From "On Problem Solving" by K. Duncker, 1945, *Psychological Monographs, 50*, (5). Copyright 1945 by *Psychological Monographs*. Adapted with permission.

···

Were you able to come up with a way to mount the candle on the wall? The solution was easy if you realized that the box holding the thumbtacks could serve as a minishelf. Tack the box onto the wall, set the candle into the box, and there you have it. The problem is that many people think of the box only as a container for the thumbtacks, and this perception keeps them from seeing the possibility to use it as a shelf. The phrase *functional fixedness* has been coined to describe this tendency to see objects or experiences from a single, everyday point of view (Duncker, 1945). Functional fixedness is one way that knowledge hinders transfer (Salomon & Perkins, 1989); the result is **negative transfer.** In this case knowledge hurts performance (Holyoak & Thagard, 1997).

Much of the research on transfer has been done in the fields of mathematics and science, yet transfer is also a factor in ill-structured domains, as illustrated by an example from recent history. During Lyndon Johnson's presidency, the United States leadership agonized over a strategy for dealing with the ongoing and increasingly unpopular Vietnam War. The president and his key advisors drew on earlier experiences in the Korean War as their strategic model for conducting the war in Vietnam. In effect, they transferred their knowledge of the Korean War to the Vietnam War. The problem, which became apparent in ensuing years, was that the conflicts in Vietnam and Korea were unique situations. The strategy that worked for the United States in Korea only escalated the conflict in Vietnam.

It may be impossible to avoid negative transfer, even for individuals trying to be open-minded and perceptive (Bereiter, 1995). However, the goal of educators remains **positive transfer,** which is the ability to use existing knowledge to facilitate learning and development in new and varied contexts (Marini & Genereux, 1995). Students must develop a capacity for positive transfer because teachers cannot teach them everything they need to know (Detterman, 1993), and students must be able to apply school-based knowledge in other contexts. Educators teach their students to think and perform well in domains like reading, mathematics, and history because they want them to carry that knowledge with them across content domains, across grades, and into the world outside the classroom. Educators aim for positive transfer at many levels.

Near and Far Transfer

Even when positive transfer does occur, it does not always happen in leaps and bounds, but often in small steps. Transfer that occurs in small steps across tasks that are highly similar is called **near transfer** (Salomon & Perkins, 1989). For example, when the 5-year-old moved from counting attribute blocks to counting teddy-bear counters, she was likely exhibiting near transfer. Likewise, a second grader who was taught how to solve addition problems in a vertical format— for example,

$$\begin{array}{cccc} \mathbf{6} & \mathbf{3} & \mathbf{1} & \mathbf{7} \\ \underline{+2} & \underline{+3} & \underline{+5} & \underline{+1} \end{array}$$

but who then independently solved problems in a horizontal format—for example,

$$5 + 2 = \qquad 8 + 1 = \qquad 6 + 5 = \qquad 2 + 1 =$$

would be showing evidence of near transfer.

When the distance is greater between what has been taught and what is required for the new application of knowledge—that is, the resemblance of the tasks performed is much less direct—a student manifests **far transfer** (Salomon & Perkins, 1989). For example, a student may have been taught procedures for sourcing historical texts, determining whether a source is primary or secondary and what the authors' potential biases or positions may be. Later, when searching online to find materials for a science project on black holes, that student begins to question whether the Internet sites he is using are good. To make that determination, he decides to use a variation of the sourcing procedure he learned in history. Not only are the surface features of these two tasks different (i.e., traditional history texts versus hypermedia Websites), but so are some of their underlying demands (e.g., ascertaining authorship). This student is engaged in far transfer.

E. L. Thorndike (1924), one of the founding fathers of American psychology, conceptualized the distance between what is taught and what is applied somewhat differently. Instead of near and far transfer, Thorndike spoke of *specific* and *general* transfer. His research, conducted early in the 20th century, set out to test the popular notion that studying certain demanding subjects—such as Latin, philosophy, or rhetoric—would result in a general improvement in students' thinking and academic performance. Thorndike called this **general transfer**—the positive and global effect on general academic performance as a result of learning one body of rigorous content.

To test for general transfer, Thorndike (with Woodworth, 1901) worked with some people who had taken "mind-expanding" courses such as Latin and with others who had not. They taught all participants to estimate the size of squares that ranged between 10 and 100 cm² in size. Once participants learned this task adequately (sometimes after thousands of trials), they were asked to estimate the size of rectangles between 20 and 90 cm² in size. In addition, Thorndike and Woodworth had participants do the same thing with a variety of shapes other than squares or rectangles. And participants in one experiment tried out their newly acquired estimation skills on squares larger than 100 cm² (Thorndike & Woodworth, 1901). Through such research Thorndike reported no significant differences in transfer performance between participants who had taken the mind-expanding courses and those who had not. The performance of the former was unimpressive, especially when varied shapes or larger squares were used. Thus, Thorndike and colleagues concluded that general transfer did not occur, and others have come to similar conclusions (Detterman, 1993).

In Thorndike's studies training that was effective at all tended to be for shapes that were very similar, such as squares and rectangles. Thorndike (1924) called these cases **specific transfer.** Thus, studying Latin probably will not translate into better performance in history or writing, but it might prove useful in learning another Latin-based language such as Spanish.

Although most educational researchers believe that far, or general, transfer is difficult to achieve, they do not consider it an impossibility. Some believe that more distant transfer can be accomplished through effective training and priming of appropriate thought processes (Holyoak & Thagard, 1995, 1997). For instance, researchers had college students read the tumor problem presented in the Thought Experiment: Finding the Cure (Gick & Holyoak, 1980). Take a minute to read the problem and see whether you can propose a solution.

Thought Experiment ....

Finding the Cure

Directions: Read the following problem. Then see whether you can devise some means to destroy the tumor without unduly injuring the patient in the process.

Suppose you are a doctor faced with a patient who has a malignant tumor in his stomach. It is impossible to operate on the patient, but unless the tumor is destroyed, the patient will die. There is a kind of ray that can be used to destroy the tumor. If the rays reach the tumor all at once at a sufficiently high intensity, the tumor will be destroyed. Unfortunately, at this intensity, the healthy tissue that the rays pass through on the way to the tumor will also be destroyed. At lower intensities the rays are harmless to healthy tissue, but they will not affect the tumor either. What type of procedure might be used to destroy the tumor with the rays and at the same time avoid destroying the healthy tissue?

Note: From "Analogical Problem Solving" by M. L. Gick and K. J. Holyoak, 1980, *Cognitive Psychology*, *12*, pp. 307–308. Copyright 1980 by *Cognitive Psychology*. Adapted with permission.

•••

If you were like the college students in the study, you found it difficult to find an effective solution to this perplexing problem; only 10% were able to come up with a workable answer. However, the results were much better for students who first had the opportunity to read a seemingly unrelated problem, "The Fortress Story," and who were told that this story might prove useful to them as they confronted other problems. Stop and read "The Fortress Story" in the Thought Experiment: Fortifying Response and then reconsider the tumor problem (Gick & Holyoak, 1980).

Keith Holyoak's creative tasks have contributed to understanding of transfer.

Thought Experiment ....

Fortifying Response

Directions: What follows is a story about a general's attempt to storm an impenetrable fortress. You may find some ideas here that will be advantageous to you as you try to tackle other problems.

A small country fell under the iron rule of a dictator. The dictator ruled the country from a strong fortress. The fortress was situated in the middle of the country, surrounded by farms and villages. Many roads radiated outward from the fortress like spokes on a wheel. A great general arose who raised a large army at the border and vowed to capture the fortress and free the country from the dictator. The general knew that if his entire army could attack the fortress at once it could be captured. His troops were poised at the head of one of the roads leading to the fortress, ready to attack. However, a spy brought the general a disturbing report. The ruthless dictator had planted mines on each of the roads. The mines were set so that small bodies of men could pass over them safely, since the dictator needed to be able to move troops and workers to and from the fortress. However, any large force would detonate the mines. Not only would this blow up the road and render it impassable, but the dictator would destroy many villages in retaliation. A full-scale direct attack on the fortress therefore appeared impossible.

The general, however, was undaunted. He divided his army up into small groups and dispatched each group to the head of a different road. When all was ready, he gave the signal, and each group charged down a different road. All of the small groups passed safely over the mines, and the army then attacked the fortress in full strength. In this way, the general was able to capture the fortress and overthrow the dictator.

Note: From "Analogical Problem Solving" by M. L. Gick and K. J. Holyoak, 1980, *Cognitive Psychology*, *12*, p. 311. Copyright 1980 by *Cognitive Psychology*. Reprinted with permission.

• •

After reading "The Fortress Story," were you better prepared to solve the tumor problem? Did you realize that the doctor, like the general, could attack the target from multiple directions simultaneously? With this technique the full intensity of the invading forces (i.e., rays) could hit the target (i.e., tumor) without damaging the surrounding area or tissues. In the original study, 75% of the college students who read "The Fortress Story" first and received the prompt to think about this information when confronting the tumor problem came up with this solution (Gick & Holyoak, 1980). Of course, 25% of the college students still did not engage in transfer, even when they were prompted to do so. Transfer is *not* easy to achieve!

Teaching for Transfer

Gick and Holyoak's (1980) study offers some cause for optimism regarding the likelihood of transfer, but the possibility of transfer simply cannot be left to fate. There seems to be no question that transfer is an essential dimension of competent performance in any complex domain: Students cannot achieve competence in history, mathematics, reading, or any other field without applying knowledge across tasks and across contexts (Alexander, 1997b; VanSledright, 1996). Thus, teachers must ensure that the conditions for transfer are more commonplace in learning environments.

Two researchers, Gavriel Salomon and David Perkins (1989) have actually mapped out two distinct paths to achieve transfer in classrooms—the low road and the high road. The low road to transfer is reminiscent of Detterman's (1993) admonition: If you want students to learn something, then teach them. **Low-road transfer** is a mindless transfer of the nearest kind, achieved by the continued, routine practice of problem-solving skills. The tasks that are the focus of low-road transfer show a great deal of surface similarity and have highly consistent underlying procedures. The objective is to make the transfer virtually effortless. For instance, for a 5-year-old to improve her phonological abilities, her teacher might concentrate on word families, beginning with *it*. Once the child learned to recognize and pronounce *it*, the teacher would have her repeatedly add familiar initial sounds to this stem, such as *hit*, *sit*, *fit*, and *bit*. The teacher could eventually introduce her to another word family, such as *an*, which she would practice in the same way—*fan*, *tan*, and *man*.

The other path to transfer, the high road, goes beyond explicit surface-level elements and direct comparisons. The focus moves instead to deep concepts, underlying principles, and foundational procedures. **High-road transfer** requires mindful and reflective exploration of complex problems encountered from diverse perspectives. For example, once LeeAnn Delli's students grasp the idea that animals can be classified according to their internal biological structures, she can help them use that principle in other domains. She might present her students with a variety of plant specimens and see whether they could apply their new understanding of internal structures to classifying those plants (e.g., those with divided or undivided leaves). This would be a case of high-road transfer.

Salomon and Perkins (1989) consider Matthew Lipman's (1991) Philosophy for Children program to be an effective example of high-road transfer. In this program students read short stories and use the story content as the basis for discussion of philosophical issues cast around social, moral, and political dilemmas. Data show that students participating in this program show higher performance in general reasoning, reading, and mathematics than nonparticipants. Counter to Thorndike and Woodworth's (1901) findings reported almost half a century earlier, these results seem to suggest that general transfer effects are possible after all.

Such effects are not achieved without concerted efforts, however. Programs that report low-road transfer and certainly those that can boast high-road transfer are orchestrated toward those ends. Among the characteristics of programs that lead to transfer are adequate time for and attention to central concepts, multiple and varied opportunities for transfer, instruction in basic problem-solving procedures or strategies, and use of pedagogical procedures that promote meaningful interaction with content. The following guidelines promote transfer in classroom settings.

Devote Sufficient Instructional Time to Concepts and Procedures   Before transfer can occur, students must possess a body of knowledge that can be fluidly and flexibly applied in alternative contexts or to novel problems. In other words, students must know something before transfer in any form is possible (Reeves & Weisberg, 1994; Thagard, 1991). This depth of knowledge cannot be expected from instructional environments in which content is treated superficially. Because inert knowledge is a barrier to transfer (Whitehead, 1929/1967), educators committed to transfer work to ensure that concepts and procedures are well taught and well learned.

However, transfer is not promoted simply by achieving time on task. Two groups of students can spend equivalent time on a particular concept or procedure yet one group may use that time in rather rote, mindless activity, whereas the other may be engaged in mindful and reflective analysis (Salomon & Perkins, 1989). Particularly if high-road transfer is the aim, teachers must work to stimulate the mindful engagement of students. In other words, they must do more than *mention* content. They should provide rich and diverse examples, promote student discussion and explanation, and reinforce students' attempts to look into the heart of the problem or task at hand. In other words, they should teach for principled understanding (Gelman & Greeno, 1989), as the Gestalt psychologists recommended half a century ago (Wertheimer, 1945/1959).

Concentrate Educational Energies on Concepts and Principles That Are Foundational   Research studies have raised questions about the concepts that teachers stress or even choose to mention in classrooms: Are the central concepts and procedures that contribute to a body of principled knowledge (Gelman & Greeno, 1989) necessarily given more weight instructionally than tangential notions (Thagard, 1991)? For example, researchers have described teachers who were highly effective at capturing student interest and attention in science classrooms and who devoted sufficient instructional time to the activity at hand but who chose to build their instructional time around content that is interesting yet quite peripheral to the central topic (Jetton & Alexander, 1997). When students were learning about astronomical phenomena such as black holes and singularities, for instance, some teachers elected to spend significant instructional time on Stephen Hawking's personal life and a Disney movie on black holes. As a result, the subsequent perform-

ance of their students on related tasks was impeded. If teachers are to give greater weight to important content, they must understand a topic or domain sufficiently to know what constitutes foundational knowledge (Singley & Anderson, 1989).

This issue of the centrality of instructional content is essential, not only because students need to know certain things in the immediate context but also because core concepts and foundational principles transfer better than concepts or processes that are more tangential (Alexander & Murphy, 1999b). When teachers treat content superficially or devote important instructional time to irrelevant information rather than to key concepts, their students are less likely to form the principled body of knowledge needed for transfer (Alexander, 1997a). As one researcher recommends, teachers should consider teaching more about less (diSessa, 1989), with sufficient time on key concepts, they may be better able to create a foundation for transfer. Moreover, when educators are free to teach more about less, they can revisit central notions under varying conditions and in diverse fashions, thereby promoting transfer. The instructional time that LeeAnn Delli devoted to the central concept of vertebrates and invertebrates not only deepened her students' understanding of this idea, but also exposed those students to a wealth of related ideas and experiences.

Present Key Concepts and Procedures in Multiple Forms and Varying Contexts   The lesson illustrated by the previous challenge to attach a candle to a wall, using a box of thumbtacks, highlights an important principle—that knowledge actually can hinder transfer. That is, the more that students are exposed to instructional content framed in nearly identical fashion and the more that they are asked to replicate given instructional conditions, the less likely they are to use knowledge and skills flexibly or innovatively (Salomon & Perkins, 1989). In effect, when learning becomes a habit, it may work against transfer.

For example, on a standardized test administered in one state, students are scored on their ability to write a good paragraph. The score for this task depends on whether they include an explicit introductory statement, several supporting-detail sentences, and a summary or concluding sentence. The sandwich format is what students and teachers aptly call this writing structure. To improve students' performance on this major test, teachers in many classrooms have adopted the sandwich format as their sole model of good writing. The good news is that this obsessive focus has raised students' scores on the statewide assessment. The bad news is that this approach to writing has been so entrenched in students' thinking that even prompts to be creative or to deviate do not result in novel or innovative forms of writing. Students have been taught well—maybe *too* well (Sternberg, 2003).

This example illustrates the low road to transfer and its residual effects. Because students rely on the sandwich format in much of their writing, some measure of transfer has occurred. However, the predominance of this one model may well block subsequent attempts to teach students alternative writing models or to have them see the sandwich

> *Sheer imitation, dictation of steps to be taken, mechanical drill may give results most quickly and yet strengthen traits likely to be fatal to reflective power.*
>
> J. Dewey, 1991, p.51.

model as just a starting point for their writing. It could well become an obstacle to deeper and more general forms of transfer (Alexander, 1998c).

Teachers should make it their goal to revisit fundamental concepts and procedures often and in diverse ways. Embodied learning, which uses all of students' senses meaningfully, promotes the reflection and analysis required for transfer—whether learners are 8 or 80.

Teach Students to Think Analogically   Research has shown that the processes involved in transfer and those required to reason analogically are similar. In fact, researchers have argued that transfer is a special case of analogical reasoning (Alexander & Murphy, 1999b). **Analogical reasoning** is based on the process of discerning relations among aspects of two seemingly dissimilar ideas, objects, or events (Alexander, Willson, White, & Fuqua, 1987). This process usually entails applying the characteristics of a known area, the source, to an unfamiliar or dissimilar area, the target. Detterman's (1993) comparison of transfer to volcanoes and earthquakes and Gentner and Markman's (1997) use of comets and planetary movements as illustrations of transfer are both examples of analogical reasoning. In these cases researchers used familiar physical events, such as earthquakes and planetary movement, to explain a less concrete, less known construct, such as transfer. Similarly, pointing out various similarities, as well as certain differences, in the two literatures on conceptual change and on persuasion also represents analogical reasoning. And learning to think analogically was likewise at the heart of the students' experience in LeeAnn's project on animal classification. They had to learn to group animals as vertebrates or invertebrates, irrespective of other apparent similarities or differences.

If learners fail to see the similarities between particular tasks or contexts, it is improbable that they will engage in the mindful transfer of conceptual or procedural knowledge across tasks or contexts (Kolodner, 1997).

Helping students to compare and contrast concepts and procedures as they are learning, both within and across content fields, is an effective method for priming analogical thought (Schunn & Dunbar, 1996). Chapter 7 looks more extensively at strategies and at specific recommendations for teaching analogical reasoning. Overall, the more comfortable students are with such reflective and comparative thinking and the more cognizant they are of procedures that facilitate comparison and contrast, the more apt they are to

exhibit what Bereiter (1995) calls a disposition to transfer. Examining how some new idea, object, or event compares to what is already known can become almost second nature when students learn to think analogically.

Prompt Students' Thinking and Build Bridging Activities into Instruction   Another step that is effective in promoting transfer was illustrated in the tumor/fortress study encountered earlier (Gick & Holyoak, 1980): The researchers achieved a fairly good level of transfer among undergraduates when they provided them with a priming story and reminded them to think about that story later when confronted with a new problem. Thus, a teacher can set the stage for transfer by calling students' attention to topics and concepts that have potential linkages to forthcoming areas of study (Garner, 1990). When that new task or topic is introduced, teachers can question students to see whether anything they have learned earlier pertains to the task or topic at hand. Setting the stage for later transfer is called **bridging** because it provides students with a pathway from old to new content (Campione et al., 1995). The reminders offered by teachers to encourage students to reach back into prior content are called **prompting.**

Bridging and prompting allow teachers to be models of transfer (Alexander & Murphy, 1999b). In essence, they show students that teachers are reflecting on the relationships that exist in content across instructional episodes. In addition, these pedagogical techniques signal to students that such comparative and integrative thinking is valued in the classroom.

Effective bridging does not always involve current and future content, bridging is also valuable in linking current to past learning, as well as in-school content to out-of-school experiences. For instance, rather than seeing geography, history, sociology, and economics as completely independent fields of studies, high-school students can be helped to form cross-domain associations. They can then recognize how thriving cultures took the topography of the land into account and how events in their histories of those cultures were driven as much by the search for material goods and economic prosperity as by concern for the general welfare of the population. Further, students can be prompted to look for similar cross-domain associations in contemporary societies and current events.

As a complement to prompting and bridging for transfer, teachers should provide students with effective feedback. Effective feedback is much more than documenting whether students have discovered relevant relations or taken advantage of a transfer opportunity. Effective feedback illustrates for students what they have done well and where they can improve their performance. It suggests points in students' analyses where they should go deeper or think more broadly, and it highlights links that may have been overlooked or not considered (McKeough et al., 1995). Such feedback can strengthen the linkages within and across topics and domains of study.

The students in Chambliss's study may have realized that the argument structures in their science and social studies texts were similar, but perhaps they should have been alerted to the fact that similar structures can be found in all of their subjects if they look for them. Or in writing persuasive paragraphs, these fourth and fifth graders may have been particularly strong in stating their claims in science and social studies, but their performance may have illustrated that they are less clear as to what constitutes evidence in science, as compared to that in social studies. Detailed and informative feedback from their teacher might have given these students an opportunity to improve on their transfer performance (McKeough et al., 1995).

Create a Learning Environment That Supports the Sociocultural Dimensions of Transfer To this point, the suggestions for teaching for transfer have stressed cognitive and rather individualistic conditions, yet there are critical sociocultural dimensions that merit teachers' concern. Just as teachers can foster a disposition toward transfer for individual students by promoting the knowledge, strategies and motivational conditions that are the seeds of transfer, teachers can also do so for the community of learners. One approach is to use small group, discussion, and collaborative activities that encourage a rich exchange of ideas (M. C. Linn et al., 1996; Webb & Palincsar, 1996). As discussed in chapter 11, one of the advantages of shared learning is that new information and alternative perspectives can be introduced into the classroom environment that may not have emerged for students working independently. Further, because students may make their ideas public and understandable to others, there may be more need to recast ideas in new ways or to find connections and applications not previously considered. In effect, rich social exchanges can be fertile ground for transfer (Greeno, Smith, & Moore, 1996).

> *[The student's] chief concern is to accommodate himself to what the teacher expects of him, rather than to devote himself energetically to the problems of subject-matter.*
>
> J. Dewey, 1910/1991, pp. 49–50.

It is essential for teachers to set aside more didactic approaches to instruction when transfer is the goal. Even though a principled knowledge base supports the transfer of ideas, that knowledge base need not come at the expense of students' exploration or exchange of ideas (Perkins, 1992). The open exchange of ideas around complex and relevant problems that defy quick and simple solutions can create a climate for transfer among students (Cognition and Technology Group at Vanderbilt, 1996; Goldman, 1996). Further, when the social norm in the classroom is the application of previously learned knowledge and processes to novel or unfamiliar contexts, transfer is far more likely to

occur (Perkins, 1992; Salomon & Perkins, 1989). In such a probing environment, teachers and students might commonly ask questions like these (Fogarty, Perkins, & Barell, 1992): Is there another way we can do this problem? Does this current situation remind us of anything we have already learned?

Consider the Multidimensional Character of Successful Transfer The knowledge and reasoning skills needed for transfer are not a guarantee that transfer will occur. Sometimes students' demonstration of transfer comes down to their motivation to do so (Pintrich et al., 1993). Mindful transfer, after all, is effortful transfer (Salomon & Perkins, 1989). Teachers must focus on the learner, the task, and the context and acknowledge that the solution to a transfer problem depends upon knowledge, strategy, and motivational training (Griffin et al., 1995). And all of these dimensions must be considered simultaneously in the learning environment (Alexander & Murphy, 1999b). As in the tumor/fortress example, transfer must be approached from all sides. In addition, teachers must not expect that raising the issue of transfer only periodically will result in frequent and spontaneous application.

At a minimum a disposition toward transfer requires a rich and cohesive body of domain knowledge, a well-honed strategic repertoire, and personal investment in an academic topic or domain (Bereiter, 1995). These are what Alexander and Murphy (1999b) call the seeds of transfer. These seeds, unlike Jack in the Beanstalk's magic beans, cannot spring forth overnight into some monumental structure capable of transporting students into the realm of transfer. Only a long-term commitment to nurturing these seeds has any real hope of producing students with a propensity toward transfer. All the guidelines forwarded in this discussion are critical aspects of that nurturing and should be characteristics of education across the grades and across domains.

A multidimensional approach to teaching for transfer also needs to reflect the differences that exist among students at varying stages in their academic development (Alexander, 1997b; Lupart, 1995). For instance, students who are new to a particular domain need a foundation of relevant subject-matter knowledge to use as a springboard for transfer (Chi et al., 1988). These novice learners may also require more explicit and repeated instruction in the processes underlying transfer, as well as more prompting and bridging. However, even novice students can be prompted to make comparisons and contrasts between their current and past learning and between their world inside and outside the classroom (Alexander, 1997b; Roth, 1990).

Reward Occasions of Transfer Until transfer becomes a valued and rewarded component of the learning environment, many students who can engage in mindful transfer will fail to do so. Students are relatively effective at determining what is valued in the classroom context (Alexander & Jetton, 2003; Alexander, Jetton et al., 1994; Schellings et al., 1996). Further, they are surprisingly strategic at altering their behavior to conform to this instructional importance (Jetton & Alexander, 1997). Thus, teachers should seek ways to reward evidence of transfer not only through their words, but also in their evaluations. After all, what gets taught and what gets tested are what students ultimately learn.

■ Summary Reflections

Why is it sometimes difficult to alter students' naive conceptions?

- Life may simply overwhelm schooled knowledge; common sense, physical evidence, even popular culture may subordinate intellectual logic and rational theorizing.
- Conceptual change occurs on different levels.
  - Accretion is the elaboration or extension of existing knowledge structures.
  - Through a weak restructuring of mental frameworks, or tuning, conceptions can take on new and more sophisticated dimensions through maturation and everyday modifications.
  - Radical restructuring is an adjustment so profound that it entails an ontological shift, an altering of fundamental world views before powerful and irrefutable evidence (e.g., Gordian misconceptions).
- Researchers have identified the reasons people resist contradictory information.
  - Background knowledge may make it impossible to confront any one erroneous concept that is part of an overall world view.
  - A new theory might not be compelling, or it might allow for alternative viewpoints, making conviction difficult.
  - The quality of the evidence, if not compelling and if not offered by multiple sources, may make it harder to overcome conceptual resistance.
  - People may cling to existing ideas if their processing of new information is superficial.
  - Students may not be open to change or purposeful in pursuing knowledge.
  - The sociocultural climate may not support reflection and questioning.

How can students' knowledge and beliefs be profoundly changed?

- The insights gained from the literatures in conceptual change and persuasion can enrich understanding of change and expand approaches to prompt it.

- These two literatures complement each other in terms of their principal foci, typical domains and problems, primary paths to change, and key research findings.
  - Particularly effective in persuading readers is refutational text.
  - In two-sided refutation both sides of an issue are weighed, but the arguments on one side are refuted.
- Models that depict the change process are especially helpful to teachers.
  - They illuminate the factors underlying transformations in students' knowledge and beliefs.
  - They suggest steps that teachers can take to promote profound and enduring change.
- Guidelines for promoting change that are based on one particular model can help teachers be more effective at dislodging ideas or attitudes that interfere with optimal learning and development in their students.

What can be done to promote the transfer of knowledge?

- Some see occurrences of transfer as rare and thus believe that if you want students to learn something, you must teach it to them.
- Others see evidence of transfer everywhere and thus see vast areas in which transfer is not problematical at all.
- Transfer assumes multiple forms—brilliant flashes of perspicacity, or extraordinary transfer, and more numerous, less dramatic occasions of everyday transfer.
- Negative transfer can blind individuals to learning opportunities.
- Near transfer is distinguished from far transfer.
  - The former occurs in small steps across tasks that are very similar.
  - The latter requires a new application of knowledge at a greater distance from what has been taught.
  - General transfer is difficult to achieve but may be prompted through effective training and priming of appropriate mental processes.
- Teaching for transfer must be a focus of classroom efforts: Students simply cannot achieve competence in any field, inside or outside school, without applying knowledge across tasks and across contexts.
  - To promote transfer, teachers must be thoroughly grounded in their subject matter and disciplined in their focus on essential concepts.
  - They must help students learn to think analogically, prompt students' thinking by building bridging activities into instruction, create a learning environment that supports the sociocultural dimensions of transfer, and provide a multidimensional learning environment that rewards instances of transfer.

■ Solution to Thought Experiment: Trying Your Hand at a Puzzling Task

1. The successful transferrors in Wertheimer's study transformed the parallelograms into rectangles, as indicated. When faced with familiar rectangles, they could then recall that the area is found by multiplying the length (l) times the width (w).

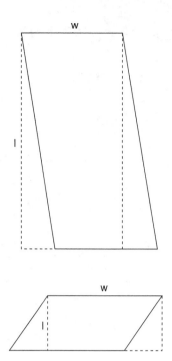

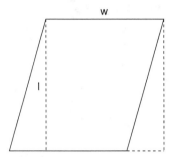

Chapter 7

Strategic Learning and Strategic Teaching

GUIDING QUESTIONS

■ What does it mean to be a strategic learner?

■ How do strategic abilities vary across domains and contexts?

■ What can teachers do to help students become more strategic?

IN THEIR OWN WORDS..

*P*am Gaskill has been a second-grade teacher for more than 20 years. Before that, she spent years tutoring children and youth with learning problems.

As an experienced teacher of second graders and learning-disabled children, I have acquired a deepening curiosity about how children learn and, perhaps more important, what teachers can do to facilitate each child's academic growth. My pursuit of this knowledge has led me to explore the influence of *self-efficacy* (i.e., how we judge our competence) and *self-regulated learning* (i.e., how we control the quality of our own work). Both of these forces are grounded in beliefs about self as agent. Access to specific learning strategies seems to give children the tools they need to gain more control of their learning and, in doing so, see themselves as more capable and successful learners. This was an idea I wanted to test.

Second graders in our school were already well acquainted with many kinds of strategies. We work on problem-solving strategies in mathematics, strategies for decoding and comprehension in reading, spelling strategies, and even desk-organizing strategies. We assume that access to these strategies helps the children to perform better.

But I wanted to design a study that would have concrete, measurable results to see if knowing a specific strategy could really improve my students' learning. I selected a very simple strategy—sorting or categorizing—to see if it would increase my second graders' ability to memorize word lists.

On the first trial, I showed the children a set of 16 words on index cards and asked them to predict how many of the words they would remember after 2 minutes. The words could easily be sorted into four groups (e.g., colors) of four related words (e.g., yellow, purple, white, and orange). But I presented the words to the children in a random order. After they made their predictions and studied the 16 words, I asked the children to write down as many of them as they could.

Only Terry figured out that the words could be grouped. He used that strategy the very first time he tried the task. Other students attempted all sorts of strategies, some of which were effective (e.g., alphabetizing) and some of which were relatively useless (e.g., rehearsal). For example, when asked what they did to help themselves remember, some students said "I kept going over and over and over the words," "I read them four times and then put them in my head," or "I just looked at the letters and knew I could remember it." Others said they "looked at the beginning letters," "looked for little words in the big words," or "read the words back and forth and then up and down." Clearly, these students innately understood that they had to try something. But the strategies they employed were typically not very helpful.

Because the words were so familiar to the children and the groups seemed so obvious, I was very surprised that only Terry thought of putting the related words together. While they practiced saying the words, some of the children even spontaneously sorted the words into related groups. However, they seemed unaware of what they were doing or why it might be helpful.

On the second trial, half of the students were taught the sorting strategy and actually laid the 16 cards out in groups of related words before they studied. The other children simply repeated the prediction/study/recall activity as before. What an amazing difference teaching the strategy made! While two thirds of the trained students were able to list all 16 of the words by using the sorting strategy, only one of the comparison children was that successful. The children who had successfully used the strategy were very pleased and were confident that they could do just as well if given another chance.

When they came back the next week for a third trial, the trained students remembered and used the categorizing strategy without any prompting. When the children in the comparison group came back, however, they appeared frustrated and discouraged. Their actual numbers of words recalled were lower on Trial 3 than they were on Trial 1. The trained children's mean scores nearly doubled. Untrained children were still saying things like "I looked at the words and tried to sound them out," as they explained how they had tried to remember.

Perhaps the biggest revelation for me was the fact that so few of the children used the strategy before training, even though it seemed obvious and was easily in their grasp once it was pointed out to them. I think that gives us teachers an important message concerning the assumptions we make about our students. We need to take the extra time to point out the use of strategies, not just assume that our students are aware of them, if we want to help them to become confident, self-regulated learners.

What Does It Mean to Be a Strategic Learner?

Pam Gaskill has come to two conclusions that are paramount for optimal learning: (a) Effective learning demands effective strategic thinking, and (b) strategic processing can be improved through strategic teaching. A wealth of evidence indicates that people who are thoughtful and reflective and who behave in reasoned rather than haphazard or impulsive ways have the edge in responding to the many situations that confront them every day, in part because they can evaluate the triviality or significance of each (Garner, 1990; Weinstein & Mayer, 1986).

Such reflective individuals not only achieve well in school, but they also perform well in life (Ennis, 1987; Pugh, Pawan, & Antommarchi, 2000). These people do not just worry about events; they weigh situations, decide on a course of action, and then act (Bransford & Stein, 1984).

When thoughtfulness and reflection are accompanied by some plan of action, we say that the individual is behaving *strategically* (Alexander, Graham, & Harris, 1998). When those second graders in Pam's classroom applied their rather rudimentary techniques, like rehearsal, to help them remember their 16 words, they were trying to take some control of their situation. They were, in effect, acting strategically.

Strategies are essentially mental operations or techniques that are employed to solve problems or to enhance performance (Alexander & Jetton, 2000). Certain strategies are quite specific to a domain or task within that domain, which is why they are referred to as **domain specific** (Bruning, Schraw, & Ronning, 1999). An example of a domain-specific strategy is the FOIL method illustrated in Figure 7–1. Other strategies have broad applicability across various domains and tasks and are thereby termed **general strategies** (Alexander & Judy, 1988; Paris, Wasik, & Turner, 1991). Some are particularly useful at helping people capture and organize information (Armbruster, 2000) or understand and remember what they read or hear (Pressley et al., 1989) or keep them focused and motivated in their learning (Winne, 1985; Zimmerman, 2001). Table 7–1 identifies specific examples of general strategies.

As the Thought Experiment: Planning—Getting It Done seems to suggest, strategic thinking can occur in all facets of life. Unfortunately, many teachers and most students have misguided notions about thinking and problem solving that detract from their performance, several of which came to light in Pam's in-class experiment. This chapter seeks to dispel four common myths about strategies and strategic thinking:

1. Strategic thinking is merely skillful performance.
2. Good strategic thinking develops naturally.
3. An individual is equally strategic in all domains.
4. Teachers can do little to help their students become strategic.

Strategic Thinking Is More Than Skillful Performance

Occasionally, in educational exchanges the phrase *strategic thinking* is described as "skillful performance" or vice versa (Alexander, Kulikowich, & Schulze, 1994). Indeed, strategies and skills have certain characteristics in common. Both are forms of procedural knowledge, they involve a sequence of actions undertaken to complete a cognitive goal. Further, to achieve academic success in any field, students must exhibit both strategic and skillful behavior. Nonetheless, strategies and skills are not equivalent notions. They differ in at least two significant ways, which have serious implications for instruction and learning. The differences lie in how *conscious* or *purposeful* the use of particular cognitive and affective procedures is (Alexander, Graham, & Harris, 1998; Nist & Holschuh, 2000).

The FOIL method is a procedure for solving mathematical problems of the form $(4x + 3)(2x + 9)$.

FOIL is a mnemonic that stands for *first, outside, inside,* and *last.* The steps of the procedure are as follows:

1. Multiply the *first* terms. $(4x + 3)(2x + 9)$
   $8x^2$

2. Multiply the *outside* terms. $(4x + 3)(2x + 9)$
   $36x$

3. Multiply the *inside* terms. $(4x + 3)(2x + 9)$
   $6x$

4. Multiply the *last* terms. $(4x + 3)(2x + 9)$
   27

Solution: $(4x + 3)(2x + 9) = 8x^2 + 36x + 6x + 27 = 8x^2 + 42x + 27$

■ **FIGURE 7–1   An example of a domain-specific strategy.**

Table 7–1	Examples of general learning and study strategies.
Category	**Strategy**
Capturing and retaining information	Underlining or highlighting Notetaking Information search Questioning
Improving memory	Rehearsal Sorting and categorizing Method of loci Mnemonics Keyword mnemonics Analogical reasoning
Comprehending and recalling text	Identifying important ideas Predicting Summarizing Clarifying Elaborating Reaccessing text Transforming text
Organizing information	Outlining Conceptual mapping
Motivating performance	Goal setting Positive self-talk Self-rewarding
Monitoring and regulating learning	Task analysis Self analysis Help seeking Formative self-evaluation

Thought Experiment ....

Planning—Getting It Done

Directions: Imagine that it is Saturday and you have a long list of chores to complete. Devise a plan for completing these chores in the most efficient way. The map provided should help you work out your approach strategically. The star on the map marks your home. Number the chores in the order in which you will complete them.

_____ Prepare breakfast for the family

_____ Pick up clothes at the dry cleaners before 5:00 p.m. (Longmire and Deacon)

_____ Get kids to soccer practice by 8:30 a.m. (Brothers and Sonoma Circle)

_____ Get kids from soccer practice at 10:00 a.m.

_____ Straighten house (1 hour)

_____ Pay bills

_____ Do grocery shopping (Treehouse)

_____ Get medicines from the pharmacy (Rio Grande and Airline)

_____ Go to exercise class at 1:00 p.m. (Longmire and Deacon)

_____ Go by video store and pick up movies for the kids (Brothers and Deacon)

_____ Take package to the post office (Rio Grande and Airline)

_____ Do laundry (1 hour)

_____ Pick up babysitter (San Benito Dr.)

_____ Meet friends for dinner at 7:30 p.m. (Rio Grande and 2818)

_____ Take babysitter home

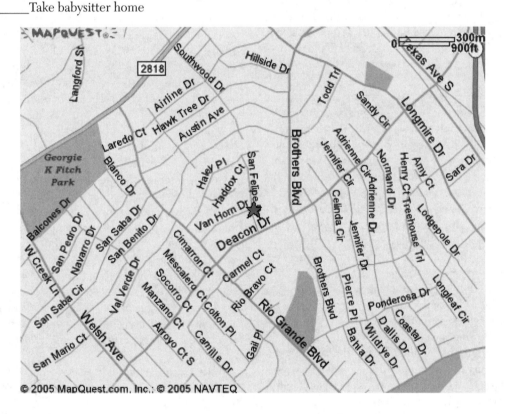

....

Simply stated, **skills** are procedures that have been routinized or habitualized; they are generally operating at an unconscious level. William James (1890) would classify skills as mental habits—actions typically taken in the face of simple and highly familiar situations. Ann Brown (1975) describes skillful performance as thinking that occurs on automatic pilot. Thus, skills are not innate abilities but are techniques acquired over time and honed until they become habits of the mind, requiring minimal cognitive energy.

The ability to read is an illustrative case of skillful performance. By definition, skillful readers routinely perform basic literacy procedures (e.g., decoding, inferencing, or rereading) fluidly and effortlessly with only a minimal expenditure of cognitive effort (Paris et al., 1991). Nonskillful readers, in contrast, labor over letter-sound combinations and have difficulty making sense of individual sentences. The surface-level processing of text requires so much of their cognitive capacity that they have little mental energy to think deeply about what is written (Britton, 1981).

A great deal of instructional attention is directed toward promoting skillful behavior in students. The fundamental processes involved in mastering any field must be grasped and practiced well before much else can be accomplished. For this reason, early literacy programs in reading and mathematics at the elementary levels (Hiebert & Taylor, 2000) and remedial and developmental courses for older students (Weinstein, Goetz, & Alexander, 1988) typically aim to make students skillful. These educators may mistakenly talk about promoting strategic learning, but they are actually guiding students toward skillful performance.

However, even skilled learners become confused or encounter obstacles to optimal performance from time to time. Skilled readers may occasionally come across unfamiliar words or concepts that require more than their typical reading routine. At such times students must take their processing off automatic pilot and make their actions conscious and purposeful (Alexander, Graham, & Harris, 1998) so that they can regulate and monitor their performance (Lanehart & Schutz, 2001; Winne & Perry, 2001). The remedies that students consider and implement—whether broad in application or particular to the task—are strategies.

This distinction between strategies and skills holds for both domain-specific and general strategies. Chapter 5 discussed certain underlying processes critical to each academic domain. For example, in history, students must develop conceptions of time and causality and be able to engage in document searching, interpretation, and reconciliation. In science those underlying processes include observing and chronicling, inquiring and discovering, as well as formulating and testing hypotheses. When consciously and purposefully invoked, the procedures that learners initiate to facilitate those central domain processes represent domain-specific strategies.

Student success in history, mathematics, or any other academic domain also depends on the execution of general strategies, such as self-questioning, summarizing, paraphrasing, and self-monitoring. Because the key myths of strategic processing pertain to both general and domain-specific strategies and because the number of domain-specific strategies would be too great, this discussion will focus on general strategies pertinent to student learning.

Good Strategic Thinking Needs to Be Nurtured

It is one thing to use strategies but quite another to use them well. Even individuals who tend to act strategically without much direct prompting are not naturally or instinctively *good* strategic thinkers. Good strategic thinking is a learned and practiced process that requires planfulness, effort, and persistence on the parts of both students and teachers (Weinstein et al., 1988). Research comparing the performance of good and poor problem solvers highlights a number of characteristics that should be weighed when judging the effectiveness of strategic thinking.

Efficiency and Effectiveness

One of the simplest criteria for evaluating strategic thinking is the quality of the outcome. For many of Pam Gaskill's second graders, reading and rereading the words (i.e., rehearsal) was not getting the job done. There were simply too many words for this rudimentary strategy to work. However, the children could see for themselves how useful a sorting strategy was when they easily conquered a comparable set of 16 words. I, too, typically introduce a unit on strategic processing with a similar activity. I present college students with 28 words, all beginning with the same letter, and give them 10 minutes to memorize all of them. It might surprise you to know that many of my undergraduates employ the same rehearsal strategy that Pam's second graders used—with about the same results. So much for the myth that good strategic behavior develops naturally!

These illustrations do not mean that rehearsal or rereading cannot be helpful tools. How and when such strategies are used and whether they are combined with more sophisticated techniques are the key issues. For example, if Pam's second graders had first "chunked" their words into meaningful groups and then rehearsed them, they would certainly have done much better on their memory task. Indeed, most people have used rehearsal to keep an important name or number in mind. The efficiency and effectiveness of the strategy is what matters.

Good strategic thinking should not be judged simply on the completion of a given task but on the "elegance" of the outcome as well (Alexander, Graham, & Harris, 1998). For example, Pam's student Terry hit upon the sorting strategy right away and was able to remember the list rather easily. What if another student was able to remember all 16 words by merely rehearsing—but it took her 40 minutes longer than it Took Terry? Are their two strategies equally successful? Terry's approach was far more efficient and given the limited time and energy people have to expend on most tasks, strategic efficiency is invaluable (Alexander & Judy, 1988).

What about the strategic effort required to complete the set of chores described in the Thought Experiment on planning? Did you get all of your Saturday chores accomplished? How efficient were you in plotting your solution path? Did you organize your chores by time *and* location so that you were not backtracking or wasting time? Were there alternative routes that you considered before you settled on the final solution? In effect, did you meet the effectiveness *and* efficiency criteria?

Planfulness

When Alan Schoenfeld (1988) looked closely at the students in his mathematics courses at Berkeley, he realized that

Alan Schoenfeld

the mind—then they are behaving skillfully rather than strategically.

Nonetheless, it is possible that some individuals do have a combination of motivational and cognitive traits that make it more likely that they would put forth strategic effort prior to, during, and after task performance (Ackerman et al., 1989). Their planfulness, although commonplace in novel or demanding contexts, might remain conscious and intentional, suggesting a disposition toward strategic behavior. However, this notion of strategic disposition remains largely hypothetical and requires further investigation before it can be more strongly argued (Alexander, Graham, & Harris, 1998).

Conditional Strategy Knowledge

Chapter 4 explained that conditional knowledge refers to one's understanding of when and how knowledge should be brought to bear in a given situation (Paris, Lipson, & Wixson, 1983). It is one aspect of reflection that good strategy users invoke before and during task performance. Not only do good strategic thinkers take time to analyze a situation or problem, but they also consider the strengths and weaknesses of various strategies in light of this task analysis (Palmer & Goetz, 1988).

For example, most students have outlined information at some point in their academic careers. Certainly, it is valuable for students to have a procedure for outlining that works for them. But students must also understand that outlining is not always wise. For example, research suggests that outlining does not enhance students' learning when the amount of information is limited (Caverly, Orlando, & Mullen, 2000). Further, unless students have sufficient knowledge of the subject matter or text structure to distinguish between main and supporting ideas, then the value of outlining, which is essentially a hierarchical summary of text, is questionable (Lipson, 1995).

Sometimes the conditional knowledge that students need to ponder has more to do with themselves as learners than with the material they are reading or studying. For example, two very different students might be taking the same high-school biology class. One might need to get an A on his unit test to pass the first quarter of the course, the other might be able to get a 40 on her test and still get an A. It would make little sense for the second student, who already knows this content well, to spend hours outlining those chapters.

Personalization and Modification of Strategies

Educators concerned with students' academic learning have devised techniques to guide learners in their studying. For example, in 1946 Robinson came up with a general approach to studying called SQ3R, which stands for *survey, question, read, recite*, and *review*. SQ3R is still taught in college reading and studying courses, even though extensive reviews have not produced strong evidence of its overall effectiveness (Caverly & Orlando, 1991; Tadlock, 1978).

those who did well shared a common characteristic. They took noticeably more time before they started to work on their test problems or assignments than other students in the course did. Less effective students, on the other hand, seemed to jump right into the task with little or no deep analysis of the problem. In fact, many of Schoenfeld's otherwise bright students believed that if they could not solve a problem in 10 minutes, they had no chance of solving it at all. Armed with such limiting beliefs, these less effective students frequently gave their assignments only a cursory analysis. They often focused on less relevant aspects of the problem and consequently selected inaccurate or less effective strategies.

The problem Schoenfeld (1988) identified was not strictly his students' fault. Those students had learned to value speed over reflection in part because of how mathematics is typically taught. Schoenfeld set out to persuade his students that faster is not always better. Just as Pam did with her second graders, Schoenfeld began to show his students how more front-end planning translated into more successful outcomes. For Schoenfeld's students, seeing was believing. Like the children in Pam Gaskill's classroom, these college students became more mindful and reflective about their problem solving and saw for themselves that thinking before acting enhances overall achievement.

The criterion of planfulness raises the issue of disposition toward strategic thinking (Ackerman, Sternberg, & Glaser, 1989). Questions have been raised about whether some individuals are more prone to engage in strategic processing than others (Alexander, Graham, & Harris, 1998). Some individuals do seem to fit this description, they are highly planful and reflect on the task at hand before they initiate specific actions. However, if these individuals really find planning to be second nature—a habit of

That finding may have something to do with the rather nonstrategic way this global strategy has been taught and implemented.

For example, students are often told to engage in this technique's five steps in the same way each time they encounter text, instead of being taught to use this technique in a conditional manner as good strategic processors do (Nist & Holschuh, 2000). Let's reconsider the cases of the two high-school biology students, described in the Thought Experiment: Strategic Conditions.

Thought Experiment ....

Strategic Conditions

Directions: Two students are enrolled in the same high-school biology class and face the same unit test. After reading these two cases, decide how these two students might adapt the SQ3R strategy.

Case A	Case B
Eddie has always found reading a chore. He would rather run laps in the sweltering heat than read some crummy textbook. He has a biology test Monday on three chapters. When his teacher, Miss Jefferson, covered the key topics in class, Eddie understood some of what she talked about but didn't really focus on what she was saying. If it weren't for his lab partner, Mary, he would never have been able to complete the related assignments. Now he is in a real fix. He has no choice but to throw himself into the reading, and he has only 2 days before this exam. If he blows the test, he will get a failing grade for the quarter.	Mary has always loved science, especially biology. Even though she is only a sophomore, Mary has already decided to become a research scientist. Biogenetics is her passion, and she reads everything she can about the subject. Needless to say, Miss Jefferson's class is a snap for her. In fact, Miss Jefferson often relies on Mary to update her on some of the content in the course textbook. With gene mapping and cloning, the field of biology is changing faster than publishers can print new editions. Even if Mary gets a 40 on this unit test, she is assured of an *A* for the quarter.

Survey _____

_____

Question _____

_____

Read _____

_____

Recite _____

_____

Review _____

_____

Survey _____

_____

Question _____

_____

Read _____

_____

Recite _____

_____

Review _____

_____

How do the academic situations of these two students differ? How should those differences be reflected in the way they implement SQ3R? Do parts of this global strategy seem unnecessary for one or both of the students? If you were Eddie or Mary, would you consider other approaches than Robinson's SQ3R technique?

Extensive Strategic Repertoire

Strategies are like tools. When there is a job to perform, individuals reach into their strategic toolboxes and select the right implements (Paris et al., 1983; Paris et al., 1991). Needless to say, they are going to be far better off if they have an extensive set of tools from which to choose. More-

Learner-Centered Psychological Principle 4

Strategic thinking. The successful learner can create and use a repertoire of thinking and reasoning strategies to achieve complex learning goals.

Learner Centered Principles Work Group of the APA Board of Educational Affairs 1997.

over, it is essential that students' strategy toolkits be stocked with both domain-specific and general strategies.

As problem-solving tools, domain-specific strategies are like the tools expressly crafted for a particular job, whereas general strategies are analogous to Swiss army knives. General strategies are essentially mental tools to keep handy and use whenever the exact tool is not available for a particular problem-solving job. These strategies are the kind taught in courses aimed at improving high-school or college students' academic performance (Flippo & Caverly, 2000). In her research with second-language learning, Rebecca Oxford (1989; Oxford & Crookall, 1989) determined that general strategies also work well with students for whom English is not a first or primary language. Perhaps this emphasis on general strategies in academic improvement programs arises from the broad applicability of such procedures; it would be almost impossible to arm students with all the domain-specific strategies they would need to succeed in high school or college.

The general learning and study strategies frequently mentioned in the research literature can be organized into six broad categories (see Table 7–1). Specifically, some strategies allow learners to locate and construct permanent records of otherwise fleeting information, whereas others let them augment or enhance their memories. Still others make text more understandable and memorable, some help individuals organize large bodies of content, and some keep people interested and focused on the task at hand. Other strategies deal with self-assessment and maintaining personal control of learning.

Capturing and Retaining Information

Some of the procedures used to learn and study are particularly useful for finding and capturing relevant content in the learning environment. Students use two such strategies, underlining (or highlighting) and notetaking, extensively (Weinstein & Mayer, 1986). In fact, nearly 97% of postsecondary students reportedly use underlining or highlighting when they study (Caverly et al., 2000). However, researchers seriously question the effectiveness of underlining as a learning strategy. Kapinus and Haynes (1983) investigated underlining among middle-school students, for example, and found that underlining was not useful for students with limited knowledge of the topic. These low-knowledge

students simply did not know enough to distinguish important from trivial information. And the performance of good readers was actually hindered by the need to underline.

So why do students fall into the routine of underlining? Many students report that underlining gives them a sense of control over written material (T. H. Anderson & Armbruster, 1984b). They believe they are monitoring their reading or studying in some manner and are marking those ideas that are important and need to be reread. Whether these strategies work depends on the actual thinking that goes into selecting the text to be underlined and the amount of text so marked.

Another common strategy, notetaking, may also be limited in its effectiveness. Ample research shows that the quantity and quality of students' class notes relate to their achievement (Kiewra, 1989), but data indicate that most students are not good notetakers (Anderson & Armbruster, 1986). Dansereau (Holley & Dansereau, 1984) and O'Donnell (with Kelly, 1994), who have researched student notetaking, offer practical guidelines for both students and teachers. For example, students are encouraged to listen for main points, write down the essence of what they hear rather than the exact words, including useful examples, and then review and reorganize those notes as soon as possible. Teachers are advised to consider the structure of their discussions, provide students a visual or graphic framework for the content, and highlight and restate key points, adding illustrative examples or cases whenever possible (Kiewra, Kauffman, Robinson, DuBois, & Staley, 1999; Robinson & Kiewra, 1995).

Students are rarely taught how to take good notes or underline effectively. However, if students are going to rely on underlining and notetaking as information-gathering strategies, then teachers should provide students with some relevant information on when, where, and how to use these techniques. Lessons in notetaking are not just for older students sitting in college lectures. Even elementary students can benefit from some simple instruction on how to write down information that they might need to review later.

Improving Memory

The ability to remember remains one of the potent differences between academically successful and unsuccessful students (Badderly, 1982). Fortunately for those without photographic memories, strategies can help them increase what they can remember. For instance, Pam Gaskill's experiment with her second graders showed how effective sorting, or **chunking,** can be with memory (Ellis & Hunt, 1983). Research on information processing (see Chapter 4) makes it clear that students' minds would quickly become saturated under the flood of content if they did not group incoming information (G. A. Miller, 1956).

Humans have long relied on various techniques to augment their memories. The ancient Greeks, for example, are credited with the method of loci. Ancient orators like Cicero used this strategy to memorize extensive public speeches (Goetz, Alexander, & Ash, 1992), associating each section of their speeches with a certain ordered location, like the rooms in a house, spots along a path, or seats at a table. As they memorized each segment, these orators would mentally place that portion of their speeches into each familiar location. Then when they delivered their speeches, they would simply conjure up the image of the familiar series of locations, and the associated words would flow more easily from memory.

If you were to apply the method of loci to recall the characteristics of good strategic thinking, you might visualize steps on a staircase. On the first step, you could put the discussion of the efficiency and effectiveness of strategies. Step two could be the location of information related to planfulness, whereas step three could hold conditional knowledge about strategies. You would continue up the staircase until all six of the stated characteristics were recalled. Try this technique if you have some ordered list of information to remember.

Keyword mnemonics is another memory strategy that relies heavily on visual imagery or mental pictures (Levin, 1981; Pressley, Levin, & Delaney, 1982). A mnemonic is a memory trick in which some word, phrase, or picture comes to represent some large body of information (Levin, 1993). For example, individuals commonly use the first-letter mnemonic *HOMES* to remember the names of the Great Lakes—Huron, Ontario, Michigan, Erie, and Superior—or a sentence mnemonic like *My Very Excellent Mother Just Served Us Nine Pizzas* to recall the nine planets in order—Mercury, Venus, Earth, Mars, Jupiter, Saturn, Uranus, Neptune, and Pluto. With keyword mnemonics students are encouraged to devise memorable visual images that cue the meaning of an unknown word. A student who wanted to learn the meaning of the word *angler* (i.e., a person who fishes) might decide on a familiar word (e.g., *angel*) that sounded similar to the new word. This familiar word would then become the student's keyword and visualizing an angel fishing would remind the student of the definition of *angler* (see Figure 7–2).

Comprehending and Recalling Text

A great deal of what is known about strategies comes from research in the 1970s and 1980s aimed at improving stu-

dents' comprehension and recall of written text (Garner, 1987; Weinstein & Mayer, 1986). Indeed, most of the experimental tasks used in memory research were text comprehension problems (Harris & Pressley, 1991). From this extensive literature, researchers and practitioners learned much about basic comprehension strategies, including finding the main idea, predicting, summarizing text, and elaborating (Paris & Winograd, 1990; Pearson & Fielding, 1991). Researchers then converted what they had learned from these studies into curricula or programs for elementary, secondary, or even college students to improve learning.

A good example of this body of research is seen in the training studies on finding the main idea reported by James Baumann in 1984. As was typical of those early strategy intervention studies, Baumann prepared detailed materials for the lesson, including training scripts like the one seen in Figure 7–3 and supporting graphics like the one shown in Figure 7–4. The training scripts ensured that students would receive explicit instruction in the target procedure.

In this first generation of strategy studies, researchers were successful at getting students to use the procedure that was being explicity and carefully taught (Nist & Holschuh, 2000). However, even though the training produced significant, immediate, and direct effects, such strategy training studies became increasingly rare by the 1990s for several reasons (Rosenshine, 1997). First, the overall approach these researchers were taking was rather nonstrategic because it permitted little personalization or self-control of the procedures (Hadwin & Winne, 1996; McKeachie, 1996). Second, these researchers showed little concern for the conditional nature of strategies or for the motivational/affective dimensions of strategic behavior (Graves, 1997). In

Phil Winne is a leading researcher in self-regulation.

essence, these researchers were treating general techniques more as skills than as strategies (Alexander, Graham, & Harris, 1998). Consequently, students often reverted to their pretraining behavior soon after the training was completed or when instructional conditions changed somewhat. Thus, the positive effects of the training did not endure or transfer (Alexander & Jetton, 2000).

Newer forms of strategy instruction are beginning to appear on the horizon. Nist and Holschuh (2000) refer to them as the second generation of strategy training. The characteristics of strategic teaching, considered later in this chapter, are reflective of this new generation of strategy instruction.

Organizing Information

Some strategies permit learners to organize bodies of information, like a chapter in a textbook or students' class notes. Outlining, whether formal or informal, is perhaps the most common example of this type of strategy (Caverly et al.,

■ FIGURE 7–2   Keyword mnemonic for *Angler.*

Introduction: "Remember last time when we learned how to find main idea sentences right in paragraphs? We called these main idea sentences *topic sentences.* Today you will learn how to find main ideas in paragraphs that do not have topic sentences; that is, paragraphs which actually do have main ideas in them, but paragraphs in which the main ideas are not stated. You will learn how to figure out these unstated main ideas by looking at the details in the paragraph and determining what all these details are talking about, and that will be the main idea. This is an important reading skill because many paragraphs have unstated main ideas, and if you can figure out what these main ideas are, you will understand and remember the most important information in the material you read."

Example: "Look at the example I have on this transparency."

> My father can cook bacon and eggs real well. He can also bake cakes that taste wonderful. He cooks excellent popcorn and pizza. The thing he cooks best of all, however, is hamburgers barbecued on the grill.

"Follow along with me silently as I read the paragraph aloud. [Teacher reads paragraph.] Notice that there is no single sentence that states the main idea; that is, there is no topic sentence. Rather, the entire paragraph consists of a series of details. That does not mean that there is not a main idea in this paragraph, however, for there is. What we will learn how to do today is to inspect paragraphs like this one that contain an unstated main idea and then figure out what that main idea is."

Direct instruction: "Let's examine this same paragraph on the transparency and see if we can determine its main idea. Remember in our last lesson, we learned to figure out the topic of a paragraph—the one or two words that tell what a paragraph is about? What would be the topic of this paragraph? Would it be 'father cooking'? [Student response.] All right, the topic of the paragraph is 'father cooking.' Now let's list on the board all the ideas that tell about father cooking. Who can help us begin? [Students respond by stating the four detail sentences in the paragraph, and the teacher writes them on the board in a numbered list.] Very good. These are the ideas that tell us about father cooking, and we learned already that we can call these ideas *supporting details.* If supporting details go with a main idea, let's inspect these details and see if we can figure out what the main idea of this paragraph is. [Teacher rereads the supporting details on the board.] Now what would be a main idea sentence we could come up with that goes with all these details? [Teacher writes student responses on the board.] Yes, there are several different ways of saying what the main idea is: 'Father can cook many different things' or 'Father is a good cook.' But the main idea tells us about all the details in the paragraph; that is the biggest, most important idea in the paragraph."

"Now look at this transparency. Who can tell me what it is? [Student response.] Yes, it is a table. Let's use this table to help us understand how main ideas and details go together. Just as a table is supported by its legs, so too, a main idea is supported by details."

■ **FIGURE 7–3   Training script on finding the main idea and supporting details in paragraphs.**

Note: From "The Effectiveness of a Direct Instruction Paradigm for Teaching Main Idea Comprehension" by J. F. Baumann, 1984, *Reading Research Quarterly, 20,* pp. 108–109. Copyright 1984 by *Reading Research Quarterly.* Reprinted with permission.

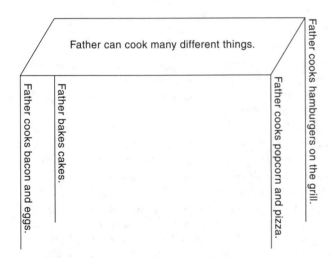

■ **FIGURE 7–4   Graphic support for strategy training in finding the main idea.**

Note: From "The Effectiveness of a Direct Instruction Paradigm for Teaching Main Idea Comprehension" by J. F. Baumann, 1984, *Reading Research Quarterly, 20,* p. 109. Copyright 1984 by *Reading Research Quarterly.* Reprinted with permission.

2000). **Outlines** are essentially hierarchical organizations that tell quickly which ideas are overarching and which are supportive. The use of outlining conventions (e.g., always having two supporting statements under each major heading) does not need to be rigorous to capture the basic structure of a text.

The concept map used to represent the notion of schemata in Figure 4–3 is another form of organizational strategy. A **concept map** is a schematic representation of information that also indicates the interrelation of the concepts displayed. Dansereau and colleagues (1983), along with others (Novak, 1998), have studied concept maps. Their findings show that concept maps enhance students' comprehension and recall of text and indicate the relative importance of ideas in text (Romance & Vitale, 1992). A concept map of this chapter might look something like the graphic in Figure 7–5. Phrases like "cases of," "characterized by," and "evidence of" denote the relation between the key concepts in this particular map.

Outlining and concept mapping are two of the general learning and study strategies commonly used in educational practice. Overall, these organizational strategies demonstrate benefits to students who use them thoughtfully and

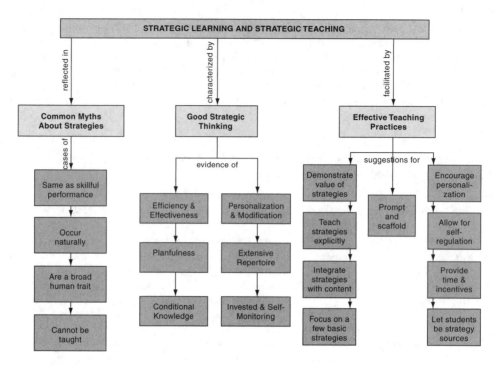

FIGURE 7–5   Partial propositional concept map for chapter 7.

selectively (Romance & Vitale, 1992). However, those benefits are not equally distributed. When Caverly et al. (2000) surveyed the research on outlining and mapping, they found that students of low to average reading ability significantly improved their learning and studying when taught to outline or map. On the other hand, as was true for underlining, outlining or mapping tended to interfere with learning and performance for high-ability students. Someone like Eddie in the Thought Experiment on strategic conditions might be well served by outlining or mapping his three biology chapters. However, for Mary this effort could prove distracting.

Caverly et al. (2000) came to two other conclusions about outlining and mapping that are pertinent to this discussion. First, they determined that students need to be taught outlining and mapping strategies. Without this instruction only high-ability students like Mary do well. Second, outlining and mapping cannot compensate for a lack of relevant knowledge; students cannot effectively outline or map if they are not also provided with some base of knowledge about the subject matter. In the case of Eddie, paying close attention to the discussions in his biology classroom would help him organize the information in the biology textbook. And without the base of knowledge provided by the classroom discussions, Eddie's outlines or maps might not translate into better test performance.

Motivating Performance

Good strategic thinkers do not rely solely on others to motivate them or let them know whether they are functioning well. On the contrary, good strategic thinkers are invested in their learning (Alexander & Jetton, 2000). They are also reflective, self-aware, and self-evaluative (Boekaerts, Pintrich, & Zeid-

ner, 2001; Winne, 1995). For example, students who are fascinated with the topic at hand or who are deeply concerned about performing well in a course are more likely to engage in course readings and assignments without the explicit directive of their teachers (Alexander & Jetton, 2003). I remember that my brother Robert, a Civil War buff even in elementary school, could not wait to open the pages of his history book, which he would scan for any section or story that mentioned this period of American history. Even when the reading was challenging for him, Robert was more than willing to exert the effort he needed to increase his Civil War knowledge. Some of the volumes he chose for school projects were clearly adult books meant for much older students, yet Robert's personal investment motivated him enough that he did not mind the literary struggles.

John Dewey (1913) would say that my brother Robert was motivated from within and that this internal drive converted work into play. Mihaly Csikszentmihalyi (1990) would agree. Csikszentmihalyi has written extensively about the concept of *flow*—the psychological state in which individuals lose themselves in some endeavor. For instance, at times I was so involved in writing this book that I forgot to stop and eat. Once I was so engrossed in my writing that I actually forgot to go and teach my class. These are instances of flow, an extreme case of self-motivation. Luckily, students do not have to be that engaged in their learning to be invested, but without some internal drive to learn deeply or perform well, they are not apt to commit the time and effort required to think and act strategically (Dweck, 1986; Palmer & Goetz, 1988). Strategic learners are invested learners.

Teachers must recognize that they cannot *make* any student think or learn strategically (Alexander, Graham, & Harris, 1998). Teachers can do much to promote good strategic processing in their students, as discussed later in this chapter. However, the choice to operate strategically ultimately rests with the learners. And being invested in the learning or in the subject matter can be a powerful spark, igniting strategic learning in individuals of any age, ability, or background (Alexander & Jetton, 2003).

Think back to the most recent Thought Experiment. Did you quickly recognize that Mary's investment in science was going to propel her forward, whereas Eddie's dislike of any reading task would likely hold him back?

Goal Setting Regrettably, students cannot always learn about or study topics with which they are already fascinated. In truth, much of schooling is spent in unfamiliar or nonstimulating territory (Alexander, 1997b). Yet no one escapes the reality of needing to perform adequately on tasks that are tedious or distasteful. Even though I am passionate about my field of educational psychology, I was not equally thrilled about writing each segment of this book. As a strategic thinker, however, I devised techniques that kept me going through the less personally exciting sections. Students like Eddie must also develop procedures or behaviors that prod them to action when they find the task at hand demanding or tiresome. This is what self-motivating learners do (Harris & Graham, 1996).

Some individuals find it helpful to set explicit overall goals and subgoals for themselves. These goals can serve as benchmarks against which learners mark their progress. For me, goal setting involved determining how many pages I would write daily and establishing dates by which I would complete particular chapters. Eddie should first be clear in his own mind about whether passing the exam really matters to him. If it does, he needs to be realistic about what he must achieve in the 2 days before the test. He might break down the big goal of passing the test into more manageable subgoals, perhaps understanding pages 46–75 of chapter 9 or relating his lab notes to chapters 9–11 of his textbook.

Positive Self-Talk **Positive self-talk,** that is, internal conversations that encourage reflection and problem solving, might also benefit Eddie. Vygotsky (1986) explained how important such private internal dialoguing can be to learning and development. But not everything individuals say to themselves is positive or motivating. For instance, Chiu and Alexander (2000) studied preschoolers' private speech as they engaged in various physical (e.g., jumping) and mental (e.g., puzzle completion) tasks. They found that some children manifested positive self-talk (e.g., "I can do this. I am a good jumper."), whereas others were more negative in their private speech (e.g., "This is too far. I won't make it."). The more the children used positive self-talk, the better they tended to do on the various tasks.

Miss Jefferson, Eddie's teacher, might be concerned about whether Eddie believes he will make sense of biology or pass the unit test. Poor-performing students like Eddie often engage in self-deprecating thinking, like "I'll never learn this stuff even if I do study" or "Things come so easy for Mary, I must just be stupid" (Manning, White, & Daugh-

erty, 1994). Instead, what Eddie needs to do is to function as his own cheerleader. He needs to remind himself that he can learn this content if he buckles down and tries hard. He should also learn to use positive self-talk to praise himself when he succeeds at relevant tasks.

Self-Rewarding Like positive self-talk, self-rewarding is an example of self-reinforcement, providing a form of positive consequence after accomplishing a particular goal or subgoal (Woolfolk, 2001). Some of my self-rewards have been small, like treating myself to a cappuccino after finishing a particular section. I have also established larger rewards for larger goals. For example, each time I finished a chapter, I put money aside to buy a painting I wanted. Eddie could also establish rewards for his goals or subgoals. Some additional time playing computer games might be a viable reward for mapping each chapter. And he might tie a passing grade in biology to the purchase of new computer equipment. However, the reward must come from Eddie and must be suitable to the accomplishments. Negative consequences can occur when students' performance is tied to external rewards set by others, as when parents pay their children for grades (Pintrich & Schunk, 2001; Ryan & Deci, 2000a).

Monitoring and Regulating Learning

Another area of strategic importance pertains to students' monitoring of their performance and regulating their learning.

Self-Analysis **Self-analysis,** or self-assessment, refers to the ability to judge one's own performance (Maehr & Anderman, 1993). Students should not depend on a teacher or some other individual to tell them whether they have done well (Zimmerman & Martinez-Pons, 1992). Instead, good strategic thinkers develop an internal gauge that signals when they must come off autopilot, and they stay in touch with that gauge so that they can act quickly when a slight glitch in performance occurs. Thus, good strategic thinkers are self-monitoring or self-regulating (Winne, 1995).

Researchers often use the term **metacognition** to describe this process of reflecting on and evaluating one's own thoughts and learning. Metacognition means thinking about thinking (Garner, 1987). Over the last several decades, another body of research pertaining to learners' self-monitoring and self-assessment has rapidly expanded; it comes from the literature on motivation and pertains to self-regulation (Iran-Nejad, 1990). Although both metacognition and self-regulation relate to cognitive monitoring, **self-regulation** is broader, for it involves the assessment and oversight of more than cognition. Theoretical models and studies in self-regulation include the self-monitoring of behavior, motivation and affect, environmental conditions, and physical circumstances (Brownlee, Leventhal, & Leventhal, 2001; Carver & Scheier, 2001; G. Matthews, Schwean, Campbell, Sklofske, & Mohamed, 2001; Schutz & Lanehart, 2002).

Students' abilities to self-evaluate or self-monitor do not come easily (Boekaerts et al., 2001). Researchers have shown that many aspects of self-regulation develop over time (Winne, 1995; Zimmerman, 1995, 2001), as students encounter more and varied tasks and have more performance history upon which to draw. Thus, with each passing year, good strategic thinkers become better at analyzing academic tasks and assessing their own strengths and weaknesses relative to those tasks (Graham & Weiner, 1996).

Help Seeking   Recognizing when outside help is needed is another important part of self-monitoring and self-regulation, and seeking such help can be a sign of good strategic behavior (Harris & Graham, 1996). McCaslin and Good (1996) call the intelligent use of this strategy **adaptive help seeking.** The difference between adaptive and maladaptive help seeking can be seen in the behavior of Eddie and Mary. Eddie has come to rely too heavily and too often on Mary to get him through, suggesting that his help seeking is maladaptive. Mary, on the other hand, has learned to ask for assistance only when the situation warrants—an adaptive approach.

Good strategic thinkers like Mary are equally thoughtful about whom they choose as helpers. Teachers are often the first people to whom students turn when seeking assistance, but peers can also be excellent sources of help in school learning (McCaslin & Good, 1996). If Eddie worked to develop a base of biology knowledge and knew how to work more collaboratively with Mary, she could prove to be an excellent ally, given her knowledge of and interest in science.

Too few students make use of this strategy, partly because students, especially those in the younger grades, often believe that help seeking is a sign of incompetence. In fact, Newman and Goldin (1990) found that 70% of a sample of third graders noted that the "dumb" or "stupid" kids in their classroom were more apt to seek help. McCaslin and Good (1996) believe these data reflect negatively on the children's learning environment; students are not shown how to engage in adaptive help seeking but are actually discouraged from turning to others for aid when questions or problems arise.

Good strategic thinkers apparently come to realize the value of seeking assistance. Of the seventh graders Newman and Goldin (1990) surveyed, 60% indicated that the "smart" students in their classes were those who asked for help, often by questioning their teachers. And as with many dimensions of good strategic thinking, help seeking can be fostered and developed in the classroom. The key is a teacher like Pam Gaskill, who does not take students' knowledge of general strategies for granted. A strategic teacher is skilled at making strategic thinking a valued and explicit component of the classroom curriculum.

How Do Strategic Abilities Vary Across Domains and Contexts?

An interesting debate took place in the educational literature during the 1980s. On one side individuals like Robert Glaser (1984) argued that general strategies, such as those just discussed are weak strategies—tools that students use when they have no clear understanding of the problem at hand or do not know the particular procedure that would produce a correct response. For example, if Pam Gaskill gives her second graders a multiplication problem to solve, they can reflect on the problem, organize the information, seek help, and motivate themselves, but they will not perform as well as students who know the mathematical procedure for solving such problems. In other words, the specific procedure for solving multiplication problems is more valuable than general learning strategies.

On the other side, proponents of general strategies, like Robert Sternberg (1985b), claimed that not all the problems students confront in schools have such clear and identifiable answers as multiplication problems. Further, even students in mathematics and science classes, where well-formed problems might be more abundant, need general strategies to perform well. They still need to analyze problems to determine what formula to apply, for instance. And almost all fields or tasks require some degree of text comprehension (Graves, 1997). Students need to read their mathematics textbooks and take notes in class if they are to learn specific problem-solving procedures.

Both sides of this debate are correct—to a degree (Alexander & Murphy, 1998b). To become competent in any field of study, students must possess general strategies as well as those that are more particular to a given domain. In science, for instance, a high-school student needs to know how to use a high-powered microscope and also needs to understand titration, the process of calculating the amount of a certain substance in a solution by systematically introducing another substance into that solution until a chemical change occurs. Students in Pam's class must learn the procedure for multiplying and dividing whole numbers. Students learning basic algebra should learn the FOIL method, the domain-specific strategy illustrated in Figure 7–1.

These processes are all examples of domain-specific strategies because they are typically applied in only one or a few fields. Such procedures stand in contrast to general strategies, like capturing and retaining information or monitoring and regulating performance, which work on a broad array of tasks in many domains. General strategies may be more pervasive in certain domains (e.g., reading, writing, or history), whereas domain-specific strategies may be more prevalent in others (e.g., mathematics or science; Spiro, Feltovich, Jacobson, & Coulson, 1992). Students need to acquire some general learning strategies to succeed academically; however, possessing only general strategies will not result in optimal achievement any more than knowing only domain-specific strategies will. Optimal academic development is dependent on both general and domain-specific strategies. Try your hand at the Thought Experiment: A Field Experience in Problem Solving to establish this point.

Thought Experiment ....

A Field Experience in Problem Solving

Pam Gaskill and her fellow second-grade teachers decide to take their students on a field trip to the local children's museum. In preparation for the trip, Pam needs to arrange for buses to transport the children, teachers, and accompanying parents to the museum. Each bus can carry 30 passengers. If all the second graders want to go, there will be 82 children, 4 teachers, and 10 parents. How many buses does Pam need to order for the field trip?

Answer_____

....

Did you have any problem doing the mathematical calculations required in the Thought Experiment? Did you add 82 + 4 + 10 for a total of 96? Did you then divide 96 by 30? If your arithmetic was flawless, you came up with 3 1/5 buses. If you were like the students in Edward Silver's studies, that is precisely where you stopped (Silver, Shapiro, & Deutsch, 1993): Pam Gaskill should order 3 1/5 buses for the field trip. But has anyone ever seen one fifth of a bus? Apparently, this reality does not occur to mathematic problem solvers who perform domain-specific procedures well but fail to reflect on the reasonableness of their solutions. Thus, general strategies remain important, even when solving relatively simple mathematical problems.

Some individuals do well at school tasks because of their general strategic abilities (Weinstein & Mayer, 1986). These good strategic thinkers generally wield their problem-solving tools thoughtfully and effectively, even when they are working in unfamiliar territory (Alexander, 1997b). Brown and Campione (1990) labeled such students intelligent novices. However, no individual is consistently effective or invested in strategic performance; many factors strongly influence students' ability to behave strategically.

Social-Contextual Forces

One reason for variability in students' strategic performance is the availability of human and nonhuman resources in their learning environment. Teachers serve as one of the most influential human resources in the educational system (Darling-Hammond & Sykes, 1999); they can do much to establish and maintain a climate for strategic thinking (Turner & Meyer, 2000; Turner et al., 2002). However, other social-contextual influences also play important roles in students' abilities to develop into problem solvers who manifest good strategic thinking (Cole et al., 1971).

Peer Interactions

As discussed in Chapter 4, a range of theories seek to explain human learning. Some of those theories place more emphasis on social interactions, but all learning theories recognize that students are influenced by their environment and by people who are part of that environment. Within the school setting, peers are significant forces in students' academic lives (Vygotsky, 1978), especially when children reach late childhood and early adolescence (Wigfield, Eccles, & Pintrich, 1996). Peer influences extend to students' strategic performance, as well (Turner & Meyer, 2000).

Specifically, peers act as *direct* and *vicarious* influences on classmates' strategic thinking (Bandura, 1977, 1993). They directly shape students' strategic thinking by modeling both adaptive and maladaptive behaviors. Peers' adaptive behaviors include publicly sharing their problem analysis, monitoring their own work, explaining their actions, probing the actions of others, and exploring alternative solution paths. Indeed, shared or cooperative learning activities, as discussed in Chapter 11, require students to make their thinking public and, thus, open to scrutiny in a manner that independent processing does not (Cohen, Lotan, Whitcomb, Balderrama, Cossey, & Swanson, 1994).

Yet peer interactions are not always conducive to better strategic processing. Sometimes peers seek quick rather than thoughtful or optimal solutions or interject inappropriate or ineffective strategies (Sharan, 1994a). There are also instances when a peer provides solutions without requiring thought or input from others, thus becoming a cognitive surrogate, doing the mental labor for others. To be helpful, peers should instigate, stimulate, or support classmates' strategic thinking, not stifle it by being too quick to take control or judge the ideas of others (Webb & Palincsar, 1996). In addition, it is not always the best strategic thinkers who command the attention and respect of peers in classroom settings. Teachers must be sure that participation patterns are sensitive to student differences (Fuchs, Fuchs, Mathes, & Simmons, 1997).

Peer influences need not be explicit or direct to shape another's strategic thinking. Students may frame certain perceptions about strategies or about themselves as strategic thinkers by watching others in their environment (Schunk, 1991). A student infers relations between peers' levels of effort and their academic success, based on what can be observed and based on teacher feedback (Bandura, 1982). By comparing themselves to their peers, students come to a determination about whether they are similarly capable of such achievement through strategic effort. In essence, the actions of peers become a source of efficacy information (Pintrich & Schunk, 2001). **Self-efficacy** refers to students' beliefs in their abilities to succeed academically in a specified domain or with a particular task (Murphy & Alexander, 2000).

Availability of Nonhuman Educational Resources

Just as human resources can alter the nature of students' strategic thinking, the availability of nonhuman resources in the learning environment can also help or hinder strategic performance. Reference materials—such as dictionaries, glossaries, encyclopedias, thesauruses, and manuals—are common aids to strategic processing (Simpson & Randall, 2000). In addition, support materials—such as pictures, charts, maps, or graphs—can assist students in their problem solving by representing content in alternative and concise ways (Kiewra et al., 1999; Shah, Mayer, & Hegarty, 1999).

Further, many students find online resources invaluable supports for their strategic performance. Online searches can provide students with rich background information about any domain or topic (Lajoie, 1993), and the Internet can give students access to those with specialized knowledge in an area of study (see Chapter 12; Bereiter, 2002). Without question my ability to locate and integrate current research into each chapter of this text was aided directly by the availability of both traditional print references and online resources. Moreover, my ability to produce text and to edit it effectively was aided by computer-based technologies. These same traditional print and hypermedia resources can prove beneficial to most students as they engage in problem solving (Salomon, 1993b).

Domain Influences

As Chapter 5 made evident, academic domains differ in significant ways (Shulman & Quinlan, 1996). Those differences can be highly influential in students' abilities to function strategically. In addition, the knowledge and interests that students bring to domains greatly affect the nature of their strategic performance.

Typical Problems and Strategic Emphases

One defining feature of academic domains is the nature of the problems used to represent those domains to students (i.e., schooled problems; Stewart, 1987). In some domains, like mathematics or science, schooled problems are often well-structured with an acceptable right answer generally derived through the application of algorithmic strategies or formulas. In other domains, like reading or history, problems are less well-structured, with many plausible responses derived from a multitude of strategies, often of a heuristic, or general guideline, nature. The well-structured and often procedurally rich domains may place greater emphasis on domain-specific rather than general strategies. In contrast, the more ill-structured domains, especially those like reading, writing, and history that are highly linguistic in nature, place greater reliance on general strategies of the type outlined in Table 7–1.

Interaction with Learner Characteristics

Beyond these features of the domains themselves, the characteristics of students relative to those domains result in quantitative and qualitative differences in their strategic thinking. These strategic variations have been well documented in studies of the model of domain learning, or MDL (Alexander, 1997b). MDL research has demonstrated that patterns in strategy use are strongly related to students' interest in and knowledge of a domain or domain-related topics (Alexander, Jetton, & Kulikowich, 1995; Alexander, Murphy, Woods, Duhon, & Parker, 1997).

According to the MDL, students progress through three stages of development within academic domains: acclimation,

competence, and proficiency/expertise. Those in acclimation are new to a field of study and consequently have limited knowledge and little personal interest or investment in that domain. Competent students, by comparison, have more integrated knowledge of the domain and are more personally interested in that field or related topics. Finally, those who reach proficiency or expertise are not only extremely knowledgeable in the domain but extensively invested in it as well.

Concomitant with these changes in knowledge and interest, students progressing from acclimation to competence and to proficiency undergo changes in their strategic abilities. Specifically, when students in acclimation are working within a domain for which their knowledge and interest are low, they are more likely to rely on surface-level rather than deep-processing strategies (Alexander, Sperl, Buehl, Fives, & Chiu, 2004). **Surface-level strategies,** such as rereading or looking up unfamiliar words, are those strategies that permit students to make initial sense of a given problem.

By comparison, **deep-processing strategies,** or higher order strategies, such as questioning the author or reframing the problem, involve a more extensive manipulation or evaluation of a specified problem (VanSledright & Alexander, 2002). As students move toward competence, displaying more knowledge of and interest in the domain, they tend to use more deep-processing than surface-level strategies (Alexander et al., 2004), a shift that continues as individuals progress toward proficiency (Alexander & Murphy, 1998b). Those who achieve proficiency rely almost exclusively on deep-processing strategies when working within their domain of expertise.

Interrelations among knowledge, interest, and strategic processing are reciprocal (Alexander, Jetton, & Kulikowich, 1995). For example, learners must dedicate a great deal of strategic time and energy to establishing a base of relevant subject-matter knowledge (Alexander, 1997b). Emerging competency does not just happen but must be sought after and worked for. Even students in acclimation must exert strategic effort if they are to establish a foothold in the domain or plant seeds of personal interest. Their reliance on surface-level rather than deep-processing strategies should not be perceived as a strategic weakness on their part (Alexander, 2003b); rather they are engaged in the type of strategic processing needed to establish a foundation of relevant knowledge. Once that relevant knowledge is formed, these students are freer to explore a topic or domain in greater depth.

Learner-Centered Psychological Principle 5

Thinking about thinking. Higher order strategies for selecting and monitoring mental operations facilitate creative and critical thinking.

Learner-Centered Principles Work Group of the APA Board of Educational Affairs, 1997.

From an educational standpoint, teachers need to ensure that their students are exposed to an array of academic domains or of topics within those domains. Teachers should aid their students in acquiring fundamental strategies so that the students will be equipped to navigate new domains with some degree of success. With these strategies students can construct a base of relevant knowledge, articulate reasonable goals, and make sound judgments about their capabilities. They will then be able to use their knowledge and strategic abilities to blaze trails toward academic development—trails that reflect their academic strengths, personal interests, values, and perceived competencies.

What Can Teachers Do to Help Students Become More Strategic?

Pam Gaskill reached two critical understandings. The first was that effective learning demands effective strategic thinking. The second was that strategic processing can be improved through strategic teaching. Teachers can do a great deal to help their students become better thinkers and problem solvers, which is what **strategic teaching** is all about—enhancing the strategic thinking that occurs in the learning environment.

Demonstrate the Power of Strategic Thinking   It is one thing to *tell* students that strategies make a significant difference in their learning and performance, but quite another to *show* them how powerful strategic thinking can be. In her second-grade classroom, Pam Gaskill did not tell her students that grouping information in meaningful ways results in better memory. She set up an experiment in her classroom so that these children could not help seeing the effect of chunking for themselves. With that personal realization, the students were ready to apply their newly learned technique again and in other contexts.

Alan Schoenfeld (1985, 1988) used the same approach with his Berkeley students. He did not tell them how valuable reflecting and planning are for mathematical problem solving. Instead, he let them discover that reality on their own. Only after they had labored ineffectively and inefficiently trying to calculate a given problem, did Schoenfeld show them how much faster and more accurately they performed when they took time to analyze the task. When the students took the time to look closely at the problem, they were able to recognize its basic structure and then rather easily apply the correct formula. As predicted, Schoenfeld's students were eager to learn more about self-monitoring and self-regulation after that demonstration. Whether the target strategy is categorizing, self-monitoring, or outlining, teachers are advised to demonstrate the effects strategies have on learning and performance.

Make Strategic Thinking an Explicit Part of the Classroom Curriculum   Many bright and capable undergraduates manage to get by with only a limited and sketchy repertoire of strategies because they have never been explicitly taught strategies for studying or for complex problem solving. How much better could they be as students if they used relevant general and domain-specific strategies?

One of the strategies that I teach my undergraduates is the steps for solving classical analogy problems similar to the ones they encounter on standardized achievement and aptitude tests (Goswami, 1992; Sternberg, 1977). I first give my students sample analogies to complete; they are usually quite confident that they have performed well—overly confident as it turns out. For instance, I might present the following problem:

HERD : COW :: FLOCK : _____

The students quickly fill in the blank with such words as *bird, birds, goose, geese, seagulls,* and *sheep.* They are then dismayed to learn that none of these words is the preferred response. Their failure to perform is rarely reflective of limited intelligence or a poor vocabulary. Rather, it is indicative of their lack of knowledge about the processes associated with analogical reasoning, which are summarized in Figure 7–6, along with the preferred answer to this problem.

It takes me 30 minutes to teach my undergraduates how to solve analogies more accurately, using the same processes that my colleagues and I have taught preschoolers, elementary students, and high schoolers (Alexander, White, & Daugherty, 1997; White & Alexander, 1986; Judy, Alexander, Kulikowich, & Willson, 1988). Understandably, my undergraduates find it disconcerting that someone did not teach them these processes years ago. Their teachers may have assumed that these steps are self-evident, but *they are not.* Perhaps their teachers had not articulated for themselves what is required to solve analogy problems well. Those who wish to teach strategically must reflect on strategies and the processes underlying them. Then they must make that knowledge public (Paris et al., 1991).

Integrate Instruction on Strategies with Academic Content in Practical and Meaningful Ways   When Sternberg and Wagner (1986) looked closely at programs specifically established to teach critical- and creative-thinking skills, they found that many of those programs were only qualified successes. The programs that characteristically taught critical and creative thinking out of the context of regular school content did not endure or transfer. Students typically displayed the processes they had been taught only when they were working directly in the same program or on variants of the contrived tasks or problems used in the training. The trained students did not apply those processes to their regular curriculum or their everyday life.

Sternberg and Wagner's (1986) analysis indicates that strategic thinking should not be taught in isolation but should be infused in the content and activities of the classroom. No one should teach children in a specialized course how to determine the main idea of text and then hope they use this strategy in school. Rather, such a procedure should be introduced when students are trying to make sense of their classroom texts or other relevant readings. As Sternberg and Wagner realized, artificiality in either the setting

HERD : COW : : FLOCK : _____

Step 1: ENCODE

Carefully consider the meaning or attributes of each term in the analogy problem.

Example: Herd is a collection of certain animals of like species, such as a herd of cows or buffalo.

Cow is a single female, domesticated animal. It is four-legged, gives milk, and bears live young. People eat the meat and use the skins of this animal.

Flock, like *herd,* is a collection of same-species animals.

Step 2: INFER

Establish the relation between the first term and the second term of the problem.

Example: A *cow* is a single, female member of a *herd.*

Step 3: MAP

Establish the relation between the first term and the third term of the problem.

Example: Herd and *flock* are both collections of animals, although they designate different species.

Step 4: APPLY

Identify the term that corresponds to the third term in the same way that the first and second terms correspond.

Example: A single female member of a flock, domesticated, milk giving, meat producing, and bearing live young . . . is a *ewe.*

■ **FIGURE 7–6   Strategy for solving classic analogies.**

or the content often works against students' ability to see a strategy as truly fundamental to their learning.

Part of infusing strategic thinking into the classroom context concerns the language and concepts teachers use during instruction. In his book, *Smart Schools,* David Perkins (1992) refers to the *language of thinking* and the *language of strategies.* He suggests that teachers find opportunities to introduce terms like *compare, predict,* and *cause/effect* in their interactions with students.

In addition, teachers can guide students as they actually do compare, predict, determine causality, and the like (Palincsar & Brown, 1984). For example, if Pam asks her second graders to compare a picture on page 3 of their reading book with a picture on page 7, she could remind the children what processes might help them make comparisons. Or when Eddie's biology teacher, Miss Jefferson, suggests that he might benefit from mapping his text chapters, she could share her approach to mapping or provide him with some useful examples. The point is that teachers who think that a particular strategy could aid students in the completion of a certain assignment should take the time to explain, reinforce, or elaborate on that strategy. They should think of it as a *strategic moment.*

Concentrate on a Few Fundamental Strategies at a Time and Teach Them Well   Michael Pressley and associates (1989) have done a great deal of research on strategies in the past decades. Based on this research, Pressley recommends that teachers be selective in the number of strategies they teach at any given time. In Pressley's opinion teachers should teach only a few strategies and cover them well, to allow students to personalize the strategies and transfer them to other tasks. For example, Pressley has suggested the four basic text-processing strategies that are part of the reciprocal teaching model (Palincsar & Brown, 1984)

as candidates for initial strategy instruction. Teachers can focus on these general strategies of questioning, predicting, clarifying, and summarizing and infuse them into the curriculum across subject-matter areas. Once these strategies are well understood and broadly practiced by students in diverse contexts, teachers can move on to other strategies. One caveat to this recommendation is that teachers must be alert to strategic moments: If the perfect assignment for introducing a new strategy arises during the course of instruction, teachers need to be prepared to take advantage of that occasion. However, new strategies remain fragile knowledge until students have repeated practice with them. In addition, teachers working with students of varying ages and abilities or with diverse subject matter must make reasoned

Michael Pressley is an advocate of teaching a limited number of key strategies.

judgments about the strategies that would prove most applicable (Alexander, 1998c). No starter set of strategies remains invariant across grades and content areas.

Prompt and Scaffold Students' Strategic Efforts As just mentioned, students' internalization of strategies remains fragile knowledge for some time. For that reason, teachers should periodically remind students to draw on their strategic knowledge, perhaps employing prompts and cues during instruction to trigger strategic thinking. Harris and Graham (1996) incorporate explicit checklists like the one shown in Figure 7–7 in their training of strategies for

Directions:

Place a check by each action that you did while writing this paper.

Time and place

_____ I set up a schedule for when I would work on the paper.

_____ I found a quiet place to work.

_____ I got started working right away.

_____ I kept track of how much time I spent working on this paper.

_____ I always had the materials ready that I needed each time.

_____ I sat down to work.

Understanding the task

_____ I read or listened to the teacher's directions carefully.

_____ I asked the teacher to explain any part of the assignment that was unclear to me.

_____ I restated what I was supposed to do in my words.

Planning

_____ I thought about who would read my paper.

_____ I thought about what I wanted my paper to accomplish.

_____ I started planning my paper before I actually started writing it.

_____ I used a strategy to help me plan my paper.

Seeking and organizing information

_____ I tried to remember everything I already knew about this topic before starting to write.

_____ I got all the information I needed before starting to write.

_____ I organized all of the information I had gathered before starting to write.

Writing

_____ I thought about what I wanted my paper to accomplish as I wrote.

_____ I thought about the reader as I wrote.

_____ I continued to develop my plans as I wrote.

_____ I made revisions in my paper as I wrote.

Revising

_____ I revised the first draft of my paper.

_____ I checked to make sure that the reader would understand everything I had to say.

_____ I checked to make sure that my goals for the paper were accomplished.

_____ I made my paper better by adding, dropping, changing, or rearranging parts of my paper.

_____ I corrected errors of spelling, capitalization, punctuation, and the like.

_____ I used a strategy to help me revise.

_____ I reread my paper before turning it in.

Seeking assistance

_____ I asked other students for help when I needed it.

_____ I asked my teacher(s) for help when I needed it.

_____ I asked my parents or other people for help when I needed it.

Motivation

_____ I told myself I was doing a good job while I was working on the paper.

_____ I rewarded myself when I finished the paper.

■ **FIGURE 7–7   Writing process checklist.**

Note: From *Making the Writing Process Work: Strategies of Composition and Self Regulation* (pp. 165–166) by K. R. Harris and S. Graham, 1996, Cambridge, MA: Brookline Books. Copyright 1996 by Brookline Books. Reprinted with permission.

Karen Harris and Steve Graham have conducted extensive research on writing strategies, especially for special populations.

composition and self-regulation. They use that particular checklist to remind students with special needs of areas that require their strategic attention during writing, such as planning and organizing information.

Harris and Graham (1996) also find that this type of checklist can be an effective tool for self-assessment. Once students have been explicitly taught how to engage in the processes listed, the checklist becomes an effective substitute for a teacher's verbal reminders of what kinds of strategic actions might be taken. Students can monitor themselves in everything from organizing their work environment (e.g., I always had the materials ready that I needed each time) and planning (e.g., I thought about who would read my paper) to self-rewarding (e.g., I told myself I was doing a good job while I was working on the paper) and help seeking (e.g., I asked other students for help when I needed it).

Even with the incorporation of prompts, such as the writing checklist, students will periodically require direct guidance and support from teachers. This support can take the form of teacher modeling, questioning, or probing. The teacher might even determine that aspects or steps of strategies need to be retaught or reinforced. In addition, the teacher might find it useful to have students demonstrate how they are performing a particular task or applying a given strategy. Listening and watching as students work through a task can give teachers valuable clues about where strategic thinking or problem solving may be faltering.

For example, Harris and Graham (1996) worked with children who had been taught a revision strategy called SCAN. With this strategy students scan each sentence they have written and ask themselves whether that sentence is (a) clear—Will a reader understand what was written? (b) useful—Does it contribute to the message or arguments? (c) complete—Are there sufficient descriptions or details? and (d) error free—Are there any spelling or syntactical problems? As Harris and Graham watched one young girl, they realized that she was systematically

dropping the last step in this process. Thus, her writing often contained mechanical errors. To help this student, Harris and Graham gave her a little booster lesson on how to identify and rectify errors, and the student's written products improved markedly. As Harris and Graham realized, even good strategic thinkers cannot be expected to perform flawlessly or effectively on every academic task. Therefore, teachers must be prepared to prompt or scaffold students' strategic efforts. However, as students become competent in a field, their need for prompting and scaffolding should decrease (Alexander, 1997b).

Encourage the Personalization and Modification of Strategic Processes   The distinctions between skills and strategies remain critical: Strategies must be intentionally and thoughtfully applied in situations where performance is less than optimal or when barriers are encountered. Researchers have realized that there is great value in teaching strategies provided that students are given control over how they conceive and implement those strategies (Randi & Corno, 2001; Weinstein, Husman, & Dierking, 2001). Students need to understand that strategies are flexible tools that learners manipulate or modify to fit the immediate context (Nist & Holschuh, 2000).

For example, Harris and Graham (1996) do not expect students to perform every one of the actions in the writing process checklist every time they write. The goal is for students to realize that these steps can be used when and if they are warranted. Students should not ask for help routinely, for instance; they should try to resolve their problems on their own first. Only if problems persist or resist self-interventions, should students turn to other classmates, teachers, or parents for assistance.

Some problems require more encoding, inferring, mapping, or applying than others (Alexander, White, Haensly, & Crimmins-Jeanes, 1987). The following two problems are a case in point.

DOG : BARK :: CAT : _____
OCEAN : BAY :: CONTINENT : _____

You probably got the answer to the first problem almost instantaneously. Thus, it would be inefficient for you to spend much time thinking through the four-step strategy in that instance. For the second problem, however, you probably needed time to encode the given terms, especially the attributes of a bay. Similarly, you probably needed to invest more effort in inferring the relationship between *ocean* and *bay* and mapping *ocean* and *continent* before you came to the answer of *peninsula*. (Note: A peninsula is an offshoot of a continent, the largest landmass, and is surrounded by water on three sides. A bay is an offshoot of an ocean, the largest body of water, and is surrounded by land on three sides.)

As these examples illustrate, strategies, especially general strategies, should be taught as performance guides, not as rigid formulas that must be followed religiously or exactly (Glynn, Duit, & Thiele, 1995; McKeachie, 1996; Nist &

Shawn Glynn has extensively researched analogies in science learning.

Holschuh, 2000). Students should be encouraged to reshape and rework these general guidelines until they become their own.

Foster Individual Goals, Self-Regulation, and Self-Evaluation Good strategic thinkers adopt a self-as-agent perspective, to use Pam Gaskill's words. That is, they understand that they have a large measure of control over their learning and development (Boekaerts et al., 2001; Iran-Nejad, 1990). Strategic teachers contribute directly and purposefully to this perception of self as agent, transferring strategic control to their students for optimal academic achievement.

Figure 7–8 briefly describes several suggestions from the writings of educational researchers—including Winne (1995), Zimmerman (1995), Pintrich and Schunk (2001), and Woolfolk (2001)—for promoting individualization, self-regulation, and self-evaluation. However, teachers must *help* students take charge of their learning and development: Merely handing over the reins to young or naive learners will not create the desired outcome (Alexander, 2003a; Graves, 1997). And such a transfer must be gradual and reasonable, accomplished in a learning environment that addresses strategic thinking in an explicit and integrated manner.

Allow Sufficient Time and Incentives for Strategic Thinking When Garner (1990) tried to uncover reasons why students were nonstrategic in their thinking and learning, she came to an important insight: Classroom climates in which most students operate do not really offer sufficient time or opportunities to think and act strategically. Performing strategically takes more time and certainly more effort than merely operating on automatic pilot. Thinking and acting strategically may cause students to raise questions or explore goals and paths other than those their teachers have in mind. Thus, as Garner (1990) deduced, even though many teachers *say* they want students to be more strategic, the teachers do not want to deal with the potential consequences of strategic thinking.

If strategic teaching is to occur, teachers must set aside their tendencies to get through the material quickly or to accept only certain results. Strategic teaching can open doors to unanticipated, but valuable, outcomes. The more teachers see their content as important and worthy of instructional investment and assessment (Chissom & Iran-Nejad, 1992), the more likely they are to give their students the time needed to explore that content deeply and richly.

Look to Students as Sources and Models of Strategic Processing Teachers must remember that they do not have to be the sole source of knowledge and guidance about strategic thinking. All learners facing challenging or novel tasks must find their own way, and the steps they take or the

---

- **Be sure that students understand the nature and purpose of academic tasks.**

  Students commonly misread the nature of academic tasks or misunderstand what their teachers want them to accomplish. Teachers should encourage students to articulate their perceptions of what is being asked and what the results should demonstrate.

- **Provide practice in task analysis.**

  Teachers can foster self-monitoring and self-regulation by helping students take a large task apart so that they can deal more effectively with its various components or dimensions. A task like writing a paper, for instance, can be subdivided into an array of subcomponents, including choosing a topic, selecting a theme, and locating good resources.

- **Describe criteria that could be used to judge various academic outcomes.**

  The more teachers explicate the specific criteria they will use to judge classroom tasks, the more students have workable models upon which to draw. Teachers should also explain their reasons for selecting those particular criteria.

- **Create opportunities for students to create individual or collective criteria for evaluating certain tasks.**

  Following their teachers' explication and modeling, students should have the opportunity to generate other criteria for use in evaluation.

- **Allow students to formulate personal goals for select learning tasks.**

  Students do not always have to have the same goal for a learning task. The inclusion of choice and personal outcomes contributes to students' investment in their learning. For example, students might choose different vocabulary words for a weekly test.

- **Give students some say in what is graded and by whom.**

  Direct student involvement can extend to grading. Occasionally giving students a choice in which products get externally evaluated and whether that evaluation comes from a teacher, peer, or self adds to an atmosphere of self-monitoring and self-regulation.

- **Promote peer collaboration and peer review.**

  Teachers who have integrated peer collaboration and peer review into the learning environment report that students are more comfortable with and prepared to engage in peer and self evaluation.

- **Have students put their plans, thoughts, and judgments in writing.**

  When goals, criteria, or evaluations are put in writing, teachers and students have a more permanent record they can discuss and use as prompts for self-monitoring or self-regulation.

■ FIGURE 7–8 Suggestions for promoting self-monitoring and self-regulation.

techniques they devise are, in effect, strategies (Alexander & Judy, 1988). The strategies may be unsophisticated or rudimentary, but they are strategies nonetheless. Thus, students can be valuable sources of and models for strategic processing.

Some of the children in Pam's class were able to group the words she had given them during rehearsal, although they did not know how to take advantage of those groupings when it came to memorization. In addition, Terry hit upon the chunking strategy on his own, suggesting that teachers do not need to be the only ones devising guidelines or heuristics that enhance thinking. Students themselves can contribute to the process. Terry could have explained to his classmates how he was able to perform so well on the recall task, and Pam could have used Terry's example as the catalyst for her categorization lesson. As students gain in competence and domain-specific knowledge, they are even more likely to construct strategic processes that their teachers have not considered (Alexander, 1997b). And by giving students a voice in articulating strategic alternatives, teachers can increase students' investment in strategic learning.

■ Summary Reflections

What does it mean to be a strategic learner?

- Optimal learning and development demand strategic thinking on the part of students and are greatly enhanced by teachers' efforts to promote thinking in their classrooms.
- Pervasive myths can be barriers to strategic learning and teaching.
  - Strategies have specific characteristics, such as consciousness and purposefulness, that differentiate them from academic skills.
  - Various characteristics of good strategic thinking can and should be nurtured in the classroom.
- Good strategic thinking involves efficient and effective thinking, planfulness, conditional knowledge of strategies, strategy modification and personalization, a rich strategy repertoire, and investment in and monitoring of performance.

- General strategies may be effective for capturing and retaining information, improving memory, comprehending and recalling text, organizing information, motivating performance, and monitoring and regulating learning.

How do strategic abilities vary across domains and contexts?

- Students are never consistently good or poor strategic thinkers but are influenced by many factors.
  - Social-contextual forces or strategic processing include peer interactions and nonhuman educational resources.
  - Domains themselves exert influence on the character of students' strategic processing.
  - As students move toward competence, they rely less on surface-level strategies and more on deep-processing strategies.
- Effective learners must be knowledgeable and competent in an array of general and domain-specific strategies.

What can teachers do to help students become more strategic?

- Teachers must *show* rather than *tell* that strategies work.
- Teachers should take time to make strategies explicit parts of the school curriculum and ensure that those strategies are integrated into instruction in practical and meaningful ways.
- Research supports the teaching of a few basic strategies at a time.
- Strategic teaching gives students' strategic efforts support and guidance in concrete and motivational ways— with prompts and cues and feedback.
- Students should be encouraged to make strategies their own by personalizing learned strategies to fit their particular goals and needs.
- Students should be guided to be self-regulating and self-monitoring.
- Effective teachers ensure that students have sufficient time and incentives to operate strategically.
- Strategic teachers see students as self-initiators and models of strategic thinking.

Chapter 8

Profiling Problem Solving in the Classroom

GUIDING QUESTIONS

■ What makes a problem a problem?

■ What is a framework for analyzing academic problems?

■ What are the guidelines for effective problem solving?

IN THEIR OWN WORDS

As a high-school physics teacher, Jennifer Gonya has discovered that her students' attitudes and perceptions can make it difficult for them to open their minds to the possibilities of physics.

So many high-school students have this stubborn idea that physics is reserved for "smart" people and that the things you learn about in physics only work in some ideal environment. Even those who enroll in my classes initially think of physics problems as these terribly sophisticated and convoluted math questions that require a plug-and-chug mentality and have nothing to do with real people or real life. I have seen over the years that my physics students initially fall into two groups. Some believe physics problems are simply impossible to solve. These students give up on the problem before they even give themselves a chance. The other students find the correct formula and do the calculations. The trouble is these students have no idea how or why the formula works—I am not sure they even care.

I know I have my work cut out for me from Day 1. I have to break through these barriers of "I can't do it" or "Just let me do the math and get the right answer—the reason be damned!" It is not an easy process. I work hard to create an environment in which it is safe to learn. In my teaching, I emphasize *process* rather than *product*. I also encourage students to take risks in their thinking, to explore alternatives, to seek justifications for their beliefs, and to be open to new possibilities. Basically, I want them to see that good problem solving in physics starts with understanding the problem on a deep level. Once they have this sense of the problem, they can formulate a strategy for solving it, take a risk and attempt a solution, analyze and evaluate their performance, and then share their results.

Still, my students easily revert to their old ways of thinking. They find it difficult to abandon their desire to find the one right answer and move on. Just the other day, we were doing an activity meant to help them discover what happens to the water level in a glass when ice melts. Before we began, I asked the students to share their predictions. Some students argued that the water level in the glass would rise as the ice melts. Arguing just as strongly on the other side were those who *knew* that the water level would remain the same. To make their cases, students on both sides searched their textbooks, computers, and resource materials for relevant data. During all of this, I served as devil's advocate, providing pros and cons for each argument the students made. After a while, the students said, "Come on, Miss Gonya. Just tell us the answer!" "Yeah, Miss Gonya, who's got it right?" But I was not about to let them off the hook.

The students then decided to have each group perform an experiment in front of the class. That way, all could see for themselves whether the water level in the glass rose or stayed the same as the ice melted. The problem was that the results of their little experiment were inconclusive. Students could make their case either way based on what they saw. Then the bell rang. My students did not want to leave until they learned "the truth." I told them they would have to wait till the next day to figure it out. I was certain that the excitement and motivation in the room would carry over into the next day's problem solving. I was also convinced that some students would leave the room and think long and hard about this little dilemma.

When class began the next day, however, no one offered new information or resurrected the debate. The excitement and passion about this question had vanished. The students' lives had moved on, and they didn't seem to care whether the water in the glass would rise or stay the same. Still, once in a while, a student like Manny will come up to me and say something like, "You know, I have been thinking about the water problem and . . ." Maybe some of my efforts are having an effect after all. It is not easy to change students' thinking about physics and physics problem solving. But I am determined to try.

What Makes a Problem a Problem?

Learning and human development are essentially lifelong experiences in problem solving. From birth individuals begin the endless process of trying to make sense of their surroundings, coping with minor and major events that disrupt the flow of their daily lives. As they mature, they even put themselves in circumstances like independent living, advanced studies, marriage, or parenting that complicate existence and exacerbate its problems. Problem solving is, thus, an integral part of the human condition (Sternberg, 1985a).

As Jennifer Gonya recognizes, problem solving is also at the very core of learning and instruction. Even everyday terms like *smart, intelligent,* and *creative* are markers for problem solving (Ennis, 1987; Sternberg & Wagner, 1986). For example, intellectual potential is typically determined by responses to a series of challenging questions (Herrnstein & Murray, 1994). The more questions individuals answer accurately and the faster they do so relative to their peers, the more intelligent they are presumed to be. Some may disagree with this manner of judging intelligence; many do (Elliott, 1987; H. Gardner, 1999). But regardless of this debate about assessment, people described as smart, intelligent, or creative in the real world have revealed their problem-solving abilities in some fashion. Maybe they know how to take command of a social situation; maybe they always respond quickly and effectively when unexpected crises arise; maybe they are inventive or exceptionally artistic. There is no way to isolate human capability from problem solving (Mayer, 1983).

It is not surprising then that education and problem solving go hand in hand. In many ways formal education is an orchestrated attempt to present students with increasingly complex and varied mental tasks and with the knowledge and strategies required to tackle such problems well (Alexander, 1997b). As Jennifer Gonya points out, problems are not always the ends of learning, but more accurately the means by which minds are stimulated and enriched. Teachers like Miss Gonya fervently hope that their students carry problem-solving knowledge into everyday situations that demand reasoned and thoughtful responses (Marini & Genereux, 1995).

The Nature of a Problem

As Chapter 7 made clear, good strategic thinking depends heavily on students' ability to judge situations accurately and to use the most effective and efficient means to improve those situations (Bransford & Stein, 1993). However, without a clear understanding of the problem, learners have little hope of analyzing situations well or acting appropriately (Polya, 1945). Moreover, if students do not have accurate knowledge of themselves as problem solvers, their efforts to be strategic processors will be greatly hampered. And same can be said for teachers, because teaching is fundamentally a problem-solving act (Alexander & Fives, 2000).

What then makes a problem a problem? A **problem** exists any time there is a discrepancy or a gap between an individual's present state and the state in which he or she wants to be (Newell & Simon, 1972). As illustrated in Figure 8–1, problems can be conceived as physical spaces, with **significance** of the problem represented by the size of the problem space—the distance between someone's current or initial state and the desired or ideal state (Simon, 1978). For example, my decision to eat cereal or eggs this morning (Figure 8–1a) was a trivial problem with initial and ideal states quite close together. Conversely, I have wrestled with the question of what information to include in this chapter and what to omit (Figure 8–1b). Thus, the size of that space was far larger, indicating that the problem was more significant.

Moreover, as Jennifer Gonya's water-level activity indicates, the size of the problem space is not fixed or consistent across individuals. During the heat of the students' debate, the problem space appeared to expand; that is, the question became increasingly important to the students as their hypotheses were publicly put to the test. However, as class ended and other events intruded on their lives, their desire to reach a solution faded, and so, too, did the significance of the problem for them. Because Jennifer mistakenly assumed that they would maintain their interest until the next class, her problem space and that of her students varied dramatically when class started the following day.

The configuration of a problem space also reflects the **complexity** of the problem, which is associated with the nature of the solution path—whether straightforward or convoluted (Simon, 1978). For instance, my breakfast dilemma had

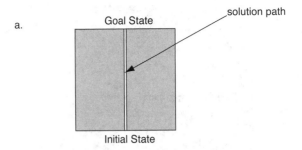

a.

Representation of a small and straightforward problem
("Shall I have cereal or eggs for breakfast?")

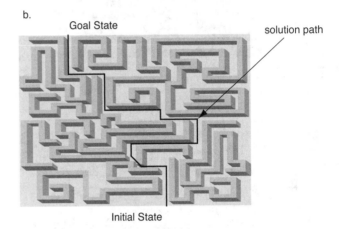

b.

Representation of a large and messy problem
("What should I include in this problem-solving chapter?")

■ **FIGURE 8–1   Understanding the problem space.**

two clear options: cereal or eggs. Thus, my path to solution—picking between the two—was quick and straightforward. In contrast, my chapter quandary had no simple solution. Consequently, my path from initial to ideal states was more convoluted and contorted. Each decision I made about content seemed to bring me to another decision point, presenting me with yet another set of options. The course of my thinking for this problem was more like that of a maze.

To illustrate further, Jennifer Gonya's students enter her physics class with the preconception that all physics problems are clear-cut and have straightforward solution paths (diSessa, 1993). They just want to find the right formula and race through the problem space. However, by emphasizing the process rather than the product, Jennifer is attempting to increase the significance of the problem and obscure the solution path so that her students explore the problem space more deeply and consider alternative solution paths.

Benefits of Classifying Academic Problems

The world offers an abundance of problems, even within the confines of the classroom. Some problems emphasize a student's ability to understand and use spoken or written

Research on problem solving owes much to the genius of Herbert Simon.

Table 8–1	Benefits of problem classification.
Beneficiary	**Benefit**
Students	Provides a means for thinking about a problem space
	Facilitates the choice of strategies for solving a problem
	Encourages students to take calculated risks
	Serves as a basis for more specific self-evaluation and self-assessment
	Moves thinking beyond global judgments of intellectual or academic capabilities
Teachers	Becomes a basis for examining instructional and assessment activities
	Reduces the likelihood of an epistemological mismatch between teachers' goals and students' perceptions
	Enriches the language of problem solving that can be used in the classroom
	Prompts review of problem-solving techniques that require explanation or elaboration
	Contributes to a more detailed understanding of students' particular strengths or needs as problem solvers

language. Others rely on alternative symbol systems, including pictures, numbers, or graphics (Kulikowich et al., 2000). Certain academic problems are routinely used in instruction (Stewart, 1987), whereas others are rarely seen in classrooms and their underlying processes are rarely taught. A system for classifying problems has many benefits (see Table 8–1) for students and teachers alike (Snow, 1981).

Learner Benefits

Logic dictates that students who know how to categorize problems should outperform those with limited knowledge of problem structures, and the research concurs (Bransford & Stein, 1993; Schoenfeld, 1985). Better problem identification and better problem solving go hand in hand, making problem identification a worthwhile enterprise at any grade level or in any content area. Sadly, the research on problem solving also reveals that critical knowledge of problem structures is scarce among young or less expert students (Mayer, 1998). Nonetheless, the specific benefits are numerous.

Conceptualizing the Problem Space

Through problem classification learners can better conceptualize a problem space. Simply grasping whether a problem likely has one or many solutions or whether the problem is more numeric than linguistic can influence the path students follow in attacking that problem. Such understanding can help students put aside their debilitating beliefs that schooled problems come in only one shape or size (Stewart, 1987). It can also help them recognize that not all problems have an unquestionable and agreed-upon right answer (diSessa, 1993; Schommer, Crouse, & Rhodes, 1992).

Making Wise Strategic Decisions

In addition, problem classification aids students in deciding which approach or strategic process works best in a given situation (Alexander & Judy, 1988). Matching strategies to problems depends greatly on conditional knowledge—knowledge about when and where to apply certain strategies (Paris, Lipson, & Wixson, 1983). Increasing students' sensitivity to distinctions among academic problems can only add to this body of conditional knowledge. Consequently, students should be better able to make thoughtful choices among their strategic alternatives (Alexander, Graham, & Harris, 1998).

Taking Calculated Risks

Risk taking involves venturing into unfamiliar academic territory. Of course, students can take more or less intelligent risks (Bransford, Brown, & Cocking, 1999), but good students are more likely to take calculated risks, which often result in positive or successful outcomes (Jetton & Alexander, 1997). The more students know about academic problems, the more able and willing they may be to engage in calculated risk taking during problem solving.

Refining Self-Evaluation

Teachers try to move students beyond global judgments about ability (e.g., "Physics is for smart people" or "I'll never be able to solve physics problems") to more specific and appropriate self-assessments (Iran-Nejad, 1990; Pajares, 1996). Understanding problem structures can be a catalyst for replacing such all-or-nothing evaluations, because more probing self-assessments result from more particular knowledge (e.g., "I am better at problems with clear right-or-wrong answers" or "I have some difficulty with tasks that require spatial reasoning").

Redefining Intelligent Behavior

Self-monitoring and self-evaluation are fundamental for optimal learning and development (Garner, 1987; Jones & Idol, 1990). However, students must be guided to the knowledge required to make such self-determinations accurately and specifically. In other words, learners must appreciate how truly complex problems and problem solving can be and abandon their notions that only certain kinds of problems and only certain modes of problem solving correspond to intelligence or smartness (Ames, 1984b; H. Gardner, 1983). Instead, students need to recognize that intelligent behavior is as varied as the problems encountered (Lampert, 1990). A framework for analyzing and discussing academic problems contributes to this understanding.

Teacher Benefits

Knowledge of problem types is just as powerful a tool for teachers as it is for students. For teachers the benefits extend to the organization of their curriculum and the way that curriculum is conveyed to students, as well as to teachers' perceptions and assessments of student learning and development.

Improving Materials for Instruction and Assessment

Jennifer Gonya is well aware of the limited view of physics problems that her students hold (diSessa, 1993) and has set out to dispel their misconceptions by incorporating varied problem-solving tasks in her curriculum (Schoenfeld, 1985). By including more open-ended, less formula-driven activities in her lessons, she hopes to disrupt her students' plug-and-chug approach to physics problems (Lampert, 1990).

The curriculum examination that prompted Jennifer to adjust her approach can benefit all teachers—not just those who teach mathematics or science. Research on students' beliefs about knowledge and knowing (i.e., epistemology) makes it painfully clear that the rather routine treatment of school subjects helps to create students' narrow perceptions of what it means to know physics, history, or other academic domains (Buehl & Alexander, 2001; Hofer, 2000). Teachers who want students to conceive of educational knowledge more broadly and flexibly should consider whether the tasks they use in instruction and assessment are sufficiently varied. A framework for analyzing problems can assist teachers in this critical analysis.

Increasing Conceptual Clarity

Knowledge of problem classification can help put teachers and students on the same epistemological page in other ways as well. For instance, Jennifer was working hard to create a learning event that she thought was open-ended and creative, but her students were envisioning a much more structured task. Figure 8–2 captures the conceptual confu-

The teacher describes the task, which should be treated as fluid, creative, and open-ended. The students expect the problem to have a clear and simple correct answer.

The teacher presents a well-specified problem and a clear solution path. The students' problem space remains convoluted and ill-formed.

■ FIGURE 8–2   Epistemological confusion.

sion that occurs in many classrooms. In both situations the beliefs of the teacher and the beliefs of the students are incongruent, which complicates both learning and teaching (M. R. Matthews, 1994). If teachers can be more specific in their communications with students about the nature of the task being introduced such epistemological confusion may be less likely to occur.

Augmenting the Language of Problem Solving

Problem classification offers another advantage that relates directly to this issue of clearer communication between teachers and students. One step toward creating smart schools, according to David Perkins (1992), is to integrate the language of thinking with the language of strategies. Having words to describe the forms or characteristics of problems expands teachers' and students' problem-solving vocabulary. Thus, learning more about problem characteristics should augment teachers' ability to speak a language of thinking and strategies that can be shared with and understood by their students.

Stimulating a Review of Students' Problem-Solving Procedures

As teachers and students become more aware of problem-solving dimensions, other benefits emerge. With an increased attention to the language of thinking and the language of strategies, greater sensitivity to the problem-solving techniques associated with varied tasks can develop.

Thus, teachers gain a platform for determining whether students' knowledge of those associated techniques is adequate to the task or requires reinforcement or reteaching (Baron & Sternberg, 1987).

Prompting More Specific Analysis of Student Capabilities

Problem classification can help teachers formulate more specific and well-founded judgments about the problem-solving abilities of their students. Teachers' knowledge of the diversity of problems and problem solving methods can diminish their tendency toward sweeping evaluations about what students know and can do academically. Part of the appeal of concepts like Howard Gardner's (1983) multiple intelligences or Robert Sternberg's (1985a) triarchic theory is that they allow educators to recognize and appreciate the variability and diversity in human learning and development. Individuals do not all need to fit the same problem-solving mold and may have multiple means of displaying their abilities. If educators know more about the structure of problems, they can more fully appreciate the diversity in human problem solving that Gardner, Sternberg, and others celebrate (Alexander, 1997a).

What Is a Framework for Analyzing Academic Problems?

To begin this discussion of problem classification, first work the problems in the Thought Experiment: Calisthenics for the Mind. You are likely to find some of the problems easier than others, and some more to your liking. Take note of your reactions as you complete each set of items. Do not worry if you cannot do all of the problems; just do your best.

Thought Experiment ....

Calisthenics for the Mind

Directions: Below are a series of problem-solving tasks. Try to complete each of the problems even though some may prove more difficult for you than others. Record your starting and ending times if you wish.

Starting time: _____

1. Complete each of the following by supplying the word, number, or picture that comes next.

    a. February January March   May April June _____

    b. 1 2 3 1 4 9 1 8 _____

    c. _____

2. Name the work in which each of the following is a main character:

    a. Tiny Tim _____

    b. Captain Ahab _____

    c. Ophelia _____

    d. Amy March _____

3. If you and a friend can make 25 party favors in 30 minutes, how many party favors can you and two friends make in 3 hours? _____

4. What is the difference between homophones and homographs?

5. On the first of the month, you deposit $1788 in a money market account that yields 4% interest per year. How much money will you have in that account after 7 months? _____

6. Three sisters—Shawn, Kim, and Karen—have three children among them—Katlin, Joshua, and Shelby. Katlin is particularly fond of playing with Kim's daughter, and Karen sometimes babysits for Shawn's children. Who is Joshua's mother?

7. Below are two patterns that are not yet complete. Draw in the missing pieces that will complete each pattern.

a.

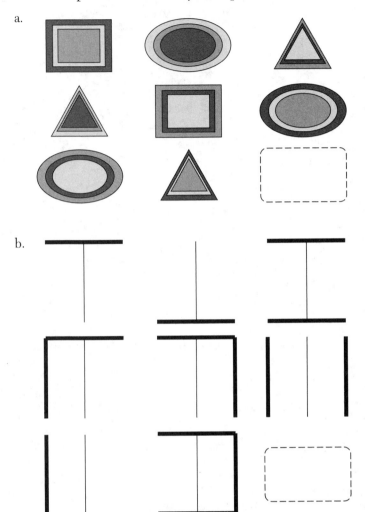

b.

8. Find at least 10 unusual uses for the styrofoam popcorn that comes in packing crates. Try to devise uses that nobody else will think of.

9. Create a unique picture using the figure below. Try to produce a picture that is highly original. (Note: Your artistic ability does not matter.)

10. Complete the following analogies:
a. Yo-Yo Ma : cello : : Andrés Segovia: _____
b. cognitive constructivism : Piaget : : social constructivism: _____
c. Christianity : Bible : : Islam: _____
d. dislike : hate : : respect _____

Ending time : _____

(Answers at the end of the chapter)

So how did this mental exercise make you feel? What does your performance teach you about problems and about you as a problem solver?

Classification of Problems

One effective problem classification scheme positions academic problems along five continua: linguistic to nonlinguistic, well structured to ill structured, schooled to unschooled, timed to untimed, and independent to collaborative. As you read the description of each continuum, think about where the various problems in the mental calisthenics activity fall.

Linguistic Versus Nonlinguistic

One dimension on which to categorize problems pertains to the symbol system(s) that are dominant in the interpretation and performance of the task. Among the symbol systems students encounter in classrooms are linguistic, numeric, and graphic/figural (Goldin, 1992). **Linguistic problems** rely on linguistic symbols in the interpretation, representation, or communication of the problems themselves or their solutions. Because so much about learning and instruction relies on verbal or written communication, many of the problems encountered in the classroom are language based to some degree (Gustafsson & Undheim, 1996).

At the other end of the continuum, **nonlinguistic problems** use alternative symbol systems in their representations or solutions. Numerical systems rely on numbers or related symbols, such as =, +, or Σ, whereas graphic/figural symbols include images, drawings, charts, or pictures. Howard Gardner's (1983) multiple intelligences theory is introduced later. It was influenced by the symbol system on which each intelligence relies.

A heavy emphasis on language can be seen in several tasks in the Mental Calisthenics activity.

> *4. What is the difference between homophones and homographs?*
>
> Linguistic ─☆──────────────────── Nonlinguistic

Not only is this a vocabulary item, which is a linguistic task, but it also queries one's knowledge *about* language. Further, the response requested is verbal. Thus, this problem falls very near the linguistic end of the continuum.

Identification of the pattern in 1.b is quite different: Performance depends extensively on number sense. Specifically, to derive the expected answer, one should know something about raising numbers to particular powers or should see, at least, a pattern of terms being multiplied. It is not necessary to explain the answer in language, only to write the number that completes the series. Thus, the problem is strongly nonlinguistic because the symbol system being manipulated is numeric. The only linguistic part of this question is the directions.

> 1 2 3 1 4 9 1 8
>
> Linguistic ────────────────☆── Nonlinguistic

Not all problems are so strongly linguistic or nonlinguistic. Many problems require both knowledge of and skill with written or oral language as well as numeric, graphic, or pictorial ability.

> *6. Three sisters—Shawn, Kim, and Karen—have three children among them. . . .*
>
> Linguistic ──────────☆────────── Nonlinguistic

In typical word problems, students' performance rests on their ability to understand the subtleties of the text (e.g., Shawn has *children*) and, if complex, to convert that text into some sort of graphic representation. As Richard Mayer (1983) and other researchers (Byrnes, 1996) have demonstrated, it is just as easy for students to get lost in the language of word problems as it is for them to misstep in the logical reasoning or mathematical calculations that follow.

Implications for Learning and Instruction

The characteristics of problems have implications for student learning and for instruction, as summarized in Table 8–2. However, nowhere are these implications more evident than in relation to the linguistic/nonlinguistic continuum. As was mentioned, much of learning and teaching relies on comprehending and communicating orally or in writing. Language even plays an important part in mathematics and science classes (Lampert, 1990).

One of the residual effects of this overlay of language is that students must learn to explain problems or justify their problem-solving approach linguistically, even when the problems are primarily nonlinguistic (Goldin, 1992). For instance, at the heart of the heated debate in Jennifer Gonya's class was her students' ability to explain and justify their positions on the water-level problem. The more students are exposed to the language of thinking and strategies, the more likely they are to have access to the words and phrases they need to make their thinking public (Paris et al., 1983; Perkins, 1992). And the more that talking about problem solving is valued in the classroom, the more practice students get in verbalizing their reasoning (Lampert, 1990). However, teachers must try to see through the language demands of problems so that they can more fully appreciate the reasoning and processing that lies beneath the surface (Kulikowich et al., 2000). Overemphasizing linguistic skills can obscure

Table 8–2   Implications of problem-solving characteristics for students and teachers.

Problem Characteristic	Influence on Student Learning	Instructional Recommendation
Linguistic v. Nonlinguistic	The need to communicate one's understanding puts greater emphasis on linguistic rather than nonlinguistic systems in the classroom. Heavy linguistic component of task may mask the thinking abilities of those less experienced or less comfortable with that linguistic system.	Emphasize the language of problems and problem solving. Try to disentangle problem-solving abilities from the ability to articulate thinking. Provide students with opportunities to demonstrate the same processes in more familiar symbol systems.
Well-Structured v. Ill-Structured	Students may believe that all problems have one best answer, especially in mathematics and science. A routine approach to problem solving often takes precedence over the exploration of alternative solution paths. Criteria for judging the quality of ill-structured problems can be fuzzy.	Share your perceptions of and objectives for various problems. Incorporate a mixture of more and less structured problems into every academic domain. Jointly construct meaningful criteria for evaluating ill-structured problems.
Schooled v. Unschooled	Novel or unschooled problem solving may be restricted to more artistic or creative activities. Students may attribute their performance to their abilities rather than to their exposure to a particular type of problem.	Encourage and reward creative solutions and add creative or novel tasks to the curriculum. Include in the curriculum the processes and procedures for solving particular classes of problems.
Timed v. Untimed	Students may have limited understanding of how to use their time effectively on timed tasks. The compartmentalization of schooling into courses and periods exacerbates the perceptions of timedness in academic tasks. Because timed tasks tend to be associated with formal assessments, they may stress students. Students may not understand the rationale behind timed versus untimed tasks.	Explain how to manage timed tasks, whether they be teacher-devised or standardized. Extend tasks across class periods and content areas for more fluid problem solving. Create as relaxed an environment as possible when students face demanding timed tasks. Inform students when you impose time limits and explain the value or purpose of those limits.
Independent v. Collaborative	Individual strengths can be difficult to ascertain during shared problem solving. Students may feel forced to engage in collaborative or independent problem solving. Group and individual differences toward independent or collaborative performance may not get adequate attention.	Include both collaborative and independent tasks in the curriculum. Articulate and document student responsibilities and contributions. Consider some varied grouping approaches during problem solving.

the thinking and reasoning capabilities of students less facile in schooled language or more comfortable with alternative representational systems (Gustafsson & Undheim, 1996). The special difficulty for students whose first language is not standard English comes not only in understanding what is being asked, but also in communicating what they know or understand in words others can comprehend (Hakuta & McLaughlin, 1996). This same kind of communication barrier can exist for students more at home in an alternative symbol system (Kulikowich et al., 2000). Many brilliant students can perform exceptionally in mathematics, art, or music but are halting and awkward when sharing their mental processes or explaining their products to others.

Teachers cannot completely remove the linguistic overlay on problem solving in classrooms, but they can lessen any undue influence it may have on students' learning and development. Teachers can prompt students to verbalize and justify their responses to certain problems—but not all of them. In addition, providing a diversity of problems that place differential emphases on language can assist in this regard (Snow, 1981).

Self-Assessment

Consider your own performance across the problems in the Mental Calisthenics activity. Carefully analyze your performance in terms of the degree to which the predominance of language or some alternative symbol system in the problem facilitated or inhibited your outcome. Then turn to the Thought Experiment: Problem-Solving Profile and plot your perceived competence along the first continuum.

Thought Experiment ....

Problem-Solving Profile

Directions: Using the definitions and examples in the text, profile your own abilities as a problem solver. Remember that you can put your X at any point on each of these continua.

Linguistic _____Nonlinguistic

Well-structured _____Ill-structured

Schooled _____Unschooled
(traditional)   (novel)

Timed _____ Untimed

Independent _____Collaborative

Well-Structured Versus Ill-Structured

Structuredness is one of the most researched characteristics of problems (Frederiksen, 1984; Spiro et al., 1992). A **well-structured problem** is one for which the problem space is well formed (Alexander & Judy, 1988). The learner has a clear sense of what an acceptable answer would be and a good understanding of what it takes to get to that answer. In other words, a well-structured problem looks more like the first problem space represented in Figure 8–1 than the second.

Question 3 in the Calisthenics Activity is a good example of a well-structured problem:

> 3. If you and a friend can make 25 party favors in 30 minutes, how many party favors can you and two friends make in 3 hours?
>
> Well-structured ☆_____ Ill-structured

Although students may follow slightly different solution paths to the target response of 225 party favors, that number remains the correct answer. Well-structured problems often entail mathematical calculations and are more apt to occur

in domains like mathematics and science (Alexander, 1998c). Of course, not every mathematics or science problem is or should be well-structured (diSessa, 1993; Lampert, 1990).

Ill-structured problems have much messier problem spaces (Alexander & Judy, 1988), like the maze in Figure 8–1. Ill-structured problems can have an untold number of acceptable responses, and the criteria for judging those responses are not simply black or white. In fact, individuals can disagree about whether an answer is acceptable (Finke, Ward, & Smith, 1992). With ill-structured problems there is no formula or algorithm students can use to get to the desired state. At best, guidelines or heuristics may improve or enhance performance on such problems, but there are apt to be as many problem-solving approaches as there are students in a classroom. When students are trying to make sense of a story, interpret a historical event, or write a persuasive paragraph, they are engaged in a task that is more ill-structured than well-structured.

Question 8 in the Calisthenics exercise is a prime example of an ill-structured task.

> 8. Find at least 10 unusual uses for the styrofoam popcorn that comes in packing crates. Try to devise uses that nobody else will think of.
>
> Well-structured _____☆_____ Ill-structured

If students have had experience with styrofoam popcorn, which may not be common in certain cultures, they should be able to come up with various uses (Hakuta & McLaughlin, 1996). Of course, the question for someone evaluating these ideas is whether they are indicative of original thought and whether they are unusual uses.

Implications for Learning and Instruction

The structuredness of problems can have significant effects on students and teachers. Because certain problem structures tend to be associated with particular fields of study (Alexander & Judy, 1988), students expect to confront more well-structured problems in mathematics and science and more ill-structured tasks in the social sciences or creative arts (Spiro & Jehng, 1990), and they often do not hold ill-structured problems in the same regard as those solved by formulas or algorithms (H. Gardner, 1999). The reason may be that teachers are more likely to use the language of thinking and the language of strategies in mathematics or science, and problem solving, thus, becomes erroneously equated with well-structured tasks (Ceci, 1990).

The literature on problem solving also focuses almost exclusively on mathematical or scientific problem solving (Byrnes, 1996; Mayer, 1983). It may be that educators intentionally or unintentionally associate well-structured problem solving with more intelligent behavior (H. Gardner, 2000). Certainly, well-structured problems are the mainstay of intelligence testing (Gustafsson & Undheim, 1996). Thus, it is not surprising that students enter classes, especially mathematics and science classes, under the misconception that academic problems have one and only one right answer (Dominowski & Dallob, 1995).

This myopic view of problems and problem solving makes it hard for students to set themselves free to explore the problem-solving space. What is the value of considering alternative solution paths if you are evaluated only on getting the one "right" word or number (Garner, 1990)? If teachers want to loosen up the boundaries of the problem space, they should take a page from Jennifer Gonya's teaching manual and give as much attention to students' thinking processes as to their responses. They should also examine their pedagogical approaches to ensure that they are not fostering students' misguided epistemological notions by supplying an unhealthy diet of highly structured problems or dismissing the importance of ill-structured tasks (M. Gardner, 1978).

In addition, it would serve both students and teachers well if criteria for evaluating ill-structured tasks were well articulated and openly discussed (Hambleton, 1996). Because it is harder to judge the quality of ill-structured tasks, model criteria would give students some sense of what to look for in their resulting products. Students could even contribute to the development of evaluative criteria. Participating in this manner might ultimately make students better able to engage in thoughtful self-assessment (Harris & Graham, 1996).

Thinking about Question 8 again, on what bases would you evaluate the uses listed? Experts in creative problem solving would consider a number of criteria for such a task (deBono, 1990; Torrance & Safter, 1999). They would certainly consider the *originality* reflected in the responses. If a number of individuals completed the same item, those uses that appear often (e.g., "Decorate the Christmas tree with them") would be scored low for originality, as compared to those that show up rarely (e.g., "Spray paint them green and use them as an artificial lawn"). *Frequency* of responses could also be factored into the score; those who produced more uses would score higher than those who listed only a few.

Creativity experts might also weigh the *elaboration*, or detailing, of an answer. For example, an answer like "jewelry" would be scored low in elaboration compared to a response like "gild a number of them, string them on a gold wire, and wear them as a necklace." Both responses deal with the same general use, but the second is much more richly described. Working together to formulate such a set of evaluation criteria could be a valuable lesson in problem solving for students (Hambleton, 1996).

Self-Assessment

Before continuing the discussion of problem classifications, take a moment to evaluate your own problem-solving capabilities on the well-structured/ill-structured continuum in the Thought Experiment. Be sure to refer to your performance on the calisthenics activity to guide you in this self-assessment.

Schooled (Traditional) Versus Unschooled (Novel)

Many of the problems students deal with in their educational experience have recognizable and routine structures whether the class is history, science, reading, or mathematics (Stewart, 1987). For example, during reading class third graders have a good idea what is going to transpire when the teacher begins to discuss a story (Alexander & Jetton, 2003). And when the teacher presents them with two-digit division problems, students have a pretty good mental model to follow (English & Halford, 1995). **Schooled** problems encompass familiar procedures or taught concepts; thus, they are also called **traditional** problems.

Question 2 in the earlier Calisthenics activity illustrates a highly schooled problem.

> 2. Name the work in which each of the following is a main character:
>
> Tiny Tim   Captain Ahab   Ophelia   Amy March
>
> Schooled ☆- Unschooled

Behind this problem is the unvoiced expectation that well-educated individuals have encountered these characters in their readings. Of course, performance requires that students retain the knowledge of these characters and their literary homes. Another indication of a schooled problem is that prior exposure is mandatory: No one could figure out the answer solely from the information given.

In direct contrast to this highly schooled problem is Question 7:

> 7. Below are two patterns that are not yet complete. Draw in the missing pieces that will complete each pattern.
>
> Schooled - ☆ Unschooled

Two aspects of this problem place it well to the unschooled end of the continuum. First, the figures used are not traditional fare in any standard academic subject (Sternberg & Davidson, 1995); students typically do not receive lessons in figural or spatial reasoning. Further, the processes that must be applied are similarly novel; students are not schooled in discerning patterns in figural arrays such as these, although they could be (Detterman & Sternberg, 1982; Dominowski & Dallob, 1995). Even though teachers sometimes focus on patterning in mathematics, the patterns they teach are typically more like a simplified version of

Question 1.c (Alexander, White, & Daugherty, 1997). Overall, problems that do not require prior or academic exposure to their underlying content or processes are **unschooled, or novel.**

Problems that are especially demanding because they place both content and process demands on respondents are classic analogies. Verbal analogy problems like those in Question 10 are one group of these classic problems that sits near the center of the schooled/unschooled continuum.

> *10. Yo-Yo Ma: cello:: Andrés Segovia:_____.*
>
> Schooled - - - - - - - - - - - - - - - - - - ☆ - - - - - - - - - - - - - - Unschooled

Verbal analogies are common measures of aptitude and achievement for good reason (Snow, 1981). Not only do they require a broad array of conceptual knowledge, but they also demand knowledge of analogical reasoning procedures (Goswami, 1992). Moreover, whereas the conceptual knowledge is presumed to result from formal learning experiences (i.e., schooled), there is little expectation that students have been explicitly taught how to reason analogically (i.e., unschooled). Thus, either individuals know who YoYo Ma or Andrés Segovia is, or they do not. But they may be able to figure out a solution strategy if that knowledge is available.

Implications for Learning and Instruction

One obvious result of the way schools treat schooled and unschooled problems can be seen in the behaviors of Jennifer Gonya's high-school students. Students view schooled problems as those that ultimately matter and are less comfortable engaging in more novel tasks (H. Gardner, 1993). This tendency seems even more pronounced in this era of high-stakes testing, when scores on formal, standardized tests shape students' futures (Paris, 2000a). Jennifer's students may have enjoyed the class debate, but their unfamiliarity with that type of activity led them to revert to more traditional, schooled behaviors as the class drew to a close. Students tend to restrict their novel problem solving to more artistic and creative venues (H. Gardner, 1983).

Teachers can increase students' comfort with unschooled tasks by including novel problem-solving activities in their curricula (deBono, 1990). On the surface this may sound paradoxical: Teachers can help students become better at novel problem solving by making such problems less novel. However, teachers can increase students' exposure to novel problems without routinizing their solution. As a result of their research on insight, Sternberg (1985a) and others (Dominowski & Dallob, 1995) recommend exactly this approach. An example of the problems that Sternberg and colleagues studied is included in the Thought Experiment: A Hare-Brained Scheme.

Thought Experiment ....

A Hare-Brained Scheme

Directions: A farmer buys nine rabbits but does not know which ones are male and which are female. Until he can find out, he wants to keep them apart. The problem is that the farmer has only one square pen. Show him how he can build two more square pens inside this large pen so that each rabbit will have its own separate area.

(Answer at the end of the chapter)

As Sternberg argues, individuals confront complex novel problems throughout their everyday lives (Baron & Sternberg, 1987); few real-life problems conform to the parameters and configurations of highly schooled problems. Therefore, the more novel problem solving is a valued educational enterprise, the more students become comfortable and competent at tackling the unique or unexpected with reason and insight (Bransford & Stein, 1993).

Some question whether all problem types that are presently novel to students should remain so. For example, analogy problems remain potent tools in gauging intelligence and academic aptitude (White & Alexander, 1986). However, because the processes for solving such problems are novel, students may be quicker to attribute their poor performance to uncontrollable factors (Weiner, 1986). In other words, when individuals have difficulty solving unschooled problems like those in Question 10 of the Calisthenics activity, they may perceive that failure as a sign of their own weak intelligence or low aptitude. In actuality, their failure to perform may reflect a lack of exposure to requisite concepts or processes, a condition that can be changed (Detterman & Sternberg, 1982).

So why are students not taught the underlying processes for problem solving when those processes could be taught? Why not expose students to the processes of analogical reasoning if analogic understanding is so critical to learning and development? One reason may have to do with the need of test developers for variable performance on achievement and aptitude measures. Students' lack of explicit instruction in certain processes or problem formats, like analogy problems, contributes to such variability (Alexander, White, & Daugherty, 1997).

Self-Assessment

Do you consider yourself to be better at solving schooled or unschooled problems? Do you enjoy working in less familiar territory, or are you like the students in Jennifer Gonya's physics class, more at home when the form and the content of an activity are fairly well known and well practiced? Or do you enjoy the challenge of both familiar and novel problems, in which case you would fall in the middle of the schooled/unschooled continuum? Use the Thought Experiment: Problem-Solving Profile to record your self-assessment.

Timed Versus Untimed

When there is a time limit or constraint established explicitly or implicitly for a given problem, that problem is **timed.** Problems or tasks that are unrestricted in the time available for solution are considered **untimed.** As a problem-solving characteristic, time plays an important role in life and in schooling. The entire educational system hinges on time. For instance, the subjects studied are typically broken down into discrete pieces and systematically introduced at particular points in students' educational experience. Students are then expected to master that material during that specified period. Thus, two-digit division might get relegated to the first half of third grade, whereas writing persuasive paragraphs gets slated for fourth grade. Even the learning that goes on in a single day is orchestrated around time units. In the upper grades, 50 minutes may be allotted for English literature, followed by 50 minutes for physics. For primary and early-elementary students, a 90-minute block of time may be set aside for language arts and a similar time for mathematics and science.

Beyond the academic structure of schools, time is a persuasive factor in human conceptions of intelligence and academic prowess (Snow, 1981), as evidenced in the very expressions used to describe more or less intelligent individuals. Someone judged as bright, for example, is described as fast or quick witted. By comparison, a person perceived as less intelligent might be called slow or delayed. This tendency to associate intelligence with time relates partially to the fact that intelligence quotients (IQs) are actually ratios (Gustafsson & Undheim, 1996). They describe how quickly or effectively a mind functions relative to others of the same age—literally, mental age in relation to a chronological age.

All of this suggests that even when teachers present students with tasks they consider to be untimed, like the water-level problem Jennifer Gonya posed to her students, some sense of time is likely still at work. Jennifer's students closed down their thinking about this perplexing problem as soon as the bell rang; even though the task itself had not come with a time constraint, physics class—and students' thinking about physics—had.

Of course, some problems or tasks come with very strict time limits. Test administrators and test takers would risk a great deal if they exceeded the time requirements on standardized tests like the SAT or Graduate Record Examination. These high-stakes tests are prime examples of timed problem sets. Students and teachers also seem to take time limits seriously during classroom assessments, although a small degree of flexibility may be present.

Other problems in educational experience are much more loosely configured with respect to time. In those cases learners need to be capable of analyzing tasks and monitoring their own time. For example, when students need to produce a research project by the end of the semester, no specific production schedule is set for them. It becomes their responsibility to break that project down into workable units to ensure its completion by the semester's end. Doctoral studies that take years to conduct and report come close to the untimed end on the timed/untimed continuum.

Implications for Learning and Instruction

Although speed and timeliness of performance are held to be important to learning and development, students are offered little explicit direction in how to manage their time when learning and being assessed (Allgood, Risko, Alvarez, & Fairbanks, 2000). Teachers can eliminate this paradoxical situation by offering students guidance in how to handle their time, especially when studying and taking tests. Currently lessons in time management are most often relegated to business settings, where consultants teach time management to improve corporate productivity, and also to college campuses, where students struggle to keep their academic heads above water. However, some research-based guidelines for coping with the time dimension of problem solving would benefit every student and every teacher (Covey, 1990; Flippo & Caverly, 2000). Such guidelines can be easily communicated to students and infused into the classroom culture.

Guidelines for Students   One of the first suggestions for students is to take time to plan. Planning does take time (Schoenfeld, 1985) but is well worth it; not taking time for planning can prove costly in the long run. Part of planning entails surveying the problem at hand to determine its nature and the best approach to dealing with it. As students engage in problem analysis, they should also consider the importance or urgency of the task. Not all tasks are of equal significance or subject to the same time pressures (Jetton & Alexander, 1997), and these differences need to be considered in the allotment of time.

Students' environment can also contribute to time management because effective learners ensure that they have the necessary materials and resources needed for task performance (Covey, 1990; Risko, Alvarez, & Fairbanks, 1991). In addition, they try to ensure that undue distractions are eliminated. Of course, what constitutes distractions will likely vary for each learner, as will the amount of time required to complete any given task. Learners should be aware of their individual academic clocks—the time frame that is most appropriate for their pace of learning and performance (Risko, Fairbanks, & Alvarez, 1991). And no matter how self-aware students are, unexpected interruptions and interferences must always be built into the management formula (Risko, Alvarez, & Fairbanks, 1991). Effective learners include some slippage in their time calculations.

In the age of cell phones, fax machines, and all manner of computer-based technologies, it is easy to accept the notion of multitasking. **Multitasking** is the idea that individuals can perform more than one mental activity simultaneously (Rubinstein, Meyer, & Evans, 2001). For example, students talk on the phone while typing a paper on the computer or do their homework while watching television. Because there is little evidence that multitasking results in effective learning or performance (accident rates for cell phone users are a case in point), students are advised to attend to one task at a time during learning and performance so that each task gets full and undivided attention (Allgood et al., 2000).

Finally, because the number of problems or tasks students face can sometimes feel overwhelming, it is advisable for students to limit, as much as possible, the tasks with which they must deal. They should also consider sharing the responsibility for demanding tasks or delegating parts to others.

Guidelines for Teachers   Time constraints frequently trigger anxiety in the classroom, perhaps because time has particular significance during assessments, especially high-stakes testing. Performance anxiety occurs even in very young children, who can become paralyzed when faced with a timed task (Mandler & Sarason, 1952). Teachers can take some simple steps to deal with such performance anxiety. For one thing, they can give students whatever time is needed for a test. Removing time as a fixed constraint gives students room to think before they write, as well as the luxury to review their answers. Teachers should also try to calculate carefully the time students will likely need to think, write, and review; cramming too much into an assessment simply increases students' performance anxiety.

In addition, teachers should encourage students to read through the entire test first and then work questions that seem easier for them so that they gain control and confidence while answering questions. Further, teachers can keep the classroom atmosphere light and relaxed when the potential for performance anxiety is high (Yerkes & Dodson, 1908). There is no need to remind students of the importance of the test, for instance, or to stand over them or pace around the room like a prison guard. And rarely is there any need to post the time, which unnerves some students.

Teachers can contribute to students' understanding of the time dimension in problem solving by making their own thinking public. At the very least, teachers should let students know when time is a factor in their performance. Teachers should also inform their students about why a particular task is being timed and what the purpose is for setting particular limits. Otherwise, decisions to time or not to time an activity or to set a particular time frame can appear capricious or arbitrary.

Jennifer Gonya's water-level experiment illustrates conflicting perceptions. Jennifer seemed to see the water-level experiment and related debate as fairly untimed. In fact, she expected her students to continue pondering the dilemma into the next class period. However, she did not expressly share this expectation with her students. Consequently, the students closed off their thinking, assuming that they had satisfied the time parameters for this problem. More explicit discussion of the time dimension might have brought Jennifer's expectations and her students' performance into closer alignment.

Self-Assessment

The Calisthenics activity gave you the option to time your problem-solving performance. Did you choose to exercise that option? Your response might provide you with a clue about whether you tend to function better under timed or untimed conditions. Do you rely on specified time constraints to motivate you or to regulate your problem solving? For some individuals open time frames are invitations to postpone or procrastinate. For others, who may be particularly good at self-monitoring and prioritizing, untimed tasks give permission to persist longer if the problem warrants it. Are you more effective and efficient when problems come with time specifications? Or do you prefer to establish your own time frame for a task, depending on its significance and complexity? After you weigh this question, position yourself on the timed/untimed continuum in the Thought Experiment profile.

Independent Versus Collaborative

Problems that are addressed without the express input or assistance of another person are **independent problems.** For instance, the directions to the Mental Calisthenics activity suggested that you work the problems on your own. Thus, that exercise represented an independent task.

At other times, however, students undertake tasks that warrant the input or assistance of others. Some of those may be group problems in which parties share the problem space, as well as the incentives for solving the problem. In those cases students are engaged in **collaborative problem solving** (Palincsar, Anderson, & David, 1993; Roschelle, 1992). Typically, when I am engaged in research, I work as a member of a team. Together my colleagues and I design a study, gather data, run the analyses, and report the outcomes. This approach clearly meets the criteria for collaborative problem solving.

Although collaborative problem solving occurs often in everyday life, it is less common in learning environments. In fact, the majority of academic problems seem to be independent in character. Educators expect students to work their problems alone, without discussion or assistance from classmates. In addition, seeking help is often frowned upon or viewed as a sign of intellectual or academic weakness (Nelson-Le Gall & Jones, 1990). Changes in educational philosophy, however, have had a dramatic effect on beliefs about independence and collaboration in problem solving (Cobb, Wood, & Yackel, 1990; Resnick, 1991). With the rise in social cognitivist and sociocultural views of learning (see Chapter 4), teachers have become more likely to incorporate collaborative activities into the classroom. As in Jennifer Gonya's physics class, students are often encouraged to tackle a problem together—to share their thoughts, strategies, and knowledge in pursuit of the answer (Cobb et al., 1990). Because of the increasing importance of collaborative or shared learning activities in today's classroom, this topic will be considered in greater depth in Chapter 11.

Sometimes either independent or collaborative problem solving makes more sense. Consider the following two problem-solving situations. The problem described in Situation 1 is broad and complex. It is the kind of real-world problem that many think is natural for collaborative problem solving (Bransford et al., 1999; CTGV, 1990). In fact, students are unlikely to achieve Miss Jamison's objectives for the water quality problem independently (CTGV, 1996).

Problem Situation 1:

Miss Jamison is a fourth-grade science teacher whose students are beginning a unit on ecology. As part of that unit, she wants her students to learn more about water quality. Specifically, she wants the class to learn about the process the local water company uses to purify the town's drinking water and verify its quality.

Problem Situation 2:

Mr. Pressman is a fourth-grade reading teacher who wants to make writing more of a priority in the curriculum. Consequently, he wants to learn more about his students' writing skills, but no specific information on their knowledge and skills is in their files.

The circumstances described in Situation 2 are quite different. Mr. Pressman has a real need to ascertain his students' individual writing skills. Perhaps, he could have his students think aloud while they engage in a carefully chosen writing task. The think-aloud information would help him determine their demonstrated skills (Coté & Goldman, 1999).

Implications for Learning and Instruction

When individuals collaborate on a task, their thinking and efforts get intermixed and intertwined, making it difficult to determine students' individual contributions to the outcome or the specific nature of their problem-solving performance. Because teachers must be cognizant of their individual students' capabilities in academic areas (Kounin, 1970), an array of both collaborative and independent tasks makes sense within the classroom environment.

During collaborative problem solving, teachers and students benefit from an initial briefing on goals and responsibilities. Teachers can share their instructional goals with students and explain clearly how students' products, both individual and collective, will be evaluated (Webb & Palincsar, 1996). In addition, group members can discuss their specific roles and responsibilities in problem solving. This clarification may make it easier for teachers to evaluate individual student's contributions to the group's performance.

Teachers must also remember that collaboration and independent problem solving are not equally attractive to all students (Lockheed, Harris, & Nemceff, 1983; Steele, 1988); they differ in their willingness and ability to be independent or collaborative. Females are perhaps more at home with collaboration than are their male classmates (Webb & Palincsar, 1996). In addition, culture affects students' tendency to collaborate. When student groups are racially mixed, minority students may be less vocal and less assertive than others (Lockheed et al., 1983). Thus, teachers must be sensitive to both individual and group differences and suitably flexible in their approaches.

Self-Assessment

Where do you fall on the collaborative/independent continuum? Do you enjoy sharing your thoughts and work with others? Or do you prefer to work on your own? Indicate your position on this dimension in the Thought Experiment: Problem-Solving Profile.

You should now have a general picture of yourself as a problem solver. These self-ratings, in essence, form your problem-solving profile. It would be interesting to see how your particular profile matches your performance on the mental calisthenics task. If you see yourself as more linguistic, well-structured, traditional, untimed, and independent, you should do well on verbal analogy problems like those in Question 10. On the other hand, a nonlinguistic, ill-structured, and novel profile fits better with problems like those in Question 7.

Another consideration is the match between individuals' profiles and the problems that dominate their chosen profession. Mechanical engineers, for example, are expected to do well at nonlinguistic, well-structured, schooled problems. By comparison, graphic artists should show some disposition toward nonlinguistic, ill-structured, and novel problems. Of course, no problem-solving profile is set in stone; profiles can be altered through relevant training, practice, and experience (Detterman & Sternberg, 1982). However, the more teachers and students understand about their current profiles, the more likely they are to seek out whatever is needed to extend or enrich their problem-solving abilities.

Interaction of Problem Solving and Intelligence

Problem solving is inextricably tied to conceptions of intelligence. However, to understand the links between the two, we need to consider the roots of the modern intelligence test, along with two contemporary theories of human intelligence.

A Historical View

The birth of the modern intelligence test has been attributed to Alfred Binet and Theodore Simon (1905/1916). In 1904 Binet was commissioned by the French government to devise some means of identifying children who were cognitively challenged so that they could be provided with suitable alternative education. Working with Simon, Binet developed the Binet-Simon scale—the first intelligence test—for that purpose. For our discussion of problem solving, what is particularly significant about this historic event is that Binet and Simon realized that they had to choose between one of two assessment methods in creating their measure: the psychological method and the pedagogical method (Ackerman, 2003). If they chose the psychological method, their assessment would focus on underlying mental facilities and processes, such as memory, judgment, and everyday knowledge. If they elected the pedagogical method, they would formulate a measure in which intelligence was equated with acquired knowledge. In effect, Binet and Simon were torn between defining intelligence in terms of schooled (traditional) or unschooled (novel) problems.

Ultimately, Binet and Simon followed the psychological route, disregarding "the degree of instruction which the subject possesses" (1905/1916, p. 42).

> It seems to us that in intelligence there is a fundamental faculty, the alteration of the lack of which, is of the utmost importance for practical life. This faculty is judgment, otherwise called good sense, practical sense, initiative, and the faculty of adapting one's self to circumstances. Indeed, the rest of the intellectual faculties seem of little importance in comparison with judgment. (Binet & Simon, 1916, pp. 42–43)

The original scale included 30 problems of increasing difficulty, some of which required the children to perform physical tasks (e.g., drawing) or to identify familiar objects (e.g., parts of the body). The researchers also incorporated tasks related to social skills (e.g., responding to a common social scenario), as well as items that tested the children's memory (e.g., repeating six random digits). By making this historic decision to focus on fundamental psychological processes, Binet and Simon influenced conceptions of intelligence for a century. Even today, there remains a great deal of relation between the early Binet-Simon scales and well-known modern intelligence tests such as the Stanford-Binet and the WISC (Ackerman, 2003).

General or Multifactorial Construct

One theme woven throughout the intelligence literature and repeated in contemporary theories and models has to do with whether intelligence is singular or multifactorial in nature. On the one side are those like Charles Spearman (1904, 1923), who argued that intelligence is fairly unitary, consisting of two factors. The general factor (g) influences all mental processing and, thus, explains human performance on a wide range of tasks (see Figure 8–3a). This g factor was presumed to be an individual difference trait, largely in place at birth (Gustafsson & Undheim, 1996; Jensen, 1998). Specific factors (s) are particular to cognitive tasks, such as linguistic or mathematical problems. Spearman believed that the g factor was most associated with intelligence because of its broad utility, and the purpose of intelligence testing was to ascertain the strength of this g factor. The concept of a general intelligence factor remains evident in many contemporary theories and research, although its nature and malleability have been widely debated (Ackerman, Kyllonen, & Roberts, 1999).

Other researchers (Guilford, 1967; Thurstone, 1938) believed that intelligence consisted of clusters of factors (see Figure 8–3b). In Thurstone's view, for example seven primary abilities were at the heart of intelligence.

1. *Number factor* (mathematical problem solving)
2. *Verbal factor* (vocabulary and general information)
3. *Word fluency* (speed of word generation)
4. *Spatial relations* (mental manipulation of pictures and images)
5. *Memory* (recall of pictures or texts)
6. *Reasoning* (inductive or deductive processing)
7. *Perceptual speed* (discrimination between pictorial, linguistic, or numeric displays)

Guilford (1959, 1967) carried this idea of primary factors to an extreme by identifying 120 cognitive factors of intelligence. He organized that multitude of factors into three dimensions: operations, content, and processes. The Struc-

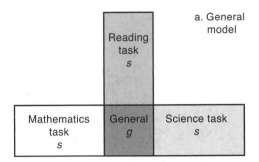

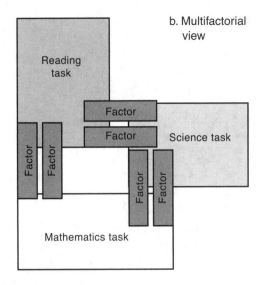

■ **FIGURE 8–3   Representations of general and multifactorial views of intelligence.**

ture of the Intellect—Learning Abilities Test (SOI-LA), based on Guilford's theory, enjoyed some popularity in the field of gifted education during the late 1970s and early 1980s (Meeker & Meeker, 1976).

Crystallized and Fluid Intelligence

The dilemma Binet and Simon faced about how to define and represent intelligence in problem form has continued unabated for almost 100 years.

This dilemma is symbolized, in part, by the degree to which the tasks chosen for assessment are commonplace and well practiced or novel and unfamiliar. To capture this distinction, researchers clustered items used to assess Spearman's g factor into two measurement groups, crystallized and fluid intelligence (R. B. Cattell, 1971; Horn, 1968; Snow, 1981).

Crystallized (G_c) intelligence can be described as the knowledge and processes that have arisen from explicit exposure, typically as a result of formal schooling. Thus, crystallized intelligence tasks correspond to the traditional or schooled problems previously discussed. An ability to name certain literary works or to calculate per annum interest is reflective of crystallized intelligence. Traditional intelligence tests, such as the Stanford-Binet and WISC, include many such schooled items, especially those that stress linguistic or mathematical abilities (H. Gardner, 1983).

Fluid (G_f) intelligence represents an ability to perform memory, reasoning, and problem-solving tasks that emphasize more inherent and less schooled abilities. Novel word problems are more representative of fluid intelligence. Although fluid intelligence is less evident in well-established measures of intelligence, there are intelligence tests that incorporate aspects of it. In fact, the Ravens Progressive Matrices (Court & Raven, 1995; Raven, 1940) are composed entirely of spatial reasoning problems similar to those in Question 7.a and 7.b in the calisthenics activity. Because of their emphasis on nonverbal and nonschooled content, the Ravens Matrices are often described as culture-fair measures (Gustafsson & Undheim, 1996).

Contemporary Perspectives

In recent years educational theorists and researchers have fueled the debate over the meaning and assessment of intelligence. The writings and research of Robert Sternberg and Howard Gardner illuminate the underlying issues in these debates and the differing perspectives on problem solving.

Sternberg: Triarchic Theory of Intelligence

Based on his extensive research in information processing, reasoning, and creativity, Robert Sternberg (1977, 1985a) articulated a general theory of intelligence that broadly encompassed facets of human thought and performance only partially addressed by Binet and Simon's scales. Sternberg argued that any theory of intelligence must account for individuals' success not only in the academic realm, but in their everyday lives as well. The conceptualization of intelligence he articulated was the **triarchic theory,** so named because of its three key dimensions or subtheories. A graphic representation of the triarchic theory is provided in Figure 8–4. Although Sternberg conceived of intelligence in terms of subtheories and components, he presented a theory that is more unitary than factorial in form.

Tenets of the Theory   Specifically, Sternberg argued that human intelligence is mental capacity reflected in componential, experiential, and contextual subtheories. The **componential subtheory** encompasses the basic mental structures and mechanisms that facilitate cognitive processing, the monitoring or self-regulation of those processes, and knowledge acquisition. This is the aspect of the triarchic theory that most closely parallels traditional views of intelligence. Sternberg attributed the outcomes of these components to **analytical abilities.**

The **experiential subtheory** addresses the nature of intelligent behavior—ranging from the most routine or automatic to the most novel and highly unfamiliar. Because this dimension of the theory involves insight, synthesis, and the ability to react to novel stimuli and situations, Sternberg has described the results of this dimension as **creative abilities.**

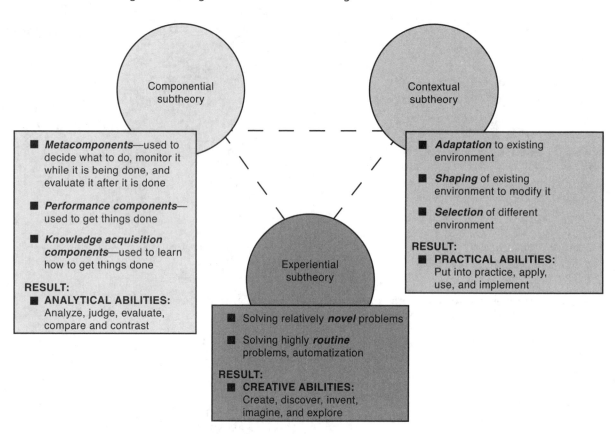

■ FIGURE 8–4   Sternberg's triarchic theory of intelligence.

Note: From *Educational Psychology* (p. 130) by R. J. Sternberg and W. M. Williams, 2002, Boston: Allyn & Bacon. Copyright 2002 by Allyn & Bacon. Adapted with permission.

Finally, the **contextual subtheory** embraces the sociocultural context in which intelligent behavior occurs and the manner in which individuals engage in that behavior. Sternberg held that individuals can respond to their existing environment by *adapting* to it, *selecting* a more suitable environment, or *shaping* or modifying that environment for their purposes. Because this contextual aspect entails an awareness of which behaviors would likely represent intelligent behavior in which situations, Sternberg has referred to its results as **practical abilities**—the street smarts that demonstrate individuals' ability to understand and solve real-life problems.

> Intelligence is the mental capability of emitting contextually appropriate behavior at those regions in the experiential continuum that involve response to novelty or automatization of information processing as a function of metacomponents, performance components, and knowledge-acquisition components. (Sternberg, 1985a, p. 128)

Assessment of the Theory   The breadth of Sternberg's definition of intelligence, which many see as its advantage over traditional definitions and models, has proven to be a stumbling block in his development of a measure to validate his theory. The Sternberg Triarchic Abilities Test (STAT, 1993) remains an unpublished instrument containing problems of both a crystallized and a fluid nature, as well as items related to social and practical intelligence.

To get at the componential dimension of his theory, Sternberg's STAT focuses on individuals' verbal compre-

Robert J. Sternberg has been a leader in the research on reasoning and problem solving.

hension skills (e.g., deriving the meaning of an unfamiliar word from contextual clues) to gauge respondents' ability to acquire new knowledge. The following paragraph is a case in point. Read it over and see whether you can deduce the meaning of the word *solecism*.

> Vocabulary skills are a crucial foundation of eloquent speech and concise prose. A good vocabulary is a powerful tool indeed, and the larger the fund of words people command, the richer will be their mode of expression. We must realize, however, that learning a new word does not entail simply the acquisition of the term's formal meaning. Moreover, dictionary definitions frequently are not sufficiently detailed to ensure proper usage. The goals must be to incorporate each new word into our active vocabularies. Words that lie gathering dust in the recesses of the mind serve no useful purpose, and a collection of half-learned words is bound to lead to *solecism*. (Sternberg, 1986, p. 195)

How did you do? Did you figure out that *solecism* refers to the incorrect usage of a words? Sternberg also included analogy and spatial reasoning problems to measure basic cognitive processes.

In order to deal with the experiential subtheory, Sternberg relied on novel questions that require insight and creative reasoning. For example, Sternberg developed novel analogies, prefacing a given analogy with an assumption that the problem solver was to take as fact, even if it violated current understandings of the world. The problem solver was then to apply that assumption if needed to solve the analogy.

1. Villains are lovable.
   HERO is to ADMIRATION as VILLAIN is to
   CONTEMPT   AFFECTION   CRUEL   KIND
2. Chowder is sour.
   CLAM is to SHELLFISH as CHOWDER is to
   SOUP   STEAK   LIQUID   SOLID
   R. J. Sternberg, 1986, p. 235

In the first problem, the prefacing statement significantly alters the emotion associated with villains. Thus, whereas heroes are admired, lovable villains would engender affection. However, the taste of chowder does not influence the relation drawn in the second problem. Just as a clam is a shellfish, chowder is a soup, regardless of its taste.

Finally, to assess individuals' sociocultural and practical abilities, Sternberg created a number of nontraditional social questions. For example, he presented a series of pictures of male/female pairs and asked respondents to distinguish real couples from fake couples. His intention was to gauge individuals' ability to read subtle social and cultural cues. Sternberg also formulated multiple-choice questions that examined individuals' responses to everyday problems. His purpose was to determine whether respondents sought to *adapt* to the given situation, *select* a more acceptable environment, or *shape* the situation to better fit their needs and desires.

Your best friend, Jill, always cheats when the two of you play tennis. She reflexively calls any ball out that falls even remotely near a line. In the face of this inexplicable ridiculousness, do you

    a. refuse to play tennis with her? After all, you have plenty of other tennis partners who do not cheat.

    b. decide that tennis is only a game to be enjoyed and, knowing in your heart that you are a better player, elect to tolerate her foolishness?

    c. take Jill aside, tell her with all the tact you can muster that this type of behavior is abominable, and make her promise to play squarely? (Sternberg, 1986, p. 318)

If your response was *a*, you selected an alternative environment, whereas *b* represented adaptation to the present situation, and *c* involved shaping that situation.

Critique of the Theory   Sternberg has devoted decades of research to the triarchic theory and the development of both classic and novel items suitable for assessing the theory's dimensions. However, limitations exist. For example, the STAT has not resulted in highly valid and reliable data that would rival more traditional intelligence tests. In effect, Sternberg has found it difficult to devise a measure with the psychometric properties that experts in test construction would deem acceptable.

Thus, neither the theory nor the related test has replaced more traditional notions of intelligence within the wider educational community, and the direct impact on educational practice has remained limited.

Gardner: Multiple Intelligences

During the period that Sternberg was doing the research leading to his triarchic theory, Howard Gardner was similarly immersed in the study of intelligence. Drawing on the literatures in development, symbolic processing, neurology,

Howard Gardner views intelligence as encompassing multiple, independent competencies.

expertise, and exceptionalities, Gardner, like Sternberg, began to question the narrowness of traditional models and measures of human intelligence. Gardner held that intelligence tests stressed "knowledge gained from living in a specific social and educational milieu" and that this bias toward crystallized versus fluid abilities came with dire consequences (1983, p. 18). However, whereas Sternberg perceived of intelligence as a relatively singular construct composed of multiple subtheories or components, Gardner's approach to intelligence—that is, multiple intelligences (MI)—had more in common with multifactorial models, like Thurstone's (1938) primary abilities perception.

> To my mind, a human intellectual competence must entail a set of skills or problem solving—enabling the individual *to resolve genuine problems or difficulties* that he or she encounters and, when appropriate, to create an effective product—and must also entail the potential for *finding or creating problems*—thereby laying the groundwork for the acquisition of new knowledge. (Gardner, 1983 pp. 60–61)

Tenets of the Theory   Gardner (1983) originally claimed that at least seven distinct, independent intelligences explained human behavior. Later, he added an eighth and potentially a ninth intelligence to that list. His criteria for what qualifies as an intelligence include the stipulations that it must do the following:

- entail an ability to solve or create problems of cultural value
- correspond to identifiable brain functions
- be evidenced at exceptional and impaired levels
- exhibit an evolutionary history in humans and other species (Checkley, 1997).

According to Gardner (1983), eight intelligences meet those criteria:

> *Linguistic*: the ability to use language(s) to comprehend others and to express oneself
> *Logical-mathematical*: the capacity to manipulate numbers, quantities, and operations, as well as a grasp of underlying principles of causality and reason
> *Spatial*: the ability to represent the physical world spatially in one's mind and to perform spatial transformations mentally
> *Bodily kinesthetic*: the capability to use one's body in problem solving or in creation or production
> *Musical*: the ability to think in music, respond to various forms of musical expression, and hear, recognize, replicate, or generate musical patterns
> *Interpersonal*: the capacity to understand others and to respond appropriately to their behaviors, affects, and motivations
> *Intrapersonal*: the ability to know oneself, including one's strengths and weaknesses, patterns of behaviors, and personal motivations
> *Naturalist*: the ability to discern patterns in nature and a sensitivity to the natural world

More recently, Gardner (1999, 2000) has considered including existential intelligence among his competencies. He describes **existential intelligence** as humans' need to posit and explore abstract, philosophical questions, such as What is intelligence? Where do I come from? What is knowledge?

Assessment and Critique of the Theory   Even though MI is a well-known and often-lauded alternative to traditional theories of intelligence, little empirical evidence substantiates its tenets (Sternberg & Williams, 2002). One reason is that Gardner, who is negatively disposed to intelligence testing, has made no attempt to devise any measure(s) to gauge the multiple intelligences he purports. In an interview with NEA Today Online (1999), Gardner made his views on intelligence testing very clear: "I'm not in favor of tests that are designed to measure people's intelligence, because frankly I don't care what intelligence or intelligences people have. I care whether they can do things which we value in our culture."

The lack of empirical evidence for MI, even after 20 years, is exacerbated by other concerns. For one Gardner's theory is predicated on multiple intelligences being quite independent. However, decades of research suggest that the intelligences Gardner has specified are correlated or overlapping rather than distinct abilities (Carroll, 1993; Sternberg, 2000). Further, neurological research is far too primitive to support Gardner's notion that each intelligence has a unique representation in the brain (Pinker, 1997). Nonetheless, such limitations have not dampened the enthusiasm for MI among educators and the general public. Educational programs, profiling activities, curricula, and the like are structured around this alternative to traditional intelligence models and assessments. It will be interesting to see whether MI endures as a viable theory of intelligence for another 20 years.

What Are the Guidelines for Effective Problem Solving?

The educational literature is replete with volumes devoted to improving student thinking and problem solving (e.g., Bransford & Stein, 1993; Lipman, 2003; Mayer, 1983). However, the multitude of suggestions and recommendations can be subsumed under four simple guidelines for problem solving, articulated by George Polya in 1945. Although Polya's recommendations were primarily devised for solving more traditional well-structured tasks, especially mathematical tasks, his four guidelines have broad applicability to the variety of problems explored in this chapter. Because Polya dealt primarily with well-structured problems, his four points are often described as steps to be followed in rather linear fashion. However, they are presented here as four interactive guidelines, as illustrated in Figure 8–5.

Understand the Problem   The first phase in effective problem solving entails the thoughtful and systematic analysis of the problem at hand. Less effective problem solvers

George Polya established the fundamentals of problem solving.

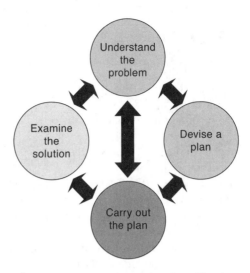

■ FIGURE 8–5   Guidelines for effective problem solving.

have a tendency to treat problems superficially making decisions only on the surface-level features of the problems (Mayer, 1983). Students must be helped to look more deeply into the problem space if they are to improve their performance. Jennifer Gonya sought this in-depth exploration of the water-level problem and thus prompted the debate in her physics class.

The various continua explored in this chapter can be useful to teachers and students for understanding the deep structure of the problems they encounter. Is this a linguistic, well-structured, traditional problem with time limits, or is it a more ill-structured and novel task that can be solved collaboratively? Problem analysis can also involve deconstructing a task into constituent parts, isolating subtasks that can be tackled separately (Gagné, 1977). In addition, Polya and others (Bransford & Stein, 1993) recommend translating a given problem into another form as a means of establishing what is known and what is unknown.

Devise a Plan   Once students have a good sense of the problem they are facing, they need to formulate their plan of attack. The strategies overviewed in Chapter 7 are of particular value in this process. Students need to decide on the optimal path through the problem space. Is this task best solved by a more direct, algorithmic path? Should the plan revolve around narrowing the problem space and finding an analogous problem that can assist in solution? Or is this a case in which the solution is best achieved by expanding the problem space, bringing more information to bear before proceeding?

In devising a plan of action, it would make sense to weigh the significance of the problem or its personal relevance. Students' goals for engaging in problem solving merit careful consideration, for not all problems warrant the same level of involvement and commitment. In fact, students' formulation of a solution plan may result in a reevaluation of the problem itself, as the arrows in Figure 8–5 suggest.

Students must also evaluate sociocontextual factors that play a role in the problem solving plan. For example, are there specific criteria that will be used to evaluate the outcome? Does the teacher encourage collaborative problem solving? What human and nonhuman resources are available for use during problem solution, and which of these would seem most pertinent for the present task?

Carry Out the Plan   The next phase in effective problem solving is carrying out the plan that has been devised. Execution of the plan encompasses the issues of time management discussed earlier in this chapter. Students must also be taught that initial plans are not always the best plans. As implementation gets underway, students should be sensitive to changes or modifications needed in the existing plan. Thus, they should be open to a reconceptualization of the problem, and they should even be willing to abandon their initial plan and start the process over.

Examine the Solution   The final phase in Polya's model involves an evaluation of the outcome of problem solving. Part of this evaluation process entails judging the plausibility or acceptability of the outcome. Has all the critical information been accounted for in this solution? Does the outcome meet the established criteria the student or others have articulated? Could a similar or the same result be reached by an alternative solution strategy?

For younger or less experienced students, the teacher may need to model and scaffold this evaluative phase of problem solving. For example, Harris and Graham's self-monitoring checklist shown in Figure 7–7 would be a useful tool for guiding students' evaluation of writing performance. Depending on the judgments students make about their solutions, they may need to reengage in one or more of the phases of problem solving.

■ Summary Reflections

What makes a problem a problem?

■ A problem exists any time there is a gap between one's present and one's ideal state.
- The significance of a problem can be judged by the size of the gap.
- The complexity of a problem relates to the simplicity or directness of the solution path.

■ Benefits accrue to students and teachers when they can classify the problems they encounter.

■ For students those benefits include conceptualizing the problem space, choosing among solution strategies, enhancing risk taking, promoting self-evaluation and self-assessment, and particularizing judgments about academic capabilities
- For teachers the benefits encompass a system for examining instructional and assessment activities, reduced incongruence between teachers' and students' perceptions of problem-solving tasks, a language for communicating about problems, a review of problem-solving techniques that need reinforcement, and diagnosis of students' problem-solving abilities.

What is a framework for analyzing academic problems?

■ Academic problems can be distinguished by the degree to which they rely on linguistic or nonlinguistic modes of inscription or communication.

■ The structuredness of tasks also influences problem-solving performance.
- For well-structured problems, the problem space is more contained, acceptable outcomes are more recognizable and readily agreed upon, and the strategies for solution are more identifiable.

- Problems that do not share these characteristics are considered ill structured.

■ Problems can be profiled in terms of their degree of familiarity or novelty.
- Familiar tasks are those that are routinely part of the school curriculum.
- Students receive little or no explicit instruction for novel or unschooled tasks.

■ Problems can be differentiated by whether they have time requirements.

■ Problems also differ in whether they are to be solved independently or with the input of others.

■ Intelligence testing has been influenced by the work of Binet and Simon.
- The question of whether intelligence is fairly unitary or consists of multiple factors remains unanswered.
- Two groups of general intelligence abilities are evident in intelligence testing and educational practice: crystallized (schooled) and novel (unschooled) abilities.
- Two contemporary and alternative perspectives on intelligence—triarchic theory and multiple intelligences—are also built on the assumption that intelligence is problem solving.

What are the guidelines for effective problem solving?

■ Effective problem solving encompasses four fundamental phases: understanding the problem, devising a plan, carrying out that plan, and examining the solution it produces.

■ By teaching students to follow these simple guidelines, and by modeling them in the classroom, educators can do much to enhance students' problem-solving performance.

■ Answers to Thought Experiment: Calisthenics for the Mind

1. a. The progression in months is 2 1 3 5 4 6, so the next month would be 8 or August.

    b. The progression is $1^1\ 2^1\ 3^1\ 1^2\ 2^2\ 3^2\ 1^3\ 2^3$, so the next number should be 3^3 or 27.

    c.

2. a. A Christmas Carol

    b. Moby Dick

    c. Hamlet

    d. Little Women

3. If 2 people can make 50 party favors each hour, then 3 could make 75 each hour for a total of 225.

4. Homophones are words that sound alike but are spelled differently (e.g., *write* and *right*), whereas homographs are words that are spelled the same but sound different (e.g., *lead*, "to direct others," and *lead*, "a certain metal").

5. You will have received 7/12 of $71.52, which is .04 of $1788, or $41.72. When added to the initial deposit, the total becomes $1829.72.

6. Shawn is Joshua's mother. (Kim has a daughter, and Shawn has children. Katlin cannot be Kim's daughter. Therefore, Shelby must be Kim's daughter, and Katlin and Joshua must be Shawn's children.)

	Katlin	Joshua	Shelby
Shawn	X	X	
Kim			X
Karen			

7. a.

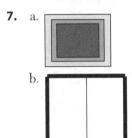

   b.

8. Answers will vary.

9. Drawings will vary.

10. a. Yo-Yo Ma plays the cello, and Andrés Segovia plays the *guitar*.
   b. Piaget's perspective on knowledge building has been called cognitive constructivism, whereas *Vygotsky* is associated with social constructivism.
   c. The religious volume central to Christianity is the Bible. The *Koran* (or *Quran*) is the holy book for Islam.
   d. Hate is a severe form of dislike, *revere* is an intense form of respect. (*Venerate* or *worship* is also acceptable.)

■ Solution to Thought Experiment: A Hare-Brained Scheme

Chapter 9

Motivation and Learning: Optimizing the Experience

GUIDING QUESTIONS

- What does it mean to be motivated?
- How do students' goals relate to their learning and achievement?
- What can teachers do to promote optimal learning?

IN THEIR OWN WORDS ....

Rich Milner spent most of his early educational life as a student in predominantly Black schools in the South. When he began his teaching career as a high-school English teacher, it was also in a Black school in the South.

At the end of my first semester at Morgan High School, Ms. Anderson, the guidance counselor, put a note in my mailbox informing me that she was placing Xavier Evans in my English II class the following term. You could not be around Morgan High and not know something about Xavier, the basketball superstar and local media darling. He was something to watch on the court! Surprised, I reread Ms. Anderson's note. "Isn't Xavier a senior this year?" I thought. "What's he doing in a sophomore English class?"

The first day of the new semester, the towering and good-spirited athlete was waiting for me at the classroom door. "Milner," he said, "Anderson told me that I need to make an appointment to talk about my grade." After school we talked, and Xavier informed me, "I have to pass this class to graduate. I've got the colleges lined up waiting for me." I assured him that he would pass the course as long as he fulfilled the requirements.

The next day Xavier was again the first to greet me. Smiling, he said, "Milner, don't call on me to read today—coach had me shooting free throws 'til 10:00 last night." Perplexed, I agreed. This and similar episodes occurred frequently throughout the semester. Other days it was, "Milner, I don't have my homework because I had to watch this basketball tape" or "I needed to work on a shot." Ms. Anderson, other teachers, and even the coach thanked me for working with Xavier. The coach kept saying things like, "In my 14 years of coaching, I have never seen a kid more motivated about the game." I was thinking, "I wish he showed some of that motivation in my class!"

As a novice teacher, I did not know what to do. On the one hand, I felt that I was being asked to put my professional beliefs aside. On the other hand, I was cognizant of Xavier's athletic potential. His ability could be a ticket out of this life of poverty and a way to get a college education. At times all of this kept me up at night. I wanted to be a motivating teacher for Xavier and challenge his mind in my English class. What was I to do?

About midway through the course, I met with Xavier. In my best big-brother/teacher voice, I asked him, "Why are you in my class? What do you want out of your life? Do you think I'm going to let you sit in my class and do nothing?" "Man," Xavier replied, "I want to be a star. This Thoreau and Whitman and Langston Hughes junk isn't going to mean anything to me when I'm making millions in the NBA." His next statement summed up his view of my class, his schooling, and his life. "You are a cool teacher, Milner, but my life can't be like your life. I can't speak proper English, drive a beat-up car, put up with all this garbage, and make $20 thousand a year." His face began to show pain as he continued, "I grew up in the ghetto, and all I can do is shoot a basketball. I want my mama to live in a house. I don't want to have to live the rest of my life in the projects. What's wrong with me wanting a good life?" And then he began to smile, "I am the man at this school."

Even now I think back to that conversation with Xavier. At what point in his life did he conclude that all he was capable of doing was shooting a basketball? Xavier had so many talents, and it disturbed me that all of that potential was overshadowed by basketball. What rewards or kudos could I dangle in front of Xavier and the hundreds of students like him that could challenge the power and allure of such things as fame, money, and adulation? Was it possible for me to help Xavier see the world differently? I didn't know what to do. I felt isolated. Everyone at the school seemed to be an unwavering fan of this young man, who would bring the school fame and victory—a championship. What was I to do?

What Does It Mean to Be Motivated?

Motivation is one of the most serious concerns of practicing teachers. It is not just a novice teacher working with poor, inner-city high school students who confronts a lack of academic interest, involvement, or engagement among students. According to national surveys and educational research, this condition is pervasive and highly resistant to intervention (Rock, Owings, & Lee, 1994). Whatever excitement or passion for learning young children bring into the classroom in their early years begins to fade as years of schooling pass by (Wigfield, Eccles, & Pintrich, 1996). A significant decline in students' interest in educational pursuits emerges in early adolescence and persists throughout the remainder of their schooling (Wigfield, 1993). As Figure 9–1 illustrates, middle-school students surveyed as part of the National Assessment of Educational Progress (Carnegie Council on Adolescent Development, 1996) became increasingly less involved in academic activities between the fourth and eighth grades.

Teachers like Rich Milner must cope with this lack of interest and involvement among their students and with the students' competing needs and goals. However, students do have a right to sense the beauty and power that deep knowledge and understanding can afford, to spend 12 years or more of their lives engaged in an educational experience they find personally rewarding, meaningful, and intellectually enriching. To transform learning into

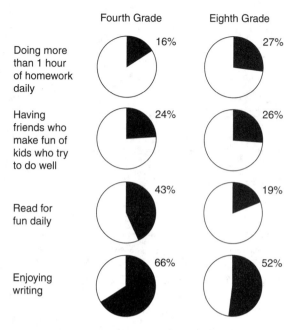

Fourth Grade   Eighth Grade

Doing more than 1 hour of homework daily   16%   27%

Having friends who make fun of kids who try to do well   24%   26%

Read for fun daily   43%   19%

Enjoying writing   66%   52%

■ **FIGURE 9–1   Patterns in students' academic pursuits during the middle-school years.**

Note: Based on 1998 National Assessment of Educational Progress.

such a positively motivating experience for all members of the classroom community, teachers must come to grips with the nature of motivation.

Defining the Construct

Motivations are the psychological processes "involved in the direction, vigor, and persistence of behavior" (Bergin, Ford, & Hess, 1993, p. 437). Motivations underlie every human action, whether that action is shooting free throws until 10:00 at night, reading Langston Hughes, or reading this text. Thus, every human being, including Xavier Evans, is motivated. In fact, Xavier is highly motivated in certain areas of his life. The issue for Rich Milner is how to direct this young man's inner energies toward academics.

Educators at all levels need to know how to tap into the desires, wants, and passions of students and channel them toward the pursuit of academic understanding so that knowledge seeking is promoted from within rather than coerced or forced from without (Dewey, 1913). Motivation is

the fuel that propels individuals through a problem space toward a desired goal or end. Individuals who are highly motivated move through that problem space with a well-honed sense of direction, energy, and commitment (Pintrich & Schunk, 2001). Less motivated individuals meander or wander aimlessly toward some vague end.

However, just as there are different theories of learning (see Chapter 4), there are varied perspectives on motivation. Much of the current research on motivation falls within a social-cognitive orientation (Pintrich & Schunk, 2001), which finds the roots of human motivation in interactions with and observations of others (Bandura, 1986). Other motivational theory and research are humanistic in orientation, internally focused and dealing with individuals striving for self-determination, personal fulfillment, or self-actualization (Deci, Vallerand, Pelletier, & Ryan, 1991). In contrast, behavioral views are externally focused and deal with the conditioning of human behavior. Behavioral researchers are concerned with the rewards and punishments that "motivate" students to behave in desired ways (Hull, 1952).

Reviewing the History

Much of this chapter draws on contemporary theory and research on motivation and thus emphasizes the social-cognitive perspective. However, the historical roots of more recent theory go back to Maslow's hierarchy of needs, an early and well-known theory representative of the humanistic perspective, and to foundational work on human needs and drives, which can be traced to a more behavioral view of motivation.

Maslow's Hierarchy of Needs

Abraham Maslow (1954, 1971) made the concept of needs central. His well-known hierarchy of needs explains that human states result from life experiences and from individuals' attempts to gain control over their situations. Maslow saw human needs as hierarchical, meaning that individuals must conquer their lower, primal needs before addressing more enriching, sophisticated ones. As depicted in Figure 9–2, Maslow places needs in two categories, deficiency needs and growth, or being, needs.

According to Maslow, those who satisfy their basic needs continue to develop and mature psychologically, whereas those who do not meet these needs ultimately suffer serious psychological consequences. Maslow believed that human development is a journey toward optimizing potential; that is, being all one can be. The term **self-actualization** applies to that optimal human state—which few individuals ever reach but to which many strive. To approach self-actualization, individuals must conquer their preoccupation with fundamental human wants or needs (**deficiency needs**) and focus on increasingly more complex and self-enriching needs (**growth needs**).

Deficiency Needs

Maslow thought that the most commonplace and primitive needs relate to physiological well-being, physical and psychological safety, and feelings of love and belonging. In his view

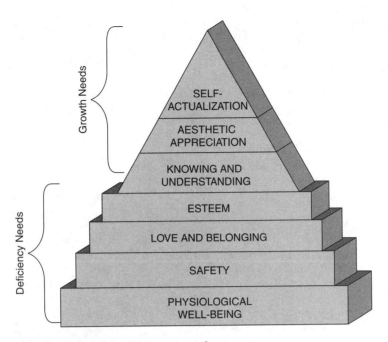

■ FIGURE 9–2   Maslow's conceptualization of human needs.

Note: From *Motivation and Personality* by A. H. Maslow, 1954, New York: Harper & Row. Copyright 1954 by Harper & Row. Adapted with permission.

the need for food, drink, shelter, and security never disappears, but the degree to which these needs define or dictate day-to-day existence changes. By positioning biological/genetic needs at the base of his psychological model, Maslow defined them as the gateway to subsequent positive growth. He believed that the more these primitive human needs go unsatisfied, the stronger their presence in people's lives.

Thus, the longer children live in a home where they do not feel safe or loved, the larger safety and belonging needs loom in their lives (Ormrod, 1998). Students like Xavier, who live their lives in the shadow of poverty, may never completely shake the feelings of hunger (physiological needs) or insecurity (safety needs) that marked their earlier development (Graham & Long, 1986). And children who are threatened with violence in schools, which should be secure havens, may never be able to feel completely safe again or concentrate effectively on their studies (Kreitler et al., 1995).

Even if students achieve some degree of financial success later on some residual of these needs can linger and prevent them from moving on to their growth needs (Graham & Weiner, 1996). As Rich came to realize, a teacher's earnest desire to help students achieve a passion for knowledge and learning can confront the reality of basic needs that must be met first. A brief summary of the ordered needs in Maslow's theory is provided in Table 9–1, along with their educational implications.

Growth Needs

Not all needs are about filling in the holes in existence. Some are about expanding or enriching life (Maslow, 1954). These needs are about growing as humans and maximizing whatever potential exists. Focusing energy on these needs

makes these areas stronger and brings individuals nearer to self-actualization (Pintrich & Schunk, 2001).

As Maslow (1971) later elaborated on his notion of growth needs, he described two steps toward self-actualization. First is a quest for knowledge and understanding, a deep-seated curiosity or interest that guides human actions (need for knowing and understanding). When this search for deep understanding of the world is largely fulfilled, individuals can devote their energies to the appreciation of beauty and order in the world at large (aesthetic need). The enrichment that comes from the continued pursuit of this growth need brings the individual closer to self-actualization.

Abraham Maslow

Table 9–1   Maslow's hierarchy of needs.

Category of Need	Specific Need	Description	Educational Implication
Deficiency	Physiological well-being	The basics needed for human survival, including food, breathable air, water, and protection from the elements	Students cannot be expected to pay attention in class or remember well what is taught when they are hungry, thirsty, or physically uncomfortable.
	Safety	Physical and emotional security, including personal safety and freedom from fear or anxiety	School environments must be perceived as safe places for students of all ages. Order and predictability in learning environments can contribute to this perception of safety.
	Love and belonging	A sense of affiliation and belonging within a family and other significant social groups; a need for personal identity	Students carry their need for belonging into the classroom. Educators need to create learning environments in which students feel cared about and cared for.
	Self-esteem	Realization of one's value or unique contributions: gaining recognition and achievement	The special qualities and abilities of each student need to be celebrated. Giving students special roles to play in the classroom can help build their self-esteem.
Growth	Knowing and understanding	Intellectual growth; the desire to understand something deeply and richly; enjoyment of knowledge for its own sake	Educators need to stress knowledge seeking as a valued end by providing students with the tools to seek knowledge of personal interest.
	Aesthetic appreciation	The pursuit of order and beauty; reaching beyond the surface to underlying qualities	Artistic appreciation and discussion of the passion and beauty found in traditional content areas can build a base for the aesthetics.
	Self-actualization	Becoming a fully functioning and fully realized individual; having no unmet needs	Educators should allow time for students to pursue areas of personal interest, areas in which students sense their personal identities and glimpse the beauty within.

According to Eggen and Kauchak (1999), individuals who approach self-actualization exhibit qualities beneficial to optimal learning: they

- Have a strong sense of reality
- Are accepting of themselves and others
- Act and think spontaneously
- Are more problem centered than ego centered
- Function independently and rather autonomously
- Promote the common welfare
- Are creative in thought and action
- Form deep and meaningful bonds with other human beings
- Experience moments of great excitement, happiness, and insight

In general, those who have reached the realm of growth needs seek intellectual challenges, find pleasure in art and music or creative pursuits, and are fulfilled by serving others.

A Developmental View

The movement from deficiency needs to growth needs in Maslow's (1954) hierarchy follows an age-related path. For example, the youngest individuals are almost exclusively focused on fulfilling their physiological needs—and rightly so. Infants understand little other than their need to be fed, rested, and otherwise physically comfortable. Soon, however, the need to be held and responded to with love and affection becomes almost as important as the desire for food or sleep.

By adolescence, children's spheres of influence and their corresponding wants have expanded. Thus, adolescents struggle to find their unique place in the world and ascertain their personal worth. Among undergraduate students the struggle for self-esteem continues. College is a critical time for them as they try to shape the future directions of their lives. The seeds of growth needs are taking root in some of them, too. Sometimes for the first time in their lives, they are invested in and excited about understanding themselves and the world around them, not just for the grades and rewards knowledge might bring, but for the sheer pleasure of knowing. Overall, the character of Maslow's hierarchy of needs makes it unlikely that young children or even young adults will have the experiences and resulting insights required to reach growth needs. Instead, the earlier, formative years of life set the stage for later growth and self-actualization.

Educational Implications

As summarized in Table 9–1, each tier of Maslow's hierarchy has educational implications. Teachers cannot assume that all students come to school adequately fed or clothed or that their students have been sufficiently loved and nurtured (Noddings, 1992). Thus, as Gage and Berliner (1998) point out, schools often have no choice but to attend to such basal needs, even if they see learning as their principal aim.

Educators can contribute to feelings of belonging and self-esteem by ensuring that students engage in group learning activities that are socially and academically reinforcing (Nichols, 1996). In addition, the contributions and potential of each student should be publicly and privately celebrated as a step toward building self-esteem (Miserandino, 1996). Moreover, to establish a foundation for students' subsequent growth and enrichment, teachers can demonstrate their own passions for knowledge seeking (Alexander, 1997b). Providing students with foundational knowledge and the strategies to seek out personally relevant information can also be advantageous.

Further, students can catch glimpses of the beauty and order in their world even if other needs intrude upon their lives. Teachers can share their own sensations of beauty with students, not merely in terms of art, drama, and music, but also in relation to traditional academic subjects. However, teachers must be purposeful about illustrating the aesthetic to those who cannot see with experienced eyes. And finally, models such as Maslow's hierarchy can be valuable tools for discussion and self-evaluation, particularly among older students. Where they see themselves in the journey toward self-actualization is a critical piece in formulating the drives and goals that move them forward.

Research into Human Needs and Drives

Many models and theories of motivation arising from different theoretical roots acknowledge certain human needs and associated drives as the foundations of motivations. However, despite the broad applicability of need and drive theories, initial research in that area was behavioral in nature. The goal was to uncover the rewards and punishments that would result in the desired performance (Hull, 1952). Those early drive researchers contended that the deficits or longings people sense (i.e., **needs**) and the way in which those deficits or longings become internalized are at the core of people's actions (i.e., **drives;** Hull, 1952; Woodworth, 1918). Thus, motivations can be understood as outgrowths or manifestations of basic human needs and drives. As illustrated in Figure 9–3, those needs, both primary and secondary, set the wheels of human behavior in motion. Needs create an imbalance or a disequilibrium—a gap between the present state and the desired state. The greater the imbalance, the more likely someone is to take action.

Primary and Secondary Needs

No living creature can exist for long without certain essentials, including food, water, air, and shelter. Such needs,

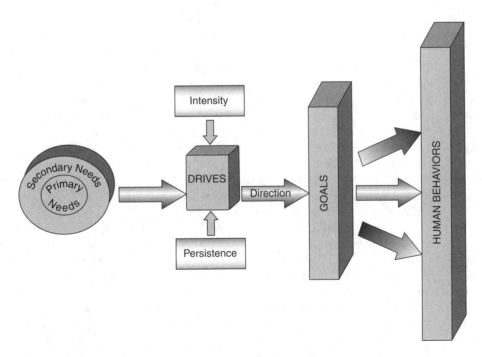

■ **FIGURE 9–3   The path from human needs to human behavior.**

which are common to all living beings, are called **primary needs** (Goetz et al., 1992). They grow out of biology, or genetic makeup, and reflect the ultimate struggle to survive. All beings, from rats in laboratory cages to educational researchers writing books about educational psychology and from minorities growing up in poverty to the wealthiest and most privileged people, share these primary needs. Xavier Evans and Bill Gates may have wildly different tastes in food or shelter, but neither can survive long without attending to those basic needs.

Not all needs arise from such primitive or basic human requirements, however, (N. E. Miller, 1948). Over time, everyone develops unique and personal wants that are not necessary for survival but are still markers by which the balance or quality of life is judged (Goetz et al., 1992). These **secondary,** or **acquired, needs**—such as the need for athletic activity, good books, or desserts—are not biological necessities, but their absence can put some individuals out of kilter.

Sometimes secondary needs are distant versions or displacements of primary needs. For instance, my friends read to their daughter, Leigh, every night at bedtime almost from the day she was born. Leigh sat on her parents' laps and snuggled close as they read her favorite books. Over time, Leigh developed a strong need for books that she carried into her adult life. Books thus became a secondary, or acquired, need for Leigh that is probably associated with the positive feelings of security and belonging she felt as a child when her parents read to her.

Advertisers certainly understand the power of acquired needs. Images of attractive adults or seemingly popular teens are systematically paired with certain products (e.g., cars, clothes, or electronic equipment). The esteem and belonging that these faces in the magazines seem to project are meant to appeal to everyone. By playing off primary needs, advertisers create a new want or desire in consumers, the need for particular symbols of health, wealth, or power.

Characteristics of Drives

When primary and secondary needs are triggered, the internal state becomes disrupted. Individuals feel internally out of sorts, and their instincts are to do something that returns them to a state of internal balance, called *homeostasis* (Pintrich & Schunk, 2001). **Drives,** the effects of needs, are the forces that propel people to act when those needs are activated, so that internal balance can be restored. For example, hunger or a fear for safety can take the form of drives for food or for protection. When that hunger is severe or when fears for safety persist, the intensity of those drives rises correspondingly and can overpower other human motives.

Drives have three essential characteristics: direction, intensity, and persistence (Bergin et al., 1993; Woodworth, 1918). **Direction,** as seen in Figure 9–3, refers to the focus or goal of a drive—the outcome that becomes the desired state (Bergin et al., 1993). Thus, a lack of food (i.e., a primary need) becomes internalized as a drive for food, which subsequently translates into a specific quest for nourishment (i.e., direction). This drive then takes shape as a specific goal (e.g., stop work and eat lunch), which can set a series of behaviors in motion (e.g., walk to the kitchen, search the refrigerator, and pull out the fixings for a sandwich).

Intensity represents the importance or urgency of a particular drive (Bergin et al., 1993). For example, if someone has not eaten since breakfast, the drive for food will be less intense than if that person had been deprived of food for several days. When a drive is low in intensity, an individual may actually choose not to act at all. On the other hand, Xavier Evans's years of feeling deprived of adequate food or shelter may help explain the intensity of his drive to become a star in the NBA.

Drives also have varying degrees of staying power or **persistence** (Woodworth, 1918). At times, for example, needs can be easily addressed. At other times needs are complex or enduring. Such differences in persistence can affect both the form and the nature of the response to primary and secondary needs, as when individuals' drives are displaced or redirected. For example, will Xavier Evans be willing to struggle for years to succeed as a professional basketball player, or will he give up when he realizes he is not "the man"?

Educational Implications

Because primary needs and their ensuing drives are ever-present forces in learning environments, their implications for teaching and learning deserve careful consideration. Educators may tend to focus on the academic dimensions of the classroom and be less attuned to the more primal needs their students project. Certainly, teacher preparation programs stress the educational mission of schools. However, educators need to be sensitive to students' primary needs, as well as their more individualistic secondary needs. Educators need to be aware that actions in classrooms that are surprising or troubling could be linked to students' primary and secondary needs. For example, teachers may fail to realize that the apathy or passivity they see is coming from unmet needs for food, security, or simple physical comfort (Stipek, 1993).

Recognizing the indicators of student need is one thing; attending to those needs is another. Trying to convince children of the merits of any particular educational content when they have not eaten or slept well is a hopeless venture. Students' primary needs for food and rest must be met first before other motivations can be activated (Gottfried, 1981). Understanding the individualistic, acquired needs of students is equally important to teachers. If they recognize what matters to their students, teachers can weave those interests into the curriculum (Gage & Berliner, 1998). And what students see as essential for maintaining balance in their lives is often revealed in their words and actions.

If Rich wants Xavier to begin to see literature as a need in his life, Rich might link literature to basketball. Of course, this association would have been much easier to accomplish before Xavier established the well-honed academic habits he now exhibits. Nonetheless, educators should take a few lessons from Leigh's parents or from advertisers and learn to couple primary needs with the needs educators want to instill in the classroom (N. E. Miller, 1948). They should cultivate secondary needs in students, instead of waiting for them to occur spontaneously, and ensure that the associations students build between primary and secondary needs are positive and frequent (Schunk, 2000a). A problem in Xavier's case is that his goals and behaviors are continually reinforced by others around him—an example of how forces, even within the educational system, can work against the establishment of secondary needs that foster higher educational goals (E. A. Skinner & Belmont, 1993). Teachers like Rich Milner cannot let such realities keep them from trying.

How Do Students' Goals Relate to Their Learning and Achievement?

Students' needs and drives must be directed toward goals before any real action occurs. In fact, some consider all motivation to be goal-directed behavior (Ford, 1992; Wentzel, 1991b). Broadly defined, a **goal** is a target to which one aspires (Pintrich & Schunk, 2001). As such, goals are natural parts of everyday existence. Some educational goals pertain specifically to learning or to school achievement (i.e., **academic goals;** Ford, 1992). Other goals relate to social

aspects of the classroom—for example, a need to please teachers, parents, or peers or to act in socially responsible ways (i.e., **social goals;** Wentzel, 1991a). The term **achievement motivation** signifies all goal-directed actions aimed at bringing about success in academic areas (Murphy & Alexander, 2000).

Carole Ames helped distinguish between learning and performance goals.

At times the academic goals students establish for themselves take on a pattern that is rather consistent across a range of academic tasks or learning situations. Such learners are said to have **goal orientations** (Ames, 1984a; R. B. Miller, Greene, Montalvo, Ravindran, & Nichols, 1996). Meece, Blumenfeld, and Hoyle (1988) consider goal orientations to be a "set of behavioral intentions that determine how students approach and engage in learning activities" (p. 514). The orientations that students manifest relate significantly to their academic achievement. Answer the questions in the Thought Experiment: Uncovering Your Goal Orientation to determine your own perspective on school tasks.

Thought Experiment ....

Uncovering Your Goal Orientation

Directions: Circle the appropriate number to indicate how much you agree or disagree with each of the following statements.

1. It's very important to me that I don't look stupid in class.

    0   1   2   3   4   5   6   7   8   9

    Strongly Disagree ....Strongly Agree

2. I want to get others to do the work for me.

    0   1   2   3   4   5   6   7   8   9

    Strongly Disagree ....Strongly Agree

3. I do my schoolwork because I am interested in it.

    0   1   2   3   4   5   6   7   8   9

    Strongly Disagree ....Strongly Agree

4. I like schoolwork best when it really makes me think.

    0   1   2   3   4   5   6   7   8   9

    Strongly Disagree ....Strongly Agree

5. I'd like to show my teachers that I am smarter than the other students in my class.

    0   1   2   3   4   5   6   7   8   9

    Strongly Disagree ....Strongly Agree

6. I wish I didn't have to do schoolwork.

    0   1   2   3   4   5   6   7   8   9

    Strongly Disagree ....Strongly Agree

7. I would feel successful in school if I did better than most of the other students.

    0   1   2   3   4   5   6   7   8   9

    Strongly Disagree ....Strongly Agree

continued

Uncovering Your Goal Orientation (continued)

8. I do my work in school because I want to get better at it.

| 0 | 1 | 2 | 3 | 4 | 5 | 6 | 7 | 8 | 9 |

Strongly Disagree ....Strongly Agree

9. I do my schoolwork so I don't embarrass myself.

| 0 | 1 | 2 | 3 | 4 | 5 | 6 | 7 | 8 | 9 |

Strongly Disagree ....Strongly Agree

10. I just want to do enough schoolwork to get by.

| 0 | 1 | 2 | 3 | 4 | 5 | 6 | 7 | 8 | 9 |

Strongly Disagree ....Strongly Agree

11. I want to do better than the other students in my classes.

| 0 | 1 | 2 | 3 | 4 | 5 | 6 | 7 | 8 | 9 |

Strongly Disagree ....Strongly Agree

12. I do my work so others won't think I am dumb.

| 0 | 1 | 2 | 3 | 4 | 5 | 6 | 7 | 8 | 9 |

Strongly Disagree ....Strongly Agree

13. I like schoolwork that I learn from, even if I make a lot of mistakes.

| 0 | 1 | 2 | 3 | 4 | 5 | 6 | 7 | 8 | 9 |

Strongly Disagree ....Strongly Agree

14. I do my work so my teachers don't think I know less than other students.

| 0 | 1 | 2 | 3 | 4 | 5 | 6 | 7 | 8 | 9 |

Strongly Disagree ....Strongly Agree

15. I want to do things as easily as possible so I won't have to work very hard.

| 0 | 1 | 2 | 3 | 4 | 5 | 6 | 7 | 8 | 9 |

Strongly Disagree ....Strongly Agree

16. I would feel really good if I were the only one who could answer the teacher's questions in class.

| 0 | 1 | 2 | 3 | 4 | 5 | 6 | 7 | 8 | 9 |

Strongly Disagree ....Strongly Agree

17. Doing better than other students in school is important to me.

| 0 | 1 | 2 | 3 | 4 | 5 | 6 | 7 | 8 | 9 |

Strongly Disagree ....Strongly Agree

18. I want to get out of doing schoolwork.

| 0 | 1 | 2 | 3 | 4 | 5 | 6 | 7 | 8 | 9 |

Strongly Disagree ....Strongly Agree

19. I do my schoolwork because I like to learn new things.

| 0 | 1 | 2 | 3 | 4 | 5 | 6 | 7 | 8 | 9 |

Strongly Disagree ....Strongly Agree

20. One of my main goals is to avoid looking like I can't do my work.

| 0 | 1 | 2 | 3 | 4 | 5 | 6 | 7 | 8 | 9 |

Strongly Disagree ....Strongly Agree

Note: Based on "Engagement in Academic Work: The Role of Learning Goals, Future Consequences, Pleasing Others, and Perceived Ability" by R. B. Miller, B. A. Greene, G. P. Montalvo, R. Bhuvaneswari, and J. D. Nichols, 1996, *Contemporary Educational Psychology*, *21*, pp. 394–395.

Academic Goals

Without question the general orientations students have toward learning translate into different learning outcomes. Motivational researchers concerned with this interplay have formulated particular models and theories to explain the potential relation. **Goal theory** seeks to position learners' goals in a comprehensive and systemic framework that encompasses such related factors as students' beliefs about themselves and learning, their expectations, and their specific academic behaviors (Pintrich & Schunk, 2001).

Mastery and Performance Goals

Carol Dweck did some of the early studies of students' goal orientations.

In the goal-theory literature, two contrasting perspectives toward academic engagement were initially identified and subsequently well researched (Ames & Archer, 1988). **Learning** or **mastery goals** (Dweck & Leggett, 1988), also referred to as *task* or *task-involved goals* (Nicholls, 1989), represent an earnest desire for increased knowledge and academic competence. In effect, one pursues knowledge for its own sake or for the inherent pleasure it brings. On the other hand, **performance goals** (Dweck & Leggett, 1988), or *ego* or *ego-involved goals* (Nicholls, Patashnick, & Nolen, 1985), signify a learner's desire to do well on a task to receive recognition and outpace others or to avoid shame or embarrassment.

Subsequent researchers differentiated between these two orientations on a number of relevant dimensions (Ames & Archer, 1988). For example, as seen in Table 9–2, students with mastery goals apply internal criteria for judging their success, willingly work toward understanding, value what they learn, and take risks to achieve their desired ends. Students with performance goals see success through competition and academic ranking. They are cautious to avoid errors or potential loss of status, and they prioritize grades over knowledge.

Work-Avoidant Goals

Over the years motivation researchers have introduced alternative orientations to academic goals and have clarified the relation between learning and performance goals. Like practicing teachers, motivation researchers are well aware that certain students have little interest in educational pursuits, whether for self-enrichment or for academic competition. Consequently, researchers added another category of goal orientation, **work-avoidant goals** (Meece et al., 1988), an intriguing but less well-established distinction. The main concern of students with work-avoidant goals is

Table 9–2	Contrasting mastery and performance goals.	
Points of Contrast	**Mastery Goals**	**Performance Goals**
How Academic Success Is Defined	Improvement in learning, knowledge gains, progress toward a deeper understanding	High grades, strong performance, especially when compared with peers; academic recognition
What Is Valued	Effort, hard work, and learning	Being perceived as smart or of high ability
What the Roots of Personal Satisfaction Are	Putting forth effort, meeting academic challenges	Doing better than others and looking good academically
How Teachers' Values Are Perceived	Concerned with students' understanding and learning	Concerned with students' output or products
How Errors and Mistakes Are Viewed	A natural step on the road to gaining understanding	Significant sources of anxiety, signs of weakness or failure
Where Attention Is Allocated	The process of learning, be it collaborative or independent	One's relative standing in competition with others
What the Reasons Are for Engagement	Achieving new understandings and new skills	Getting good grades, doing better than classmates, avoiding failure
How Performance Is Judged	Progress toward desired understanding	Outpacing others, achieving high academic standing

Note: From "Achieving Goals in the Classroom" by C. Ames and J. Archer, 1988, *Journal of Educational Psychology, 80,* p. 261. Copyright 1988 by *Journal of Educational Psychology.* Adapted with permission.

Table 9–3 **Possible explanations for work avoidance.**

Potential Factor	Illustrative Comments
Inability to see the value or meaningfulness of academic work	"Why should I bother? What good is this school stuff going to be to me when I'm playing basketball in the NBA?"
Lack of challenge	"This is the same work I've been doing since elementary school. Why should I bother? It's just busy work."
Fear or disdain of social comparison	"I don't like having my work shared. Competition makes me uncomfortable."
	"It shouldn't matter to the others what I am doing. That is my business."
Negative view of the relation between intelligence and effort	"Everything comes easy to smart people. They never have to work hard to get the grades."
Fatalistic attitude	"Why should I bother? It doesn't matter how hard I try, I am still going to end up at the bottom of the barrel."
Energies directed to more pressing and fundamental needs	"My parents are getting divorced and are fighting over visitation. How can I concentrate on schoolwork when my family is coming apart?"

Judith Meece's research has contributed to an understanding of students' work-avoidant behavior.

getting their work done with a minimum of mental or physical effort (Meece & Holt, 1993).

My son, John, and his approach to homework in elementary school illustrate this particular orientation. One day John brought home a list of words to define for social studies. The list contained terms such as *equator, Tropic of Cancer, prime meridien, longitude,* and *latitude.* After reflecting on the terms for a while, he created the same two-word definition for the entire list—"imaginary line." No coaxing or cajoling on my part could convince John that more effort on this assignment was appropriate. This minimalist orientation to schoolwork and learning in general is what marks students as work avoidant. Those who manifest this general orientation to education typically do not perform well on measures of academic achievement.

Why students develop such negative attitudes toward academic work is a question with many possible and complex responses, as indicated in Table 9–3. Some work-avoidant students may simply see no value in or purpose to their schoolwork, either for the short term (e.g., grades) or the long term (e.g., future success; Bandura & Schunk, 1981). Xavier Evans's remarks to Rich Milner reflect just such a lack of value or meaningfulness (Wigfield & Eccles, 1992). In other cases work-avoidant students may find their schoolwork monotonous or unchallenging, as gifted underachievers have reported (Stipek & Gralinski, 1996). Consistently underestimating students' abilities or failing to provide suf-

ficient challenge for extended periods of time can contribute to student disengagement or inactivity (R. B. Miller, Behrens, Greene, & Newman, 1993).

Work-avoidant students may also be socially ill at ease in the classroom and may simply withdraw. A competitive classroom atmosphere can create social tensions for some students (Ames, 1992; Nichols, 1996). Rather than participate in competitive activities, students who find comparisons with peers disconcerting may simply disengage (Nicholls & Miller, 1994).

Another potential contributor to work-avoidant goals is students' beliefs about intelligence (Dweck, 1986; Stipek & Gralinski, 1996); some elementary and high-school students hold troubling and potentially detrimental views (Alexander, 1985). Specifically, in self-reports many students equate intelligence with the ability to succeed with limited effort and thus believe that any manifestation of effort is evidence of limited intellectual capacity. These students might risk poor grades rather than call their mental abilities into question. In addition, work-avoidant students may hold fatalistic attitudes about their performance, believing that their efforts will not have any real effect on their academic success.

Finally, some students have other needs that seem far more important or pressing and therefore push schoolwork to the background (Ford, 1982; Wentzel, 1989). Students who are facing difficult situations in their family life or are struggling with serious issues of self-esteem may have only limited energy to devote to an academic agenda. Their basic needs may overwhelm higher enrichment needs, including the need to learn or understand. All in all, as these factors suggest, educators need to know much more about this particular orientation to learning (N. E. Miller, 1948).

Table 9–4	Approach/avoidance states of goal orientations.	
Orientation	**Approach State**	**Avoidance State**
Mastery	Focus on mastering task, learning, and understanding	Focus on avoiding misunderstanding, avoiding not mastering task
	Use of standards of self-improvement, progress, deep understanding of task	Use of standards of not being wrong, not doing anything incorrectly relative to task
Performance	Focus on being superior, besting others, being the smartest or best at task in comparison to others	Focus on avoiding inferiority, not looking stupid or dumb in comparison to others
	Use of normative standards such as getting best or highest grades, being top or best performer in class	Use of normative standards of not getting the worst grades, not being lowest performer in class

Note: From "An Achievement Goal Theory Perspective on Issues in Motivation Terminology, Theory, and Research" by P. R. Pintrich, 2000, Contemporary Educational Psychology, 25, p. 100. Copyright 2000 by Contemporary Educational Psychology. Adapted with permission.

Questions About Goals and Goal Orientations

When researchers took a critical look at the motivational literature, they identified several unsettling issues about goals and goal orientations that could not be easily answered by the existing literature (Murphy & Alexander, 2000). The exploration of these questions ultimately led to important clarifications and elaborations in motivation theory. Three of those questions have particular relevance to a discussion of optimal learning:

> What explains the achievement of students with performance goals?
> Are flexible and multiple academic goals possible, rather than one pervasive orientation?
> Does optimal learning come only from internal as opposed to external motivations?

Achievement and Performance Goals

According to the sharp contrasts between mastery and performance goal orientations (see Table 9–2), students pursuing mastery goals should demonstrate significantly higher levels of learning or achievement than students with performance goals. The problem is that such clear-cut differences do not consistently emerge (Elliot & Harackiewicz, 1996; Pintrich, 2000a). Students who report having performance goals can do well in school, sometimes well enough to rival students with mastery goals.

To understand this anomaly, Elliott and Dweck (1988) and Pintrich (2000a) analyzed mastery and performance goals further and broke them into two subcategories with theoretically different learning outcomes. Pintrich's (2000a) description of those subgoals appears in Table 9–4. Elliot and Harackiewicz's (1996) work in goal theory also distinguishes between efforts to make something positive occur (i.e., approach) or to keep something negative from happening (i.e., avoidance).

In sum, mastery goals can reflect active knowledge seeking, a willingness to take the risks required to understand deeply (i.e., mastery approach). However, a perfectionist might have a real desire to understand but cannot risk being wrong (i.e., mastery avoidance). Similarly, those who espouse performance goals may need to outshine and outpace others around them (i.e., performance approach). Or they may wish to get good grades because they do not want to be held up to the ridicule or abasement that can come with poor performance (i.e., performance avoidance).

In their research both Pintrich and Elliot hypothesized that students with performance avoidance goals should consistently show poor achievement relative to students with other goal orientations. To date, their data have supported their hypotheses. And this alternative interpretation has helped to explain learning outcomes that were difficult to interpret. With this more specific analysis of goal orientation, return to the Thought Experiment: Uncovering Your Goal Orientation. The procedure for scoring your responses follows. The orientation for which you receive the highest score represents your particular orientation toward schoolwork.

Answer Key to Thought Experiment: Uncovering Your Goal Orientation.............

Directions: Add the points for each of the following sets of questions. The category receiving the highest score represents your goal orientation.

Mastery Orientation

Total for Questions 3, 4, 8, 13, 19 _____

Performance Orientation: Approach

Total for Questions 5, 7, 11, 16, 17 _____

Performance Orientation: Avoidance

Total for Questions 1, 9, 12, 14, 20 _____

Work Avoidance

Total for Questions 2, 6, 10, 15, 18 _____

Flexible Goals and Multiple Goals

Are goal orientations "general traits that cut across domains" (Harter & Jackson, 1992, p. 282), or do goals vary according to the characteristics of the domain or situation? Can students engage in a learning activity for multiple reasons, or must there be only one overriding purpose? Consider your own ratings from the goal orientation experiment. Was one orientation clearly dominant in your responses? Or did you find that you scored rather high in more than one of those orientations? When you rated yourself, did you ever find yourself thinking, "That depends"?

The word *orientation* gives the impression that an individual should reflect mastery, performance, or work avoidance in almost every academic task undertaken (Silva & Nicholls, 1993). However, several factors point to the fact that goals fluctuate by academic domain (Murphy & Alexander, 2000). First, many of the motivational beliefs considered in Chapter 10, such as students' individual interests and their beliefs about their potential to succeed (self-efficacy), vary with the situation or context (Bandura, 1977). In other words, students do not feel equally invested in all subjects, nor do they feel equally capable in every academic domain (Ackerman & Woltz, 1994). Goals seem to reflect these changing interests and competency beliefs.

Second, students' reported goal orientations may result from instructional practices (Ames, 1992). For example, researchers examined the effects of cooperative groupings on students' goal orientations in Algebra II classrooms (Nicholls & Miller, 1994). They found that students working cooperatively had significant gains in their mastery-goal orientations over students who continued to learn within a traditional lecture setting.

A similar paradox arises with the possibility of multiple goals (Ford, 1992; Wentzel, 1989). Perhaps students participate in learning for more than one reason, be it personal satisfaction, enjoyment, looking smart, or gaining the approval of others (Urdan & Maehr, 1995). Conceivably students may pursue knowledge for many reasons—to achieve new understanding (mastery), to gain public or academic recognition (performance approach), and to avoid failure (performance avoidance). After all, human learning is complex; should the reasons for pursuing learning not be equally complex?

Intrinsic Versus Extrinsic Motivations

Internal versus external rewards raise another perplexing question about human goals. Must rewards always be internally derived or self-imposed to produce optimal learning? Do external reinforcements reduce individuals' engagement and enjoyment of learning experiences, as some educational researchers argue (Butler, 1993)? Or are external motivators necessary parts of today's learning environments and essential catalysts for student achievement, as some teachers contend? Explore your own views on this issue by responding to the questions in the Thought Experiment: The Ongoing Debate over Classroom Perks.

Thought Experiment ···

The Ongoing Debate over Classroom Perks

What would happen if Bonnie Nagel stopped rewarding her attentive fourth graders with tokens redeemable for bendy straws and bouncy balls? If correct answers in math didn't rate them Now and Laters? If Mrs. Nagel didn't bake them brownies for earning good-behavior points in art and gym?

"It would be like a dungeon," said Ricky Frank, 9.

"Then I'm not coming to school," said Kwabena Nimarko, 10.

"That's, like, what we live for," said Katherine Driessen, 9.

Enter just about any elementary or middle school, and you'll find that for doing well, students constantly are rewarded with stuff. McDonald's fries for good grades, pencils if they show up for standardized tests, a chance for a restaurant lunch if they do a good deed.

These incentives—descendants of the good old gold star—have proliferated in the face of highly critical research. In a slew of articles, academics say teachers' reliance on extrinsic motivators—in which the reason for doing something is a reward other than the activity itself—is an insidious cop-out that turns classrooms into game shows and forever kills children's inner enthusiasm to learn or behave.

"I've read those articles," said Nagel, a teacher at Swansfield Elementary in Columbia [Maryland] who, like many other teachers, dismisses them as poppycock.

From "The Sweet Rewards of Learning" by L. Perlstein, *Washington Post*, November 14, 1999.

Questions:

What is your impression of this classroom situation?

Do you agree with Bonnie Nagel that teachers cannot function without extrinsic motivators?

What do you think will be the long-term effect of rewarding children for participating in the learning environment?

Are there any conditions under which you believe that extrinsic motivators can contribute to an optimal learning environment?

This debate about internal or external motivation has been around for a long time and tends to cast external forces in the role of villain (Butler, 1993; Deci, 1971). Indeed, the portrayals of optimal learning assume that needs, drives, and goals must be internally instigated. **Intrinsic motivation** can be defined as the performance of an activity for its inherent satisfaction rather than for some separate consequence. **Extrinsic motivation** occurs whenever action is taken to attain some separate end, such as monetary rewards, high grades, or public praise (Ryan & Deci, 2000a).

Ryan and Deci's Self-Determination Theory

For over 3 decades, Richard Ryan and Edward Deci (e.g., Deci, 1971; Ryan & Deci, 2000a) have investigated this apparent conflict between intrinsic and extrinsic motivation. Their intensive study of the interplay of intrinsic and extrinsic goals has recently shed new light on this perplexing issue by explaining the conditions under which intrinsic or extrinsic motivation should promote optimal learning. The interplay of the two types of motivation is central to their self-determination theory (SDT), in which they present a model of human motivation as shown in Figure 9–4. This model actually places intrinsic and extrinsic motivation along a continuum from impersonal to internal.

At the far end of this SDT continuum is *amotivation,* which Ryan and Deci (2000a) describe as a lack of intention to respond or act. Reasons for amotivation, an impersonal state, could be the devaluation of an activity, feelings of incompetence, or beliefs that positive outcomes will never result. Amotivation seems similar to work-avoidance. Xavier probably operated in an amotivational state in Rich Milner's classroom; he was there in body, but not in spirit.

Edward Deci   Richard Ryan

Next comes the state of *external regulation,* the least self-determined or least autonomous form of extrinsic motivation. Students responding at this level often feel alienated because control seems to be beyond their reach. In the Perks excerpt, the children paying attention in Bonnie Nagel's class solely to earn bendy straws fall into this state of external regulation. In Ryan and Deci's model, this state corresponds to performance goals with control resting on outside forces.

One step up in Ryan and Deci's model is *introjected regulation.* In this case a bit of students' self-identity or ego is woven into task performance, although strong external pressures are still associated with that effort. If students in Rich Milner's literature class are concerned about looking smart to their peers and therefore elect to focus on their performance, they would be displaying introjected regulation. Ryan and Deci describe this as a somewhat external state. This state of extrinsic motivation shows evidence of both mastery and performance goals, although their relative force varies.

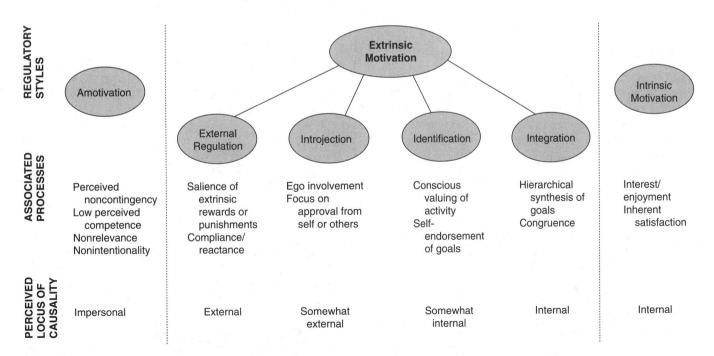

■ FIGURE 9–4   Ryan and Deci's taxonomy for extrinsic and intrinsic motivation.

Note: From "Intrinsic and Extrinsic Motivation: Classic Definitions and New Directions" by R. M. Ryan and E. L. Deci, 2000, *Contemporary Educational Psychology, 25,* p. 61. Copyright 2000 by *Contemporary Educational Psychology.* Reprinted with permission.

Identification is deeper in the realm of internal goals. Specifically, students see personal value in the activity and pursue it principally for that reason. Even though other external factors remain in play, internal forces take precedence. For example, students in Rich Milner's class may perceive the study of Black literature as emotionally and culturally valuable because it may help them understand their own perceptions of the world and give voice to some of their life experiences. However, the grades they receive from Mr. Milner and their ability to communicate effectively in class discussions may also remain important to them.

At the point of *integration*, students are functioning at the most autonomous and internal level of extrinsic motivation and feel strongly in control of their performance. The target activity has value in and of itself, but students still respond to the external rewards and reinforcements that come from task engagement. Thus, external reinforcers can have positive effects on learning when they are linked to students' strong internal motivations. In contrast, the children in Bonnie Nagel's class are unlikely to see their bendy straws or bouncy balls as linked to their internal goals or interest. The more teachers like Ms. Nagel sugarcoat content, the more students are apt to perceive their studies as painful, meaningless, or valueless.

Intrinsic motivation is at the other extreme of Ryan and Deci's taxonomy. For learners at this level, the perceived source of control is exclusively internal. All that matters to these individuals is fulfillment of personal interests, enjoyment, and inherent feelings of satisfaction. Any external reinforcers that might be present in the learning environment have virtually no effect on students' academic engagement. Overall, Ryan and Deci's taxonomy shows that there is no good/bad dichotomy between extrinsic and intrinsic motivation as it pertains to optimal learning. Extrinsic motivation that is coupled with perceived internal control can, like true intrinsic motivation, help optimize learning.

Csikszentmihalyi's Flow Theory

For several decades psychologist Mihaly Csikszentmihalyi (1982, 1985) has asked questions about happiness or contentment. What makes people happy? When do they feel most content or joyful? From the thousands of interviews he and colleagues conducted, Csikszentmihalyi articulated a theory of optimal experience, more commonly called **flow,** which he de-

fined as "a sense of exhilaration, a deep sense of enjoyment that is long cherished and that becomes a landmark in memory for what life should be like" (Csikszentmihalyi, 1990, p. 3).

Closed and Open Goals   In contrast to the early drive theorists, such as Woodworth (1918) and Hull (1952), Csikszentmihalyi (1990) posits that the primary motivation for human actions is not internal balance or homeostasis, but rather a continual pursuit of happiness. Many human needs and goals—including recognition, wealth, popularity, or power—are important only because individuals believe they will bring them happiness.

Like Maslow, Csikszentmihalyi recognizes that humans are biological entities with primitive needs that must be satisfied. Yet Csikszentmihalyi holds that people are *strivers*, as much as they are *survivors*. That is, they are on a quest for some higher state of personal fulfillment, be that self-actualization or true contentment. In fact, Csikszentmihalyi argues that the paradox of human needs is that the satisfaction of one merely causes it to be replaced with another more sophisticated and complex need. This perspective is part of the larger movement termed **positive psychology**—an effort to move the focus of psychology away from its preoccupation with the worst things in life to a focus on valued human experiences (Seligman & Csikszentmihalyi, 2000).

Unlike Maslow, however, Csikszentmihalyi does not reserve optimal experiences for only a few or for those who have conquered their more basic needs. Instead, Csikszentmihalyi (1982) believes that individuals have moments of flow throughout their lives and in many facets of their lives. What becomes important is their ability to control their lives in such a way as to make those moments of flow occur more often. For that result to occur, however, individuals must attend to two categories of human needs and associated goals referred to as closed and open systemic goals (Csikszentmihalyi, 1985).

Essentially, **closed systemic goals** entail goals beyond conscious control. These goals are comparable to primary, deficiency needs and may have either internal or external sources. For instance, closed goals can encompass a response to internal biological needs, including the nonnegotiable needs for food, hunger, and safety that fall in Maslow's deficiency category. However, closed systemic goals can also arise in response to external needs created by the sociocultural context. Such goals exist because people are essentially social creatures with needs to belong or affiliate. And these needs must be addressed if people are to function as members of complex societies with standards and codes of conduct.

In contrast, **open systemic goals** reflect purposeful control over internal or external circumstances. Such goals are related to personal values, beliefs, and interests and may deviate from social dictates (Csikszentmihalyi, 1985). For example, my brother Robert's fascination with the Civil War during elementary school was not shared by his close friends or classmates, but that fact did not deter him from his pursuits. Open goals contribute positively to feelings of fulfillment or contentment in a way that closed systemic goals cannot. These goals are about *thriving*, not simply *surviving*. In that way open systemic goals parallel Maslow's growth or

---

Learner-Centered Psychological Principle 8
Intrinsic motivation to learn. The learner's creativity, higher order thinking, and natural curiosity all contribute to motivation to learn. Intrinsic motivation is stimulated by tasks of optimal novelty and difficulty, relevant to personal interests, and providing for personal choice and control.

Learner-Centered Principles Work Group of the APA Board of Educational Affairs, 1997.

The field of positive psychology at the subjective level is about valued subjective experiences: well-being, contentment, and satisfaction (in the past); hope and optimism (for the future); and flow and happiness (in the present). At the individual level, it is about positive individual traits: the capacity for love and vocation, courage, interpersonal skill, aesthetic sensibility, perseverance, forgiveness, originality, future mindedness, spirituality, high talent, and wisdom. At the group level, it is about the civic virtues and the institutions that move individuals toward better citizenship: responsibility, nurturance, altruism, civility, moderation, tolerance, and work ethic.

M. E. P. Seligman and M. Csikszentmihalyi, 2000, p. 5.

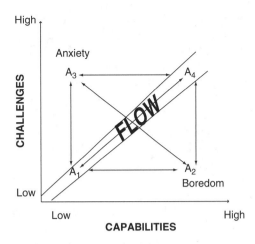

■ **FIGURE 9–5   The interplay of challenge and competency in flow experiences.**

Note: From FLOW: The Psychology of Optimal Experience, *(p. 74) by M. Csikszentmihalyi, 1990, New York: HarperCollins. Copyright 1990 by HarperCollins. Adapted with permission.*

being needs. When individuals operate in the realm of open systemic goals, they are more apt to achieve flow. In fact, when they are "in flow"—that is, deeply engrossed in a stimulating experience—they may momentarily put aside even more primary needs. Individuals may forget to eat, for instance, or may fail to notice other forms of physical discomfort. The importance of social acceptance and the need for external approval likewise decrease in power in this situation.

Contributors to Flow   Generally certain conditions must be met if flow is to result. From the self-reports of individuals across the globe and throughout the life span, Csikszentmihalyi (1990) found that people consistently mentioned four elements in their descriptions of optimal experiences. These characteristics are as relevant to optimal learning experiences in classrooms as they are to experiences outside school walls.

First, individuals must be engaged in activities that are important to them—that is, have intrinsic value. Thus, the value of these activities is not externally but internally established. In addition, the act itself must be perceived as challenging. Individuals must feel that their minds or bodies are being stretched and duly exercised—that is, a maximum challenge. Further, people must feel that they have the capabilities and competencies needed to succeed—that is, corresponding competencies. Finally, upon completion individuals must feel a sense of achievement or accomplishment—that is, a rewarding outcome. They must be rewarded for performing such a challenging task, although that reward can be completely self-determined and self-administered. External rewards, in the form of public accolades or material gain, are not necessary but may be well received if they complement the internal value and rewards individuals bestow on themselves.

Depending on the relative state of the challenge and the competency aspects of the flow experience, certain emotional states result, according to Csikszentmihalyi (1985) (see Figure 9–5). For example, even when individuals are working on a topic or task of personal value, the challenge

may outstrip their competencies or vice versa. As a case in point, inspired by the likes of Michael Jordan, Xavier might decide to enroll in business courses in college to develop the ability to manage his future career in the NBA. However, in his first business course, Xavier might feel misplaced; the content might be so far over his head that he would not know where to begin. Under these conditions, where challenge is high but perceived competencies are low, Xavier would likely experience anxiety (A_3).

However, during that same semester, Xavier might also enroll in a required physical education class. With Xavier's athletic ability, this general class would be no real challenge, but at least he would be engaged in the kind of physical activity he enjoys and might find himself in flow (A_1). Over the course of the semester, though, jogging around the field or tossing around a basketball would start to get pretty monotonous for Xavier. Even his general enjoyment of physical activity might not be enough to keep him going to class; it might be just too boring (A_2). If his attendance started becoming a problem, Xavier might be allowed to take over some coaching responsibilities in several of the education classes. Thus, he might find a new challenge that also made use of his knowledge and skills. And, pretty soon, Xavier might find that he looked forward to the coaching almost as much as playing basketball. He would then be back in flow (A_4).

Educational Implications   Csikszentmihalyi's (1982, 1990) descriptions of flow suggest that optimal experiences are challenging; students must have their minds and their thinking stretched if flow is to result. The question educators must ask is how often their students feel that they are being challenged, other than in testing situations. Students need to feel that the time they spend in classrooms is worthwhile *and* demanding.

However, teachers must also ensure that students have the foundational knowledge and skills to meet those challenges.

The objective, according to Csikszentmihalyi (1990), is to exert effort to achieve some laudable end, not to be overwhelmed by it. Little is gained from a challenge that students have very little, if any, hope of achieving. Over time, such exceedingly challenging tasks can easily erode students' self-esteem and make them feel as if they are simply incapable of performing to expected standards. They are apt to quit trying.

Further, academic tasks should be perceived as meaningful or personally valuable to students. If such value does not exist inherently, then teachers should work to establish the merits of what they ask students to do in the classroom (Dewey, 1902/1956). Learning comes more easily when both students and teachers see the worth of the information or tasks being presented. By structuring his literature class around Black writers and themes of human struggle, Rich Milner believed that he could tap into his students' values and concerns. His approach may have been successful with the students who were already in tune with such themes. But for others, like Xavier, Rich needed to be more effortful and explicit in highlighting the significance of those themes for those students' present and future lives.

When student interests already exist, teachers would be wise to make a place for them in the learning environment (Alexander, Kulikowich, & Jetton, 1994). This attempt may not always be easy, especially when students' values and interests seem tangential to the educational agenda. Yet to whatever degree possible, teachers should make room for personal exploration in the learning environment (Alexander, 1997b). Teachers should also keep in mind that not every activity or undertaking needs to be graded or rated in the same manner. Thus, on some occasions grading may be set aside, so that students can more freely explore intriguing areas or take on more challenging activities. In addition, based on the research on self-regulation and self-monitoring strategies (see Chapter 7), it is wise to encourage students to establish their own goals, criteria, and rewards for particular learning activities (Pintrich, 2000b; Zimmerman & Martinez-Pons, 1992).

Students' participation in the learning environment does not have to be an all-or-nothing situation. Student choice and self-determination can take many forms, even in mandatory assignments (Deci & Ryan, 1991; Rigby, Deci, Patrick, & Ryan, 1992). For example, if Rich Milner requires a semester project in which students explore one particular writer in depth, students could be encouraged to choose a writer of personal interest to them. And they could be given some freedom in the medium of presentation (e.g., written report, video display, or computer program). Just these allowances for student decision making and input can enhance students' pleasure and enjoyment, as well as the effort they exert and the extent to which they challenge themselves.

Finally, Csikszentmihalyi's (1982, 1985) consideration of closed and open goals should remind educators that some goals are more internal, whereas others are more socially derived. Because learning is such a social enterprise, teachers may sometimes forget that students can benefit from experiences that are not only individually conceived, but also independently performed. Some allowance for both independent and group activities in the learning environment acknowledges the need for both intra-individual and interindividual pursuits.

Social Goals

Not all the goals that learners internalize are about academic performance. Some pertain to social relationships in the learning environment or to performing in ways that are socially acceptable or socially sanctioned. These forms of human pursuits are called **social goals** (Wentzel, 1991a, 1991b). Questions that reflect students' social goals are posed in the earlier Thought Experiment on goal orientation.

For some time social influences in students' academic performance were overlooked or downplayed in the motivation literature (Schunk, 2000a). However, in the earlier discussions of human needs, drives, and academic goals, social factors were undeniable forces in academic performance. For example, the belonging need described in Maslow's hierarchy (1954) relates to students' social goals; it is often exhibited in students' efforts to understand and comply with the social codes of conduct in the classroom (Wentzel, 2000). Thus, students generally sit politely at their desks or tables, enter discussions at appropriate times, and recognize the social hierarchy. Because of these social dynamics and students' desires to be part of the school culture, misbehaviors become the exception in classrooms rather than the rule.

Kathryn Wentzel researches the power of social forces, including friendships, on students' learning and development.

The belonging need, however, also manifests itself in the relationships and friendships that students form in the learning environment (Youniss & Smollar, 1989). Such social relationships can vary in their importance from student to student and from year to year. Some students have strong needs to be well liked and socially connected to a large number of others. Other students are content with one or two close friends. Females with just a small circle of friends do well in the academic realm, especially when those friends also value learning (Wentzel, 1999).

Of course, during middle school and high school, the influence of peers increases in importance (Eccles & Midgley, 1990). What classmates think, for better or worse, colors students' views of learning and achievement. As shown in Figure 9–1, approximately one quarter of the fourth graders and eighth graders admit that their friends make fun of students who try hard in school. Such negative perceptions of academic effort among their friends may dampen students' willingness to display enthusiasm for their schoolwork.

Social forces are much more influential in students' goals than most motivational researchers acknowledge (Wentzel, 2000). Even the questions used to establish goal orientations illustrate the strong undercurrent of social forces on students' learning and achievement. When students respond that they do their schoolwork so they do not look stupid, they are showing evidence of social forces. Even those who set out to perform well so they compare favorably with their peers are responding to social factors.

Social beliefs and ensuing goals can sometimes complement students' academic goals, making learning and achievement more likely (Wentzel, 1996). For example, if students believe that popularity and high academic performance go hand in hand, they may be more apt to devote energy to learning and achievement. Or if students enjoy working collaboratively with others, their own understanding and performance might well be enhanced in such settings. On the other hand, social and academic goals can be at odds, resulting in limited engagement. For instance, students who see school as principally a place to make friends and influence people may be less likely to dedicate their energies to academic tasks, especially when they or their friends hold negative perceptions of hard-working or enthusiastic students.

With this framework in mind, consider your answers to the questions in the Thought Experiment: Social Agendas in the Classroom. Use the answer key that follows the rating scale to determine whether your social agenda is more likely to enhance or inhibit your learning and achievement.

Thought Experiment ....

Social Agendas in the Classroom

Directions: Rate how strongly you agree or disagree with each of the following statements.

1. The teacher's perception of me matters.

    | 0 | 1 | 2 | 3 | 4 | 5 | 6 | 7 | 8 | 9 |
    Strongly Disagree ....Strongly Agree

2. It is not cool to be too smart in school.

    | 0 | 1 | 2 | 3 | 4 | 5 | 6 | 7 | 8 | 9 |
    Strongly Disagree ....Strongly Agree

3. If you want to be popular, you sometimes have to put your schoolwork on the back burner.

    | 0 | 1 | 2 | 3 | 4 | 5 | 6 | 7 | 8 | 9 |
    Strongly Disagree ....Strongly Agree

4. Brighter students tend to be more popular in my school.

    | 0 | 1 | 2 | 3 | 4 | 5 | 6 | 7 | 8 | 9 |
    Strongly Disagree ....Strongly Agree

5. It is very important to me that I not look stupid to my peers.

    | 0 | 1 | 2 | 3 | 4 | 5 | 6 | 7 | 8 | 9 |
    Strongly Disagree ....Strongly Agree

6. All I need is one or two really good friends in school.

    | 0 | 1 | 2 | 3 | 4 | 5 | 6 | 7 | 8 | 9 |
    Strongly Disagree ....Strongly Agree

7. I am not about to let school interfere with my social life.

    | 0 | 1 | 2 | 3 | 4 | 5 | 6 | 7 | 8 | 9 |
    Strongly Disagree ....Strongly Agree

8. I enjoy working with other students on tasks or projects.

    | 0 | 1 | 2 | 3 | 4 | 5 | 6 | 7 | 8 | 9 |
    Strongly Disagree ....Strongly Agree

9. The only good thing about school is interacting with my friends.

    | 0 | 1 | 2 | 3 | 4 | 5 | 6 | 7 | 8 | 9 |
    Strongly Disagree ....Strongly Agree

10. Students who ask questions in class are socially out of it.

    | 0 | 1 | 2 | 3 | 4 | 5 | 6 | 7 | 8 | 9 |
    Strongly Disagree ....Strongly Agree

Note: Based on "Social-Motivational Processes and Interpersonal Relationships: Implications for Understanding Students' Academic Success" by K. R. Wentzel, 1999, *Journal of Educational Psychology, 91,* pp. 76–97.

Answer Key to Thought Experiment: Social Agendas in the Classroom ....

Directions: Add the points for each of the following sets of questions. Determine which category has the higher score to see whether your social agenda is more likely to enhance or inhibit your learning or academic achievement.

Social Enhancers

Total for Questions 1, 4, 5, 6, 8 _____

Social Inhibitors

Total for Questions 2, 3, 7, 9, 10 _____

• •

What Can Teachers Do to Promote Optimal Learning?

The power of students' needs, drives, and goals to foster learning and academic achievement is undeniable. However, the ability of students to translate those needs, drives, and goals into optimal learning depends on the nature of the learning environment (Blumenfeld, 1992; Butler, 1994). Whether the learning environment operates as a barrier to optimization or bolsters the positive motivations that students bring into the classroom depends on multiple factors, some of which are within teachers' control. Teachers can take a number of positive steps to guide students toward optimal learning and development.

Make Motivation a Primary Focus in the Learning Environment   Positive motivation does not just happen, even for teachers who are concerned about students' engagement in the learning environment (Brophy, 1998; Stipek, 1993). Teachers must be proactive and consciously and explicitly work to create learning environments that spark motivation. One important factor in this process is sensitivity to students' signals of their level of motivation. Not all students are as clear about their motivational state as Xavier Evans. In fact, many younger students lack the ability or the security to be outspoken and direct with their teachers about their needs and goals. And some students may not interpret their feelings and actions in the way an experienced, sensitive teacher can.

Thus, teachers need to be on the lookout for even subtle indicators of emerging motivational problems (Maehr, 1982). Guiding questions to help teachers are listed in Figure 9–6. These questions should be used after students have been observed on multiple occasions and under varying academic contexts. Several negative responses might suggest a budding motivational difficulty and should receive a teacher's immediate attention.

Build on Students' Existing Needs, Drives, Goals, and Personal Interests   The most potent motivational energies come from within students in the form of unvoiced needs, drives, and goals (Ryan & Deci, 2000b). They also exist as personal or individual interests, such as hobbies or avocations. Teachers who learn to tap these internal energy sources in the classroom are more likely to promote optimal learning (Hidi, 1990). As they plan and implement the curriculum, teachers should evaluate how lessons and topics match students' needs, interests, and goals.

Inventories or surveys are additional tools teachers can use to uncover students' interests and hobbies. Even a few general questions can be enlightening:

> Do you have any particular hobbies or special talents?
> What do you like to do when you have free time?
> What was the last book you read for pleasure?

More particular inventories can target specific subject-matter areas. For instance, teachers might inquire about students' reading habits or their history-related activities (Wigfield & Guthrie, 1997; VanSledright & Alexander, 2002). Csikszentmihalyi (1990) argues that what individuals do in their free time is a good indicator of their deep-seated interests. Thus, teachers should use whatever techniques they can to uncover what students enjoy in their spare time and infuse those interests into the curriculum.

Challenge Students' Minds in Meaningful Ways   For optimal learning to occur, students must engage in suitably challenging experiences. Their minds must be stretched by activities and discussions that require them to work hard to understand (Csikszentmihalyi, 1990). When students feel that their time is wasted by demeaning or worthless tasks, teachers may have to revert to educational bribery to keep them attentive and involved. However, as Ryan and Deci (2000b) make clear, the long-term consequences of the earn-as-you-learn approach exemplified by gold stars, bendy straws, or other trinkets are an erosion of the foundation of optimal learning. Dewey (1913) cautions that education should not be portrayed as simply an *end* that must be reached, but rather a *means* to higher states of human existence.

Challenge should not be misperceived as just hard work, however. It must carry with it the personal value that Csikszentmihalyi (1990) described. Moreover, students must come to that task equipped with the knowledge and skills required to meet the challenge. Teachers can demand more of students academically when teachers are there to scaffold the learning and provide information and support if and when required (Alexander, 2003b). In addition, students will accept the challenges more readily when they can take certain calculated risks and express their thoughts and wishes in the learning environment (Ryan & Deci, 2000b).

Acknowledge Students' Efforts and Accomplishments Appropriately   Part of students' willingness to take risks rests on teachers' responses to students' efforts and achievements in the classroom (Butler, 1994; Harter, 1996). Given the nature of schooling, teachers can easily convey the idea that learning is a matter of social or normative comparison.

Questions to Assess Motivation

Does the student pay attention to the teacher?

Does the student volunteer answers in class?

Does the student begin work on tasks immediately?

Does the student maintain attention until tasks are completed?

Does the student persist in trying to solve problems rather than giving up as soon as a problem appears to be difficult to solve?

Does the student work autonomously whenever possible?

Does the student ask for assistance when it is really needed?

Does the student turn assignments in on time?

Is the student's work complete?

When given a choice, does the student select challenging courses and tasks, even though he or she might not initially succeed?

Does the student accept initial errors or less-than-perfect performance as a natural part of learning a new skill?

Is the student's performance fairly uniform on different tasks that require similar skills?

Does the student's test performance reflect as high a level of understanding as his or her assignments?

Does the student engage in learning activities beyond course requirements?

Does the student appear happy, proud, enthusiastic, and eager in learning situations?

Does the student follow directions?

Does the student strive to improve his or her skill, even when performing well relative to peers?

Does the student initiate challenging learning activities?

Does the student work hard on tasks when not being graded?

■ **FIGURE 9–6   Examining students' motivations.**

Note: From *Motivation to Learn: From Theory to Practice* (p. 14) by D. J. Stipek, 1988, Englewood Cliffs, NJ: Prentice Hall. Copyright 1988 by Prentice Hall. Adapted with permission.

Because of the manner in which grades are given and large-scale tests are conducted, students may see their own learning as hinging on the success or failure of others rather than on individual achievement.

However, for optimal learning to result, students must believe their teachers attend to individual student efforts and achievements, even when those accomplishments do not reach exceptional levels on a normative scale (Eccles, Midgley, & Adler, 1984). Several questions can help teachers determine whether they are acknowledging individual efforts and accomplishments. First, are students judged on their personal progress toward established goals that are either spelled out in individual teacher-student contracts or related to independent projects and activities? And do students have opportunities to interact privately and personally with the teacher about their personal needs and goals? Teachers can use individual student conferences to promote such personal interchanges (Valencia & Calfee, 1991). Such conferences not only offer private time away from the dynamics of the classroom, but also leave students with the sense that their feelings, ideas, and personal interests matter.

Further, are some academic tasks set aside to be assessed on jointly established criteria or simply not graded at all? Within the learning environment, students must feel that their individual journeys toward self-fulfillment are not buried beneath the competition and comparison that is almost inevitable. Instead, students must feel that their individual characteristics and abilities are recognized and appreciated (Eccles, Wigfield, & Schiefele, 1998). Toward

this end, teachers might consider making individual portfolios or individual progress charts a part of their systemic evaluation plans (Valencia & Calfee, 1991). These would give teachers a basis for guiding the learning and development of each student, regardless of where the student stands on the road to self-fulfillment or self-actualization.

Conceptualize Motivation as a Continuous, Multifaceted, and Developing Process   Motivation is not an all-or-nothing phenomenon. It is a complicated, dynamic, and ongoing aspect of life (Bong, 1996; Wigfield et al., 1996). Teachers must accept the varied and fluid nature of students' motivations. All the physical, emotional, social, and cognitive changes experienced throughout life alter motivations, and no dimension is unwavering. The significance of various motivations rises and falls, as does students' ability to take control over their needs and ensuing goals.

This developmental perspective has significant implications for teachers (Stipek, 1996). First, it suggests that optimal learning is more likely to occur when teachers focus early on students' needs, drives, and goals. It is never *too* early to concentrate on students' motivational well-being. Educators must not wait until students like Xavier Evans are seniors in high school and then decide that these students need

Deborah Stipek has written extensively about motivation and classroom management.

to discover the positive character of learning. Young children's inquisitive nature and their desire to please others need to be cultivated and nurtured from Day 1 if teachers are to prevent the serious declines in motivation illustrated in Figure 9–1.

Second, teachers must realize that students will not be equally motivated in all academic domains or with all school tasks (Pintrich & Schunk, 2001). Certain learning activities will be more stimulating and rewarding, and certain domains more relevant to students than others. Such variability and fluctuation is inevitable and not necessarily detrimental. Similarly, the reasons that students perform academic tasks will vary according to the perceived value and expectancies of particular tasks. Teachers need to be prepared to reevaluate the curriculum and reinforce students' efforts so more positive strivings emerge whenever those fluctuations become significant and, thus, problematic.

Finally, academic motivations must be placed in a broad developmental context that acknowledges nonacademic needs, drives, and goals (Schunk, 2000a; Wigfield et al., 1996). By understanding the progress of cognitive, socioemotional, and physical development discussed in Chapters 2 and 3, teachers can more effectively assess the competing draws on students' motivational energies. For example, in the motivationally perplexing period of early adolescence, students' intense physical transformation may make them more susceptible to declines in academic motivation. In addition, the rise in peer influences during this same period can either inhibit or spark academic goals. Two factors in determining the positive or negative effects of these social influences are the nature of the friendships students form and learners' beliefs that their teachers care about their socioemotional well-being. Academic motivations must always be considered a part of the complex interplay of individual strivings.

■ Summary Reflections

What does it mean to be motivated?

- Maslow's hierarchy of needs is a humanistic theory that explores individuals' pursuit of self-actualization.
  - Motivations are a striving toward a higher state of existence.

- Humans must first overcome basic deficiency needs before they can pursue growth needs that bring them closer to their optimal state (i.e., self-actualization).
- Another model depicts the relations between individuals' primary and secondary needs, their goals, and the behaviors they promote.

How do students' goals relate to their learning and achievement?

- Those who have investigated students' goals for academic achievement have uncovered three primary orientations.
  - Some students seek to learn or master the content presented to them.
  - Some are more concerned with the accolades and recognition that come with academic success or the shame or difficulties that accompany failure.
  - Some seek to avoid the work that academic achievement necessitates.
- Several questions about academic goal orientations remain, including the influence of instructional interventions and the presence of extrinsic versus intrinsic motivators.
  - Ryan and Deci's taxonomy helps explain how extrinsic and intrinsic motivations can work together to foster learning.
  - Csikszentmihalyi's (1985) flow theory is a case study in intrinsic motivation.
- Researchers have also examined the social reasons for students' engagement or nonengagement in educational experiences.

What can teachers do to promote optimal learning?

- Teachers should be certain to focus on the motivational dimensions of learning.
- Teachers should also take students' drives, goals, and personal interests into account as they plan and deliver curriculum.
- Teachers should seek to make learning experiences challenging and meaningful.
- They should acknowledge students' efforts and accomplishments whenever possible.
- Educators must keep in mind that motivation is a complex process that is always in development.

Chapter 10

The Role of Student Beliefs in Learning and Achievement

GUIDING QUESTIONS

- How do students' self-perceptions influence their motivations to learn?
- How do students rationalize and internalize their academic successes and failures?
- What can teachers do to foster positive attitudes and beliefs among their students?

IN THEIR OWN WORDS ....

Connie Lutz has been teaching art for 20 years. Much of that time she has worked with exceptional and special needs populations in Alaska's Matusitka Borough School District, a district approximately the size of West Virginia.

I can hear them coming. There is an excited murmur as the sixth graders travel down the hall. They round the corner and see me welcoming them by my classroom door. "That's the art teacher," some say in knowing whispers. Anticipation for art is high for our sixth graders. We do not have art teachers in our elementary schools, so I am the first art teacher most of my students have ever encountered. And this is their first glimpse of an art classroom. As I greet each student, I watch their reactions to the art room. I learned long ago that the way students enter my art classroom telegraphs their motivations about art.

Some students, like Kenya and Michael, rush into the room. They stop midway, turn about, and gaze in wonder at the displays, artifacts, reproductions, and art materials arrayed before them. These students are highly motivated to learn. They display curiosity about art and artistic expression. Likely they felt personal pleasure or received public acclaim as a result of their art. Whatever the causes, students like Kenya and Michael come to my class to learn more.

With students like these, my job is to tap into their sense of competence, their curiosity, and their interest through stimulating lessons and thoughtful discussions that advance their skills, abilities, and understanding. Even with these motivated students, preexisting ideas about art are not always helpful. Students often equate art with free, unstructured, and unevaluated play. As a result, they sometimes balk when presented with a challenging task; their motivations wane because they are surprised that there is *work* involved in making art. In such moments, I help them understand this frustration is a natural aspect of their artistic development. When they ultimately meet these challenges, the Kenyas and Michaels in my classes acquire a personal sense of satisfaction.

Others, like Kyle and Claire, look at the art room as simply a place to make messes. These two rush into the room, heading straight for the art supplies. "When do we get to play with clay?" is always the first question. Kyle and Claire are ready to dive into the experience at a physical level. Maybe they equate art with playtime, or they have had no formal experiences in art.

They certainly have no idea about the rewards and challenges that can come from making art. They do not realize the insights about oneself and about the world that can come from exploring art across cultures and across time. With these students, my job is to channel their enthusiasm for physical experimentation into talking about and making art.

Lurking in the doorway or sulking to a table are Lei and Sebastian. They do not want to be here. For them, the idea of art conjures negative feelings. Perhaps in the past they were like Kenya and Michael, but their interests or talents were squashed or squandered by too much intervention, misguided attention, or lack of support. Maybe their excitement to experiment with materials was met with resistance or deterrence. Perhaps their negative feelings about art stem from some lethal combination of external disapproval and stifled exploration. Because of these negative motivations, I need to help redirect students' energies through supportive art education experiences. The approach I take to encourage my students or give them specific feedback on their artwork can have a great effect on them as well as others. A misplaced comment or empty praise can set them back in their art development.

At the beginning of the school year, my art room is seen as a place of magic, messes, or misery. All students entering the art room bring their previous experiences with art with them. Bundled in these experiences are their beliefs about their capabilities, their interests, and their expectations—key components of their motivations. Anticipative or apprehensive, excited or apathetic, each student arrives motivated toward or away from art. My task as their teacher is clear—to engage all my students by acknowledging their individual motivations and tailoring my art lessons to meet their individual needs. I want them to leave my classroom more knowledgeable about art and more knowledgeable about themselves as consumers and creators of art.

How Do Students' Self-Perceptions Influence Their Motivations to Learn?

As mentioned earlier, Gestalt psychologists were fascinated with human perception (Wertheimer, 1959). To these researchers what the mind perceives matters in learning and development more than what the eyes actually see. In fact, Gestalt psychologists illustrated time and again that people's minds create a vision of the world that conforms to preexisting notions or past experiences (Lewin, 1938). Because of the idiosyncrasies of human perception, some individuals can look at an ambiguous picture and see a saxophone player, whereas others see only an attractive woman (see Figure 10–1a). On other occasions, they think they are looking at a triangle, even when one does not actually exist (Figure 10–1b), or they easily read "THE CAT" despite

a. b. c.

■ FIGURE 10–1 Seeing with the mind's eye.

Note: From *The Story of Psychology* by M. Hunt, 1993, New York: Doubleday; and from *The Universe Within: A New Science Explores the Human Mind* by M. Hunt, 1982, New York: Simon & Schuster. Copyright 1993 by Doubleday and 1982 by Simon & Schuster. Adapted with permission. Also retrieved from http://encyclozine.com/Illusion/1.html.

what is really printed on the page (Figure 10–1c). Optical illusions are more than magic tricks; they remind us that important differences can exist between the worlds outside and inside the mind (Heider, 1958).

In the classroom the inner world of a student's mind places its stamp on every aspect of learning and development. For instance, the self-perceptions of Connie Lutz's students as art consumers and creators will unquestionably affect their eagerness or hesitancy to participate (R. B. Miller et al., 1996). Self-perception deeply influences human learning and development.

Self-Perceptions

According to the principles of Gestalt psychology, individuals interact with the world based on their perceptions, including perceptions of self (Heider, 1958). **Self-perceptions** are fundamental internal models people construct about who they are (Bryne, 1984). The term **self-concept** broadly applies to those perceptions. Some aspects of those mental models lie buried in the unconscious. Other aspects can be made explicit and, thus, thought about and talked about (James, 1890). Self-perceptions can be more influential than any reality they presumably reflect, as indicated by Figure 10–2. That is, the needs that are felt, the drives that are internalized, and the goals that are set are reactions to what a situation is believed to be, whether that belief is accurate or not (Lewin, 1951).

A sense of self also colors how individuals interpret their own actions and those of others (Weiner, 1972). Because self-perceptions are rarely precise internalizations of the outside world, humans cannot help seeing with a biased eye; their self-perceptions slant their interpretations in one direction or another. A disparity also exists between what individuals believe they are revealing about themselves to the world and the impressions others receive.

The way some individuals perceive themselves is very similar to the way other people perceive them. In contrast, what

■ FIGURE 10–2 The difference between self-images and the images others see.

some people hold to be true can be significantly different from what others perceive (Lewin, 1938). Lei, for instance, may perceive herself as enthusiastic or hard working in art class, whereas Connie Lutz sees a hesitant or reluctant student. Similarly, Kyle may consider himself to be poor at art even though he receives positive feedback from Ms. Lutz.

Historically, research on self-concept tended to portray beliefs about self as quite global (i.e., nondifferentiated) and more inherent than dynamic in nature (see Harter, 1986; Wigfield & Karpathian, 1991). Recent research, however,

> *Properly speaking, a man has as many social selves as there are individuals who recognize him and carry an image of him in their mind.*
>
> W. James, 1890, p. 294.

Paul Pintrich conducted groundbreaking research on self-schemas.

has brought these views into question. Ideas about self are increasingly more domain specific and highly dynamic (Harter, 1985; Marsh, 1990). The academic and social experiences students have significantly bear on the views they form about themselves as learners and as members of learning communities.

Whenever the topic of self arises, there is a common tendency to confuse the concept of *self-esteem* with other self terms, such as *self-concept, self-perception,* or *self-schema.* **Self-esteem,** or *self-worth,* deals with individuals' affective evaluation of themselves (Harter, 1985). In essence, self-esteem is an emotional reaction to self. Terms like *self-schema, self-concept, self-perception,* and *self-efficacy* are more cognitive understandings or appraisals—whether accurate or inaccurate.

Although the cognitive and affective aspects of self-understanding and self-evaluation are intertwined, self-esteem research has followed a different course from that of the more cognitive studies and is differentially related to school achievement. Specifically, self-esteem has been approached as a more global, less particularized concept (Harter, 1990), whereas the cognitive terms are more domain and task specific (Pintrich & Schunk, 2001). In addition, the relations between cognitive self-assessment and school achievement have been well established, whereas self-esteem has not been strongly linked to academic success.

The reason for the precarious association between self-esteem and school performance becomes clearer in the case of Sebastian, one of Ms. Lutz's reluctant students. Sebastian may not perceive himself as very good or very interested in art, but that cognitive judgment may have little effect on his overall sense of worth. Or Sebastian may not perceive himself as very good in art but may simultaneously not consider art very valuable. Therefore, his self-esteem remains high regardless of his class performance or his perceived artistic abilities.

Self-Schemas

Self-perceptions are at the core of self-schemas. As described in Chapter 4, a schema is an organized body of conceptual knowledge held in memory. **Self-schemas,** or schemata, are the conceptual knowledge or beliefs individuals possess about themselves. They are generalizations about who people are in different facets of their being (e.g., physical or emotional) and in varying contexts (e.g., family member or student; Pintrich, 1994). These understandings can also be accurate or inaccurate.

According to Paul Pintrich (1994; Pintrich & Schunk, 2001), self-schemas are analogous to the knowledge individuals have about academic topics or domains; that is, they are generally explicit and statable knowledge. The difference is that this knowledge pertains directly to who people are, rather than to some academic subject. If Connie Lutz decided to start her classes each year by having students talk about themselves, the information they would share would reveal part of their self-schemas.

Working Self-Concepts and Future Selves

Self-schemas relate not only to the past, but to the present and the future as well. Self-perceptions about who individuals are at this moment are called **working self-concepts** (Schunk, 2000a). However, these present-time perceptions always have temporal links to the past and the future. They are tied to the past because self-perceptions form from past events (Garcia & Pintrich, 1994). For instance, Connie Lutz suspects that the reluctance or apathy toward art class that she senses in Lei and Sebastian is a manifestation of previous unpleasant or unrewarding experiences.

In addition, current perceptions contribute to future goals and judgments. These future conceptions are *possible selves* (Markus & Narius, 1986), which include notions of what individuals will likely become—for better or worse. Within these possible selves are also ideas about what individuals could ideally become (Markus & Wurf, 1987). The activity in the Thought Experiment: Declaring Your Current and Ideal Selves can assist you in uncovering information about your working self-concept and your possible ideal selves.

Thought Experiment ....

Declaring Your Current and Ideal Selves

Directions: For each of the areas specified, record five words or phrases that describe your sense of self now (current self) and the way you would ideally want to be in the future (ideal self).

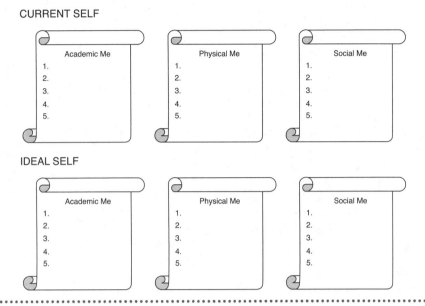

Looking back at your self-schema, now consider the following questions:

- Were certain facets of your self-image easier to articulate than others?
- Were the descriptions you gave for your current self generally positive or negative?
- Were you more critical about one facet of your self-schema than another?
- How easily did the ideal descriptions come to you?
- How disparate are the current and the ideal images you generated?

Future Time Perspectives

A **future time perspective (FTP)** can also be telling (Lens, 1986). Those who have studied FTP point out that some individuals are more oriented toward the future than others. This orientation is referred to as a **time attitude** (Nuttin & Lens, 1985). Some students have their eye on high school graduation, college entrance, or the job they will get when they finally finish school. Other students function more in the now; they rarely envision themselves or their lives in the near or distant future.

Some valuing of the future is critical to learning and achievement (Husman & Lens, 1999). For instance, goal setting is about future performance (Gjesme, 1975). If people had no concern for the future, they would have little reason to set goals (Lens & Decruyenaere, 1991). A concern for the future is also linked to mastery, or learning goal orientations, self-regulation, and academic involvement (Husman, Shell, & Just, 1996). Students who think only about the now usually do not engage fully in their learning

and are thus handicapped educationally. On the other hand, highly effective students must not simply wait and hope for the tomorrows in their academic lives. They must remain attuned to the state of their lives in the present. Effective future perceptions and the goals and actions that follow them must be predicated on accurate interpretations of present conditions.

Look again at your own ideal-self statements in the Thought Experiment. As you envisioned your ideal selves, were you thinking 1 year, 5 years, or further into the future? Are your ideal self-perceptions reflective of both near and distant futures? Self-regulating learners have self-goals that are both near *(proximal)* and far *(distal)* in time (Bandura & Schunk, 1981; Raynor, 1981). This approach makes it more likely that they will achieve their goals by establishing various benchmarks for improvement, which can be evaluated as the need arises.

Cognitive Dissonance

Self-schemas, based on explicit and shareable knowledge and beliefs, are the frameworks used to guide and organize life experiences (Markus & Narius, 1986). In general, people

> *In each kind of self, material, social, and spiritual, men distinguish between the immediate and actual, and the remote and potential.*
>
> W. James, 1890, p. 315.

try to orchestrate their lives to conform to their self-perceptions in a type of self-fulfilling prophecy (Pajares, 1996). For example, a student who considers herself to be mathematically inclined is apt to take more mathematics courses or pursue a career in mathematics. Those actions support or reinforce her self-judgments. Even middle-school students like those in Connie Lutz's classes have probably formed some rudimentary ideas about their abilities. And those perceptions contribute to the positive, negative, or apathetic reactions teachers everywhere face.

However, life does not always play out as expected; sometimes experiences conflict dramatically with the beliefs individuals hold about themselves. The result is **cognitive dissonance,** a tension between the perceived self and actual events. Perhaps a college senior who has always believed himself to be an intelligent person does extremely poorly on an important job aptitude test. The result is tension between his existing self-beliefs and the test results. When such tensions arise, individuals work to reestablish harmony between their perceptions and their actions by following one of several paths.

Ignoring Discrepant Events

One possible path is to ignore the seemingly discrepant experience. In other words, the surprised college senior can close his mind to any further consideration of whether failing the test is a reflection of his general intelligence. Or if Kenya and Michael do become frustrated, they may just let that momentary frustration slip from their memories when they become engaged in challenging but rewarding activities.

Devaluing the Event

Another way to reinstate balance is to acknowledge the event as relevant but devalue its overall importance. In this case, the college senior might admit to himself that the job aptitude test is a gauge of intellectual processing, but one that is not particularly central to mainstream notions of intelligence. "Yes, this is a measure of intellectual processing on which I performed poorly, but the kinds of questions they asked on the test were just bizarre." And Kenya and Michael might conclude that this one frustrating art assignment is just one of many activities their teacher will give them, so it becomes no big deal. All three of these students could simply rationalize these conflicting episodes as flukes, random occurrences.

Altering Self-Perceptions

When cognitive dissonance occurs and experiences are severe enough or repetitive enough, individuals can alter or abandon their existing self-perceptions. For instance, Sebastian, the seemingly disengaged student in Connie Lutz's art class, may have believed that only mathematics and science were important to him. However, through Connie's expert teaching, Sebastian might come to see the beauty in art and also find pleasure in creating art himself. At that point he would alter his beliefs about the value of art in his life, and his self-schema would undergo marked change.

Development of Self-Schemas

Just like other schemata, self-schemas develop over time. Among the significant changes that occur are increased realism, heightened abstraction, and increased differentiation by dimensions and domain (Marsh, 1992; Reeve, 1996; Stipek & MacIver, 1989).

Increased Realism

Very young children tend to make sweeping and glowing self-judgments (Marsh, 1992): "I know everything about dinosaurs" or "I am a good girl." These less-than-sophisticated analyses may be due to a number of factors. For example, very young children do not necessarily have the cognitive abilities needed to reason and reflect on their personal characteristics (Harter, 1990). They may simply not have reached the developmental stage that allows for reasonable and realistic judgments. In addition, these children are limited in their interactions with the world (Wigfield et al., 1996). Many of their interactions are with parents and family, who often project biased and positive views of them (Reeve, 1996). Don't parents frequently tell their children they are the cutest, the smartest, the sweetest children in the whole world? And why should these children not believe these assessments?

By virtue of their growing mental maturity, expanding life experiences, and increasing social interactions, children and youth begin to make more specific and more critical self-assessments (Wigfield et al., 1996). They begin to talk about the subject areas in which they perform better or worse (Buehl & Alexander, 2000) and position themselves relative to other children and youth in their classes (Ruble, Boggiano, Feldman, & Loebl, 1980). Along with enhanced specificity and greater social comparison, however, comes greater negativity (Graham, Taylor, & Hudley, 1998). Young people begin to recognize their weaknesses along with their strengths, coming close to identifying their true selves (Harter, 1996).

Heightened Abstraction

Most motivational and self-concept researchers agree that individuals' self-perceptions fall into at least the three areas represented in the Declaring Your Current and Ideal Selves Thought Experiment: academic, physical, and social (Harter, 1981; Marsh, 1990). The academic self encompasses ideas about school and one's performance in various academic subjects (e.g., mathematics, reading, and science). The physical self involves perceptions of physical appearance or attractiveness, along with competencies in physically related activities. Perceptions about interactions with others—including relationships with peers, parents, and teachers—fall in the social arena (Wentzel, 1999; Wentzel & Berndt, 1999).

From a developmental standpoint, the ideas expressed by young children tend to focus on external or surface-level attributes in these three areas. The physical self of very young children may be the most developed (e.g., "I have blue eyes" or "I can jump on one foot"), but their social and academic responses will also stress observable and concrete aspects. Thus, they might say "I can count to 10" or "I have a friend, Joey."

By the time students approach adolescence, their self-judgments begin to become more abstract (Harter & Jackson, 1992; Wigfield, 1993). At this stage abstraction may come in the form of general trait-like statements. Instead of saying "I have blue eyes" or "I can count to 10," middle-school or high-school students might make statements like "I am ugly" or "I am smart." Social and academic arenas may also become more central to the self-judgments of these older children and youth. However, their self-perceptions are still apt to take the form of global pronouncements, such as "I am friendly" (Pintrich & Schunk, 2001).

This trend toward abstraction continues into adulthood with two potential distinctions. From late adolescence into adulthood, self-perceptions and self-judgments become increasingly complex and conditional (Reeve, 1996). Adults externalizing their self-schemas are less likely to say they are attractive, smart, or friendly. Rather they would probably offer qualifiers and parameters to these assessments, such as "I have nice eyes, but my nose is too broad" or "I am particularly good at mathematical reasoning tasks but have problems with spatial orientation." In addition, older adolescents and adults pay far more attention to the internal, psychological state of their beings than younger individuals do.

Increased Differentiation

Such general developmental changes hint at the growing differentiation that occurs in self-schemas over time (Markus & Narius, 1986) and that is nowhere more apparent than in the area of academic self-knowledge. When students enter preschool, they operate from what Reeve (1996) calls "an undifferentiated self" (p. 140). These young children do not yet have the cognitive wherewithal or the experiences to make particular or accurate judgments about themselves as learners.

New studies show that self-awareness and accompanying differentiation begin to take shape soon after children start school. As a matter of fact, second graders have no problem evaluating themselves or others in certain academic domains (Buehl & Alexander, 2000). These children make determinations about their relative standing among classmates in mathematics, for instance, readily naming the best math student or the classmate who is having problems learning mathematics. And even though the children could make similar judgments in social studies, this academic domain was less formed in their minds, according to Buehl and Alexander.

By the time Connie Lutz encounters her middle schoolers, their academic self-perceptions have become even more specific and potentially more negative (Graham et al., 1998). Because of continued academic exposure and explicit or vicarious feedback from teachers, peers, and parents, students make more particular assessments (Marsh & Yeung, 1997a, 1997b). Their self-judgments cross domains (e.g., "I am much better in reading than writing") and occur within domains (e.g., "Word problems throw me, but I do fine otherwise in math class").

Susan Harter (1981, 1990) and Herbert Marsh (1992) are leaders in the study of the differentiation of self-schemas. According to Harter, students can make rather precise evaluations about their academic performance and the internal or external catalysts for such performance (Harter & Jackson, 1992), and she has developed several scales to tap into these self-judgments. Harter's intrinsic/extrinsic motivation scale examines differences in five areas of self-perception: (a) preference for challenge; (b) curiosity- and interest-based learning; (c) independent mastery; (d) independent judgment; and (e) internal criteria for success or failure. The organization of this scale and a sample item for each of the five dimensions are displayed in Table 10–1.

By applying this scale, Harter (1981) found significant changes in the aforementioned dimensions between third and ninth grades. Specifically, she reported that measures of preference for challenge, curiosity and interest, and independent mastery declined during this period. In contrast, scores for independent judgment and internal criteria for success or failure increased. This pattern suggests that students in upper elementary to early high school feel more personally in control of their judgments but overall less invested and challenged academically.

Herbert Marsh has also explored students' domain-specific concepts and the relation between those concepts and academic achievement. For this purpose he developed his Academic Self-Description Questionnaire (ASDO), which poses questions like those in Figure 10–3 (Marsh & Yeung, 1997a). Marsh's research looks at preadolescent, adolescent, and adult perceptions of capabilities in eight core academic subjects: English, foreign languages, history, geography, commerce, computer studies, science, and mathematics.

Several outcomes of Marsh's studies are important for this discussion. First, he determined that a reciprocal relation exists between students' academic self-concepts and their academic achievement. Not only does prior achievement in specific school subjects influence students' self-perceptions, but their academic self-concepts also affect their subsequent achievement. This finding suggests that teachers cannot simply help students feel good about themselves without improving their knowledge and skills in school subjects. Further, it suggests that focusing on students' academic skills can have positive effects on their beliefs about themselves.

Second, Marsh (1992) determined that the relation between academic self-concept and domain-specific achievement varies by subject. Specifically, students' overall self-concepts relate to their subsequent achievement in English and science. Also, students' prior conceptions about their mathematics abilities related to later mathematics achievement. The differences in school subjects are reflected in how broadly past achievements influence an overall sense of self (Marsh & Yeung, 1997b). But teachers need to understand that students' self-perceptions by academic domain do affect their achievement.

Table 10–1   Sample items from Harter's self-report scale.

Really True For Me	Sort of True For Me	Intrinsic/Extrinsic Motivation		Sort of True For Me	Really True For Me
4	3	**Preference for challenge** Some kids like to go on to new work that's at a more difficult level.	**Preference for easy work** Other kids would rather stick to assignments that are pretty easy.	2	1
1	2	**Pleasing teacher/ getting grades** Some kids do extra projects so they can get better grades.	**Curiosity/ interest** Other kids do extra projects because they learn about things that interest them.	3	4
1	2	**Dependence on teacher** When some kids get stuck on a problem, they ask the teacher for help.	**Independent mastery** Other kids keep trying to figure out the problem on their own.	3	4
1	2	**Reliance on teacher's judgment** Some kids think the teacher should decide what work to do.	**Independent judgment** Other kids think they should have a say in what work they do.	3	4
4	3	**Internal criteria** Some kids know whether or not they're doing well in school without grades.	**External criteria** Other kids need to have grades to know how well they are doing in school.	2	1

Note: From "A New Self-Report Scale of Intrinsic Versus Extrinsic Orientation in the Classroom: Motivational and Informational Components" by S. Harter, 1981, *Developmental Psychology, 17*, pp. 300–312. Copyright 1981 by *Developmental Psychology*. Adapted with permission.

Instructional Influences of Self-Schemas

In keeping with Harter's and Marsh's research, Jere Brophy (1998, 1999) believes that individuals who possess well-articulated self-schemas have a firmer foundation for academic success. He refers to such self-knowledgeable individuals as *schematic learners*. By comparison, Brophy believes that students lacking rich and accurate self-understanding face serious difficulties in learning and development. Brophy calls these less-well-positioned students *aschematic learners*. The adaptive and maladaptive processes Brophy attributes to schematic and aschematic learners are summarized in Table 10–2.

Overall, schematic learners are much more in touch with their general cognitive strengths and weaknesses than aschematic learners are. Thus, schematic students would be expected to be more in tune with their problem-solving profiles (see Chapter 8), and they would be perceptive about their relative standing among peers academically, physically, and socially. Moreover, schematic learners positively value the self-knowledge they possess and trust the judgments that arise from such self-understanding. Aschematic students, by

Jere Brophy

Compared to others my age I am good at history.

1	2	3	4	5	6
false	mostly false	more false than true	more true than false	mostly true	true

I get good marks in geography.

1	2	3	4	5	6
false	mostly false	more false than true	more true than false	mostly true	true

Work in mathematics classes is easy for me.

1	2	3	4	5	6
false	mostly false	more false than true	more true than false	mostly true	true

I am hopeless when it comes to English.

1	2	3	4	5	6
false	mostly false	more false than true	more true than false	mostly true	true

I learn things quickly in science.

1	2	3	4	5	6
false	mostly false	more false than true	more true than false	mostly true	true

I have always done well in computer science.

1	2	3	4	5	6
false	mostly false	more false than true	more true than false	mostly true	true

■ **FIGURE 10–3   Sample items from Marsh's Academic Self-Description Questionnaire.**

Note: From "Causal Effects of Academic Self-Concept on Academic Achievement: Structural Equation Models of Longitudinal Data" by H. W. Marsh and A. S. Yeung, 1997, *Journal of Educational Psychology, 89*, p. 44. Copyright 1997 by *Journal of Educational Psychology*. Adapted with permission.

Table 10–2   Comparison of schematic and aschematic learners.

Schematic Learners	Aschematic Learners
Understand their general cognitive strengths and weaknesses	Cannot clearly articulate their overall strengths or weaknesses as learners
Value their self-knowledge	Do not value their self-knowledge
Trust their self-perceptions	Are unsure about their self-judgments
Have a strong sense of their domain-specific abilities	Have a vague notion of their domain-specific abilities
Make quick and accurate judgments about academic tasks	Do not apply self-knowledge in appropriate learning situations
Use self-knowledge to adapt their academic goals for varied tasks	Are relatively inflexible in their academic goals
Learn well from academic experiences	Do not take advantage of academic experiences or the information they provide
Retrieve relevant information for the domain or task in question	Do not activate relevant knowledge for the domain or task at hand

Note: Based on *Motivating Students to Learn* (p. 216) by J. Brophy, 1998, Boston: McGraw-Hill.

comparison, often do not value the self-knowledge they possess, nor do they trust whatever knowledge they have.

Not only do schematic learners have clearer understandings of their general abilities, but they are also more aware of their aptitudes in specific academic domains. In other words, schematic students would be more accurate in their responses to Harter's motivation scales relative to performance or to Marsh's academic self-concept measures. In addition, they would use their domain-specific perceptions to perform more quickly and accurately on domain-specific tasks. Moreover, schematic students' academic goals are more flexible than those of aschematic students, reflecting a greater sensitivity to their subject-specific strengths and weaknesses.

Perhaps the relation between academic self-awareness and academic achievement that Marsh found comes from the fact that schematic learners take greater advantage of educational opportunities to acquire even more academic self-knowledge. Aschematic students, on the other hand, see academic tasks as experiences to get through, not necessarily to learn from. Schematic students have a good sense of what information about self and academics matters and what information is apt to be tangential or irrelevant. Regrettably, the same cannot be said for aschematic learners.

How Do Students Rationalize and Internalize Their Academic Successes and Failures?

Among the different theoretical perspectives on human learning and development is the belief that just the right dose of reinforcement and punishment applied over an appropriate period of time will create desired outcomes in students (Schunk, 2000b). Known as **operant conditioning,** this belief, which is part of the broader theory of behaviorism, focuses on changing (i.e., *conditioning*) human behav-

Dale Schunk has been a pioneer in motivation research.

Bernard Weiner

ior through the systematic application of desirable or aversive contingencies—that is, reinforcers or punishment (Watson, 1924). The guiding principle is that reinforcement increases desired behaviors, whereas punishment decreases or eliminates unwanted behaviors (Skinner, 1958). To a strict behaviorist, students' interpretations, explanations, or rationalizations of perceived reinforcers or punishers are of little or no consequence.

Motivational researchers—such as Rotter (1954), Weiner (1986), and Bandura (1986)—recognized that this direct and simple relation between reinforcements or punishments and students' performance was faulty. Indeed, the judgments and interpretations that students form about why good or bad things happen to them have a great deal to do with the responses they make. This realization became the basis for aggressive research in causal attributions and efficacy judgments and led to important insights about human learning. Simply stated, whenever students face surprising or significant outcomes, they cannot help reacting emotionally and cognitively (Weiner, 1991). And how they react not only signals their motivational state, but also hints at their academic self-concepts and their likelihood of later achievement.

The Dimensions of Causality: Taking Credit or Placing Blame

The rationalizations and justifications students make to explain life events are called **attributions** (Weiner, 1986). Attributions are causal judgments about the conditions that underlie apparent successes or failures. According to attributional researchers, or those who study this rationalization process, all individuals are basically miniscientists (Schunk, 2000a; Weiner, 1994). When events occur—whether positive or negative—they try to fit them into their existing beliefs about themselves and the world. Students attempt to make sense of academic events by taking credit or placing blame in accordance with their preconceptions about themselves as learners. The credit they take and the blame they place are the foundations of their causal attributions (Weiner, 1972).

After studying students' attributions for years, Bernard Weiner (1991) developed a theory that explains the nature of these causal judgments. From his extensive research, Weiner identified three critical components in students' attributions: locus, stability, and controllability. These dimensions are displayed in Table 10–3.

Locus

One of the most potent characteristics of causal judgments deals with where students place credit or blame. **Locus** is the specific term identifying the location of responsibility. Either students see the cause as within themselves (i.e., **internal locus**), or they attribute the cause to external forces (i.e., **external locus**). For example, if Michael thinks that his strong performance results from his artistic talent, he is crediting an internal condition, artistic ability. If Sebastian credits his less-than-stellar performance to poor teaching in the past, his is an external attribution that places blame on an outside force, his former teachers.

Individuals who tend toward internal rather than external judgments typically believe that their behaviors are meaningfully linked to resulting outcomes (Graham & Weiner, 1996). These internally oriented students (i.e., **internals**) see their rewards and punishment as reflections of their efforts, skills, or abilities. Those who tend to focus on external causes (i.e., **externals**) are more apt to see the outcomes of their actions as somewhat capricious or haphazard. They are more apt to call upon fate, luck, or other people when rationalizing their performance (Weiner, 1986).

Stability

When Weiner and colleagues looked closely at internal and external judgments, they recognized that not all internal attributions were the same (Weiner, Frieze, Kukla, Reed, Rest, & Rosenbaum, 1971). They determined that attributions related to ability had another aspect—stability—that distinguished them from attributions of effort. When students talk about ability or potential, they are basically talking about a factor that they see as fixed or resistant to change. Effort, on the other hand, is typically portrayed as more temporal and modifiable.

Because of this important distinction, Weiner (1972) added the dimension of **stability** to his attributional dimensions. Because **stable** factors, like aptitude or personality traits, are more fixed and unwavering, they should be predictable and reliable features of learning or the learning environment. Effort, on the other hand, is more closely related to the situation or context and is therefore not as consistent as potential. **Unstable** causes are quick to change and are thus highly unpredictable. Thus, even stable personality traits can experience swings in moods. Or generally healthy individuals can be affected by illness or accident. Moods and illness are two examples of unstable conditions.

Even though effort has typically been associated with unstable attributions, Pintrich and Schunk (2001) argue that there are actually two types of effort. First is the typical effort that students exhibit in instructional contexts. Students like Kenya consistently put forth high levels of effort, whereas others like Lei are predictably work avoidant. These typical levels of effort are quite stable. However, students do exhibit situational or temporal effort, triggered by specific tasks or classroom conditions. For instance, Lei may find a particular art assignment more to her liking and may work harder for the moment. This situational or temporal effort would be more in keeping with Weiner's characterization of an unstable attribution.

Controllability

When researchers first talked about the locus dimension, they used the phrase "locus of control." But Weiner (1972) holds that this concept actually has two separate dimensions, locus *and* control. **Controllability** identifies whether students see the factors associated with their success or failure as within their personal control (i.e., **controllable**) or outside their direct control (i.e., **uncontrollable**). If Michael believed that he could have done better on his art project if he had just spent more time on it, he would be framing a controllable explanation. In contrast, if Claire believed that her performance was due to her lack of fine motor coordination, she would be identifying an uncontrollable causal condition.

Table 10–3 The three dimensions of attributions: locus, stability, and controllability.

STABILITY	LOCUS			
	Internal		External	
	Controllable	Uncontrollable	Controllable	Uncontrollable
Stable	Typical effort	Aptitude/ability	Instructor bias	Task/instructional conditions
Unstable	Immediate effort	Mood/illness	Teacher/peer assistance	Luck

Note: From *Attribution Theory of Motivation and Emotion* by B. Weiner, 1986, New York: Springer-Verlag. Copyright 1986 by Springer-Verlag. Adapted with permission.

Motivational researchers still debate the controllable/external issue (Stipek, 1988). Can a factor be external to the individual and still be perceived as controllable? According to Weiner, some situations can be both controllable and external (Weiner, 1991). For example, if Connie Lutz scored Lei's art project low because she was biased toward this student, the circumstance would be external to Lei but would be within Connie's control to eliminate. Stipek (1988) and others disagree with this analysis and argue that any external cause must be judged uncontrollable by default.

One other perspective on this controversy over the controllability of external causes acknowledges the complexity of this issue. From this vantage point, the value of attribution theory lies in understanding how *students* perceive the circumstances of their successes or failures. That is, to be judged controllable, the situation must be in the students' control and not in the domain of others like teachers, parents, or peers. Thus, if teacher bias is at the heart of Lei's causal attribution for a poor grade, she is unlikely to perceive that circumstance as within her control, making teacher bias uncontrollable.

Such judgments can be affected by the degree to which students perceive themselves to be active participants in their learning. In classroom environments where students feel able or even encouraged to express their views on important academic matters, such as grading, they may be apt to perceive more control over external influences on their learning and performance. For example, if a student does not do well on a mathematics quiz because her teacher did not explain a formula well but the student believes that the teacher would have clarified the formula if she had asked for assistance, this external factor is within the student's perceived control to a certain extent. Similarly, in classrooms where cooperative and shared learning are commonplace, a student could see peer assistance as an external but controllable condition.

With this foundation try your hand at analyzing students' explanations for their academic triumphs or tribulations. Turn to the Thought Experiment: Plotting Students' Attributions for Success or Failure, where you will find various statements made by students enrolled in a high-school chemistry class. See whether you can place their rationalizations in the appropriate cell of the locus/stability/controllability matrix. Remember to think in terms of the students' perceptions as you make your judgments. After you have made your designations, check your responses against those listed at the end of the chapter.

Thought Experiment ....

Plotting Students' Attributions for Success or Failure

Directions: Following are various statements made by students after Mr. Jervis, their teacher, hands back a chemistry test. Decide what each statement represents in terms of *locus* (*I* = internal; *E* = external), *stability* (*S* = stable; *US* = unstable), and *controllability* (*C* = controllable; *UC* = uncontrollable). Try to analyze the statements from the students' points of view.

1. "I have always done well in chemistry. This stuff is second-nature to me—a snap!"
2. "Mr. Jervis asked the wrong questions on this test. Just my luck!"
3. "All I have to do is look at a chemistry test, and I *freeze*!"
4. "I had the state wrestling tournament this week and didn't have time to study. I'll ace the next one."
5. "Chemistry is for geniuses. It doesn't belong in high school."
6. "I was down with the flu for 3 days. Who can think with a fever of 102?"
7. "Myron kept tapping his pencil the whole time. It was driving me crazy. I should have asked Mr. Jervis to move me."
8. "There's no point in studying. I am just plain stupid."
9. "I go over my notes and problems every day after class. I earn my grades."
10. "Thank goodness I asked Mr. Jervis to explain isotopes again. I got those problems right on this exam!"

(Answers at the end of the chapter)

....

Common Attributional Biases

In an innovative analysis of attributional research, Pintrich and Schunk (2001) identified five common schema or inference rules that lead students or teachers to make erroneous and potentially harmful attributions. Building on the research of Fiske and Taylor (1991), Nisbett and Ross (1980), and others (Covington, 1992), Pintrich and Schunk call these undesirable situations *common attributional biases.* They are summarized in Table 10–4.

Fundamental Attribution Error

Students sometimes attribute outcomes to dispositional or trait-like factors, such as physical appearance or sociocultural factors, overlooking conditions within the immediate situation or context. Jumping to conclusions based on the external features of those involved is a common case of **fundamental attribution error.** For example, by generalizing from one art teacher to all art teachers, Kyle might let his negative opinion of his previous art teacher influence his reaction to Ms. Lutz. Conversely, Connie Lutz might interpret students' physical restraint as evidence of passivity or work avoidance and thus form a negative judgment about Lei or Sebastian that would color her assessment of their performance.

Actor-Observer Perspective

When an **actor-observer perspective** arises, students or teachers see their own behaviors as appropriate for the current situation or context but regard the actions of others as indicative of their dispositions or traits. Thus, Claire might

Table 10–4 Common biases in attributions.

Attribution Problem	Student Bias	Teacher Bias
Fundamental attribution error: Attribute other's behavior to a disposition or a trait	Student perceives all teacher behavior as a function of disposition: *Ms. Baker is always mean.* *Mr. Smith is prejudiced against minorities and women.*	Teacher perceives all student behavior as a function of disposition: *Sam is just a lazy person. He never tries hard.* *Sally has no aptitude for science.*
Actor-observer perspective: Attribute other's behavior to disposition but one's own behavior to the situation	Student perceives his behavior as a function of the situation but attributes teacher's behavior to disposition: *I hit him because he was bugging me, but now you are punishing me because you don't like me and always pick on me.*	Teacher perceives her behavior as a function of the classroom but attributes students' behavior to disposition: *You are a very aggressive boy, and I'm just trying to keep control of my class.*
Self-serving bias: Accept personal responsibility for success but deny responsibility for failure	Student perceives her successes as due to her behavior, but failures are due to other factors: *I did well in math because I'm smart at that, but I did poorly in English because the teacher can't teach it well.*	Teacher perceives his success as due to his behavior but attributes failures to other factors: *I did a great unit in math, but the students just aren't motivated to study English literature.*
Self-centered bias: Regardless of success or failure, accept more personal responsibility for a jointly determined outcome	Student perceives that he is more responsible for an outcome even when it is due to his and others' behavior: *I did more of the work on this project than all the other students in my small group.*	Teacher perceives that she is more responsible for an outcome even when it is due to her and others' behavior: *Third period class discussion was excellent. I'm a really good facilitator of discussions.*
False consensus effect: Assume that one's beliefs and behavior are typical of most people	Student perceives that her beliefs or behaviors are representative of most students: *I hate math and most girls hate it just like me.* *All the other kids are cheating, so I can, too.*	Teacher assumes that his beliefs or behaviors are representative of most teachers: *Like all the other teachers in this building, I think the biggest problem is that the kids are just not motivated.*

Note: From *Motivation in Education* (p. 119) by P. R. Pintrich and D. H. Schunk, 1996, Englewood Cliffs, NJ: Merrill/Prentice Hall. Copyright 1996 by Prentice Hall, Inc. Adapted with permission.

think that art should be fun rather than work but then get upset with classmates who do not work hard enough on a group project. Or Connie might believe that schools put too much emphasis on grades yet see her own grading system as an essential ingredient in student learning.

Self-Serving Bias

Another common problem, **self-serving bias,** is a pattern of accepting responsibility for one's successes but attributing failures to external forces. This tendency has also been called the *ego* or *self-protective bias* because it allows students or teachers to maintain their self-esteem in the face of failure. Pintrich and Schunk (2001) point out that this bias is pervasive outside the classroom as well, in athletics and politics especially. Thus, Claire might attribute her A on an art project to her own hard work. When she gets a B-, however, she claims that Ms. Lutz did not explain well enough what she wanted. In the same way,

Connie Lutz might attribute her students' overall strong performance on a test to the effectiveness of her teaching. However, if a number of students perform poorly on one question on that test, she might rationalize that they did not listen well in class when she went over that information.

Self-Centered Bias

Some individuals demonstrate a **self-centered bias.** That is, they see themselves as the source of all the good or bad that befalls them, even when other parties are involved. For example, when the students get feedback on a group activity, Kenya might feel that the grade reflects her creativity and hard work in the group, ignoring the contributions of others. Or Connie might perceive the positive academic growth of her students as largely attributable to her emphasis on art, overlooking the contributions of the other teachers at the middle school.

False Consensus Effect

Sometimes attributional biases result from evoking an everyone-else-does-it rationale, the **false consensus effect.** For example, adults who fudge on their income taxes may explain their behavior by claiming that everyone else does it. Students and teachers also fall back on false consensus effects in their attributions and justify situations by folding them into a sweeping generalization. Thus, Kyle might explain that he does not do as well as Kenya because "girls are just better at artsy stuff." And Connie might explain away her students' lack of interest in art history by pointing to their preadolescent self-centeredness, overlooking other significant factors.

In the Thought Experiment: Spotting Cases of Attributional Bias, you will find various statements made by students and teachers. See whether you can spot the attributional biases being expressed.

Thought Experiment ....

Spotting Cases of Attributional Bias

Directions: Below are statements made by students and teachers when they were asked to explain their academic successes or difficulties. Decide whether each statement is a case of *fundamental attribution error (FA), actor-observer perspective (AO), self-serving bias (SS), self-centered bias (SC),* or *false consensus effect (FC).* If you believe that there is no bias in the response, mark the statement *NB.*

1. "I'm not surprised there are so few women in my engineering classes. They're just not equipped to handle the math."
2. "No, I didn't study for Mr. Morgan's biology test. Nobody studies in that class anyway."
3. "The students in my American literature course just want to be entertained. It doesn't matter that I developed a dynamite lesson on Hawthorne."
4. "If it wasn't for me, our team would never have won the school geography bee."
5. "These geometry proofs are really hard for me."
6. "I can't help it that Mary Elizabeth isn't getting along in her small group. She is just hardheaded and won't listen."
7. "Yes, I've skipped PE classes. Who hasn't?"
8. "Mr. Jackson had no right to keep me after school for that hall fight. I don't care what the rules are—Malcolm deserved what he got after what he said about me!"
9. "The reading problems that some of my students have are making it difficult for them to get much out of their history text."
10. "Those science fair judges don't know a thing about science. I should have won that competition. I won last year."

(Answers at the end of the chapter)

Consequences of Attributions

The attributions that students and teachers make tell a great deal about their views of the world (Stipek, 1988). Such rationalizations reveal whether they feel personally responsible for academic outcomes and also hint at whether they believe they are in control of causal conditions and can modify those conditions (Weiner, 1972). In addition, attributions have important consequences.

Emotional/Affective Consequences

When individuals succeed or perform well, they tend to feel happy or pleased. When they fail or perform poorly, they generally experience sadness or displeasure. Such reactions are likely regardless of the explanations or rationalizations of those successes or failures. Beyond such global responses, however, the emotional reactions people display appear to be linked to the attributions they make (Weiner, 1980).

Consider the emotions of surprise, anger, frustration, resignation, guilt, shame, pride, or gratitude in relation to the locus/stability/controllability matrix (see Table 10–5). To determine the conditions under which these emotions would likely appear, go back to the responses the chemistry students offered in the Thought Experiment on plotting attributions and explore the related emotions. How was the student who said, "Chemistry is for geniuses" feeling when he was handed the D on his chemistry test? Because he attributes his performance to the nature of the domain, a stable and uncontrollable condition, he likely felt resignation at the expected outcome (Stipek, 1996). For the student who proclaimed that chemistry is "second nature to me," how might he have felt if he got a C on the next test? Shame would be a reasonable emotional response for a student who has failed to live up to his own expectations (Weiner, 1980).

And how about the student who got the "wrong questions" as a result of bad luck? What if she got a B on that next text? Surprise would be a reasonable emotional reaction for someone who thought success was outside her control (Weiner et al., 1971). On the other hand, surprise would not be expected from the student who felt she earned her good grades through hard work. In that case pride would be an appropriate reaction—her hard work paid off.

Weiner (1994) found that students are more apt to display anger or guilt when their negative outcomes arise from controllable conditions. Thus, the student who was bothered by his classmate's incessant tapping but did not take steps to rectify the situation might be susceptible to guilt. Or the young man who did not study because he was preoccupied with the wrestling tournament might have displayed anger that he did not perform to his usual expectations (Bandura & Adams, 1977; Weiner, Graham, & Chandler, 1982). Another group of learners see the help of others as important to their success, as was the case of the student who got valuable assistance on isotopes from Mr. Jervis. In this scenario the student was probably grateful for that as-

Table 10–5   Emotions and associated attributions.

STABILITY	LOCUS			
	Internal		External	
	Controllable	Uncontrollable	Controllable	Uncontrollable
Stable	Pride	Shame	Gratitude/regret	Apathy/resignation
Unstable	Anger	Frustration	Guilt	Surprise/relief

Note: From *Attribution Theory of Motivation and Emotion* by B. Weiner, 1986, New York: Springer-Verlag. Copyright 1986 by Springer-Verlag. Adapted with permission.

sistance. On the other hand, if she could have asked for help but did not, she might well regret her inaction.

These patterns suggest that students' emotions are meaningfully linked to the attributions they make about themselves and the conditions of their learning. Teachers should promote desirable emotions such as pride or gratitude (Bandura, Adams, Hardy, & Howells, 1980). However, they should be careful not to convey emotions like sympathy when it comes to academic performance, because that would imply that students' performance is out of their immediate control (Graham, 1984). Such emotion could constrain students' willingness to try harder in the future (Bandura et al., 1980).

Behavioral Consequences

What if you believed strongly that nothing you did as a student could help you to learn, that your fate as a low-performing student was sealed? How would you feel as a student, and how would you behave? Unfortunately, a small percentage of students carry around such negative beliefs about themselves and their place in the learning community (Maier & Seligman, 1976). A belief in an endless cycle of failure and negative emotions or attributions is called **learned helplessness** (Peterson, Maier, & Seligman, 1993). How this cycle begins is not clear, but students with learned helplessness come to perceive each failure as undeniable evidence that their mental aptitudes are low (Seligman, 1975). Even when they succeed, these students' attributions contribute to their negative conditions. That is, they may attribute their success to luck or to an overly easy task, rather than to effort or skill. Over time, these students come to expect failure and, thus, respond to challenges with apathy or resignation.

The contrast between these students and highly successful, learning-oriented students can be quite dramatic (Schunk, 2000b) and can extend to almost every dimension of learning, from perceptions of intelligence and beliefs in effort to a valuing of knowledge and challenge. Distinguishing features of learned helplessness, as listed in Table 10–6, include seeing intelligence as fixed and unchanging, effort as ineffective, and knowledge as personally meaningless.

Learning-oriented students, by comparison, believe that they can improve through hard work and by learning more.

Moreover, students with learned helplessness do not expect much of themselves and easily give up when difficulties arise, whereas learning-oriented students maintain high expectations of themselves and are persistent even in the face of significant difficulty (Reeve, 1996). Because students with learned helplessness do not know how to help themselves and have a repertoire of strategies that is limited and ineffective, they avoid potentially challenging situations and experience pervasive failure and high anxiety. Learning-oriented students, on the other hand, are well equipped strategically to deal with problem situations and, thus, seek out challenge and infrequently face failure or experience high anxiety.

Ways to Help the Helpless

Researchers who work with students with learned-helplessness offer several valuable recommendations for helping them (Diener & Dweck, 1978; Dweck & Reppucci, 1973). Their suggestions can also be useful with a broader population of students who have more negative than positive attributions or who do not possess the necessary self-help strategies (I. W. Miller & Norman, 1981; Orbach & Hadas, 1982).

Demonstrate the Effect of Effort   In her 20 years as a teacher, Connie Lutz has encountered more than one student with learned-helplessness, but Marcia is a good example of them all. Her apathy masks her academic despair, which is strengthened by her belief that effort can never translate into better performance (Diener & Dweck, 1978). And merely telling her that effort can help will not persuade her to alter that deeply held belief. If Connie wants Marcia to start believing that effort will improve her performance, Marcia must see this causal relation played out in the flesh and in nontrivial ways (I. W. Miller & Norman, 1981). Resistant students like Marcia must see that wisely exerting effort can reliably produce deeper understanding and higher achievement (Schoenfeld, 1988), and they need to see that effect on multiple occasions with varied tasks.

Table 10–6   Distinguishing a learning-orientation from learned-helplessness.

Characteristic	Learning Orientation	Learned Helplessness
View of Intelligence	Perceives intelligence as malleable and changeable	Considers intelligence to be a fixed, unwavering capacity
Belief in Effort	Sees an undeniable link between effort and academic success	Sees effort as basically unrelated to academic outcomes
Valuing of Knowledge	Places a high value on academic knowledge	Perceives knowledge as relatively worthless or personally meaningless
Pursuit of Challenge	Looks forward to challenging tasks that demand thought	Avoids challenge, prefers tasks that are easy or routine
Level of Expectation	Holds high expectations of academic success	Has no expectation of academic success, only of continued failure
Persistence	Displays a stick-with-it attitude toward difficult or challenging tasks	Gives up quickly when any difficulty arises
Strategic Processing	Has rich and effective strategies that encourage multiple solution paths	Possesses few strategies for dealing with gaps in understanding or performance
Failure Pattern	Faces performance problems only infrequently or with specific domains or tasks	Experiences failure frequently and in many academic areas
Task Anxiety	Experiences low anxiety even when tasks are complex or novel	Feels anxious when presented with seemingly demanding or unfamiliar tasks

Note: Based on *Learning Theories: An Educational Perspective* (3rd ed.) by D. H. Schunk, 2000, Upper Saddle River, NJ: Merrill/Prentice Hall. Copyright 2000 by Prentice Hall, Inc.

Perhaps Connie could convince Marcia to work with her to establish a performance contract, which could include a clear goal statement, timeline, and performance criteria (Graham & Harris, 1993). Then, during the 2 weeks that the class is working on their self-portrait projects, Connie and Marcia could meet regularly to talk about her progress. In the end Marcia should be able to see that this focused effort resulted in a highly evaluated art project of which both she and Ms. Lutz can be proud.

Set More Precise Goals   Connie has learned through experience not to hand students like Marcia nebulous assignments like "create a self-portrait." To these students such an assignment is vague and daunting, and its novelty is apt to induce high anxiety (Convington, 1992). Students with learned helplessness simply do not know where to begin with such an assignment or where they should end up. Thus, to work independently and effectively on Ms. Lutz's art project, Marcia needs a more precise target for her often-limited academic energies (Goetz et al., 1992)—something around which she can wrap her mind and energies.

This target can be accomplished in several ways (Reeve, 1996). First, Connie should use precise words to specify what she means by art project (e.g., a drawing, a sculpture, a collage). Also, she should share any particular criteria or parameters she will use to judge the final project (e.g., originality or personal relevance). She might also present students with product models, along with explanations about why these works are good examples.

Once this stage setting is complete, Connie should take time to meet individually with each student to specify what

he or she envisions as a desirable end product. During these meetings Connie can help Marcia and any other students frame their ideas in the form of a goal statement (e.g., "I will paint a water color that shows me in my room"). Connie should also be sensitive to Marcia's particular strengths and needs in judging whether her stated goals are indeed reasonable, adequately challenging, and feasible. Has Marcia worked well with watercolors before? Does she know some of the tricks in producing definition with this medium? Finally, the consensus that Connie and Marcia reach should be written down and should serve as the beginning of Marcia's performance contract.

Break Tasks into More Manageable Parts   As part of the work contract for students like Marcia, the end goal should be broken down into smaller and thus more manageable and trackable components (Goetz et al., 1992). For instance, Connie could work with Marcia to formulate a timeline for the self-portrait art project, (e.g., develop a sketch for the watercolor by October 6, do background wash by October 9). Connie and Marcia can then monitor progress at each point on the timeline. In this way Marcia does not have a large deadline looming sometime in the future. Rather, she has more specific and proximal performance goals that she can discuss and evaluate with Ms. Lutz.

Provide Explicit Strategy Training   As Chapter 7 made clear, not all students come equipped with the tools they need to rectify academic problems or enhance their performance (Wigfield et al., 1996). Students like Marcia often become paralyzed when difficulties arise (Peterson et al.,

1993). Consequently, because strategies are essential to problem solving in all domains, teachers must contribute to these students' problem-solving repertoire by teaching them specific techniques that fit the task at hand (Alexander, Graham, & Harris, 1998).

In assisting Marcia with her self-portrait project, Connie might consider what general or specific art techniques would make for a better outcome. Are there techniques that could help Marcia with the perspective and the color of her composition? What about some strategies for enhancing color when working with water-based paints? Rather than assume that Marcia knows these strategies or will discover them, Connie should take the time to review them or teach them to her. Perhaps she and Marcia could jointly construct a checklist of strategic reminders to guide Marcia during project development.

Attribute Success to Effort and Ability, Failure to Controllable Conditions Two recommendations for aiding students with learned helplessness focus on the feedback they receive from their teachers. In effect, Connie needs to work to reshape Marcia's attributions for both the successes she experiences and the problems or failures she encounters (Skinner & Belmont, 1993). Reshaping requires convincing Marcia and others like her that successes are not random occurrences but are the consequence of effort or aptitudes and skills brought to the task (Weiner et al., 1971).

If students begin to believe that successes have discernible causes, they cannot ignore their contributions to these positive outcomes. Similarly, when problems arise, students must be helped to identify potential causes that fall within the controllable portions of the attributional model (see Table 10–3; Covington, 1984). A checklist of actions to be taken during task performance could serve as a reference point in a task debriefing: Did you establish a specific goal for the task? Did you gather all the materials and information needed to perform the task effectively? Such a checklist has been very successful with students with special needs (Harris & Graham 1996).

Self-Efficacy

Motivational researchers have identified another influential set of beliefs that students hold, which are formed in part by the attributions they make. Those beliefs are essentially judgments that students form about their ability to perform or execute a task from a specific domain or with particular characteristics. Bandura (1977) refers to these as **self-efficacy** beliefs.

Albert Bandura

Although attributions and efficacy beliefs are both cognitive self-assessments, they are distinct in several important ways. First, self-efficacy represents beliefs about future success, whereas attributions involve interpretations of past actions. Thus, self-efficacy is future oriented (Bandura, 1982). Second, whereas attribu-

tion theory explains how individuals determine whether events are within or outside their control, efficacy beliefs determine whether those individuals expect to do well or poorly at the tasks for which they assume responsibility.

In effect, efficacy beliefs answer the how-well questions about student performance, rather than the how-come questions of attribution theory. If Claire makes a judgment about why she did not do well on Ms. Lutz's art project, she is attempting to justify or rationalize what has already occurred (i.e., attribution). If, on the other hand, she decides that she is not going to do well on the next art project because it is a time-consuming task, she is determining how she is likely to perform (i.e., efficacy).

Sources of Efficacy Beliefs

The simplified model in Figure 10–4 suggests that certain student characteristics influence their cognitive functioning, including their efficacy judgments. Among those characteristics are students' cognitive aptitudes and abilities, their task or domain knowledge, and their task or domain beliefs (Ackerman et al., 1999; Snow, Corno, & Jackson, 1996). Sebastian is a case in point. He has high aptitude for mathematics and science, and his verbal skills, both written and oral, are above average as well. As for his beliefs about knowledge and academic domains, Sebastian believes that there should be clear right and wrong answers to school

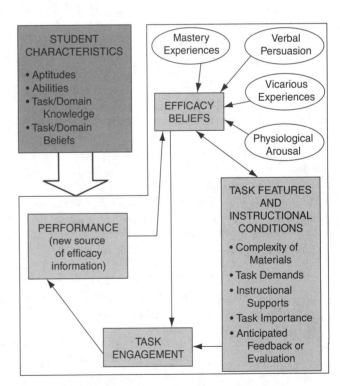

■ **FIGURE 10–4   The sources and effects of self-efficacy beliefs.**

Note: Based on research by Fives (2003), Pintrich and Schunk (2001), and Tschannen-Moran and Woolfolk (2001).

problems and that art, as a domain, is neither particularly rigorous nor important. Such characteristics clearly affect how deeply and how well Sebastian engages in self-assessment, and they are likely to bias whatever interpretations or judgments Sebastian makes about his potential to succeed in Ms. Lutz's class.

Rather stable characteristics, like aptitude, interact with students' efficacy judgments, which are activated during the performance of a specific task. These efficacy beliefs arise from multiple sources.

- *Verbal persuasion*—the comments or feedback students receive from others, including teachers, peers, or parents. What do others say to students about their capabilities or incompetencies?
- *Mastery experiences*—the past successes or failures students have had with the target domain or with similar tasks. When confronted with a similar situation, did the student experience success or difficulty?
- *Vicarious experiences*—the reactions students have from observing others in their academic, social, or cultural circles. What do students see happening to others with whom they relate, or what do they hear said to those with whom they identify?
- *Physiological arousal*—students' biological reactions or their physical states. Do students' hearts race or their palms sweat when presented with certain tasks? (Bandura & Schunk, 1981)

Existing efficacy beliefs continually interact with the specific features of the domains and tasks students confront, as well as with instructional conditions. Among such features and conditions are the complexity of the educational or instructional materials; the task demands; the nature and quality of the instructional support given by teachers, peers, or others; the relative importance of the task or the value of the related domain to the student; and the nature or significance of the feedback or evaluation.

This interaction between existing efficacy beliefs and the task and instructional conditions guides students' engagement in the task at hand. Whatever outcome results (i.e., performance) will influence future efficacy judgments about similar tasks and domains. Thus, current performance functions as a new source of efficacy information, affecting future judgments about similar tasks and domains (Fives, 2003).

Even though the idealized model in Figure 10–4 is described in terms of students' efficacy beliefs, it is also relevant to teachers and their instructional performance. The writings of Anita Woolfolk-Hoy and colleagues (e.g., Tschannen-Moran & Woolfolk, 2001; Tschannen-Moran, Woolfolk-Hoy & Hoy, 1998) have helped to translate the efficacy literature into teacher practice.

Woolfolk-Hoy

Effects of Efficacy Beliefs

The effects of efficacy beliefs on student learning and achievement have been well documented (Pintrich & Schrauben, 1992; Schunk, 1991). One of those effects has to do with students' academic choices and career paths (Betz & Hackett, 1983). As Bandura (1986) hypothesized, students tend to engage in those tasks or pursue those fields for which they feel relatively efficacious, and they often avoid tasks or domains for which their self-efficacy is low. Such decisions can have significant and lasting effects on student learning and development. For example, Sebastian's positive beliefs about his mathematical ability may prompt him to take more advanced courses during high school and college and may lead him toward a mathematics-related career. Kyle's negative beliefs about his mathematical skills may mean that he avoids similar opportunities.

Self-efficacy beliefs have also been linked to students' effort and persistence (Bandura & Cervone, 1986; Schunk, 1991). When students have more positive efficacy beliefs, they are more likely to stay with a task or field even if they encounter difficulties or face setbacks. However, when faced with similar problems, students with low efficacy are more apt to quit or withdraw. The difficulties low-efficacy students encounter may only reinforce their existing notions that they do not have what it takes to succeed even if additional effort or strategies are employed. High-efficacy students, by comparison, may become more strategically involved in what they perceive as difficult but doable tasks. Indeed, Pintrich and colleagues (Pintrich & deGroot, 1990; Pintrich & Schrauben, 1992) found that the nature of strategic processing and the level of student engagement were correlated with self-efficacy; higher efficacy was tied to higher levels of strategy use and engagement.

Like attributions, self-efficacy beliefs are associated with differing emotional responses, depending on **outcome expectations,** which are anticipations of success. High outcome expectations mean that success is anticipated, whereas low outcome expectations mean that success is unlikely. Generally, there is a strong, positive correlation between students' efficacy beliefs and their outcome expectations; those who feel efficacious also anticipate success. However, this is not always the case, and the different relations between self-efficacy and outcome expectations can produce intriguing behavioral or affective responses, as shown in Table 10–7.

When self-efficacy beliefs and outcome expectations are both high, for example, students display self-assurance and are highly engaged in the task. When both self-efficacy beliefs and outcome expectations are low, emotions and behaviors are similar to those of learned helplessness; students are resigned, apathetic, or withdrawn in school. In less common instances, when efficacy beliefs remain high but outcome expectations are low, students may display activism or protest existing conditions. Thus, Sebastian might question Ms.

Table 10–7   Affective and behavioral reactions to high and low self-efficacy beliefs and outcome expectations.

Self-Efficacy Beliefs	Outcome Expectations	
	High	**Low**
High	Self-assured High engagement	Activism Protest Grievance
Low	Self-devaluation Depression	Resignation Apathy Withdrawal

Note: From "Self-Efficacy Mechanism in Human Agency" by A. Bandura, 1982, *American Psychologist, 37*, p. 140. Copyright 1982 by *American Psychologist.* Adapted with permission.

Lutz's approach to art projects and her evaluation; he might seek more acceptable and definitive parameters for judging the quality of students' work. And adults in high-efficacy/low-outcome situations might find themselves strongly supporting unpopular or risky causes. Finally, when students manifest low self-efficacy beliefs but high outcome expectations, they may feel little sense of accomplishment, devaluing whatever success they experience. They could even find themselves depressed when success is expected for tasks in which they perceive themselves as relatively incompetent.

What Can Teachers Do to Foster Positive Attitudes and Beliefs Among Their Students?

As Jacquelynne Eccles and colleagues (1989) have emphasized, aspects of students' self-beliefs do not exist as independent dimensions. As shown in Figure 10–5, students' self-schemas, goals, and interpretations of success are parts of a complex motivational/instructional system. For example, learners' aptitudes and prior achievements directly influence their causal attributions and sense of academic control, which in turn help to shape their short-term and long-term goals (Wigfield & Eccles, 1992, 2000). Similarly, the cultural milieu, or the atmosphere in which students live and learn, is strongly linked to their perceptions of themselves as males or females or as members of particular cultural or ethnic groups (Eccles et al., 1989). These perceptions affect not only learners' attributions, efficacy beliefs, and goals, but also the value learners assign to academic content.

Although the role of teachers is not specified in this expectancy-value model of achievement motivation, their influence is pervasive nonetheless. That influence is seen in the general atmosphere or milieu of the classroom and is apparent in the expectations teachers convey through their feedback and in their treatment of students (Ginott, 1972). Further, the value that students place on academic content rests, in part, on the ability of the learning environment to amplify the interest and value of the instructional content (Wigfield & Karpathian, 1991).

Create a Positive Learning Environment Devoid of Gender and Cultural Stereotypes

Motivational researchers recognize that the academic beliefs of males and females differ (Entwisle & Baker, 1983; Frey & Ruble, 1987), as do those of certain sociocultural groups (Graham, 1994; McInerney, Roche, McInerney, & Marsh, 1997). More important, students' beliefs do not always coincide with their actual performance.

Gender Patterns in Perceptions and Performance

Perceptions of gender and ethnic differences can be strong even when those differences are weak or statistically nonexistent (Byrnes, 1996). For example, study after study has found that females rate their competencies in language-related tasks or domains (e.g., English and writing) higher than males rate theirs (Halpern, 1992; Hyde & Linn, 1988). Males, on the other hand, consider themselves more competent in mathematics, physical ability, and physical appearance (Eccles, Adler, & Meece, 1984; Wigfield, Eccles, MacIver, Reuman, & Midgley, 1991). Overall, males have higher self-perceptions than females have by ninth grade. (Phillips & Zimmerman, 1990). In some studies females had lower self-perceptions by the early elementary grades (Frey & Ruble, 1987).

However, these differences tend not to coincide with actual performance differences for females and males. For example, females apparently have as much natural mathematical ability as males do (Byrnes, 1996). Females also generally get higher grades than males in mathematics courses (Eccles, Adler, & Meece, 1984), although they may perform differently on certain mathematics achievement tests and on experimental measures (Hyde & Linn, 1988). However, even those differences exist more among young precocious students or older students engaged in problem solving (Hyde, Fennema, & Lamon, 1990).

A similar gap between perception and performance appears in other content areas as well. For instance, males may

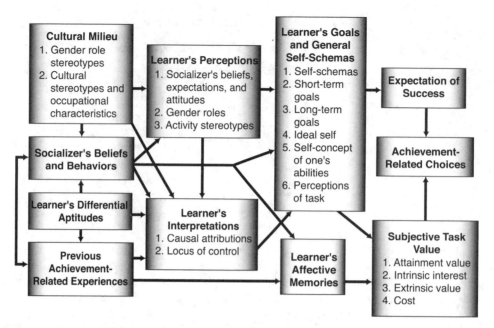

■ FIGURE 10–5   Expectancy-value model of achievement motivation.

Note: From "Expectancy-Value Theory of Achievement Motivation" by A. Wigfield and J. S Eccles, 2000, *Contemporary Educational Psychology, 25,* p. 69. Copyright 2000 by *Contemporary Educational Psychology.* Adapted with permission.

believe they are more competent in science but perform only slightly better on large-scale measures (Byrnes, 1996). Likewise, females' stronger feelings of competence in reading and writing correspond to only a slight difference on most standardized tests (Hyde & Linn, 1988). Thus, it would seem that females and males do feel different about their inherent abilities in a number of academic subjects even though only moderate differences actually exist.

Ethnic Patterns in Perceptions and Performance

Perceived differences between sociocultural groups present an equally perplexing picture. According to performance data across cultural groups, differences consistently arise. Overall, Caucasian students perform substantially better on large-scale achievement measures than do either African American or Hispanic students (Byrnes, 1996). Whether minority students have lower self-concepts is a difficult question to answer, in part because relevant studies are limited and ethnic differences are intertwined with socioeconomic factors (Pintrich & Schunk, 1996). Thus, it is hard to separate effects directly attributable to ethnicity from those more rightly attributable to the culture of poverty.

Sandra Graham (1994; Graham et al., 1998) has done extensive research on the motivational characteristics of African American students. Her findings point to a complex relation between self-perception and academic performance. In fact, Graham (1994) found that African American students had higher expectations of success than Caucasian students did in 12 of 14 studies she analyzed. In 18 studies of self-concept, Graham again found that 7 studies reported higher ratings for African American students; only 2 studies had results that were higher for Caucasians, with the remaining investigations reporting no differences or mixed re-

sults. The bottom line is that African American students generally report higher levels of competency and self-esteem than one might expect, given their lower performance on achievement measures.

Interpretation of Gender and Ethnic Patterns

What are educators to make of these intriguing but counterintuitive self-beliefs? One explanation of gender differences in self-beliefs rests in the broad stereotypes that override actual performance outcomes. For instance, females may rationalize their higher grades as a case of greater effort or chance instead of higher ability (Eccles, Adler, & Meece, 1984; Wigfield et al., 1996). Males, on the other hand, may attribute lower grades to a lack of personal effort, or they may devalue the academic content (Halpern, 1992; Reeve, 1996). There may also be a higher need for females to comply socially in the classroom, whereas males may feel greater social freedom to resist academic engagement (Wentzel, 1991a).

When it comes to ethnic differences, Graham (1994) and others (e.g., Crocker & Mayor, 1989) offer several explanations for the seemingly contradictory patterns in self-perception of African Americans. First, the researchers point to the possibility that African American students compare themselves to others in their ethnic group rather than to those in other cultural groups. Like males in general, African Americans may also be able to maintain positive self-esteem by devaluing school and school-related achievement (Crocker & Mayor, 1989). In addition, African Americans may attribute lower performance on tests and grades to an inequity of opportunity and to substandard education (Rosenberg & Simmons, 1971), conditions substantiated in the research literature (Byrnes, 1996).

Claude M. Steele

Implications for Teachers

Motivation researchers like Graham (1994), Pintrich (2000a), and Schunk (2000a) recommend that teachers look beyond gender or ethnic identifications as much as possible. Differences *within* any gender or sociocultural group, after all, are far greater than the reported differences *between* the genders or the sociocultural groups. Teachers should focus their instructional energies on individual students and on their particular strengths, interests, values, and beliefs.

Claude Steele (1997) has offered an alternative solution to perceptual and performance conflicts for African American students. His recommendation is to aim for positive stereotyping as a way to instigate more reinforcing attitudes and increased effort. For instance, Steele found that when African American students were told that their ethnic group does well on certain kinds of academic tasks, the performance of this group on those tasks actually improved. However, evoking any stereotypical perceptions, even in positive ways or for desirable ends, remains a risky and questionable practice (Alexander, 1996). Thus, teachers who use this approach with gender or sociocultural groups must remember that stereotypes can carry serious negative consequences.

Because of this negative potential, teachers should try to confront stereotypical notions that arise in the classroom, even if those stereotypes might work to the students' advantage. Educational discussion about girls, boys, African Americans, Asians, or any other group should be replaced with references to individual students' abilities, efforts, and needs (Graham, 1994). The learning environment should be a place of opportunity and possibility for all students, not a place where stereotypes are played out or given voice.

Unearth Students' Beliefs, Perceptions, Goals, and Values

Students are not typically forthcoming about their beliefs or their personal interests and values. It is likely that students have not even expressly considered these important dimensions in connection with their learning or achievement.

Thus, if teachers are to succeed in creating a positive and enriching learning environment that targets individual strengths and needs, they must become skilled at uncovering students' beliefs, perceptions, goals, and values (Alexander & Dochy, 1995). Connie Lutz can speculate on Lei's, Sebastian's, or Kenya's perceptions of their artistic aptitudes, for instance. She can infer Michael's or Claire's beliefs about the value of art from their actions and verbal statements. However, if she wants more direct access to such information, she must ask questions or pose situations that speak to internal beliefs and perceptions (Murphy, 1998).

Of course, self-report data are not flawless or unquestionable (Ericsson & Simon, 1980; Pressley & Afflerbach, 1995). Students may respond in ways they see as socially acceptable, even though they do not represent an honest reflection of their personal views. Nonetheless, well-phrased questions such as those presented throughout this chapter can prove useful, especially when there is a pattern to what students reveal. Figure 10–6 presents additional questions teachers can pose to gauge students' academic, sociocultural, and expectancy beliefs. These questions have been used effectively to explore learners' expectations as well as their beliefs about gender or activity stereotypes (Wigfield & Eccles, 2000). Such perceptions influence students' goal setting and causal attributions, as shown in Figure 10–5.

Bandura and Schunk (1981) have used other approaches to examine students' self-efficacy beliefs—approaches that teachers can apply in classrooms. Specifically, they have presented students with a particular task, such as a series of word problems, and have asked the students how successful they think they will be at solving those problems. Using this approach, Connie Lutz could present students like Kyle or Marcia with sample art projects and ask them how capable they feel about creating a comparable project. Connie could then gauge the amount of self-assurance students feel and the amount of support or scaffolding she might need to provide.

However teachers go about it, they must secure meaningful and useful information about their students' belief systems (Alexander & Murphy, 1998a). Then they must make effective use of that information as they plan their curriculum and evaluate their students' progress.

Treat All Students Equitably

Teachers must be sensitive to their own instructional biases toward students who are perceived as less competent or less capable (Allington, 1980; Brophy, 1998). Educators cannot help forming broad ability judgments about their students, mentally sorting students into more or less capable categories based on performance or sometimes other more insidious characteristics, including physical appearance or socioeconomic status. And these categorizations influence the way teachers unconsciously treat their students' instruction (Brophy, 1999).

For instance, observational studies illustrate the ways teachers unconsciously treat females and males differently in their classrooms (Sadker & Sadker, 1994; Sadker, Sadker, & Klein, 1991). Teachers consistently report that girls participate more in their classrooms than boys do. However, the

Ability Beliefs

How good are you in science?

0	1	2	3	4	5	6	7	8	9

Terrible .... Excellent

If you were to line up all the students in your class from the worst to the best in reading, where would you stand in the lineup?

0	1	2	3	4	5	6	7	8	9

The Worst .... The Best

Do students do well in mathematics because of hard work, or were they just born that way?

0	1	2	3	4	5	6	7	8	9

Born That Way .... Hard Work

Compared to the other subjects you take in school, how good are you in history?

0	1	2	3	4	5	6	7	8	9

A Lot Worse .... A Lot Better

Sociocultural Beliefs

Compared to the girls in your school, how do boys do in history?

0	1	2	3	4	5	6	7	8	9

A Lot Worse .... A Lot Better

How much does your teacher care about your understanding of mathematics?

0	1	2	3	4	5	6	7	8	9

Very Little .... A Great Deal

How do you think that students from other countries do in science compared to students in this country?

0	1	2	3	4	5	6	7	8	9

A Lot Worse .... A Lot Better

Expectancies

How well do you think you will do in science this year?

0	1	2	3	4	5	6	7	8	9

Not Well At All .... Very Well

Compared to your other subjects, how well will you do in history this year?

0	1	2	3	4	5	6	7	8	9

A Lot Worse .... A Lot Better

■ **FIGURE 10–6   Questions used to gauge learners' ability, sociocultural, and expectancy beliefs.**

Note: From "The Development of Achievement Task Values: A Theoretical Analysis" by A. Wigfield and J. S. Eccles, 1992, *Developmental Review, 12.* Copyright 1992 by *Developmental Review.* Also from "Expectancy-Value Theory of Achievement Motivation" by A. Wigfield and J. S. Eccles, 2000, *Contemporary Educational Psychology, 25,* p. 70. Copyright 2000 by *Contemporary Educational Psychology.* Adapted with permission.

videotapes of classroom instruction reveal quite a different story. In reality, the teachers tend to call on the males more than on the females, give the boys more general, abstract questions to answer and a longer time to answer them, and let the males try again if they are unable to respond correctly at first.

This differential treatment has also been documented in teachers' interactions with students thought to be low in academic ability (Allington, 1980). As summarized in Table 10–8, teachers react differently to presumed low-ability students in the pattern of questions asked, the assignments made, and the opportunities for choice and personal expression provided (Ryan & Deci, 2000b). Teachers might publicly proclaim that these students are able to learn, but their actual behaviors send a very different message to those students (Entwisle & Baker, 1983)—a message likely to reinforce any negative self-beliefs the students harbor.

Teachers must be concerned that all students have sufficient time to think before responding and chances to rephrase or reevaluate their answers (Allington, 1980). All students must have a voice in classroom discussions and the occasion to explore tasks of personal value and interest (Alexander, 1997b). Moreover, all students need to feel that they are valued members of the classroom community who can sometimes work without direct supervision (Miserandino, 1996).

Table 10–8 How teachers communicate their expectations to low versus high achievers.

Teacher Behavior	Low Achievers	High Achievers
Wait Time	Given limited time to think through or weigh a question before answering	Allowed extended time to think before answering a question during discussion
Instructional Content	Presented with simplistic and routine tasks	Given challenging and abstract tasks as part of the curriculum
Seating Pattern	Seated away from the center of classroom activity	Positioned prominently at the front and center of instructional activity
Student Questioning	Called on infrequently in class	Relied on to provide answers during classroom recitation or discussion
Level of Questioning	Typically asked declarative-knowledge questions with right/wrong answers	Asked more complex, abstract questions requiring extended responses
Responses	Receive no feedback or terse responses about the correctness of their statements	Get positive or reflective comments and reactions to their answers
Probing	Receive no follow-up to a given response or comment, especially when answer is judged incorrect	Receive additional questions or comments, even if response is incorrect
Discussion	Given limited time for open-ended discussion	Given time in both teacher-led and student-led discussions
Student Choice	Have little if any opportunity to pursue topics or tasks of personal interest	Allowed to work on projects or tasks they choose
Attentiveness	Get less of the teacher's attention	Often have the teacher's attention, either through eye contact or physical proximity
Trust	Have their actions or products doubted or questioned	Given the benefit of the doubt when issues arise
Task Completion	Not expected to complete their work or do it well	Held to high standards for work completion and quality
Frequency of Criticism/Praise	Often criticized, even publicly, for poor work or praised for mediocre outcomes	Rarely criticized for inappropriate behaviors and praised only when performance is truly praiseworthy
Supervision	Made to work under direct supervision	Permitted to work independently or without direct supervision

Use Feedback That Highlights Student Effort and Control

Like their behaviors, teachers' verbal feedback to students can mold their attributions and self-competency beliefs (Brophy, 1998). Teachers' evaluative comments can either promote feelings of control and increased effort or exacerbate negative attributions (Graham, 1984; Weiner et al., 1982). Effective feedback does not need to avoid critical comments; students need to understand what they are doing well and what they need to improve (Bangert-Drowns, Kulik, Kulik, & Morgan, 1991; Elawar & Corno, 1985). However, evaluative comments should be positively and sensitively framed.

Even praise can be rightly or wrongly given (Ginott, 1972). Specifically, praise that is offered at the wrong time, as when work is mediocre or is below students' capabilities, or praise that is framed in the wrong way can lead to negative attributions, lower expectations of success, and reduced valuing of academic tasks (Maier & Seligman, 1976). Table 10–9 summarizes the distinguishing characteristics of effective and ineffective praise (Brophy, 1998). For example, effective feedback to students should regularly and systematically follow their actions and should address specific aspects of their performance (e.g., "Marcia, you have produced very rich colors in your self-portrait"; Nafpaktitis, Mayer, & Butterworth, 1985). Further, feedback should refer directly to agreed-upon performance criteria (e.g., "Marcia, you remember that we discussed having a sketch of your self-portrait project completed by October 18?"; Brophy & Good, 1986).

In addition, for feedback to enhance students' performance, it should offer clear information about the students' competence on specific tasks (Kohn, 1993). The teacher also needs to compare students' current performance with what they did in the past (e.g., "Marcia, you are getting much better at creating perspective in your sketches") as opposed what other students have done (Brophy & Good, 1986). Moreover, the teacher needs to praise students' efforts, along with their abilities, particularly when the task is difficult and when some success is realized (e.g., "Your extra effort and your original idea for this self-portrait really came together in this creative work, Marcia"; Natriello & Dornbusch, 1985). If students accept such feedback, they may feel in greater control of their learning and be more willing to work hard in the future (Weiner, 1994).

Table 10–9   Effective and ineffective praise.

Effective Praise	Ineffective Praise
Is contingent on performance	Is delivered randomly or unsystematically
Specifies the particulars of the accomplishment	Is restricted to global positive reactions
Shows spontaneity, variety, and other signs of credibility; suggests clear attention to the student's accomplishment	Shows a bland uniformity that suggests a conditioned response made with minimal attention
Rewards attainment of specified performance criteria	Rewards mere participation, without consideration of performance processes or outcomes
Provides information to students about their competence or the value of their accomplishments	Provides no information at all or gives students information about their status
Orients students toward better appreciation of their own task-related behavior and thinking about problem solving	Orients students toward comparing themselves with others and thinking about competing
Uses students' own prior accomplishments as the context for describing present accomplishments	Uses the accomplishments of peers as the context for describing students' present accomplishments
Is given in recognition of noteworthy effort or success at difficult tasks	Is given without regard to the effort expended or the meaning of the accomplishment
Attributes success to effort and ability, implying that similar success can be expected in the future	Attributes success to ability alone or external factors such as luck or minimal task difficulty
Fosters endogenous attributions (students believe that they expend effort on the task because they enjoy the task and/or want to develop task-relevant skills)	Fosters exogenous attributions (students believe that they expend effort on the task for external reasons—to please the teacher, win a competition or reward, etc.)
Focuses students' attention on their own task-relevant behavior	Focuses students' attention on the teacher as an external authority figure who is manipulating students
Fosters appreciation of, and desirable attributions about, task-relevant behavior after the process is completed	Intrudes into the ongoing process, distracting attention from relevant behavior

Note: From *Motivating Students to Learn* (p. 115) by J. Brophy, 1998, Boston: McGraw-Hill. Copyright 1998 by McGraw-Hill. Reprinted with permission.

Further, when teachers make evaluative comments to students, they should talk in terms of the students' actions and skills, not in terms of their own actions or interpretations (Wlodkowski, 1985). The feedback is about the students, not the teacher. Thus, rather than a comment like "Marcia, I gave you this grade because . . . ," Connie should put the responsibility on Marcia's shoulders—"Marcia, you earned this grade because. . . ."

Finally, the teacher should be careful not to disrupt students' performance during processing, distracting them from their immediate goals (Brophy, 1998). Instead, attributional feedback should be rendered once that phase of the process is completed. This recommendation is more easily accomplished when a formidable task is broken into components with an associated timeline. Teachers and students can then discuss task performance at each of those designated points during the process without disrupting the students' thinking or learning.

Concentrate on Domain-Specific Competencies and Beliefs

If there is one lesson to be learned from the research on self-schemas and self-efficacy, it is the difficulty of trying to alter students' global self-esteem or overall self-concept (Schunk, 1991). Educational interventions aimed at pro-

ducing such broad transformations have not been very successful. Teachers can be more influential when they target students' specific self-beliefs in relation to particular academic tasks or domains (Pajares, Miller, & Johnson, 1999; Randhawa, Beamer, & Lundberg, 1993). In other words, Connie Lutz should not expect to see sweeping changes in Sebastian's self-esteem as a consequence of art education. However, she can hope to change his perceptions of art and his views of himself as an artist or art consumer.

Domain- and task-specific beliefs should become the focus of teachers' efforts for several reasons. For one, those beliefs are explicitly related to classroom activities. Because teachers have a mission to improve students' knowledge and skills in academic subjects (Alexander, 1997b), they have greater opportunities to promote positive self-beliefs that are related to those academic subjects. In addition, teachers are rarely trained counselors and should concentrate on those areas in which they have expertise, such as the subjects they teach. If teachers understand their content domains, they will be equipped to recognize students' particular strengths and needs (Shell, Colvin, & Bruning, 1995). Those strengths and needs can then be reflected in teachers' positive expectations and explicit feedback.

The most important reason to maintain a domain-specific or task-specific focus relates to the idea of grounded competency beliefs. It makes no sense to inflate students' judgments about their abilities and competencies beyond actual knowledge and skills. Connie Lutz could succeed in making Marcia feel better about her artistic talents, but if Connie does not ensure that Marcia acquires basic artistic knowledge and skills, then Marcia's positive feelings will eventually collide with harsh reality. **Grounded competency beliefs,** by comparison, more accurately align with domain- or task-specific abilities. They appropriately reflect the aptitude and efforts students bring to the learning environment. If teachers contribute to students' knowledge and skills, then students will have realistic reasons to feel a heightened sense of competency and value.

Create an Environment That Accentuates the Interest and Value of What Is Taught and What Is Learned

When Connie Lutz described her educational mission, she spoke passionately about creating an environment that would welcome and stimulate her students. She used words like *curiosity* and *challenge.* Connie was right to be concerned about the climate in her classroom. Environments that stimulate student interest and curiosity and highlight the value of what is taught foster positive motivations (Ainley, 1998; Reio & Wiswell, 2000). That is, when students are interested in or curious about instructional content, they are more apt to be instructionally involved. This enhanced involvement, in turn, increases knowledge and raises self-perceptions of competency and esteem (Wigfield et al., 1991). Further, when students recognize the importance and value of the content, they are more likely to persist in the face of challenge and hold themselves to higher performance standards (Jetton & Alexander, 1997).

Attainment Value

Wigfield and Eccles (1992) hold that the value of an academic task consists of at least four components: attainment value or importance, intrinsic interest, extrinsic value, and cost (see Figure 10–5). **Attainment value,** or **importance,**

Allan Wigfield has focused much of his research on the motivations of middle-school students.

describes how important it is for students to do well at a task or domain. For example, Michael is a member of an artistic family; his mother is a commercial artist, and his sister has won art competitions. Thus, doing well has particular importance to Michael from the standpoint of his family identity. Kenya also wants to do well in Connie Lutz's class. She has always considered herself to be an excellent student and a high achiever. Doing well in art class will allow Kenya to maintain her grade point average and her self-perception.

Attainment value can also work against student engagement, however. Sebastian might believe that art is a "fluffy" subject. Thus, if he were to invest himself in art, he would be operating counter to his epistemological beliefs and related values. This potential becomes yet another reason to disassemble stereotypes in the classroom. Questions that Wigfield and Eccles (1992) have used to tap into students' attainment value are included in Figure 10–7.

> **Learner-Centered Psychological Principle 9**
> *Effects of motivation on effort.* Acquisition of complex knowledge and skills requires extended learner effort and guided practice. Without learners' motivation to learn, the willingness to exert this effort is unlikely without coercion.
>
> Learner-Centered Principles Work Group of the APA Board of Educational Affairs, 1997.

Intrinsic Interest Value

The **intrinsic interest value** component of Eccles and colleagues' expectancy-value model is the personal pleasure or enjoyment students experience when engaged in a given task or domain. Michael, for example, pursues art as an avocation. He and his family regularly go to art museums, and Michael is taking private art lessons. Therefore, he has a high level of intrinsic interest in art. Defined in this way, intrinsic interest relates to individual or personal interest (Hidi, 1990; Jetton & Alexander, 1997) and to the construct of intrinsic motivation described by Ryan and Deci (2000a).

Teachers often talk about interest in terms of external stimulation from the environment (Mitchell, 1993; Schraw, Bruning, & Svoboda, 1995). This extrinsic, or situational, dimension of interest is undeniably important but is quite different from the intrinsic interest Wigfield and Eccles (1992, 2000) represent in their model, which is reflected in the measures in Figure 10–7.

Extrinsic Utility Value

Extrinsic utility value is the usefulness of the task or domain from the student's perspective (Wigfield & Eccles, 1992). It indicates what the student gains from success with a particular task or domain. The knowledge and skills that Michael gains from Ms. Lutz's class, for instance, can help

---

Attainment Value/Importance

In order to do well in the world, you need to know mathematics.

| 0 | 1 | 2 | 3 | 4 | 5 | 6 | 7 | 8 | 9 |

Strongly Agree ....Strongly Disagree

The time we spend on history in school is well worth it.

| 0 | 1 | 2 | 3 | 4 | 5 | 6 | 7 | 8 | 9 |

Strongly Agree ....Strongly Disagree

It is important for me to do well in science.

| 0 | 1 | 2 | 3 | 4 | 5 | 6 | 7 | 8 | 9 |

Strongly Agree ....Strongly Disagree

Interest

Overall, I find the work in science boring.

| 0 | 1 | 2 | 3 | 4 | 5 | 6 | 7 | 8 | 9 |

Strongly Agree ....Strongly Disagree

I look forward to the activities we do in mathematics.

| 0 | 1 | 2 | 3 | 4 | 5 | 6 | 7 | 8 | 9 |

Strongly Agree ....Strongly Disagree

When I have free time, I enjoy reading books about history.

| 0 | 1 | 2 | 3 | 4 | 5 | 6 | 7 | 8 | 9 |

Strongly Agree ....Strongly Disagree

Usefulness (Utility)

There will be many opportunities for me to use my knowledge of reading outside class.

| 0 | 1 | 2 | 3 | 4 | 5 | 6 | 7 | 8 | 9 |

Strongly Agree ....Strongly Disagree

I will be able to use what I learned in history in other classes.

| 0 | 1 | 2 | 3 | 4 | 5 | 6 | 7 | 8 | 9 |

Strongly Agree ....Strongly Disagree

There are practical uses for the science content taught in school.

| 0 | 1 | 2 | 3 | 4 | 5 | 6 | 7 | 8 | 9 |

Strongly Agree ....Strongly Disagree

Cost

It takes years of hard work to become good in mathematics.

| 0 | 1 | 2 | 3 | 4 | 5 | 6 | 7 | 8 | 9 |

Strongly Agree ....Strongly Disagree

To do well in science, I have to give up other activities I enjoy.

| 0 | 1 | 2 | 3 | 4 | 5 | 6 | 7 | 8 | 9 |

Strongly Agree ....Strongly Disagree

■ **FIGURE 10–7   Sample statements related to aspects of task value.**

Note: From "The Development of Achievement Task Values: A Theoretical Analysis" by A. Wigfield and J. S. Eccles, 1992, *Developmental Review, 12.* Copyright 1992 by *Developmental Review.* Also from "Expectancy-Value Theory of Achievement Motivation" by A. Wigfield and J. S. Eccles, 2000, *Contemporary Educational Psychology, 25,* p. 70. Copyright 2000 by *Contemporary Educational Psychology.*

him pursue a career in commercial art like his mother. For Kenya Ms. Lutz's class should be useful when she takes the test battery to enroll in the magnet program for gifted students because the test includes a measure of visual creativity.

Recently, Husman (1998) has looked at this component of task utility somewhat differently from the view of Eccles and Wigfield. Specifically, she talks about two forms of instrumentality, endogenous and exogenous, which compare the value of the present task with future goals. **Endogenous instrumentality** occurs when the current task and future goals align. For Michael, performing well on the tasks in Ms. Lutz's class is in accord with his long-term goal of being an artist, a case of endogenous instrumentality. On the other hand, Kenya's valuing of Ms. Lutz's art class is more tangentially related to her goal of getting into the magnet program. The association between task and long-term goal is somewhat removed; Husman would it call **exogenous instrumentality.** Sample questions associated with the utility dimension also appear in Figure 10–7.

Cost

Finally, there is the component of **cost,** or what is required to complete a given task (Wigfield & Eccles, 2000). Costs can be both cognitive and emotional. For instance, to accomplish her goal of top grades on her art assignments, Kenya must invest a great deal of time and energy. She will have to give up some extracurricular activities she enjoys because art is not as easy for her as it is for Michael. Michael, by comparison, easily finds the time required for his art assignments. However, because of his sister's artistic successes and the level of expectations in his family, Michael will experience a higher level of performance anxiety on Ms. Lutz's major projects.

Implications for Teachers

Several recommendations are relevant to the four task-value components.

- Maintain high expectations for achievement within a risk-taking environment.
- Link academic tasks to students' espoused interests or everyday activities.
- Establish the relevance of academic tasks to students' short-term and long-term goals.
- Teach what seems to be valued content.
- Explicitly consider the cognitive effort required of task performance.
- Put the costs of academic tasks in perspective.

For example, attainment value rests on creating within students a real need for doing well (Wigfield & Eccles, 2000). Students who are members of classroom communities in which high achievement expectations are the rule and students who are encouraged to take reasoned risks are more likely to manifest high attainment value. Thus, in creating an environment of achievement orientation coupled with the freedom to attempt challenging, but risky tasks, teachers enhance the attainment value of academic tasks (Ryan & Deci, 2000b; Wigfield et al., 1991).

Another implication for teachers pertains to the relevance of the tasks undertaken in the learning environment (Jetton & Alexander, 1997). That relevance should be established on multiple levels. First, teachers should routinely link ongoing learning to activities and concepts that already matter to students (Wade, Buxton, & Kelly, 1999). This approach instantaneously increases the intrinsic value of the task or domain at hand. For example, if Connie Lutz knows that Michael's family is artistic and that Michael also aspires to be an artist, she can build associations between class tasks and commercial art.

In addition, teachers should build on their students' short- and long-term goals. Understanding Kenya's goal to attend the district's magnet program, Ms. Lutz can explain how current tasks serve that particular end. Teachers should also help students realize how the information or skills they are learning today will connect to what will be taught tomorrow, next week, or next year. When teachers make these curricular linkages apparent, students may become more invested in performance (Jetton & Alexander, 1997).

Teachers find it easier to convey the relevance of content when they themselves perceive its merits (Alexander, Murphy, & Woods, 1996). Yet teachers sometimes take the value of basic content for granted. Perhaps because its utility or relevance seems so obvious to them, teachers mistakenly presume that the merits are equally apparent to their students. In some cases teachers include certain content merely because it appears in the textbook or curricular documents, without considering the basic utility of that knowledge and those skills. Under these circumstances it may be harder for students to independently recognize the potential value of the academic content (Alexander, 1997b), which, in turn, can decrease their pursuit of knowledge and achievement.

Experienced teachers typically operate with an awareness of what effort or energy particular tasks will require. That realization is not true for many students, however. Often, when teachers present them with tasks, like Connie's self-portrait project, they cannot realistically conceive of the time or effort required (Brophy, 1998). Therefore, teachers should take the time to discuss the parameters of the assignments they make. Overall, the more students understand about the requirements of academic tasks, the better equipped they will be to make a reasonable determination about the cognitive costs involved. Teachers should also explain the intrinsic and extrinsic benefits of those tasks (Eccles & Midgley, 1989). By bringing these two components into juxtaposition, teachers help students place the activity in a broader perspective. For instance, students may be more willing to engage in tasks that require a great deal of effort if those tasks have high intrinsic value. As in other aspects of life, costs are easier to pay when the value of the commodity is evident.

■ Summary Reflections

How do students' self-perceptions influence their motivations to learn?

- ■ Self-beliefs are multifaceted, encompassing physical, academic, and social dimensions of self.
  - Self-schemas are time oriented.
  - Self-schemas involve beliefs about who one currently is (i.e., a working self-concept), as well as who one will become (i.e., future self).
- ■ Self-perceptions may or may not be well grounded in reality.

- With time and experiences, students' self-perceptions should become more realistic and more abstract.
- Students' self-perceptions should also become increasingly more differentiated.

■ Students' self-schemas have instructional influences.
- Self-knowledgeable students trust and value their self-judgments and use them to shape their academic goals and approaches to instructional tasks.
- Self-knowledgeable students learn from academic experiences, extracting relevant information that can further enrich their self-understanding.

How do students rationalize and internalize their academic successes and failures?

■ Certain attributions have been tied to academic achievement, whereas others are indicative of learning problems.
- Students may attribute success or failure to forces within themselves or in the outside world (i.e., locus).
- Students see these influential forces as stable or unstable and controllable or uncontrollable.

■ Students and teachers may make erroneous or harmful attributions for one of five common reasons: fundamental attribution error, actor-observer perspective, self-serving bias, self-centered bias, and false consensus effect.

■ Attributions come with consequences.
- Attributions are tied to human emotions and affect.
- There are behavioral consequences of students' attributions.
- Students with learned helplessness have entered into an endless cycle of failure and negative attributions.
- Teachers can take steps to help students with learned helplessness reframe their attributions.

■ Self-efficacy beliefs have been repeatedly associated with student success at specific tasks or in particular domains.
- Several differences exist between self-efficacy beliefs and attributions—their time orientation and their specificity.
- Self-efficacy beliefs influence student learning and development.

What can teachers do to foster positive attitudes and beliefs among their students?

■ Teachers can eliminate gender or cultural stereotypes from the learning environment—a critical step toward the development of positive self-perceptions.
■ Various techniques and measures can aid teachers in uncovering students' buried beliefs, perceptions, goals,

and values so that these belief systems can be effectively addressed in the classroom.
■ Teachers should maintain high expectations for all students.
■ Teacher feedback is a powerful tool for stimulating student effort or facilitating students' sense of control.
■ Teachers should be domain and task specific in their efforts to promote positive self-beliefs.
■ The environment should accentuate the interest and value of what is taught and what is learned.

···

■ Answer Key to Thought Experiment: Plotting Students' Attributions

1. Ability—I, S, UC
2. Luck—E, US, UC
3. Ability—I, S, UC
4. Immediate effort—E, US, UC
5. Task/domain characteristics—E, S, UC
6. Health—I, US, UC
7. Instructional conditions—E, US, C
8. Ability—I, S, UC
9. Typical effort—I, S, C
10. Teacher assistance—E, S, C

···

■ Answer Key to Thought Experiment: Spotting Cases of Attributional Bias

1. FA
2. FC
3. SS
4. SC
5. NB
6. FA
7. FC
8. AO
9. NB
10. SS

···

Chapter **11**

Shared Learning and Shared Instruction

GUIDING QUESTIONS

- In what ways is learning shared or distributed?
- How do the principles of shared understanding extend to teachers as well as to students?
- How does socially shared education translate into better learning for all students?

IN THEIR OWN WORDS ....

*A*s a master high-school mathematics and computer science teacher, Janet Seipel understands the shared nature of learning and instruction. Through an innovative program called the Academy Period, she has seen the positive effects of approaching mathematics as a collaborative and integrated problem-solving process. At Grove City High School, the Academy has been a truly positive experience for students others would categorize as at risk.

This year I am teaching in the Academy, an experiment in intercurricular cooperative teaching and learning. Alice Brooker, Connie Chiu, Gordon Radcliffe, and I work together to teach 32 ninth graders. Many of these students, academically at risk because of learning and behavioral problems, study mathematics, English, social studies, and science together as part of thematic units. They also have an extra period that alternates between a keyboarding class and a special tutoring session. We call this support time the Academy Period.

The Academy demands cooperation. The students not only take all their classes together, but also work together on their daily assignments and theme-related projects. We teachers stress the importance of education and personal responsibility. Over the year, the students have come together. They obey classroom rules, contribute ideas and opinions, and help one another meet their individual and group goals.

We teachers collaborate as well. Each themed unit reflects a tremendous amount of joint planning. We want our individual content areas to be effectively represented, but we want that done within the framework of a thought-provoking and important issue or topic. We also share a lunch and a planning period. We use this time to discuss problems, student absences, and intercurricular projects. We also jointly handle most of the discipline problems that occur within the Academy.

The parents are part of our collective, too. We send them letters several times a year, and we talk with them on the phone and during school conferences. The cooperation and support we have received from them has been exceptional. Positive outcomes have emerged from this experience—and one negative one. On the positive side, the students repeatedly refer to our group as a family. The only disadvantage has

been that they get tired of seeing the same people all day and tempers can flare with so much closeness.

One of the most interesting learning experiences occurred during an intercurricular project about travel and culture. For this activity, students worked in pairs to find tourism information over the Internet. Each pair had a country to research. They had to locate several Websites with information about transportation, lodging, tourist attractions, and currency exchange.

The students did find a variety of sources. But the sources often contradicted one another. The question became which site contained valid information. The discussion that followed covered determining which sources were reliable and what motivates a source to make accurate statements and give reliable information. We discussed the effects inaccurate information could have on tourists in foreign countries. We also considered the importance of reading anything reported to be fact with a certain level of skepticism. Finally, we discussed how to compare information from several sites and make intelligent decisions. While these students may never travel to Singapore or the Ukraine, the critical thinking skills they developed will be useful for the rest of their lives.

Next year we are moving to tenth grade with our Academy. We believe the program helped the students' transition to high school occur with less difficulty and gave them a strong group identity. They became a family within a sea of 2,000 adolescent faces.

We teachers have also had a true learning experience. We have learned about each other's subjects, and we have built a professional working relationship we can build on over the next few years. One of the difficulties in teaching is isolation. We used to work alone in our classrooms throughout the day with very little opportunity for professional conversation with peers. Having a structure for professional cooperation has given us a new respect for teachers in other subject areas, allowed us to renew our enthusiasm for teaching, kept our work fresh, and given us the incentive to keep current with trends in our fields. We have become better teachers, while helping our students to become better learners.

In What Ways Is Learning Shared or Distributed?

During the 1970s and 1980s, a great deal was made of the critical differences between strict behavioral views of human learning and development and the views of information-processing researchers (Jenkins, 1974). To behaviorists following in the footsteps of John Watson (1926) and B. F. Skinner (1968), humans are animals who respond to the

stimuli in their environments. For behaviorists, instruction is about devising and administering the right sequence and proportion of pleasant and unpleasant stimuli, and learning is essentially being trained to react in desired ways (Skinner, 1984). What occurs in the black box of the human mind is of little or no consequence to strict behaviorists (Watson, 1926). In fact, dwelling on the thoughts or emotions of a student would only serve to distract educators from the science of teaching, that is, conditioning (Skinner, 1953).

When cognitive science and information-processing theory appeared on the scene, the emphasis in education shifted dramatically from the external world of visible behavior to the internal world of mental processing (see Chapter 4; Baars, 1986; Neisser, 1967). Understanding the inner workings of the mind became central to understanding human learning and development (R. C. Anderson, Spiro, & Anderson, 1978). Investigations of stimulus/response, punishment, reinforcement, and schedules of conditioning gave way to explorations of knowledge acquisition, memory, and individual problem solving.

However, despite their clear and powerful differences, behaviorism and cognition, as represented by information-processing theory, share two undeniable attributes. First, both theories and their prescriptions for learning and development focus on the individual in relative isolation from others (Cole, Gay, Glick, & Sharp, 1971). Behaviorism set out to alter the actions of an individual, whereas information processing sought to change an individual's knowledge or mental processing. Both behaviorism and information-processing theory overlooked the fact that humans are fundamentally social beings—not just in their actions, but in their thoughts (Resnick, 1991). Second, both behaviorists and information-processing theorists overlooked the power of the social contexts in which humans live and learn (Suchman, 1987). Thus, information-processing theory had taken educators one step away from behaviorist notions that students are merely reactionary creatures who need conditioning, but it failed to account for the social and interpersonal nature of learning and instruction.

Learning does not take place in a vacuum (APA Board of Educational Affairs, 1995); it requires human interaction in a stimulating and supporting social environment (Alexander & Murphy, 1998b). Learning is fundamentally a socially shared enterprise because schools are social institutions where culturally valued content is shared (Cole et al., 1971). Likewise, classrooms are social gatherings where the thoughts, ideas, and actions of one individual are reciprocally influenced by the thoughts, ideas, and actions of others. Every person in Grove City High School's Academy Period shapes the learning of all the others. Thus, understanding and expertise cannot be thought of as the sole property of any one person, understanding is essentially distributed among all Academy participants (Hastie & Pennington, 1991). Seen in this light, all learning is to some extent socially shared and socially distributed.

Further, learning happens at a specific time and in a specific place, and the characteristics of that time and place matter greatly in how students learn and develop (Wertsch, 1985). It clearly matters whether Academy students study mathematics, English, social studies, and science separately or as part of an integrated curriculum. It also matters whether their teachers are committed to this partnership and are capable of meeting the goals of the experimental program. These environments are more than stimuli to which humans react, and they are more than sources of information that people input into their mental computers. Learning environments are social, dynamic, and reciprocal (Alexander & Murphy, 1998b).

In recent years educators have become increasingly aware of the importance of the social and contextual dimensions of learning (Wertsch, 1985). Today, most educational psychologists and expert teachers like Janet Seipel understand how important it is for teachers to build effective learning environments that take advantage of the social and contextual character of human learning and development (Brown, Collins, & Duguid, 1989). Many educators have put aside past instructional models that set out to eliminate or control any student-to-student interactions in the classroom for the sake of order. Instead, they have replaced such ideas with models that promote verbal exchanges and shared thinking between teachers and students (Cazden, 1988; Mehan, 1979). They have also put away antiquated notions that teachers should be the sole source of relevant academic content and the ultimate judge of what is taught and what is learned (Kantor, Green, Bradley, & Lin, 1992). Instead, instructional approaches and techniques today allow students to raise questions and seek knowledge, becoming partners in setting the academic agenda (Lemke, 1990; Palincsar & Brown, 1984).

Although there is general agreement within the research community about the value of socially shared learning and about the power of contextual factors, educators differ widely in the emphasis they place on these factors (Lave & Wenger, 1991). As discussed in Chapter 4, some see social and contextual influences as contributing to or shaping individual thinking and behavior (Alexander & Jetton, 2003). For them, thoughts and knowledge remain personal and idiosyncratic, even though the processes of learning and instruction are basically social acts. Cognitive constructivists following in the tradition of Piaget fall within this group of educators (Piaget, 1926). Others, who are more influenced by the writings of Vygotsky (1978) and Lave (1988), think learning and development are all about the group or collective. Thus, they regard any discussion of individual thinking, knowledge, or beliefs as of limited value (Cole & Engeström, 1993). To these educators, knowing, or the process by which groups form meaning and understanding, is of greatest importance—not its product, that is, knowledge (Sfard, 1998).

This discussion assumes a moderate stance about shared learning and shared instruction. It examines approaches that intentionally use social interactions to optimize human learning and development without overlooking the contributions of each individual student or the teacher. An array of interactional forms and models

---

Learner-Centered Psychological Principle 11

Social influences on learning. Learning is influenced by social interactions, interpersonal relations, and communication with others.

Learner-Centered Principles Work Group of the APA Board of Educational Affairs, 1997.

should be a part of any teacher's pedagogical repertoire and elements in any systematic approach to optimizing learning.

The Theory Behind Social Interaction

Among the educational philosophers and theorists who helped to bring the notion of situation and context into the limelight was Lev Vygotsky (1978), a Russian psychologist. Before his early death at the age of 38 in 1934, Vygotsky and his colleagues extensively studied the language and cognitive development of children. Decades after his death, Vygotsky's writings became widely available in the West and helped to change the thinking about the role of social interactions in human learning and development (Cole et al., 1971; Wertsch, 1985). One of Vygotsky's most influential concepts was the **zone of proximal development (ZPD)** Vygotsky described the ZPD as "the distance between the actual developmental level as determined by independent problem solving and the level of potential development through problem solving under adult guidance or in collaboration with more capable peers" (1978, p. 86).

A simple but powerful principle lies behind ZPD: When aided by a more knowledgeable or skillful peer or teacher, the level or quality of students' thinking and performance is markedly above their thinking or performance when working independently (Loent'ev, 1981). It is this distance between assisted and independent thinking that constitutes the zone in ZPD (see Figure 11–1). A student's zone varies, depending on the familiarity or complexity of the task and the effectiveness of the support or guidance that is given.

Many of the instructional techniques discussed in this chapter build directly on this fundamental principle. David Perkins (1992) suggests that educators embrace the notion

PERSON-SOLO

Placing all the weight and responsibility for learning or performance on an individual student creates strain. The outcome reflects only that student's thoughts and experiences.

PERSON-PLUS

When students are allowed to work collaboratively, thinking and responsibilities are distributed, and the strengths and experiences of each individual become instructional resources that are applied to each task. The results are typically superior to anything an individual student could accomplish alone.

■ **FIGURE 11–2   The merits of person-plus over person-solo.**

of *person-plus* over *person-solo* learning environments and create smart schools. Person-plus learning environments offer numerous benefits for students and teachers. For one, the cognitive responsibilities involved in any academic task are not borne by one student but are distributed among individuals (Perkins, 1993). What might be stressful or overwhelming for any one student becomes reasonable and possible with the assistance and support of others, as illustrated in Figure 11–2. Also, when learning occurs in a person-plus environment, the understanding and skills reflected in the activity or assignment are those of all participating students. The mental sharing and collective thinking that transpires in a person-plus environment is called **distributed** or **shared intelligence** (Salomon, 1993a).

The person-plus environment can be seen in Janet Seipel's Academy. The intentional and valued interactions take place not just among the students, but among the teachers as well. Vygotsky's idea of the ZPD and Perkins's person-plus ideology are both at work in the Academy as Janet Seipel's students collaborate on their intercurricular tourism project. One student's strength in mathematics complements his part-

Level of Assisted or
Scaffolded Performance

ZONE OF PROXIMAL
DEVELOPMENT

Level of Independent
Performance

■ **FIGURE 11–1   Vygotsky's zone of proximal development.**

David Perkins

Table 11–1	The language of social interaction.	
Term	**Description**	**Example**
Competition	A student's performance or standing in the class is determined through direct or implied comparison with others.	Periodically, the students in the Academy take part in academic contests like team spelling games or geography bees that fit with their themed unit. These competitive activities prompt student review and heighten excitement.
Discussion	Verbal interactions between two or more students mix together words and thoughts about topics or issues.	At least once every themed unit, Academy teachers set aside time for students to share their ideas on a stimulating but puzzling issue. Even though this discussion typically involves the whole class, the teachers use small groups and dyads to ensure that the students have sufficient opportunity to share and reflect.
Cooperation	A group of students functions as a unit to perform some specific task or activity. Group members are often evaluated on the group outcome.	Today, three students are sitting at the back table editing each other's section of a report on Rome. When they are done, the three pieces will be assembled into their tourism presentation.
Collaboration	Typically applied to decision making, collaboration entails a form of consensus building regarding an agreed-upon outcome for a group.	For some of the Academy assignments, like a group essay exam, students are expected to create responses with which all group members agree. To produce these responses, students continue to discuss and debate until a shared answer results.

ner's travel experiences. Another's inquisitive nature and facility in surfing the Internet for information works well with her partner's strong comprehension abilities. The reports these student pairs produce should be noticeably better than any report created alone.

Further, the planning and support Janet Seipel can offer the 32 ninth graders in the Academy Period is greatly enhanced by the contributions of three other capable and concerned teachers. Each teacher's subject-matter expertise and instructional experiences are woven into a curricular program that makes the Academy innovative and successful.

The Basics of Shared Learning

The education literature is filled with terminology related to shared learning. The key concepts, described in Table 11–1, capture a range of social exchanges, from rather individualistic interactions to large group collaborations. Each signifies some level of shared learning and can be found in some form in today's schools (Webb & Palincsar, 1996).

Competition Versus Shared Learning

Most often, shared instruction and learning suggest an alternative to competitive educational models (Deutsch, 1949; Heath, 1991). **Competition** is an educational orientation whereby teachers assess student performance by comparing it to that of others (Slavin, 1995). Performance thus becomes contingent on the level of performance of others within the comparison group. A competitive incentive structure "exists when any one individual can attain his or her goal only if other participants do not obtain theirs" (Graham & Weiner, 1996, p. 79).

The American educational system relies heavily on competition in the grading and placement of students (McCaslin & Good, 1996; Webb & Palincsar, 1996). Many educators support some level of competition in learning environments. Some argue that competition is a biological, primary drive for humans (Berger, Rosenholtz, & Zelditch, 1980). However, the fact that some cultures, like certain Native American tribes, frown on competition calls the universality of competition into question (E. G. Cohen, 1986; Vasquez, 1993). Other educators claim that because competition is part of real life (McCaslin & Good, 1996), students should learn to deal with competition in the educational environment. Still other proponents see competition as a motivating factor that propels students to higher levels of achievement (Oakes, 1990).

Despite these arguments the potential side effects of competition have been well established. Morton Deutsch (1949, 1993), who compared competitive with cooperative approaches for more than 50 years, found that competition increases anxiety, lowers students' self-esteem, limits creativity, creates negative feelings among classmates, and makes students feel less responsible for their classmates' success or well-being. Motivation researchers have also identified negative consequences of competition (Ames, 1984b; Nicholls, 1989):

- contributing to unwanted or nonproductive behaviors (e.g., cheating)
- presenting more problems for females and for certain cultural groups
- promoting performance goals (i.e., getting the task done or looking good to peers) over mastery goals (i.e., learning the content for its own sake)

- giving rise to causal attributions that stress ability over effort
- resulting in lower grades and less valuing of learning

With all these negative consequences, is there any place for competition in schools? In reality, until schools are completely reconfigured and the rating and ranking of students are eliminated, competition will always be present in schools (Nicholls, 1989). However, for teachers like Janet Seipel, who are working to build a sense of family and community, explicit or intentional competition should be kept to a minimum. Teachers should generally avoid pitting students against one another for the sake of academic achievement (Pugach & Johnson, 1995).

Several of the formal approaches to cooperative learning discussed in this chapter introduce small measures of competition (Slavin, 1978). However, in these cases competition is essentially team-based or involves students of similar achievement levels who compete for team points. In addition, the games or contests that are part of those approaches build on instructional materials that are learned cooperatively.

Discussions

At the heart of all shared learning and instruction are the verbal interactions that occur between students and teachers. **Discussion** refers to constructive conversation between students and teachers who are willing to listen and learn from one another (Lemke, 1990). For social constructivists and socioculturalists, what is important about discussions is not just that multiple speakers interject their individual thoughts and ideas, but that those ideas become intertwined and interwoven together as shared understanding (Jetton & Alexander, 2000). Teachers and students in the Academy typically engage in a verbal exchange around themed issues. For the tourism unit, discussion focused on the problem of inconsistent information on the Internet, which students found when exploring sites covering their chosen countries. Although particular students voiced certain experiences or opinions, the understanding that arose through the discussion reflected the students' collective thinking.

Even though large group discussions are the most typical form of verbal interaction in classrooms, especially in the upper grades, two individuals can exchange ideas in pairs called **dyads** (G. M. Phillips, 1973), which can be either public or private. For example, Janet Seipel talks privately with each Academy student to discuss how she can best incorporate that student's particular interests and needs within the Academy curriculum. Also, students in the Academy often break into pairs to do peer editing and evaluation of written products or to discuss assigned readings.

Social psychologists who study group dynamics and communication see discussion as an invaluable educational tool with numerous benefits (Mishler, 1978; G. M. Phillips, 1973):

- helping students explore the personal relevance of issues or content

- making students more active participants in the learning process
- putting greater responsibility for learning on students' shoulders
- improving social skills
- giving teachers clues about what students think or believe

However, if discussions are to achieve these laudable ends, teachers must understand certain basic principles of human communication that underlie effective verbal interchanges.

Establish Goals and Standards of Conduct

Teachers cannot expect students who have spent most of their time in traditional classrooms to know instinctively how to engage in a meaningful discussion (Jetton, 1994; Luft, 1970). Students must acquire good discussion skills through instruction and modeling, as well as guided practice (Lipman, 1991). One of the first steps in this learning process is to understand the goals or purposes of any discussion. For example, as part of their themed unit on tourism, the Academy teachers wanted students to share their views on and experiences with finding accurate information on the Internet. Consequently, the teachers specifically told the students that the goal of the discussion was to come up with guidelines they could apply to ascertain the credibility of an Internet source and the information it provided.

Further, students should know and abide by simple rules of acceptable conduct during discussions. Some of the characteristics of acceptable discussion that are frequently mentioned in the communications literature (e.g., E. G. Cohen, 1994) include these:

- listen carefully
- make your ideas known
- support your opinions
- take turns speaking
- show mutual respect
- participate but do not dominate
- refrain from personal remarks

I have also found that students have a tendency to direct their remarks to the teacher, even when they respond to their classmates. This pattern may reflect the students' need for teacher approval or their efforts to read the teacher's reaction to what they say (Alexander, Jetton, Kulikowich, & Woehler, 1994). For this reason I remind my students that they are to speak to and look directly at one another—not me. In addition, I physically arrange the classroom so that students can see one another better, and I remove myself from easy view to affirm my intent that the students engage one another in this verbal exchange.

Select Discussible Questions or Issues

Questions that work best for classroom discussions have several key characteristics. First, they are suitably controversial or open-ended (Phillips, 1973). Thus, ample room is available for multiple perspectives and ideas, and some justification of one's position would be expected (E. G. Cohen,

1994). Second, students have sufficient knowledge and experience to bring to bear in the discussion (Alexander & Jetton, 2003). Finally, questions are appropriate for students' ages and backgrounds (G. M. Phillips, 1973).

It made sense for Academy teachers to discuss the reliability and accuracy of information on the Internet. The students had just confronted problems with contradictory information in their online searches. Also, they needed to understand why people might put misleading information about countries online. The students' experiences and interests made this question very discussible.

Create a Sanction-Free Environment

For effective discussions to occur, students should feel that they can put their ideas and beliefs forward without concern for teacher reprimand or peer ridicule (Lampert, 1998). As long as the rules of appropriate conduct are followed, students should be free to say or react honestly and frankly. For example, during their discussion of Internet accuracy, Salvador might have reacted strongly, saying that it was stupid for the students to be talking about tourism when most of them did not have the money to take a bus to the next town. The teachers would have been careful to make no emotional or verbal response to Salvador's seemingly antagonistic reaction. In fact, his point had merit and certainly deserved to be voiced. Any reaction to such an opinion should have come from other students, not the teachers.

However, if something was said or done in the context of discussion that Janet Seipel and the Academy teachers felt must be addressed, they should have dealt with that issue privately and without rancor. As long as the discussion does not deteriorate into a verbal or physical confrontation, teachers should reserve their interventions or evaluative comments for less public venues.

Establish an Atmosphere of Openness and Trust

Teachers need to go beyond removing fears of public reprimand and strive to create a context in which students express their honest views—not those that they feel will win teacher approval (Alexander, Jetton, et al., 1994). Students want to gain approval from their teachers for good reason; teachers remain the principal authorities and evaluators in the classroom. Thus, if students believe that there is a true position or stance that their teacher wants promoted in discussion, many will bend their comments to fit that preferred position.

Students generally learn quite quickly the difference between open discussions and those meant to reinforce a teacher's biases or beliefs. Consequently, teachers should avoid entering a discussion in too strong or direct a manner. Important differences exist between facilitating class discussions and directing or controlling them. It is one thing for teachers to prompt student responses, seek clarification, or reflect on a stated opinion; these are tools of effective facilitation. It is another matter to offer side comments or interject supporting examples that frame the discussion in a certain way or sway it to one side. If teachers want to aid students during discussion, they should be careful to offer general support that does not reveal the teachers' views.

As the Academy students worked through their guidelines for judging what is true in tourism, Janet and her fellow teachers generally remained on the sidelines, transferring leadership to the students. To facilitate this transfer of leadership, teachers might have taught the students how to assume the roles of discussion leader or recorder. Discussion leaders have the responsibility of calling on classmates, including those who seem reluctant to share. They also remind others that they have had sufficient time to express themselves on the discussion topic. It is the recorder's job to maintain a list of the positions or ideas the classmates express.

Use Discussion as One Aspect of the Instructional Program

Even though discussions are invaluable tools in building shared understanding in the classroom, they cannot generally serve as the sole or primary mechanism for content delivery (Jetton & Alexander, 1997). The effectiveness of discussions rests on a breadth or depth of knowledge and on adequate interest in the topic or issue. Thus, discussion is a useful complement to other forms of social interaction considered later in this chapter. One important point on which educational researchers tend to agree is that discussion is suitable for all subject matter areas, including mathematics and science (Cobb, Wood, & Yackel, 1991; Lemke, 1990). Certainly, in the integrated learning environment that Janet and her fellow teachers have orchestrated, discussion would be a wonderful method for amplifying or extending the issues that students research.

Be Flexible

Effective discussions do not always fall within precise time limits (Kagan & Kagan, 1994). When ideas begin to flow, students want to explore them further. For elementary teachers a discussion might carry over briefly into the time set aside for another subject. For middle- or high-school teachers whose students change classes, it may be necessary to carry discussions into the next session. Of course, it is not always easy to maintain student interest and involvement under those circumstances (Webb, 1989), and steps must be taken to reenergize or reconstitute the discussion when such a lapse in time occurs.

In addition, the physical arrangement in the learning environment can reinforce or undermine the teacher's goal of promoting the social exchange of ideas among students. That arrangement sends a message that certain procedures or rules of conduct are in place as the discussion unfolds. Thus, teachers need to try various physical arrangements to find configurations that work for their students and their goals (Kagan & Kagan, 1994). For example, to cope with her large high-school literature classes, Tamara Jetton used an arrangement she calls inner-outer circle. The students formed two concentric circles with their desks; those seated in the inner circle begin the discussion, while those on the outer circle observe or make notes. Then, when signaled, the students shift positions, and those seated on the outside move into the inner circle to carry on the discussion, making references to the issues and arguments their classmates have already put forward. Other classroom arrangements that can be used during large group or small group discussions are examined later in this chapter.

Seek Full Participation

Discussion is most effective when all participants believe they have a role and a voice (Fuchs, Fuchs, Mathes, & Simmons, 1997). Some students find it hard to speak out during discussions, whereas others find it hard to hold back so that others can share. Part of the learning process for both teachers and students is finding appropriate ways to promote balanced student involvement. Whatever actions teachers take, they need to ensure that all students participate in some manner during discussions (Kagan & Kagan, 1994).

The teachers and students in the Academy created a simple guideline to deal with this concern. Their rule of thumb was that all students had to contribute at least one thought or opinion to the discussion, and no student was to make more than three comments unless leading the group. The discussion leaders monitored the extent of classmates' participation. Over the course of the year, as students became comfortable with open discussion, Janet Seipel discovered that students rarely needed to be reminded about their level of participation.

Cooperation

Most educators conceive of cooperation as the opposite of competition (McCaslin & Good, 1996). Broadly defined, **cooperation** exists when students come together to work toward some common academic goal or end (Webb & Palincsar, 1996). In cooperative systems each student's academic success depends to some degree on the success of his or her classmates.

Cooperation and cooperative learning are generic terms that encompass innumerable approaches to teaching and learning. According to David and Roger Johnson (1994, 1999; Johnson, Johnson, & Stanne, 2000), leading advocates of cooperation, several cooperative learning models are well researched and show positive learning outcomes. A comparison of seven such models is provided in Table 11–2.

Learning Together

Johnson and Johnson promote the **learning together and alone (LT)** model in which four or five students of differing abilities work together on well-chosen assignments with clearly specified goals (Johnson & Johnson, 1999). The students turn in one assignment, which becomes the basis for feedback and evaluation. Teachers who adopt the LT model spend a great deal of time in team-building activities with student groups. Through team building, group members learn to take on different roles in the group, such as reporter or questioner (Johnson & Johnson, 1994).

As discussed earlier, it is easier for students to work effectively in groups when they have particular roles. From

Roger and David Johnson

studying students' interactions in cooperative groups, Spencer Kagan (1992) devised a colorful list of cooperative learning roles, including cheerleader, coach, and material monitor (see Table 11–3). Even though Janet Seipel may not find the LT model particularly relevant to the project-based Academy, she still uses some roles like question commander and recorder during open discussions and group activities.

Student Teams–Achievement Divisions

Slavin and colleagues (1978, 1995; Slavin, Karweit, & Madden, 1989) have emphasized cooperative learning models in their efforts to improve basic reading and mathematics performance in the early and intermediate grades. One of the models they devised is the **student teams–achievement divisions (STAD)** approach (Slavin & Oickle, 1981). STAD involves four steps:

- *Teach*: Teacher presents the content.
- *Team study*: Students work on a related written assignment.
- *Test*: Teacher presents individual quizzes or assessments.

Robert Slavin

Table 11–2   A comparison of well-researched cooperative learning techniques.

Technique	Description	Benefits
Learning Together & Alone (Johnson & Johnson)	Four or five students of mixed ability work in groups; team-building activities are stressed; evaluation occurs at the group level.	Attends to the noncognitive aspects of grouping; focuses on well-specified tasks; is effective with young learners or those in need of basic skill instruction
Student Teams–Achievement Divisions, STAD (Slavin)	Four or five students of mixed ability, gender, and ethnicity work together on specific assignments, following a teacher's directed lesson.	Evaluates the continued improvement of individual group members; effective in teaching basic skills
Team-Assisted Individualization, TAI (Slavin, Leavey, & Madden)	Following group work, students work in pairs on programmed, individualized materials; students are evaluated individually.	Provides for both individualized instruction and evaluation of well-structured problems
Teams-Games-Tournament, TGT (DeVries & Edwards)	Three students of similar achievement level take turns being the reader or challenger; groups change weekly; individual and team scores are reported.	Allows students of high ability to work together; offers opportunity for competition
Cooperative Integrated Reading & Composition, CIRC (Stevens & Slavin)	Students in four-member groups work on a variety of literacy skills, including reading comprehension, writing mechanics, and spelling.	Targets writing composition along with comprehension; gives opportunities for peer evaluation
Jigsaw (Aronson)	This project-based approach puts four to six students on a team; each student is assigned a specific aspect of the project; all students working on the same aspect meet together and then return to their home groups as experts.	Appropriate for older students and varied subject-matter areas; seeks to ensure that students have knowledge to share
Group Investigation (Sharan & Sharan)	Students form their own groups of two to six and work on related topics chosen with teacher guidance; they give a summary report to the class.	Introduces more student choice into the structure of the groups and into the focus on the project content

- *Team recognition*: Teacher calculates team scores based on student improvement and recognizes achievement (e.g., certificates).

In the STAD model, four students of mixed achievement levels, gender, and ethnicity work on an assignment, following the teacher's explicit instruction (Slavin, 1978). The teacher calculates students' baseline achievement level by averaging their last three quizzes. Structured worksheets and regular quizzes are a big part of STAD. Figures 11–3 and 11–4 present a segment of an intermediate grade worksheet on compound sentences and several corresponding questions.

Even though teachers test students individually on the lesson's content, they determine their grades by how well

Table 11–3   Students' roles in cooperative groups.

Role	Description
Encourager	Encourages reluctant or shy students to participate
Praiser/cheerleader	Shows appreciation of others' contributions and recognizes accomplishments
Gatekeeper	Equalizes participation and makes sure no one dominates
Coach	Helps with the academic content, explains concepts
Question commander	Makes sure all students' questions are asked and answered
Checker	Checks the group's understanding
Taskmaster	Keeps the group on task
Recorder	Writes down ideas, decisions, and plans
Reflector	Keeps group aware of progress (or lack of progress)
Quiet captain	Monitors noise level
Materials monitor	Picks up and returns materials

Note: From Cooperative Learning by S. Kagan, 1994, San Clemente, CA: Kagan Cooperative Learning. Copyright 1994 by Kagan Cooperative Learning. Reprinted with permission.

Student Team Learning: **Subject:**

Segment of the intermediate language arts worksheet:

Objective XIII: Compound sentences

Topics: Form compound sentences from two independent clauses, using coordinating and correlative conjunctions or using a semicolon. Identify the correct use of coordinating and correlative conjunctions in compound sentences.

Correctly punctuate compound sentences.

Introduction: This worksheet will help prepare for the Compound Sentences Game Quiz.

1. A compound sentence consists of two or more simple sentences joined together.
2. They are joined either with coordinating conjunctions or with correlative conjunctions.
3. Coordinating conjunctions used in compound sentences are *and, but, or, nor, for, yet.*
    Example: Terri loves to go swimming, but she doesn't like to go to swimming class.
4. Correlative conjunctions are always used in pairs. The most common correlative conjunctions used in compound sentences are *either-or* and *neither-nor.*
    Example: Either you take back what you said, or I will not stay here tonight.
5. A compound sentence can be formed without a conjunction by using a semicolon.
    Example: One of my favorite sports is hockey. Another is baseball.
          One of my favorite sports is hockey; another is baseball.

Instructions: Correctly punctuate the following compound sentences.

1. I studied all day but I failed the test.
2. Provide an example from your own experience or provide one from your textbook.
3. It rained all day and it thundered all night.
4. Sally understood the problem but she raised her hand to ask a question.
5. He cleans and she cooks.
6. Either Mr. Jones was not trying hard enough or he was having bad luck.
7. Every time I took the test I failed but I kept taking it.
8. My uncle gave me advice about fishing but I did not listen to him.
9. Elm Street is lined with maples and Maple Street is lined with elms.
10. Alice worked hard in school for she was eager to learn.

(Answers at the end of the chapter)

■ **FIGURE 11–3   Sample STAD worksheet.**

Note: From *Cooperative Learning* (2nd ed., p. 172) by R. E. Slavin, 1995, Boston: Allyn & Bacon. Copyright 1995 by Allyn & Bacon. Reprinted with permission.

group members have progressed since their last test. Slavin, Leavey, and Madden (1985) have specific criteria for awarding improvement points.

Quiz Performance	Improvement Points
More than 10 points below the base score	5
1 to 10 points below the base score	10
0 to 10 points above base score	20
More than 10 points above the base score	30
Perfect paper (regardless of base)	30

In this way, students are held responsible for the learning of the others in their group. Students remain in these mixed-ability groups for approximately 5 to 6 weeks. Then new teams are formed.

Team-Assisted Individualization

The **team-assisted individualization (TAI)** model, which is used to teach mathematics, combines individualized instruction with cooperative group work (Slavin et al., 1985). The prescriptive and programmed nature of the mathematics curriculum used with TAI makes this approach quite manageable for teachers. Specifically, students work in mixed-ability groups of four or five, similar to those described for STAD. However, students first study with one other group member on programmed instructional materials. The pair reads, completes assignments together, and grades one another's work and tests. If the team improves, as indicated by increases in individual test scores, the group receives formal recognition.

Student Team Learning:

Segment of the Subject: Intermediate language arts

Game Quiz: **Objective XIII: Compound sentences**

Instructions: Correctly punctuate the following compound sentences.

1. He likes catsup on hamburgers but on hot dogs he likes mustard.
2. Jimmy lives in the country and he plays in the woods.
3. Either the lightbulb burned out or the switch is not working.
4. Neither did the girls play basketball nor did they go hiking.
5. To get exercise, Dorothy plays tennis for an hour or she swims for two hours.
6. I have studied the problem for two days yet I have not come up with a solution.
7. Either there will be food at the picnic or there will be a trip to McDonald's at lunchtime.
8. Donna arrived early for she didn't want to miss the opening ceremonies.
9. Mr. Goldsmith tried the front door but it was locked.
10. Eddie will not work after school nor will he work on the weekends.

Instructions: Correctly combine the simple sentences into a compound sentence by using a semicolon.

11. Roy liked the spotted dog best. It reminded him of Spooky.
12. Martha passed the test. She did not miss a single question.
13. Don't be afraid of the dog. His bark is worse than his bite.
14. It wasn't a flying saucer that you saw. It was a shooting star.
15. I prefer the red candy. It tastes sweeter.

(Answers at the end of the chapter)

■ **FIGURE 11–4   Sample STAD game/quiz questions.**

Note: From *Cooperative Learning* (2nd ed., p. 175) by R. E. Slavin, 1995, Boston: Allyn & Bacon. Copyright 1995 by Allyn & Bacon. Reprinted with permission.

Teams-Games-Tournaments

Teams-games-tournaments (TGT) is another cooperative learning approach that is often used in conjunction with STAD to interject some competition into students' cooperative learning (DeVries & Edwards, 1974; Slavin, 1994). In this model three students from different STAD groups who are at similar achievement levels compete in an academic game intended to reinforce prior learning. In turn, each of the students serves as the Reader, Challenger 1, or Challenger 2. The Reader picks a question and attempts to answer it. Challenger 1 either accepts the Reader's answer or offers an alternative response. Challenger 2 then reads the correct response. The Reader gains a point for each correct answer, whereas Challenger 1 loses a point for questioning a correct response.

Unlike STAD groups, which remain fairly stable over an extended period, TGT groups are reconfigured regularly (DeVries & Edwards, 1974). As seen in Figure 11–4, the questions used in TGT are well structured and well practiced. However, some modification of TGT could be useful in less directed situations. Even within the Academy, where much of the work relates to a particular theme, teachers could use some form of the TGT model. For example, Janet and her fellow teachers could construct questions about the knowledge or skills practiced in groups. Or the students could write competition questions based on their theme-related research.

Cooperative Integrated Reading and Composition

For the most part, the cooperative models previously described are used in the early elementary to intermediate grades to teach specific skills or simple concepts in reading and mathematics (Stevens, Madden, Slavin, & Farnish, 1987). Stevens and Slavin (1995) modified the principles of STAD to work with reading and writing in the upper elementary grades; the result was the **cooperative integrated reading and composition (CIRC)** technique. In CIRC, students work in groups of four and participate in various literacy activities, including reading to one another, writing about their readings, and sharing drafts. In addition to trying to improve comprehension and composition, the students monitor one another for mechanics such as spelling, vocabulary, and grammar. The team also produces and shares its own books (Stevens et al., 1987).

CIRC could be of use to Janet Seipel with students who need help with particular literacy skills. Muriel, for instance, who has problems with writing mechanics and spelling, could be part of a small group that focuses on basic composition skills or processes. To be consistent with the philosophy of the Academy, the writing and peer editing that occurs must be explicitly related to the learning theme. Consequently, instead of composing storybooks, the students could produce travel books or brochures, and Muriel's contributions could be orchestrated around the cause/effect or explanatory paragraphs that have proven to be a problem for her. In this way Muriel would not only get the practice and direction she needs, but would also engage in activities that are relevant to the entire learning community.

Jigsaw

Elliot Aronson and his colleagues (e.g., Aronson, 1978; Aronson, Blaney, Sikes, Stephan, & Snapp, 1978; Aronson & Patnoe, 1997) devised a cooperative

Elliot Aronson's research, including studies of social interaction, has shaped knowledge of human motivation.

learning approach that is particularly useful for older students and for a variety of content areas. Aronson called the procedure **jigsaw** because it involves assembling bodies of related content, much like assembling a jigsaw puzzle. When applying the jigsaw model, Academy teachers would first decide on an appropriate topic or theme (e.g., tourism). They then would break that topic into approximately six subtopics (e.g., tourist attractions, customs, or modes). At that point they would organize the class into teams of approximately six students. Each team member would select one of the subtopics to research independently. The students researching the same subtopic (e.g., customs and rituals) would eventually get together and share the results of their independent research. These students would then return to their base groups and serve as experts on that subtopic.

Group Investigation

Like the jigsaw approach, **group investigation (GI)** is a project-based cooperative technique in which students work together to complete a project they select (Sharan, 1994b; Sharan & Sharan, 1992). The GI approach varies from the jigsaw method in that students form their own groups of two to six. Then, with teacher guidance each team selects an aspect of the broader class topic it wishes to research. After completion, the group shares the results with the whole class.

If Janet Seipel wanted to use GI in the Academy, her 32 students would be free to decide what facet of tourism they would research. They would also decide what final product they would present to the rest of the class. For example, three friends might decide to concentrate on Rome. Following their research, they might create a travel brochure that covers tourist attractions and important festivals. Another Academy group might settle on wilderness tours as their topic and prepare a PowerPoint slide show as their final project.

With this information about seven of the best known forms of cooperative learning, see whether you can decide which approach the teachers or students are describing in the Thought Experiment: Putting a Name to Cooperation. Keep in mind that teachers sometimes modify basic procedures to fit their particular classrooms or content needs.

Thought Experiment ....

Putting a Name to Cooperation

Directions: Below are descriptions of cooperative approaches applied by teachers and students in K–12 settings. Decide which model of cooperative learning is being described in each case. Remember that these can be modifications of the formal models.

a. Learning together
b. Student team—achievement divisions
c. Team-assisted individualization
d. Teams-games-tournaments
e. Cooperative integrated reading and composition
f. Jigsaw
g. Group investigation

_____ 1. Morgan, Barbara, and Fallon decided to investigate black holes as part of their physical science project. With Mr. Jensen's approval, the three classmates will create their own video about black holes to accompany their written report.

_____ 2. After her group studies the material on percentages, Zena will represent her team in a competition against Malcolm and Nancy. She has reviewed the unit worksheets to get ready.

_____ 3. Once Pat Ritcher finishes explaining auxiliary verbs, her third-grade students will move into their groups to practice what she just taught. This practice involves completing a worksheet on auxiliary verbs.

_____ 4. Manny and Hanna are reading the drafts of each other's stories. They and their other classmates will eventually read their stories to their school's second graders.

_____ 5. Edith Byrnes structured her current American history unit so that each group will investigate a different major battle of the Civil War. Within these groups each student will learn about a particular facet of those historic battles, including commanders/generals, strategies, and personal interest stories.

_____ 6. To provide her second graders with additional practice on their basic reading skills, Annie Pool has them work in pairs on special worksheets. The students help each other complete the worksheet and then grade each other's work.

_____ 7. The four-person teams in Adam Steinman's sixth-grade class are working on their science unit—local plants and animals. Their assignment requires them to learn about a set number of plants and animals indigenous to the upper New York region. The number and types of species assigned varies by the group's ability level. Every team member gets the same final grade on the group's report.

(Answers at the end of the chapter)

Collaboration

In the past decade, a particular form of cooperation, called **collaboration** or **collaborative learning,** has appeared in the educational literature (Cohen, 1994). Collaboration differs from other forms cooperation in that students are to achieve consensus or agreement as a result of the collaborative process. The outcome of collaborative interaction is a co-constructed understanding, rather than an external product that is evaluated by others, typically teachers. For this reason, much of a group's collaborative activity centers on externalizing, confirming, clarifying, and acknowledging their shared understandings. Two forms of shared learning fit this description.

Reciprocal Teaching

Reciprocal teaching (RT) is a text-based instructional approach in which groups of students work together to make sense of texts on specific subject matter (Brown & Palincsar, 1987). RT is unique in having one of the group's members act as the facilitator after receiving instruction from the teacher in how to perform this role. The actions of the group center on four general comprehension strategies described in Chapter 7: summarizing, questioning, clarifying, and predicting.

In *summarizing,* students try to capture the main idea of a text segment by answering the guiding question: What is the author trying to say? *Questioning* is used to probe members' understanding of specific elements of text. For example, while discussing a passage on the American colonies, the student facilitator might say, "What did the authors mean when they said there was taxation without representation in the Colonies?" *Clarifying* helps group members try to clear up any confusing points in the text. A story on Eskimo's hunting practices, for example, might elicit the question, "How does the Eskimo know the seals are migrating?" Finally, *predicting* allows students to think ahead and make reasoned guesses about what the author will share in the next segment. For example, as they continue reading the passage about seal hunting, students might say, "Since the authors just told us about Eskimos

leaving for the hunting ground, I think we are going to read about seal hunting."

By applying these four strategies, members of the student-led groups jointly build an understanding of the text the teacher has selected (Palincsar & Brown, 1984). That is, by learning how to make predictions, pose questions of the text or of group members, seek clarification, and summarize the collective understanding, students make the text meaningful. Much of the research on RT has involved materials from science or social studies textbooks, like the segments shown in Figure 11–5. RT seems to be helpful to students who have difficulty comprehending such material. Further, because students assume the role of the teacher, RT apparently contributes to their positive feelings of efficacy and competence.

Palincsar and Brown (1984) describe RT as *scaffolded* instruction because the amount of teacher direction usually decreases over time as the students' knowledge and skill increase. This phasing out of the teacher's direction puts RT in accord with Vygotsky's concept of the zone of proximal development (Dixon-Kraus, 1996). Although RT groups do not always include the more capable other that Vygotsky envisioned, group members work under the watchful eye of the teacher. This scaffolding helps move students closer to their optimal level of performance within their zones. The excerpts in Figure 11–5 illustrate how that teacher supports his students as they develop their text processing skills. Notice how the students become more skilled at summarizing the text segment and predicting what might follow. Also, see how the teacher becomes less directive over time, restricting his role to periodic reinforcement. RT has been used most frequently with students in the elementary grades (Rosenshine & Meister, 1994). Clearly, RT's four core strategies, along with its use of student facilitators, have broad appeal.

Some variation of this collaborative approach could easily be introduced into the Academy. During the research phase of their projects, students could work reciprocally in groups to ensure that all members reach a shared understanding of the informational texts. Janet and the other Academy teachers could guide and scaffold the groups' interactions as needed.

Scripted Cooperation

Another well-researched collaborative technique is **scripted cooperation (SC)** (O'Donnell & Kelly, 1994; Spurlin, Dansereau, Larson, & Brooks, 1984). Developed by Dansereau, O'Donnell, and colleagues, SC has certain features in common with RT. As with RT, SC is a student-led approach. The teacher remains on the periphery, offering support and assistance as needed. Also, the overall goal of SC is to ensure that group members build a shared understanding of the text, problem, or writing assigned to them (O'Donnell & Kelly, 1994). These collaborative techniques have been widely used in subject-matter areas like reading and social studies, where the demands for text comprehension can be great (Spurlin et al., 1984).

Early Lesson	Later Lesson
Spinner's mate is much smaller than she, and his body is dull brown. He spends most of his time sitting at one side of her web.	*The second oldest form of salt production is mining. Unlike early methods that made the work extremely dangerous and difficult, today's methods use special machinery, and salt mining is easier and safer. The old expression "back to the salt mine" no longer applies.*

Early Lesson

Student: (No question)

Teacher: What's this paragraph about?

Student: Spinner's mate. How do spinner's mate …

Teacher: That's good. Keep going.

Student: How do spinner's mate is smaller than … How am I going to say that?

Teacher: Take your time with it. You want to ask a question about spinner's mate and what he does, beginning with the word *how*.

Student: How do they spend most of his time sitting?

Teacher: You're very close. The question would be, How does spinner's mate spend most of his time? Now, you ask it.

Student: How does spinner's mate spend most of his time?

Later Lesson

Student A (group leader): Name two words that often describe mining salt in the old days.

Student B: Back to the salt mines?

Student A: No, Angela.

Student C: Dangerous and difficult.

Student A: Correct. This paragraph is all about comparing the old mining of salt and today's mining of salt.

Teacher: Beautiful!

Student A: I have a prediction to make.

Teacher: Good.

Student A: I think it might tell when salt was first discovered … well, it might tell what salt is made of and how it's made.

Teacher: OK. Can we have another teacher?

■ **FIGURE 11–5   Excerpts from two reciprocal teaching lessons.**

Note: From "When the Student Becomes the Teacher" by President and Fellows of Harvard College, March 1986, *Harvard Education Letter, 2*(3), pp. 5–6. Copyright 1986 by *Harvard Education Letter.* Adapted with permission.

However, there are important distinctions between RT and SC, as shown in Table 11–4. First, in SC, students work in pairs rather than in small groups. One member of the pair starts out as the recaller, while the other takes the role of listener. Second, the student pairs follow a general script, like the one in Figure 11–6. The script cues these novice facilitators to the steps they should follow. The students begin by reading a prescribed amount of text defined by the teacher. Then the recaller offers a summary of the content, which the listener corrects or expands.

Angela O'Donnell's research has shown the benefits of scripted cooperation.

Directions: As you work together on today's assignment, be sure to follow these steps.

1. Decide by flipping a coin who will be the recaller and who will be the listener.
2. Read silently until you reach the end of a section.
3. Recaller: Summarize aloud what was read, without looking back. Try to include all of the main ideas and important facts in your summary.
4. Listener: Use the text to do the following:
   a. Increase your own and your partner's understanding of the text by improving your partner's summary. You can do this by adding any main ideas or essential facts that may not have been mentioned or by correcting any misunderstandings.
   b. Help you and your partner remember the content by thinking of a clever way to memorize the important ideas and facts. Maybe you could draw a picture, make a chart, or create a picture in your mind.
5. Recaller: Help the listener improve the summary.
6. Complete and discuss the summary, and then switch roles.
7. Repeat this process as you read the next section of the chapter.

■ **FIGURE 11–6   A sample script for scripted cooperation.**

Note: From "Cooperative Learning Strategies in Processing Descriptive Text: Effects of Role and Activity Level of the Learner" by G. E. Spurlin, D. F. Dansereau, C. O. Larson, and L. W. Brooks, 1984, *Cognition and Instruction, 1.* Copyright 1984 by *Cognition and Instruction.* Adapted with permission.

Table 11–4   Distinguishing between reciprocal teaching and scripted cooperation.

Characteristic	Reciprocal Teaching	Scripted Cooperation
Grouping Pattern	Students work in small groups of 4 to 6.	Students work collaboratively in pairs.
Educational Applications	This is particularly useful in processing science and social studies textbook materials.	Although used primarily with subject-matter texts, this has been applied in mathematical problem solving and writing.
Instructional Processes	Students use four general comprehension strategies: summarizing, questioning, clarifying, and predicting.	A shared understanding emerges from the students' summarizing and questioning; student pairs also elaborate on the text by creating a picture or chart, for example.
Teacher Role	The teacher initially explains and models the basic strategies and then scaffolds instruction as needed.	The teacher remains available to guide or assist student pairs when required.
Student Roles	One student serves as group leader or facilitator for the lesson.	Student pairs alternate in the roles of recaller and listener.
Age Range	This is used most often in elementary and middle school.	This is an effective collaborative approach with middle-school, high-school, and college students.
Ability Levels	Research has targeted students with special learning needs, such as those identified as learning disabled.	Studies have included older students at varying levels of reading ability.

Another unique feature of the SC approach is its built-in elaboration (Spurlin et al., 1984). After the recaller and the listener work together to establish the important content, they are cued to do something additional to improve their memory, such as creating a picture on paper or in their minds. Described in Chapter 7, such elaborative strategies are helpful additions to any students' collection of academic tools. In SC, students also move back and forth between the roles of recaller and listener. This provision could heighten their willingness to participate and affords them more opportunities to take on the leadership role (O'Donnell & Kelly, 1994).

Because large amounts of text can be involved, SC is even useful with college students (Dansereau, 1988). The cues provided in SC are global; once students understand the recaller-listener routine, the script is no longer necessary except to set the page limits. These characteristics suggest that SC would fit nicely with the instructional goals of the Academy. The nature of the assignments could vary by student pairs, giving the students in the Academy a chance to work on more specialized tasks or individualized objectives.

between teachers and students and among students themselves (Cole et al., 1971; Resnick, 1991). Certainly, Janet Seipel and her fellow teachers in the Academy operate on that premise, and the result for them is an innovative learning environment in which at-risk students do well. But another secret to the success of the Academy is often overlooked: Optimal learning also demands cooperation and collaboration among teachers (Sharan, 1994a). The opening scenario clearly shows that the Academy teachers engage in significant and varied shared teaching, from combining their subject-matter expertise when devising the Academy's curriculum to team teaching the 32 students.

Other teachers who embrace shared learning and implement cooperative and collaborative techniques in their classrooms often operate independently and individualistically themselves (Joyce, Weil, & Showers, 1992). As a result, group thinking and shared understandings among teachers can be highly informal and haphazard.

Lauren Resnick is a leader in shared learning.

How Do the Principles of Shared Understanding Extend to Teachers as Well as to Students?

The unwavering message of shared learning is that optimal learning cannot occur without meaningful social interaction

The Basics of Shared Teaching

A discussion of shared teaching includes a number of key terms, which are summarized in Table 11–5. Four concepts deserve attention: individualized instruction, cooperative teaching, collaborative consultation, and coteaching.

Table 11–5   The vocabulary of socially shared teaching.

Term	Explanation	Instructional Illustration
Individualized Instruction	Each student has a unique set of objectives or goals and is often evaluated without direct comparison to other students. More formal individualized programs come from extensive collaboration among teachers, students, parents, and other professionals	Muriel, like the other students in the Academy, has a unique set of goals or tasks that are laid out in an individualized education program (IEP). These goals have been expressed for her in a learning contract.
Cooperative Teaching	Two or more teachers share educational ideas or materials; it can be limited or extensive, formal or informal, and can occur regularly or infrequently.	Martha Griffin, the special education teacher at Janet's school, works with the Academy teachers to ensure that the instructional objectives for students with special needs, like Muriel, are addressed. To make this work, Martha and Janet meet weekly to discuss and organize lesson plans, class assignments, and tests.
Collaborative Consultation	Groups of educators with particular expertise come to consensus on the best way to build on students' identified strengths and needs—a rather formal process.	To determine how best to serve Muriel's educational needs, a group of concerned educators, including Janet and Martha, meet with others (e.g., Muriel's father). Together they come to consensus on Muriel's situation and then lay out an instructional program consistent with their assessments.
Coteaching Approaches	Two or more educators coordinate their instructional activities in a single learning environment, such as a classroom or a resource room.	The four Academy teachers find a number of ways to share the responsibilities for instruction in the Academy. Sometimes one provides information to the whole class while others assist. At other times they each take a particular group and work on specific skills or aspects of the themed project.

Individualized Instruction

Individualized instruction creates unique educational goals and objectives for each student (Johnson & Johnson, 1974). At first glance individualized instruction seems to be the antithesis of shared learning and teaching. To some educational researchers, it may well be (Heath, 1991). But in reality, students achieve their personal goals with the support and guidance of teachers, parents, and other professionals.

Further, when individualized instruction is a systematic part of the educational program, as often occurs in special education, it reflects a great deal of shared thinking and decision making (Alexander & Jetton, 2003). And although students may work independently on special assignments or activities, individualized instruction does not preclude them from participating in varied forms of socially shared learning (Jetton & Alexander, 2000).

In programs serving students with special needs, the **individualized education program (IEP)** is required by law (Semmel, Gerber, & MacMillan, 1994). The goals and objectives outlined in an IEP should arise from assessment, analysis, and conversations among the teacher, parents, and relevant professionals like the school psychologist (Fuchs & Fuchs, 1989). An IEP should encompass not just students' cognitive needs but any pertinent social, emotional, or motivational ones as well (Turnbull, Turnbull, Shank, & Leal, 1999a, 1999b). Individualized plans can be created for students of any age, including the ninth graders in the Academy. Figure 11–7 displays an IEP developed for Muriel, who has been identified as learning disabled and has partic-

ular needs in mathematical computation, writing mechanics, and spelling. The special education teacher, Martha Griffin, and Janet Seipel work together to address these special needs through Academy activities and assignments.

Individualization does not have to be as formal as Muriel's IEP. As Janet Seipel explains in her opening scenario, every student in the Academy has individual goals. The students meet with the four Academy teachers and, together, write a contract that specifies particular educational skills that need attention. Franklin, for example, reads the words on the page fairly accurately but often does not understand what those words mean. Thus, his goals stress comprehension strategies like determining the main idea and summarization. Molly, on the other hand, tends to get lost when searching the Internet. For her, online navigational strategies are appropriate as individual goals.

Cooperative Teaching

The overarching concept in shared teaching terminology is **cooperative teaching,** which refers to any arrangement in which two or more teachers work together to plan or deliver instruction (Thousand, Villa, & Nevin, 1994). Because these working relationships can be formal or informal and cursory or extensive, cooperative teaching covers a wide array of teacher-to-teacher interactions (Hertz-Lazarowitz & Calderón, 1994). They can range from simply exchanging educational ideas and materials to actually sharing the instructional responsibilities in a particular learning environment.

Student: Muriel Tolman	Date of Birth: 8-2-1991	Age: 14.2	Grade: 9	Date: 10-4-2005

Committee: Roger Bergen, Principal
Martha Griffin, Sp. ed. teacher
Jordan Strum, School psychologist

Janet Seipel, Math/Academy teacher
Forrest Tolman, Parent
Muriel Tolman, Student

Current Placement: Regular classes (100%)

Unique Characteristics and Needs: Mathematical computation

Strengths:
a. Performs well on measures of mathematical and spatial reasoning
b. Demonstrates interest and positive self-efficacy on most mathematical activities

Needs:
a. Frequently makes computational errors on problems that are familiar
b. Does not complete all assigned work
c. Has difficulty with more algebraic expressions

Annual Goal: Student will significantly improve in mathematical computation on teacher-made tests and on the 10th-grade standardized assessment (CAT).

Instructional Objectives	Assessment Criteria	Instructional Responsibility
When presented with mathematical tasks in Algebra 1 or the Academy Period, Muriel will complete the entire assignment within the designated time frame with an accuracy of 80% or higher.	Teacher-made assignments/tests	Special education teacher Mathematics/Academy teacher
Muriel will take responsibility for mathematical portions of group projects in the Academy Period 50% of the time and with 90% accuracy.	Class or group projects	Mathematics/Academy teacher
After 3 months of explicit instruction, the student will be able to solve for one or two unknowns with 80% accuracy.	District competency test; teacher-made tests	Special education teacher Mathematics/Academy teacher

Unique Characteristics and Needs: Writing mechanics/spelling

Strengths:
a. Displays creativity in narrative writing samples
b. Demonstrates competence in noun/verb agreement

Needs:
a. Construction of compound/complex sentences below criterion
b. Difficulty in constructing cause/effect or explanatory text
c. Frequent misspellings in written compositions

Annual Goal: After 7 months student will perform at criterion level on the state writing performance measure and in the 50th percentile or above on the WRAT Spelling Test.

Instructional Objectives	Assessment Criteria	Instructional Responsibility
Following 5 months of assisted instruction, Muriel will be able to compose a 400-word expository text with complex and compound sentences.	Teacher-made assessments	Special education teacher English instructor
Student will independently produce a 600- to 800-word report with 85% correct spelling and punctuation.	Classroom assignments/projects District writing measure	Mathematics/Academy teacher
After 3 months of explicit instruction, Muriel will produce cause/effect and explanatory paragraphs with 80% accuracy.	Teacher-made assessments	English instructor Mathematics/Academy teacher

■ **FIGURE 11-7 Example from an individualized education program.**

Two educational movements have fueled the growing interest in cooperative teaching. The first, which is part of the Academy, is the movement toward integrated, thematic, or interdisciplinary teaching (Harris & Alexander, 1998). Although the words *integrated, thematic,* and *interdisciplinary* actually have somewhat different meanings, they all describe a combination of particular bodies of subject-matter knowledge in instruction (McGonagill, 1995). For example, teachers in the Academy intentionally combine their mathematics, English, social studies, and science lessons around captivating themes, such as tourism. As interest in integrating content areas has grown, so has the focus on teacher cooperation.

The second educational thrust comes from the field of special education—the movement known as inclusion (Stainback & Stainback, 1992). **Inclusion** arose out of **mainstreaming,** the effort to make students with special needs members of regular learning environments to the greatest extent possible (Sailor, 1991). The goal of inclusion is to integrate students with special needs into regular classrooms to an even higher degree than was typical under mainstreaming. The hope is that special students can attend their neighborhood schools with their peers, instead of being isolated in special classes or wings of the schools (National Association of State Boards of Education, 1992).

Advocates describe two forms of inclusion: partial and full inclusion. **Partial inclusion** means that students may leave regular classes to receive special services (Kaufman, Gotleib, Agard, & Kukie, 1975). For example, some students at Janet's school receive physical therapy or hearing and speech training during the school day. Trudy, an Academy student with muscular dystrophy, spends 80% of her time in regular classes and 20% in the resource room, where her physical needs are attended to. In **full inclusion** students spend the entire day in regular classes (Friend & Bursuck, 1996). For instance, as her IEP states, Muriel spends 100% of her time in regular classrooms. Thus, Martha Griffin must come to the Academy Period to help Muriel, whereas Trudy goes to Martha for help in the resource room. Because regular and special education teachers must coordinate their efforts, especially when there is full inclusion, cooperative teaching must occur.

However, cooperative teaching should be everywhere in schools, in every learning context, and the every grade, not relegated to individualized programs mandated by law. Like their students teachers must learn to work effectively and efficiently with other teachers. They need to adapt simple guidelines, such as those outlined in Table 11–6, which can improve the outcomes of shared teaching.

Collaborative Consultation

Collaborative consultation is a form of cooperative teaching developed for special education (Kampwirth, 1999) and is typically associated with the development of individualized education programs like the one shown in Figure 11–7. However, the term applies to all joint planning and decision making that takes place among educators who bring their diverse expertise and perspectives to bear on students' cognitive, affective, and social needs (O'Shea & O'Shea, 1997).

Effective IEPs, such as the one devised for Muriel, result from extensive consultation, planning, and problem solving among concerned and invested parties (Idol, 1997; Idol, Nevin, & Paolucci-Whitcomb, 1994). Thus, collaborative consultation fits the criteria for collaboration previously established. In addition, group members must continue to participate actively in the guidance and support of various students' learning and development. In other words, Janet Seipel is not finished when she signs her name to that IEP. She has committed herself to working with Martha Griffin to build on Muriel's strengths and address her needs.

Coteaching Approaches

Because of the movements toward integrated instruction and full inclusion, it is now more common to find multiple educators or instructional personnel (e.g., aides or parents) **coteaching,** or sharing the instructional responsibilities, in a single learning environment (Friend & Bursuck, 1996). When coteaching is part of an IEP, the special education teacher often works in a regular classroom to help that teacher work on the specific instructional objectives of iden-

tified students. When the focus is on integrated instruction, coteachers can be regular classroom teachers with different subject-matter expertise.

Both types of coteaching have been incorporated into the Academy Period at Grove City High School. Janet, Alice, Connie, and Gordon regularly share the teaching, and Martha, the special education teacher, frequently joins them. Even though Martha is there specifically for Muriel and other students with identified special needs, she willingly helps others when she can. On occasion parents also volunteer their time to assist with certain Academy activities. During the unit on personnel health and safety, for instance, Hector's mother, a registered nurse, donated several days of her time to teach lifesaving skills, including CPR, to the class. The Academy teachers feel strongly about encouraging this kind of parent participation because effective schools report high levels of positive parental involvement (Joyce et al., 1992).

Coteaching typically follows one of five common models, depicted in Figure 11–8. In **whole class instruction** (see Figure 11–8a), one teacher takes the instructional lead while the others provide individual student support as required. For example, Janet, Alice, Connie, or Gordon might alternately take center stage in the classroom. The lead teacher is responsible for introducing new concepts, sharing materials, demonstrating new computer programs, or conducting science experiments in class while the other three assist. This approach is not used often in the Academy, but this arrangement does help when novel or complex content has to be explicitly shared with the class.

Sometimes teachers work together to deliver instruction to the entire class in a **team teaching** arrangement (see Figure 11–8b). For example, Janet, Alice, Connie, and Gordon can work as a kind of instructional tag team, with all four freely contributing to the lesson presentation as it unfolds. Knowing each other as well as they do makes this shared teaching approach work for them. They find team teaching most effective when a new theme is being overviewed for the class, and each teacher can illustrate the particular role of mathematics, English, social studies, science, or computers in the area under study.

On other occasions teachers may actually divide the class for instruction, each taking responsibility for a particular group of students, all of whom are working on the same task. This approach is known as **parallel teaching** (see Figure 11–8c). Academy teachers make frequent use of this arrangement because project-based learning commonly entails small group work. At times the four randomly choose which group they will scaffold; at other times they instruct the group of students with the special needs they can best serve. For instance, during the tourism assignment, four students worked on the computers and needed assistance in identifying some critical wilderness tour sites. Thus, it made sense for Janet to work with them.

In certain situations, where small groups or learning centers or areas are used, teachers use **station teaching** (see Figure 11–8d), aiding students in the groups or at the centers. Station teaching is a more common form of coteaching in the early-childhood and elementary grades, where classrooms include a number of learning stations or centers, and students frequently spend time in the reading or writing

Table 11–6 Guidelines for effective teacher cooperation.

Guideline	Explanation	Example
Establish a clear purpose or goal for the cooperation	Cooperation among teachers works best when all parties understand the reason for sharing their thoughts and ideas. These stated purposes or goals can guide judgments about whether the cooperation is successful.	Janet Seipel and her colleagues created the Academy to improve learning for students considered at risk in multiple subjects. Rather than work on these subject-matter areas independently, the four teachers decided to pool their efforts to provide the assistance needed in a thematic, integrated curriculum.
Ensure that participants understand their roles and responsibilities	Just as with student groups, teachers working together need a sense of their roles or duties: Who is going to take charge of what, or what expertise does each bring to the table?	In the Academy Janet serves as lead teacher and takes primary responsibility for mathematics and computer keyboarding. Gordon focuses on English, whereas Alice oversees social studies and scheduling. Connie Chiu contributes to the science segments. As the most artistic of the teachers, Connie also maintains the bulletin boards and helps students with the artistic/creative sides of their projects. All four must agree on any major issue, such as project grades, and they meet jointly with students' parents.
Respect the positions and knowledge of each contributor	All cooperating teachers must feel that they bring something valued to the exchange. Thus, all views and expertise must be heard and weighed during discussion.	The Academy teachers were selected because of their teaching skills and their complementary areas of expertise. Janet, Gordon, Alice, and Connie had worked together previously on school initiatives, and they held one another in high esteem. This mutual respect has contributed to the success of the Academy.
Consider a time frame or schedule for shared actions	Teaching is more apt to be cooperative when participants understand when their goals should be met or when particular tasks should be accomplished.	Janet, Gordon, Alice, and Connie maintain a master schedule that documents what needs to be done and who is primarily responsible for that action. This schedule serves as a constant and simple reminder of upcoming assignments.
Monitor the group's progress	Periodic evaluation allows cooperative teachers to assess whether they are moving toward their desired goals.	The four Academy teachers have daily conversations about what is working or not working in the Academy. They also conduct a more formal evaluation of the Academy curriculum and procedures at the end of each themed unit. This review allows them to fine tune the program as warranted.
Celebrate the joint effort	Educators should acknowledge their cooperative successes and should celebrate these occasions publicly and enthusiastically.	Janet, Gordon, Alice, and Connie take every opportunity to praise their joint efforts and to point out the successes of the Academy to colleagues. They see this not only as a way to reinforce their tireless efforts, but also to model effective cooperation.

center, library corner, science center, or art area. Children may also play in designated areas, like the home center or big block area (White & Coleman, 2000).

Nonetheless, station teaching also works well in the middle grades or in high school when there are specialized content or task areas within a learning environment. In the Academy, for instance, the computers are in the back corner, allowing some students to work at the computers while the rest of the class engages in other activities. In a form of station teaching, Janet sometimes takes a group of students to the computer area to work on special skills or tasks while the other teachers work with the remainder of the class.

One other approach can be applied when a small number of students require individualized instruction or special assistance that is not necessarily tied to a particular learning area. In that case one teacher may elect to work with those students while the other teachers oversee instruction for the rest of the class. This approach is called **alternative teaching** (see Figure 11–8e). Because the Academy has four master teachers, alternative teaching is a popular coteaching approach. If a student or two need help in English, for example, Gordon works with them. Alice and Connie do the same when the problem area is social studies or science. Students realize and appreciate that they are getting assistance from a teacher with particular expertise.

With this brief introduction, see whether you can identify which of the five patterns is being described in the Thought Experiment: Testing Your Coteaching Knowledge. Again, remember that these arrangements may include regular and special teachers, as well as other instructional personnel such as parent volunteers.

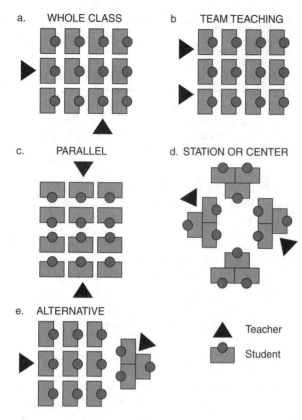

■ FIGURE 11–8 Coteaching approaches within inclusive classrooms.

Note: From Including Students with Special Needs: A Practical Guide for Classroom Teachers, by M. Friend and W. Bursuck, 1996, Boston: Allyn & Bacon. Copyright 1996 by Allyn & Bacon. Adapted with permission.

Thought Experiment ....

Testing Your Coteaching Knowledge

Directions: Below are descriptions of classroom situations in which two or more educators or instructional personnel are teaching together. Match each situation with one of the five forms of coteaching listed underneath.

a. Whole class
b. Team teaching
c. Parallel
d. Station or center
e. Alternate

_____ 1. The honors group at Macmillan High School takes part in a special fine arts program that combines art, music, and drama in one course. For this course the three instructors typically share the lecturing and demonstrations.

_____ 2. Evert Miles and April Knowles teach in a combined fourth-fifth-grade classroom. For today's science period, Evert will work with the 11 fourth graders to prepare for the upcoming state competency test while April works on writing with the 9 fifth graders.

_____ 3. Nancy Abel is a local artist. Once a week she volunteers in Bunny Jackson's third-grade class as an art teacher. Each week she introduces the children to a famous artist and then lets them experiment with that artist's style of painting or drawing. During these weekly art lessons, Bunny sits with the children to ensure that they are paying attention or understanding Mrs. Abel's directions.

_____ 4. In language arts classes at Stony Brook Middle School, students routinely work in areas of the room set aside for writing, reading, and listening. Two aides help the teacher with the instruction, and they each generally take responsibility for the students working in a particular area.

_____ 5. Mr. Atkinson is an old-school teacher. When the high school moved to full inclusion, he was skeptical. However, when Dennis Reilly, the resource teacher, comes to his English class, Dennis does not intrude. He sits near Hattie Prine, a student with cerebral palsy, and helps her and others with their reading and writing assignments.

_____ 6. Stephanie and Pat are two mathematics teachers who enjoy collaborating. This year they convinced their principal to let them coteach Algebra I and II. Their styles are so compatible that they freely share the teaching duties. They have even been known to finish one another's sentences. The students love their banter and enthusiastic style.

_____ 7. Bruce Wigfield believes in hands-on science. That means that students can often be found working on experiments or discovery activities at the tables in his classroom. Sometimes Karen O'Dell, the resource teacher, comes to Bruce's room to work with three of his eighth graders who have learning disabilities. Karen sits and works with these students at a table in the rear of the classroom.

(Answers at the end of the chapter)

....

The Merits of Shared Teaching

When educators undertake shared teaching realistically and willingly, students are not the only ones who benefit (Dishon & O'Leary, 1984). Teachers realize many advantages as well, several of which Janet Seipel describes in her opening scenario:

• an increased sense of community and a reduced feeling of instructional isolation

- enhanced expertise both in subject-matter areas and in the science of teaching (i.e., pedagogy)
- a sharing of educational responsibilities that exist within an educational unit
- diversity of opinions and perspectives on educational topics or issues

Reduced Isolation

Just like their students, teachers function best when they feel that they are part of a professional community (Lieberman, 1988). As Janet Seipel comments, teaching can be very isolating, especially when shared teaching is limited or is not endorsed in the instructional institution. Under those circumstances teachers often feel that they must shoulder the full educational burden. They also can feel that they do not have others upon whom they can rely for either educational or emotional support (Sharan, 1994a).

Having colleagues like Alice, Connie, and Gordon with whom to commiserate or celebrate reduces this feeling of isolation for Janet Seipel. Together these four teachers have become an educational support group for one another. Shared teaching and the professional community it fosters can enrich the lives of many other teachers (Lieberman, 1988).

Shared Expertise

One of the obvious advantages of shared teaching is shared expertise (Salomon, 1993a). Even the best of teachers cannot know it all. When teachers put their heads together, the shared intelligence that results can be a boon to students and teachers alike. As Janet Seipel states, the quality of education the Academy students receive is a direct reflection of the cumulative expertise available in that environment. But as Janet makes clear, she and the other teachers also learn a great deal as a result of their collaboration. Janet's English, social studies, and science knowledge has grown, as have her pedagogical knowledge and skills. All four Academy teachers are better educators as a result of this shared experience.

Teachers benefit from their colleagues' expertise even when the level of cooperation is more casual and limited than that of the teachers in the Academy (Perkins, 1993). Fellow teachers who share instructional materials or offer educational advice can gain from even this rather cursory form of shared teaching. The benefits, of course, increase as cooperation and collaboration expand.

Distributed Responsibilities

Shared teaching does even more for participants, whether the educational unit is the classroom, the grade level, or the school (Perkins, 1992). In classroom situations where coteaching exists, instructional responsibilities that would otherwise fall on the shoulders of one person are distributed. In Janet Seipel's description of the Academy, the four teachers use a lunch and a planning period to tackle academic and behavioral problems.

More and more, teachers are discovering the value of shared teaching (Senge, 1990). In grade level and departmental meetings, for instance, teachers jointly plan the curriculum, discuss student academic strengths and needs, and address disciplinary problems. Of course, the merits of such cooperation depend greatly on the effectiveness of the educational collaboration. If one individual sets out to control the interaction or resists the notion of shared teaching, the benefits can be diminished.

Multiple Perspectives

Through shared teaching a diversity of views or opinions can emerge (Alexander, Fives, Buehl, & Mulhern, 2002). Teachers may see problems or issues from the perspective of others whose personal and professional experiences differ from their own. The validity of this premise is quite apparent in the Academy. These four teachers come from markedly different academic disciplines, as detailed in Chapter 5. Their differences have influenced the way that Janet, Alice, Connie, and Gordon view learning, teaching, and problem solving. Diverse opinions were also at work in the group that framed Muriel's IEP. And all concerned parties will benefit from their varied contributions.

Even when personal or professional differences are not so evident, a diversity of views can still arise. By soliciting and appreciating alternative perspectives on academic, social, or motivational issues, educators can amplify the diversity the educational environment offers (Fuchs & Fuchs, 1989).

How Can Socially Shared Education Translate into Better Learning for All Students?

For all the rhetoric about shared learning and teaching, skeptics remain. In fact, one frequently asked question about socially shared education is whether it actually translates into better learning for all students. The answer is it depends.

Overall, research suggests that cooperation or collaboration contributes to increased student achievement and to more positive learning climates (Slavin, 1990). Such practices contribute to both cognitive and motivational improvement (Johnson & Johnson, 1994). Slavin (1990), for example, reports significant achievement gains in reading and mathematics, increased time on academic task, and a greater sense of learner control, as well as improved intergroup relations and positive social behaviors among students. These advantages are more often found for well-specified techniques, like STAD or TGT, than for project-based approaches like jigsaw (Aronson, 1978) and group investigation (Sharan, 1994b). And the positive results are generally reported for more basic skills in reading, writing, and mathematics.

However, these benefits are not always equally distributed among students of differing abilities and backgrounds (Oakes, 1990; Webb, 1989). For instance, more positive evidence for socially shared education exists in the early-elementary through middle-school grades than in the high-school years (Johnson, Johnson, & Stanne, 2000). In addition, low-ability students appear to gain the most from mixed-ability groupings (McCaslin & Good, 1996), seemingly because they draw on the knowledge and skills of students of higher ability (Azmitia, 1988). This pattern supports Vygotsky's theory of the zone of proximal development because more capable students scaffold those who are less capable (Webb, 1991). Some are concerned that less capable students may rely too heavily on advanced students (Renzulli, 1986). High-ability students do as well in mixed-ability as in same-ability groups, but studies rarely contrast the performance of high-ability students learning alone with those working in either mixed-ability or similar-ability groups. Thus, the question of whether or when socially shared education is most beneficial to advanced learners remains largely unanswered.

Moreover, individual and cultural differences affect students' preference for group work. From an affective standpoint, some students seem more disposed to either competition or cooperation (Kagan, 1992). Thus, classrooms in which group learning is the mainstay of instruction may either complement or conflict with these students' general dispositions. Achievement and motivational outcomes also differ for certain ethnic and cultural populations (E. G. Cohen, 1994). For example, African American and Hispanic students show more affinity for cooperative grouping, whereas European Americans seem to prefer more traditional, competitive classroom structures (Kagan, 1992). Some support also exists for the contention that females may be more comfortable with shared learning, whereas males may be more inclined toward competitive educational models (Belensky, Clinchy, Goldberger, & Tarule, 1986).

Although this research is not definitive, it points to two important conclusions. First, socially shared practices generally promote students' learning and development (Slavin & Oickle, 1981). Second, the benefits of such practices cannot simply be taken for granted (Sharan, 1994b). Just putting students in groups guarantees nothing. Socially shared learning and teaching must be implemented intelligently, with an eye toward the cognitive and motivational effects on every member of the classroom community. Three key factors, summarized in Figure 11–9, affect the results of socially shared education.

Apply Social Interaction Patterns That Match Instructional Goals

Advocates of cooperative learning have devised varied grouping techniques—such as learning together, STAD, and TGT—to allow for flexibility in student interactions (Slavin, 1995). However, being an intelligent user of social-learning models means more than deciding whether to use jigsaw, STAD, TAI, or some other technique (Cohen, 1994). Skillful coordination begins with awareness that all forms of social interaction have potential instructional advantages and disadvantages (Jetton & Alexander, 2000), which become more evident when the fundamental patterns of social interaction are compared (Alexander, Jetton, et al., 1994). The six basic patterns are illustrated in Figure 11–10.

These six interaction patterns are basic to any formal or informal approach to socially shared learning (Alexander & Jetton, 2003). Thus, one or more of these patterns can be

---

- · $\mathcal{A}$pply social interaction patterns that match instructional goals.

  Social interactions in classrooms tend to fall into one of six patterns: recitation, open exchange, student-directed learning, group-interactive learning, peer tutoring, and peer learning. Each one of these patterns tends to serve varied instructional purposes and has its own set of possible disadvantages. Educators should be sensitive to these uses and limitations as they manage the learning environment.

- · $\mathcal{B}$ase judgments about socially shared practices on valid and reliable evidence.

  Teachers cannot rely on speculation or intuition when deciding whether their instructional decisions are benefiting students. As professionals they need reliable information they can analyze and weigh. Although that information can come from many sources and take many forms, data-based decision making remains essential to confirm the quality of social interactions in the classroom.

- · $\mathcal{C}$onsider the configuration and consistency of cooperative and collaborative groups.

  Teachers must foster the ongoing and continued academic and social health of classroom groups. Up-front planning about group membership and duration is important. Decisions about group membership and longevity should support the instructional agenda.

■ FIGURE 11–9   The ABCs of effective cooperation and collaboration.

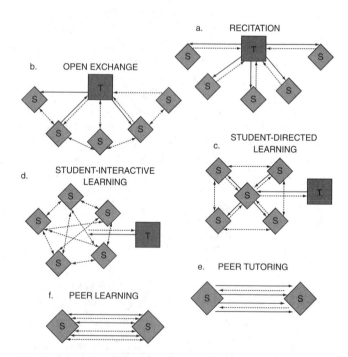

■ FIGURE 11–10   The shape of social interaction.

Note: Based on *Teachers' and Students' Understanding of Scientific Exposition: How Importance and Interest Influence What Is Accessed and What Is Discussed* by T. L. Jetton, 1994, unpublished doctoral dissertation, Texas A & M University, College Station, and *The Nature of Student Involvement: Discussions That Occur in Science Classrooms* by T. L. Jetton and P. A. Alexander, 2000, unpublished manuscript.

Table 11–7 Comparison of six interactional arrangements.

Pattern	Description	Advantages	Disadvantages
Recitation	The teacher is the primary authority, who presents content and directs questions to students as a way to review content or assess student understanding.	Delivers a large amount of information in a short period of time; can be helpful in introducing a new topic or procedure or for reviewing	Limits participation of students to answering questions; can deal with content superficially; restricts alternative perspectives and healthy skepticism
Open Exchange	Often sparked by a question or dilemma the teacher poses, students are encouraged to converse with one another with periodic interjections from the teacher.	Allows teachers and students to examine multiple sides of an unresolved, ambiguous, or controversial subject; permits more in-depth examination of a topic or issue	Allows less control of academic content; permits inaccurate or misleading notions to seem verified or unwavering; is affected by students' verbal ability and knowledge
Student-Directed Learning	Following teacher modeling and explanation, a student leads a small group; the teacher assists as needed but limits direct involvement.	Distributes the academic load from whole class to smaller instructional units; can enhance the lead student's feelings of competence	Allows variable quality of instruction within groups; favors students equipped to take an instructional role
Student-Interactive Learning	Groups of students work together to complete an academic task; no particular student leader need be designated.	Permits more differentiation of instruction in the classroom; is useful for problem-based activities; can change bases for grouping	Disperses teacher's guidance over multiple groups; can be hard to regulate or evaluate student behavior, input, and participation
Peer Tutoring	A student with particular knowledge and skills provides one-on-one instruction to another student in need of assistance.	Can provide added reinforcement, practice, or assistance for individual students with particular needs	Must have a peer with the requisite knowledge or skill and the ability to teach that to another classmate; must have a willing partner
Peer Learning	Two students work together as partners to complete a task or acquire certain knowledge or skills.	Is useful for smaller projects or assignments for which content or skills have been previously taught	Depends on the specific pairing for the quality of the learning; can be hard to maintain teacher attention on pairs

found in each of the techniques for cooperation and collaboration already examined in this chapter. For example, reciprocal teaching typically begins with some manner of recitation and then moves into student-directed learning; scripted cooperation relies on a peer learning pattern. In addition, a number of these patterns can emerge within a single class period (Jetton, 1994). Janet and the Academy teachers might start class with recitation, move to an open exchange, and then move back to recitation. And none of these patterns should be considered inherently good or bad (Alexander & Jetton, 2003). The merits of each depend on whether the pattern is thoughtfully and purposefully instituted and flexibly applied to meet instructional conditions (Mishler, 1978). Table 11–7 compares the six patterns.

Recitation

One of the most pervasive forms of social interaction observed in educational settings is **recitation** (Alvermann, O'Brien, & Dillon, 1990; Lampert, 1998). Recitation occurs when one person, typically the teacher, dominates the class-room interactions (see Figure 11–10a). **Expository teaching** and **lecture** are other common labels for this interaction pattern. Occasionally in expository teaching, the teacher directs questions or comments to students but still retains control of the flow of content. Few, if any, student-to-student exchanges take place (Jetton & Alexander, 2000).

Advantages of Expository Teaching Advocates of socially shared learning occasionally portray expository teaching or lecturing as a detrimental pattern of interaction, especially when it is the only or the predominant mode of exchange (Alvermann et al., 1990). However, the use of expository teaching has clear advantages when it is suitably and well applied (Alexander & Jetton, 2003). For example, teachers may use this form of interaction to give an overview of content because it allows for the delivery of large amounts of information in a short time (Jetton, 1994). Further, expository teaching permits the repetition of important content in multiple formats, as when the teacher not only explains a particular concept verbally but also illustrates it graphically or pictorially (McKeachie, Pintrich, Lin, & Smith, 1990). Expository teaching can also be used in reviewing previously covered content (Gage & Berliner, 1998).

Janet Seipel and her fellow teachers often use expository teaching at the beginning of class. Janet might spend the first 10 minutes demonstrating a new software package or reviewing the mathematical procedures covered the previous day. When responses and reactions convince Janet that the students can handle the new software or retain their understanding of the formula, she can shift to an alternative mode of interaction. Thus, expository teaching need not occupy an entire class session but can be combined with other interaction patterns.

Guidelines for Effective Expository Teaching

As with any form of teacher-student interaction, students may feel disengaged if teachers apply an expository teaching approach too long, too often, or indiscriminately (Broadwell, 1980; Luft, 1970). Also, content covered in this way might receive superficial treatment because it leaves little time or opportunity for the teacher and students to play with ideas (Lampert, 1998). Several guidelines for expository teaching are recommended in the literature to ensure that teachers apply this form of interaction pattern more effectively (Armbruster, 2000; Gage & Berliner, 1998; Ormrod, 1998).

- Make personal connections between the content and the students, such as referencing topics of particular interest to the students.
- Preview the content, perhaps through the use of a graphic organizer that visually summarizes the key ideas and displays their relations.
- Signal important ideas or relevant sequences through linguistic cues (e.g., *most important*, *first*, or *next*), repetitions, or graphic displays.
- Question periodically to maintain students' attention, assess understanding, spark their interests, solicit personal examples, or review content.
- Model salient procedures or useful strategies that support content.
- Offer appropriate and varied examples that reinforce the content.
- Alter the pacing of content delivery to adjust to the complexity of the material and to maintain momentum.
- Summarize the main ideas that have been covered during the lecture.

The point that must be emphasized is that recitation, as exemplified in expository teaching or lecturing, should not be dismissed as an inappropriate or ineffective form of teacher-student interaction. Expository teaching or lecturing is an invaluable tool in teachers' pedagogical repertoire when it is reasonably and suitably matched to the instructional goals, the task, and the audience (Broadwell, 1980; Gage & Berliner, 1998).

Open Exchange

In the case of **open exchange,** the teacher is less dominant but still oversees the exchange of ideas in the classroom (Cobb et al., 1991). Typically, teachers initiate this pattern when they pose open-ended, controversial, or stimulating questions to their students. In addition, teachers give students some explicit or implicit indication that they are free to pursue those questions verbally, with limited input from the teacher. Thus, this pattern shows increased participation among students (see Figure 11–10b), but the teacher has a clear role in the exchange. That role might involve clarifying, giving feedback, elaborating on a point, or redirecting the exchange. What teachers may call free or open discussion fits within this pattern (Alvermann et al., 1990).

Academy teachers intentionally use open exchange when they want to go deeper into a particular topic, especially one that students find ambiguous or troubling (G. M. Phillips, 1973). For example, because students held different opinions about the truthfulness of information on the Internet and were confused by the seemingly contradictory information they were finding for their tourism project, an open exchange proved valuable. Of course, open discussion has shortcomings, too, including the fact that more opportunity exists for behavioral disruption, especially when students are not well versed in the etiquette of open discourse (Kagan & Kagan, 1994). Open exchange also provides more opportunities to introduce misleading or inaccurate content because students are free to share any of their thoughts or perceptions. And many teachers find this form of social interaction particularly time-consuming (Jetton, 1994).

Student-Directed Learning

Student-directed learning offers a modification of the recitation pattern within student-led groups (Alexander & Jetton, 2003). The flow of interaction moves back and forth from an appointed or emergent student leader (see Figure 11–10c), with the teacher taking a supportive role (Jetton, 1994). Just as the teacher does in recitation, this student leader directs questions and comments to the group members. There may be some student-to-student exchanges, but these tend to be limited (Jetton & Alexander, 2000).

Even though the teacher does not directly regulate student interchanges in student-directed learning the teacher often organizes these groups, assigns the tasks, and oversees the work of the surrogate (Webb & Palincsar, 1996). The extent of the teacher's oversight depends on both the skill of the group leader and the capability of group members to function independently. Student-directed learning is at the center of the RT approach described earlier (Palincsar & Brown, 1984).

Academy teachers occasionally use student-directed learning to allow students to practice or review content that has been covered. In this way student leaders are better equipped to guide group interactions because they understand the content well enough to maintain the group's focus. Janet likes student-directed interaction because it distributes instructional responsibility, giving her and the other Academy teachers the freedom to work with individual students or groups. It also instills a sense of competence in student leaders when the group performs well (Brown & Campione, 1990). However, Janet has learned that a great deal of preparation is needed to make these student-led groups work well. If the personality mix is wrong or the students do not understand the content or process well, student-directed learning is not effective.

Student-Interactive Learning

As with student-directed learning, **student-interactive learning** is learner-centered. However, in this pattern group exchanges are not directed by one student but move freely among group members (see Figure 11–10d). This pattern suits the more collaborative models of shared understanding because no single student directs the actions of the others (Perret-Clermont, Perret, & Bell, 1991; Resnick, 1991). But the potential for confusion and disruption in these student groups is greater than in student-directed learning groups. Students do not have specialized roles that help to structure their interactions, allowing these groups to operate in very diverse ways (Jetton, 1994). This unpredictability complicates the teacher's role because the attention each group requires can vary markedly.

On the other hand, the discovery character of this social pattern makes it useful in problem-based learning, the predominant model in the Academy (Lemke, 1990). Thus, student groups have a general idea about what they are to explore or analyze but are relatively unconstrained in the procedure they use to achieve that end. Each group may perceive the problem somewhat differently and, therefore, may interact somewhat differently. During the travel and culture unit, for example, Janet's students knew that they had to work in groups and that each group was to contribute to the Academy's Top Ten List of Travel Spots. Which students formed the groups, how they chose their travel spot, and how they assembled their class presentation were decisions left up to the students.

Peer Tutoring and Peer Learning

Two social interaction patterns are based on one-to-one exchanges. In the case of **peer tutoring,** one of the two students in the exchange has more advanced knowledge or skills than the other (Fuchs et al., 1997). That more knowledgeable or skilled student assumes responsibility for aiding the peer in learning. Peer tutoring (see Figure 11–10e) is widely used in classrooms to reinforce and enhance important educational content (Cohen et al., 1994). Precisely because this interaction occurs in pairs, a wide range of instructional objectives can be addressed in a single classroom (O'Donnell & Kelly, 1994). However, the viability of peer tutoring rests on having peers in the classroom who not only possess the requisite knowledge and skills, but also have the ability and willingness to teach someone else. In addition, the tutee must be willing to receive assistance from a peer.

On occasion Janet and the Academy teachers have turned to peer tutoring when there was a suitable match between the needs of certain students and the abilities of others. However, because all students assigned to the Academy have significant academic, social, or emotional problems, Academy teachers do not routinely rely on peer tutoring during the regular class period. Sometimes students from the advanced placement classes volunteer to work with Academy students before or after school, and that form of peer tutoring has proven very helpful to the teachers and students alike.

Most often in the Academy, students get into pairs to work on a project or assignment without any expectation that one of them will teach the other. Instead, they assume that they will be working with a peer of comparable knowledge and skills and will consolidate their abilities to complete the task at hand. This type of one-on-one interaction is known as **peer learning** (see Figure 11–10f; Spurlin et al., 1984). One advantage of this pattern is that pairings can be readily formed and can work well with common tasks or well-practiced procedures (Dansereau, 1988). On the downside, however, the quality of work done in these peer groups can vary (Kagan & Kagan, 1994). And teachers must be able to monitor quite a number of pairs simultaneously. As a result, the attention each pair receives can be sporadic and superficial (E. G. Cohen, 1994).

Academy students often form pairs to work on assignments and projects. In the opening scenario, Janet describes one of those occasions when students worked with a partner to surf the Internet for information about particular countries. With four teachers in the classroom, this pattern operates well because Janet, Alice, Connie, and Gordon can move easily about the room to provide guidance or monitor the students' learning. Scripted cooperation, which builds on this interaction pattern, has also been an effective model for the Academy because it allows students to work together on problems that are not too complex or too novel. The students feel more in control of their learning in these cases because they are free to choose their own learning partners and have a general script to guide them (Spurlin et al., 1984).

Janet Seipel has learned that selecting the right social interaction patterns is a critical first step in making the Academy curriculum function smoothly and effectively. Consequently, as she and her colleagues plan the content and objectives of their curriculum, they also discuss which social interaction patterns will be most effective. They even code their lesson plans to suggest which of the patterns matches the particular objective. In the Thought Experiment: Being Social, you have the opportunity to consider interaction patterns relative to educational goals.

Thought Experiment ....

Being Social

Directions: Select the form of social interaction you think is most suitable for the situation Janet, Alice, Connie, and Gordon are describing.

a. Recitation
b. Open exchange
c. Student-direct learning
d. Student-interactive learning
e. Peer tutoring
f. Peer learning

_____ 1.   Muriel and Hector need some individual help on their prefixes and suffixes. Do you think Sasha and Linda could work with them?

_____ 2.   After reading those group reports, I think we need to spend more time teaching the students some basic steps for summarization.

_____ 3.   I would like to try some of the peer editing techniques I have been reading about. They sound like a good way to help the students improve their writing. I think it would be fine if they chose to work with a friend for the first couple of tries.

_____ 4.   Did you see how well Edmundo explained the graphing problem to Omar? I would like to have him lead a group when we do those review problems next week.

_____ 5.   I have those worksheets on calculating distances between famous cities ready for the tourism unit. I think we could let the students do those in groups, as long as we select good group leaders.

_____ 6.   Do you think the students are ready to carry on an intelligent conversation about truth on the Internet? This whole business about online veracity seems to have them frustrated. If you agree, we should schedule that before they finish their Top 10 project.

_____ 7.   I have a couple of science experiments that I can work into the tourism theme, like lift and drag on airplane wings. Instead of just giving the students the formulas, I would like to let them figure out the relationship through group experimentation.

_____ 8.   Tomorrow, when the students finish presenting their tourism projects, I would like to use the remaining time to review the key concepts and procedures they should have learned. Does that work for you?

(Answers at the end of the chapter)

....

Base Judgments About Socially Shared Practices on Valid and Reliable Evidence

Teachers cannot simply guess whether the social interaction patterns they institute are working; they need to monitor the positive and negative effects on students' academic, social, and emotional well-being (Fuchs, Fuchs, Hamlett, & Stecker, 1991; Hertz-Lazarowitz & Calderón, 1994). Valid and reliable evidence about what is or is not working allows teachers to fine tune their socially shared educational practices (Kampwirth, 1999). It also provides them with important insights about what types of instructional tasks or activities work well with what types of classroom configuration.

Several of the popular programs of cooperative learning introduced earlier have very specific mechanisms for student evaluation (Johnson & Johnson, 1999; Slavin, 1995). In the STAD and TGT programs, for example, structured assessment procedures make use of the worksheets and games that are part of everyday instruction (Slavin, 1994). Another unique feature of approaches like STAD or TGT is that students' achievement scores depend on the performance of their group members, along with their individual progress.

Whatever pattern of social interaction teachers employ, a wide range of assessment practices can help them gauge its effects. Those assessments can be informal and target students' motivation, as the team rating form in Figure 11–11 does, an appropriate form for young children. The teachers in the Academy also administer an evaluation instrument at the end of each themed unit. Students are allowed to rate each of the activities included in the unit on a 1-to-10 scale. They can also suggest ways to improve the activities and list the most important ideas or skills they acquired from each one.

When group work is involved, Academy students also have the chance to assess their own and each member's contributions. For example, when students used the group investigations procedure for one of their tourism projects, the teachers supplied them with an evaluation checklist. The checklist outlined each of the areas for which they would be evaluated (e.g., adherence to the theme, organization, and inclusion of important content), along with the points allotted for each area. In this way, students were prepared for the feedback that teachers gave them. Also, the students had a chance to rate themselves on each of those dimensions. Con-

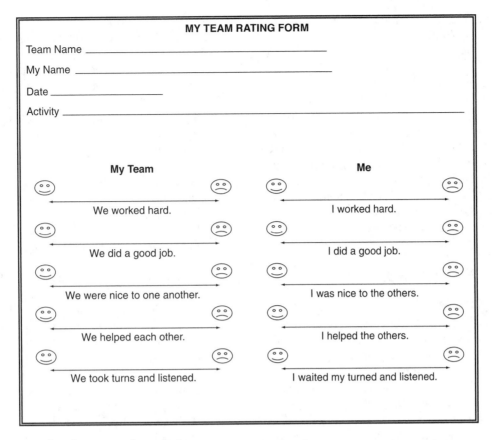

MY TEAM RATING FORM

Team Name _____

My Name _____

Date _____

Activity _____

My Team

We worked hard.

We did a good job.

We were nice to one another.

We helped each other.

We took turns and listened.

Me

I worked hard.

I did a good job.

I was nice to the others.

I helped the others.

I waited my turned and listened.

■ **FIGURE 11–11 Evaluating group interactions.**

sequently, when the teachers met with the students, they could discuss the similarities and differences in their ratings.

It is also important to judge whether students of various ability, gender, and ethnic groups share equally in the learning (Azmitia, 1988; Slavin & Oickle, 1981). This information is particularly important to the Academy teachers, whose students have confronted failure far too often in the past. Even though it is unrealistic to assume that all students will benefit equally from each and every instructional activity, any discernible pattern of inequity that arises can seriously damage students' continued development and must not be tolerated (DeVries & Edwards, 1974). Certainly, the collection of academic, motivational, and social data takes time. However, such data help educators identify the various conditions under which social practices operate optimally and the conditions that should be modified or avoided in the future.

Consider the Configuration and Consistency of Cooperative and Collaborative Groups

Nothing is more frustrating or aggravating than getting stuck in a group that is not functioning well, especially when performance is judged on the basis of everyone's contributions. Unfortunately, some group members assume the unhealthy roles of slacker, resister, or dominator (Kagan, 1992). Consequently, teachers should take great care when forming groups, especially when those groups will be evalu-

ated as a whole or when they will remain intact for any length of time (Johnson & Johnson, 1974). Ample evidence indicates that groups formed with sufficient attention to ability, personality, gender, and ethnic differences among individual members generally work best (Fuchs et al., 1997).

The cooperative techniques developed by Slavin (1995), Johnson and Johnson (1999), and others have rather specific procedures for forming mixed-ability and same-ability groups. Most of these procedures rest on recent academic achievement. Janet Seipel has occasion to work with ability groups in the Academy as well, and student performance on class activities is a criterion she and the other teachers use to form ability groups. Because the Academy is interdisciplinary, the teachers sometimes groups students whose subject-matter strengths vary. However, the teachers are just as likely to create special interest groups for certain tasks. For instance, because several students in the Academy are involved in music, it would seem appropriate to allow them to delve into music collectively as part of a themed task. Allowing students to form their own groups, select their own tasks, or evaluate their own performance can introduce variety into classroom structures and promote self-determination.

However, groups that are not functioning well need to be assessed quickly so that suitable adjustments can be made. For example, Janet has learned from experience to avoid placing Jesse and Molly in the same group, because both are extremely chatty and have a great need to be in control. Having both of them in one group is too much for the other students to handle. Of course, groups of ninth graders require some time to solidify and settle in, so Janet and the others are careful not to shuffle their groups too quickly when a minor problem or issue arises (Sharan, 1994a).

Periodic reassessment of group membership also allows for changes in interaction patterns (Hertz-Lazarowitz & Calderón, 1994). How long a group stays together should depend on the tasks to be accomplished and the ongoing health and well-being of the group members. A certain degree of fluidity in grouping procedures can help maintain student motivation and offset complacency, stereotyping, or routinization (E. G. Cohen et al., 1994; Dishon & O'Leary, 1984). In general, the degree of fluidity or consistency must be appropriate to the age and ability of the students.

■ Summary Reflections

In what ways is learning shared or distributed?

- Teachers must understand and target at the social and contextual nature of learning if students are to thrive.
  - An array of cooperative and collaborative procedures are well researched and have promising results.
  - Teachers need to consider educational goals and instructional content, as well as the age, ability, and ethnicity of students.
  - They need to be prepared to teach students how to be appropriately social—how to work well with their classmates to accomplish the tasks at hand.
- Some educational researchers and practitioners see many limitations and shortcomings in cooperation and collaboration.
  - Group learning may become an occasion for social loafing.
  - Shared intelligence may become shared ignorance.

How do the principles of shared understanding extend to teachers as well as to students?

- If optimal learning and development is a real goal for schools, then educational institutions need to become teaching communities.
  - Teachers should be as free as their students to share relevant professional knowledge and skills with others.
  - They should welcome occasions to meet with other concerned parties to work toward consensus on issues of importance to them and their students.
- Shared teaching is fostered when those involved are committed to dismantling perceptions of teaching as an isolated act.
  - It is more successful when differences of opinion and alternative instructional perspectives are welcome.
  - Shared teaching needs external encouragement and support if it is to endure.

How can socially shared education translate into better learning for all students?

- The effectiveness of socially shared educational practices rests on the shoulders of the teachers who implement them.
  - The teachers should consider the particular advantages and disadvantages of different social interaction patterns.
  - Teachers should initiate socially shared approaches with these advantages and disadvantages in mind.
- Teachers must secure evaluative information they can trust to determine whether their pedagogical decisions are wise and their social practices are achieving instructional goals.
  - Useful data can be found in the course of day-to-day instruction, in the form of documented achievements and in motivational, social, and behavioral data.
  - Evaluative information can be rather formal, like test scores, or informal, like observations of student behavior and student self-reports.
- Effective socially shared education requires teachers to consider the structure and consistency of student groupings.
  - Those questions need to be carefully considered, along with issues of academic progress.
  - Socially shared education involves far more than putting desks or students together.

■ Answers to Figure 11–3

1. I studied all day, but I failed the test.

2. Provide an example from your own experience, or provide one from your textbook.

3. It rained all day and it thundered all night.

4. Sally understood the problem, but she raised her hand to ask a question.

5. He cleans and she cooks.

6. Either Mr. Jones was not trying hard enough, or he was having bad luck.

7. Every time I took the test I failed, but I kept taking it.

8. My uncle gave me advice about fishing, but I did not listen to him.

9. Elm Street is lined with maples, and Maple Street is lined with elms.

10. Alice worked hard in school, for she was eager to learn.

■ Answers to Figure 11–4

1. He likes catsup on hamburgers, but on hot dogs he likes mustard.

2. Jimmy lives in the country, and he plays in the woods.

3. Either the lightbulb burned out, or the switch is not working.

4. Neither did the girls play basketball, nor did they do hiking.

5. To get exercise, Dorothy plays tennis for an hour, or she swims for two hours.

6. I have studied the problem for two days, yet I have not come up with a solution.

7. Either there will be food at the picnic, or there will be a trip to McDonald's at lunchtime.

8. Donna arrived early, for she didn't want to miss the opening ceremonies.

9. Mr. Goldsmith tried the front door, but it was locked.

10. Eddie will not work after school, nor will he work on weekends.

11. Roy liked the spotted dog best; it reminded him of Spooky.

12. Martha passed the test; she did not miss a single question.

13. Don't be afraid of the dog; his bark is worse than his bite.

14. It wasn't a flying saucer that you saw; it was a shooting star.

15. I prefer the red candy; it tastes sweeter.

■ Answers to Thought Experiment: Putting a Name to Cooperation

1. g
2. d
3. b
4. e

5. f
6. c
7. a

■ Answers to Thought Experiment: Testing Your Coteaching Knowledge

1. b
2. c
3. a
4. d
5. a
6. b
7. e

■ Answers to Thought Experiment: Being Social

1. e
2. a
3. f
4. c
5. c
6. b
7. d
8. a

Chapter 12

Technology and the Educational Process

GUIDING QUESTIONS

- How has technology changed learning and instruction?

- How can teachers keep up with the ever-changing world of technology?

- What principles underlie optimal learning in a technologically rich society?

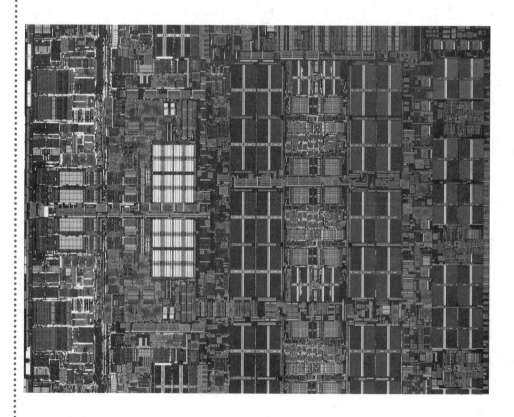

IN THEIR OWN WORDS ....

As an instructional technology specialist for Austin High School, Kim Taber shares her knowledge and expertise with teachers and students alike. Whether modeling lessons in classrooms, conducting minitraining sessions for teachers and staff, or troubleshooting mechanical or instructional problems, Kim witnesses both effective and ineffective uses of technology.

The computer, like any other tool used in teaching, is only as good as the teacher using it. Some educators see technology as a dynamic and interactive tool that enhances learning, while others see it as an easy way out. Almost daily I encounter three types of technology users—the good, the bad, and the ugly.

Last Monday I arrived at school to help our French teacher, Diane Lemmonier, set up the projector and the Smart Board so her students could work with the interactive compact disc that comes with their textbook. The students love using the interactive board, and it allows them a hands-on approach to learning. I then met with an English teacher, Mr. Stuart, who needed the digital camera so that his students could take pictures for their PowerPoint presentations. Later, several teachers arrived at the minitraining session on Excel that I am running during their off periods. Then I stopped at Lilli Wong's room to check out the videoconference her class is having with the author of the book they just finished reading. At the same time, the Spanish teacher, Mrs. Savia, in the lab across the hall has constructed an Internet scavenger hunt to introduce her students to the countries in South America.

These teachers make my days enjoyable. They challenge me to use technology to engage and interest their students. I consider these teachers to be experts in their fields. In all cases they use the power of technology to enhance student learning.

But then I got a call from Mr. Smart, who wanted to know if the technology lab was available. At Austin High, teachers can check the schedule of the computer lab from any classroom and reserve it for a particular time. Therefore, even getting this call was not a good sign. I asked Mr. Smart if his students would need assistance in the lab. He told me that he would be grading papers while his students surfed the Web. As you might imagine, we encourage teachers NOT to allow students simply to roam the Internet. I reminded Mr. Smart that he should have instructional sites for his students to browse and that he should monitor the students. He responded, "Oh, of course!" Later, when I went by the lab, I saw the students printing pictures of half-naked people. I also noticed that most of the screen savers displayed beer and marijuana ads. I call this the babysitting approach to computer use. Mr. Smart always assures me that his students are very mature and can handle such unstructured computer use. All in all, I consider him an example of a bad technology user.

Just when I thought things couldn't get worse, I ran into the teacher who is too smart for his own good. Mr. Smug brought his English class to the lab to do structured Web searches. His class was well behaved in the lab. However, on closer inspection I realized that several students were fixated on their computer screens. They were playing the computer game Dune, which Mr. Smug had illegally loaded onto the computers. The district has questioned the appropriateness of this particular game, and its use during class time could cost Mr. Smug his job.

If that weren't enough, Mr. Smug had bypassed the computer safeguards so the students did not have to log on. This makes everything in the school's database, from scheduling to student grades, accessible. It is safe to say that Mr. Smug will be sitting in my principal's office at the end of the day having a little chat. His use of the computer was beyond bad. It was downright ugly.

The experiences of this single day reminded me how strong a presence technology has in today's schools. Yet it also reminded me that technology does not ensure that students learn better. As I said, the computer and all the media devices in wired schools like Austin High School are ultimately only as good, bad, or ugly as the teachers who use them.

How Has Technology Changed Learning and Instruction?

Historical/Philosophical Background

The term **technology** encompasses all types of tools that humans have created to serve them in their work and play (Salomon, 1993b). That technology can range from a simple device (e.g., a wheel) to rather sophisticated mechanisms (e.g., combustible engines or nuclear reactors). Historical evidence indicates that each generation is shaped by the technologies it develops (Postman, 1993), whether that technology is the alphabet, the printing press, the automobile, or the computer (Nix, 1990; Reinking, 1998). Just think about how society has been transformed by the discovery of flight or nuclear energy. The influences of technology reach even beyond the broader society into its educational institutions, changing the very nature of learning and instruction—sometimes for better and sometimes for worse (Lajoie & Derry, 1993; Lemke, 1998).

Educational Technology

Some of the tools and devices that societies create are especially relevant to the processes of learning and teaching. Because of their instructional purpose, devices such as pencils, books, desks, and overhead projectors are referred to as **educational technology** (Bransford, Brown, & Cocking, 1999; Kerr, 1996). For the most part, educational technologies are commonplace in schools and classrooms—so much so that their presence and their power are simply accepted without question or reflection (Bruce & Hogan, 1998). However, this chapter focuses on one class of educational technology that remains sufficiently novel and complex that its effect on learning and instruction is only beginning to take shape (Meyrowitz, 1996; Zhao & Conway, 2001).

Computer-Based Technologies

The phrase **computer-based technologies** signifies not only the computers themselves, but all the peripheral or related devices used with them (Alexander & Wade, 2000). The Smart Board used by Diane Lemmonier's French students, the videoconferencing equipment at work in Lilli Wong's classroom, and the digital camera used by Mr. Stuart are all computer-based technologies.

Computer-based technologies are not new to education. They have been in educational institutions since the 1950s (Segal, 1996). However, computers have become increasingly more common educational tools in the last 2 decades (Salomon & Perkins, 1996), and their form, ease of use, and purpose have changed dramatically. Even a cursory examination of computer-based technologies reveals how far they have come in the past 20 years—from rarity to commonplace, from machines for drill and practice to devices for navigating the world, and from monstrous room-sized structures to hand-held tools (U.S. Congress Office of Technology Assessment, 1988).

As Kim Taber's experiences make apparent, today's educators have no choice but to become familiar with new, computer-based technologies. Her tongue-in-cheek reference to the good, the bad, and the ugly at Austin High School serves as a potent reminder that technology is neither savior nor satan. Technology, in and of itself, lacks the power to transform ineffective teachers into effective ones or vice versa. Instead, technology can amplify or intensify whatever fundamental traits and patterns already exist in the learning environment (Lajoie, 2000).

No one makes this point any more eloquently than Neil Postman (1993). In the opening pages of *Technopoly*, a volume that sometimes casts computer-based technology in an unflattering light, Postman describes computers as friend *and* enemy—both a blessing *and* a burden to humanity. Postman argues vehemently that the question is not *whether* technology will change the way individuals acquire and use information, but rather *how* it will change these fundamental processes. That premise characterizes this discussion.

Multimedia to Hypermedia

One of the changes that comes with computer-based technologies is the movement from multimedia to hypermedia (Bolter, 1991). Throughout the centuries students have relied on various forms of communication, both oral and written. In the past century, however, students and teachers have become accustomed to learning in environments where multiple media—involving spoken words, pictures, text, and graphics—are used in combination to enhance student understanding. Thus, learning and instruction have become a **multimedia** process (Shah, Mayer, & Hegarty, 1999).

With the influx of computer-based technologies, multimedia processing has risen to a new level. **Hypermedia** involves the full integration of multiple media forms (e.g., words, pictures, and videos) by means of networked systems that allow the users to select the representations they prefer (Alexander, Kulikowich, & Jetton, 1994; Britt, Rouet, & Perfetti, 1996). Thus, students in Mrs. Lemmonier's French class not only read their computer-enhanced books on the Smart Board, but also link to related videos or click on *hot words*—highlighted vocabulary words that are pronounced and defined for them. At the same time, students in Jerry Stuart's English class can download their digital pictures to create pictorial essays. And Antonia Savia's Spanish II class can conduct their online scavenger hunt, which incorporates whatever forms of representation the students choose to access via the computer network.

Although this movement from multimedia to hypermedia is only one of the many transformations taking place in today's schools, it is a reminder of the instructional differences computer-based technologies bring. The educational community must recognize these differences and deal with them effectively and efficiently if optimal learning and development are to occur (Reinking, Labbo, & McKenna, 1997).

Components of Effective Computer-Based Instruction

Despite the expanding versatility of computer-based technologies, several key and unwavering elements guide their optimal use. According to the Cognition and Technology Group at Vanderbilt (CTGV, 1996), leaders in educational technology research and development, the key components of the effective application of computer-based technologies are the technologies themselves, theories of learning, and educational practices. As depicted in Figure 12–1, all three must mesh well if teachers and students are to realize the promise of technology and sidestep its pitfalls.

Technology

Technology is obviously an essential component of optimal computer-based instruction. Although computer use has steadily risen in recent years (U.S. Department of Commerce, 2000), many schools and classrooms still have little or no up-to-date computer technology (U.S. Department of Commerce, 1999, 2000). In fact, the phrase *digital divide*

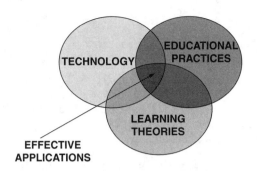

■ FIGURE 12–1   Key components of effective technology use.

Note: From "Looking at Technology in Context: A Framework for Understanding Technology and Education Research" by Cognition and Technology Group at Vanderbilt in D. C. Berliner and R. C. Calfee (Eds.), *Handbook of Educational Psychology* (p. 808), 1996, New York: Macmillan. Copyright 1996 by Macmillan. Adapted with permission.

has been coined to signify the extensive gap between the technology haves and have nots (U.S. Department of Commerce, 1995). Even more problematic, however, is the fact that many of the underequipped schools falling on the have-not side of this digital divide serve diverse populations, rural areas, or low socioeconomic neighborhoods—the very populations that often have less access to technology outside school.

Nonetheless, merely having the requisite computer hardware or software in a school or classroom is not enough to bring about effective learning. Computer-based technologies are too often underutilized, sitting in closets or in the back corners of classrooms gathering dust rather than opening students' minds. These instructional environments apparently lack educators with knowledge of the learning theories or educational practices needed to use that technology effectively.

Learning Theories

The effective application of computer-based technologies relies on teachers' understanding of human learning (CTGV, 1996). As discussed in Chapter 4, all educators have a conception of learning that affects the way they approach teaching—and therefore teaching with technology. For example, some educators hold that learning is a social constructivist process—a building of understandings through social and cultural interactions (Kafai & Resnick, 1996; Perkins, 1991). For these educators technology-rich environments may not only increase access to information but also provide multiple avenues for social exchange and knowledge building. In the hands of these teachers, technology becomes a platform for student cooperation and collaboration.

Those with situated cognitive views of learning care about the meaningfulness and effectiveness of the thinking and problem solving triggered by these technologies (Kulikowich & Young, 2001; Stevens & Hall, 1998). Within this theoretical framework, a richness in human and nonhuman resources within the classroom stimulates or prompts deeper processing among participants. Thus, to these situ-

ated cognitivists, technology-rich environments become wonderful problem posers and links to other human and nonhuman resources beyond the classroom walls (Clancey, 1993). In addition, technology becomes a way to off-load cognitive demands—from information storage to mathematical computations (J. S. Brown, Collins, & Duguid, 1989). In other words, computer technologies can perform tasks that students would otherwise perform so that the students can go deeper into the problem at hand (Young & Barab, 1999).

Although recent applications stress the social aspects of learning, computer-based technology can complement any theoretical view of learning and development. Even the strict behaviorist, who believes in the power of stimulus/ response and positive reinforcement, can find multiple uses for technology in the classroom. In fact, drill-and-practice exercises, which fit nicely within this theoretical model, remain a common application of technology (Lajoie, 2000).

The question here is not which theoretical perspective is right or wrong but whether educators are making sound decisions in applying computer technologies based on whatever theoretical orientations they hold. The more teachers see technology as a tool for realizing their particular vision of optimal human learning, the more apt they will be to apply it effectively (Derry & Lajoie, 1993).

Educational Practices

Teachers must make reasoned and thoughtful pedagogical choices about what form of technology they will apply and how that tool will contribute to student learning and development (Salomon & Perkins, 1996). These choices include the model of classroom interaction teachers will pursue (e.g., recitation or student-led interactions), the specific content they will target, and the type of assessment they will employ (Alexander, Kulikowich, & Jetton, 1994; Lesgold, 1993). Teachers should consider what their overall goal for a lesson is and how computer-based technologies can contribute to that goal. Further, they should decide how much time they want to devote to a particular task or lesson and whether the use of computer-based technologies will fit within that time frame (Chipman, 1993; Mandinach & Cline, 2000). In addition, teachers must plan how they will measure student performance and what role computer-based technologies can play in that assessment (Alexander & Wade, 2000).

Some guiding questions that teachers might ask themselves as they develop their lessons appear in Table 12–1. These questions and their accompanying classroom examples target a range of pedagogical issues that teachers need to weigh as they attempt to integrate technology into the learning environment and their class content. Collectively, these questions address all three of the components that CTGV and others have found essential for effective technology use.

Perplexing Questions and Potential Solutions

Technology is dramatically changing the world in which we live (Bolter, 1998; Papert, 1980). Chapter 1 introduced several

Table 12–1	Considerations to guide effective technology-based instruction.	
Issue	**Prompts**	**Classroom Case**
Learning Goals	*What academic knowledge or skills will this lesson reinforce?* *How will the inclusion of technology contribute to my academic, social, or motivational goals for this lesson?*	For the unit on prose and politics, Jerry Stuart wants his students to understand the persuasive and provocative effects political writings can have. He also hopes to encourage his students to become more politically active. He sees the appeal of the Internet as an aid in this process.
Content Familiarity	*How much background do my students have for this content?* *Will this problem or task be particularly challenging or routine for my students?*	In Mr. Stuart's judgment, his students understand little about the genres of political writing from classical (e.g., tracts or treatises) to modern forms (e.g., commercials). They understand even less about the online forms of political persuasion they encounter.
Technological Tool	*What equipment or software do I need to carry out this lesson?*	For this lesson Mr. Stuart's students will need access to digital cameras, computers, conversion software, a desktop publishing program, PowerPoint, and color printers.
Technological Familiarity	*Will I require assistance to integrate this technology into my lesson?* *What experiences have my students had with this technology?*	All but one or two of Jerry Stuart's students have used the requisite technology before. Mrs. Taber also offers students a workshop on desktop publishing.
Interaction Pattern	*Are the goals of this lesson best achieved by peer learning or through a student-interactive approach?* *Should I begin with recitation and move to student-directed learning?*	Using a recitation model, Mr. Stuart will show students examples of past (e.g., Paine's *Common Sense*) and recent political prose. Then he will move to small groups for project planning on the Internet.
Special Needs	*Do any students in the classroom require special assistance to complete the task or use the technology effectively?*	Fred Dyer is a student with visual impairments. Kim Taber has adaptive equipment that Fred can use to complete his project.
Time Frame	*How long will the entire process or assignment take?* *Does the use of the technology add additional time to the overall task?*	Based on last year's performance, this pictorial essay will require a week for completion. However, Mr. Stuart is prepared to extend the time if needed.
Planning/ Coordination	*What arrangements do I need to make to ensure that the tools or supports are available?* *Are other people or classrooms involved in this lesson?*	Mr. Stuart needs to schedule the use of the digital camera and the production lab with Mrs. Taber to ensure that his students have access not only during class, but also before or after school.
Extension or Follow-Up	*What is the best way to build on the knowledge or skills students gain from this activity?* *Should the product be teacher-determined or student-selected?*	One of the extensions that Mr. Stuart has planned for this lesson is to have his students prepare fliers in support of school or local issues of importance to them.
Assessment Method	*How will I decide whether the students achieved my goals for this lesson?* *What kinds of information can I gather during and after the lesson?*	Because the project focuses on a pictorial essay, each group will be judged on its quality. Students will be given the scoring criteria beforehand.

of the unsettling but unavoidable consequences that arise when computer-based technologies move into learning environments. For instance, some students inevitably get lost as they try to navigate this technological world (Hooper & Hannafin, 1991). In addition, students often have more computer knowledge and expertise than their teachers do (Means et al.,

1993). And quality control for online information is basically nonexistent (Purves, 1998).

Because these concerns are relatively new, educational researchers and practitioners have had only limited opportunity to study them and to pose workable solutions. Nonetheless, they need to be discussed because they are

Table 12–2   Educational options for potential technological concerns.

Dilemma	Instructional Issues	Educational Responses
Virtual Reality/Virtual Learning	It is difficult to ascertain whether learning is occuring.	Consider the effects of learning with (assisted) and learning from (residual) technology.
		Explore alternative definitions and measures of learning.
	The validity or authority of online information is questionable.	Use site filters or lists of approved Websites to guide students' Internet navigation.
		Teach students how to judge the credibility of online information.
Instructional Novelty/Enduring Pedagogy	Newness of computer-based technology may give rise to temporary arousal instead of sustained interest.	Define learning goals and expressly share them with students before engagement.
		Keep substantive content or meaningful problems front and center in instruction.
	Teachers may not have well-established educational techniques to complement emerging technologies.	Apply and evaluate various instructional approaches.
		Use new technologies in situations where traditional teaching approaches do not work well.
Electronic Equalizer/Digital Divider	Students who are already technologically versed have a learning edge.	Form dyads and groups to distribute technological expertise.
		Complement computer capabilities with instruction in online strategies.
	Women and minorities may feel technologically detached.	Ensure greater access to technological training for women and other underrepresented groups.
		Select educational tasks or problems that are particularly relevant to females and minorities.
Human Connection/Human Isolation	Extensive time online is sometimes associated with loneliness and depression.	Encourage students to work with others and discuss their thoughts and ideas during processing.
		Nurture direct human contact, even in wired learning environments.

omens of what lies ahead as computers and related technologies become entrenched in educational environments. Table 12–2 looks at four educational dilemmas raised by computer-based technologies.

Virtual Reality/Virtual Learning

On the surface, technology appears to be a blessing to educators and students because it affords almost instantaneous and seemingly limitless access to a universe of information on any conceivable topic. With the click of a few keys, students at Austin High School can explore Greece, tour the Prado museum in Madrid, watch the weather unfold in their neighborhoods, or investigate Elizabethan England. More subject-matter content can be downloaded from a computer disk than can be stored in even the most weighty school textbook. Further, these disks come with animation and audio tracks that traditional books lack (Anderson-Inman & Reinking, 1998). Many students who would be reluctant to open their French books look forward to using the Smart Board in Mrs. Lem-

monier's classroom. Hearing the text and seeing the video clips makes the reading more enjoyable. However, this world of virtual learning, with its universe of information and its audiovisual appeal, raises at least two concerns for teachers.

Assessing Learning Outcomes

How can teachers be confident that student engagement with computers actually fosters deep and enduring understanding? This fundamental concern affects educators working with computer-based technology, even in innovative and well-conceived programs (Alexander & Wade, 2000).

Like the members of the Computer Club at Austin High School, students often come together after school to design Websites, share programs, inventory equipment, repair computers, publish original stories, play games, and chat online (Resnick & Rusk, 1996; Zhao, Mishra, & Girod, 2000). Students who participate in such activities report a sense of heightened engagement and enthusiasm, but program developers infrequently provide clear definitions or specific measures of student learning, even though student learning is among their stated goals (Gallego & Cole, 2000). In some cases developers argue that the hours spent in chat rooms or playing games are themselves valid indicators of learning and achievement (Grosshandler & Grosshandler, 2000).

Mr. Smart and Mr. Smug, the bad and the ugly examples Kim Taber described, might agree with an extremely liberal definition of learning. Maybe they would hold that playing Dune, downloading racy screen savers, or accessing restricted records are signs of learning. However, most educators want more for their investment of time and money. They want to feel secure that their students are acquiring valuable knowledge and skills that will survive when the computer is turned off. Researchers offer two responses to this concern.

Residual Effects of Computer-Based Instruction
One insightful response to this dilemma comes from Salomon, Perkins, and Globerson (1991), who distinguish between the effects *with* and *of* technology. Effects *with* technology include the empowerment afforded students during processing. In this sense the computer technology assists the learner, operating like a more intelligent other in Vygotsky's (1934/1986) zone of proximal development. For example, Manny, a student in Del Torres's Geometry I class, does fairly well on geometric proofs when using a tutoring program, but not yet on his own. Manny's performance with the assistance of this program demonstrates his abilities *with* computer technology (i.e., **assisted effects**).

Salomon et al. (1991) see the effects *of* technology as the **residual effects,** what remains after the technology has been used. Effects *of* include whatever enhanced knowledge or processes students gain from computer-based learning opportunities. Mr. Torres assumes that after using the proofs tutorial for some time, Manny and the other students in his class will understand proofs well enough to make that tutorial program unnecessary. In other words, Mr. Torres is anticipating that residual effects *of* computer technology will emerge. If this anticipated outcome does not occur with time and exposure, then Mr. Torres should question whether the proofs tutorial is serving his educational goals. Similarly, if Mr. Smart or Mr. Smug cannot document residual, positive outcomes from students' downloading provocative screensavers or playing Dune, then they, too, must acknowledge that these activities are not worthwhile.

Alternative Definitions and Measures
Even though both assisted and residual effects of computer-based technologies contribute to student learning, many educators, like Del Torres, focus on the long-lasting, residual effects (Salomon et al., 1991). The problem is that traditional measures of learning do not effectively capture even what students are doing online, much less what remains later (Alexander & Jetton, 2003). Thus, it is hard to know whether internalized knowledge and skills have been acquired or whether students like Manny remain dependent on the assistance the computer provides. The differences in learning with and learning from computers demand that

---

Learner-Centered Psychological Principle 6
Context of learning. Learning is influenced by environmental factors, including culture, technology, and instructional practices.

Learner-Centered Principles Work Group of the APA Board of Educational Affairs, 1997.

---

alternative definitions and measures be developed and used in educational settings (Barab, Fajen, Kulikowich, & Young, 1996).

Despite the complexity of gauging online processing, classroom teachers *can* assess student learning. Teachers should be sure to note the nature and quality of student performance under both assisted and residual conditions (Perkins, 1992). For example, if Mr. Torres wants to see whether the proofs tutorial has enduring effects, he could test his students on proofs before introducing the tutorial program. This would give him baseline information about his students' abilities. Then he could test his students again as they solve the problems with the aid of the tutorial. This would assess their assisted performance. Later in the school term, he could retest the students with similar problems but without the aid of the computer tutorial. This would become his measure of the residual learning effects. With these data in hand, Mr. Torres could make a reasonable decision about whether the proofs tutorial improves student performance while it is being used and whether it fosters enduring change.

Preventing the Erosion of Authority

Online credibility is another nagging problem (Purves, 1998). The computer, which serves as a gateway to untold information, comes with no guarantees that the information it provides has any validity or significance. Anyone—regardless of experience, intention, or bias—can become an author on the Internet. Thus, students can be easily flooded with fragmented, irrelevant, and misleading information (Postman, 1993).

Some researchers relate this flood of questionable online information to an *erosion of authority*—a tendency for students to view everything presented to them with skepticism or apathy (Purves, 1998). According to Bolter (1991):

As long as the printed book remains the primary medium of literature, traditional views of the author as authority and of literature as monument will remain convincing for most readers. The electronic medium, however, threatens to bring down the whole edifice at once. It complicates our understanding of literature as either mimesis or expression, it denies the fixity of the text, and it questions the authority of the author. (p. 153)

Educators must also be concerned about less experienced or novice users, who are more likely to perceive trivia as relevant or important and mistake fictitious, erroneous, or misleading content for accurate information (Alexander, Kulikowich, & Jetton, 1994). Given these two realities, teachers must be prepared to serve as online guides for their students and teach them how to judge the credibility of specific sites or online content.

Guiding Students' Online Journeys In her dealings with colleagues, Kim Taber offers one strategy for preventing students from meandering into unsavory or questionable territory on the World Wide Web. She recommends that teachers provide students with a list of appropriate or helpful Websites for their projects.

Some schools and other public institutions like libraries have gone one step farther. They have installed electronic devices or software that blocks access to questionable Websites (Roblyer, 2001). These devices can block access by keywords (e.g., *breast* or *beer*) or by specific sites (e.g., www.hate.com). Not everyone supports the use of such monitoring devices (Rich, 1996). For example, such software left students in Kristen Marks's health class unable to do online research on breast cancer and sexually transmitted diseases. Some people hold that blocking devices infringe on free speech; others believe that they unduly restrict student access. Still others claim that blocking mechanisms impede students' and teachers' rights to self-regulate.

Whether the monitoring comes from an electronic device or through personal vigilance, teachers remain responsible for the activities of their students during instruction (Westbrook & Kerr, 1996). Therefore, they cannot ignore their role in providing reasonable guidance, as Mr. Smart and Mr. Smug apparently have done.

Teaching About Sourcing and Credibility Regardless of teachers' good intentions and vigilance, they cannot be with students every time they surf the Web. For this reason it seems wise to teach students how to make their own informed and intelligent decisions about online content. Some of the foundational guidelines for judging Internet content come from research on sourcing in history (see Chapter 5; VanSledright & Frankes, 1998; Wineburg, 1991b) and research on persuasion (see Chapter 6; Hynd, Alvermann, & Qian, 1997; Petty & Cacioppo, 1986). Table 12–3 displays several simple suggestions that can be introduced even in the elementary grades when students first begin to use the Internet to locate relevant content or to prepare their own material.

Instructional Novelty/Enduring Pedagogy

Computer-based technologies can carry individuals to places only imagined before (Bereiter & Scardamalia, 1989; Garner & Gillingham, 1998). Jerry Stuart is always surprised at how much rich and relevant information the Web offers on William Shakespeare and Elizabethan England. Virtual libraries of information, more than he could ever hope to physically amass for his students, are only a click away. These technologies can bring educational experiences to people and locations previously cut off from access because of physical and economic constraints (Purves, 1998). How

exciting for students of English literature to interact directly with a Shakespearean scholar from Oxford or to take a virtual tour of the Globe Theatre!

These new technologies can pique students' interest and stimulate their engagement (Zhao et al., 2000). But what happens when Smart Boards become as commonplace as chalkboards or when computers are as abundant as radios or televisions? Computer-based technologies will not always be the educational novelties they are now. Soon, books on psychology in learning and instruction will not need to set aside a separate chapter on technology.

Converting Temporary Interest to Sustained Learning

The novelty of computer-based technologies will eventually wear off. Already new schools, just like new homes, are being constructed with hypermedia technology in mind. However, most schools still need specialists like Kim Taber to infuse these technologies into traditional classrooms. And students still find computer-based instruction a pleasing diversion from traditional modes of teaching and learning (Grosshandler & Grosshandler, 2000).

A question remains about whether students' technological interests lead them to use technology to foster learning or to satisfy more tangential goals (Chipman, 1993). For example, in a critique of after-school computer programs, researchers found that students seemed to prefer playing games, surfing the Web for entertaining content, and sitting in chat rooms creating alter egos (Alexander & Wade, 2000; Bruce & Bruce, 2000). There are two steps that teachers can take to harness students' interest and the potential power of the Internet.

Setting Clear Educational Goals In the dynamic environment of hypermedia learning, students can easily get sidetracked or distracted (Lawless & Kulikowich, 1996). For that reason, students should know from the outset the specific goal or purpose of a lesson or activity (Azevedo, Verona, & Cromley, 2000). They also need to understand how the computer is expected to serve that instructional end. In surfing the Web for scantily clad women or beer ads, Mr. Smart's students have clearly put their personal entertainment at the forefront and have lost any sense of a learning objective, if one ever existed.

In contrast, Antonia Savia's students understand that their online scavenger hunt is not the end but the educational means. That is, the students are clear about why they are playing this enjoyable game and what they are seeking to learn as a consequence. For these students learning is in the foreground, and the computer is just the tool that makes the activity possible, as well as enjoyable (Lajoie, 2000; Mandinach & Cline, 1994). Before they began, Antonia told them that this activity would not only help them learn interesting tidbits about the history, geography, and culture of Spanish-speaking countries, but also allow them to create a catalogue of helpful Websites for future classes.

Building on Meaningful Content Because students can become lost or readily distracted when they surf the Internet and because it is hard for them to distinguish between

Table 12–3   Questions for online authors.

Guiding Question	Explanation
What is the nature of the online site from which this information is drawn?	Students should be sensitive to whether the information comes from a named organization, an institution, or an individual's personal Website.
Is the site or message free of inflammatory, derogatory, or inappropriate content?	As soon as students encounter inappropriate visual or written content, they should block any further access to that site or the messages it contains.
Are the authors specifically identified?	Anonymity on the Internet can be a license to say whatever one wants, regardless of its veracity. Students should, thus, be leery of any content that is not attributed to an author or sponsoring organization.
What are the authors' credentials?	Determining credibility online can be aided by determining the background and experiences of the authors. Do these individuals have the expertise to make their claims or statements?
Are the ideas documented or supported with credible evidence?	It is one thing to make a statement and another thing to support that claim with some form of evidence. Students should always look for substantiation of information and should not accept it on blind faith.
Do the authors have a particular position or viewpoint?	Particular sites or authors can reflect a narrow or biased perspective. Therefore, students should consider whether the authors have a reason to slant their information.
Are alternative arguments or positions addressed?	Balanced authors look at issues or events from multiple perspectives. Is only one side of a topic or issue presented, or are the authors open to a variety of views?
What are the nature and quality of the other sites to which this one is linked?	One way to judge the validity or credibility of a site is to see how it is linked to other sites. Links indicate what the authors perceive as relevant content and viable sources.
Has the same point or issue been raised and supported by others or in alternative ways?	Before students accept an idea or position as credible or factual, they should seek confirmation from other sites or sources. Supporting or confirming information may appear in different forms as well. An idea presented in textual form on one site might correspond with graphic or visual information on another site.

important and trivial content, teachers must model intelligent technology use for their students (Alexander, Kulikowich, & Jetton, 1994). Teachers should discuss their criteria for selecting educational tasks and online content with their students (Garner & Gillingham, 1998). In addition, teachers should help students see the relevance of the task or problem at hand to their learning and their lives (Bransford et al., 1999; Gallego & Cole, 2000).

Lilli Wong helps her students stay focused during computer-based instruction by framing lessons and activities in a broader educational context. She also works as a partner with students in their working groups; she sits with them and thinks through problems with them. And she encourages them to explain what they are doing and thinking. At first the students were a bit nervous having her sit in their groups. However, they now look forward to being the chosen group for the day. The students get to see how Miss Wong weighs issues and evaluates content, and Lilli learns a great deal from the students who are more technologically adept than she is.

Identifying Effective Teaching Approaches

Some researchers see the relative newness of computer-based technologies as advantageous to students and teachers. For example, when students have trouble learning in traditional classrooms with traditional materials like text-

books, the pedagogy and materials used to deliver the content are less frequently seen as the source of the problem. Instead, the onus for performance tends to rest squarely on students' shoulders (Bruce & Hogan, 1998). However, because computer-based technologies are still making their way into schools and classrooms and because educators are less oriented toward technology-enhanced instruction, teachers may look at student problems with technology differently (Tierney & Damarin, 1998). They are more likely to blame problems in student learning and performance on the technologies themselves or on the teachers' attempts to use those technologies (Bruce & Hogan, 1998). This tendency suggests that educators have a unique opportunity to look critically at technology-based education before that technology becomes an invisible part of the instructional equation.

Teachers can ask themselves two basic questions about their instructional approach to computer-based technologies: Have I adjusted my teaching approach to fit with the technology in use? Does the task or lesson benefit from these technological enhancements?

Fitting the Instructional Approach to the Technological Tool   The range of technological tools is quite extensive and their applications very diverse (Derry & Lajoie, 1993). Choosing an appropriate tool is only the first step;

just as important is deciding how to meld that technology into the learning environment to meet the needs of the particular students engaged in a specific task (Leu et al., 1998; Mandinach & Cline, 1994).

Some goals are better met by allowing students to work independently with well-structured, computer-based tutorials (CTGV, 1996). Other ends are better served when groups of students labor together over complex, open-ended problems (Koschmann, Myers, Feltovich, & Barrows, 1994; Young & Barab, 1999). Such decisions cannot be made serendipitously; they should arise from thoughtful reflection.

Teachers must later determine whether the technology adequately fit the lesson (Askov & Bixler, 1998; Lajoie, 1993). Evaluating what worked and what did not work helps teachers make more wise pedagogical decisions in the future. Such reflective practice can go a long way toward harnessing the energy and interests in the classroom, while also achieving critical educational goals.

Benefiting Fully from Technological Enhancements

Advocates of educational technologies often state that the choice of instructional task has much to do with whether student interest and engagement translates into positive learning (Bransford et al., 1999). The more personally relevant or meaningful the task and the more central the content, the more students ultimately gain from their participation in technology-based learning (CTGV, 1997; Rubtsov & Margolis, 1996).

Patsy Dingle, the geography teacher at Austin High School, can help illustrate this point. Last year, when her class studied Africa, Patsy took them to the technology lab to search for information on selected North African countries. She gave each pair of students a list of questions to answer from content in three prechosen Websites. Patsy used this same activity in her other classes without the aid of computers. Instead, she assembled texts and reference materials such as atlases, books, and magazines that contained similar content on the selected countries. This year Patsy presented her students with a more complex and less direct question to answer: How does the geography of Africa contribute to the significant differences between northern and sub-Saharan Africa? For this task students worked in teams of four and were free to use whatever suitable Internet files they wished.

Even though both of Patsy's tasks related to her curriculum and resulted in learning, the second assignment is preferable for study with technology for several reasons. First, Patsy's North Africa task could be completed with or without the computer. Further, it is a rather closed activity, requiring students only to locate, read, and record explicit content—something of an online, fill-in-the-blank test. The comparison task takes fuller advantage of the technology, allowing students to use their resources creatively (Gillingham, Young, & Kulikowich, 1994; Harper, Hedberg, Corderoy, & Wright, 2000). Moreover, because there is no singular or simplistic answer to the comparison question, it requires the students to think critically and to synthesize information from various sources and domains, including geography, politics, history, and economics.

Teachers who wish to build on students' technological skills and interests should carefully consider whether they are using computers as instructional window dressing or are truly tapping their benefits (Chipman, 1993; CTGV, 1997). Simply putting a task on a computer does not make it better, as researchers found when they compared the effects of reading persuasive articles online and in hard copy. Murphy, Long, Holleran, and Esterly (2000) learned that students found the printed version more persuasive, more interesting, and more memorable than the onscreen versions. Thus, computerizing instruction is not always desirable.

Electronic Equalizer/Digital Divider

If futurists are to be believed, the 21st century holds great promise for those who can harness the power of computer-based technologies (Means et al., 1993; Sutton, 1991). But technology can also contribute to the creation of a new underclass (U.S. Department of Commerce, 1995). The more technology becomes an integral component in learning and performance, both in school and out of school, the more concern increases about the growing disparity between the technological haves and have nots (Reinking, 1998).

Such disparity may already exist for individuals of different ages, genders, and social classes (American Association of University Women, 1998) and may have far-reaching consequences, especially if these gaps are allowed to widen (Means et al., 1993). Thus, it becomes essential for educators to explore how to close existing technology gaps and ensure that learner differences do not unfairly penalize women and other underrepresented groups (U.S. Department of Commerce, 1995).

Closing the Technology Gap

The differences between the haves and the have nots in technology have been well documented (Sutton, 1991; U.S. Department of Commerce, 2000). Students attending schools serving poor and mostly minority populations have significantly less access to computer technologies overall than students in richer or nonminority communities (Educational Testing Service, 1998). Even more problematic, students with prior exposure often have the instructional edge in a wired society and a wired classroom (Salomon & Perkins, 1996). Such inequities extend to particular forms of technology as well, including Internet, videodisc and CD-ROM technologies. Educators like Diane Lemmonier are concerned that some students are already falling behind the technology curve— one reason she frequently uses computers in her classroom.

Without equity of access, students—especially those from poor or minority communities—may find themselves locked out of educational and career opportunities that other students can take for granted. Although they are not in a position to wire schools and invest in computer hardware and software, teachers like Diane Lemmonier can prevent the digital divide from widening. Specifically, they can consider grouping arrangements that build on students' existing knowledge and skills, and they can provide explicit online strategy instruction for those less familiar with online processing.

Grouping Techniques   Chapter 11 discussed differing cooperative and collaborative grouping techniques that teachers use to promote learning (Johnson & Johnson, 1999; Sharan, 1994a). Several of the better researched approaches, such as STAD, are based on the thoughtful formation of groups (Slavin, 1990). Educators intentionally distribute high achievers among those of average and low achievement across classroom groups, allowing students to benefit from the knowledge and skills of their peers. This same distribution principle can be applied to technological diversity in classrooms. Thus, teachers can distribute students' technological expertise across groups in the same way they distribute subject-matter expertise.

This pedagogical approach requires teachers to determine what kind of technological knowledge or expertise their students possess (Newsom, 1996; Zhao, 1998). To get at this information, Patsy asks her students to rate their familiarity or ability with various functions and features of technology (e.g., e-mail, Web pages, or PowerPoint). She then refers to this information when creating work groups. Simple survey questions like those in Figure 12–2 can tap relevant technological areas.

Online Processing Instruction   When students are relatively unfamiliar with computer-based technologies, they can benefit from explicit instruction in the processes underlying these technologies (Azevedo et al., 2000; Leu & Reinking, 1996). That instruction should focus on the fundamental mental processes that improve online performance (i.e., strategies). Chapter 7 made clear that effective learning depends on strategic processes, which allow learners to overcome obstacles to optimal performance (Guthrie, 1988). The same is true for online learning. In fact, for students relatively unfamiliar with hypermedia, the need for strategic processing is apt to be great (Alexander, Kulikowich, & Jetton, 1994).

Although research on online strategic processing is only beginning to take shape, several processes should be part of any students' problem-solving repertoire. These processing strategies appear in Table 12–4 and serve three basic purposes: locating, accessing, and applying information (Azevedo, Guthrie, Wang, & Mulhern, 2001; Lawless & Kulikowich, 1996).

Locating strategies, such as orienting and navigating, permit students to situate themselves in the virtual universe of the World Wide Web and to move within that universe in a purposeful and intentional way (Guthrie, 1988; Roblyer, 2001). **Accessing strategies** give students the tools for searching among the innumerable sites (i.e., *isolating*), making intelligent choices (i.e., *sourcing*), and then evaluating the utility and veracity of the information they have found (Alexander, Kulikowich, & Jetton, 1994; Barab et al., 1996). In addition, accessing requires students to control the many resources they find at various sites (i.e., *resourcing*). For example, many sites offer links to related sites that users may want to survey. As discussed later, programmers also create a wide array of online supports, such as audio segments or video clips, vocabulary screens, or auxiliary information (Anderson-Inman, & Reinking, 1998). Learning when to access these resources often distinguishes more and less successful learners (Lawless & Kulikowich, 1996).

Finally, **application strategies** include taking information off the web (i.e., *downloading*) or adding information to it (i.e., *uploading*; Harper, Hedberg, Corderay, & Wright, 2000; Lehrer, 1993). Students must learn various procedures for downloading online content that can be incorporated into class projects or applied to instructional tasks. Students in Jerry Stuart's literature class and Antonia Savia's Spanish course cannot complete their assignments without downloading or uploading online information.

Students need to learn how to become online authors, contributing to the ever-expanding world of the Internet (Garner & Gillingham, 1996; Lehrer, 1993). Whether that authorship involves communicating via e-mail or Web pages or modifying existing online sites, students must have the procedural knowledge, and they must learn to operate in the new

---

How experienced and how interested are you in each of the following?	
MY EXPERIENCE	**MY INTEREST**
Web surfing	*Web surfing*
1 2 3 4 5	1 2 3 4 5
excellent good OK weak poor	excellent good OK weak poor
e-mailing	*e-mailing*
1 2 3 4 5	1 2 3 4 5
excellent good OK weak poor	excellent good OK weak poor
Web page development	*Web page development*
1 2 3 4 5	1 2 3 4 5
excellent good OK weak poor	excellent good OK weak poor

■ **FIGURE 12–2   Simple technology survey.**

Table 12–4   Tools for online learning.

Goal	Process	Definition	Explanation
Locating	Orienting	Situating or locating oneself within the informational Web of the Internet	Even before students try to maneuver within the Web, they must understand how it is configured. By grasping the role of nodes, links, and pages, students can locate themselves more effectively in hyperspace.
	Navigating	Moving from one node or site on the Web to another effectively and efficiently	To benefit from the wealth of information on the Web, students must understand how to travel in virtual space. They need to know how to identify useful sites and how to access them.
Accessing	Isolating	Narrowing the pool of sites to those most likely to provide needed information	Because of the untold number of sites related to any topic, students must be able to set adequate parameters for online searches. They must also learn to scan information on potential sites to make their search time and effort manageable.
	Sourcing	Judging the relevance of suitability of Internet sites and content	Students must scrutinize selected sites thoughtfully and weigh their content for accuracy and bias. Knowing about the source of a site and its content can help students in these deliberations.
	Resourcing	Taking advantage of the supports, associated links, and resources found at select Internet sites	Successful online learners use available resources selectively and purposefully. Students need to learn when and how to use those resources.
Applying	Downloading	Transferring information from selected sites or locations on the Internet	For students one of the values of hypermedia comes in applying the information computers make available. Students must have strategies that allow them to take useful content off line and put it to work for them in alternative forms.
	Uploading	Contributing information or creating nodes and links on the Internet	The Internet allows anyone with the appropriate hardware and software to become an online contributor or author. Students must learn how to be responsible and effective contributors to the World Wide Web.

social environment of the Web. They need to establish criteria for personal communication, just as they develop guidelines for judging the contributions of others (Bolter, 1998).

Creating a Supportive Technology Environment for Girls and Minorities

The digital divide reflects more than varying exposure to computers; it also has to do with how computers are used. The good news for females and minorities is that some of the technological inequities that once existed are less evident because of focused efforts at the federal, state, and local levels (Newsom, 1996; U.S. Department of Commerce, 2000). The bad news is that girls and minorities still do not take full advantage of computer-based technologies.

A recent report by the American Association of University Women's (1998) Educational Foundation raised concerns about differences in how females and males use technology. According to this report, 25% of female high-school students enroll in computer science courses, as compared to 30% of the males. Only 2% of these females take computer application courses, as compared to 6% of their male classmates. Further, females are more likely to use computers for word processing, whereas males engage in

more problem-related activities. The AAUW leadership is concerned about this differential usage and fears that it may leave females less able to compete with males in the career markets of the 21st century. The outcome in their judgment is a virtual ceiling that may hold females back, professionally and economically, in the years to come.

Educators who are determined to create a supportive environment may wish to consider two actions that promote high-quality engagement with technology among females and minorities. The first is to offer training on technological products and processes; the second involves focusing on meaningful problems and academic tasks.

Offering Technological Training   Providing access to computers during class time is simply not enough to ensure that girls and minorities realize the full advantage of modern technologies. Often these learners do not have the detailed knowledge and skills they need to use computer-based technologies effectively and efficiently (Alexander, Kulikowich, & Jetton, 1994). Teachers can assist these students by including explicit technology instruction in content lessons (Bruce & Bruce, 2000). Such explicit instruction can be about various computer programs (e.g., PowerPoint or tutorials), online supports (e.g., video clips), or strategic processes (e.g., navigating techniques). Students in a history class, who are learning about primary and secondary sources might be shown how to locate primary documents online. Students learning about geometric proofs might be taught how to use a specific tutorial program that aids problem solving. In both examples content and online learning can be blended effectively.

Those less familiar with technology may require more out-of-class time to sharpen their skills and deepen their interest in hypermedia (Zhao, 1998). Despite the proliferation of computers, Kim knows that many of Austin High School's students do not have access to computers at home or in their neighborhoods. For that reason, she reserves several lab computers for classwork before and after school hours. She has also worked with the school's librarians to ensure that students can get time on the computers there. Austin has even instituted a computer loaner program that permits families to check out computers for home use.

The goal of increasing before- and after-school access was behind the creation of programs like Kids Learning in Computer Klubhouses, or KLICK! (Garner & Zhao, 2000), Fifth Dimension (Gallego & Cole, 2000), and Project SEARCH (Bruce & Bruce, 2000). KLICK! is a consortium of computer clubhouses across the United States in which students gather to play and work in a technology-rich environment under the supportive guidance of knowledgeable adults (Zhao et al., 2000). Students are given the chance to learn new programs, create their own Web pages, produce newsletters, inventory and repair computers, and create games and tutorials.

The Computer Club at Austin High School follows a similar model. Kim, along with other teachers and students, contributes her time and expertise so that interested students can gain valuable knowledge and increase their interest in technology. Club members inventory, repair, and update donated computers that become part of the school's computer check-out program (Gillingham & Youniss, 2000). The skills and sense of community that students gain from working with computer hardware and their enhanced interest in technology bring them richer opportunities. Similar activities occur in computer clubs nationwide, and many have been shown to benefit females and minorities (Gallego & Cole, 2000; Gillingham & Youniss, 2000).

Focusing on Meaningful Problems and Tasks   Educational researchers and practitioners have found that focusing on the content of computer activities helps to address the technological gender gap. By applying their technology-based instruction to problems of particular importance to females or minorities (Goldman, 1996), teachers are motivating student's who might otherwise not be drawn to technology. These students begin to find the technology invaluable because it helps them address real issues (CTGV, 1990). And as the computer becomes the means rather than the end students develop an abiding interest in technology.

Reston Tepper, who teaches political science at Austin High School, has found that many of his female students are concerned about the environment and many of his African American students are interested in social justice. Reston has used this knowledge to create projects like those suggested by the CTGV, which link the content of his political science course with his students' activism. The students are free to formulate their own projects around local or state issues. One group of students, for instance, is studying environmental initiatives affecting the aquifer that supplies water to their entire region. Another group has taken on the topic of racial profiling. The Internet is the students' link to extensive data on legislation, court cases, and statistics and has allowed them to prepare impressive reports and presentations.

Susan Goldman has been a strong voice for the effective use of computer-based technologies in classroom learning.

Human Connection/Human Isolation

The rapid rise of computer-based technologies in the last several decades has brought about new modes of human communication. Where postal addresses or telephone numbers were once sufficient to locate individuals in the global society, today many also require e-mail addresses, fax numbers, Websites, and cellular phone numbers to mark their place. In addition, through the creation of virtual communities, it is now possible to connect with others from across the globe who share similar interests or concerns (Kerr, 1996). With all of these new avenues of communication, one would expect computer-based technologies to foster increased human contact. Indeed, some evidence supports this expectation (Bereiter, & Scardamalia, 1989; Garner & Gillingham, 1996).

However, intense Internet use may actually heighten feelings of loneliness, depression, and isolation (Granovetter, 1973; Kraut et al., 1998). Some researchers have suggested that when online contact becomes extensive, individuals may disengage from the world around around them (Granovetter, 1973). Others have uncovered an unexpected link between heavy Internet use and growing feelings of social isolation and depression (Heim, 1992). Greater Internet use has also been associated with a decrease in communication and a narrowing of individuals' social circles (Kraut et al., 1998).

Although the reasons are not known for this seeming paradox of connection causing isolation, certain explanations are plausible. For instance, some speculate that weak online friendships substitute for strong, everyday relationships (Granovetter, 1973); students who do not have strong friendships may fill their emptiness with superficial associations in hyperspace. Moreover, without face-to-face contact, it is impossible to know the extent to which online relationships are built on contrived or intentionally misleading information (Heim, 1992). In fact, research on after-school computer programs suggests that students set free to engage in online chats often create false identifies or fictitious life stories (Alexander & Wade, 2000). These students may think they need virtual selves that are more exciting, fulfilling, and desirable than their real selves. But individuals who maintain online associations developed on such unsound or false grounds may feel guilt or remorse or may experience a decline in self-esteem (Kraut et al., 1998). Such feelings may affect intimacy and meaningful friendships.

Getting Meaningfully Connected

Because educators must be as concerned about their students' social and emotional well-being as they are about their academic development (Gresham, 1981), these potential disadvantages must be taken seriously. There are two ways that teachers can promote meaningful online communications in their classrooms.

Combining Direct and Virtual Communication. It appears that communicating via computers in moderation and as a complement to everyday, real-life interactions enhances social connections and mitigates social isolation (Garner & Gillingham, 1996). Thus, it makes sense for teachers to promote direct social contact via computers—contact that involves rich verbal exchanges among students.

In many ways computer technologies can be natural catalysts for direct social interactions in the classroom (Salomon et al., 1991). For instance, classrooms rarely come equipped with enough computers for independent use by all students. Therefore, two or three students usually gather around a computer terminal, working collaboratively on academic tasks. Many technology advocates believe strongly that cooperation and collaboration should be centerpieces of computer-based instruction, precisely because of the shared communication computers stimulate (Bereiter & Scardamalia, 1989; CTGV, 1990). Indeed, shared learning around computer-based technologies seems to foster community among students and lessens students' needs to rely on contrived or superficial online relationships (Brown & Campione, 1990).

Establishing Guidelines for Positive Online Exchanges
Educators know that rules of conduct must be established

Carl Bereiter and Marlene Scardamalia have explored interclassroom communications around culturally rich, complex problems.

for classroom behavior, but they are not as aware that this need pertains to online communications as well. Just as with other realms of human learning and development, students are aided by the sensitive and well-informed guidance of others, like their teachers (Perkins, 1992). Part of that guidance can come from principles for positive online exchanges that teachers and students construct together (Bruce, Peyton, & Batson, 1993; KLICK!, 1998).

Leaders in after-school and out-of-school computer programs worked with students to create the KLICK! handbook (1998), which establishes a Bill of Rights for all participants, as well as a code of ethics. This document guarantees students the right to be treated with dignity and to participate in a well-maintained, safe, and healthy environment. Site coordinators promise to ensure that activities under their control make student welfare a priority. Similar documents can be coconstructed by other teachers and students involved in computer-based learning and can speak directly to their personal responsibilities as well as their collective rights.

To revisit and review the different pedagogical dilemmas considered in this section, try your hand at the Thought Experiment: What's the Problem Here?

Thought Experiment ....

What's the Problem Here?

Directions: Kim Taber regularly meets with Austin High School teachers to discuss the situations that arise in their classrooms. Below are specific questions or concerns these teachers have shared. Try to determine which of the technology dilemmas fits each situation.

Possible Dilemmas

> Virtual reality/Virtual learning
> Instructional novelty/Enduring pedagogy
> Electronic equalizer/Digital divider
> Human connection/Human isolation

1. Jerry Stuart has worked hard to bring technology into his classroom in positive ways. And he has seen positive effects from his effort, for example, improved student projects and reports. However, one of his students, LeShaunda, claims that her project grade was negatively affected because she could not work online from home as her classmates could. Jerry worries that there are other LeShaundas in his classes.
   Problem? _____

2. Mary Celina shares with Kim Taber a concern about the endless hours her ninth graders spend in chat rooms—especially her female students. They talk openly and animatedly about the fake personae they have created for these online chats. Several have even mentioned certain crazy or sick characters they have met in these chat rooms.
   Problem? _____

(continued)

3. Even though her students jump at the chance to work online in her classroom, Patsy Dingle is concerned that this interest is more in the technology than in the academic content. When it comes down to it, Patsy is not sure that students' geography learning is really any better than it used to be when there were no computers in her room.
Problem? _____

4. Greg Picket had an interesting discussion with one of his brighter history students, Marcus Jones. Marcus told Mr. Picket that most of his technology-assisted projects at Austin have been lame. Marcus wanted to know why teachers could not get into real issues that relate to the students' lives instead of the tired and noncreative assignments they always give. Even in history Marcus said he was hoping for something more than the study of dead white men and their white-washed stories.
Problem? _____

5. When Reston Tepper started grading his students' political science projects, he was shocked by what some of his students accepted as factual information (e.g., "There is some evidence that the events of the Holocaust were exaggerated for political reasons") and which Websites they listed as their key sources for the report (e.g., the Drudge Report).
Problem? _____

6. In her meetings with teachers, Kim finds that very few find any need to teach students how to use hypermedia to support their learning. In fact, both the teachers and the students seem to assume that there are really no differences between online learning and traditional print or oral modes of instruction.
Problem? _____

(Answers at the end of the chapter)

How Can Various Technologies Help Individual Students Learn?

Kim's opening scenario spoke of Smart Books, digital cameras, computer labs, videoconferencing facilities, and more—a reminder that the variety of computer-based tools is not only extensive but also expanding by the minute. If teachers are to deliver effective computer-based instruction, they must be able to deal with this vast array of technologies in modern schools.

Computer-based technologies can be classified in a number of ways. For instance, researchers might group them by the manner in which they are assessed. In fact, researchers at Vanderbilt University have used this scheme to overview trends in technology research and practice (see CTGV, 1996). Although it is useful for educators to understand the different ways that researchers assess the effectiveness of technology, few practitioners have the time or inclination for such systematic analysis. An alternative classification scheme considers the instructional purpose of the technology, identifying four types of educational goals.

Computer-Assisted Instruction

Computer-Assisted Instruction (CAI) is a stand-alone system that not only presents content to students but also assesses their performance and provides corrective feedback. CAI supplements teachers' lessons effectively and efficiently by serving as a computerized aide or tutor (Askov & Bixler, 1998). Drill-and-practice exercises that present students with a series of problems or tasks are perhaps the simplest form of CAI (Chipman, 1993). More sophisticated

CAI programs include tutorial programs often designed to approximate expert problem solving (Lajoie, 1993).

Drill and Practice

When technology was first introduced into classrooms, CAI often took the form of drill-and-practice exercises—electronic worksheets (Kerr, 1996). It is easy to understand why drill-and-practice exercises dominated early computer instruction: They were relatively simple to create, easy to use, and not prohibitively expensive (J. R. Anderson, 1991). Drill-and-practice programs remain common and often criticized forms of CAI. Critics portray drill-and-practice as a mindless and ineffective use of sophisticated technologies that targets lower order mental processes (Kerr, 1996). According to these critics, drill-and-practice programs do not really teach; they just deliver questions or problems (Streibel, 1986).

Others find some advantages in CAI. They argue that providing students with opportunities to practice fundamental skills in a nonthreatening setting has merit (U.S. Congress, Office of Technology Assessment, 1993). In fact, reviews have documented some positive learning outcomes for CAI (Hasselbring, Going, & Bransford, 1988; Kulik, Kulik, & Cohen, 1980), although the benefits do come with certain qualifiers.

- CAI works best with younger or less able students.
- Documented gains over traditional instruction tend to be low or modest.
- More structured programs do better than less structured programs.
- Cost effectiveness remains an issue.

It is easy to see how educators could convert some of the worksheets used in cooperative learning into computerized form (see Figure 11–3), allowing for ease of delivery and feedback. In addition, newer versions of drill-and-practice programs are more appealing visually and offer more immediate feedback and detailed record keeping than their predecessors (Askov & Bixler, 1998). When teachers use these exercises in a limited and well-chosen manner, drill and practice can facilitate students' independent practice and meet individual needs (Hasselbring et al., 1988).

Tutorial Systems

Tutorial systems are more advanced forms of CAI. Many of them came out of work in artificial intelligence (AI) and are founded on the assumption that machines can be programmed to model complex human thinking. Thus, they are called intelligent tutoring systems. The goal is to create a nonhuman processor that acts like a knowledgeable and patient human tutor, responding directly to students' questions or reacting to their errors or lack of understanding (Reusser, 1993). Researchers program these expert tutors with extensive content and procedural (i.e., how to) knowledge, as well as the ability to make that knowledge available to others (Derry & Lajoie, 1993).

As one might guess, it takes great skill, time, and money to develop expert tutoring systems. Consequently, many of the most tested systems are not in schools, but are in workplaces supporting complex or sensitive tasks. The Sherlock system, for instance, is a tutoring program that teaches Air Force technicians how to troubleshoot electronic problems in machinery with thousands of parts (Lesgold, Lajoie, Bunzo, & Eggan, 1992). The researchers who worked on the first of these systems determined that 25 hours of Sherlock training is comparable to 4 years of on-the-job instruction. Another expert tutoring system is used in medical diagnosis to help technicians learn to spot potential problems in mammograms. This system poses problems and offers respondents immediate guidance and feedback (Lajoie & Azevedo, 2000).

Tutoring systems are finding their way into schools, especially mathematics and science classrooms. The geometry tutor, for instance, teaches high-school students how to solve geometric proofs (J. R. Anderson, Boyle, & Yost, 1986), and PAT (PUMP Algebra Tutor) tutors students in the fundamentals of algebra (Koedinger, Anderson, Hadley, & Mark, 1997). Like their human counterparts, these computer tutors provide scaffolding that might not be available from peers. The developers of these intelligent tutoring systems report impressive results from their use. In studies of the geometry tutor, for example, students in an urban high school had marked increases in their interest in geometry and their feelings of self-competence (Wertheimer, 1990). Similarly, urban high-school students who used PAT along with their regular algebra curriculum gained impressively on a number of algebra and problem-solving measures (Koedinger et al., 1997).

However, such glowing reports need to be carefully considered. The computer tutor supplements instruction delivered by well-trained teachers—but does not substitute for it (Chipman, 1993). Also, these computer tutoring systems are much more useful in well-structured and procedurally rich domains, like geometry, algebra, or physics. They are less useful in fields like literature, history, or psychology, where tasks are fuzzier and are less driven by specific formulas and procedures (Wineburg, 1991a).

Educational Implications

Human and computer tutors offer decided advantages (Derry & Lajoie, 1993; Salomon, 1993b). Table 12–5 contrasts the two on a number of characteristics. Before someone like Kim Taber would invest in expert tutoring systems, she and her fellow teachers should weigh the pros and cons carefully. That is, they should consider how well human tutors or computerized tutors can assess the knowledge and emotional reactions of students. Teachers need to decide whether the almost continuous diagnosis, feedback, and record keeping of these tutorial systems adequately compensate for their lack of pedagogical flexibility, authoritativeness, and emotional responsiveness.

Computer-Mediated Communication

Computer-mediated communication (CMC) is another class of technology that has altered teaching and learning. With CMC individual computers are networked, linking students and teachers to human and nonhuman resources outside the classroom (Walther & Tidwell, 1996). The key to CMC is the Internet and supporting systems. Through the Internet students can engage in e-mailing and videoconferencing, or they can participate in Web-based, Web-enhanced, or distance learning courses (Bransford et al., 1999). In particular, three forms of CMC are available in wired schools like Austin High School: synchronous, asynchronous, and mixed communication.

Synchronous Communication

Synchronous CMC allows individuals to exchange information or thoughts in real time (Beach & Lundell, 1998). For example, videoconferencing allowed Lilli Wong's students to chat online with the authors of books they were reading; both the authors and the students had immediate visual and verbal access to one another. Lilli also uses online journaling in her literature classes. After completing assigned readings, students sign into a designated chat room, where they can freely and anonymously share their reactions and responses spontaneously and simultaneously. Only Lilli knows which students have posted which messages. She uses this approach to allow less assertive students to take the floor in class. Consistent with research studies (Schallert et al., 1996), Lilli finds that students open up in these chat rooms in a different way than they do in traditional class discussions. Perhaps students are less fearful of peer reaction or ridicule when online.

Overall, data on CMC have been positive. Videoconferencing brings needed expertise into learning environments

Table 12–5   A critical look at human and computer tutors.

Function	Human	Computer
Diagnosis	Builds on overt student responses, subtle physical and emotional reactions, and explanations; relies on performance expectations and error detection skills	Based on prototypic analysis of correct or incorrect responses; organized around detailed knowledge of naive and expert response patterns
Attention	Can waver; tends to focus on only a few performance elements at a given time	Is consistent; can examine multiple factors or elements simultaneously
Feedback	Can be spontaneous and personal; may vary in frequency and quality	Occurs according to a fixed schedule; delivers preset comments and may seem canned
Motivation	Depends on the willing engagement of tutor and tutee; presents opportunities for positive and negative emotional reactions	Can motivate with initial novelty; provides no physical or direct emotional support
Record Keeping	May require additional time and attention from the tutor	Can generate continuous records automatically
Credibility	Depends on personal characteristics of the tutor	Has no authority or emotional connection
Delivery	Can have flexible teaching approaches or models	Relies on an established written text and set programming parameters
Content	Represents a combination of formal training and everyday common sense	Constructed around expert models that rely solely on formal knowledge and procedures

and stimulates students to explore topics in depth (Baym, 1995). And researchers find that online journaling improves literacy skills and fosters student engagement in academic activities (Jackson, 1992; Staton, Shuy, Peyton, & Reed, 1988).

Asynchronous Communication

Asynchronous CMC also exchanges information, but not in real time (Beach & Lundell, 1998). One of the services instituted at Austin High School, for example, is a school Website. Links on this Website allow teachers to post daily assignments or notes about upcoming classroom activities, which parents and students can then access at their leisure. Also, by logging onto the Website, parents and students can contact any teacher at Austin via a personal e-mail if they want more information or have questions. Kim Taber works with the students in the Computer Club to maintain the school's Website.

In addition, both the students and the teachers at Austin take advantage of the Internet and its nearly limitless information. During their scavenger hunt, for example, Antonia Savia's students uncovered specific historical facts about select countries in Central and South America, located menus from restaurants in Mexico City, and found maps written in Spanish for the Prado Museum in Madrid. Even though similar searches could have been conducted in the absence of computer technology, the Internet allowed Antonia's class to perform these tasks in their own classroom with an ease and speed of access unmatched in the print world (Bereiter & Scardamalia, 1989).

Mixed Approaches

Web-based, Web-enhanced, or distance learning courses often incorporate both synchronous and asynchronous elements—thus, they are **mixed approaches.** Although all of these forms of mixed communication depend on computers to some extent, they are distinguished by their differing degrees of reliance on that technology.

For example, **web-based** courses are online offerings that require no face-to-face contact between teachers and students (CTGV, 1996). **Web-enhanced** courses, by comparison, often involve some traditional class time. At Vanderbilt University, for instance, John Bransford offers a course on How People Learn (Bransford et al., 1999). Most of his interactions with his undergraduate students take place over the Internet, although they have periodic face-to-face class meetings.

The oldest form of computer-based instruction is distance learning. With **distance learning** the instructor and the students might have established class meetings, but the instructor may be in a room hundreds of miles away (Barker, Frisbie, & Patrick, 1989). Their exchanges are aided by technology that gives them both audio and visual access to one another. In some cases an on-site facilitator works with student groups, or the instructor may periodically travel to the students' location. For the most part, distance learning courses rely heavily on recitation models (see Chapter 11), in which the teacher delivers content to students at multiple sites with limited student engagement (Moore, 1989). Researchers are critical of distance learning

(Garner & Gillingham, 1998; Walther, & Tidwell, 1996), but it is just as good as classroom instruction that relies predominante on recitation (Moore, 1989).

The number of CMC courses is growing exponentially, prompted by an increased ease of development, accessibility, and cost efficiency (Beach & Lundell, 1998). Almost every university in this country and abroad offers some coursework of this type. State education agencies and local school districts are joining in the Web-based course movement as well. Catalysts for Web-course development in K–12 institutions include teacher preparation needs; teacher shortages, especially in science, mathematics, and second-language learning; and increased student diversity (Means et al., 1993).

Educational Implications

Several of the promises and pitfalls of CMC are outlined in Table 12–6. For instance, researchers have found that synchronous forms of CMC allow less vocal students to find their voice (Schallert et al., 1996; Staton et al., 1988), although the potential anonymity may lead to less realistic or less authentic exchanges (Purves, 1998). Further, with synchronous communication students are free to express themselves without some of the social or peer constraints they face in traditional classroom exchanges. However, lifting these social constraints can also open the door to unwanted or inappropriate remarks that cannot be easily screened or filtered (Kraut et al., 1998).

With asynchronous CMC students and teachers are free to send or receive messages at any time to or from any spot on the globe (Bereiter & Scardamalia, 1989). A possible downside is that individuals, including students in classrooms, can find themselves flooded with irrelevant messages of questionable veracity. In addition, online communications come without the vocal intonations, facial expressions, and body language that enrich vocal or direct human exchanges (Derry & Lajoie, 1993).

The potential benefits of Web-based, Web-enhanced, or distance learning courses are easy to recognize. Technology-based courses put content or expert teachers in reach of those who otherwise might not have access to them (Streibel, 1986). Some online courses also permit students to work at their own pace, and the delivery system is cost-efficient. It can put one person in contact with large numbers of students scattered across the city, state, or globe (Bereiter & Scardamalia, 1989). However, data are limited on the overall effectiveness of such courses in comparison to more traditional instructional models (CTGV, 1996). In addition, less self-regulating students can get lost in this virtual classroom, to say nothing about the potential for feelings of social disconnectedness (Alexander, Kulikowich, & Jetton, 1994).

Educators must consider all of these pluses and minuses if they are to integrate the various forms of CMC into learning environments. No one can ensure that all pitfalls will be avoided, but teachers are able to decrease their occurrence and lessen their impact. Just as Kim reminds the uncooperative Mr. Smart, teachers must be vigilant about the use of technology in the classroom, and they must not exacerbate technology's shortcomings.

Computer-Integrated Instruction

Computer-integrated instruction (CII) puts students into a virtual problem-solving environment. Two forms of CII finding their way into schools are simulations and microworlds. This educational technology allows Diane Lemmonier's French class to travel to a virtual café on the

Table 12–6	Promises and pitfalls of CMC formats.	
Form	**Promises**	**Pitfalls**
Synchronous Exchanges	Allow less assertive or vocal students to take the floor at any time	Could result in less linear or coherent exchange of ideas
	May promote less constrained sharing, especially when participants' identities are masked	May open the door to less authentic or honest exchanges
Asynchronous Exchanges	Permit individuals to send or receive messages at any time and any place	Create the possibility of unwanted or irrelevant information
	Open the classroom to exchanges with individuals from diverse regions and backgrounds	May integrate exchanges devoid of vocal and nonverbal indicators of affect or emotion
Web-Based or Web-Enhanced Courses	Bring content or expertise to those who might not otherwise have access	Lose the advantages that come from direct human-to-human contact
	Let instruction be self-paced to some extent	May give less self-regulated students more problems staying motivated and engaged
	Can be a cost-effective way to deliver instruction	Have less evidence of cognitive and affective advantage over traditional courses

Rue de la Seine, Nassem Assad's science class to see the climatic effects of deforestation, and Del Torres's geometry class to apply their learning to real-world problems.

Simulations

Computer simulations are programs that model real-world problem-solving situations and contexts (Chipman, 1993; Lesgold, 2000). Educational simulations are basically computer-generated experiential contexts in which students can become immersed (Harper et al., 2000). Students are encouraged to think and operate within that virtual environment as they engage in complex tasks, often in cooperative or collaboration groups.

Simulations have been important learning tools outside the classroom for years; they have been widely used in areas where real environments or actual problems are dangerous or inaccessible (Askov & Bixler, 1998). For instance, astronauts experience hundreds of hours of simulation training in preparation for their missions. And many other professionals who perform highly intricate, messy, or dangerous tasks—such as police, firefighters, pilots, and medical personnel—rely on simulations to model the conditions and contexts they will likely experience. Simulations can also illustrate how particular situations may unfold over time if certain actions or conditions occur (Swaak & de Jong, 1996). For example, the spread of infectious agents, like particular strands of flu virus, can be simulated via computer technology. The environmental effects of global warming or the traffic patterns resulting from housing or industrial developments can also be simulated and studied before they actually happen.

Ton de Jong is an expert in simulation learning.

Even though simulations are far less frequently used in schools, they are found there (Lajoie, 2000). Existing simulations allow students to explore changes in the Amazon rain forest, create new animals, or study a village as it evolves into a city (National Geographic Society, 1991; Salisbury, 1995). As technologies advance, so does the sophistication of educational simulations. For example, Exploring the Nardoo is a simulation designed to allow high school students to explore the relationship between living organisms and the geographic, physical, and chemical environments in which they exist (Harper et al., 2000). By means of simulations, students can tackle complex problems like the one shown in Figure 12–3.

To assist them in their ecological problem solving, students using the Nardoo simulation have access to extensive amounts of data and visual and graphic resources like the Water Research Centre. At the Centre students can examine a book containing descriptions of plant and animal life in or around the Nardoo River. They can replay television and radio shows, read newspaper stories, or examine technical reports housed in the Centre. All of these technological tools support the students as they investigate and solve the problems before them.

Water Plants and Weeds

Hugh Smythe captains a riverboat that ferries passengers up and down the Nardoo River. As the river is the key to his livelihood, he has become concerned about the rampant growth of weeds and willows that have begun to obstruct parts of the river in recent months.

Your task: Investigate the extent to which the river is affected by the weed and willow growth. Keep a journal of the information that you find and try to reorganize your information to clearly recount the history of the weed problem.

■ **FIGURE 12–3   A sample simulation problem.**

Note: From "Employing Cognitive Tools Within Interactive Multimedia Applications" by B. Harper, J. Hedberg, B. Corderoy, and R. Wright in S. P. Lajoie (Ed.), *Computers as Cognitive Tools: No More Walls*, (p. 233), 2000, Mahwah, NJ: Lawrence Erlbaum. Copyright 2000 by Lawrence Erlbaum. Reprinted with permission.

Microworlds

Seymour Papert (1980), one of the creative minds in modern educational technology, coined the term **microworlds,** which are similar to simulations in presenting students with rich problems to explore via the computer (Askov & Bixler, 1998). In Papert's Logo microworlds, students' attempts to make two turtles perform particular functions in their computer-created environment are the catalyst for learning basic physics principles. Another microworld helps students learn geometry as they locate and design a bridge in an urban area (Salisbury, 1995).

Although some use the terms *simulations* and *microworlds* interchangeably, educational technologists see important distinctions between them. Microworlds are less extensive environments than simulations and typically focus on well-defined principles or rules that experts see as central to particular domains, such as science or mathematics

Seymour Papert

(Rieber, 1992). Thus, instead of creating a virtual ecological community along a river basin as in Nardoo, a microworld would target specific principles of ecology that students must use in problem solving. In addition, microworlds are generally designed so that students can enter the program at a point appropriate to their knowledge or ability level (Rieber, 1993). In other words, the microworld adapts to its user. By comparison, most simulations have no such adaptive function but require the user to adapt to the demands of the simulation (Askov & Bixler, 1998).

Educational Implications

Proponents of CII see many educational benefits in these new technologies (Rieber, 1993; Swaak & de Jong, 1996). Among the benefits, which are summarized in Table 12–7, is the potential for students to experience people, places, and events that would not otherwise be available to them (CTGV, 1996). A few of Diane Lemmonier's students may actually travel to France and walk along the Rue de la Seine, but none of Nassem Assad's students are apt to have the opportunity to study the effects of deforestation along the Amazon River.

In addition, when problems are cast in a resource-rich setting that students can control themselves, they have many opportunities to become actively engaged in the tasks at hand (Lesgold, 2000). It also helps that the problems that frame many of these CII programs mirror those in the world outside the classroom (Harper et al., 2000). Thus, strategies for locating, analyzing, and reporting data are not taught in isolation but become meaningfully linked to the resolution of a particular problem, like controlling the spread of an infectious agent (Bransford et al., 1999).

Further, CII can be a catalyst for cross-disciplinary studies in schools (CTGV, 1997) because the extensive problems these programs pose can rarely be explored deeply or effectively without bringing multiple subject areas together. For example, the Nardoo simulation addresses geography and ecology (Harper et al., 2000), and Bio-World combines biology and mathematics (Lajoie & Azevedo, 2000). The more complex the problems these simulations and microworlds tackle, the greater the possibility for content integration. When done well, CII programs help students see how certain conditions and factors give rise to specific consequences (Papert, 1980). Cause-and-effect relation can come to life in these technological learning environments to a degree not possible in more traditional educational contexts.

But educational researchers and practitioners perceive some problems and shortcomings with CII, too (Azevedo et al., 2001). For one thing teachers cannot simply put students and simulations together and expect outstanding results (Kerr, 1996). Although the data on the educational effectiveness of CII remain limited, positive outcomes are more likely when teachers are well versed in their content and are also technologically competent (Askov & Bixler, 1998; Chipman, 1993). These can be complex programs, which are often costly and time-consuming (Lesgold, 2000). In addition, evidence shows that students gain more from CII when teachers reinforce central content and provide explicit instruction in relevant strategies (Rieber, 1992).

Roger Azevedo looks at the benefits of computer-integrated instruction.

The best outcomes for CII have been reported in those contexts where this mode of learning is infused in the school environment and is well supported by teachers and school administration (CTGV, 1997; Lesgold, 2000). The Schools for Thought project offers a prime example of just such a fully integrated CII application (Bruer, 1993). Schools for Thought was intended to restructure the entire learning environment for middle-school students in different cities across the country. The participating schools and classrooms were reframed around highly student-centered

Table 12–7 The pros and cons of computer-integrated instruction.

Academic Asset	Curricular Concern
Lets students have experiences that might not otherwise be available to them	Requires a teacher who is not only technologically able but also knowledgeable in relevant subject-matter areas
Actively involves students in the learning process	Can be costly to purchase and maintain programs and equipment
Situates academic knowledge and skills in the context of real-world problem solving	Requires an extensive amount of instructional time to pursue problems deeply and fully
Links various subject-matter areas	Is supported by limited data on the overall academic effectiveness of these forms of hypermedia
Offers opportunities to hone problem-solving strategies in a more student-controlled approach	Functions best with complementary instruction on content and strategies
Can reinforce cause-effect relation not evident in traditional instructional approaches	Functions best when simulations and microworlds are fully integrated into the overall school environment

and problem-based learning in which technology was a centerpiece. The classrooms were also networked so that ideas and programs could be shared. Thus, students in Nashville, Tennessee, tackling questions of local water purification, could be linked to middle-school students in Berkeley, California, who were collectively investigating contaminants in the local water supply. At the same time, students in Ontario, Canada, could be discussing the effect of industrialization in their region on the overall ecology. Not only do students in various classrooms in the same school gather, discuss, and synthesize data, but they also share their new understandings and ideas with students at other sites (Bereiter & Scardamalia, 1989).

As this example illustrates, schoolwide investments in computer-integrated approaches involve time, money, and personnel. Schools for Thought and similar computer-integrated projects have been conceived and maintained by some of the best minds in educational research and have been funded by research grants. Whether similar or scaled-down models of these CII projects could prove successful in Austin High School or other wired school communities remains to be demonstrated (Chipman, 1993; Mandinach & Cline, 2000).

Computer-Adaptive Instruction

Computer-Adaptive Instruction (CADI) uses technologies to assist learners with special needs (Hornbeck, 1990; Horney & Anderson-Inman, 1995). The adaptations that computers can offer teachers and students can be quite extensive. For example, Stephen Hawking, one of the greatest scientific minds of the 20th century, suffers from Lou Gehrig's disease, which causes progressive deterioration of the nervous system. Hawking's disease has progressed to the point that he can no longer move most of his muscles, not even his vocal chords. Yet his mind remains sharp. Hawking now spends much of his day in a specially equipped computerized wheelchair that allows him to speak through a computer activated by eye movements. Thus, he can still give lectures and hold meetings because of these advancements.

Technology also assists students with special needs (Anderson-Inman & Horney, 1998; Mansoor, 1993), such as those with psychomotor problems, visual difficulties, or hearing impairments (MacArthur & Haynes, 1995; Prinz, 1991). Devon Jones, a student at Austin High School, has motor problems that make it hard for him to write, but he still dreams of being a sports writer. To compensate for his problem, Devon takes a small laptop computer to classes and uses the modified keyboard to take notes and write papers. Max Martin is a visually impaired student who uses a computerized pen to convert text into spoken words and an electronic keypad to take notes in braille. Mimi Valencia is a hearing-impaired student whose teachers use a special microphone during instruction to augment their voices. This microphone transmits directly to computerized earphones that Mimi wears.

Computer-Adaptive Testing

Computer assistance is available for students who cannot perform well under traditional high-stakes testing conditions or who have specific reading problems (Mansoor, 1993). Computer-adaptive testing has been in use for years (Snow, Corno, & Jackson, 1996), and more and more high-school and college students now take tests like the Scholastic Aptitude Test online. Thus, students who suffer from test anxiety or have certain learning problems can benefit from controlled, private, or adapted settings (Snow et al., 1996).

Adaptations in testing can involve more than just the setting, however. Adaptive tests can also individualize questioning for students (MacArthur & Haynes, 1995). Depending on how well a student responds to a set of items, the computer can immediately adjust, presenting easier or harder questions (C. R. Reynolds, 1994). Such computer-adaptive testing is already used for high-stakes or highly specialized testing but requires more money and expertise than most teachers or school districts have available. Instead, educators must learn how to make their own adaptations in student assessment with assistance from computer technology in delivery and record keeping (Prinz, 1991).

Supportive Texts

Supportive texts are another form of CADI; they are electronically enhanced versions of traditional text (Anderson-Inman & Reinking, 1998). The enhancements support the reading and learning of students who might not perform as well when texts are presented in their normal, unembellished format (Anderson-Inman & Horney, 1998). Supportive texts do much more than display pages on a computer screen, they include an array of auditory and visual tools, as well as auxiliary information. For example, a video can run on a split screen, displaying an American Sign Language translation of either oral or written text (Hornbeck, 1990). Another option might allow students to click on marked words in the text to hear those words pronounced or to have them defined. Some supportive texts have also been developed with strategic cues that prompt students to apply appropriate cognitive or self-regulatory strategies (Lawless & Kulikowich, 1996).

David Reinking's research focuses on the role of technology in literacy learning.

In addition, some supportive texts allow students to go beyond the text when they require help comprehending. This help can come in the form of supplementary materials, such as background information, reference materials, graphic displays, or summary statements (Azevedo et al., 2001). Instructional resources can also include follow-up examples, guiding questions, and notational resources (MacArthur & Haynes, 1995). Moreover, minilessons may be wrapped into the text to reinforce key concepts and to offer students opportunities to practice what they are learning (Young & Barab, 1999). An example of supportive text is shown in Figure 12–4.

Educational Implications

Various researchers have reported positive outcomes for these hypermedia alternatives for at-risk readers, which include learning disabled, visually or hearing-impaired, or second-language learners (Horney & Anderson-Inman, 1995). At the

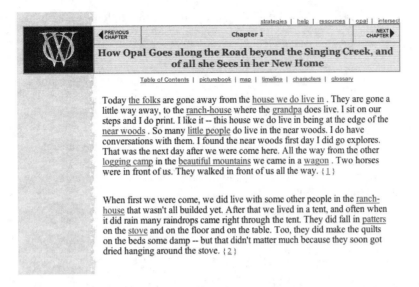

■ FIGURE 12–4   Sample of a supportive text.

Note: From *The Diary of Opal Whiteley*. First published in the Atlantic Monthly Magazine in 1920. This digital edition is part of the Intersect Digital Library, 2001. http://intersect.uoregon.edu/opal/Action.lasso?-database=opal&-layout=standard&-op=eq&pg5=1&-response=format/opal5fmt. html&maxRecords=100&-noresultserror=isp/sorry.html&-search

Center for Electronic Studying at the University of Oregon, middle-school students considered at risk often showed improved comprehension and motivation when working with supportive versus traditional texts (Anderson-Inman & Horney, 1998). However, these benefits were not universal and depended on whether students took appropriate advantage of these resources (Lawless & Kulikowich, 1996).

Students who make the most of computerized supports have some level of knowledge, interest, and strategic ability (Alexander, Kulikowich, & Jetton, 1994), along with defined goals for learning or performing well (Azevedo et al., 2001).

Teachers cannot just place these electronic resources in front of students and assume that optimal learning will result (Chipman, 1993). Instead, students need to be taught how to make intelligent use of them. By modeling how to apply these tools, teachers can increase the likelihood of their being well used and, thus, educationally valuable (Mandinach & Cline, 2000).

The Thought Experiment: Making Wise Technological Choices includes brief descriptions of instructional situations for which Kim Taber recommended a particular classification of technology. See whether you can determine what she recommended.

Thought Experiment ....

Making Wise Technological Choices

Directions: Kim Taber is frequently called upon to help teachers select technological options to fit particular instructional conditions. See whether you can determine which category of hypermedia technology Kim recommended for each of these situations.

_____ 1.   Betsy Chambers must deal with great diversity in her creative writing class. Several students have wonderful imaginations, but their mechanics—especially their spelling ability—are atrocious. To make matters worse, their handwriting is so bad that it is hard to know what these creative students have written until they read their papers aloud. Is there anything that can help these special students?

_____ 2.   Fort Bend School District, which includes Austin High School, wants to find a way to serve highly gifted mathematics students. To date, there are 8 students distributed across the three high schools who qualify for college-level course work in mathematics, but there is no way for them to attend a college or university in the area. What approach makes sense?

_____ 3.   Campbell Finch has to stay home for at least 4 weeks because of a highly infectious illness that requires quarantine. Campbell needs to stay up with his studies because he is being considered for several academic scholarships. Is there some way that Linda Hoffman, Austin's itinerant teacher, can connect with Campbell and assist him with his classwork for the next 4 weeks?

a. Computer-assisted instruction

b. Computer-mediated communication

c. Computer-integrated instruction

d. Computer-adaptive instruction

(continued)

_____ 4. Greg Picket, the history teacher, is worried about a number of his students who cannot manage their textbook. They struggle to get the ideas and are losing ground as a result. What can be done to help these students get more out of their readings?

_____ 5. Several of the science and mathematics teachers at Austin would like to learn more about problem-based programs like those talked about in Schools for Thought. Kim does not feel equipped to help but knows of some experts who have the information her teachers need. But these experts are halfway across the country and cannot travel to Austin to meet face-to-face with the teachers. What can they do?

_____ 6. Del Torres finds that proofs are very tough for some of his geometry students to master. He has tried peer tutoring to provide the extra help these students need, but the peers do not have the level of skill that the strugglers require. Del cannot tutor these students himself. What other options are there for his students?

_____ 7. Some of the experiments that Sasha O'Malley would like to conduct with her chemistry students are too expensive and too dangerous. What can she do?

(Answers at the end of the chapter)

What Principles Underlie Optimal Learning in a Technologically Rich Society?

Whether teachers settle on assisted, mediated, integrated, or adaptive technologies, they must adhere to fundamental psychological principles that remain consistent across the categories. There are four principles, well supported by empirical research. Some principles are used as general guidelines that should be evident in all educational environments. As illustrated in Figure 12–5, these principles build directly on the key components of effective technology use that were introduced earlier.

Conceptualize Technology as a Tool

For all their promises and perils, computer-based technologies are nothing more than tools for teaching and learning (Lajoie, 2000; Lajoie & Derry, 1993). Those who portray computer-based technologies as a panacea for education or conceive of them as the devil incarnate have lost sight of this most fundamental notion (Cuban, 1986). Like tools computer-based technologies have no intrinsic value (Salomon, 1993b) but attain value from the services they provide. Like pencils, automobiles, or microwave ovens, computers sit inactive and powerless until humans give them life. If computers are to be valuable in educational settings, experienced teachers and their students must implement these tools effectively. Computers can be good tools when they serve student learning and development or when they enhance teachers' abilities to serve their students better (Lesgold, 1993).

Of course, the better the tool, the more impressive or creative the products and services that may result (CTGV, 1996). But what makes a good computer tool? Salomon (1993b) suggests one valuable criterion for evaluating a computer tool: Does it upgrade students' thinking? Quality computer tools promote better, deeper, or richer thinking among students (Bransford et al., 1999; CTGV, 1997). They should aid students in their own mental operations but should not do all the processing, conceptualizing, or manipulating for the students. This principle holds true whether the tool is a drill-and-practice program for a mathematics class or a supportive text for students learning English (Askov & Bixler, 1998; Horney & Anderson-Inman, 1995).

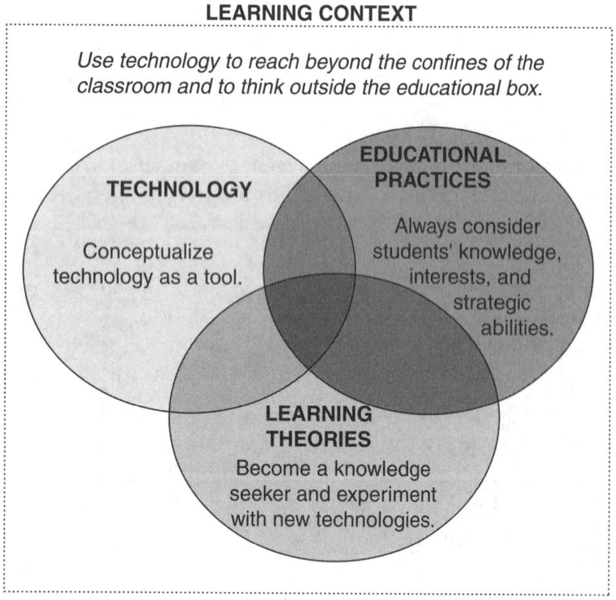

LEARNING CONTEXT

Use technology to reach beyond the confines of the classroom and to think outside the educational box.

TECHNOLOGY
Conceptualize technology as a tool.

EDUCATIONAL PRACTICES
Always consider students' knowledge, interests, and strategic abilities.

LEARNING THEORIES
Become a knowledge seeker and experiment with new technologies.

■ **FIGURE 12–5   Four principles for technology-based education.**

It is not the computer that should be doing the diagnosing, the goal-setting, and the planning, it is the student.

M. Scardamalia, C. Bereiter, R. S. McLean, J. Swallow, and E. Woodruff, 1989.

Always Consider Students' Knowledge, Interests, and Strategic Abilities

When Alexander and colleagues analyzed the research on learning with computer-based technologies (Alexander, Kulikowich, & Jetton, 1994), it became apparent that some base of relevant knowledge, interest, and strategic ability was requisite to positive outcomes. However, it was also evident that researchers often either assumed that these requisites were in place or focused on advanced populations. But teachers are responsible for providing the best possible guidance to *all* students, many of whom come into the classroom lacking the background knowledge, interest, or skills needed to navigate the complex world of the Internet (Resnick & Rusk, 1996; Zhao, 1998) or to learn in the world of hypermedia (Reinking, 1998). Thus, teachers must first gauge students' underlying knowledge, interest, and abilities and then take whatever steps are necessary to shore up those fundamentals.

Jonna Kulikowich, along with Kim Lawless, investigates students' computer-based strategies.

Educators should teach students techniques for assessing the nature and validity of the flood of information they will encounter online (Murphy, Long, Holleran, & Esterly, 2000). Studies in text processing and written communication that examine text structure, main ideas, persuasion, and argument can prove helpful (Goldman, 1996; Lawless & Kulikowich, 1996). Also helpful is the research from history, library sciences, and social psychology that speaks to the source and validity of documents (VanSledright & Frankes, 1998) as well as to author credibility (Lehrer, 1993). The bottom line, however, is that these basic concepts must be explicitly taught, rather than left to be discovered.

Educators should also explicitly instruct students about how to navigate and search hypermedia (Azevedo et al., 2001). Educators should demonstrate procedures for locating pertinent information sources online and identifying relevant, accurate, and important content within those sources (Alexander & Jetton, 2000). Research on text searches could serve as a starting point for these lessons (Guthrie, 1988), although teachers will want to extend and modify the suggested techniques based on the technologies and tasks they choose.

Beyond the general background knowledge that students may or may not possess, they also need to acquire basic knowledge about computer-based technologies. Organizations like the International Society for Technology Education (1998) have established standards for students in grades K–12, which can serve as a starting point (see Figure 12–6). With the assistance of knowledgeable colleagues and a supportive school administration, teachers must work to ensure that all students acquire these competencies, regardless of their gender or socioeconomic background (Sutton, 1991).

Student interest is another key component of this effort to maximize technological learning experiences. Teachers

---

Basic operations and concepts

- Students demonstrate a sound understanding of the nature and operation of technology systems.
- Students are proficient in the use of technology.

Social, ethical, and human issues

- Students understand the ethical, cultural, and societal issues related to technology.
- Students practice responsible use of technology systems, information, and software.

Technology productivity tools

- Students use technology tools to enhance learning, increase productivity, and promote creativity.
- Students use productivity tools to collaborate in constructing technology-related models, preparing publications, and producing other creative works.

Technology communication tools

- Students use telecommunications to collaborate, publish, and interact with peers, experts, and other audiences.
- Students use a variety of media and formats to communicate information and ideas effectively to multiple audiences.

Technology research tools

- Students use technology to locate, evaluate, and collect information from a variety of sources.
- Students use technology tools to process data and report results.
- Students evaluate and select new information resources and technological innovations based on the appropriateness to specific tasks.

Technology problem-solving and decision-making tools

- Students use technology resources for solving problems and making informed decisions.
- Students employ technology in the development of strategies for solving problems in the real world.

■ FIGURE 12–6   Technology standards for all students.

Note: From *National Educational Technology Standards* by International Society for Technology Education, 1998, retrieved from http://cnets.iste.org/index

---

should be prepared to support students' technological interests and creativity, allowing them to pursue related topics or to employ technology in projects and assignments. For example, Mr. Stuart encourages his students to present their class projects using computers, and he permits students with special needs to bring their laptops to his class to take notes or complete their exams. He has also found that allowing students to compose and edit on computers improves their writing; the research on writing and literacy development is in agreement with his experience (Kamil & Lane, 1998; Lemke, 1998).

These technological ventures are natural opportunities for problem solving and for student cooperation and collaboration. Indeed, several collaborative approaches, such as jigsaw (Brown & Campione, 1990) and computer-supported international learning environment (Scardamalia et al., 1989), rely on computer-based technologies to enhance students' research and presentation of selected topics and to create virtual learning communities. By encouraging students to explore the benefits of computer-based technologies independently, teachers can build on their interests and curiosity (Rubtsov & Margolis, 1996).

Become a Knowledge Seeker and Experiment with New Technologies

Researchers report a striking contradiction between the growing presence of computers in everyday life and teachers' limited use of computer-based technologies in their classrooms (Leu et al., 1998). Although various circumstances contribute to this dilemma, including a lack of appropriate software and competing instructional initiatives, teacher preparation remains a defining factor (Kinzer & Risko, 1998). Preservice teacher education currently offers little explicit instruction on the effective application of computer-based technologies (Garner & Gillingham, 1998). Further, those teaching preservice courses infrequently employ computer-based technologies in the delivery of their course content (Kinzer & Risko, 1998). As a result, students in these classes do not have the creative and effective technology models they need and deserve.

If teachers are to guide students effectively in a postindustrial society, they must become technological learners themselves. They must seek professional opportunities to expand their knowledge of computer-based technologies and must then include these technologies in their instructional programs (Kerr, 1996). In studying six teachers' attempts to integrate technology into their classrooms, Garner and Gillingham (1998) witnessed much positive technological and pedagogical advancement in their classrooms as soon as the teachers embraced their own professional opportunities.

The International Society for Technology Education, in conjunction with the National Council for Accreditation of Teacher Education (1997), has outlined basic technological competencies for teachers. These competencies appear in Figure 12–7 and should be viewed as foundational. Over time teachers should seek to move beyond these basics and explore new computer-based technologies with which they can experiment in creative and novel ways.

Of course, not every foray into the world of technology will be successful or fully satisfying. Learning and teaching in any complex domain, including computer-based technology, requires time, patience, and some risk taking (Alexander & Fives, 2000). Teachers must allow themselves to be novices with respect to these new technologies and strive over time to reach technological competence. They should

- Operate a computer system to use software successfully.
- Evaluate and use computers and other technologies to support instruction.
- Explore, evaluate, and use technology-based applications for communications, presentations, and decision making.
- Apply current instructional principles and research and appropriate assessment practices to the use of computers and related technologies.
- Demonstrate knowledge of uses of computers for problem solving, data collection, information management, communications, presentations, and decision making.
- Develop student learning activities that integrate computers and technology for a variety of student grouping strategies and for diverse student populations.
- Evaluate, select, and integrate computer/technology-based instruction in the curriculum in a subject area and/or grade level.
- Demonstrate knowledge of uses of multimedia, hypermedia, and telecommunications tools to support instruction.
- Demonstrate skills in using productivity tools for professional and personal use, including word processing, database management, spreadsheet software, and print/graphic utilities.
- Demonstrate knowledge of equity, ethical, legal, and human issues of computing and technology use as they relate to society and model appropriate behavior.
- Identify resources to keep current in applications of computing and related technologies in education.
- Use technology to access information to enhance personal and professional productivity.
- Apply computers and related technologies to facilitate emerging roles of learners and educators.

■ FIGURE 12–7   Technological competencies for practicing teachers.

Note: From International Society for Technology in Education and National Council for Accreditation of Teacher Education, 1997, retrieved from http://cnets.iste.org/index

be well supported in these efforts by the broader educational community (Newsom, 1996).

Use Technology to Reach Beyond the Confines of the Classroom and to Think Outside the Educational Box

Computers have wide-ranging applications, but as long as educators and students see computers as a technological add-on and fail to reconceptualize their teaching and learning accordingly, the promise of the computer cannot be realized.

If nothing significant changes in the classroom save the introduction of a tool, few if any important effects can be expected. . . . If the tool is to be effective, most everything in the learning environment ought to change. (Salomon, 1993, p. 189)

What kinds of systemic transformations should occur in learning environments to take full advantage of computer-based technologies? First, the curriculum should be altered to focus on problems or tasks that are worthy of the information and expertise that come into the classroom via the Internet.

Specifically, worthy tasks

- benefit from an influx of information into the learning environment (Bransford et al., 1999; Salomon, 1993b)
- can be examined from multiple perspectives and can have varied acceptable solutions or resolutions (Garner & Gillingham, 1998)
- spark the construction of new knowledge or the formation of new associations for existing knowledge (Salomon & Perkins, 1996)
- demand deep and extended mental processing that cannot be performed as well in the absence of technology (Lajoie, 2000)
- support and extend key concepts and principles in academic domains (Alexander & Wade, 2000; Bruce & Bruce, 2000)
- foster collaboration and cooperation within the learning environment (Lemke, 1998; Tierney & Damarin, 1998)
- relate to society at large and to students in particular (CTGV, 1997)

Further, worthy tasks should be complemented with appropriate shifts in grouping arrangements (e.g., small group or whole class), discourse patterns (e.g., student-directed or recitation), assessment practices, and the like (Salomon & Perkins, 1996). When both the technology and the content are novel and the task is challenging, students often find themselves confused and overwhelmed (Alexander, Kulikowich, & Jetton, 1994). Therefore, teachers should ensure that students are adequately grounded in either the target subject matter or the chosen technologies before proceeding. Alternatively, teachers may consider grouping arrangements that allow for such competencies to be developed within the student collective (Lesgold, 2000).

■ Summary Reflections

How has technology changed learning and instruction?

- Three fundamental factors are required for the effective application of computer-based technologies in classrooms: technology, knowledge of learning theories, and appropriate educational practices.
  - Effective technology-based instruction needs more than good equipment.

- It demands knowledgeable and committed teachers who grasp the fundamentals of human learning and seek intelligent ways to use technology in educational settings.
- Even when teachers are capable, technology available, and support forthcoming, four dilemmas can confront students and teachers; virtual reality/virtual learning; instructional novelty/enduring pedagogy; electronic equalizer/digital divider; and human connection/human isolation.
  - Educators should keep learning goals paramount, consider the validity of online information, and explore ways to sustain student interest in technology.
  - Teachers should take advantage of technological skills in group settings and provide explicit instruction in online strategies.
  - They should focus on computer projects particularly motivating to females and minorities and encourage positive and honest online communications.

How can various technologies help individual students learn?

- One way for educators to cope with the expanding world of hypermedia is to think in terms of the pedagogical functions such technological tools perform.
  - Technologies meant to serve as surrogate teachers or tutors are called assisted.
  - Technologies intended to connect students to human or informational resources outside the classroom are termed mediated.
  - If computers are designed to put students into a hypermedia environment that reaches broadly into the curriculum, the technology is integrated.
  - Technologies that meet the learning and assessment needs of students who require special support are adaptive.
- Each use of computer-based technologies has its own advantages and disadvantages.
  - Intelligent use requires teachers and school administrators to weigh costs and benefits.
  - No technology is complete in and of itself but requires knowledgeable and committed teachers to apply the tools wisely.

What principles underlie optimal learning in a technologically rich society?

- Educators must keep in mind that computers are only tools waiting to be activated by capable teachers and students.
- Student knowledge, interest, and strategic processing must be monitored and nurtured.
- Teachers must attend to their own technological knowledge and skills, seeking professional opportunities that further their development.
- A learning context that allows for a richer and fuller implementation of new information technologies will require teachers and students to alter their beliefs about learning and rethink traditional modes of learning.

■ Answers to Thought Experiment: What's the Problem Here?

1. Electronic equalizer/digital divider
2. Human connection/human isolation
3. Instructional novelty/enduring pedagogy
4. Electronic equalizer/digital divider or instructional novelty/enduring pedagogy
5. Virtual reality/virtual learning
6. Virtual reality/virtual learning

■ Answers to Thought Experiment: Making Wise Technological Choices

1. d or a
2. b
3. b
4. d
5. b
6. a
7. c

Chapter 13

The Role of Assessment in Learning and Instruction

GUIDING QUESTIONS

■ How does assessment contribute to improved learning and instruction?

■ What forms of academic assessment are better than others?

■ What do teachers need to know about assessment?

IN THEIR OWN WORDS ....

Shirley Herrin has been a dedicated middle-school and high-school teacher for more than 2 decades. For the last 4 years, she has been teaching economics to students at Dumfries High School.

You never stop trying to improve your teaching. When you think you know it all as a teacher, then that's the time to hang up your certificate and look for another career. My students' opinions on my course and my teaching can help me make those improvements, since I always learn something from their comments and reactions. That is why I ask my students to evaluate my economics class at the end of each school year: What did you see as the strengths of the course? What changes would you make in the course content, the assignments, and the tests?

The students know that I pay attention to their recommendations and make changes in next year's curriculum based on what they tell me. This last time, I also included a general question about assessment: How have the assessment practices at Dumfries affected your education? I figured these students had been going through assessments all their lives and would certainly have opinions on the matter.

When I began reading the students' answers, some things caught me by surprise. When I asked them what changes I could make for next year's economics classes, they suggested more essay tests and group projects. They felt that essays gave them more opportunity to show what they know, and they liked the opportunity to collaborate on "meaty" problems.

Those recommendations made sense to me. But the students also expressed concern over cheating on assignments and tests. They wanted safeguards that their classmates could not steal their answers on exams, especially the multiple-choice portions. They also wanted more assurance that those who did little on joint projects would not get the same grade as those doing the yeoman's share of the work. Over and over again, there was this concern for honesty and fairness in their comments. It just never occurred to me that those were big problems in my classes.

Of all the responses I got on this year's survey, the one that shocked me the most was the students' reaction to my general question on assessment. The bottom line was they had no clue what I was talking about. Before they could respond, I had to define assessment for them. These were good students, many from advanced and advanced placement classes, who have been assessed all their lives. But they did not know what the word *assessment* meant.

As I tried to explain the word, a few students chimed in, "You mean standardized tests!" Even though I said that assessment is bigger than that and involves all the ways that we measure and evaluate them, most of the students focused on standardized tests in their answers. They told me that regurgitating information for the sole purpose of a school's ranking in the community or state disenchanted them. They felt that standardized tests were far too stressful to be of any value and that these tests were something they did because they were required, not because they believed in them.

My students' lack of assessment knowledge made me realize I was assuming too much of them. It was clear that repeated exposure to assessment does not ensure that you understand the idea behind it. That made me wonder what other students, parents, and my fellow teachers understand about assessment. Are their perceptions as narrow and negative as my students'?

How Does Assessment Contribute to Improved Learning and Instruction?

For Shirley Herrin's high-school students, assessment is a fuzzy concept. For them assessment equates to high-stakes, high-pressure tests of the sort associated with sealed booklets and #2 pencils. **High-stakes tests** are those used to make critical decisions about students and teachers—decisions about promotion, retention, and graduation (American Educational Research Association, 2000). Many students, teachers, and the general public equate assessment with formal, high-stakes tests, and it is almost impossible to imagine today's schools devoid of such measures.

The testing movement remains a relatively new dimension in education, a 20th century phenomenon (Paris, 2000a). However, formal tests, and even informal ones, are only one dimension of academic assessment, which encompasses an array of measurement tools and techniques (American Psychological Association, 1985, 1995). Rather than being valueless, as Shirley's students claim, effective assessment is integral to education and requisite for optimal learning and development. Of course, the operative word here is *effective* (Linn & Gronlund, 2000).

Of all the terms that pertain to judgments about learner understanding and performance, *assessment* is the most general and most encompassing (APA, 1995). Any time teachers formally or informally set out to gather information about their students and use that knowledge to inform their actions, they are engaged in assessment. When Shirley Herrin surveyed her students about their experiences and asked their views of assessment, she was actually engaged in assessment. Her questions and the students' responses sparked insights into the students' thinking about learning, evaluation, and testing. And according to Shirley, those

[Assessment is] the process of obtaining information that is used to make educational decisions about students, to give feedback to the student about his or her progress, strengths, and weaknesses, to judge instructional effectiveness and curricular adequacy, and to inform policy.

American Federation of Teachers, National Council of Measurement in Education, and National Educational Association, 1990, p. 1.

questions and responses will change her curriculum and her teaching in the coming years. Effective teachers rely on assessment to make decisions that they believe will serve their students better in the future.

Effective teaching cannot exist without some manner of assessment. However, inappropriate, flawed, or inadequate assessment can actually impede instruction. Consequently, it is essential to determine the characteristics of appropriate, valid, and sufficient assessment. *Measurement, evaluation,* and *tests* represent three dimensions of the broader concept of assessment.

Measurement

Frequently, when educators engage in assessment, they convert the information they collect into numbers that substitute for that information. For example, Shirley gave every student in her regular and advanced economics classes a particular score on their global economy unit test. Those numbers represented the students' knowledge of the unit content. **Measurement** is this process of converting information into a numeric representation; it is the quantification of an educational event (McMillan, 2001). This conversion allows educators to collect and summarize their experiences and observations—to make them manageable and analyzable (Sprinthall, 1997).

The numbers chosen to represent educational experiences often convey information about *how often, how much,* or *how well* (Lind & Gronlund, 2000), thereby allowing for the comparison or differentiation of students. One student's grade on Shirley's unit test was 94, another received an 85, and another a 76. Those numbers made it possible for Shirley to judge the students' level of understanding about economic concepts (Glass, 1978).

Whenever measurement is involved in the assessment process, the number assigned is of critical importance. When students' experiences, attributes, or abilities become coded as numbers, those numbers must be meaningful representations. When I look at my checkbook and see $500 written there, I expect a corresponding amount of money to be in my bank account. Likewise, when a student receives an 89 on Shirley's economics test, that 89 should correspond

in some real way to what that student actually knows about global economies.

The quantification of educational experiences helps teachers interpret what is occurring in classrooms so that they can respond appropriately (Shepard, 1995). When done well, measurement becomes a tool for identifying patterns that might not otherwise be noticed. For example, it might be possible for Shirley to teach economics without using any form of grades or numeric evaluations, but it would be difficult to know how individual students were doing over time. Even teachers who might applaud a moratorium on national or state tests would not necessarily want to give up their grade books or student report cards.

However, as they engage in academic quantification, teachers need to be aware that the numbers they assign to educational outcomes may not be of equal mathematical value (Brookhart, 1999) and should then be treated differently. Replacing different kinds of outcomes with numbers can involve four levels of measurement: nominal, ordinal, interval, and ratio. These **levels of measurement** constitute a hierarchy of numeric representation that specifically delimits the mathematical interpretations of academic experiences (see Table 13–1).

There are several reasons that teachers need to recognize the level of measurement they are using as part of an assessment process (Goetz, Alexander, & Ash, 1992). First, these levels of measurement signify varying levels of numerical sophistication; a 5 on a nominal scale is simply not the same as a 5 on an interval scale. Because the numbers teachers use to represent students' learning and development fall at varied points in this measurement hierarchy, teachers need to appreciate the differences in measurement levels. Second, the value of measurement lies in the interpretations it allows educators to make. Unless teachers understand the relation between levels of measurement and data analysis, they can form misguided and misleading interpretations about their students (Brookhart, 1997; Kubiszyn & Borich, 1996).

Nominal

The least sophisticated level of measurement is nominal. With **nominal** data a number is substituted for a category or a name; thus, nominal data are referred to as *categorical data.* Like the names assigned to objects in the environment, any number can theoretically serve the purpose. My parents could just as well have named me Eloise when I was born, instead of Patricia. Similarly, the number 6 is just as good to categorize Democrats, Republicans, or Independents as a 3 or a 1. Nominal data are a useful tool for summarizing descriptive information about individuals, including their gender, ethnicity, or political affiliation.

For example, the administrators at Dumfries High School wanted to know the religious orientation of their students. Consequently, the administration included the following question on the registration form that students complete at the start of each school year:

Scale	Description	Example
Table 13–1	**The subtleties of measurement scales.**	
Nominal	This is the least sophisticated level of measurement, in which a number simply takes the place of a name and can be randomly assigned. Beyond looking at how often these categories occur, few analyses are appropriate for this level of measurement.	When the students at Dumfries High School register in the fall, they mark 1 for female and 2 for male on the form. Because the 1 and 2 are just name substitutes, these are nominal data.
Ordinal	This level of measurement has the characteristic of order not present in nominal data; the assigned numbers must be similarly ordered. Few analyses beyond frequency can be done with these data.	When the students at Dumfries complete their registration form, they mark 1 to 4 depending on whether they are a freshman, sophomore, junior, or senior, respectively. The meaningful order of those numbers makes them ordinal data.
Interval	Not only do interval data have order, but the units that separate those numbers—the intervals—are equivalent. This characteristic permits more sophisticated analyses and comparisons of the data.	One question on the registration form asks students to list their date of birth. Because the intervals between dates on a calendar are consistent, this represents interval data.
Ratio	The most sophisticated level, but one rarely encountered in educational assessment, requires a zero to represent the true absence of the factor. Complicated comparisons are possible at this level.	Another question on the registration asks students to list their height and weight. Because there can be a true absence of height and weight, these are ratio measures.

What is your religious affiliation?

___ 1. Buddhist

___ 2. Catholic

___ 3. Hindu

___ 4. Muslim

___ 5. Protestant

___ 6. Jewish

___ 7. Other _____

___ 8. None

This scale is nominal because there is no particular order or meaningful association between the assigned numbers and the religions. The numbers are simply labels. The assignment of 1 to Buddhists does not imply that this religion is better or worse than 2 Catholics.

Because nominal data are the least sophisticated, little more can be done with them than to explore patterns in occurrence, or **frequency** (i.e., how often a certain category appears). For example, the administration at Dumfries may have wanted to know which religions are the most prevalent among the student population. Or administrators may have wondered whether any noticeable changes have occurred in those affiliations in the past few years. Both of these questions could be answered with nominal data.

Ordinal

The **ordinal** level of measurement has one characteristic that nominal data lack—a meaningful order or rank. Ordinal data convey information about the relative position of an experience or an event and are often associated with compar-

ative words like *more/less, greater/lesser,* or *higher/lower.* The assignment of the number at this level is not arbitrary, but must intentionally reflect the order of the information.

On Dumfries High School's yearly registration form, students are asked about their class rank:

Indicate your class designation:

___ 1. Freshman

___ 2. Sophomore

___ 3. Junior

___ 4. Senior

When the administration created this question, the order of the information was important. In this case freshman is a lower academic rank than sophomore, and juniors have less educational experience than seniors. However, as with nominal data, educators can do little with ordinal data other than look at frequency or relative order.

Teachers use ordinal data in their classes when they use grading systems like A, B, C, and D, pass/fail, or satisfactory/unsatisfactory. Those systems allow someone to say that students who earned an A, a pass, or a satisfactory performed better than students who received a B, a fail, or an unsatisfactory. Teachers can also determine whether there were more As, Bs, Cs, Ds, or Fs in economics. However, they cannot specifically determine how much better someone is at economics who got an A, as opposed to someone who received a B, C, D, or F.

Interval

Adding one more attribute to the measurement scales—consistent distances between scores—produces **interval** data. Interval data allow Shirley Herrin to know who ranks higher on her global economy test and by how much. Thus, she knows that a grade of 94 is higher than an 85, specifically 9 points higher.

On the Dumfries registration form, the students also record their birth dates. Calendar dates are a common form of interval data because the distances between days or portions of days are mathematically constant. Thus, the distance between March 15, 2001, and March 15, 2002, is the same as the distance between April 1, 1875, and April 1, 1876. Similarly, the time that elapses between 6:00 a.m. and 6:00 p.m. on December 2 and on August 9 is the same. Once educators reach this level of measurement, they can perform a variety of analyses that allow for more sophisticated interpretations.

Ratio

For all their refinement, interval data lack one critical attribute: There is no true zero for this scale. In other words, 0 does not signify a true absence of the factor being measured. Only **ratio** data can claim to have a true zero point, making it the most sophisticated level of measurement. A true zero on a scale is important because it gives a clear starting point from which to gauge performance and thus allows ratio or proportional comparisons (e.g., Norman is two times faster than Mavis).

To understand this distinction between interval and ratio data, consider the difference between a 0 on Shirley Herrin's unit test and a 0 in my checkbook. If a student in Shirley's class actually managed to get a 0 on the economics test, we could not assume that the student had absolutely no knowledge about the global economy—just that the student did not produce any correct answers on that particular exam. On the other hand, a zero in my checkbook means that there is simply no money in that account—an absolute zero.

Ratio data are extremely rare in academic assessment (D. E. Tanner, 2001). A true absence of some abstract educational construct, like knowledge or intelligence, may well exist, but no measurement tools are available to make such determinations. Consequently, ratio data are more often associated with physical measurements like height, weight, volume, speed, or length.

Evaluation

Lorrie Shepard's research has focused on program and school evaluation.

Whereas measurement deals with the quantification of assessment, evaluation focuses on its application. **Evaluation** occurs when educators make specific judgments or decisions based on their assessments (Stiggins, 1993); evaluation is thus the interpretations made during assessment. Effective teachers are continually involved in evaluation, at least informal evaluation (Shepard, 1993). They read students' reactions during instruction, for example, and make minor or major adjustments in their lesson as a consequence.

Some evaluations take the form of scores, notes, or grades, which teachers record for subsequent analysis. Shirley's end-of-the-year survey of her students and her subsequent modification of her curriculum is a case of evaluation. Evaluation relates to the purposes teachers have for gathering assessment data and the approaches they take to discerning their meaning. Without evaluation academic data would remain nothing more than marks on a page or numbers in a grade book.

Purposes for Evaluation

When educators engage in evaluation, both formally and informally, they do so for a variety of reasons. Generally speaking, those purposes fit one of four categories: formative, summative, diagnostic, and placement (Linn & Gronlund, 2000). A description of these four categories appears in Table 13–2.

Formative

Gary Phye explores the relationship between assessment and learning.

Evaluation is called **formative** when its purpose is to monitor progress so that needed modifications can be instituted (Phye, 1996). Because formative evaluation contributes to changes in ongoing instruction, it typically relies on informal assessment techniques such as observation, questioning, and teacher-made tests geared to instruction (Airasian, 1997). The resulting information can be quickly and easily put to use.

Shirley Herrin asks students questions during class and gives them weekly assignments because their oral and written responses are important clues to their understanding and performance. Based on what the students say or do, Shirley can judge whether they are getting the content or struggling with particular concepts or procedures. Then she can make whatever midcourse or midyear adjustments are necessary.

Summative

With **summative** evaluation the purpose of the judgment is to arrive at some terminal decision regarding students or instruction (Bloom, Hastings, & Madaus, 1971). In other words, have teachers, students, or educational programs achieved their academic goals? At the end of the year, when Shirley Herrin records the final grades for the students in her economics classes, she is making a summative evaluation. Teachers and schools can also be the recipients of summative evaluations. For instance, in this era of **accountability,** student scores on high-stakes tests are routinely used to evaluate individual teachers, schools, states, and even the national education system (Fiske, 1988; Stiggins, 2001).

Diagnostic

Chapter 3 discussed the groundbreaking work of Alfred Binet, when he and his colleague Simon set out to create a

Table 13–2	Reasons to evaluate.	
Type of Purpose	**Explanation**	**Example**
Formative	Conducted to inform ongoing practice; tends to rely on more informal procedures, such as questionnaires or observations	Shirley Herrin's questioning of her economics students about the curriculum serves to guide midyear revisions in that program.
Summative	Leads to a terminal decision based on relevant information about students or instruction; used to determine whether goals have been met	At the end of the year, Shirley records economics grades for her students, indicating the degree to which they have attained course objectives.
Diagnostic	Undertaken to pinpoint particular strengths or needs; may involve special measures or personnel with specialized knowledge	The counselors at Dumfries High School are trained to give career placement tests that suggest career options based on students' academic preferences and demonstrated abilities.
Placement	Intends to place students initially in the appropriate educational environment so that optimal learning and development result; a special form of diagnosis	Before students can participate in advanced placement classes at Dumfries High School, they need to demonstrate certain levels of ability and motivation.

measure that would screen French children for serious mental problems (Binet & Simon, 1905). It is still common educational practice to use assessment for **diagnosis,** that is, for the purpose of screening students (Airasian & Madaus, 1972). For example, once every year, the students at Dumfries High School undergo a physical screening. They parade to the gym, where volunteers record their heights and weights. Someone else looks in their ears and down their throats, checks their reflexes, and has them read an eye chart. The goal of this exercise is to spot any students with obvious physical problems that warrant further examination.

Students can also be screened for potential cognitive or psychosocial conditions that might require intervention (Hallahan & Kauffman, 2000). When I was a reading specialist, teachers often sent students to me whom they suspected of having reading problems. I would give the students tests that would tell me whether the teachers' suspicions were well founded and would help us identify the nature of the students' reading abilities. Other personnel—like the school psychologist, mathematics specialist, or hearing and speech specialist—perform related diagnoses, which may become the basis for specialized instructional plans.

Placement

According to Robert Linn and Norman Gronlund (2000), there is yet another reason for evaluation—a special case of diagnostic assessment called **placement.** Through assessment educators can gain information about students' initial levels of knowledge and skill and can then use that information to place students in appropriate learning environments. Before students can enroll in Shirley Herrin's advanced placement economics class, they have to score well on an initial economics examination. Thus, that examination serves a clear placement purpose. Similarly, before students

can take part in her advanced economics classes, Shirley considers their prior grades and work samples to determine the suitability of that placement.

These four purposes for evaluation typically operate interactively in the educational environment. Diagnostic evaluation might contribute to an initial placement decision. And once students are placed in an instructional environment, their progress might be gauged through formative evaluation (Phye, 1996). On the other hand, once a summative evaluation is rendered, that outcome might inform subsequent placement decisions.

Quantitative Interpretation

Regardless of the purpose of evaluation, it often requires teachers to make sense of data that have been numerically represented (Lyman, 1991). However, making sense of pages of numbers can be a daunting task. This was the dilemma that Francis Galton faced (see Chapter 3) when he wanted to interpret his thousands of observations about human characteristics. What could all of those measurements of height, weight, and speed tell him about the human species? Just as Galton (1883) performed certain mathematical calculations that allowed him to describe and summarize those data, teachers can make similar calculations. Rather simple procedures can show teachers the degree to which students' scores are typical or the pattern of their variation (Stiggins, 1991).

Measures of Central Tendency

When educators want to pinpoint the scores that best typify a group of scores, they turn to measures of **central tendency.** The three most common measures of central tendency are mode, median, and mean. Each one of these measurements allows teachers to make certain interpretations about the typicality of student data.

Mode   One question that educators ask about student data is what category or score occurs most often. The **mode** is just that—the most frequently occurring category or score. This particular statistic applies to all levels of measurement, including nominal data. For instance, one could identify the mode for the religious affiliation data collected at Dumfries High School even though the data are only categorical. Whichever category had the greatest number would be the modal religion at Dumfries. Or perhaps Shirley was interested in calculating the mode for the unit test she gave her second-period class. The scores for that class are listed here:

SECOND PERIOD ADVANCED ECONOMICS

Student	Score	Student	Score
Calvin	100	Marcus	92
Louise	100	Dan	89
Dell	99	Patrick	88
Alice May	98	Dennis Paul	86
Corbin	98	Andy	86
Warren	98	Ernie	85
Kevin	96	Renee	76
Jenny	92	Sasha	68
		Frank	52

Thus, the mode would be 98—a very high score. If Ernie's 85 had been an 86, there would have been two modes for this set of scores—a **bimodal distribution.**

Median   Teachers may also want to know which score falls at the midpoint of a data set, that is, the **median.** The median physically splits a distribution into two equal portions. An educational researcher or practitioner can use a median to make some rough comparisons between the two groups. However, because scores must be in a meaningful order before the median can be calculated, data must be at the ordinal level of measurement or higher.

Perhaps Shirley wanted to calculate the median for her fourth-period class. Those scores are listed here:

FOURTH PERIOD ADVANCED ECONOMICS

Student	Score	Student	Score
Agnes	98	Hector	85
James	94	Jennifer	85
Gina	94	Grant	85
Samson	91	Michael	82
Jeff	89	Nancy	81
Daniel	89	Elmer	80
Anabell	87	Norman	76
Theodore	86	Doris	69
Mavis	86	Betty	65

With 18 students in the class, the midpoint would fall between the 9th and 10th scores in the ordered distribution, that is, between Mavis's 86 and Hector's 85. Since these two scores are different, the median would be midway between them—at 85.5.

Mean   The final measure of central tendency is the **mean,** which is the statistical average of all scores in a distribution. Although the mean is the most sophisticated measure of central tendency, it is also the one with which most educators are familiar. It is calculated by adding up all scores and dividing by the number of scores in that distribution. For example, for Shirley's fourth-period class, all 18 scores add up to 1522 points. When this total is divided by the number of scores, the mean is 84.56.

The statistical mean has certain noteworthy characteristics (Goetz et al., 1992). First, this particular measure requires either interval or ratio data. Second, because the mean is based on every score in a distribution, a shift in any one changes the outcome. Third, the mean can be strongly influenced by one or two extreme scores. For instance, when Shirley Herrin tested all 80 of her regular and advanced economics students, their average score was 80.6. However, if one student's 0 was dropped, the mean would jump to 81.6. Educational researchers have to look carefully at their data so that such statistical outliers do not lead them to erroneous interpretations. And finally, even though the mean takes every score into consideration, the resulting average does not have to be a number in that distribution.

Measures of Dispersion

Measures of **dispersion** reveal information about differences among scores (Townsend & Burke, 1975). Three measures of dispersion are frequently used in academic assessment: range, variance, and standard deviation.

Range   The simplest measure of dispersion is **range,** the span of scores for a particular distribution. The range of any set of data is found by subtracting the lowest score from the highest. Thus, the range of scores for Shirley's second-period class was 100 − 52, or 48. The spread of scores for her fourth-period class was 98 − 65, or 33. These numbers indicate more dispersion, or variability, among the second-period scores.

Variance and Standard Deviation   Educational researchers are generally concerned with the dispersion of scores occurring around the mean. Two measures, in particular, are basic to understanding dispersion in human performance: variance and standard deviation. Both of these measures are based on a **deviation score,** the distance a particular score is from the mean. In general, the **standard deviation** is an average of deviation scores. Thus, the greater the standard deviation, the greater the differences among the data being analyzed. The **variance** is determined by squaring the standard deviation.

Phillip Ackerman has used assessment to explore individual differences.

With this overview try your hand at the formula for finding the standard deviation in the Thought Experiment: Interpreting the Variability of Scores. Do the calculation now before moving on.

Without variance and standard deviation, educators and researchers could not discuss individual differences from a statistical standpoint (Ackerman, Kyllonen, & Roberts, 1999).

Indeed, Galton's notion of eminence and many of the legal definitions of exceptionality discussed in Chapter 3 are built around the concept of statistical deviation. Specifically, those who display attributes or abilities more than one standard deviation from the mean are significantly above or below average. For Shirley's fourth-period class, the calculations in the Thought Experiment found a mean of 84.56 and a standard deviation of 8.13. Thus, any score that is more than 8.13 points above or below the mean is significantly varied. That criterion puts Agnes's 98 well above the average and Doris's 69 and Betty's 65 well below the average.

The Shape of Distributions

The measures of central tendency and dispersion can provide teachers with valuable information about students' academic performance (Townsend & Burke, 1975). When scores are graphically represented in either a bar graph or a frequency distribution, those measures and other characteristics can become more evident. Both bar graphs and frequency distributions account for all scores in a distribution and are particularly useful when a large number of scores are examined. The bar graph in Figure 13–1 is similar to the one Shirley would have developed for her four economics classes after their unit test. The normal

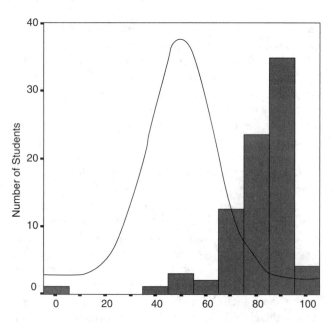

■ FIGURE 13–1   A bar graph with normal distribution superimposed.

Thought Experiment ....

Interpreting the Variability of Scores

Directions: See whether you can determine the standard deviation for Shirley Herrin's fourth-period class.

To calculate the standard deviation, follow these steps:

1. Calculate the mean $(\overline{X})$ of the distribution
2. Calculate the deviation score by subtracting the mean from each score: $(X - \overline{X})$
3. Square the deviation scores so that they are all positive: $(X - \overline{X})^2$
4. Sum (Σ) the squared deviation scores: $\Sigma (X - \overline{X})^2$
5. Divide this sum by the total number of scores (N) in the distribution: $\dfrac{\Sigma (X - \overline{X})^2}{N}$
6. Find the square root of the resulting number $\sqrt{\dfrac{\Sigma (X - \overline{X})^2}{N}}$

Here are the scores the fourth-period students received. The first two calculations have been done for you.

Scores	Deviation Score	Deviation Score Squared
98	$98 - 84.56 = 13.44$	180.63
94	$94 - 84.56 = 9.44$	89.11
94		
91		
89		
89		
87		
86		
86		
85		
85		
85		
82		
81		
80		
76		
69		
65		

$$\Sigma(X - \overline{X})^2 =$$

$$\frac{\Sigma (X - \overline{X})^2}{N} =$$

$$\sqrt{\frac{\Sigma (X - \overline{X})^2}{N}} =$$

(Answer at the end of the chapter)

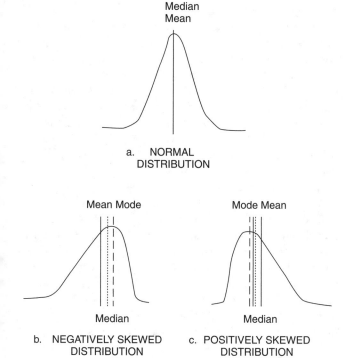

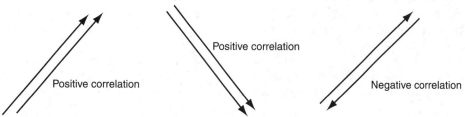

■ FIGURE 13–2   Normal and skewed distributions.

bell-shaped distribution that is superimposed shows that scores are clearly skewed toward the upper end of the scale.

In a perfectly proportioned normal distribution, the mode, median, and mean are all the same number (see Figure 13–2a). However, for Shirley's 80 economics students, the mean for her test was 80.6, and the mode and the median were 85. Thus, her test distribution was **negatively skewed** (see Figure 13–2b), with a noticeable number of scores falling above the mean. Had the reverse been true—with more students' scores falling below the mean—her distribution would have been **positively skewed** (see Figure 13–2c).

There are several plausible explanations for the results on Shirley's test, only one of which is potentially worrisome for her. First, such a distribution could result if the unit test was well coordinated to her classroom instruction and she is simply a great teacher. Students who pay close attention and do all the required work should score high on a unit test. In addition, two of Shirley's classes are advanced sections; thus, a good number of those students *should* score well above average. If either of these explanations fits Shirley's situation, she should not be concerned with this negatively skewed distribution.

However, it is also possible that Shirley has written an exam that is simply too easy for most of her students. Perhaps her treatment of global economies was superficial, and test items

did not require students to think deeply or creatively about the topic. In that case students in Shirley's classes would have been able to score high even though their knowledge of the topic was neither deep nor extensive. Before Shirley can feel good about her students' overall performance, she must be able to reject this possibility. She must be convinced that her test adequately covered the content and was suitably thought provoking and challenging for these high-school students.

Whenever the majority of scores on a measure are below average, or are positively skewed, it is conceivable that the test was too difficult or too demanding for students. It is also possible that the students are below average in the characteristic or ability that was tested. In addition, it is possible that the language or the experiences tapped by the measure were ill-matched to the student group and thus underestimated the students' actual potential.

Measures of Association

Sometimes educators want to explore the relations between two distributions so that they can determine how closely two characteristics or measures relate or can gauge how consistently students are performing. They then turn to **correlation analysis,** a statistical procedure that results in a measure of association between paired distributions, which are two sets of scores for the same group of people. One example might be the scores of Ms. Herrin's advanced placement students on her economics final and on the formal advanced placement economics test.

The concept of correlation was introduced in Chapter 2 with the discussion of individual differences. Galton (1883) initially conceived of the procedure so that he could examine relations between select human characteristics, such as people's height and weight. Because he believed these characteristics were linked, he needed to prove an association between them. If an association exists, then as people get taller, they should also tend to get heavier. The measurement procedure he devised to answer this question was correlation analysis, which other scholars subsequently refined.

When correlation analysis is applied, a number called the **correlation coefficient** is obtained, which tells about the direction and the strength of association between any two paired distributions. The correlation coefficient can fall anywhere between -1 and $+1$. The $-$ or $+$ before the number indicates the **direction** of the relation, whether the scores in the two distributions move in similar or dissimilar directions. If students receiving higher scores on Ms. Herrin's AP economics final exam also tended to get higher scores on the AP economics test and those receiving lower scores on her exam generally got lower scores on the AP test, then the direction of association would be positive $(+)$. That is, the distributions

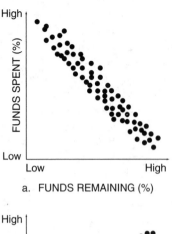

a. FUNDS REMAINING (%)

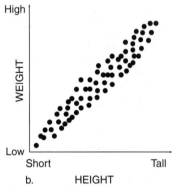

b.   HEIGHT

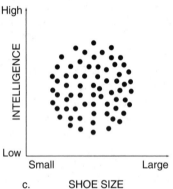

c.   SHOE SIZE

■ **FIGURE 13–3   Scatterplots of near-perfect and random associations.**

tion (+1). As individuals physically mature, they simultaneously tend to get taller and heavier.

At the other extreme, when there is no meaningful or discernible relation between paired distributions, the correlation coefficient is 0. If individuals' shoe sizes and IQ scores were plotted, the association should be random or meaningless (see Figure 13–3c), with a coefficient approaching 0. Scatterplots are useful graphic depictions of scores that show the relative strength or weakness of paired distributions.

Most associations fall somewhere between these two extreme points. Correlations above .70 are referred to as strong; those below .30, as weak. But again, these coefficients can be either positive (+) or negative (−) in direction. Thus, if researchers collected information on individuals' height and their mathematical achievement, they might find a weak, positive correlation. The reason the relation would not be random is that people tend to get taller as they get older—to a point—and achievement tends to go up with age—again, to a point. By comparison, a strong, positive correlation would be expected between individuals' IQ scores and their academic achievement. The rationale is that higher IQs make learning easier, resulting in higher achievement. Even though correlation analysis cannot explain why relations exist or what caused them, this procedure is invaluable in exploring questions of association in student performance, as well as consistency across time and situations.

Tests

Tests have become a mainstay of formal education in most industrialized countries (Resnick & Resnick, 1990; Sacks, 2000). At its simplest, a **test** is a sampling of human behavior or attributes (Alexander & Parsons, 1991). If Shirley wants to know about her students' understanding of economics, she asks questions or makes observations that sample that domain. For most people the word *test* suggests a written instrument or device that is converted into numbers, like Shirley's unit test. However, tests come in a multitude of forms, serving a variety of educational goals. An overview of those forms appears in Table 13–3.

Maximum Versus Typical Performance

Lee Cronbach (1990), one of the leaders in educational assessment, categorized tests into two broad classes based on the nature of the performance they reveal—maximum or typical. Measures of **maximum performance,** according to Cronbach, seek to uncover students' potential in a given area, particularly when the stakes for performing well are high. It is an effort to catch students at their best. Measures of **typical performance,** aim to profile students under usual or everyday conditions—in their classroom setting when the stakes for performing are routine and resources are variable.

Cronbach's (1990) distinction between maximum and typical performance rests on the assumption that maximum performance results when significant consequences are

moved in a similar direction. On the other hand, if those getting higher scores on Ms. Herrin's final tended to receive lower scores on the AP exam, or vice versa, the nature of association would be negative (−) because scores in the distributions moved in opposite directions.

Strength indicates how strongly these two distributions are associated. A perfect correlation produces a coefficient of 1; it results when changes in one set of scores are matched exactly by changes in the other. For example, the relation between individuals' expenditures and their remaining income generally approaches a near perfect, negative correlation of −1 (see Figure 13–3a); that is, as their expenditures go up, their remaining income comes down. On the other hand, the association between height and weight (see Figure 13–3b) should approach a perfect, positive correla-

Table 13–3 Forms of tests.

Form	Description	Example
Maximum Performance	Assesses students with high-stakes measures under conditions that are likely to produce positive outcomes or favorable results; catches learners at their best	Before Dumfries students take the AP economics test, they have taken Ms. Herrin's AP course and several practice exams. They know that they will be receiving college credit for their work if they perform at a satisfactory level on the AP exam.
Typical Performance	Uses measures of a more informal nature that demonstrate how students generally perform under normal, everyday conditions	As part of the AP class, students complete daily assignments, weekly quizzes, and periodic unit tests. These measures offer a picture of students' typical performance in economics.
Norm-Referenced	Measures performance against that of a selected norm group; shows relative performance contingent on the profile of that norm group	Dumfries students who take the AP economics test are judged against the scores of the norm group for that same test.
Criterion-Referenced	Judges performance against an established, absolute standard or criterion	To gauge reading ability, students answer a series of questions related to basic skills. Those who score 75 % or better on the items associated with each skill are judged to be competent in that area.
Self-Referenced	Uses the students' own performance history as the base of comparison	In certain cooperative learning programs, students' grades are determined by the gains they show over past performance.
Standardized	Routinizes procedures for administering, scoring, and interpreting students' performance	Students at Dumfries take various achievement and aptitude tests, like the SAT I, which are given at specified times and places under highly controlled conditions.

Lee Cronbach

involved—as in the case of high-stakes testing (A. S. Cohen, 2000). Achievement and aptitude tests administered nationally or districtwide fit this notion of maximum performance. **Achievement tests** focus on demonstrated knowledge and abilities, whereas **aptitude tests** target potential or the ca-

pacity to learn (McMillan, 2001). For these tests students should be motivated to put forth their best effort, resulting in their best results. In contrast, measures of personality, attitude, and interest are designed to be representative of students' everyday thoughts and feelings, making them measures of typical performance according to Cronbach.

With contemporary theories of knowledge and learning (see Chapter 4), alternative perspectives on maximum and typical performance have emerged (Ackerman & Heggestad, 1997; Alexander & Murphy, 1999a). According to those who embrace sociocultural views of development, maximum performance is unlikely to result when students are placed under high-stress conditions and are asked to perform unfamiliar tasks (Bronfenbrenner, 1989). Instead, best performance is apt to occur when students work in familiar and comfortable settings on interesting and meaningful tasks (Gelman, 1979; White & Alexander, 1986). Vygotsky (1978) would argue that maximum performance results when a more knowledgeable adult or peer guides or scaffolds student performance.

Typical performance from the sociocultural perspective is likely collaborative, because individuals rarely labor independently in the world of work (Resnick, Levine, & Teasley, 1991). Thus, work samples from classrooms might include both independent and collaborative measures.

Sociocultural researchers would agree with Cronbach that it is difficult to capture typical performance in a single instance (Madaus & Kellaghan, 1993). Thus, profiling students' thinking and emotions over time and under varying circumstances is more apt to reveal typicality (Alexander & Murphy, 1999a).

Norm-, Criterion-, and Self-Referenced Assessments

Whenever a test is created to sample students' abilities or characteristics, someone must decide what point of reference will be used to score and interpret the outcomes: the performance of others, an absolute standard, or the students' past performance. Each of these forms comes with its own set of advantages and disadvantages.

Norm-Referenced Testing

The basis of interpretation for **norm-referenced** tests is the individual's standing relative to an established comparison group (Terwilliger, 1989). The scores for that comparison group, which can be national or local, become the target distribution and the basis for measures of central tendency and dispersion. The comparison group is referred to as the **norm group** (Ebel & Frisbie, 1991), and each student's performance on the test is plotted against this norm group.

One clear advantage of norm-referenced testing is that it allows for a definitive ranking of students (Petersen, Kolen, & Hoover, 1989); their performance can be described as average or markedly above or below the norm. Consequently, commercial test developers typically rely on norm referencing when they want to make broad comparisons among students, often at a national level. However, one serious concern about norm-referenced testing is whether the norm group was carefully and appropriately chosen (Smith & Rottenberg, 1991). If the developer gave too little attention to gender, ethnicity, culture, age, socioeconomic status, or geographic region, then it may not be appropriate to compare certain groups of students to the norming sample (Sattler, 1992; Willingham & Cole, 1997).

During their senior year, students at Dumfries take the Scholastic Aptitude Test I (SAT I), frequently used in college admission decisions. The SAT I consists of a verbal and a math portion, each with scores that range from 200 to 800. Each portion has a mean of 500 and a standard deviation of 100. Marcus, a Caucasian male, received scores of 475 verbal and 510 math on the SAT I. Chuck, an African American male, received scores of 632 verbal and 645 math. Those scores put Marcus within the average range of performance for both segments of the SAT I, whereas Chuck is more than one standard deviation above the mean for the entire norm group. However, when Chuck's performance is compared to that of other African American males in the norm group, his scores on both the verbal and the math portions are almost two standard deviations above the mean. Thus, the level of Chuck's performance would be underestimated if it is compared only to that of Caucasian males, without an adequate sampling of African American males.

If Shirley Herrin were to use norm-referenced testing in her economics classes, she would take all her students' scores on the global economy unit test and manipulate them mathematically until they conformed to a normal distribution. That manipulation might mean that only students who received scores of 98 to 100 would get As, instead of the school's usual standard of 94 to 100. Similarly, students with scores of 85 to 90 might get Cs, rather than the school's standard of 75 to 85. In effect, one student's grade would depend on the performance of all 79 classmates. The relative nature of norm-referenced tests explains why some educators view them as inappropriate and objectionable measures of student learning and development (Crouse & Trusheim, 1998; Heubert & Hauser, 1999).

Criterion-Referenced Testing

The relative standard in norm-referenced testing is replaced by an absolute standard in criterion-referenced testing. Robert Glaser (1963) is credited with coining the term *criterion-referenced testing,* which is also referred to as *standards-based, objectives-based,* or *domain-referenced testing.* Specifically, in **criterion-referenced testing** students' performance is judged against an accepted standard or prototype. The idea underlying criterion-referenced testing is that learning is about students reaching a desired standard in performance (R. A. Berk, 1984). How those students stack up against one another or how many students achieve particular rankings is not central.

When Shirley Herrin created her global economy unit test, she allocated certain point values to each question. For the short answer and essay portions of her test, she also developed a response protocol that indicated what information was required for a thorough and complete answer. As she graded students' exams, she compared their answers against this response prototype. It made no difference to Shirley how many students got As or Cs. What

Robert Glaser

mattered was whether the students demonstrated mastery of the content. Thus, she took a criterion-referenced approach to this particular test. Many teachers take a similar approach to testing in their own classrooms when they establish absolute standards for student performance.

Despite the broad appeal of criterion-referenced testing, it has its limitations (Nitko, 1984). Specifically, the credibility of criterion referencing rests on the standard established. However, it may not be easy to determine what the prototypic response should be or what level of performance should serve as the threshold for mastery. Moreover, the all-or-nothing nature of criterion-referenced testing leaves little opportunity for ascertaining student growth toward mastery.

Self-Referenced Testing

A third option for scoring and interpreting tests is **self-referenced testing,** in which the point of comparison is

Learner-Centered Psychological Principle 14

Standards and assessment. Setting appropriately high and challenging standards and assessing the learner and learning process—including diagnostic, process, and outcome assessment—are integral parts of the learning process.

Learner-Centered Principles Work Group of the APA Board of Educational Affairs, 1997.

the individual student's prior performance (Linn & Gronlund, 2000). Because the goal is to motivate students by crediting their improvement, self-referencing has also been called *growth-based* or *change-based* evaluation.

Some critics of self-referenced testing argue that it benefits those with the least knowledge or skill at the outset and penalizes students who are already highly knowledgeable or skilled (Nitko, 2001; Terwilliger, 1971). Advocates of self-referenced testing, like Robert Slavin, have attempted to circumvent this problem. Slavin's (1994) approaches to cooperative learning, including the Student Teams-Achievement Divisions discussed in Chapter 11, assign a set number of points based on documented improvement. However, perfect papers also receive the highest number of improvement points, allowing highly knowledgeable and skilled students to maintain their academic edge if they continue to perform well.

Standardized Tests

The majority of commercial, high-stakes tests that students take are standardized measures (Mehrens & Lehman, 1987). Although most teachers and students are quite familiar with standardized tests, few can explain the attributes of these tests (Carey, 1994; Stiggins, 1991). **Standardized tests** are so named because there are uniform procedures for their administration, scoring, and interpretation that must be followed. Aspects of this standardization include not only explicit directions to test takers, strict timing parameters, and conditions for administration (e.g., group or individual settings), but also specific guidelines for when in the school year such tests should be given.

Standardized tests must be rigorously and uniformly scored as well. Regardless of where or by whom standardized tests are taken, the same responses should result in the exact same score. Consequently, most standardized tests rely on multiple-choice questions, which can be scored easily and objectively. However, standardized tests can theoretically include any measure of question (e.g., essay or matching) and can be either norm-referenced or criterion-referenced.

Perhaps the greatest appeal of standardized tests is their consistency. When students at Dumfries High School take the SAT I each spring, it is exactly the same test as the SAT I being administered in Minnesota, Maryland, or Mississippi. Students at Dumfries hear the same directions, work under the same conditions and constraints, and use the same resources as students in other locations. For that reason, Chuck's 632 verbal and 645 math scores can be confidently compared to those of students from any state or school in the country. Of course, whether those standardized tests meet other standards for consistency, appropriateness, and truthfulness remains to be seen. Standardization procedures alone cannot address such critical indicators of test effectiveness and suitability (Hambleton, 1996; Shepard, 1989).

What Forms of Academic Assessment Are Better Than Others?

Education and assessment are truly wedded. However, that marriage can periodically suffer from external circumstances and internal conditions (Shepard, 1995). Sometimes the relation suffers from a lack of clarity, appropriateness, or stability, just a few of the external circumstances that can threaten the union (Smith & Rottenberg, 1991). Two time-honored indicators of a viable and meaningful relation between education and assessment are validity and reliability.

Evaluating the Legitimacy of Assessment Practices

Validity represents the legitimacy (i.e., appropriateness and suitability) of assessment practices, specifically in relation to the interpretations and applications of resulting data. Strong validity is the ultimate goal of assessment practices. If assessment data do not meet the tests of appropriateness and suitability for the targeted purposes and the desired conditions, then they are significantly flawed and are of questionable educational merit (Messick, 1980).

The Nature of Validity

As Shirley Herrin realized in her brief survey, high-school students' knowledge of assessment is very limited. However, evidence suggests that those students are not alone. Many practicing educators have rather limited and sometimes misguided ideas about validity—one of the most important markers of assessment quality. Linn and Gronlund (2000) outline five cautions about validity that educators at all levels must bear in mind.

Suitability of Practice

Educators and educational researchers often speak about the validity of a test or measure. Despite such statements validity is not a characteristic inherent in any test or measure. No assessment tool, in and of itself, is valid or invalid. Instead, validity rests in the soundness or legitimacy of the judgments made from the information these tools provide. This distinction is important because it creates a more contextualized and dynamic notion of validity (Cronbach &

Meehl, 1955). It ties decisions about assessment adequacy, trustworthiness, and legitimacy to the manner in which information from such measures is collected and used.

Matter of Degree

Novices in educational assessment are prone to characterize assessment practices as either valid or invalid. However, validity is not a simple and dichotomous condition. The interpretation and application of assessment data should be conceptualized on a continuum from more valid to less valid (Moss, 1992), encouraging educators to find ways to improve their assessment practices, rather than feeling helpless in the face of difficulties (Shepard, 1995).

For example, the scores from Shirley Herrin's unit test may have raised questions in her mind. Only those students in her two advanced classes demonstrated the level of conceptual understanding she anticipated. Rather than dismiss the scores from the other classes as invalid, Shirley might consider a variety of instructional and measurement options that could result in more valid distributions for her other classes. For instance, she might find that particular items on the test corresponded better with the content emphasized in the advanced classes. Or she might ascertain that the writing components of her essay items masked the content knowledge of her regular students, bringing down their overall score. If she had thought of validity in black and white terms, she might not have weighed these assessment alternatives.

Situation-Specific Evaluation

Validity judgments can be rendered only when educators consider outcomes in the broader educational context (Shepard, 1989). No abstract determinations apply to validity. Experts can scan a test and make a surface-level judgment about whether that test seems to be a reasonable measure of the content, a form of judgment known as **face validity** (D.E. Tanner, 2001). However, more in-depth analyses must be specific to the situation and to the context in which those data were gathered. For instance, Shirley Herrin cannot determine whether her test produced valid information until she weighs students' scores in light of her goals for the unit, the content domain, the quality of her instruction, and student behaviors.

Unitary Construct

Educators no longer think of validity as having multiple forms (APA, 1985, 1995). Instead, it is a singular or unitary construct. What were once considered the different forms of validity are now viewed as multiple sources of evidence that allow educators to judge the levels of validity. Further, because of the situation-specific nature of validity judgments, particular sources of evidence may carry greater weight in some situations than in others (Messick, 1994).

Global Judgment

Even though educators must carefully weigh whatever relevant evidence is available to them, they must eventually reach a global determination about the validity of their assessment practices (Linn & Gronlund, 2000). They must ultimately decide the level of validity attained in the acquisition, interpretation, and application of assessment information. Once Shirley Herrin had scored her unit tests, considered outcomes in relation to students' class performance, and looked at error patterns, she had to decide the degree to which those outcomes were a suitable reflection of her students' economics knowledge. That validity judgment should then have guided the subsequent actions she took.

Sources of Validity Evidence

Relevant evidence comes in four forms, summarized in Table 13–4: content, construct, criterion, and related consequences (Linn & Gronlund, 2000). Each of these sources affords educators a unique perspective on the legitimacy of assessment practices by highlighting a different facet of that process.

Content Evaluations

One source of evidence about the appropriateness and suitability of assessment practices focuses on the match in content between the measurement tool and the domain or curriculum being assessed. **Content validity** refers to the degree to which the academic domain is adequately represented on a particular assessment measure (Fiske, 1988). It also pertains to the degree to which a certain measure duly reflects the particular topics or subjects emphasized in the classroom curriculum. Because tests are inevitably a sampling of human abilities or characteristics, it is critical to ask questions about how well sampled particular domains or topics have been (Popham, 1998). Two examples help to illustrate the value of this source of evidence for both commercially produced and teacher-made measures.

W. James Popham

Some students at Dumfries High School enroll in Shirley Herrin's AP economics class so that they can earn college credit for their high-school work. They realize that they must inevitably score well on the AP economics test (College Board, 2005) before that college credit is awarded. In the AP manual for this program, the developers describe in detail how the content of the course and the subsequent measure have been derived. They establish a valid correspondence between the content included in the AP program and test and the content that economics experts see as central to the domain of economics. They also establish an association between introductory college courses in economics and the content of the AP program and test. In establishing the courses and examinations, the AP Development Committee on Economics surveyed the economics departments of the 200 institutions receiving the most AP grades in economics. Using the information ob-

Table 13–4	The sources of validity.	
Source	**Explanation**	**Guiding Questions**
Content	The degree of association evidenced between assessment tools and the academic domain or educational curriculum being sampled	What concepts or skills are considered important in these measures? How do those concepts and skills compare to my goals as a teacher and to the curriculum being taught? Is the subject well represented or narrowly assessed? How is students' understanding gauged, and does this match my educational objectives?
Construct	Evidence that the idea or conceptualization underlying a measure is viable	Does performance of these items or tasks reflect the intended characteristic or ability? Can student performance be explained by other factors than the one targeted? How do I expect to see this characteristic or ability manifest in my students, given their age and experiences?
Criterion	Use of an external standard or criterion to establish the appropriateness or legitimacy of assessment practices	Were the judgments made about students on these data upheld by their later performance? Would a similar judgment be reached about my students if an alternative measure were used?
Related Consequences	Evidence that the assessment practices have acceptable benefits and costs for students	Are my students benefiting from my approach to assessment? What affective and cognitive costs come with my assessment practices? Are those costs manageable or acceptable?

tained about the content of typical introductory college courses, the Committee developed the course outline and had the multiple-choice questions covering the outline pretested on college students enrolled in the appropriate economics courses. The AP course descriptions and examinations are thus representative of college courses and are, therefore, considered appropriate for the measurement of skills and knowledge in the fields of introductory microeconomics and macroeconomics (College Board, 2005).

When Shirley Herrin creates her own AP economics tests and evaluates the results, she also considers content validity issues. She has built her AP economics course around the AP program course description provided by the College Board (2005), which is foundational to the AP test. Her instruction and tests reflect selected economics concepts spelled out in the AP program. Shirley actually develops a **table of specification** for each unit, which is essentially a curricular blueprint (McMillan, 2001). That blueprint, illustrated in Table 13–5, outlines key concepts, specifies the level of processing desired, and establishes the relative weight (i.e., number of questions) for each concept in the course assessment.

Such a preparatory step does not eliminate Shirley's need to weigh the match between test results and her teaching (Shepard, 1995). However, it does increase the likelihood that she will give due attention to those concepts that are central to students' understanding of economics. As part of her ongoing assessment practices, Shirley makes it a habit to think back over the daily interactions. She carefully monitors whether she covered the topics to the breadth and depth she had intended. Further, she makes notes about

which concepts may require additional explanation and exploration if they are to be well understood. To judge the overall validity of her assessment practices for this unit, Shirley will weigh all of this content-related evidence.

Construct Judgments

A **construct** is a trait or characteristic presumed to underlie human personality or performance (Cronbach & Meehl, 1955). Unlike external physical characteristics, such as height or weight or running speed, constructs like intelligence, reading ability, or mathematical reasoning cannot be directly measured or weighed. However, these constructs are foundational to human learning and development. Consequently, when educators gauge the degree of validity in their use and interpretation of assessment data, they must decide the degree to which they effectively represented the construct of concern (Moss, 1992; Popham, 1998). The evidence they consider relates to **construct validity.**

To gather construct-related evidence, educators need to explore two complementary questions. First, how well do the measures represent the constructs of interest? Both Shirley Herrin and the College Board purport to have developed measures that gauge high-school students' economics knowledge. Before they can feel confident about those measures, both Shirley and the College Board must be able to demonstrate that the topics and items on those measures are indeed indicative of economics knowledge.

The second question educators should pose is whether performance can be explained by other factors or constructs not targeted by a measure—an all-too-common testing concern (Haladyna, Nolan, & Haas, 1991; Heubert & Hauser,

Table 13–5   Content specifications for an AP economics unit on the global economy.

Concept	Factual	Inferential	Application	Elaborative
	Weight Per Level of Mental Processing			
Bases for international trade	1	2		1
Functions of a global economy	2		2	
International exchange rates	1	1	1	
International trade policies	1		1	2
Global banking practices	1		1	1
Global market interdependencies	2	1		1

1999). For example, two of Shirley Herrin's AP students are immigrants for whom English is not the first language. When Shirley examines the results of her AP test, she needs to examine how much students' scores can be attributed to their language processing rather than to their economics knowledge. She does not want her economics tests to become English language tests.

To make this determination, Shirley should consider those students' in-class oral performance on the targeted concepts in comparison to their written test performance. She should also look at scoring patterns on selected-response questions (e.g., multiple-choice items) as compared to constructed-response questions (e.g., essay items). Her purpose is to ensure that she is not unintentionally penalizing those students for their writing.

Criterion Considerations

As discussed earlier, a **criterion** is essentially a standard against which student ability or performance is judged. Such standards are important tools for gathering evidence about the appropriateness of assessment practices. Two forms of criterion-related evidence are commonly used when weighing validity decisions—concurrent and predictive (Glass, 1978). What differentiates the two is the time frame in which they operate. One way to validate assessment decisions is to compare outcomes from one measure to the outcomes for another measure, which is considered a legitimate indicator of that domain or construct (Messick, 1994). When one measure is compared to an accepted standard within a relatively short time span, the process is referred to as **concurrent validity.**

For example, the school administration at Dumfries might want to determine whether their locally developed mathematics achievement test will produce data comparable to that of a more expensive commercial measure they have given in the past. To make that determination, the administration could give all high-school freshmen both tests in the early fall. If the local measure is functioning well, students should perform comparably on both measures. Students would not necessarily get the same scores on the two measures, but those who score above average, average, or below average on one measure should perform similarly on the other. If no such discernible correlation results, the Dumfries administration would need to reevaluate the validity of the data resulting from their locally created measure.

Sometimes educators want evidence that current assessment data predict later performance or behavior (Messick, 1980). When the standard applied in validation is future performance, the concept is known as **predictive validity.** Because the AP economics test is based on college economics curricula, there should be a strong, positive relation between students' performance on the AP economics test and their subsequent performance in college economics courses.

Similarly, the reason many colleges and universities rely on screening measures like the SAT I is that they assume a relation between higher verbal and mathematics scores and subsequent success in college—an assumption being heatedly debated in the literature (Crouse & Trusheim, 1998). This issue relates to personality measures as well. There should be some evidence that individuals classified as adjusted or maladjusted on such measures eventually manifest traits or conditions consistent with the earlier diagnosis. If not, there would be little justification for administering such measures or bestowing such labels.

Consequence Issues

When researchers discuss validity evidence, they typically focus only on content-, construct-, and criterion-related information. However, some like Stanley Messick (1994), an expert in educational assessment, argue for yet another evidentiary source. It is Messick's contention that validity determinations deal with the uses and interpretations made of assessment outcomes. Therefore, it makes sense to consider the consequences of those uses and interpretations on students and the educational process. That is, it is critical for educators to gather **consequence-related** evidence (Smith & Rottenberg, 1991). Consequence-related analysis is analogous to a cost-benefit evaluation. The educator catalogs the positive results of assessments and weighs those against any potential negative effects. If the costs of current assessment practices outweigh their perceived benefits, those practices should be seriously reconsidered.

Ms. Herrin might want to ascertain the merits of continuing the AP economics program at Dumfries to be sure that the demands of the program and the stress of the final AP exam are not exacting too high a toll on the students, relative to any benefits they are receiving. As data sources Shirley could survey past students to find out whether the content of the economics course prepared them well for their college classes. She could also interview current students about their interests in economics and any performance anxieties they might be feeling.

In light of the emphasis placed on testing and accountability in today's schools, it is understandable that concerns about assessment consequences are growing (Paris, 2000b). Many educators are aware of the degree to which measures meant to document the outcomes of the educational process are now dictating or constraining instructional content. To gather consequence-related information, educators need to explore the positive and negative results of assessment practices, and that exploration should extend beyond classroom practices to the systemic nature of assessment at the local and state levels as well. To be valid, the outcomes of these practices should contribute to students' learning and development and should not distract from it.

Guidelines for Enhancing Validity

Based on the literature in educational assessment (e.g., Popham, 1998; D. E. Tanner, 2001), several guidelines can enhance the validity of assessment practices. These guidelines (see Table 13–6) have value for classroom teachers who are directly involved in the assessment of students.

They are also valuable for educational researchers who create measures for commercial use or for study purposes.

Carefully Specify the Content or Task to Be Assessed
Taking time to specify the core concepts and principles in a domain can increase the likelihood that relevant content is taught and subsequently tested (Shepard, 1995). Educators with principled knowledge of the subjects they are teaching are more likely to represent critical concepts adequately and give suitable weight or attention to central versus tangential content. Commercial test developers can turn to recognized experts to contribute to content specification; individual teachers can turn to established sources like professional communities or research organizations for such guidance.

Consider the Cognitive and Affective Processes Involved in Task Performance Task analysis has always been a useful tool in a teacher's arsenal. In **task analysis** educators sketch out the basic concepts and processes that underlie performance of a certain task (Goetz et al., 1992). For example, Goldin (1992) sought to capture the forms of representational thinking required in mathematical problem solving; his analysis is graphically represented in Figure 5–2. Shirley Herrin could offer a much simpler analysis of the processes affecting performance on her unit test (see Figure 13–4).

Shirley recognizes that, to some degree, her students' scores on the unit test can be attributed to their general reading abilities because her students must process the material in their course textbooks and outside readings. The

Table 13–6 Guidelines for improving validity.	
Guideline	**Illustration**
Carefully specify the content or task to be assessed	When Shirley Herrin wrote the curriculum for her regular economics course, she turned to several sources for assistance, including the state's curriculum guide. She used these established sources to help create her course specifications.
Consider the cognitive and affective processes involved in task performance	Shirley recognizes that cognitive and affective processes influence her students' performance. Consequently, she considers such factors as the students' reading and study abilities and their interests in the subject matter.
Compare the scores for particular groups	Shirley has come to expect some performance differences between her regular and advance students. As long as those differences are not extreme or in conflict with in-class behaviors, she sees them as acceptable and predictable. However, she also analyzes her performance data to ensure that other group differences do not mar the process, such as those between males and females or between minority and nonminority students.
Analyze scores that occur before and after relevant experiences or interventions	Shirley gives a test at the beginning and the end of her economic courses. She expects changes in student performance to correspond to relevant educational experiences (e.g., class attendance and active participation), but not to tangential events (e.g., weather or unrelated activities).
Compare scores to those for related measures	For evidence that assessment practices result in meaningful and valid information, Shirley looks at her AP students' performance on the formal AP economics test. She expects those who do well in her class to do well on that exam.

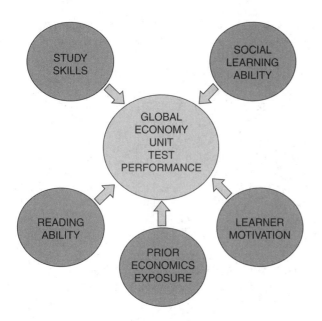

■ FIGURE 13–4   An analysis of students' performance on a global economy test.

students must also know how to study and prepare for their exams. Thus, differences in study skills would naturally affect scores. In addition, Shirley has found that students perform differentially because of their motivations, including their interests and self-efficacy beliefs (see Chapter 10). Further, Shirley's curriculum involves various group activities reflected on the test. Thus, students' abilities to work in social groups could impact their test performance. Finally, Shirley has found that some students come to her classes with prior exposure to economics, and that background knowledge can play a significant role in test performance.

Compare the Scores for Particular Groups   Another important consideration in making validity judgments is between-group performance. Under most circumstances teachers expect students to perform differently on educational measures. The critical question from a validity standpoint is whether student groups are behaving as expected (Messick, 1980).

For instance, in educational research differences in performance are expected between younger and older students. Because of their varied experiences, older students should generally outperform younger students. Similarly, we might anticipate that the advanced students, who may be more motivated to earn higher grades and who may see economics as more relevant to their lives, might outperform regular students on Ms. Herrin's unit test. Unwanted or unexpected group differences, such as those between minority and nonminority students, can point to problems with current assessment practices (Haladyna et al., 1991; Heubert & Hauser, 1999).

Analyze Scores That Occur Before and After Relevant Experiences or Interventions   Some teachers administer a test on the first day of class to survey their

students' knowledge of the particular domain. They then give that same test at the conclusion of the course, expecting that their teaching and the other experiences of the course will be reflected in the students' scores in predictable ways (Messick, 1994). For instance, students who attended regularly and participated actively should have appreciable gains in their knowledge. However, if students with low attendance, minimal participation, and poor daily grades scored well on the exit exam, it would raise doubts about the validity of the teachers' practices.

Overall, if practices are truly grounded in the construct, then positive outcomes should result when experiences are provided or conditions are altered directly relevant to that construct (Cronbach & Meehl, 1955). Conversely, no marked changes should occur in students' performance as a result of experiences or conditions that are tangential or irrelevant. Students' participation in the school's music program should not have any dramatic or predictable effect on performance in Shirley Herrin's economics course, for instance. By tracking relevant transformations in outcomes, teachers can have a better idea of whether their assessment practices are legitimate (Moss, 1992).

Compare Scores to Those for Related Measures   Another source of validation evidence can be found in comparing performance on construct-related measures (Fiske, 1988). In other words, if outcomes can be trusted, students should manifest similar performance patterns on measures that claim to tap the same underlying constructs. For example, Shirley would be concerned if AP students who received high scores on her final examination did not generally do well on the AP economics test. Because Shirley's course is based on the AP curriculum and the specifications that frame the AP economics test, there should be a strong, positive relation between performance on her final exam and the commercially produced test.

This correlation does not mean that every student getting an A on Shirley's test should score in the upper portion of the AP distribution. Nor does it mean that every student who does poorly in Shirley's course would perform similarly on the AP test. But there should be sufficient correspondence in students' scores on these two measures to reinforce Shirley's judgment that her assessment practices are targeting the same content as the AP exam.

Judging the Consistency of Assessment Practices

Although validity remains the penultimate judgment in the evaluation of educational assessment, its complement is reliability. **Reliability** deals with the stability and consistency of assessment outcomes (Algina, 1992). In essence, reliability is a necessary but not sufficient condition for determining validity. If educators are confident that their measures result in stable and consistent data, they can then turn to the issue of whether those outcomes are legitimate.

The Nature of Reliability

Like validity, reliability does not rest in any measures or procedures, but in the data they produce (Feldt & Brennan, 1989; Traub, 1994). Reliability analysis informs assessment decisions in multiple ways. First, it can help educators determine whether students' performance on a particular measure was stable from the beginning to the end. Second, it can reveal whether students' scores on the same or related tests stayed relatively consistent over time. Finally, reliability analysis can show whether two measures are behaving similarly for a group of students.

Correlation analysis, discussed in the prior section, is the basis for determining whether outcomes are highly consistent or not. When scores are highly reliable, the distributions compared should result in a strong, positive correlation coefficient (+.70 or greater). Four common methods of reliability analysis are used in educational research and practice. As summarized in Table 13–7, these types vary in terms of the number and the form of the measures administered and the time frame in which testing occurs.

Split-Half

Sometimes educators want to know whether scores from a particular test are reliable indicators of student characteristics or abilities. That is, they want to gauge the **internal consistency** of a selected measure, such as Shirley Herrin's global economy test. One method for making this determination is the **split-half** procedure. Because reliability methods involve correlation analysis, there must be two paired distributions to compare. Thus, with only one measure given only one time, it is necessary to make two tests out of one and then calculate the direction and the strength of their association. If a test results in a relatively consistent performance for students, it should show fairly similar scores on the two test halves.

Shirley used this method for her unit test by separating her multiple-choice, short-answer, and essay questions into two parts (A and B). She then paired students' scores for Part A with their scores from Part B. The resulting scores for her fourth-period class are listed in the box on the right.

When Shirley performed a correlation analysis, she found that the correlation coefficient for these two parts was

FOURTH PERIOD ADVANCED ECONOMICS					
Student	Part A	Part B	Student	Part A	Part B
Agnes	50	48	Hector	43	42
James	47	47	Jennifer	44	41
Gina	49	45	Grant	41	44
Samson	45	46	Michael	41	41
Jeff	45	44	Nancy	42	39
Daniel	43	46	Elmer	42	38
Anabell	44	43	Norman	38	38
Theodore	46	40	Doris	33	36
Mavis	44	42	Betty	31	34

.77. Thus, this teacher-developed unit test had a high level of internal consistency, which should make Shirley feel good about the consistency of her scoring practices.

Test-Retest

Sometimes educators want to explore the stability of scores for a particular measure over a span of time. In this case a **test-retest** procedure applies. For this method students are given a test and are then given that same test again after some lapse of time. As mentioned earlier, some teachers give students a general test at the beginning of a course and then administer that same test at the end. Because they expect the intervening instruction to have a significant effect on the students, the teachers look for some variation (i.e., instability) in students' performance from the beginning to the end of the course. Students who come into class with higher levels of related knowledge are apt to gain more from the course than students with no background knowledge of the subject. However, depending on students' motivation and effort, some students with initially low scores may show substantial gains. Therefore, with a test-retest analysis, teachers might expect a moderate to low positive correlation between pretest and posttest scores, with coefficients typically falling between .30 and .50.

Table 13–7	Forms of reliability analysis.
Method	**Procedure**
Split-Half	Take one test and divide it into two theoretically equivalent parts. Correlate students' performance on one part to their performance on the second part.
Test-Retest	Administer one test twice with some lapse of time between first and second administrations.
Alternate-Forms	Use two versions of a test built on the same table of specifications. Administer those two versions at approximately the same time or after some lapse of time. The length of time between testings will influence the strength of the correlation expected.
Interrater	Have two or more individuals score the same measure or experience. If these raters' scorings are consistent, those markings should be strongly, positively correlated.

Alternate-Forms

Commercial test developers often want to develop more than one version of a measure for reasons of diversity and security. Although these developers base their alternate versions on the same table of specifications and expert analyses, they still must ensure that these two versions are statistically equivalent. Thus, they must show that these two forms produce comparable scores among respondents. The **alternate-forms** (also called *parallel* or *equivalent*) method permits educators to estimate the degree of reliability between two versions of a select measure.

Educators can perform alternate-form analysis in two ways that vary in the time interval. In the standard alternate-form analysis, the two test versions are given to a number of individuals at approximately the same time. The respondents' scores on these two versions are then submitted to correlation analysis. If the two versions perform as expected, the outcome is a significant positive correlation coefficient. In the other procedure, which approximates the test-retest method, the same respondents take one of the versions at some point in time and then take the other version after a specified time interval. Linn and Gronlund (2000) consider this to be the more rigorous and thereby sounder procedure for ascertaining equivalence because of the the added condition of a time interval. According to Linn and Gronlund, the span of time influences the strength of the expected coefficient, the longer the interval between testings, the smaller the anticipated coefficient.

Interrater

As an educational researcher, I often need to confirm that my methods of scoring data are not idiosyncratic but would be independently reached by others with highly comparable outcomes. The **interrater** method, which systematically compares the scores of one qualified rater to those of another for the same set of measures, allows for this type of analysis (Traub, 1994). Interrater analysis is not just of value to researchers, however. With the rise in assessment measures that are more subjective or judgmental in nature, teachers like Shirley Herrin can also benefit from procedures that confirm the consistency of their grading practices. For example, they might occasionally ask another qualified individual to score their class projects or essays against a rubric and then compare the ratings to judge the consistency in interpretations.

Guidelines for Enhancing Reliability

Educators should consider several guidelines, which are illustrated in Table 13–8, to enhance the consistency and stability of their assessment data (Linn & Gronlund, 2000; Messick, 1980).

Include an Adequate Sampling of Items and Cases
When it comes to making sound reliability judgments, it helps to have a sufficient sampling of items to evaluate (Algina, 1992; Feldt & Brennan, 1989). With only one question or task on which to base a judgment, there is more chance for an error. It is also hard to know whether assessments result in stable outcomes if results are compared for only a few individuals. The more cases that are considered, the clearer the picture of consistency that is achieved.

Eliminate Extraneous Factors or Conditions
When the stability of measurement outcomes matters, it is important that no irrelevant factors or conditions significantly affect the outcomes (Algina, 1992; Popham, 1993). For example, if the fire alarm goes off during Shirley Herrin's third-period class, as students are in the midst of their global economy test, they might be required to go outside and stand in the cold before they can return to the exam. Even if this distraction takes only 10 minutes, it could seriously affect the consistency of those students' performance on the remaining items. Extraneous factors such as testwiseness, time, anxiety, and mental disruptions can make the outcomes of any measure unstable (Cannell, 1988). To reduce the potential for such extraneous effects, high-stakes measures like the SAT I or the AP economics test are standardized (Madaus & Kellaghan, 1993).

Determine the Strength and Direction of Association Appropriate for the Context
Commercial test developers are understandably invested in creating measures that are highly reliable, as well as valid. For these companies strong positive correlation coefficients need to be documented for multiple forms of reliability (Traub, 1994). However, in other situations the strength and direction of correlation coefficients can legitimately vary (Nitko, 2001). For example, when significant interventions are meant to change individuals' physical, cognitive, or psychosocial characteristics, there may well be shifts in pretreatment and posttreatment performance, which would directly change the strength and direction of assessment data (Linn & Gronlund, 2000).

In certain classroom situations, marked shifts in assessment outcomes are desirable. For instance, as mentioned earlier, when teachers administer an initial test and then readminister it at the end of the course, with an instructional intervention between the testings, they would not expect to find a strong, positive correlation. A moderate-to-low positive correlation would be quite acceptable in this situation. Educators must weigh the conditions under which they assess their students and must ascertain what forms and level of reliability evidence they would accept as confirming their assessment practices (Algina, 1992).

Clearly Delineate and Illustrate the Bases for Scoring
It obviously enhances reliability when responses on assessment measures can be readily judged (Messick, 1994; D. E. Tanner, 2001). Not surprisingly, most commercial measures consist of selected-response items like multiple-choice questions. Given an answer key, most individuals score such items identically. However, constructed-response items can be more consistently scored when the basis for scoring is carefully delineated (Ebel & Frisbie, 1991). A response pro-

Table 13–8 Guidelines for improving reliability.

Guideline	Illustration
Include an adequate sampling of items	When it comes to making reliability judgments, Shirley Herrin knows that she needs to have a sufficient number of items, tasks, or students to evaluate. Consequently, she often includes some selected-response as well as constructed-response items on her tests.
Eliminate extraneous factors or conditions	Shirley always tries to keep the climate in her classroom quiet and orderly during testing. She also tries to ensure that her students understand the test directions and have sufficient time to answer all questions.
Determine the direction and strength of association appropriate for the context	Shirley expects that each test she administers will be internally consistent. However, she recognizes that her essay and application questions are more challenging and often result in more variable scores than her multiple-choice items.
Clearly delineate and illustrate the bases for scoring	Shirley establishes clear scoring criteria, especially for her constructed-response items. She also checks her results periodically for interrater agreement by comparing her markings against those of a colleague familiar with her scoring procedures and rubrics.

tocol that outlines the contents of a good answer or a scoring rubric with examples that illustrate the differences in scoring levels can significantly improve reliability.

When multiple raters are used, it is important to ensure that those raters receive training (Stiggins, 2001), part of which should entail clear explanations and models to follow. In our research my colleagues and I train raters until they meet a particular performance criterion before we allow them to score data independently. These same cautionary steps can be instituted in K–12 classrooms, as well.

What Do Teachers Need to Know About Assessment?

Because assessment is integral to optimal learning and development, teachers at all levels need foundational knowledge of and skills in educational assessment. Moreover, those competencies need to encompass the breadth and the depth of educational activities. That is, those competencies must acknowledge the many forms and purposes of assessment discussed earlier.

Recognizing the influential place of assessment in student learning, several leading educational organizations jointly studied this topic and produced *Standards for Teacher Competence in Educational Assessment of Students* (AFT, NCME, & NEA, 1990). The framers of that document wanted those assessment standards to serve multiple purposes for multiple audiences.

- A guide for teacher educators as they design and approve programs for teacher preparation
- A self-assessment guide for teachers in identifying their need for professional development in student assessment

- A guide for workshop instructors as they design professional development experiences for in-service teachers
- An impetus for educational measurement specialists and teacher trainers to conceptualize both student assessment and teacher training in student assessment more broadly than has been the case in the past

The resulting standards, or competencies, can be stated as guiding principles covering seven broad areas in educational assessment.

Teachers Should Be Skilled in Choosing Assessment Methods Appropriate for Instructional Decisions

Education and assessment should operate in communion (Gellman, 1995; Shepard, 1995). What occurs in the classroom should inform assessment practices, just as assessment practices must reflect classroom activities. However, there are many purposes for and forms of assessment, just as there are many factors that can influence the quality of such assessments. Teachers must understand these forms, purposes, and factors if they are to make wise assessment choices. For example, teachers must be able to judge the validity and reliability of assessment outcomes, and they must be able to use whatever valid and reliable information they garner about students and about their teaching to enhance the learning environment (Brookhart, 1999).

Moreover, teachers need to consider the physical, cognitive, and psychosocial characteristics of their students when they weigh their many assessment options (Hambleton, 1996; Popham, 1998). What evidence is there that developers took steps to avoid biased content or unsuitable language in the tests? Did they administer the test to diverse groups and report that information in their manuals? What modifications or alternatives did these developers make available for students with particular physical, cognitive, or psychosocial conditions? Are these learner conditions discussed in the administration procedures or reflected in the norms?

Teachers' goals also come into play in their decision about what assessment methods seem viable for a given situation (McMillan, 2001; Nitko, 2001). Are teachers seeking a broad assessment of students' knowledge and skills in a particular content area, or are they seeking to make more specific, individualistic determinations about students' needs, characteristics, or aptitudes? The many assessment options include an assortment of norm-referenced tests, as well as performance measures, writing samples, portfolios, and surveys and questionnaires, all of which are more criterion-referenced and self-referential (Hambleton, 1996).

In many cases the selection of appropriate assessment is not the decision of an isolated teacher; it often involves groups of teachers, administrators, and evaluation experts working collaboratively. Nonetheless, those educators concerned with identifying appropriate tests should take certain steps to ensure a more viable decision.

- Clearly specify the purpose for testing, as well as the population being tested
- Identify tests that match both the purpose and the target population
- Examine sample questions and consider the procedures involved in administering each identified test
- Search manuals for evidence that the tests result in valid and reliable outcomes
- Look at critiques and reviews from external sources other than the publisher
- Select the measure that most closely matches instructional goals, student population, and teacher expertise

Given the untold number of tests from which teachers may choose, where can teachers turn for guidance on picking valid and reliable measures? They certainly do not have time to secure samples of every possibility and comb through the manuals for validity and reliability data. Fortunately, key sources provide useful summaries and critiques of many published tests. The Buros Institute, for example, annually publishes the *Mental Measurements Yearbook,* which includes descriptions of tests and relevant technical information as well as informative critiques by assessment experts. In addition, PRO-ED, an educational publisher, offers a series of volumes entitled *Test Critiques,* which summarizes and reviews measures used in psychology, education, and business. These and other sources can give educators access to the information they need to make wise choices in test selection.

Teachers Should Be Skilled in Developing Assessment Methods Appropriate for Instructional Decisions

Despite the many externally produced tests that are part of the school experience, it is teacher-developed measures that remain the linchpin of educational assessment. For that reason, teachers must be competent in developing the assessment methods that result in effective decision making. Chapter 14 focuses specifically on teacher-made measures and methods for improving both the variety and validity of such measures. However, classroom-based assessment goes beyond teacher-made tests; it encompasses all forms of information-gathering that teachers employ on a daily basis (Alexander & Parsons, 1991). When Shirley Herrin observes her students, listens to their comments, or analyzes their responses, she is extracting meaningful information from those common experiences and is engaging in valuable assessment practices.

Teachers Should Be Skilled in Administering, Scoring, and Interpreting the Results of Both Externally Produced and Teacher-Produced Assessment Methods

Selecting or devising valid and reliable measures is one thing, but teachers must also be skilled at administering, scoring, and interpreting the results of assessment practices, whether they are externally produced or teacher made (Brookhart, 1997). With teacher-produced measures, teachers should take the time to calculate and examine the measures of typicality, dispersion, and association explored earlier in this chapter. These procedures can unearth patterns in student performance that speak not only to the characteristics and abilities of the students themselves, but also to the effectiveness of instruction and assessment practices.

For standardized tests like the SAT I or the AP economics test, teachers' roles are primarily those of administrator and interpreter of outcomes (Lyman, 1991; Nolen, Haladyna, & Haas, 1992). When the tests are standardized, any variation in administration could have a significant effect on the validity or reliability of results. If students are to be judged on the basis of such tests, educators must ensure their validity and reliability.

A good part of interpreting externally produced tests entails making sense of the types of test norms developers have used and the scores derived from those norms (Diekhoff, 1992; Mehrens & Lehman, 1987). When students take standardized tests like the Iowa Test of Basic Skills (ITBS), their performance is described in multiple forms, including percentile ranks, grade equivalents, and standard scores. All of these methods, overviewed in Table 13–9, involve transforming students' raw scores or adjusted raw scores into a system that allows for normative comparisons.

Base Scores

A **raw score** is simply the number of items that a student answers correctly. If there are 100 questions on the AP economics test and Tony misses 32, his raw score is 68. If test developers want to discourage guessing, they can penalize students for each incorrect answer by subtracting from the raw score some fraction of the number of incorrect answers. This procedure results in an **adjusted raw score.** If test de-

Table 13-9 A glossary of scoring terms.

Category of Scores	Form	Description
Base Score	Raw score Adjusted raw score	The number of items a respondent answered correctly The raw score minus some portion of incorrect answers
Ordinal Transformation	Percentile ranking Grade equivalent	Individual's relative standing within a normal distribution that has been divided into 100 parts Student's performance converted into an integer corresponding to years and months of schooling
Standard Score Transformation	Stanines Z-score T-score Normal curve equivalent	The nine parts into which a normal distribution is divided, with a mean of 5 and a standard deviation of 2 A scale with a mean of 0 and a standard deviation of 1 A conversion of z-scores with a mean of 50 and a standard deviation of 10 A scale with a mean of 50 and a standard deviation of 21.06, to parallel percentile rankings at the endpoints (1 and 99) and the midpoint (50) of the distribution

velopers subtracted one-quarter point for each of Tony's wrong answers (not those he just left blank) and he answered 28 of the questions incorrectly, his adjusted raw score would be $68 - (28 \times .25)$ or 61.

Ordinal Transformations

Whether based on raw or adjusted raw scores, each manner of score comes with certain uses and limitations that teachers must understand.

Percentile Ranks   Percentiles are one of the most widely used and easily understood methods of reporting test performance. **Percentiles** essentially divide the normal distribution into 100 parts; the resulting ranking tells the percentage of the norm group that a particular student outscored (Diekhoff, 1992). Thus, Mary Sanders's national percentile rank (NPR) for reading on the ITBS (see Figure 13–5) means that 53% of the norming group scored at or below her in that subject area. Even though percentiles are easy to grasp, they are only ordinal measures; that is, the differences between percentile ranks, such as between 53 and 54, are not necessarily consistent or particularly meaningful.

Grade Equivalent Scores   Another score transformation that was once quite popular and is deceptively easy to interpret is the grade equivalent (Goetz et al., 1992). With **grade equivalents** a student's performance is expressed as an integer representing years and months of schooling. For example, a 6.9 means the ninth month of sixth grade and represents that point in schooling when students in the norming group would typically receive a comparable score. When Mary's 53 in reading was converted to a grade equivalent of 3.8, it meant that her level of performance was typical for students in the norming group who were in the eighth month of third grade.

Even though grade equivalents seem to be clear and precise measures, they are not (Linn & Gronlund, 2000). Test developers have started moving away from their use in standardized testing because they can be readily misinterpreted by teachers, parents, and the lay public. Serious measurement problems are associated with these score transformations (Reynolds, 1982; Wright & Isenstein, 1977).

- Grade equivalents tend to exaggerate rather small differences in performance, particularly in the upper grades. In some cases a difference of one or two items could translate into almost a year's increase.
- Grade equivalents assume that the rate of learning during the academic year remains constant, with no appreciable losses or gains during intervening periods like summer vacation. Anyone who has ever taught school knows how variable the rates of learning are, both from month to month and from year to year.
- The meaning of grade equivalents can vary dramatically as a consequence of the test itself, as well as the skill or domain tested. Because grade equivalents are based on the performance of a specific norming group, they will differ from test to test. In other words, Mary's 3.8 on reading for one standardized test may have little in common with the 3.8 in reading on another published measure. Similarly, Mary's 4.8 for reading comprehension would not be equivalent to a 4.8 in vocabulary or a 4.8 in mathematical computation. Grade equivalents have no consistency of scale even for skills within a domain like reading, much less across domains such as reading and mathematics.
- Grade equivalents are not viable tools for grade placement. Perhaps the most common misconception about grade equivalent scores is that they indicate where a student should be placed for instruction. However, grade equivalents were never meant to serve that type of

PRIMARY READING PROFILE FOR MARY SANDERS
Iowa Tests of Basic Skills® (ITBS®)

IOWA TESTS

Student: Sanders, Mary   Student ID: 1234567890
Class/Group: Clark
School: Central Elementary   Form/Level: A/9
School Code: 99C00212   Test Date: 04/2001   Report Date: 04/26/01
District: Spring Lake   Norms: Spring 2000
Order No.: 002-A7000028-0-002   Page: 1   Grade: 3

A student's ability to read is related to success in many areas of school work. This Reading Profile combines information from the reading and reading-related skills measured by various tests in the Iowa Tests of Basic Skills.

Reading Profile Summary

NATIONAL PERCENTILE RANK (NPR)

TESTS	NPR
Vocabulary	31
Word Analysis	30
Spelling	48
Listening	60
Reading Comprehension	71
Reading Profile Total	52

The Vocabulary test measures knowledge of words important in the comprehension of all kinds of reading materials. This test is also the best single measure of general verbal ability in the entire test battery. Vocabulary development contributes to a student's understanding of spoken and written language encountered both in and out of school.

The Word Analysis test measures a student's awareness of sound-to-symbol relationships that play an important role in early literacy development. It also tests a student's ability to identify and analyze word parts. Word Analysis is a particularly useful part of the Reading Profile for students whose comprehension-related skills in reading and/or listening are relatively weak.

The Spelling test measures a student's understanding of how the sounds of spoken English are encoded into written words. Weaknesses in spelling can provide insight into aspects of the reading process that involve word attack skills or the ability to sound out and comprehend unfamiliar words.

The Listening test measures many of the same comprehension skills as a reading test, but for spoken rather than written language. These comprehension skills range from understanding factual details in a story to making inferences, predicting outcomes, and understanding sequences or new concepts. The Listening test is a especially useful indicator of comprehension skills for students whose ability to decode written language is limited.

The Reading Comprehension test measures the ultimate goal or reading: the understanding of written language in a variety of fiction, nonfiction, and poetry. Factual details as well as inferences and generalizations based on stories are tested.

Tests and Skills	Total Num. Items Att.	%C Stu.	%C Nat.	Diff.
VOCABULARY				
Vocabulary	29 29	62	67	-5
WORD ANALYSIS				
Phonological Awareness and Decoding	11 11	63	60	+3
Initial Sounds	4 4	75	70	+5
Medial Sounds	4 4	50	83	-33
Final Sounds	3 3	67	76	-9
Identifying and Analyzing Word Parts	24 24	84	78	+6
Silent Letters	4 4	75	60	+15
Initial Syllable	5 5	60	83	-23
Final Syllable	5 5	80	62	+18
Suffixes	5 5	60	62	-2
Compound Words	5 5	100	80	+20
SPELLING				
Vowels	9 9	66	77	-11
Consonants	8 8	63	63	0
Vowel Consonant Combinations	4 4	50	60	-10
Affixes	3 3	67	62	+5

Tests and Skills	Total Num. Items Att.	%C Stu.	%C Nat.	Diff.
LISTENING				
Literal Comprehension	16 14	69	55	+14
Literal Meaning	4 4	50	64	-14
Following Directions	4 3	75	60	+15
Visual Relationships	3 3	67	87	-20
Sustained Listening	5 4	80	83	-3
Inferential Comprehension	15 15	64	68	-4
Inferential Meaning	4 4	75	60	+15
Concept Development	3 3	67	67	0
Predicting Outcomes	3 3	67	54	+13
Sequential Relationships	5 5	60	72	-12
READING COMPREHENSION				
Factual Understanding	17 16	86	71	+8
Inference and Interpretation	12 12	74	66	+8
Analysis and Generalization	8 8	100	66	+34

* A plus sign (+) or a minus sign (-) in the difference graph indicates that the bar extends beyond +/- 20.

■ FIGURE 13–5   Individual student report.

Note: From Iowa Tests Individual Student Report. Copyright 2001 by Riverside Publishers.

diagnostic function. At best, they are extremely rough estimates of a student's performance level that must be treated with a great deal of suspicion and caution.

Standard Scores

The third category of score transformations that educators encounter are standard scores, or *scaled* scores. Although they come in various forms, **standard scores** are all based on measures of dispersion, especially the standard deviation (Diekhoff, 1992). Standard scores generally tell how far a given score is from the mean. Further, they all involve the mathematical transformation of test data to a common and consistent metric that can be easily grasped and communicated.

The SAT I is an example. The range on the verbal or mathematics portion of that test is 200 to 800 with a mean of 500 and a standard deviation of 100. There are certainly far fewer than 800 verbal or 800 mathematical items on the test. And it is not by chance that the mean and the standard deviation from year to year are 500 and 100, respectively. The true mean and standard deviation are made to fit that certain scale by applying a particular formula, which determines the form of standard score that is applied to the test. The most common forms of standard scores, summarized in Table 13–9, are stanines, z-scores, T-scores, and normal curve equivalents.

Stanines With **stanines,** a term that comes from the phrase "standard nines," the normal distribution is divided into nine parts, each of which corresponds to different per-

centages of the distribution. For this particular scale, the mean is 5 and the standard deviation is 2. In other words, Stanine 5 sits at the midpoint of the distribution. Stanine 9, which is two standard deviations above that mean, is the highest point of the scale. Similarly, Stanine 1 is the lowest point, two standard deviations below the mean. Because stanines are normalized, Mary's 5 in reading on the ITBS can be compared to her 4 in vocabulary. In addition, Mary's overall reading stanine of 5 can be compared to Jason's 3, which suggests that he may require special assistance in this area.

Z-score One of the best known standard scores is the **z-score**. This scale is based on a mean of 0 and a standard deviation of 1. A negative z-score indicates performance below the mean, whereas a positive z-score marks performance above the mean. Thus, if Mary received a +1 for the social studies portion of the ITBS, her score would be one standard deviation above the mean for that subject area. The formula for obtaining z-scores is rather simple and can be easily applied to interval data, such as scores on Shirley Herrin's global economy unit test.

$$\text{z-score} = \frac{X - \overline{X}}{\text{SD}}$$

X = any raw score

$\overline{X}$ = mean of the raw score

SD = standard deviation of raw score distribution

T-score For **T-scores** the scale has a mean of 50 and a standard deviation of 10. To obtain a T-score, one must first convert raw scores to z-scores and then apply the following formula: T-score = 50 + 10(z). Thus, Mary's +1 for social studies on the ITBS would convert to a T-score of 60.

Normal Curve Equivalent Another form of standard score that is commonly reported for standardized tests is the normal curve equivalent. The **normal curve equivalent (NCE)** has a mean of 50 and a standard deviation of 21.06. This metric sets the range of the NCE from 1 to 99. Thus, the NCE score and a student's percentile rank will be comparable at the two extremes (1 and 99) and at the midpoint of the distribution (50).

Teachers Should Be Skilled in Using Assessment Results When Making Decisions About Individual Students, Planning Instruction, Developing Curriculum, and Targeting School Improvement

Students and teachers are well aware of the power that assessment plays in formal learning. Students are frequently placed in groups, classes, and special programs as a result of assessment practices (Hallahan & Kauffman, 2000). Educators are expected to make appropriate modifications in the lessons for individual students or classes based on reliable and valid information (Ebel & Frisbie, 1991; Shepard, 1995). Even entire schools and school districts institute programs or modify their structures based on the outcomes of large-scale assessments. In several states, for example, schoolwide data from tests like the ITBS have compelled state education offices to demand significant improvements in schools' overall performance. Without evidence of such improvement, targeted schools may be subjected to various penalties, up to the complete restructuring of their personnel and programs.

At every educational level, the decisions made are only as good as the information guiding them (Stiggins, 1993). From teachers to school administrators to state and national education officials, there is a responsibility to gather the most appropriate evidence possible and ensure that such information is valid, reliable, and relevant to the situation at hand. Clearly, teachers cannot make critical decisions about their students based solely on intuitions or gut feelings. They should be able to produce viable evidence that supports those intuitions. And the same is true at every level of the educational enterprise.

Teachers Should Be Skilled in Developing Valid Pupil Grading Procedures That Use Pupil Assessments

Nothing is as common or as frustrating to the teaching profession as the task of grading students' work (Kubiszyn & Borich, 1996). Teachers find grading frustrating for many reasons, including the ambiguity that the resulting numbers, letters, or checkmarks convey and the internal philosophical conflicts grading may engender (Ebel, 1979). However, students need some indication of how they are progressing, as do parents, who are partners in their children's academic development (Gellman, 1995). Educators

can follow certain guidelines to reduce the ambiguity and conflicts that come with the evaluative dimension of assessment (Brookhart, 1997; Wiggins, 1998).

- Develop grading practices that are in concert with educational goals and instructional philosophies. Although teachers must work within the educational system, they retain latitude in the grades they report. Shirley Herrin may be required to work within Dumfries High School's numerical grading system, but she decides who receives the 95, 85, or 75 and what the bases are for those grades. In other words, Shirley can decide how much effort, knowledge demonstration, or collaboration matters and how these factors will figure into students' grades.

- Consider the various purposes of assessment when grading student work. Grades are not all of equal importance, nor do they serve the same functions. When the purpose of grading is more formative, teachers must ensure that the grading procedure encompasses rich and informative feedback from which students can learn and grow. In the case of summative evaluation, grades and their consequences must be thoughtfully weighed and sensitively communicated.

- Base grades on solid and converging evidence of students' capabilities. Grades should afford a portrait of students and reflect a pattern in characteristics or behavior. One test or score that is unusually high or low for a given student should be treated as an outlier. Unless that performance can be confirmed with other valid and reliable sources of information, it should be rightly perceived as an academic aberration. For example, if Frank's 52 on Ms. Herrin's unit test is the only time he has ever scored below a 85, Shirley's instructional alarm should sound immediately. She should sit down with Frank and discuss this unexpected and uncharacteristic event rather than simply record it in her grade book without a second thought.

- Employ multiple assessment approaches that tap into varied processes and emphasize differing performance criteria. There is a remarkable variety of traditional and alternative assessments that teachers can introduce into the learning environment. By using a variety of such measures and the related grading procedures, teachers afford their students diverse venues for displaying their abilities and capabilities.

- Allow students and parents to be participants in the assessment process. Teachers do not need to shoulder the burden of grading alone. They should seek opportunities to bring other stakeholders, including the students themselves, into the decision-making process when reasonable. This approach can be particularly educational for students, who must acquire the ability to self-evaluate if they are to become competent in any academic domain. Allowing students and parents to participate in decision making—providing self-evaluations, articulating criteria, or selecting works to be assessed—can make them partners in this process.

Teachers Should Be Skilled in Communicating Assessment Results to Students, Parents, Other Lay Audiences, and Other Educators

Another important role that teachers must play is that of communicator. A teacher's job is not done when the tests have been selected or developed, administered, and scored. The interpretation of the outcomes to educational stakeholders is essential if assessment practices are to serve their intended goal of improving student learning and development (Brookhart, 1999; Nolen et al., 1992). Most textbooks on educational assessment talk about the communication role of teachers in terms of parent-teacher conferences or the few times a year when high-stakes test results or report cards go home. Although these are certainly important assessment events, they cannot be the sole bases for effective communication between home and school or school and community. Just as assessment is much broader than testing or evaluation, so, too, the lines of communication between school and home must entail more than a discussion of major tests or summative grades.

Particularly during the early years of schooling, regular written communication must occur between teachers and parents (Goetz et al., 1992; Nitko, 2001). Those written communications should seek to keep parents or guardians informed about upcoming educational experiences and instructional objectives. These communications should also give parents or guardians opportunities to contribute their time and expertise to the classroom community. Whether written or oral, the messages that teachers share with students, parents, and the public are more likely to have the desired effect when teachers follow certain recommendations.

- Be well versed in assessment and knowledgeable about each student
- Frame interactions positively and informally
- Provide suggestions or recommendations for contributing to student learning and performance
- Use clear and understandable language
- Listen and learn from others who care about students' well-being

Teachers Should Be Skilled in Recognizing Unethical, Illegal, and Otherwise Inappropriate Assessment Methods and Uses of Assessment Information

The byword in educational assessment should be fairness (Heubert & Hauser, 1999). Simply stated, **fairness** means that every individual has the right to be judged fairly and equitably (Popham, 1998). Fairness in assessment practices generally falls into four broad areas: absence of bias, procedural fairness, opportunity to learn, and equity of results (Linn & Gronlund, 2000). An **absence of bias** means that assessment methods and measurements must not inappropriately value the knowledge and abilities of one group over those of another. Intelligence tests, for instance, should

value mental processes as manifested in diverse sociocultural groups. The abilities or experiences of the nonminority cultural group must not determine what counts as good thinking, reasoning, or the like.

Procedural fairness deals with the equity of treatment afforded individuals during the assessment process. For example, is there evidence that Shirley followed equitable procedures in preparing and scoring the essay questions for her two advanced sections and her two regular sections? Another problem occurs when certain groups of students do not have the opportunity to learn or experience essential knowledge or skills sampled on assessment measures. This situation represents a violation of the **opportunity-to-learn** aspect of fairness, which seeks equity of academic exposure.

An additional concern relates to comparability in performance for diverse groups. This is the **equality-of-results** dimension of fairness. On most standardized tests, there are frequently differences in the average performance of nonminority and minority cultures. Various explanations are put forward for such cultural bias.

- Inappropriate test content—The information or processes tested are not oriented to the lives and the experiences of diverse cultures (Alexander & Parsons, 1991; Haladyna et al., 1991).
- Inappropriate standardization samples—Diverse groups are underrepresented in the norming sample (Mehrens & Lehman, 1987).
- Examiner or language bias—Either the examiner is ill-equipped to understand and interpret the responses of diverse students, or the language of the test precludes a fair measurement of the targeted knowledge or skills (Cannell, 1988).
- Inequitable social conditions—Students from diverse backgrounds may feel ill at ease in the testing environment or uncertain about the purposes for such assessments (Willingham & Cole, 1997).
- Weak construct validity—What is perceived as the construct of interest for the majority culture (e.g., intelligence) may not be comparably perceived by a diverse culture (Shepard, 1989, 1993).
- Poor predictive validity—Measures that may suitably predict subsequent performance for the nonminority culture may underestimate the future performance of those from diverse backgrounds (Crouse & Trusheim, 1998; Sacks, 2000).

■ Summary Reflections

How does assessment contribute to improved learning and instruction?

- Educational assessment involves the gathering of information to guide academic decision making.

- Measurement is the translation of human characteristics and abilities into numerical form.
  - Nominal data are merely numbers substituted for a categorical name.
  - Ordinal data signify the ranking or order of the information.
  - An interval scale makes the distance between measurements consistent and meaningful.
  - Ratio data have a true zero point.
- The evaluation component of assessment encompasses the specific judgments derived from academic information.
  - Those judgments can be classified according to their underlying purpose.
    - Those that are meant to shape or inform the ongoing process are formative.
    - Those that signify the degree of attainment of desired goals or objectives are summative.
    - Those that identify or profile learners' particular strengths or needs are diagnostic.
    - Those that ensure that students are placed in a suitable learning environment are placement.
  - The decision-making process requires educators to organize and summarize their information.
    - Measures of typicality allow them to identify the most frequently occurring score (i.e., mode) or the physical midpoint of a distribution (i.e., median) or the numerical center or average (i.e., mean) of that distribution.
    - Measures of dispersion tell about the differences among scores; the range, or overall spread of the distribution; the variance and standard deviation, or distance between a particular score and the mean, and the shape of the distribution, whether normal or positively or negatively skewed.
    - Measures of association examine the relation between two paired distributions, correlation analysis looks at the direction and the strength of that relation.
- Tests involve the development of measures to sample human characteristics and abilities.
  - Tests of maximum performance measure the upper bounds of human characteristics or abilities, whereas tests of typical performance capture normal or everyday behavior.
  - Norm-referenced tests use an established norm group for comparison, whereas an absolute standard is used for criterion referencing and an individual's performance history is the baseline in self-referencing.
  - Many commercial tests are standardized; that is, highly regulated in their administration, scoring, and interpretation.

What forms of academic assessment are better than others?

- The quality of assessments is most often judged by analyzing the legitimacy (i.e., validity) and the stability (i.e., reliability) of information they produce.
- The validity of efforts is judged by considering evidence from four basic sources.
  - Content-related evidence looks carefully at the content sampled on the measures.
  - Construct evidence questions the way characteristics or abilities have been operationalized in those measures.
  - With criterion-related validity, evidence turns to external standards, such as a related test or future performance.
  - The consequences of practices on students and their learning can be weighed to ascertain the level of validity achieved.
- Several statistical methods help educators judge the stability or consistency of their assessments.
  - They can consider the stability in students' performance on one particular measure (i.e., split-half).
  - They can use the same test to track stability across time (i.e., test-retest).
  - They have the option of creating two versions of a measure and using students' performance on both testings to evaluate consistency (i.e., alternate-forms).
  - They can compare their markings or interpretations with those of other trained or expert raters (i.e., interrater).
- Teachers can follow various guidelines to enhance the quality of their assessment decisions.

What do teachers need to know about assessment?

- Teachers must be competent in all facets of the assessment process.
  - Teachers should be skilled in choosing the right assessment methods for each instructional decision.
  - They need to be competent in giving, scoring, and interpreting measures that are either commercially produced or teacher made.
  - Teachers' competencies extend to their use of resulting information in instructional decision making and their development of grading procedures that are valid and reliable.
  - Teachers need to be skilled at communicating their actions and the resulting outcomes to students, parents, and school personnel.
  - They must be able to recognize and avoid all unethical or inappropriate methods.
- Because optimal learning and development cannot occur without effective assessment, the educational community must be willing to do whatever it takes to provide teachers with professional development opportunities that will promote the attainment of such competencies.

··

■ Solution to Thought Experiment: Interpreting the Variability of Scores

Scores	$(X - \overline{X})$ Deviation Score	$(X - \overline{X})^2$ Deviation Score Squared
98	$98 - 84.56 = \quad 13.44$	180.63
94	$94 - 84.56 = \quad 9.44$	89.11
94	$94 - 84.56 = \quad 9.44$	89.11
91	$91 - 84.56 = \quad 6.44$	41.47
89	$89 - 84.56 = \quad 4.44$	19.71
89	$89 - 84.56 = \quad 4.44$	19.71
87	$87 - 84.56 = \quad 2.44$	5.95
86	$86 - 84.56 = \quad 1.44$	2.07
86	$86 - 84.56 = \quad 1.44$	2.07
85	$85 - 84.56 = \quad 0.44$	0.19
85	$85 - 84.56 = \quad 0.44$	0.19
85	$85 - 84.56 = \quad 0.44$	0.19
82	$82 - 84.56 = -2.56$	6.55
81	$81 - 84.56 = -3.56$	12.67
80	$80 - 84.56 = -4.56$	20.79
76	$76 - 84.56 = -8.56$	73.27
69	$69 - 84.56 = -15.56$	242.11
65	$65 - 84.56 = -19.56$	382.59
		$\Sigma 1188.38$

$$\frac{\Sigma (X - \overline{X})^2}{N} = \frac{1188.38}{18} = 66.02$$

$$\sqrt{\frac{\Sigma (X - \overline{X})^2}{N}} = \sqrt{66.02} = 8.13$$

Standard deviation $= 8.13$

··

Chapter 14

Traditional and Alternative Approaches to Teacher-Made Tests

GUIDING QUESTIONS

- How can teachers improve the quality of their traditional assessments?
- What alternatives to traditional measures should teachers consider?
- What are the fundamental principles of effective classroom assessment?

IN THEIR OWN WORDS

Gregg Ponitch came to education from the world of business, where success was a rather straightforward matter of profit and loss. As a math and social studies teacher at Sacred Heart Academy, Gregg feels a sense of fulfillment he never experienced as a financial analyst. However, assessing middle-school students' performance is a much tougher business than he ever imagined.

When I first began teaching, I did not give much thought to testing. Testing was just another part of the job I was hired to perform. You teach and then you test the students over what you taught—no big deal, right? I credit some of my early naiveté about testing to my preparation program. I never had a class where we specifically dealt with test construction or test interpretation. No one ever presented me with guidelines or the do's and don'ts of testing. I was virtually flying by the seat of my pants. I don't think I am alone in this situation, either. I can understand why some of the teachers I work with depend on those test banks that come with their books. They do not know where to begin, and they do not have the confidence in their abilities as test creators.

In some ways, my lack of training left me with the impression that test development should be simple and uncomplicated. As long as students and parents were not complaining, and as long as the grades made sense in terms of students' in-class performance, then everything was fine. Only now, after 8 years of experience, do I recognize how misguided those impressions were.

When I began teaching, I only had my personal experiences to guide me when I prepared exams or quizzes. As a student, for example, I hated multiple-choice, true/false, and completion items. They were often poorly written and misleading. I cannot tell you how many times I got those kinds of questions wrong, even though I really knew the material. I do not want that to be the case for my students. So I do not use multiple-choice, true/false, or completion questions on any of my social studies tests.

Essays are another matter, though. I have always been a pretty good writer, so I usually scored well on essays—even when I was not well versed in the content. But I still do not use essay questions much in my teaching. They are too hard to grade. I am never sure if I am evaluating students fairly. I do not want to be misled by lots of words and nice handwriting, the way many of my teachers were. At the same time, I want students to express themselves well and to make important connections in the material. That is why I use short-answer questions. I get the best of both worlds. They are not wordy but do give students more opportunities to show what they know. And they are easier to grade than essays.

In my math classes, assessment is less of a concern for me. I just stick to problems that parallel those we work in class or the students do for homework. I always make students show me their work, even when they use calculators. When students list out their steps in solution, I have a chance to give them partial credit even when the final answer is wrong.

Through the years, I have also picked up helpful hints from fellow teachers who are more masterful and self-assured than I am. Mrs. Dench, the language arts teacher and my mentor, told me that she works hard to match the content of her tests to the content of her teaching. That rang true with me. I remember how unjust it was for teachers in high school and college to include test items over material they never even mentioned in class. Or they would have six items on a concept that got maybe 2 seconds' worth of class time. Mrs. Dench also told me that students do better if the test questions are in the same order as class instruction. I am not sure if that is true, but I do follow that advice.

Honestly, I know I am a good teacher. I am just not sure I am a great test writer. I do pretty well, though, considering I had to figure this process out on my own. For example, I know that it is poor practice to use the questions that come with the textbooks unless they match your content and your instructional goals. I also have learned that students can read a question differently from the way you intended, so you cannot be afraid to rethink your scoring. In addition, I recognize that some students will get overly anxious and blow tests even when they know the material well. That means you have to find different ways to let students show you what they know and can do. I also know that traditional tests are not the only way to evaluate students. There are always projects and in-class assignments. These are a few of the guidelines I now share with others.

The trouble is that I know there is much more about testing that I do not know. Testing is still too much of a mystery for me and for most of the teachers I know. That is not the way it should be. I cannot help but wonder how much better a teacher I would have been and how much better off my students would have been, if someone had enlightened me about this whole testing process.

How Can Teachers Improve the Quality of Their Traditional Assessments?

Gregg's apprehensions about constructing and interpreting tests are not surprising. In fact, they are all too common (Alexander & Parsons, 1991). When I first began my career as a university professor, guiding the development of future teachers, I was struck by the lack of attention assessment was given in preparation programs. Despite all their years of taking tests and despite the fact that these young women and men would soon be responsible for their own classrooms, they often knew relatively little about sound assessment practices. In fact, future teachers often have little, if any, opportunity to prepare their own tests, much less grade and interpret the results (Stiggins, 1993).

Nonetheless, this lack of direct assessment experience does not prevent these soon-to-be teachers from espousing some strong beliefs about teacher-made tests (Nitko, 2001). Like Gregg they internalize certain notions about tests and testing from their own test-taking days or from watching others. The trouble is that many of these notions are misguided and maladaptive (Alexander & Parsons, 1991; Murphy & Alexander, 2002a).

Understanding Traditional Assessments

If you were to ask family and friends to describe different approaches to measuring academic knowledge and skills, you would probably end up with a familiar listing of formats: multiple choice, completion, true/false, matching, short answer, and essay questions. Precisely because such formats are so commonplace and have been part of the school culture for more than a century, they are called **traditional assessments** (Greeno, Collins, & Resnick, 1996; D. E. Tanner, 2001).

Despite the agreement about what types of measures are traditional, there is disagreement about their fundamental value in uncovering students' knowledge and skills (Baker & O'Neil, 1993; Haladyna, Nolan, & Haas, 1991). Perhaps because traditional items have become strongly aligned with high-stakes, high-pressure assessment practices, they have been stigmatized (American Educational Research Association, 2000; Paris, 2000a). For whatever reason, there is an undercurrent of belief within the educational community that traditional assessments are outmoded, old-fashioned, and detrimental to student learning (Aschbacher, 1997). There is also the perception among some novice and experienced educators that traditional assessments are inherently narrow and fatally flawed indicators of students' academic abilities (Wiggins, 1991).

However, there are advantages and disadvantages to every form of assessment, whether traditional or nontraditional (Cizek, 1991; Hambleton, 1996). Effective teachers should not arbitrarily accept or reject any assessment approach, nor should they assume that ongoing problems with testing in general are solely or primarily attributable to the method of assessment. Instead, knowledgeable teachers must understand the relative merits of each approach and must make reasoned and reasonable choices when they create and implement tests in their own classrooms (Linn & Gronlund, 2000).

Categories of Traditional Assessments

The traditional assessment approaches just identified can be categorized in two ways. One system is based on the responses students provide—responses that have been either selected or constructed (Linn & Gronlund, 2000). The other system looks at how those responses are scored—whether they are objectively or subjectively marked (Popham, 2002).

Selected-Response Versus Constructed-Response Items

Among the traditional assessment formats are those that require students to choose an answer from among given options. These are **selected-response** items (McMillan, 2001), the most common of which are multiple-choice, true/false, and matching items. Figure 14–1 displays the typical structure of these items. Each involves an item **stem,** which is the basic statement of the question. This statement comes with two or more **response options,** which serve as potential answers to the posed question. One of the options is the correct response; the other(s) serve as **distracters.** The more plausible the distracters, the more difficult the item becomes because selection requires more effort and is less certain.

Other questions require students to compose an answer instead of picking from specified options. Such questions are **constructed-response** items (Nitko, 2001). Among constructed-response questions, certain item types—such as completions, analogies, and modified true/false items—require students to answer in only a few words. These are called **restricted** forms of constructed-response questions (Linn & Gronlund, 2000); examples appear in Figure 14–2. Other constructed-responses formats, such as short-answer and essay questions, require written answers of more than a few words. They are referred to as **extended** forms of constructed-response questions (Linn & Gronlund, 2000).

Objective Versus Subjective Items

The other common method for categorizing traditional assessments focuses on the manner in which responses are scored. Those items that provide response options can be directly and readily marked according to a coding scheme. This category of questions sits at one end of the scoring continuum shown in Figure 14–3 and is called **objective** (Popham, 1998; D. E. Tanner, 2001). In essence, anyone who can read and follow directions can consistently convert objective responses to numerical scores, resulting in an interrater reliability that is nearly perfect. All the item formats shown in Figure 14–1 fit this category because they generally have a single correct option that can be easily scored.

Some educational researchers find the label *objective* unsuitable, because it "connotes an absence of subjectivity in development or use" (Stiggins, 2001, p. 120). In fact, all the items that teachers or test developers create carry some degree of subjectivity because certain content and particular perspectives are given more emphasis than other content and other perspectives. These concerns serve as a reminder that the objective classification deals solely with the manner of scoring such items and not with either their construction or the selection of certain items for certain tests.

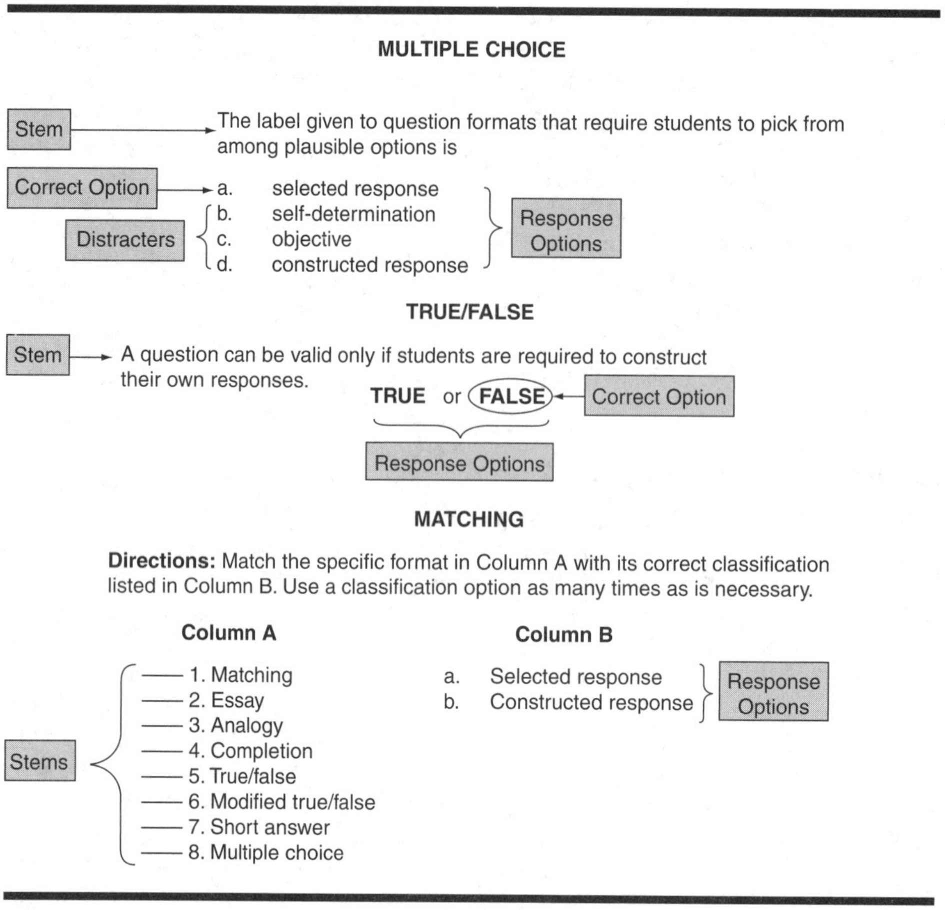

MULTIPLE CHOICE

Stem ⟶ The label given to question formats that require students to pick from among plausible options is

Correct Option ⟶ a. selected response
Distracters ⟶ b. self-determination
c. objective
d. constructed response
} Response Options

TRUE/FALSE

Stem ⟶ A question can be valid only if students are required to construct their own responses.

TRUE or (**FALSE**) ⟵ Correct Option

} Response Options

MATCHING

Directions: Match the specific format in Column A with its correct classification listed in Column B. Use a classification option as many times as is necessary.

Column A

Stems {
—— 1. Matching
—— 2. Essay
—— 3. Analogy
—— 4. Completion
—— 5. True/false
—— 6. Modified true/false
—— 7. Short answer
—— 8. Multiple choice

Column B

a. Selected response
b. Constructed response
} Response Options

■ **FIGURE 14–1   Common forms of selected-response questions.**

At the other extreme of the scoring continuum are the extended-response questions—short-answer and essay—which can result in a wide range of acceptable answers (Nitko, 2001). When Gregg Ponitch includes short-answer questions on his test, he should expect a different response from each of his 22 students, and any number of those answers could be acceptable. Constructed-response questions can result in highly variable evaluations and are thus considered **subjective** items (D. E. Tanner, 2001).

Somewhere between the most objectively and most subjectively scored items are those traditional questions that may have more than one accepted response, although the range of correct answers remains limited (Goetz, Alexander, & Ash, 1992). The restricted form of constructed-response items would fit this description. Because students must supply an answer to completion questions, analogies, and modified true/false items, there is some room for scoring variability. Thus, these questions reflect a moderate level of objectivity and subjectivity.

The objective/subjective character of teacher-made questions is important for several reasons. For one, the objectivity/subjectivity of tests relates to the consistency or reliability of scoring associated with each measure (Algina, 1992). With greater subjectivity comes the potential for more fluctuation or error in the evaluation each student receives (D. E. Tanner, 2001). In addition, increased subjec-

tivity opens the door to variability in scoring from test to test and from rater to rater (Popham, 2002), decreasing the possibility of a high reliability of scores (see Chapter 13; Linn & Gronlund, 2000).

Advantages and Disadvantages of Traditional Assessments

No form of assessment should be routinely and unceremoniously excluded from the classroom (Kindvatter, Wilen, & Ishler, 1996). Gregg Ponitch may well have personal reasons to dislike multiple-choice, true/false, and matching questions, but he should consider their potential utility and place in his assessment practices nonetheless (Phye, 1996). He should be able to see their potential value to him and his students, even as he recognizes their shortcomings. Indeed, all educators need a deep understanding of every form of traditional and nontraditional measurement tool (Popham, 2000). Table 14–1 offers a summary of the pluses and minuses of both selected-response and constructed-response questions.

Selected-Response Items

Advantages   Many of the pluses and minuses of selected-response items revolve around their defining feature. First of all, when teachers mark selected-response items, they need only check to see whether the right options have been

RESTRICTED FORMS

COMPLETION

Those questions that require students to formulate their own answers
without the aid of options are called ____ *(constructed-response)* ____ items.

ANALOGIES

Few words : restricted-response form: : many words : *(extended-response form)* ____

MODIFIED TRUE/FALSE

Directions: For each of the following items, indicate whether the given statement
is true or false. Provide a justification for your decision.

Constructed-response questions require that students provide an extended
written answer.   **TRUE** or (**FALSE**)

Justification: ____ *(Can be either restricted or extended in form)* ____

____

____

EXTENDED FORMS

SHORT-ANSWER

Describe how traditional assessment can be categorized, based on the character
of student responses.

*(Selected-response items involve picking from among given options, whereas
constructed-response questions entail generating an answer. Constructed
responses can be either restricted or extended in form).*

ESSAY

Every form of teacher-made assessments comes with its own set of advantages
and disadvantages. When it comes to the primary forms of traditional
assessment, what key advantages and disadvantages should teachers consider
when applying each of these approaches?

■ **FIGURE 14–2   Restricted and extended forms of constructed-response questions.**

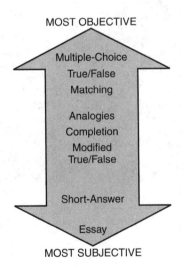

MOST OBJECTIVE

Multiple-Choice
True/False
Matching

Analogies
Completion
Modified
True/False

Short-Answer

Essay

MOST SUBJECTIVE

■ **FIGURE 14–3   The scoring continuum of question
types.**

marked on student papers (McMillan, 2001). Therefore, the
scoring of these items is a relatively quick and easy process.
In fact, tests that consist entirely of selected-response items
can be machine scored and analyzed—one reason they are
so popular with commercial test developers.

This ease of scoring brings other advantages pertaining to
reliability (see Chapter 13). When answers are readily scored
as right or wrong, there is greater likelihood that the scoring
is consistent from beginning to end (Kubiszyn, & Borich,
1996). Thus, the internal consistency of data from these
measures should be stronger than it is for measures with
more extensive and subjectively scored responses (Traub,
1994). Reliability advantages extend to interrater agreement
as well (Linn & Gronlund, 2000); multiple evaluators, armed
with an accurate answer key, should arrive at the same results.

Consistency in administration and interpretation also
goes in the plus column for selected-response items (D. E.
Tanner, 2001). As Chapter 13 made clear, it is critical to administer a test in exactly the same manner from time to time
and from place to place if student results are being compared (Goetz et al., 1992). The same is true for classroom
teachers who have multiple classes with the same content
and who want to use the same test for those classes. Slight

Table 14–1   The advantages and disadvantages of traditional assessment formats.

Format	Pluses	Minuses
Selected-Response Items	Are easy to score	Are hard to construct
	Tend to have high reliability indicators	Give credit for only the one right answer
	Can be more readily standardized procedurally	Can discount or overlook certain abilities or aptitudes not easily cast into such a format
	Have more straightforward interpretation of results	Can result in highly contrived, abstract orientation toward learning
	Prompt memory of the content	Can be overly influenced by testwiseness
	Allow for breadth of coverage for a content area	Provide little chance for respondents to go deeply into any topic or ability
Constructed-Response Items	Give students a chance to explore a topic in some depth	Can result in knowledge telling or can trigger anxiety in students with language production problems
	Allow for greater creative license	May be impacted by extraneous factors, such as grammar or handwriting
	Place value on higher-level thinking skills, such as synthesis and summarization	May hold students accountable for strategic processes that have not been effectively modeled or taught
	Prompt the evaluation of bigger ideas through content integration	May be equally well cast as selected-response items
	Open the door for multiple correct answers and varied interpretations	Have potential for scoring error and bias

variations in the testing conditions or the class environment can mean that identical scores are not equivalent. However, when students select responses rather than construct them, it can be easier for teachers to standardize the administration and scoring (Ebel & Frisbie, 1991). Response time is less of a problem with selected-response items than it is with short-answer or essay questions, for which some students require much more time to get their thoughts down on paper or to revise their answers (Eisner, 1999).

Of course, standardization of this type is much more important to commercial test developers than to classroom teachers (Gronlund, 1993). Test companies must be able to assure consumers that the test given on Monday in San Diego is administered and interpreted in just the same way as the test given in Syracuse on Tuesday. Without this assurance normative comparisons would be inappropriate (Popham, 2002).

Another advantage of selected-response items has to do with students' memory of the material. In effect, the structure of selected-response items prompts students' memory or allows them to compare their recollections to the various options given (Goetz et al., 1992). Therefore, these items may be less taxing on students' memories and potentially less anxiety producing than questions that require students to conjure up information from long-term memory and weave it into a coherent written response (Culler & Holahan, 1980). When students talk about what they like most about selected-response questions, this issue of recognition versus recall of information is typically at the top of the list.

Elliott Eisner has explored the assessment of complex thinking.

Another plus for selected-response items may not be as apparent to students and teachers. That advantage pertains to information coverage (D. E. Tanner, 2001). Because selected-response items like multiple-choice and matching questions need much less response time than short-answer and essay questions, many more items can be included on an exam. Thus, teachers can cover a broader span of content than would be possible with constructed-response questions. This superior coverage of content can be invaluable when a general assessment of a domain, topic, or skill is desired (Gronlund, 1993).

Disadvantages With all these clear advantages, why would so many teachers like Gregg Ponitch avoid using selected-response items on their own tests? The fact is that each of these potential-advantages of selected-response items has an associated disadvantage (see Table 14–1). And those associated disadvantages can overshadow any possible benefits for teachers (Airasian, 1997). For example, as Gregg realized, multiple-choice and true/false questions may indeed be easy to score, but good ones are hard to construct (Haladyna, 1999; McMillan, 2001). Just putting stems and options together does not translate into an effective measure of students' knowledge and skills.

Moreover, even though the reliability of selected-response items is strong, that reliability can come at a cost. One of the costs is that students come to see much of school knowledge as having an obvious and simple right and wrong that can be captured in a few words or phrases (Kulikowich & Alexander, 1994). That perception does not just apply to mathematics or other well-structured subjects, but also to highly interpretable domains such as history or literature (VanSledright, 1996; Wineburg, 1991b). There is no room for grays or for conflicting interpretations when students are selecting a, b, c, or d or marking true or false (Buehl, Alexander, & Murphy, 2002).

In short, the need to dichotomize students' answers as right or wrong overlooks the complexity and ambiguity that exists in all domains of knowledge, even mathematics and science (Alexander, 1998c). Getting beyond the notion that school questions have one and only one right answer (Schommer, 1993) and valuing students' thinking are reasons that Gregg prefers short-answer questions and awards partial credit on his mathematics tests.

The consistency and reliability of scores associated with selected-response questions may also miss critical abilities or aptitudes that cannot be readily captured in question stems and options (Wiggins, 1991). Gregg believes that selected-response items afford students little opportunity to explain their answers or to pose alternatives. Marking options rather than constructing a response does not allow them to draw on their strengths of writing, argumentation, and synthesis. Certainly, there is no opportunity for students to apply their linguistic skills, go into depth, or play with ideas when tests are composed entirely of selected-response items (Airasian, 1997).

Some students like my son, John, prefer selected-response questions for some of the same reasons that Gregg dislikes them. I often describe John as extremely testwise—a multiple-choice genius. He consistently performs extremely well on tests composed of selected-response items. He seems to have a way of reading into the questions and drawing on related knowledge to choose the correct option. The problem is that his testwiseness, and that of other students, can result in an inflated score, as well as an inflated sense of what he or they know well or can do effectively (Sarnacki, 1979). In John's case his test-taking ability led to his being placed in two advanced classes in his freshman year of college—engineering and calculus—for which he was not well prepared.

Finally, because selected-response items offer a broad, if somewhat surface-level view of a domain or topic, there can be a tendency to emphasize more factual or declarative knowledge (Sacks, 1999). As many critics of these traditional items argue, this orientation can give students a highly contrived perspective of a field of study—one greatly removed from the practice of that domain in the world outside schools. For example, students often perceive history as the study of famous people, places, and dates (Wineburg, 1991a). The idea that social studies involves an exploration of the present through accounts of the past and a consideration of multiple interpretations through primary and secondary sources can be easily lost (VanSledright, 1996).

Constructed-Response Items

With multiple-choice, true/false, and matching questions, the advantages and disadvantages revolve around the restricted nature of responses (Linn & Gronlund, 2000). With constructed-response items, the pluses and minuses arise from just the opposite situation. That is, students must construct either a limited or an extended answer to each question (McMillan, 2001). This requirement can be advantageous to students who have a depth of topic knowledge and a creative take on the question, as well as an ability to express themselves in writing (Alexander, 1997b). However, constructed-response questions can be problematic for students who lack one or more of those attributes (Hiebert & Raphael, 1996; Kubiszyn & Borich, 1996). And these questions can be headaches for teachers in terms of time and consistency in scoring.

Advantages One of the obvious advantages of constructed-response items is that they do not give away too much information to students (Goetz et al., 1992). Instead, students must pull that information from memory and build their responses from those recollections. Thus, a teacher can feel more confident that students' correct responses represent their understanding of the content and not simply their skill at picking from among plausible options (Sarnacki, 1979). Further, the structure of constructed-response questions means that teachers can test more than students' factual or declarative knowledge easily and effectively (Hiebert & Raphael, 1996). They can go more deeply into students' conceptual understanding and examine their ability to make connections within and across topics.

Precisely because constructed-response questions are conducive to measuring conceptual understanding, they are effective tools for tapping students' critical thinking and reasoning (Eisner, 1999). When well formed, these items demand summarization or synthesis of relevant subject matter (Aschbacher, 1997; Baker & Niemi, 1996), ideas must be woven together to form a coherent and meaningful response. Teachers who place a premium on such complex thinking would understandably be drawn to constructed-response items (Hiebert & Raphael, 1996).

Constructed-response questions can also be a useful tool for promoting students' creative processing (Quellmalz & Hoskyn, 1997). If well written and appropriately scored, constructed-response questions, particularly essay items, can afford students greater license to play with ideas. Such questions can stimulate students to derive unique solutions or forge alternative perspectives on an issue—to think outside the box (Terry, 1933). The open-ended character of these items can allow students greater creative license.

Finally, that open-ended format can have positive effects on students' epistemological beliefs (Buehl et al., 2002); that is, their beliefs about the nature of knowledge (see Chapter 4). Because students are not forced to pick from among a narrow range of options, they may be less prone to perceive schooled knowledge in simplistic terms of right or wrong. Instead, they may see knowledge as complex, ambiguous, and multifaceted. This development of more sophisticated views of knowledge is important to students' optimal learning; research has shown that more sophisticated beliefs about knowledge are related to higher achievement (Schommer, 1993). Beliefs in the complexity and ambiguity of knowledge are also linked to more strategic and critical thinking (Schommer, 1990; Schommer, Crouse, & Rhodes, 1992).

Disadvantages So why would teachers not embrace all forms of constructed-response approaches to assessment? For one thing it takes a long time to grade constructed-response questions, especially essays, and even more effort to ensure that the outcomes are consistent from student to student and from class to class (Frisbie, 1988). There is no question that short-answer and essay questions permit students and teachers to probe deeply into students' understanding and thinking. But many teachers, like those that Gregg had as a student, can be unduly influenced by other factors than knowledge and understanding when they are marking students' papers (Braun, Bennett, Frye, & Soloway, 1990). A relation exists between how much students produce and how neatly they write and the score they receive on constructed-response questions (Linn & Gronlund, 2000). Some of that score may have little to do with the substance of students' answers.

Savvy students know this reality all too well. Many of my college students think that if they just write down everything remotely related to the topic—what has been termed knowledge telling (Bereiter & Scardamalia, 1989)—and if they do so neatly, they will get a good grade on short-answer and essay questions. This point was made clear to me several years ago when I was scoring essay questions on an educational psychology test—the first one of the semester. As I was grading an extended answer from one of my bright, engaged students, I came across this sentence buried in the middle of a generally well-conceived and well-argued essay: "I know that this has nothing to do with the question, but I wonder if professors really read these papers closely." You can imagine my surprise. Of course, from my written comments throughout the essay, as well as

my direct response to her inquiry, the student realized that I did, indeed, read those papers closely. But what was even more interesting to me was that the student admitted to inserting a similar sentence in essays in other classes without receiving any feedback from her professors, other than her usual A.

This story is very telling not only because it illustrates a student's misguided notion that more is better when it comes to constructed-response questions. It also emphasizes how extraneous factors can influence teachers' grading of short-answer and essay questions (Ebel & Frisbie, 1991). Gregg is correct in his observation that grading essay questions is tough business. Internal consistency and interrater reliability for both short-answer and essay items can be poor. Teachers need to manifest greater care and thoroughness in their grading practices, whether they are teaching young children or college students.

Another minus of constructed-response questions is that on many occasions questions cast as constructed-response items go no deeper and make no more conceptual connections than do selected-response questions (McMillan, 2001). They only put more demands on students' memory and writing production. The following question is a case in point:

What are three forms of selected-response items?

Although this question is structured as a constructed response, it targets factual, declarative information that could be as readily written as a selected-response item:

Which of the following formats would be considered selected-response items? (Check all options that apply.)

  a. completion
  b. true/false
  c. short-answer
  d. matching

As these examples indicate, just framing a question in a construction format does not mean that teachers are necessarily assessing students' complex thinking and creativity. They may simply be putting more demands on students' memory and language production (Eisner, 1999).

The idea of language production raises yet another concern about constructed-response questions. They can underestimate the knowledge and thinking of students who are less comfortable or facile with written language (Popham, 1998). For example, students who speak or write in non–Standard English or for whom English is not their primary language are apt to be at a serious disadvantage when responding to short-answer or essay questions (Phye, 1996). The construction of answers for these students will likely be more time-consuming and effortful than for others, even when their command of the content is solid and their language relatively strong (Goetz et al., 1992). When tests are timed, as most are, this disparity can become a serious handicap in students' performance.

Finally, when well conceived and well written, constructed-response questions require students to forge conceptual relationships or draw insights from the content. Therefore, in order to perform well on constructed-response questions, particularly those requiring extended answers, students must engage in strategic processes such as analysis, synthesis, and summarization. (See Chapter 7 for a more detailed discussion of strategies.) The problem is that many students have not been taught how to analyze, synthesize, and summarize, and they have been unable to self-instruct themselves in these fundamental strategies (Weinstein & Mayer, 1986). Thus, these students are being held responsible for a level of processing for which they may have been insufficiently prepared.

Improving the Quality of Selected-Response Items

Teachers can take steps to build on the positive attributes of traditional items while lessening the effects of any negative features.

Creating Better Multiple-Choice Items

Multiple-choice questions are hard to create, but teachers can make them more effective and can reduce the probability that students will rely on their testwiseness rather than their knowledge of the content to perform well.

Be Sure That the Problem Is Simply and Clearly Stated

If teachers want to feel more confident that multiple-choice questions are truly tapping students' requisite knowledge, they must be sure that the problem posed in the stem is clearly stated. Consider the following question:

Poor:

There are many issues that can be involved when teachers try to construct good multiple-choice questions. Among those issues some pertain specifically to the way in which the options are put together. Which of the following is most likely to be a problem in wording multiple-choice questions?

   a. There are too many choices.
   b. There are too few choices.
   c. The material was not taught.
   d. There are clues in the stem.

Students trying to answer this question have to work through unnecessary and confusing verbiage to get to the basic problem. This careless wording would put even more burden on students with language differences or difficulties (Popham, 1998). The same question can be rephrased in a much more concise manner, putting the real problem up front:

Better:

Which of the following is a common problem in the wording of multiple-choice items?

   a. There are too many options.
   b. There are too few options.
   c. The material was not taught.
   d. There are clues in the stem.

Remove All Extraneous Clues in the Stem or the Options

Part of my son's testwiseness had to do with his skill at looking for the clues that inexperienced, and sometimes experienced, test developers unintentionally inserted in the stems and the options of multiple-choice questions. One such clue is the inclusion of some form of the target response in the problem stem (Linn & Gronlund, 2000). For example, in the item below, the word *select* gives away the expected response:

Poor:

What do we call the category of questions for which students are required to select from among viable alternatives?

   a. true/false
   b. constructed-response
   c. selected-response
   d. short-answer

The teacher should replace the word *select* with a workable alternative.

Better:

What do we call the category of questions for which students are required to pick from among viable alternatives?

   a. true/false
   b. constructed-response
   c. selected-response
   d. short-answer

Other common errors made in the construction of multiple-choice questions are grammatical flaws or clues that reduce the viability of response options (McMillan, 2001). In the following sample item, an astute student will realize that the correct answer has to begin with a vowel.

Poor:

The part of a multiple-choice question that presents a response alternative is an

   a. stem
   b. option
   c. distracter
   d. problem

A simple change can remove the clue:

Better:

The part of a multiple-choice question that presents a response alternative is a(n)

   a. stem
   b. option
   c. distracter
   d. problem

It is equally important that all the options are grammatically plausible responses to the question poised in the stem.

Poor:

The quality of multiple-choice questions can be improved by

   a. eliminating clues in the stem
   b. easy-to-spot distracters
   c. wordy problem statements
   d. textbook phrases

Better:

The quality of multiple-choice questions can be improved by

   a. eliminating clues in the stem
   b. including easy-to-spot distracters
   c. using wordy problem statements
   d. selecting phrases directly from the textbook

Novice test writers also have a tendency to put more verbiage in their correct options than in their distracters (Goetz et al., 1992).

Poor:

Which of the following item characteristics is likely to improve the performance of testwise students?

   a. There are more than four options.
   b. The question material was never taught.
   c. There is noticeably more information in the correct answer than in distracters.
   d. The options are similar in wording.

Better:

Which of the following item characteristics is likely to improve the performance of testwise students?

   a. There are more than four options.
   b. The question material was never taught.
   c. The options differ in length.
   d. The options are similar in wording.

Make Sure That the Distracters Are Sufficiently Distracting   If teachers want to make their multiple-choice questions more discriminating and more revealing, each distracter must be plausible (D. E. Tanner, 2001). If Gregg Ponitch were to include the following item on one of his social studies exams, his students would probably not find every option feasible:

Poor:

The president of the Confederacy was

   a. Thomas Edison
   b. Robert E. Lee
   c. Jefferson Davis
   d. Bozo the Clown

However amusing the inclusion of Bozo the Clown may be, it is a throwaway option. Even Thomas Edison is not particularly plausible for most middle-school students. Thus, most students will narrow their options down to two, Robert E. Lee and Jefferson Davis, giving them a 50-50 probability

that will contribute to inflated scores on Gregg's exam. Gregg should stick with famous leaders and generals of the Civil War period to improve the attractiveness of his options:

Better:

The president of the Confederacy was

   a. William Sheridan
   b. Robert E. Lee
   c. Jefferson Davis
   d. Thomas Hooker

In their research Alexander and colleagues created a number of tests that could be given to elementary, high-school, and college students to evaluate their subject-matter knowledge (Alexander, Kulikowich, & Schulze, 1994; Alexander, Pate, Kulikowich, Farrell, & Wright, 1989). In those survey tests, they went beyond plausible distracters, beyond simple right and wrong, so that a degree of correctness was represented in each option (Alexander, Pate, et al., 1989). They created a response model that was appropriate for the age and experience of their participants and then applied that model to each question they wrote. The models Alexander et al. followed in creating human biology/human immunology tests for sixth graders and for high schoolers are shown in Figure 14–4. Sample questions developed for the sixth-grade model are shown in Figure 14–5.

Creating multiple-choice questions in this way proved advantageous for two reasons. First, they could award students partial credit for answers because there were actually degrees of incorrectness in the tests. For instance, the sixth graders might have received 4 points for each correct human-biology response, 2 points for each incorrect human-biology option, and 1 point for each incorrect science option. Second, they were able to look at the pattern in the students' errors for clues about the cohesiveness of their topic or domain knowledge. Specifically, they found that most student errors fell into one of the response option levels, which reflected the cohesiveness of their understanding. For example, Mark and Sue both got 17 of the 35 questions correct. But 75% of Mark's errors were at the human biology level, whereas 70% of Sue's errors were in the nonscience category. Thus, Mark's knowledge of human biology was more principled, more tightly integrated than Sue's (Alexander, Pate, et al., 1989).

Teachers can employ a similar procedure by creating response options that represent levels of correctness. However, they must be sure that they choose distracter levels that are plausible for the age and experience of their students.

Avoid Unnecessary Confounds   When they create multiple-choice questions, some commercial test writers insert into their stems negative words or phrases such as *except* or *not*, as in this question:

Poor:

All of the following are forms of constructed-response items *except*

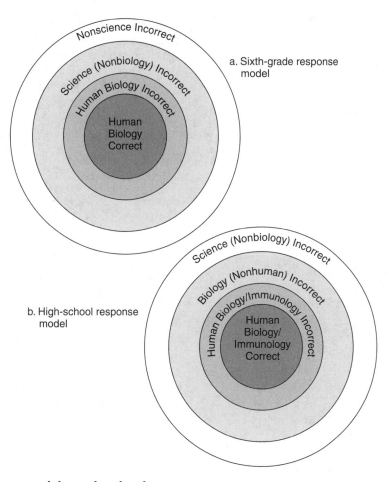

■ FIGURE 14–4   Response models used to develop two tests.

    a. essay questions
    b. analogies
    c. short-answer questions
    d. matching items

They also use response options that consist of qualifying phrases, such as *all of the above* or *none of the above* or combination options like *a and b* or *b and c.*

Poor:

Which of the following qualify as constructed-response items?

    a. essay questions
    b. analogies
    c. short-answer questions
    d. *a* and *c*
    e. all of the above

Commercial test developers use negating words and qualifying statements in their multiple-choice questions because their presence increases the difficulty of such items without making the core content more difficult. These test developers want to make normative comparisons (see Chapter 13); thus, they need to ensure a sufficient spread of scores among respondents. And adding words and phrases like *except* and *none of the above* complicates the processing, thereby increasing the error rates

among students (Linn & Gronlund, 2000), especially students who have language difficulties or for whom English is not their first language. Teachers should avoid using such complicating language in their tests. Their aim is to test, not trick.

Writing More Discriminating True/False Items

Many teachers and students find limited appeal in traditional true/false items. From the teachers' standpoint, students have a 50-50 probability of getting the right answer even when they have no knowledge of the content. In addition, writing good items that pose feasible questions without giving too much away is tricky business (Phye, 1996). From the students' perspective, there is no opportunity to explain their reason for a true or a false judgment, even though the statements they are given may be ambiguous. Teachers can take two important steps to convert traditional true/false items into more informative and useful assessment tools.

Be Sure That Statements Are Complete, Clear, and Precise   The stems of true/false items are central to their effectiveness and are often the source of their problems (McMillan, 2001). The stem must be able to stand on its own. In other words, teachers cannot simply pick up a sentence or a phrase from the textbook or from classnotes and assume that it will work well in a true/false format. Many of

Omnivore is

   a. a breakfast dish made with eggs (NSI)

   b. an animal that has a trunk (SI)

   c. the lining of the stomach (BI)

   d. an organism that eats plants and animals (BC)

Inhale means

   a. to take oxygen into the lungs (BC)

   b. large pieces of ice that fall from the sky (SI)

   c. the flow of blood into the heart (BI)

   d. to salute or recognize a superior (NSI)

Sperm means

   a. the rejection of a hypothesis (SI)

   b. a curly hairstyle (NSI)

   c. the male reproductive cell (BC)

   d. bacteria that destroy white blood cells (BI)

Epidermis is

   a. the outer covering of the kidney (BI)

   b. an electric blanket (NSI)

   c. a disease of plants (SI)

   d. the top layer of skin (BC)

Pancreas is

   a. an elevated plain in higher altitudes (SI)

   b. a muscle used in breathing (BI)

   c. an organ that releases digestive enzymes (BC)

   d. an all-purpose solution (NSI)

Legend

BC = Biology Correct

BI = Biology Incorrect

SI = Science Incorrect

NSI = Nonscience Incorrect

■ **FIGURE 14–5   Sample questions from a sixth-grade human biology test.**

the sentences or phrases in textbooks and notes have the benefit of surrounding context to help with their interpretation. However, the stems of true/false questions must function without such a context and must make a statement that is readily classifiable as correct or incorrect.

Consider these two examples:

True/false items involve no response construction.

One advantage of constructed-response items is that they are easy to score.

At first glance, these seem to be reasonable true/false items. However, with the first item, some variations of true/false questions actually encourage students to justify their answers. Knowing that would make it harder to respond *true* and acknowledge no room for student construction. The second item is less unwavering in its wording. Because ease of scoring is a known problem for constructed-response items, the truthfulness of this item should be clearer to the respondent.

Avoid Absolute Words   Testwise students like my son, John, quickly learn that absolute or extreme words—such as *always, never, every,* and *none* are generally surefire signals that an item is false (Sarnacki, 1979). Unconditional or unqualified truths are rare in the real world, just as they are in the classroom. Questions containing these giveaway words can be easily rewritten to convey a more typical or realistic condition, as the following example illustrates:

Poor:

True/false items never involve response construction.

Better:

True/false items typically involve no response construction.

The first version of the question is relatively easy to reject. The rewritten statement that talks about the "typical" condition not only is more appropriately worded, but also requires a deeper understanding of true/false item constructions.

Consider Signaling Key Words or Phrases for Young or Novice Learners   One technique that is effective in true/false item construction, particularly in working with young or novice students, involves highlighting key words or phrases in the stem. When I was a student answering true/false questions, I often wondered which concepts or words in the item stem my teacher had targeted in writing the question. Part of my dislike of true/false items came from my concern that my teachers were trying to be intentionally vague or tricky in their wording. And one way to be tricky is to target seemingly trivial words in the stem, figuring that students will focus on more central concepts.

Poor:

One advantage of selective-response items is that they are easy to score.

Many students reading this item would ponder whether selected-response items are actually easy to score. They would miss the fact that this question says "selective-response" instead of "selected-response," thereby making a "true" response wrong. If teachers sincerely want to evaluate students' understanding of important concepts, they should not target such wording trivia. In fact, teachers could scaffold students' thinking about the content by highlighting words that are pivotal to judging the accuracy or inaccuracy of true/false statements.

Better:

One advantage of *selected-response items* is that they are *easy to score.*

Effective pedagogical scaffolding, such as this type of signaling, should be dependent on the knowledge and skill of the student population (Goetz et al., 1992). For example, such a technique should not be necessary with college students, who have a sufficient base of content knowledge and years of experience taking traditional tests. But for young children or for novices in a field, such signaling can ensure that they attend to the relevant features of the item and do not get hung up on unimportant or trivial words (Nitko, 2001).

Provide Opportunities for Student Justification or Rationalization Perhaps the most annoying aspect of true/false items is that students have no mechanism for explaining their true or false markings. The single word *true* or *false* reflects none of the thinking that went into that selection (Airasian, 1997). To circumvent this frustration, teachers may want to consider using modified true/false items, as illustrated in Figure 14–2, which elicit students' thoughts on the accuracy or inaccuracy of each statement. The earlier item dealing with the nature of true/false questions could be rewritten as follows:

Better:
True/false items involve no response construction.

Justification: _____ (Depends on whether you are using the traditional or modified form.) _____
_____

Of course, if teachers take this approach, they will have converted their traditional selected-response questions into more open-ended, subjective items. But there are two advantages to this modification. First, teachers can get a clearer picture of what students understand about the concept under assessment—subtleties that would be lost with traditional true/false questions (Kubiszyn & Borich, 1996). Second, teachers have the opportunity to give partial credit for students' responses, because they can score not only the accuracy of the decision but also the students' justification of that decision.

Producing Better Matching Questions

Although less utilized than multiple-choice questions, matching items can be useful assessment tools if teachers adhere to certain guidelines.

Ensure Sufficient Imbalance Between the Number of Stems and the Number of Options One of the most common problems with the matching questions that appear on teacher-made tests is that students can often use a process of elimination to answer correctly even if their background knowledge is limited (Goetz et al., 1992). Consider the following example:

Poor:
Directions: Match each item in Column A with the correct term in Column B. Use the terms in Column B only once.

Column A	Column B
___ 1. The portions that state the problems	a. options
___ 2. All possible responses	b. distracters
___ 3. The incorrect responses	c. stems
___ 4. The desired responses	d. answers

If students are sure of only two of these items, they still have a high probability of matching the remaining two options correctly, simply by a process of elimination. To prevent this common problem, teachers should develop matching questions with a significant imbalance between

stems and options. This imbalance can be achieved in several ways. First, teachers can include many more options than will be required, making it harder for students to identify answers through a process of elimination (Nitko, 2001).

Better:
Directions: Match each item in Column A with the correct term in Column B. Use the terms in Column B only once.

Column A	Column B
___ 1. The portions that state the problems	a. objectives
___ 2. All possible responses	b. items
___ 3. The incorrect responses	c. stems
___ 4. The desired responses	d. answers
	e. distracters
	f. terms
	g. options

Another technique to increase item difficulty is to keep the number of options limited but allow students to use those options as many times as they wish (Stiggins, 2001). This approach is illustrated in Figure 14–1. In that example students must carefully consider each of the stems and repeatedly decide between option *a* or *b*. This technique can be very effective in assessing students' understanding of related concepts. However, this approach also points to the importance of clear directions for matching items, always specifying whether options can be used once or more than once.

Make Sure Stems and Response Options Fit Together Unambiguously Students can experience frustration when they attempt to answer matching questions with stems for which multiple options seem to apply (MacMillan, 2001). Teachers can remedy this situation by creating stems that are brief but fully comprehensible without surrounding context. For example, an undergraduate education student produced the following matching questions:

Poor:
Directions: Match the specific item stems in Column A with their correct response options in Column B. Use the options in Column B as often as is necessary.

Column A	Column B
___ 1. Same test given twice after some delay and correlation between scores compared	a. Interrater reliability
___ 2. Comparison of data from independent observers	b. Test-retest reliability
___ 3. The consistency of results over time or between measures or observers	c. Reliability
___ 4. Scores from two equivalent test versions compared	d. Alternate-form reliability
___ 5. Scores from two different but related tests compared	

At first glance this seems like a reasonable set of items. The stems are fairly well written and can stand alone. Also, the options, although not numerous, can be repeated. One significant problem is that the student included Option c. Reliability is an overarching concept that subsumes all the other categories of reliability that are listed. Thus, respondents could actually use Option c for all of the stems and be theoretically correct. The student could easily improve this exercise by keeping all the options at the same level of specificity.

Use Stems and Options Within Similar Categories of Information   Robert Linn and Norman Gronlund (2000), who are among the leading authorities in test construction, offer one more recommendation for improving the quality of matching items. According to these experts, the most important rule of quality construction for such items pertains to their focused emphasis. Effective matching items target content within a similar or homogeneous category of information, such as machines and their uses or dates and their associated historical events. Various relations that Linn and Gronlund identify as viable for matching items are listed in Figure 14–6.

Such cohesion among matching questions is important because it increases the reasoning and discrimination in which students must engage (Nitko, 2001). They must carefully explore subtleties if they are to make the correct selection. Here again it is important for teachers to include directions that make clear whether options can be used only once or more than once. Figure 14–7 gives a checklist of all the suggestions to improve selected-response items.

Improving the Quality of Constructed-Response Items

Teachers can implement recommendations to enhance the quality of both restricted and extended forms of constructed-response questions. Here again, the point of

---

A Checklist for Writing Better Selected-Response Items

Multiple-Choice
✓ Keep the problem statement simple and clear.
✓ Remove any unnecessary clues in stems and options.
✓ Be sure the distracters are sufficiently distracting.
✓ Avoid unnecessary confounds (e.g., *none of the above* or *except*).

True/False
✓ Ensure that the problem statements are complete, clear, and precise.
✓ Avoid absolute words (e.g., *always, never, every,* and *none*).
✓ Consider highlighting key words or phrases for young or novice students.
✓ Give students the chance to explain their decisions.

Matching
✓ Provide sufficient imbalance between stems and response options.
✓ Be certain that stems and options fit together unambiguously.
✓ Select stems and options from the same category of information.

■ **FIGURE 14–7   Suggestions to improve selected-response items.**

---

the recommendations is to take advantage of the general strengths of these items, such as their ability to explore complex issues in some depth, while avoiding their associated pitfalls, such as inconsistency in scoring.

Restricted-Response Questions

Formulating Effective Completion Items

The restricted-response question with which students are most familiar is probably the completion item (Hopkins, Stanley, & Hopkins, 1990). Basically, these items take the form of a sentence with a missing word or phrase, as seen in Figure 14–2. It is the student's task to write in the word(s) that would render the statement complete and accurate. The brevity in both the given material and the response is at the heart of the advantages and disadvantages of these traditional items (Nitko, 2001). The steps that teachers can take to make completion questions more sound and more appropriate in gauging students' knowledge are summarized in Figure 14–8.

Craft Root Statements That Are Comprehensible on Their Own   The nucleus of any effective completion item is the problem statement (Popham, 2002). Students must be able to read those statements with a part missing and grasp what is being asked.

Use of verbatim sentences from textbooks is one of the common mistakes made by novice test developers. Sen-

---

Persons	Achievements
Dates	Historical events
Terms	Definitions
Rules	Examples
Symbols	Concepts
Authors	Titles of books
Foreign words	English equivalents
Machines	Uses
Plants or animals	Classifications
Principles	Illustrations
Objects	Names of objects
Parts	Functions

■ **FIGURE 14–6   Desirable relation for matching items.**

Note: From *Measurement and assessment in teaching* (8th ed., p. 187) by R. L. Linn and N. E. Gronlund, 2000, Upper Saddle River, NJ: Merrill/Prentice Hall. Copyright 2000 by Prentice Hall. Reprinted with permission.

A Checklist for Writing Better Constructed-Response Items
Restricted Form
Completion
√ Formulate root statements that stand on their own.
√ Target declarative information that can be specified in a word or two.
√ Put the missing term(s) at the end of the sentence.
√ Provide blanks of consistent and adequate length.
√ Eliminate unnecessary textual clues.
Analogies
√ Maintain balance in the two portions of the problem.
√ Award variable credit for demonstrated knowledge and strategic effort.
Extended Form
√ Target deep mental processing.
√ Be certain that students understand the scope of the expected responses.
√ Give sufficient time and space for student response.
√ Prepare a response protocol that outlines critical content.
√ Preestablish criteria for evaluation.
√ Score each question separately and blindly.

■ **FIGURE 14–8 Suggestions to improve constructed-response items.**

tences in texts are often complex and linked together in such a way that they are not clearly understandable on their own. Consider these two sentences selected from this chapter:

> The consistency and reliability of scores associated with selected-response questions may also miss critical abilities or aptitudes that cannot be readily captured in question stems and options.
> The restricted-response question with which students are most familiar is probably the completion item.

Although each sentence discusses an important idea, neither would be particularly good as the basis for a completion question as presently written. The first is too wordy and is a follow-up to something else, as indicated by *also*. Thus, it does not stand alone, and it also lacks a singular focus that could be readily tested by inserting a blank or two.

In the second sentence the word *probably* makes this a conditional sentence. Completion questions are not the place for ambiguity. Instead, students need definitive, independent statements that clearly and briefly establish the problems to be addressed (Linn & Gronlund, 2000). If this sentence is going to serve as the foundation for a completion item, it needs to be rewritten.

Focus on Specific, Declarative Information That Can Be Captured in a Word or Two Because completion items have to be tightly worded and unambiguous, they work best with content that is more factual or declarative in nature (Hopkins et al., 1990). Definitions, principles, important names, and critical dates are examples of the straightforward subject matter that works well in completion form (McMillan, 2001). In addition, the categories of material that work well for matching items (see Figure 14–6) also work well for completion questions. Some sample completion items are given here that could work well for Gregg Ponitch's social studies and mathematics tests:

> The expression the Patriots used as their rallying cry for the Boston Tea Party was ___(no taxation without representation)___
> The branch of government responsible for interpreting and upholding the laws of our country is the ___(judiciary)___.
> The sum of all internal angles of a triangle is ___(180 degrees)___.
> The formula for finding the area of a circle is ___(πr^2)___.

Position the Missing Word(s) at the End of the Sentence Several other features of completion questions are important for creating items that effectively assess students' understanding. Experts recommend positioning the blank signifying the missing word(s) toward the end of the sentence (Ebel & Frisbie, 1991). When the blank is at the end of the sentence, students are better able to interpret the problem statement than they are when their reading is interrupted (Linn & Gronlund, 2000). Compare these two completion items to see the difference:

> Poor:
> One advantage of ___(selected-response)___ items is that they are easy to score.

> Better:
> Ease of scoring is one advantage of ___(selected-response)___ items.

Keep the Length of All Blanks Consistent and Adequate in Length Another simple recommendation is to keep the length of all blanks identical. This practice ensures that students do not look to the blank itself for clues to the expected response (Goetz et al., 1992). Previous examples illustrate an appropriate and consistent use of blanks. Of course, if students are expected to write in the missing words, the teacher must be certain to insert a blank of sufficient length.

> Poor:
> The two forms of constructed-response questions are ____ and ____. (restricted/extended)

> Better:
> The two forms of constructed-response questions are ___(restricted)___ and ___(extended)___.

Guide Students Toward the Expected Response Without Including Unnecessary Textual Clues   The lengths of the blanks are not the only clues that teachers might inadvertently insert into completion items. Some of the same problems that plague poorly written multiple-choice questions also surface in completion questions. Unnecessary clues include grammatical hints (Ebel & Frisbie, 1991) or signaling words (Linn & Gronlund, 2000):

> Poor:
> The part of a multiple-choice question that serves as a response alternative is called an ____(option)____.
> The constructed-response questions that result in more extensive written answers are described as ____(extended)____ in format.

These items can be easily rewritten to eliminate both clues but retain the items' integrity.

> Better:
> Those parts of multiple-choice questions that serve as response alternatives are called ____(options)____.
> The constructed-response questions that require more involved or elaborate written answers are referred to as ____(extended)____ in format.

Constructing Analogies That Work

Too few teachers have discovered the value of analogy problems as classroom assessment tools. Although analogies have long been a mainstay of achievement, aptitude, and intelligence tests (Sternberg, 1977), they can be just as useful at uncovering students' understanding and strategic thinking in any subject-matter area (Alexander, Murphy, & Kulikowich, 1998). Chapter 7, describes the processes underlying analogical reasoning in some detail. One of the greatest assets of analogy problems is that they combine students' knowledge of content with their ability to analyze and synthesize (Alexander, Murphy & Kulikowich, 1998). Thus, even though these items are rather limited in their response requirements, they can reveal quite a bit about students' knowledge and reasoning (Alexander, Pate, et al., 1989). However, like multiple-choice items, classic analogy problems must be carefully constructed and appropriately scored.

Be Certain That the Two Sides of the Analogy Problem Are Completely Proportional   Classic analogies are essentially verbal ratio problems—A:B::C:(D), read as "A is to B as C is to (D)" (Alexander, White, & Daugherty, 1997). The A:B side of the problem must be fully balanced or proportional with the C:D side, in terms of both the relations they represent and their grammatical structure (Sternberg, 1997). Further, each pairing in the problem, including the pivotal relation between the A and C terms, must be as comparable as possible.

> Poor:
> multiple-choice : selected-response :: constructed-response : (____e.g., essay____).

This problem violates one of the fundamental rules of analogies: The relation specified in the A:B pairing must be replicated in the C:D pairing. In this example the relation in A:B, which is an example-to-category association, is mistakenly reversed on the C:D side. In a well-constructed analogy problem, the A and C terms should represent similar concepts, as should the B and D terms.

> Better:
> selected-response : multiple-choice :: constructed-response : (____e.g., essay____)

Simply reordering the three terms of this analogy restores the required balance.

Another kind of imbalance can be seen in the following example:

> Poor:
> selected-response : ease of scoring :: strong reliability : ____(e.g., speed of response)____

Whoever created this question meant to assess students' understanding of the advantages/disadvantages of selected-response items but did not frame the problem proportionally. In fact, the relation between the A and C terms is a simple repeat of A and B. There are several ways that this item could be rewritten to improve its assessment ability:

> Better:
> Selected-response advantage : ease of scoring :: Selected-response disadvantage : ____(e.g., difficulty in constructing)____
> (or)
> selected-response : ease of scoring :: constructed-response : ____(e.g., ease of constructing)____

The proportionality of analogies extends to their grammatical structure as well. Any deviation in that structure also results in an imbalance and a less-than-perfect item. Thus, the pairings must be equivalent with regard to part of speech, tense, and number (i.e., whether singular or plural).

> Poor:
> completion : restricted-response form :: essays : ____(extended-response form)____

Even though the intention of this analogy seems clear, it is not a completely balanced question. The problem is that the A:B pairing is singular in form, whereas the resulting C:D pairing is plural. This error may seem somewhat trivial in this instance, but slight variations can be more significant problems in other items or in other domains (Alexander, Willson, White, & Fuqua, 1987). In addition, these minor flaws can be reflected in the scores students receive (Alexander, Murphy, & Kulikowich, 1998). The good news is that this type of error can be easily corrected:

> Better:
> completion : restricted response :: essay : ____(extended response)____

Create a Grading Scheme That Awards Partial Credit for Student Responses   Another advantage to analogy problems is that student responses can be treated as more than simply right or wrong answers (Kulikowich & Alexander, 1994). Variable scoring rubrics, like the ones Gregg Ponitch uses in his mathematics classes, can be applied to analogies in any academic subject. How complex the scoring rubrics should be is up to individual teachers. Alexander and colleagues created a seven-level scoring system that allows fine-tuned evaluations of students' answers (Alexander, Murphy, & Kulikowich, 1998), responding to both effort and accuracy. That scoring system and a sample item from human biology are shown in Table 14–2.

Classroom teachers may not find it useful to be this specific in their grading of analogies. However, they are advised to look for patterns in students' analogy answers and to make use of those patterns in their evaluations. They may at least look at variants of the expected response (i.e., target variant), topic- or domain-relevant answers (i.e., domain response), answers that fall outside the central topic or domain (i.e., nondomain response), and nonresponses.

Extended-Response Questions

Extended-response questions give teachers the chance to go more deeply into a specific topic, issue, or procedure. However, because they require more than a word or two of written response, the scoring of such questions can be both time-consuming and inconsistent from student to student and even from question to question. Teachers can apply the guidelines summarized in Figure 14–8 to maintain the advantages of short-answer and essay questions, while enhancing the reliability of scores for such item types.

Building Better Short-Answer and Essay Questions

Thought-provoking and informative short-answer and essay questions generally target two general areas: the thinking processes they instigate and the response parameters they involve (McMillan, 2001; Popham, 2002). The following guidelines harness the potential of extended-response questions to probe students' understanding as well as their ability to construct rich interpretations of learned content.

Focus on Deep Mental Processes That Cannot Be Tapped with Other Question Formats Teachers have little reason to subject themselves to the rigorous scoring and analyses required of extended-response questions unless they and their students reap the benefits these items afford with regard to deep mental processing (Linn & Gronlund, 2000). Effective short-answer and essay questions produce more than added verbiage. What is important is the thinking that those words represent.

The following short-answer item illuminates this point:

Poor:
In multiple-choice questions, what is the stem?

This question could easily be converted to some form of selected-response question without any loss of information:

Better:
The part of a multiple-choice question that poses the question to be answered is called the

   a. stem
   b. option
   c. distracter
   d. alternative

Table 14–2 An assessment system for analogy responses.

Score	Category	Example	Explanation
0	No response	Alike : Different :: Homozygous: _____	An absence of response represents the least amount of effort on the part of the respondent. It is the lowest category of scoring.
1	Repetition	Alike : Different :: Homozygous: *Different*	The duplication of one of the three given terms demonstrates limited knowledge and effort by the student.
2	Nondomain response	Alike : Different :: Homozygous: *Odd*	Although the student constructs a response, it falls outside the target topic or domain.
3	Structural dependency	Alike : Different :: Homozygous: *Nonhomozygous*	The student uses the root word to help construct a seemingly plausible response.
4	Domain response	Alike : Different :: Homozygous: *Fetus*	This represents another error but one that is domain specific.
5	Target variant	Alike : Different :: Homozygous: *Heterozygote*	The student has a good grasp of the content, but the response is the wrong part of speech.
6	Correct response	Alike : Different :: Homozygous: *Heterozygous*	This is the target response. The student receives the maximum number of points for this answer.

Note: From "What responses to domain-specific analogy problems reveal about emerging competence: A new perspective on an old acquaintance" by P. A. Alexander, P. K. Murphy, and J. M. Kulikowich, 1998, *Journal of Educational Psychology, 90*, p. 399. Copyright 1998 by *Journal of Educational Psychology*. Adapted with permission.

However, this more effective short-answer question calls for analysis and interpretation on the student's part that could not be easily addressed in a selected-response question.

> Short-answer item:
> Describe three conditions for which selected-response items would be preferable to constructed-response items? (*e.g., need to test for breadth of understanding, reliability of major importance, standardization of test administration, interest in students' factual knowledge*)

Most test construction experts agree that mental processes—such as comparing, justifying, persuading, analyzing, and synthesizing—are the mainstay of extended-response questions (Stiggins, 2001). These are processes referred to in the literature as higher-order, complex, or critical-thinking processes (Linn & Gronlund, 2000). These higher-order processes, along with sample questions associated with each, are listed in Table 14–3.

Among the distinctions between short-answer and essay items are the number of these processes explicitly involved in the answer construction and the scope of that processing. Compare the prior short-answer question with an essay item that explores some of the same territory but in a more extensive and intensive manner.

> Essay item:
> Gregg Ponitch is a middle-school science and mathematics teacher who is concerned about the use of essay questions in his evaluations. He believes that they take too long to grade and are simply too unreliable. What would you advise Gregg about the appropriate use of essay questions in his courses? Are there situations in which essays would be more effective assessment tools than other forms of selected-response or constructed-response questions? Explain.

At a minimum this question requires the respondent to articulate a number of principles that frame the appropriate

Table 14–3   Deeper mental processing involved in short-answer and essay questions.

Cognitive Process	Sample Question Stems
Comparing	Describe the similarities and differences between. . . Compare the following two methods for. . .
Relating cause and effect	What are the major causes of. . . What would be the most likely effects of. . .
Justifying	Which of the following alternatives would you favor, and why? Explain why you agree or disagree with the following statement.
Summarizing	State the main points included in. . . Briefly summarize the contents of. . .
Generalizing	Formulate several valid generalizations from the following data. State a set of principles that can explain the following events.
Inferring	In light of the facts presented, what is most likely to happen when. . . How would Senator X be likely to react to the following issue?
Explaining	Why did the candle go out shortly after it was covered by the jar? Explain what President Truman meant when he said, "If you can't stand the heat, get out of the kitchen."
Persuading	Write a letter to the principal to get approval for a class field trip to the state capital. Why should the student newspaper be allowed to decide what should be printed without prior approval from teachers?
Classifying	Group the following items according to. . . What do the following items have in common?
Creating	List as many ways as you can think of for. . . Make up a story describing what would happen if. . .
Applying	Using the principle of. . . as a guide, describe how you would solve the following problem situation. Describe a situation that illustrates the principle of. . .
Analyzing	Describe the reasoning errors in the following paragraph. List and describe the main characteristics of. . .
Synthesizing	Describe a plan for proving that. . . Write a well-organized report that shows. . .
Evaluating	Describe the strengths and weaknesses of. . . Using the given criteria, write an evaluation of. . .

use of essay questions and then to draw explicit comparisons between essays and alternative-question formats.

Ensure That Students Have an Explicit Understanding of the Breadth and Depth of Response That Is Expected

The effectiveness of extended-response questions is increased when students have a good sense of what teachers expect of them (Airasian, 1997). Explicit indicators of the expected breadth and depth of responses should be part of a well-written item. The following short-answer and essay items let students know how many issues or factors are anticipated in a complete response, the specific source of desired information, and the number of points each question has been allocated.

Short-answer item: (15 points)
Compare the perceived advantages and disadvantages of selected-response and constructed-response items in at least 3 areas.

Essay item: (30 points)
Of all the issues we have considered in this course, what do you see as the 5 most important factors in determining the form and content of the tests you administer in your own classroom? What makes these 5 factors more influential than all the others we have weighed? Be sure to support the choice of each factor with clear and convincing evidence from class discussion and from the assigned readings.

Students answering this short-answer item know that they are to provide at least three issues of comparison. Similarly, those answering the essay item recognize not only that five specific factors must be identified and defended, but also that their defense must draw on information presented in class discussions and in the relevant course readings. In addition, students recognize that their performance on the short-answer question can merit up to 15 points, whereas the essay can garner up to 30 evaluation points. These insertions make teachers' expectations more transparent to students and thus help them interpret questions better and frame their responses more appropriately (Kubiszyn & Borich, 1996).

Provide Sufficient Time and Space for Each Extended Response

Even the best crafted short-answer and essay questions can prove problematic for students if they do not have the time or space they need to answer them well. Often, novice teachers have a tendency to include too many items on their exams, forcing students to rush or leave questions unfinished (Nitko, 2001). These teachers forget that younger or less experienced minds than theirs will need more time to ponder questions, formulate answers, and then compose and revise those answers (Popham, 2002). Teachers should work under the assumption that their students will need twice the time they do to answer their test questions.

In their research on studying, Alexander and colleagues uncovered what they call the space-filling phenomenon in students' performance (Alexander, Hare, & Garner, 1984). Specifically, students see the amount of space that teachers provide them on written tests as an important clue to the extensiveness of the response expected. For example, a student who receives the following item on a test would probably use the size of the designated response space to signal the extensiveness of the written answer. The issue, of course, is whether that response space is truly adequate for the depth of answer the teacher has in mind. Teachers should err on the side of caution; that is, students should be given more response space than teachers think they will require (Alexander et al., 1984).

> Compare the perceived advantages and disadvantages of selected-response and constructed-response items in at least 3 areas.

Evaluating Short-Answer and Essay Questions

Like Gregg Ponitch many teachers find the thought of grading essays, and even short-answer items, daunting (McMillan, 2001). The bottom line is that extended-response questions do require much more time to score than selected-response or limited-response questions. Even though there is no way around this time commitment, three simple guidelines, summarized in Figure 14–8, should maximize the accuracy and reliability of the resulting scores.

Prepare a Protocol That Specifies the Critical Content Expected in a Thorough Response

The first key to scoring extended-response items reliably is to specify the content that applies. The key ideas that teachers expect should be included in a **response protocol,** which is essentially an outline of the desired content (Linn & Gronlund, 2000). This protocol should be created when items are first written. For instance, a partial protocol for the previous short-answer question might take the following form:

Short-answer item:
Compare the perceived advantages and disadvantages of selected-response and constructed-response items in at least 3 areas.

Potential Areas	Selected	Constructed
Scoring	Easy	Effortful
Nature	Objective	Subjective
Reliability	Strong	Variable
Focus	Breadth	Depth
Knowledge	Factual	Procedural/ conditional
Mental processes	Lower order	Higher order
Related factors	Memory	Writing ability

With a protocol in hand, teachers can then check students' written answers against the outlined information. Protocols help to ensure higher reliability in scoring because teachers can search for the presence or absence of particular ideas or principles in each response (Stiggins, 2001). In addition, response protocols can lessen the impact that extraneous factors, such as handwriting or word usage, have on students' scores (Nitko, 2001). And when protocols are prepared as questions are initially written, they help teachers decide on the number of issues or factors to specify in each item and the number of points to assign (McMillan, 2001).

Clearly Specify the Criteria for Evaluation and the Value of Each Question   Frequently, students' performance on extended-response questions is not dependent solely on the articulation of specific principles, issues, or facts. At times teachers either intentionally or unintentionally take students' writing proficiency, spelling ability, handwriting, and other criteria into account as well. When teachers factor such noncontent elements into students' evaluations, the students should be made aware of that fact prior to response generation (Linn & Gronlund, 2000). And the teachers should consider how much such noncontent elements will figure into the students' final scores (Kubiszyn & Borich, 1996). Some measurement experts, like Richard Stiggins (2001), even argue that students should have a voice in what factors count in the final score.

Gregg, for example, might decide that up to 5% of a student's score can be influenced by noncontent factors, ensuring that more evaluative weight is given to knowledge of social studies instead of writing facility. This evaluation issue hit close to home when my son, John, received a D on one of his essay tests in elementary school. It was not the grade alone that shocked me. It was the teacher's written feedback. On the top of the paper, she wrote: "This was one of the most creative and thoughtful exams I have ever read." The problem was that she deducted 1 point for each misspelled word or grammatical error on the test. On the next essay test for this teacher, John produced a very limited, highly controlled response, using only words he knew he could spell correctly and very simple sentence structures. The result for this far-less-inspired exam was a B. Clearly, teachers must put the appropriate emphasis on the most critical factors.

Score One Question at a Time Without Knowledge of Respondent   Teachers might find it helpful to institute the following six-step procedure, which has been shown to increase the accuracy and consistency of their scoring (Linn & Gronlund, 2000; McMillan, 2001; Nitko, 2001).

1. Focus on one question at a time, and try to score the item blindly that is, without an awareness of who wrote it.
2. Read through all students' responses to the question first without recording any specific scores, to gain a sense of the class's overall approach to this item and the general quality of responses.

3. Reorder students' papers and begin the scoring process, using a response protocol. (Some evidence shows that teachers grade the first and last papers differentially from those in the middle of a distribution.)
4. Provide students with written feedback on their performance on this item as appropriate. This feedback should reveal the reason for their score and should guide them in improving their performance on subsequent tests.
5. Evaluate this item for any other criteria prespecified as important.
6. Repeat this cycle for each extended-response item on the test.

These six steps give teachers a firmer basis for the grades they assign to students' work on short-answer and essay questions. Linking numeric or letter grades to protocols and criteria reduces the likelihood of bias that might color judgments about what students know and can do. Thus, these steps help to ensure that the content is being evaluated and not the student or the student's academic history (Stiggins, 2001).

What Alternatives to Traditional Measures Should Teachers Consider?

In the past few years, teachers and educational researchers have rallied against the emphasis placed on traditional assessments in the school environment (Paris, 2000a). As mentioned earlier, part of this growing reaction against such common assessment tools comes as a result of their association with high-stakes testing (Hiebert & Raphael, 1996; Sacks, 1999). More and more, students' academic futures hinge on their ability to perform well on multiple-choice, analogy, completion, and true/false items (Paris, 2000b).

One outcome of this rising concern over traditional testing is a growing interest in alternative assessment approaches (Resnick & Resnick, 1991). **Alternative assessment** implies evaluation techniques that differ from traditional testing formats (Popham, 2002). Other terms have been applied to these nontraditional formats, most notably **authentic assessment** (Valencia, Hiebert, & Afflerbach, 1994). However, there are good reasons to avoid the label *authentic* when discussing this category of assessment tools. No form of measurement is inherently authentic or inauthentic (Hambleton, 1996); the genuineness, value, and quality of any assessment approach rest on teachers' instructional and evaluation goals and on the care and intelligence they apply in constructing and interpreting assessment measures.

Performance-Based Assessments

Performance-based assessments are evaluation measures that emphasize students' application of knowledge (Dunbar, Koretz, & Hoover, 1991). The traditional assessment items previously considered are of greatest value in gauging students' conceptual knowledge, especially their declarative or factual knowledge (Wiggins, 1998). With performance-based assessments, students are required to carry out a designated, sometimes physical, hands-on task, like the one displayed in Figure 14–9. Like portfolios performance-based measures have been around for a long time (Greeno, Collins, & Resnick, 1996). In fact, in some fields performance-based measures are quite commonplace. For instance, those who want to evaluate the competencies of auto mechanics have long relied on hands-on, physical tasks rather than paper-and-pencil, traditional tests. They want to be sure that mechanics can actually fix cars and not just answer questions about them. However, performance-based assessment represents a rather new wave in classroom evaluation (Stiggins, 2001), and it comes with particular advantages and disadvantages.

Advantages

Complexity

When students are dealing with complex notions that cannot be easily captured in a few words or simple examples, it may make sense to turn to performance-based assessments (Hiebert & Raphael, 1996). These assessments work well with intricate, multilayered ideas, especially when hands-on, physical components are involved. For example, the goal of the activities depicted in Figure 14–9 is to help middle-school students explore complex scientific concepts, such as animals' adaptations to their habitats (Guthrie et al., 1998). But complexity pertains to more than the intricacy of the ideas being taught; it also relates to the mental processes required to carry out the designated tasks. Even more than essay questions, performance-based items often involve higher-order mental processes, such as those outlined in Table 14–3.

For this reason John Guthrie and his colleagues rely heavily on performance-based measures as part of their concept-oriented reading instruction (CORI), a well-researched approach instituted in science classrooms. As an example of the different processes involved, their CORI ponds-and-deserts task requires students to explain, justify, and create, as well as summarize and analyze relevant information. In addition, search and research skills are key components of this program (Guthrie et al., 1998). Guthrie and colleagues build performance-based evaluations to complement the forms of research and hands-on experimentation that are centerpieces of such thematic units.

Procedural Orientation

Performance-based assessments are especially effective when teachers want to evaluate students' procedural or how-to knowledge, as well their factual understanding (Hambleton, 1996). In other words, with a CORI approach, students not only have to comprehend the characteristics of ponds or deserts as habitats, but also must put that knowledge to work. They must produce written explanations, create informative drawings, and even transfer their understanding to a novel situation.

Understanding Ponds and Deserts

Prior Knowledge Phase

Directions: Here are various pictures of ponds and deserts. Based on what you already know or see in these pictures, explain in writing how ponds are different from deserts. What is a pond like? What is a desert like? How are they different?

Information Search Phase

Directions: Using any of the materials available to you, see what new information about ponds and deserts you can uncover. Fill out the search log to show where you looked and what you found.

Production Phase

Directions: Based on all that you now know about ponds and deserts, draw a picture to show how ponds are different from deserts. Be sure to label the important parts of your drawing. Also, write an explanation of your drawing that tells how ponds are different from deserts.

Transfer Phase

Directions: Suppose people drank all the water from a pond one day. Would the pond then be like a desert? Explain your answer.

■ **FIGURE 14–9 A hands-on performance task.**

Note: Based on "Does concept-oriented reading instruction increase strategy use and conceptual learning from text?" by J. T. Guthrie, P. van Meter, G. R. Hancock, S. Alao, E. Anderson, and A. McCann, 1988, *Journal of Educational Psychology, 90,* pp. 261–278.

John Guthrie

Depth of Exploration

Another advantage of performance-based assessments is that they allow teachers to explore certain topics or processes in far more depth than is possible with traditional measurements (Dunbar et al., 1991). The student evaluation in Figure 14–9, for instance, represents the culmination of 3 weeks of student reading, discussion, and experimentation on the central theme. By the conclusion of the unit, students should have constructed a rich, integrated body of scientific knowledge about varied environs and animals' adaptations to them (Valencia et al., 1994).

Student Engagement

With performance-based assessments students have extensive roles to play in their own evaluation. Those roles can be either independent or collaborative in nature; they frequently involve jointly performed tasks. That kind of engagement can be seen in the CORI science activity in Figure 14–9. To complete the evaluation, students must participate in independent reading and reporting and must have previously engaged in collaborative problem solving. Guthrie et al. (1998) believe that this level of engagement is a critical factor in building student motivation, which they have found to contribute to students' performance.

Disadvantages

Despite their advantages certain shortcomings are linked to performance-based measures (Dunbar et al., 1991; Hambleton, 1996).

Limited Scope

Because performance-based assessments entail the extended examination of select concepts or processes, they do not permit the kind of broad-based evaluation that traditional measures do (Eisner, 1999). And this trade-off between depth and breadth can be problematic. By the conclusion of this CORI project, for example, students should have developed a rich understanding of ponds and deserts. However, unless that conceptual understanding is well linked to their general science learning, its value as a 3-week instructional focus may be questioned.

Under a best case scenario, the students' newly acquired understanding of the differences between ponds and deserts will contribute to a wider understanding of habitats and biomes (Guthrie et al., 1998). And the students' engagement in this extended, hands-on project will spark their interest in science and reinforce their complex thinking (Linn, Songer, & Eylon, 1996). However, if the learning is not well integrated, students will have devoted a great deal of their instructional and assessment energy to rather minor content or concepts (Dunbar et al., 1991). Consequently, it is essential that teachers involved in such a project choose themes that are not only broad in scope, but also key to principled knowledge and abilities in the target domain.

Production Demands

The execution of performance-based assessment requires students to invest a good amount of time and energy in the orchestrated tasks (Bond, 1995). This involvement may be a positive feature of these alternative evaluations because students must employ higher-order thinking and problem-solving skills (D. E. Tanner, 2001). However, the reading, researching, writing, and other productions involved in these assessments can overburden students who do not possess the requisite knowledge or strategic abilities (Cizek, 1991; Dunbar et al., 1991). For example, students with reading and writing problems may be handicapped in their ability to show what they know (Popham, 2002).

To hold production demands in check, teachers must be ready to provide whatever scaffolding or support students of varying abilities require (Valencia et al., 1994). The inclusion of the drawing task in the CORI assessment (see Figure 14–9) is one approach to reduce the burden placed on linguistic abilities, while permitting students to express themselves in varied ways (Guthrie et al., 1998). Also, carefully orchestrated partnerships or teams can decrease production demands (Resnick & Resnick, 1991). Teachers can form student groups with an eye toward the kind of knowledge and skills that specific performance tasks require. Perhaps stronger readers and writers can be grouped with students who require more assistance with such literacy tasks (Slavin, 1995; Stevens & Slavin, 1995). Guidelines for creating peer work groups can be found in Chapter 11.

Scoring Difficulties

Scoring performance-based assessments carries many of the same problems discussed with extended-response traditional questions (Braun et al., 1990; Goetz et al., 1992). Thus, teachers need to consider the techniques that contribute to a more accurate and reliable scoring of short-answer and essay questions before tackling the scoring demands of performance-based assessments (Linn & Gronlund, 2000). Experts in this area often turn to rubrics as a way to specify the criteria and values associated with these evaluation measures (Herman, Aschbacher, & Winters, 1992). A **rubric** is a scoring framework that typically includes an ordered set of verbal performance descriptions and associated values (Andrade, 2000; McMillan, 2001). Rubrics can be of two forms.

With **analytic rubrics** the characteristics or criteria are first specified that would be indicative of competent performance, much as was discussed with extended-response traditional items (Gearhart, Herman, Baker, & Whittaker, 1992). Then separate scores are assigned to the levels of quality for each characteristic, as seen in Table 14–4. Thus, for this particular rubric, developed for scoring expository essays, the teacher is concerned with the characteristics of focus and organization, language, elaboration, and adherence to grammar and mechanics.

The teacher must then decide what would be indicative of exceptional, commendable, adequate, marginal, limited, and minimal performance in each of those four characteristics. Once the characteristics are separately analyzed, the teacher can determine what level of performance the cumulative, or overall, score represents. For instance, for the expository essays being evaluated in Table 14–4, the teacher might establish the following levels of performance:

Table 14–4   A sample analytic scoring rubric for expository essays.

Score	General Achievement	Focus/ Organization	Language	Elaboration	Mechanics
6	Exceptional	• Clearly stated main idea • Unified focus and organization • Effective orientation of reader	• Specific and concrete expression • Details consistent with intent • Clear, vivid images	Extended elaboration of one main point	• One or two minor errors • No major errors
5	Commendable	• Stated or implied main idea • Focused and organized • Effectively oriented	• Specific sensory details • Most details consistent with intent	Full elaboration on one main point	• A few minor errors • No more than one major error
4	Adequate	• Main idea present but inconsistent focus • Some orientation of reader	• Some specific details • Details usually clear • Generally clear images	Moderate elaboration of main point	• Some minor errors • One or two major errors that do not cause reader confusion
3	Marginal	• Main idea not clear • Some digressions from the topic	• Few or inconsistent details • Some details in appropriate	Restricted elaboration of main point	• Some minor and major errors • Error interference with reader understanding
2	Limited	• Vague indication of main idea or focus • Significant digressions • No sense of closure	• Limited concrete language • Simple or generic naming	Limited elaboration of main point	• Many minor and major errors • Error interference with reader understanding
1	Minimal	• No apparent main idea • No apparent plan or coherence	• No concrete language	No elaboration of any point or central statement	• Many major errors causing reader confusion

_____ Student summary score

Note: From *Writing portfolios at the elementary level: A study of methods of writing assessment* (CSE Technical Report 337) by M. Gearhart, J. L. Herman, E. L. Baker, and A. K. Whittaker, 1992, Los Angeles: University of California, Center for Research on Evaluation, Standards, and Student Testing. Retrieved from http://www.cse.ucla.edu. Copyright 1992 by University of California. Adapted with permission.

Overall Evaluation	Score
Excellent	21–24
Commendable	17–20
Adequate	13–16
Marginal	9–12
Limited	5–8
Minimal	0–4

Holistic rubrics treat together the various criteria that might be involved in assessment (Nitko, 2001). As a result, the description accompanying each score level addresses multiple factors, as seen in Figure 14–10. Holistic rubrics of this type have been applied to the performance-based assessments used in the CORI project previously described (Guthrie et al., 1998). For the rubric in Figure 14–10, scores are reflective of students' response to the specific problem, their use of appropriate sources, their knowledge of the topic, their ability to organize and communicate that content effectively, and their effective collaboration.

Student Portfolios

A **portfolio** is a purposeful, organized collection of work that is presumed to represent certain knowledge, skills, or abilities (Arter & Spandel, 1992; Baker & O'Neil, 1993) and often to show maturity in the field or development. Portfolios are intended to showcase an individual's or group's accomplishments or capabilities in a general domain, such as science knowledge (Farr & Tone, 1994). Like performance-based assessments, portfolios have long been applied in certain fields, such as graphic or performing arts. However, their application in K–12 classrooms represents a relatively

Performance-based task: In your study groups, research the following question, using at least three suitable sources. Then create a written report based on that research. Be sure to indicate your information sources. Feel free to include charts, illustrations, or pictures to accompany your written text.

Research question: In what different ways has the animal life in deserts adapted to the surroundings?

Score	Criteria
5	*Problem focus:* Students focused clearly and specifically on the given problem. *Research sources:* Multiple and appropriate information sources were used in topic research. *Major and relevant data:* Important and relevant information was included in the response (textual and graphic). *Writing quality:* The response was well organized, well written. *Student collaboration:* Students collaborated well in preparing their response.
4	All but one of the above criteria were met.
3	All but two of the above criteria were achieved.
2	Two of the above criteria were met.
1	Only one of the criteria was achieved.

■ **FIGURE 14–10   A holistic rubric for a performance-based measure.**

Eva Baker is an internationally distinguished educational test expert and the director of UCLA's Center for the Study of Evaluation.

new and promising evaluation avenue (Aschbacher, 1997). Although some states (e.g., Kentucky and Vermont) and some school districts (e.g., Pittsburgh Public School District) have moved to portfolios as a primary means of judging students' academic progress, this discussion focuses on the use of portfolios at the classroom level, where they are more common.

Even though there is no limit to the potential uses of portfolios in classroom-based assessment, such applications often fall within two broad categories: (a) best work and (b) growth and learning progress (Nitko, 2001). **Best-work,** or **showcase,** portfolios provide evidence of students' accomplishments or achievements (Farr & Tone, 1994). The works collected for these portfolios are meant to showcase students' demonstrated strengths or competencies. An individual seeking a job as a technical writer might want to compile work samples that demonstrated competence and versatility in that area and would appeal to a prospective employer. A best-work portfolio would make sense in that case.

Growth and **learning-progress** portfolios are documentations of the development students make over time in a particular academic domain (Nitko, 2001). For example, if Gregg Ponitch wanted to highlight the changes in students'

mathematics knowledge and skills over the course of the school year, he might consider having his middle schoolers prepare growth and learning-progress portfolios. Gregg and his students might collaborate to decide which kinds of mathematical knowledge and skills should be emphasized. Next, they could discuss the kinds of work samples, like those outlined by Stenmark (1991) in Table 14–5, that would highlight the targeted mathematical competencies. Gregg should then be sure that he and the students collect those work samples at different times during the school year so that the students can demonstrate how their performance has changed with continued instruction and effort.

Advantages

Organizing and maintaining student portfolios is no small feat. For teachers and students to invest in this form of alternative assessment, there must be obvious advantages to the use of portfolios—and there are (Stiggins, 2001).

Self-Assessment Opportunities

More than any of the other forms of traditional or alternative assessment discussed in this chapter, portfolios are unique for the amount of self-determination and self-evaluation they allow students (Nitko, 2001). With the help of their teachers, students select work samples for their portfolios that meet preestablished criteria or purposes. The students are also responsible for justifying the inclusion of each work sample, as well as for analyzing the specific strengths and weaknesses of each entry (Airasian, 1997).

Table 14–5 **Documentation of mathematics competencies through portfolios.**

Sample Work Products	Sept.–Dec.	Jan.–June
• A solution to an open-ended question done as homework • A mathematical autobiography • Papers that show the correction of errors or misconceptions • A photo or sketch of work with manipulatives or with mathematical models of multidimensional figures • A letter to the reader of the portfolio, explaining each enclosed item • A report of a group project, with comments on the individual's contributions • Work from another subject area that relates to mathematics, such as an analysis of data collected and presented in a graph for social studies • A problem made up by the student • Artwork done by the student, such as string designs, coordinate pictures, and scale drawings or maps • Draft, revised, and final versions of student work on a complex mathematical problem, including writing, diagrams, graphs, charts, • A description by the teacher of a student activity that displayed understanding of a mathematical conception or relation		

Note: From *Mathematics assessment: Myth, models, good questions, and practical suggestions (p. 37)* by J. K. Stenmark, 1991, Reston, VA: National Council of Teachers of Mathematics. Copyright 1991 by National Council of Teachers of Mathematics. Adapted with permission.

Learner-Centered Psychological Principle 14

Standards and assessment. . . . Performance assessment can provide other sources of information about the attainment of learning outcomes. Self-assessments of learning progress can also improve students' self-appraisal skills and enhance motivation and self-directed learning.

Learner-Centered Principles Work Group of the APA Board of Educational Affairs, 1997.

Teachers can facilitate student engagement and self-assessment by requiring students to complete a well-structured cover sheet, like the one shown in Figure 14–11, for each portfolio entry (Linn & Gronlund, 2000). Such a cover sheet requires students to furnish basic information about the entry, including a clear description of its contents and an explanation of how it relates to preset purposes for the portfolio. The sheet also asks students to evaluate the perceived strength of the work and its implication for their subsequent performance.

Individualization

In portfolio assessment each student ends up with a unique representation of his or her knowledge, skills, or abilities

(Farr & Tone, 1994). Thus, more than any other mode of assessment considered here, portfolios result in a highly individualistic evaluation. Because students are free to choose products that they and the teacher believe match instructional and assessment goals, no two portfolios incorporate the same entries. For instance, Gregg Ponitch's middle-school students independently decided how they were going to demonstrate that they could perform complex mathematical processes, and they were free to create any kind of mathematical problem they wanted for their portfolios. They knew that both they and Mr. Ponitch would judge the appropriateness and the quality of their entries and that the portfolio would be used to judge their progress in mathematics learning across the school year.

Sheila Valencia is recognized for her research on literacy portfolios.

This unprecedented degree of individualization is by many accounts both the greatest asset and the greatest liability of portfolio assessments (Farr & Tone, 1994). The creativity, self-determination, and variability permit students to show what they know or can do without limiting constraints or fear of peer comparisons. Of course, this freedom makes it extremely difficult for teachers to maintain consistency in their evaluations or to make normative comparisons (Cizek, 1991).

Student name _____

Student Comments

Description of the entry:

Why did I choose to include this entry? How does it relate to class goals?

What do I consider to be the strength of this entry?

What does this entry show about my learning (competencies)?

Based on this entry, what do I hope to learn or accomplish in the future?

Teacher Comments

What do I see as the strength of this entry?

Based on this entry, what knowledge or skills might the student emphasize in the future?

■ **FIGURE 14–11   Entry cover sheet and self-evaluation form.**

Accumulated Evaluations

Another advantage of portfolios is the assessment interval they allow (Nitko, 2001). In the case of traditional tests, students complete a series of items within a limited time frame of hours or days. The assessment interval is relatively short with performance-based measures, as well (Valencia et al., 1994). Even for the CORI project, which is a rather extended form of performance-based assessment, students complete their multilevel tasks within a few weeks' time (Guthrie et al., 1998).

But the assessment interval associated with portfolios can easily extend across months and even years (Farr & Tone, 1994). It is easy to see how Gregg Ponitch could use portfolios to document what his students have learned in their

sixth-grade mathematics classes. In addition, colleges and universities are now using portfolios as part of their application process and as a means of evaluating the competencies of preservice teachers before they are awarded teaching certificates. The work samples or entries in these two cases could conceivably be collected over the course of years. This long-term feature can be very useful, whether one is creating a best-work portfolio or documenting progress in an academic domain (Nitko, 2001).

Disadvantages

Clearly, portfolios can serve as a versatile and creative means of assessing students, but their advantages can come with certain undesirable side effects.

Sampling Problems

Sampling, or selecting from among existing possibilities, is a serious concern for both students and teachers when it comes to assembling portfolios (Linn & Gronlund, 2000). To appreciate this problem from a student's perspective, imagine that you are a sixth-grade student in Gregg Ponitch's class, facing the daunting task of selecting work samples to demonstrate your mastery of mathematics competencies. How would you decide which products or creations best demonstrated those specified competencies? You are not an expert in mathematics and certainly have a slanted perspective on your own work. But picking the most appropriate samples of your work is serious business—your grade depends on it.

From the teacher's perspective, this issue of sampling is likewise problematic (Airasian, 1997). Teachers must allow students freedom in their selection of portfolio entries; exerting too much authority eliminates one of the strongest assets of this assessment approach—student choice and self-evaluation.

This situation can result in biased evaluations (McMillan, 2001). Because of their lack of organizational skills or motivation, some students may fail to assemble appropriate work samples. Consequently, the judgments that teachers make about students' learning and development based on those samples will be flawed. Or samples may be poorly selected or misrepresentative of students' abilities and efforts, even when students include a suitable number of entries. Again, teachers would end up making important academic judgments based on weak evidence (Eisner, 1999). There are simply no guarantees that the works included in portfolios are good representations of students' knowledge, skills, and abilities (Dunbar et al., 1991).

However, there are guidelines that teachers can follow to enhance the quantity and quality of the work students add to their portfolios and to improve the validity of academic decisions teachers make about those portfolios (Farr & Tone, 1994; Nitko, 2001). Those guidelines are summarized in Figure 14–12.

First of all, students are apt to do a better job of assembling and maintaining their portfolios when the teacher takes time to discuss the value of portfolios in their academic development (Nitko, 2001). Specifically, students need to know whether they are compiling a best-work or a growth portfolio, because this decision has a significant bearing on the samples collected. Second, it helps if students grasp the intended purpose for each portfolio entry (Stenmark, 1991). The more specific the information students have, the more reasoned their individual choices can be. Toward that end, teachers should supply students with a clear set of goals and provide them with prototypes or well-executed models they can follow. For instance the preservice teachers in the University of Maryland's teacher preparation program are required to develop a teaching portfolio as part of their educational program. Their goal is to demonstrate to their university professors and their school-based mentors the extent of their subject-matter and pedagogical knowledge and

Guidelines for More Effective Student Portfolios

√ Be sure students have a firm grasp of the value and the nature of portfolios.
√ Clearly specify the purposes or goals for each portfolio entry.
√ Allow both teacher and student to be contributors to the portfolio.
√ Collect relevant work samples from which students can make their selections for particular entries.
√ Institute regular teacher-student conferences regarding the content and progress of the portfolio.
√ Create specific and detailed scoring criteria for entries or for the overall portfolio.
√ Reevaluate students' work after a reasonable interval.
√ Be as organized as possible.
√ Set aside regular class time for portfolio work.
√ Alert students to time requirements of their entries.

■ **FIGURE 14–12 Suggestions to improve the quality and utility of portfolios.**

skills. The portfolios have also proven useful to the students as they showcase their abilities to prospective employers.

Third, even though students should play the dominant role in the compilation of their portfolios, it is good practice for teachers to participate directly and meaningfully in its development (Arter & Spandel, 1992). Teachers can contribute student work samples to the portfolios, thereby increasing the likelihood of sufficient quantity and quality of work in each student's portfolio. In addition, with younger students or those with special needs, some assessment experts recommend that teachers systematically collect student work and then collaborate with students in picking entries from among those collected samples (Farr & Tone, 1994). These students would still be making decisions about their entries, but they would be doing so under constraints appropriate for their developmental abilities.

Finally, regardless of the age or presumed ability of the students, teachers should confer with them on a regular basis (Wiggins, 1998). During those conferences teachers and students can discuss such issues as specific work samples, the maintenance of the portfolio, potential revisions, and overall academic progress. These one-to-one meetings are among the heralded advantages of portfolios over traditional assessments (Hiebert & Raphael, 1996). Particularly when working with younger students or those with special needs, teachers may also find it useful to meet with parents, as well as the students themselves.

Scoring Consistency

Another reason that some educators avoid the use of portfolios has to do with the bias that can easily result in scoring and interpreting them (Linn & Gronlund, 2000). In fact, one recent analysis of Vermont's portfolio assessment program reported low interrater agreements among scorers for both mathematics and writing portfolios (Koretz, Mc-Caffrey, Klein, Bell, & Strecher, 1993). Even though very general criteria and inadequate training of scorers may have accounted for the low interrater reliabilities in that study, some degree of subjectivity seems inherent in portfolio assessment (Eisner, 1999; Jamentz, 1994). Teachers cannot generally create answer keys or response protocols in advance, nor can they score students' entries blindly, as they can for extended-response questions. In addition, there is intentional variability in the specific entries students choose for inclusion in their portfolios. Because of these potential threats to reliability, it is very difficult to make comparative decisions based solely on student portfolios.

Even though this problem cannot be completely eliminated, teachers can take steps to make more reliable and defensible judgments when evaluating student portfolios. For example, teachers are wise to use well-specified, detailed criteria or rubrics when scoring students' work (Andrade, 2000). The more specific and detailed the criteria, the less room for scoring bias. Linn and Gronlund (2000) provide such a scoring scale in Table 14–6. The scale not only targets important skills and abilities, but also focuses on the growth students show from the first to the end of the school year.

To increase consistency, teachers should also consider scoring entries or entire portfolios twice (McMillan, 2001). After works have been scored once, teachers should set those evaluations aside for a reasonable interval, then reorder, and score them again. They can then compare the two sets of scores to ensure that there are no noticeable discrepancies. If discrepancies are found, those entries or portfolios can be reevaluated, perhaps with the assistance of a knowledgeable colleague. In schools where portfolios are accepted practice, teachers can collaborate in the scoring process. Collaborating teachers can independently score students' work samples and then compare their scores to gauge interrater agreement. When there are marked differences in scores, the teachers can discuss their ratings and reach agreement on the final outcome (Arter & Spandel, 1992).

Time Demands

Educators who want to make portfolios part of their assessment repertoire must accept one fundamental fact: The development, maintenance, and interpretation of portfolios are time-consuming activities. As James McMillan (2001) makes clear, portfolios are much more than folders containing student work. Implementing portfolios appropriately and effectively requires a considerable investment of time. That time is associated not only with designating entries, designing criteria, and scoring or rescoring student work samples, but also in pursuing the professional development teachers need to implement portfolios.

Nonetheless, teachers can take steps to control the time demands that come with portfolio assessments. Those steps, summarized in Figure 14–12, include being organized, setting aside specific class time for portfolio work, and associating time frames with particular entries. Teachers who are better organized devote less time to portfolio assessment than teachers who have difficulty physically ordering and maintaining students' materials or who have not sufficiently prepared themselves for evaluating each entry (Valencia & Calfee, 1991).

In addition, when teachers and students have designated time during the week to work on the portfolios and to confer about their content and evaluation, both are better equipped to use their available time to fuller advantage (Valencia et al., 1994). Moreover, students are helped by having some notion of how much time and effort a given entry should require. For instance, students in Gregg Ponitch's class know that one of their entries for the fall and the spring will be a problem of their own creation. They have also been given the criteria that Mr. Ponitch will use to evaluate their problems. However, it would be even more helpful to both Mr. Ponitch and the students to have some sense of the time they should expect to devote to this one component of their portfolio. To assist them,

---

Table 14–6   Rating scale for a growth portfolio in mathematics.

Development of Mathematics Understanding	Unsatisfactory Progress				Satisfactory Progress
Progress from early to late problem sets	1	2	3	4	5
Improvement in ability to formulate and solve problems	1	2	3	4	5
Reduction in errors in computation	1	2	3	4	5
Increased ability to make connections	1	2	3	4	5
Improvement in ability to communicate mathematical results to others	1	2	3	4	5
Increased ability to estimate and to check solutions for reasonableness	1	2	3	4	5
Increased skills in using charts and graphs	1	2	3	4	5

Note: From *Measurement and assessment in teaching* (p. 310) by R. L. Linn and N. E. Gronlund, 2000, Upper Saddle River, NJ: Merrill/Prentice Hall. Copyright 2000 by Prentice Hall. Reprinted with permission.

Mr. Ponitch might show them some good examples and discuss the approximate number of hours these prototypes might take (e.g., 2 to 3 hours from conception through revision).

What Are the Fundamental Principles of Effective Classroom Assessment?

Whatever tools or formats classroom teachers choose to gauge student learning and development, their actions should reflect certain fundamentals grounded in the assessment literature. Those guiding principles have implications for educational practice.

Embrace a Systemic Approach to Student Assessment

One of the lessons to be learned from an exploration of classroom-based assessments is that there is no perfect mode of measurement and evaluation (Alexander & Parsons, 1991). Despite the rhetoric or passion that surrounds both traditional and alternative approaches, no one manner of assessment can do it all. Each form of assessment comes with certain assets and its own potential liabilities. Consequently, teachers should consider adopting a systemic approach to assessment—one that encompasses a variety of traditional and alternative assessment techniques used for specific purposes (Airasian, 1997).

Teachers who continually rely on only one or two assessment formats are unquestionably hampered in their professional role. Instead, teachers should be equipped with a rich repertoire of assessment tools they can competently and confidently ply. Otherwise, they may find themselves wielding an assessment hammer when a screwdriver is required.

Moreover, teachers should embrace a variety of assessment approaches so that students have multiple avenues for demonstrating what they know and can do (Aschbacher, 1997). Teachers who routinely employ only a narrow range of assessment measures may unintentionally hamper their students' academic progress by overlooking areas of strength or need (McMillan, 2001). Certainly, any who have

taught can appreciate Gregg Ponitch's hesitancy to try a wider variety of measurement tools when he feels so confident about one or two forms. But there are ways around Gregg's concerns and very valid reasons that he should consider items other than short-answer questions or computational problems. With continued professional development, committed teachers like Gregg may set their hesitancies aside and engage in the systemic, varied assessment needed for optimal learning and development.

Make Assessment Decisions Based on Instructional Goals and Student Characteristics

Two issues should lie at the heart of teachers' decisions about which manner of assessment tool to implement in a given situation (Linn & Gronlund, 2000; Nitko, 2001). The first is their instructional goals: What am I trying to accomplish through this particular academic experience, and how will my choice of assessment approach complement those intentions? The second is their students' capabilities, experiences, and propensities.

McMillan (2001) cautions that these concerns about goals and student characteristics must be weighed not only *before* but also *during* and *after* instruction. This ongoing attention to instructional goals and student characteristics is well depicted in McMillan's model of the preinstruction, during-instruction, and postinstruction stages of assessment decision making shown in Figure 14–13. The choice of assessment approach should begin long before lessons get underway, as teachers reflect on their students' existing knowledge or ponder the nature of chosen activities.

Such analysis should also continue as those lessons unfold. For instance, teachers must weigh students' responses to ongoing activities and decide on appropriate feedback for the students. In addition, decisions about assessment continue to take shape after the activity has concluded and should inform teachers' subsequent goals and instructional planning. In other words, assessment decision making is a continuous process. It should never become an academic afterthought or simply a reflexive response. As an aid to teachers, McMillan frames leading questions and associated assessment

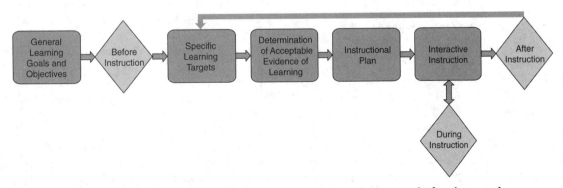

■ **FIGURE 14–13   The stages of assessment decision making: before, during, and after instruction.**

Note: From *Classroom assessment: Principles and practice for effective instruction* (2nd ed., p. 7) by J. H. McMillan, 2001, Boston: Allyn & Bacon. Copyright 2001 by Allyn & Bacon. Adapted with Permission.

Table 14–7   Questions to guide classroom-based assessment decision making.

Stage	Questions	Assessment Information
Before instruction	How much do my students know?	Previous student achievement; test scores; observations of student performance
	Are my students motivated to learn?	Observations of student involvement and willingness
	Are there any exceptional students? If so, what should I plan for them?	Student records; conference with a special education teacher
	What instructional activities should I plan? Are these activities realistic for these students?	Overall strengths and needs of students; comments from previous teachers; evaluations of previous teaching
	What homework assignments should I prepare?	Student progress and level of understanding
	What is acceptable evidence that students have attained desired proficiencies?	Determination of which assessment methods will provide needed evidence
During instruction	What type of feedback should I give to students?	Quality of student work; type of student
	What questions should I ask?	Observations of student understanding
	How should a student response to a question be answered?	Potential for this student to know the answer
	Which students need my individual attention?	Performance on homework; observations of work in class
	What response is best to student inattention or disruption?	Effect of the student on others
	When should I stop this lecture?	Observation of student attention
	How well have my students mastered the material?	Achievement test results in relation to a specified level
	Are students ready for the next unit?	Analysis of demonstrated knowledge
After instruction	What grades should the students receive?	Tests; quizzes; homework; class participation
	What comments should I make to parents?	Improvement; observations of behavior
	How should I change my instruction?	Diagnosis of demonstrated learning; student evaluations

Note: From *Classroom assessment: Principles and practice for effective instruction* (2nd ed., p. 6) by J. H. McMillan, 2001, Boston: Allyn & Bacon. Copyright 2001 by Allyn & Bacon. Reprinted with Permission.

information teachers may want to consider at each of the three stages of assessment decision making (see Table 14–7).

Move Beyond Simplistic Notions of Right or Wrong

Teachers should be concerned about students' strong beliefs about tests and testing, which can interfere with their optimal learning and development (Alexander & Parsons, 1991; Buehl et al., 2002). Central among those beliefs is the common conviction that there is one and only one answer that counts in school performance (Schommer, 1993; Schommer et al., 1992). Under this belief system, the students' primary task is to figure out what that singular right answer is. Even when teachers turn to performance-based or portfolio assessments, students may still hold to the belief that their responses or entries are fundamentally good or bad, right or wrong.

In reality, there are inevitable degrees of correctness or incorrectness inherent in any mode of evaluation, even those held to be highly objective (Alexander, Murphy, & Kulikowich, 1998). Educators should embrace this fact, not just theoretically but also in terms of their scoring systems (Kulikowich & Alexander, 1994, in press). For example, they should consider using graduated responses, as well as awarding partial credits (see Figure 14–5). Shades of right and wrong can also be reflected in the rubrics teachers devise (see Table 14–4).

In addition, teacher and student discussions about the strengths and weaknesses of particular answers—from selected-response to constructed-response formats and from performance-based to portfolio alternatives—should be routine classroom events (Stiggins, 2001). Through such discussions students may come to realize that concepts of right and wrong are never as simplistic as they sometimes appear on teacher-made or formal assessments. As discussed in Chapter 6, these more sophisticated and relativistic understandings about knowledge and learning are important for many reasons, not the least of which is their link to students' self-competence, their problem solving, and even their achievement (Schommer, 1990).

Ensure That Assessment Outcomes Actually Reflect Understanding and Ability

One principle that should always guide teachers' actions is the recognition that assessment in all its many forms and variations is intended to promote student learning and development. Assessment must remain a *means* and not an *end*. Those in public and policy sectors may see tests as catalysts for more acceptable instruction or as mechanisms for punishing or rewarding teachers, schools, or school districts. However, effective and meaningful assessment should ultimately exist to *serve* learning and instruction, not to dictate to or regulate them (Wolf, Bixby, Glenn, & Gardner, 1991). When tests or test developers try to dictate to or regulate learning and development, curriculum becomes distorted (Paris, 2000a). Students may come to learn what is on the tests, but they will fail to achieve the understandings or abilities that such measures purport to gauge.

Further, when teacher-made tests are poorly conceived or poorly interpreted, they, too, may misdirect students' efforts or learning (Wiggins, 1991). Or they may only superficially measure what students know and can do (Valencia et al., 1994). Thus, if teachers are going to invest in the construction and implementation of both traditional and alternative assessments and if students are going to exert thought and effort in responding to those measures, it is critical that assessment outcomes correspond well to the knowledge, skills, and abilities deemed valuable.

Involve Others in the Assessment Process

Teachers need not shoulder the entire burden of assessment, nor is it healthy for them to do so (Stiggins, 1993). It has become clear that students benefit greatly when they are real participants in the entire assessment process (Hiebert & Raphael, 1996). Students can participate in many ways (Nitko, 2001):

- help to frame classroom assessment goals
- create possible measurement items or tasks
- share in the construction of evaluation criteria and rubrics
- assist in the selection of work for evaluation
- judge the strengths and weaknesses of their own performance

Depending on the age and the background of the students, teachers should also consider involving parents in the classroom assessment process. Parent-teacher conferences are one way to maintain open lines of communication with parents about their children's progress (Popham, 2002). Parents should also be kept informed about instructional goals and upcoming activities. In addition, parents can play a direct role in assisting in classroom evaluation tasks and in selecting works for their children's portfolios.

Moreover, assessment is enhanced when teachers share their thoughts and efforts with colleagues (Valencia & Calfee, 1991). Teachers can benefit from shared discussions about assessment goals and approaches, just as Gregg Ponitch benefited from Mrs. Dench's mentorship. Together teachers can formulate specific items or tasks, discuss the match between goals and measurement tools, and share in the scoring of student work.

Base Decisions on Patterns in Student Performance

Teachers should keep in mind that student performance can vary on any given day and with any specific task (Airasian, 1997). Thus, if teachers are going to make valid judgments about students and then make the appropriate shifts in learning targets that those judgments suggest (see Figure 14–13), they must depend on reliable evidence (McMillan, 2001). And reliable evidence means patterns in student performance that represent true strengths or needs—strengths or needs that do not quickly disappear when the school day comes to an end or when certain features of a task change.

Teachers can be more confident about the fundamental character of students' knowledge, skills, and abilities if predictions about students' strengths and needs are upheld across a number of testing occasions and assessment formats (Alexander, Murphy, & Kulikowich, 1998). For instance, students with difficulties comprehending text should manifest that basic problem whether they are reading essay questions or responding to performance-based assessments (Valencia et al., 1994). Likewise, if students lack a deep understanding of central concepts in history, mathematics, science, or other academic subjects, that deficit should be evident whether the assessment tool is traditional or alternative. But if the same problems arise across distinct modes of assessment, teachers can feel quite confident that their judgments about students are credible and worthy of instructional intervention (Alexander & Parsons, 1991).

....

■ Summary

How can teachers improve the quality of their traditional assessments?

- ■ Traditional items can be classified in terms of their scoring or their expected responses.
  - Objective items have generally agreed-upon answers, whereas subjective items have multiple acceptable interpretations.
  - Students need only choose from several options for selected-response items, whereas they must provide some form of written answer for constructed-response items.
  - Objective and selected-response items include multiple-choice, true/false, and matching questions.

- Subjective and extended-response items include short-answer and essay questions.
- Question formats that involve a limited written answer and introduce a degree of subjectivity are called restricted-response and include completion, analogies, and modified true/false questions.

■ Each type of traditional test item comes with its own set of advantages and disadvantages, which teachers must carefully consider when preparing classroom-based assessments.

■ If teachers understand these advantages and disadvantages and take the necessary steps to ensure that common disadvantages are circumvented, traditional question forms can remain effective tools in their assessment repertoire.

What alternatives to traditional measures should teachers consider?

■ Performance-based assessments ask students to engage in a task that demonstrates their understanding and skills in a particular area.

- Performance-based assessments permit teachers to evaluate complex ideas and processes that cannot be readily cast in multiple-choice or short-answer formats.
- They can also tap into students' procedural or how-to knowledge, which is typically overlooked by traditional items.
- This alternative can be effective at prompting deeper and richer exploration of academic topics and domains.
- It also gets students actively and meaningfully engaged in the learning and assessment process.
- But performance-based assessments are less effective at evaluating academic domains or topics broadly.
- The additional reading and writing can prove problematic for students with less developed literacy skills.
- The complexity of performance-based assessments introduces much more ambiguity and error into teachers' evaluations.

■ Well-specified criteria and carefully constructed rubrics can help.

■ Nothing can completely eliminate the subjectivity that comes with performance-based measures.

■ Portfolios are purposeful collections of student works that set out to either showcase the best of students'

knowledge, skills, and abilities or demonstrate how the students have grown and progressed over time.

- Students have a continual and direct role to play in collecting and judging entries in their portfolio—a level of participation unique to this mode of evaluation.
- The very nature of portfolio assessments means that the works teachers use to judge the learning and development of students differ for each.
- With portfolios students and teachers have the luxury of weeks, months, or even years to collect the desired work samples that establish students' capabilities or demonstrate their achievements.

What are the fundamental principles of effective classroom assessment?

■ Teachers should institute an approach to assessment that encompasses a variety of both traditional and alternative measures, enabling them to formulate a richer and more comprehensive portrait of students' capabilities and associated instructional needs than would result from reliance on only one or two methods.

■ Teachers must make thoughtful decisions about the choice of assessment tools for particular tasks; the key should be the goals teachers are pursuing and the specific characteristics of the students involved.

■ There are really no simple right or wrong answers, but shades and grades of correctness or incorrectness, a principle that should be evidenced in the measures teachers construct and the interpretations they make from them.

■ The one valid reason for investing classroom time and effort in assessment practices is student learning and development.

- Teachers must use methods that reach to the heart of student understanding and ability.
- Superficial measurements or assessments employed to prod teachers or hold them accountable will not have the desired effect.

■ Teachers are wise to involve others in the assessment process—the students in the classrooms, their parents, and fellow teachers, all of whom have a real stake in the outcome of classroom assessments.

■ Teachers need to be in search of reliable assessment data, reflecting patterns in performance that emerge across tasks and occasions and reveal students' academic strengths and specific instructional needs.

References

Ackerman, P. L. (2003). Cognitive ability and non-ability trait determinants of expertise. *Educational Researcher, 32*(8), 15–20.

Ackerman, P. L., & Heggestad, E. D. (1997). Intelligence, personality, and interests: Evidence of overlapping traits. *Psychological Bulletin, 121,* 219–245.

Ackerman, P. L., Kyllonen, P. C., & Roberts, R. D. (1999). *Learning and individual differences: Process, trait, and content determinants.* Washington, DC: American Psychological Association.

Ackerman, P. L., Sternberg, R. J., & Glaser, R. (1989). *Learning and individual differences: Advances in theory and research.* New York: Freeman.

Ackerman, P. L., & Woltz, D. J. (1994). Determinants of learning and performance in an associative memory/substitution task: Task constraints, individual differences, volition, and motivation. *Journal of Educational Psychology, 86*(4), 487–515.

Actions for Healthy Kids. (2003). *Taking action for healthy kids: A report on the healthy schools summit and the Actions for Healthy Kids initiative.* Retrieved from *http://www.actionforhealthykids.org*

Adams, M. J. (1990). *Beginning to read.* Cambridge, MA: MIT Press.

Adams, M. J., Treiman, R., & Pressley, M. (1998). Reading, writing, and literacy. In I. Sigel & A. Renninger (Eds.), *Handbook of child psychology: Child psychology in practice* (Vol.4, pp. 275–355). New York: Wiley.

Afflerbach, P. A., & VanSledright, B. (2001). Hath! Doth! What! The challenges middle school students face when they read innovative history text. *Journal of Adolescent and Adult Literacy, 44,* 696–707.

Ainley, M. D. (1998). Interest in learning in the disposition of curiosity in secondary students: Investigating process and context. In L. Hoffman, A. Krapp, K. Renninger, & J. Baumert (Eds.), *Interest and learning: Proceedings of the Seeon Conference on interest and gender* (pp. 257–266). Kiel, Germany: IPN.

Airasian, P. W. (1997). *Classroom assessment* (3rd ed.). New York: McGraw-Hill.

Airasian, P. W., & Madaus, G. J. (1972). Functional types of student evaluation. *Measurement and Evaluation in Guidance, 4,* 221–233.

Alexander, P. A. (1983). Comprehension instruction in a reading clinic: Comparison of clinic and classroom practices. *Reading Psychology, 4,* 169–180.

Alexander, P. A. (1985). Gifted and nongifted students' perceptions of intelligence. *Gifted Child Quarterly, 29,* 137–143.

Alexander, P. A. (1996). *Cognition and multicultural education: Contributing to the goals of knowledge construction and prejudice reduction.* Report for the Carnegie Foundation Funded Project, The Synthesis and Dissemination of Knowledge about Multicultural Education. New York: Carnegie Foundation.

Alexander, P. A. (1997a). Knowledge-seeking and self-schema: A case for the motivational dimensions of exposition [Special issue]. *Educational Psychologist, 32,* 83–94.

Alexander, P. A. (1997b). Mapping the multidimensional nature of domain learning: The interplay of cognitive, motivational, and strategic forces. In M. L. Maehr & P. R. Pintrich (Eds.), *Advances in motivation and achievement* (Vol. 10, pp. 213–250). Greenwich, CT: JAI Press.

Alexander, P. A. (1998a). Knowledge and literacy: A transgenerational perspective. In T. Shanahan & F. Rodriguez-Brown (Eds.), *Forty-seventh yearbook of the National Reading Conference* (pp. 22–43). Chicago: National Reading Conference.

Alexander, P. A. (1998b, April). Knowledge seeking: Toward a new model of domain learning. In G. Sinatra (Chair), *New models and metaphors for conceptualizing knowledge.* Address at the annual meeting of the American Educational Research Association, San Diego, CA.

Alexander, P. A. (1998c). The nature of disciplinary and domain learning: The knowledge, interest, and strategic dimensions of learning from subject-matter text. In C. Hynd (Ed.), *Learning from text across conceptual domains* (pp. 263–287). Mahwah, NJ: Lawrence Erlbaum.

Alexander, P. A. (2000). Toward a model of academic development: Schooling and the acquisition of knowledge: The sequel. *Educational Researcher, 29*(2), 28–33, 44.

Alexander, P. A. (2001). Persuasion: Rethinking the nature of change in students' knowledge and beliefs: Introduction to special issue on persuasion. *International Journal of Educational Research, 35,* 629–631.

Alexander, P. A. (2003a). The development of expertise: The journey from acclimation to proficiency. *Educational Researcher, 32*(8), 10–14.

Alexander, P. A. (2003b). Profiling the developing reader: The interplay of knowledge, interest, and strategic processing. In C. M. Fairbanks, J. Worthy, B. Maloch, J. V. Hoffman, & D. L. Schallert (Eds.), *The fifty-first yearbook of the National Reading Conference* (pp. 47–65). Oak Creek, WI: National Reading Conference.

Alexander, P. A., & Dochy, F. J. R. C. (1995). Conceptions of knowledge and beliefs: A comparison across varying cultural and educational communities. *American Educational Research Journal, 32,* 413–442.

Alexander, P. A., & Fives, H. (2000). Achieving expertise in teaching reading. In L. Baker, M. J. Dreher, & J. T. Guthrie (Eds.), *Engaging young readers: Promoting achievement and motivation* (pp. 285–308). New York: Guilford Press.

Alexander, P. A., Fives, H., Buehl, M. M., & Mulhern, J. (2002). Teaching as persuasion. *Teacher and Teacher Education, 18,* 795–813.

Alexander, P. A., Graham, S., & Harris, K. (1998). A perspective on strategy research: Progress and prospects [Special issue]. *Educational Psychology Review, 10,* 129–154.

Alexander, P. A., Hare, V. C., & Garner, R. (1984). Effects of time, access and question type on the response accuracy and frequency of lookbacks in older, proficient readers. *Journal of Reading Behavior, 16,* 119–130.

Alexander, P. A., & Jetton, T. L. (1996). The role of importance and interest in the processing of text. *Educational Psychology Review, 8*(1), 89–122.

Alexander, P. A., & Jetton, T. L. (2000). Learning from text: A multidimensional and developmental perspective. In M. L. Kamil, P. B. Mosenthal, P. D. Pearson, & R. Barr (Eds.), *Handbook of reading research* (Vol. 3, pp. 285–310). Mahwah, NJ: Lawrence Erlbaum.

Alexander, P. A., & Jetton, T. L. (2003). Learning from traditional and alternative texts: New conceptualization for an information age. In A. Graesser, M. Gernsbacher, & S. Goldman (Eds.), *Handbook of discourse processes* (pp. 199–241). Mahwah, NJ: Lawrence Erlbaum.

Alexander, P. A., & Jetton, T. L. & Kulikowich, J. M. (1995). Interrelationship of knowledge, interest, and recall: Assessing a model of domain learning. *Journal of Educational Psychology, 87,* 559–575.

Alexander, P. A., & Jetton, T. L., & Kulikowich, J. M., & Woehler, C. (1994). Contrasting instructional and structural importance: The seductive effects of teacher questions. *Journal of Reading Behavior, 26,* 19–45.

Alexander, P. A., & Judy, J. E. (1988). The interaction of domain-specific and strategic knowledge in academic performance. *Review of Educational Research, 58,* 375–404.

Alexander, P. A., & Knight, S. L. (1993). Dimensions of the interplay between learning and teaching. *Educational Forum, 57,* 232–245.

Alexander, P. A., & Kulikowich, J. M. (1994). Learning from physics text: A synthesis of recent research. *Journal of Research in Science Teaching: Special Issue on Print-Based Language Arts and Science Learning, 31,* 895–911.

Alexander, P. A., & Kulikowich, J. M. (2002). Commentary: Crossing lines. In R. Garner (Ed.), *Hanging out: Community-based after-school programs for children* (pp. 153–166). Westport, CT: Bergin & Garvey.

Alexander, P. A., Kulikowich, J. M., & Jetton, T. L. (1994). The role of subject-matter knowledge and interest in the processing of linear and nonlinear texts. *Review of Educational Research, 64,* 201–252.

Alexander, P. A., Kulikowich, J. M., & Schulze, S. K. (1994). How subject-matter knowledge affects recall and interest. *American Educational Research Journal, 31,* 313–337.

Alexander, P. A., & Murphy, P. K. (1998a). Profiling the differences in students' knowledge, interest, and strategic processing. *Journal of Educational Psychology, 90,* 435–447.

Alexander, P. A., & Murphy, P. K. (1998b). The research base for APA's learner-centered principles. In N. M. Lambert & B. L. McCombs (Eds.), *Issues in school reform: A sampler of psychological perspectives on learner-centered school* (pp. 25–60). Washington, DC: American Psychological Association.

Alexander, P. A., & Murphy, P. K. (1999a). Learner profiles: Valuing individual differences within classroom communities. In P. L. Ackerman, P. C. Kyllonen, & R. D. Roberts (Eds.), *Learning and individual differences: Processes, traits, and content determinants* (pp. 413–431). Washington, DC: American Psychological Association.

Alexander, P. A., & Murphy, P. K. (1999b). Nurturing the seeds of transfer: A domain-specific perspective. *International Journal of Educational Research, 31,* 561–576.

Alexander, P. A., & Murphy, P. K., Buehl, M. M., & Sperl, C. T. (1998). The influence of prior knowledge, beliefs, and interest in learning from persuasive text. In T. Shanahan & F. Rodriguez-Brown (Eds.), *Forty-seventh yearbook of the National Reading Conference* (pp. 167–181). Chicago: National Reading Conference.

Alexander, P. A., Murphy, P. K., Kulikowich, J. M. (1998). What responses to domain-specific analogy problems reveal about emerging competence: A new perspective on an old acquaintance. *Journal of Educational Psychology, 90,* 397–406.

Alexander, P. A., Murphy, P. K., & Woods, B. S. (1996). Of squalls and fathoms: Navigating the seas of educational innovation. *Educational Researcher, 25*(3), 31–36, 39.

Alexander, P. A., Murphy, P. K., Woods, B. S., Duhon, K. E., & Parker, D. (1997). College instruction and concomitant changes in students' knowledge, interest, and strategy use: A study of domain learning. *Contemporary Educational Psychology, 22,* 125–146.

Alexander, P. A., & Parsons, J. L. (1991). Confronting the misconceptions of testing and assessment. *Contemporary Education, 62,* 243–249.

Alexander, P. A., Pate, P. E., Kulikowich, J. M., Farrell, D. M., & Wright, N. L. (1989). Domain-specific and strategic knowledge: Effects of training on students of differing ages or competence levels. *Learning and Individual Differences, 1,* 283–325.

Alexander, P. A., Schallert, D. L., & Hare, V. C. (1991). Coming to terms: How researchers in learning and literacy talk about knowledge. *Review of Educational Research, 61,* 315–343.

Alexander, P. A., Sperl, C. T., Buehl, M. M., Fives, H., & Chiu, S. (2004). Modeling domain learning: Profiles from the field of special education. *Journal of Educational Psychology, 96,* 545–557.

Alexander, P. A., & Wade. S. E. (2000). Contexts that promote interest, self-determination, and learning: Lasting impressions and lingering questions [Commentary to special issue]. *Computers in Human Behavior, 16,* 349–358.

Alexander, P. A., White, C. S., & Daugherty, M. (1997). Children's use of analogical reasoning in early mathematics learning. In L. English (Ed.), *Mathematical reasoning: Analogies, metaphors, and images* (pp. 117–147). Mahwah, NJ: Lawrence Erlbaum.

Alexander, P. A., White, C. S., Haensly, P. A., & Crimmins-Jeanes, M. (1987). Training in analogical reasoning. *American Educational Research Journal, 24,* 387–404.

Alexander, P. A., Willson, V. L., White, C. S., & Fuqua, J. D. (1987). Analogical reasoning in young children. *Journal of Educational Psychology, 79,* 401–408.

Algina, J. (1992). Reliability of measurement. In M. C. Alkin (Ed.), *Encyclopedia of educational research* (6th ed., pp. 1090–1093). New York: Macmillan.

Allgood, W. P., Risko, V. J., Alvarez, M. D., & Fairbanks, M. M. (2000). Factors that influence study: In R. F. Flippo & D. C. Caverly (Eds.), *Handbook of college reading and study strategy research* (pp. 201–219). Mahwah, NJ: Lawrence Erlbaum.

Allington, R. (1980). Teacher interruption behaviors during primary-grade oral reading. *Journal of Educational Psychology, 71,* 371–377.

Alvermann, D. E. (2001). Teaching as persuasion: The worthiness of the metaphor. *Theory into Practice, 40,* 278–283.

Alvermann, D. E., & Hayes, D. A. (1989). Classroom discussion of content area reading assignments: An intervention study. *Reading Research Quarterly, 24,* 305–335.

Alvermann, D. E., O'Brien, D. G., & Dillon, D. R. (1990). What teachers do when they say they're having discussions of content area reading assignments: A qualitative analysis. *Reading Research Quarterly, 25,* 297–322.

Alvermann, D. E., Smith, L. C., & Readence, J. E. (1985). Prior knowledge activation and the comprehension of compatible and incompatible text. *Reading Research Quarterly, 20,* 420–436.

American Academy of Pediatrics. (2003). Prevention of pediatric overweight and obesity: Policy statement. *Pediatrics, 112*(2), 424–430. Retrieved from *http://www.aap. org/policy/s100029.html*

American Association for the Advancement of Science. (1993). *Benchmarks for science literacy: Project 2061.* New York: Oxford University Press.

American Association of University Women. (1998). *Gender gaps: Where schools still fail our children.* New York: Author.

American Educational Research Association. (2000). *AERA position statement concerning high-stakes testing in preK–12 education.* Retrieved from *http://www.aera.net/ about/policy/stakes.htm*

American Federation of Teachers, National Council of Measurement in Education, & National Educational Association. (1990). *Standards for teacher competence in educational assessment of students.* Washington, DC: American Psychological Association.

American Psychological Association. (1985). *Standards for educational and psychological testing.* Washington, DC: Author.

American Psychological Association. (1995). *Standards for educational and psychological testing.* Washington, DC: Author.

American Psychological Association Board of Educational Affairs. (1995, Dec.). *Learner-centered psychological principles: A framework for school redesign and reform.* Washington, DC: American Psychological Association. Also retrieved from *http:// www.apa.org/ed/lcp.html*

Ames, C. (1984a). Achievement attributions and self-instructions under competitive and individualistic goal structures. *Journal of Educational Psychology, 76*(3), 478–487.

Ames, C. (1984b). Competitive, cooperative, and individualistic goal structures: A motivational analysis. In R. Ames & C. Ames (Eds.), *Research on motivation in education* (Vol. 1, pp. 177–207). New York: Academic Press.

Ames, C. (1992). Classrooms: Goals, structures, and student motivation. *Journal of Educational Psychology, 84,* 261–271.

Ames, C., & Archer, J. (1988). Achievement goals in the classroom: Students' learning strategies and motivation processes. *Journal of Educational Psychology, 80*(3), 260–267.

Anderson, J. R. (1983). *The architecture of cognition.* Cambridge, MA: Harvard University Press.

Anderson, J. R. (1990). *Cognitive psychology and its implications* (3rd ed.). New York: Freeman.

Anderson, J. R. (1991). *Technology and adult literacy.* New York: Routledge.

Anderson, J. R., Boyle, C. F., & Yost, G. (1986). The geometry tutor. *Journal of Computer Assisted Learning, 8,* 221–230.

Anderson, L. M., Blumenfeld, P., Pintrich, P. R., Clark, C. M., Marx, R. W., & Peterson, P. (1995). Educational psychology for teachers: Reforming our courses, rethinking our roles. *Educational Psychologist, 30*(3), 143–157.

Anderson, R. C. (1977). The notion of schemata and the educational enterprise. In R. C. Anderson, R. J. Spiro, & W. E. Montague (Eds.), *Schooling and the acquisition of knowledge* (pp. 415–431). Hillsdale, NJ: Erlbaum.

Anderson, R. C., Pichert, J. W., Goetz, E. T., Schallert, D. L., Stevens, K. V., & Trollip, S. R. (1976). Instantiation of general terms. *Journal of Verbal Learning and Verbal Behavior, 15,* 667–679.

Anderson, R. C., Reynolds, R. E., Schallert, D. L., & Goetz, E. T. (1977). Frameworks for comprehending discourse. *American Educational Research Journal, 14,* 367–381.

Anderson, R. C., Spiro, R., & Anderson, M. C. (1978). Schemata as scaffolding for the representation of information in connected discourse. *American Educational Research Journal, 15,* 433–440.

Anderson, T. H., & Armbruster, B. B. (1984a). Content area textbooks. In R. C. Anderson, J. Osborn, & R. J. Tierney (Eds.), *Learning to read in American schools* (pp. 193–224). Hillsdale, NJ: Lawrence Erlbaum.

Anderson, T. H., & Armbruster, B. B. (1984b). Studying. In P. D. Pearson, R. Barr, M. L. Kamil, & P. Mosenthal (Eds.), *Handbook of reading research* (Vol. 1, pp. 657–679). White Plains, NY: Longman.

Anderson, T. H., & Armbruster, B. B. (1986). *The value of taking notes* (Reading Education Report No. 374). Champaign: University of Illinois at Urbana-Champaign, Center for the Study of Reading.

Anderson-Inman, L., & Horney, M. A. (1998). Transforming text for at-risk readers. In D. Reinking, M. C. McKenna, L. D. Labbo, & R. D. Kieffer (Eds.), *Handbook of literacy and technology: Transformations in a post-typographical world* (pp. 15–43). Mahwah, NJ: Lawrence Erlbaum.

Anderson-Inman, L., & Reinking, D. (1998). Learning from text in a post-typographic world. In C. R. Hynd (Ed.), *Learning from text across conceptual domains* (pp. 165–191). Mahwah, NJ: Lawrence Erlbaum.

Andrade, H. G. (2000). Using rubrics to promote thinking and learning. *Educational Leadership, 57*(5), 13–18.

Applebee, A. N., Langer, J. A., Mullis, I. V. S., & Jenkins, L. B. (1990). *The writing report card, 1984–1988: Findings from the national assessment of educational progress.* Princeton, NJ: Educational Testing Service.

Armbruster, B. B. (2000). Taking notes from lectures. In R. F. Flippo & D. C. Caverly (Eds.), *Handbook of college reading and study strategy research* (pp. 175–199). Mahwah, NJ: Lawrence Erlbaum.

Aronson, E. (1978). *The jigsaw classroom.* Beverly Hills, CA: Sage.

Aronson, E., Blaney, N., Sikes, J., Stephan, C., & Snapp, M. (1978). *The jigsaw classroom.* Beverly Hills, CA: Sage.

Aronson, E., & Patnoe, S. (1997). *The jigsaw classroom* (2nd ed.). New York: Longman.

Arter, J. R., & Spandel, V. (1992). Using portfolios of student work in instruction and assessment. *Educational Measurement: Issues and Practices, 11*(1), 36–44.

Aschbacher, P. (1997). New directions in student assessment. *Theory into Practice, 36*(4), 194–272.

Askov, E. N., & Bixler, B. (1998). Transforming adult literacy instruction through computer-assisted instruction. In D. Reinking, M. C. McKenna, L. D. Labbo, & R. D. Kieffer (Eds.), *Handbook of literacy and technology: Transformations in a post-typographical world* (pp. 167–202). Mahwah, NJ: Lawrence Erlbaum.

Astington, J. W. (1993). *The child's discovery of the mind.* Cambridge, MA: Harvard University Press.

Azevedo, R., Guthrie, J. T., Wang, H., & Mulhern, J. (2001, April). *Do different instructional interventions facilitate students' ability to shift to more sophisticated models of complex systems?* Paper presented at the annual meeting of the American Educational Research Association, Seattle, WA.

Azevedo, R., Verona, M. E., & Cromley, J. G. (2000). *Fostering learners' collaborative problem solving with RiverWeb.* Paper submitted for presentation at the 10th International Conference on Artificial Intelligence in Education, San Antonio, TX.

Azmitia, M. (1988). Peer interaction and problem solving: When are two heads better than one? *Child Development, 59,* 87–96.

Baars, B. J. (1986). *The cognitive revolution in psychology.* New York: Guilford.

Badderly, A. D. (1982). *Your memory: A user's guide.* New York: Macmillan.

Baker, E. L., & Niemi, D. (1996). School and program evaluation. In D. C. Berliner & R. C. Calfee (Eds.), *Handbook of educational psychology* (pp. 926–944). New York: Macmillan.

Baker, E. L., & O'Neil, H. F., Jr. (1993). Policy and validity prospects for performance-based assessment. *American Psychologist, 48,* 1210–1218.

Bakhtin, M. M. (1981). *The dialogic imagination* (M. Holquist, Ed.; M. Holquist & C. Emerson, Trans.). Austin: University of Texas Press.

Ball, D. (1993). With an eye on the mathematical horizon: Dilemmas of teaching elementary school mathematics. *Elementary School Journal, 93,* 373–397.

Bandura, A. (1977). Self-efficacy: Toward a unifying theory of behavioral change. *Psychological Review, 84,* 191–215.

Bandura, A. (1982). Self-efficacy mechanisms in human agency. *American Psychologist, 37,* 122–147.

Bandura, A. (1986). *Social foundations of thought and action.* Englewood Cliffs, NJ: Prentice Hall.

Bandura, A. (1993). Perceived self-efficacy in cognitive development and functioning. *Educational Psychologist, 28,* 117–148.

Bandura, A., & Adams, N. E. (1977). Analysis of self-efficacy theory of behavioral change. *Cognitive Therapy and Research, 1,* 287–308.

Bandura, A., Adams, N. E., Hardy, A. B., & Howells, G. N. (1980). Tests of the generality of self-efficacy theory. *Cognitive Therapy and Research, 4,* 39–66.

Bandura, A., & Cervone, D. (1986). Differential engagement of self-reactive influences in cognitive motivation. *Organizational Behavior and Human Decision Processes, 38,* 92–133.

Bandura, A., & Schunk, D. H. (1981). Cultivating competence, self-efficacy, and intrinsic interest through proximal self-motivation. *Journal of Personality and Social Psychology, 41,* 586–598.

Bangert-Drowns, R. L., Kulik, C. C., Kulik, J. A., & Morgan, M. (1991). The instructional effect of feedback in test-like events. *Review of Educational Research, 61,* 213–238.

Banks, J. A. (1993). The canon debate, knowledge construction, and multicultural education. *Educational Researcher, 22*(5), 4–14.

Barab, S. A., Fajen, B. R., Kulikowich, J. M., & Young, M. F. (1996). Assessing navigation through Pathfinder: Learning from dribble files. *Journal of Educational Computing Research, 15*(3), 175–195.

Barker, B. O., Frisbie, A. G., & Patrick, K. R. (1989). Broadening the definition of distance education in light of the new telecommunications technologies. *American Journal of Distance Education, 3*(1), 20–29.

Barnes, D. (1986). Brain architecture: Beyond genes. *Science, 233,* 155–156.

Baron, J. B., & Sternberg, R. J. (1987). *Teaching for thinking.* New York: Freeman.

Barrows, J. D. (1998). *Impossibility: The limits of science and the science of limits.* Oxford, England: Oxford University Press.

Bartlett, F. C. (1932). *A study in experimental and social psychology.* London: Cambridge University Press.

Baumann, J. F. (1984). The effectiveness of a direct instruction paradigm for teaching main idea comprehension. *Reading Research Quarterly, 20,* 93–115.

Baxter, G. P., Elder, A. D., & Glaser, R. (1996). Knowledge-based cognition and performance assessment in science classrooms. *Educational Psychologist, 31*(2), 133–140.

Baym, N. (1995). The emergence of community in computer-mediated instruction. In S. Jones (Ed.), *Cybersociety: Computer-mediated communication and community* (pp. 138–163). Thousand Oaks, CA: Sage.

Bazerman, C. (1995). *The informed writer* (2nd ed.). Boston, MA: Houghton Mifflin.

Beach, R., & Lundell, D. (1998). Early adolescents' use of computer-mediated communication in writing and reading. In D. Reinking, M. C. McKenna, L. D. Labbo, & R. D Kieffer (Eds.), *Handbook of literacy and technology: Transformations in a post-typographical world* (pp. 93–112). Mahwah, NJ: Lawrence Erlbaum.

Beason, L. (1993). Feedback and revision in writing across the curriculum classes. *Research in the Teaching of English, 27,* 395–422.

Beck, I. L., & McKeown, M. G. (1989). Expository text for young readers: The issue of coherence. In L. B. Resnick (Ed.), *Learning to read in American schools* (pp. 47–66). Hillsdale, NJ: Lawrence Erlbaum.

Beck, I. L., McKeown, M. G., & Gromoll, E. W. (1989). Learning from social studies texts. *Cognition and Instruction, 6,* 99–158.

Beck, I. L., McKeown, M. G., Sinatra, G. M., & Loxterman, J. A. (1991). Revising social studies text from a text-processing perspective. Evidence of improved comprehensibility. *Reading Research Quarterly, 26,* 251–276.

Begley, S. (1979, December). Twins: Nazi and Jew. *Newsweek,* p. 139.

Beilin, H. (1992). Piaget's enduring contribution to developmental psychology. *Developmental Psychology, 28,* 191–204.

Belensky, M. F., Clinchy, B. M., Goldberger, N., & Tarule, J. (1986). *Women's way of knowing: The development of self, voice, and mind.* New York: Basic Books.

Bell, J. C. (1917). The historic sense. *Journal of Educational Psychology, 5,* 317–318.

Bell, J. C., & McCollum, D. F. (1917). A study of the attainments of pupils in United States history. *Journal of Educational Psychology, 8,* 257–274.

Ben-Zvi, R., Eylon, B., Silberstein, J. (1987). Students' visualization of a chemical reaction. *Education in Chemistry, 24*(4), 117–120.

Bereiter, C. (1994). Constructivism, socioculturalism, and Popper's World 3. *Educational Researcher, 23*(7), 21–23.

Bereiter, C. (1995). A dispositional view of transfer. In A. McKeough, J. Lupart, & A. Marini (Eds.), *Teaching for transfer: Fostering generalization in learning* (pp. 21–34). Mahwah, NJ: Lawrence Erlbaum.

Bereiter, C. (2002). *Education and mind in the knowledge age.* Mahwah, NJ: Lawrence Erlbaum.

Bereiter, C., & Scardamalia, M. (1989). Intentional learning as a goal of instruction. In L. B. Resnick (Ed.), *Knowing, learning, and instruction: Essays in honor of Robert Glaser* (pp. 361–392). Hillsdale, NJ: Erlbaum.

Berger, J., Rosenholtz, S. J., & Zelditch, M. (1980). Status organizing processes. *Annual Review of Sociology, 6,* 479–508.

Bergin, D. A., Ford, M. E., & Hess, R. D. (1993). Patterns of motivation and social behavior associated with microcomputer use of young children. *Journal of Educational Psychology, 85,* 437–445.

Berk, L. E. (1999). *Infants and children: Prenatal through middle childhood* (3rd ed.). Boston: Allyn & Bacon.

Berk, R. A. (1984). *A guide to criterion-referenced test construction.* Baltimore: Johns Hopkins University Press.

Berliner, D. C. (1987). Knowledge is power: A talk to teachers about a revolution in the teaching profession. In D. C. Berliner & B. V. Rosenshine (Eds.), *Talks to teachers: A festschrift for N. L. Gage* (pp. 3–33). New York: Random House.

Berliner, D. C. (1993). The 100-year journey of educational psychology: From interest, to disdain, to respect for practice. In T. K. Fagan & G. R. VandenBos (Eds.), *Exploring applied psychology: Origins and critical analysis.* Washington, DC: American Psychological Association.

Berliner, D. C., & Biddle, B. J. (1995). *The manufactured crisis: Myths, fraud, and the attack on America's public schools.* Reading, MA: Addison-Wesley.

Berninger, V. W., & Corine, D. (1998). Making cognitive neuroscience educationally relevant: Creating bi-directional collaborations between educational psychology and cognitive neuroscience. *Educational Psychology Review, 10,* 343–354.

Berninger, V. W., & Richards, T. L. (2002). *Brain literacy for educators and psychologists.* San Diego, CA: Academic Press.

Betz, N. E., & Hackett, G. (1983). The relationship of mathematics self-efficacy expectations to the selection of science-based college majors. *Journal of Vocational Behavior, 28,* 329–345.

Bidell, T. R., & Fischer, K. W. (1992). Beyond the stage debate: Action, structure, and variability in Piagetian theory and research. In R. J. Sternberg & C. A. Berg (Eds.), *Intellectual development* (pp. 100–140). Cambridge, England: Cambridge University Press.

Binet, A., & Simon, T. (1905). Méthodes nouvelles pour le diagnostic du niveau intellectual des anormaux [New methods for diagnosing the intellectual level of abnormals]. *Année Psychologique, 11,* 191–336.

Binet, A., & Simon, T. (1916). *The development of intelligence in children.* Baltimore, Williams & Wilkins. (Original work published 1905; reprinted 1973, New York: Arno Press; reprinted 1983, Salem, NH: Ayer).

Bloom, B. S., Hastings, J. T., & Madaus, G. E. (1971). *Handbook on formative and summative assessment of student learning.* New York: McGraw Hill.

Blumenfeld, P. C. (1992). Classroom learning and motivation: Clarifying and expanding goal theory. *Journal of Educational Psychology, 84*(3), 272–281.

Boekaerts, M., Pintrich, P. R., & Zeidner, M. (2001). Self-regulation: An introductory overview. In M. Boekaerts, P. R. Pintrich, & M. Zeidner (Eds.), *Handbook of self-regulation* (pp. 1–11). San Diego, CA: Academic Press.

Bolter, J. D. (1991). *Writing space: The computer, hypertext, and the history of writing.* Hillsdale, NJ: Lawrence Erlbaum.

Bolter, J. D. (1998). Hypertext and the question of visual literacy. In D. Reinking, M. C. McKenna, L. D. Labbo, & R. D Kieffer (Eds.), *Handbook of literacy and technology: Transformations in a post-typographical world* (pp. 3–13). Mahwah, NJ: Lawrence Erlbaum.

Bond, L. (1995). Unintended consequences of performance assessment: Issues of bias and fairness. *Educational Measurement: Issues and Practice, 14*(4), 21–24.

Bong, M. (1996). Problems in academic motivation research and advantages and disadvantages of their solutions. *Contemporary Educational Psychology, 21,* 149–165.

Bouchard, T. J., Jr. (1984). Twins reared apart and together: What they tell us about human diversity. In S. Fox (Ed.), *The chemical and biological bases of individuality.* New York: Plenum Press.

Bouchard, T. J., Jr., & McGue, M. (1981). Familial studies of intelligence: A review. *Science, 212,* 1055–1059.

Bransford, J. D., Brown, A. L., & Cocking, R. R. (1999). *How people learn: Brain, mind, experience, and school.* Washington, DC: National Academy Press.

Bransford, J. D., & Johnson, M. K. (1973). Consideration of some problems of comprehension. In W. G. Chase (Ed.), *Visual information processing* (pp. 383–438). New York: Academic Press.

Bransford, J. D., & Stein, B. S. (1984). *The IDEAL problem solver.* New York: W. H. Freeman.

Bransford, J. D., & Stein, B. S. (1993). *The IDEAL problem solver* (2nd ed.). New York: W. H. Freeman.

Bransford, J. D., Zech, L., Schwartz, D., Barron, B., Vye, N., & the Cognition and Technology Group at Vanderbilt. (1996). Fostering mathematical thinking in middle school students: Lessons from research. In R. J. Sternberg & T. Ben-Zeev (Eds.), *The nature of mathematical thinking* (pp. 203–250). Mahwah, NJ: Lawrence Erlbaum.

Braun, H. L., Bennett, R. E., Frye, D., & Soloway, E. (1990). Scoring constructed responses using expert systems. *Journal of Educational Measurement, 27,* 93–108.

Bredekamp, S. (1987). *Developmentally appropriate practices in early childhood programs serving children from birth through age 8.* Washington, DC: National Association for the Education of Young Children.

Bredo, E. (1996). The social construction of learning. In G. D. Phye (Ed.), *Handbook of academic learning: Construction of knowledge* (pp. 3–45). San Diego, CA: Academic Press.

Britt, M. A., Rouet, J.-F., & Perfetti, C. A. (1996). Using hypertext to study and reason about historical evidence. In J.-F. Rouet, J. J. Levonen, A. P. Dillon, & R. J. Spiro (Eds.), *Hypertext and cognition* (pp. 43–72). Mahwah, NJ: Lawrence Erlbaum.

Britton, B. K. (1981, April). *Use of cognitive capacity in reading.* Paper presented at the annual meeting of the American Educational Research Association, Los Angeles.

Broadbent, D. E. (1938). *Perception and communication.* New York: Pergamon Press.

Broadwell, M. M. (1980). *The lecture method of instruction.* Englewood Cliffs, NJ: Educational Technology Publications.

Bronfenbrenner, U. (1979). *The ecology of human development.* Cambridge, MA: Harvard University Press.

Bronfenbrenner, U. (1989). Ecological systems theory. In R. Vasta (Ed.), *Annals of child development: Vol 6. Six theories of child development: Revised formulations and current issues.* Greenwich, CT: JAI Press.

Brookhart, S. M. (1997). A theoretical framework for the role of classroom assessment in motivating student effort and achievement. *Applied Measurement in Education, 10,* 161–180.

Brookhart, S. M. (1999). Teaching about communicating assessment results and grading. *Educational Measurement: Issues and Practice, 18*(1), 5–13.

Brophy, J. (1998). *Motivating students to learn.* Boston: McGraw-Hill.

Brophy, J. (1999). Toward a model of the value aspects of motivation in education: Developing appreciation for particular learning domains and activities. *Educational Psychologist, 34,* 75–85.

Brophy, J., & Good, T. (1986). Teacher behavior and student achievement. In M. Wittrock (Ed.), *Handbook of research on teaching* (3rd ed., pp. 328–375). New York: Macmillan.

Brophy, J., & VanSledright, B. (1997). *Teaching and learning history in elementary schools.* New York: Teachers' College Press.

Brown, A. L. (1975). The development of memory: Knowing, knowing about knowing, and knowing how to know. In H. W. Reese (Ed.), *Advances in child development and behavior* (Vol. 10, pp. 103–152). New York: Academic Press.

Brown, A. L., & Campione, J. S. (1990). Communities of learning and thinking, or a context by any other name. *Contributions to Human Development, 21,* 108–126.

Brown, A. L., & DeLoache, J. S. (1978). Skills, plans, and self-regulation. In R. Siegler (Ed.), *Children's thinking: What develops?* (pp. 3–35). Hillsdale, NJ: Lawrence Erlbaum.

Brown, A. L., & Palinscar, A. S. (1987). Reciprocal teaching of comprehension strategies: A natural history of one program for enhancing learning. In J. Borkowski & J. D. Day (Eds.), *Cognition in special education: Comparative approaches to retardation, learning disabilities, and giftedness.* Norwood, NJ: Ablex.

Brown, J. S., & Burton, R. R. (1978). Diagnostic models for procedural bugs in basic mathematical skills. *Cognitive Science, 2,* 155–192.

Brown, J. S., Collins, A., & Duguid, P. (1989). Situated cognition and the culture of learning. *Educational Researcher, 18*(1), 32–42.

Brown, R., & Kulik, J. (1977). Flashbulb memories. *Cognition, 5,* 73–99.

Brownlee, S., Leventhal, H., & Leventhal, E. A. (2001). Self-regulation and construction of the self in the maintenance of physical health. In M. Boekaerts, P. R. Pintrich, & M. Zeidner (Eds.), *Handbook of self-regulation* (pp. 369–416). San Diego, CA: Academic Press.

Bruce, B. C., & Hogan, M. P. (1998). The disappearance of technology: Toward an ecological model of literacy. In D. Reinking, M. C. McKenna, L. D. Labbo, & R. D Kieffer (Eds.), *Handbook of literacy and technology: Transformations in a post-typographical world* (pp. 269–281). Mahwah, NJ: Lawrence Erlbaum.

Bruce, B. C., Peyton, J. K., & Batson, T. (1993). *Network-based classrooms: Promises and realities.* New York: Cambridge University Press.

Bruce, S. P., & Bruce, B. C. (2000). Constructing images of science: People, technologies, and practices. *Computers in Human Behavior, 16,* 241–256.

Bruer, J. T. (1993). *Schools for thought: A science of learning in the classroom.* Cambridge, MA: MIT Press.

Bruner, J. S. (1961). The act of discovery. *Harvard Educational Review, 31,* 21–32.

Bruner, J. S. (1974). *Relevance of education.* New York: Penguin.

Bruner, J. S., Goodnow, J. J., & Austin, G. A. (1956). *A study of thinking.* New York: John Wiley.

Bruning, R. H., Schraw, G. J., & Ronning, R. R. (1999). *Cognitive psychology and instruction* (3rd ed.). Columbus, OH: Merrill.

Bryk, A. S., & Weisberg, H. I. (1977). Use of nonequivalent control group design when subjects are growing. *Psychological Bulletin, 85,* 950–962.

Bryne, B. M. (1984). The general/academic self-concept nomological network: A review of construct validation research. *Review of Educational Research, 54,* 427–456.

Buehl, M. M., & Alexander, P. A. (2000, August). *Young Children's conceptions of schooled knowledge and learning.* Paper presented at the annual meeting of the American Psychological Association, Washington, DC.

Buehl, M. M., & Alexander, P. A. (2001). Examining beliefs about academic knowledge: Domain general or domain specific? *Educational Psychology Review, 13,* 385–418.

Buehl, M. M., & Alexander, P. A., & Murphy, P. K.(2002). Beliefs about schooled knowledge: Domain specific or domain general. *Contemporary Educational Psychology, 27,* 415–449.

Burtt, E. A. (1939). *The English philosophers from Bacon to Mill.* New York: Modern Library.

Butler, R. (1993). Effects of task- and ego-achievement goals on information seeking during task engagement. *Journal of Educational Psychology, 65,* 18–31.

Butler, R. (1994). Teacher communications and student interpretations: Effects of teacher responses to failing students on attributional inferences in two age groups. *British Journal of Educational Psychology, 64,* 277–294.

Butterworth, B. (1999). *What counts: How every brain is hardwired for math.* New York: Free Press.

Byrnes, J. P. (1996). *Cognitive development and learning in instructional contexts.* Boston: Allyn & Bacon.

Byrnes, J. P. (2001). *Cognitive development and learning in instructional contexts* (2nd ed.). Boston: Allyn & Bacon.

Cambel, A. B. (1993). *Applied Chaos Theory: A paradigm for complexity.* Boston: Academic Press.

Campione, J. C., Shapiro, A. M., & Brown, A. L. (1995). Forms of transfer in a community of learners: Flexible learning and understanding. In A. Mckeough, J. Lupart, & A. Marini (Eds.), *Teaching for transfer: Fostering generalization in learning* (pp. 35–68). Mahwah, NJ: Lawrence Erlbaum.

Canfield, R. L., & Smith, E. G. (1993, April). *Counting in early infancy: Number-based expectations.* Paper presented at the annual meeting of the Society for the Study of Child Development, New Orleans, LA.

Cannell, J. J. (1988). Nationally normed elementary achievement testing in America's public schools: How all 50 states are above the national average. *Educational Measurement: Issues and Practice, 7*(2), 5–9.

Carey, L. M. (1994). *Measuring and evaluating school learning* (2nd ed.). Boston: Allyn & Bacon.

Carey, S. (1985). *Conceptual change in childhood.* Cambridge, MA: MIT Press.

Carey, S., Evans, R., Honda, M., Jay, E., & Unger, C. (1989). An experiment is when you try it and see if it works: A study of grade 7 students' understanding of the construction of scientific knowledge. *International Journal of Science Education, 11,* 514–529.

Carnegie Council on Adolescent Development. (1996). *Great transitions: Preparing adolescents for a new century* (Abridged Version). New York: Carnegie.

Carr, E., & Ogle, D. (1987). K-W-L Plus: A strategy for comprehension and summarization. *Journal of Reading, 30,* 626–631.

Carraher, T., Carraher, D., & Schlieman, A. (1985). Mathematics in the streets and in the schools. *British Journal of Developmental Psychology, 3,* 21–29.

Carroll, J. B. (1993). *Human cognitive abilities.* Cambridge, England: Cambridge University Press.

Carver, C. S., & Scheier, M. F. (2001). On the structure of behavioral self-regulation. In M. Boekaerts, P. R. Pintrich, & M. Zeidner (Eds.), *Handbook of self-regulation* (pp. 42–85). San Diego, CA: Academic Press.

Case, R. (1985). *Intellectual development: Birth to adulthood.* New York: Academic Press.

Case, R. (1992). *The mind's staircase: Exploring the conceptual underpinnings of children's thought and knowledge.* Mahwah, NJ: Lawrence Erlbaum.

Case, R., & Griffin, S. (1990). Child cognitive development: The role of central conceptual structures in the development of scientific and social thought. In C. A. Hauert (Ed.), *Developmental psychology: Cognitive, perceptuo-motor and neuropsychological perspectives.* Amsterdam: North-Holland.

Case, R., & Okamoto, Y. (1996). The role of central conceptual structures in the development of children's numerical, literacy, and spatial thought. *Monographs of the Society for Research in Child Development* (Serial No. 246).

Cattell, R. B. (1971). *Abilities: Their structure, growth, and action.* Boston: Houghton Mifflin.

Caverly, D. C., & Orlando, V. P. (1991). Textbook study strategies. In R. F. Flippo & D. C. Caverly (Eds.), *Teaching reading and study strategies at the college level* (pp. 86–165). Newark, DE: International Reading Association.

Caverly, D. C., Orlando, V. P., & Mullen, J. L. (2000). Textbook study reading. In R. F. Flippo & D. C. Caverly (Eds.), *Handbook of college reading and study strategy research* (pp. 105–147). Mahwah, NJ: Lawrence Erlbaum.

Cazden, C. (1988). *Classroom discourse: The language of teaching and learning.* Portsmouth, NJ: Heinemann.

Ceci, S. J. (1990). *On intelligence . . . more or less: A bio-ecological treatise on intellectual development.* Englewood Cliffs, NJ: Prentice Hall.

Chambliss, M. J. (1995). Text cues and strategies successful readers use to construct the gist of lengthy written arguments. *Reading Research Quarterly, 30,* 778–807.

Chambliss, M. J., & Garner, R. (1996). Do adults change their minds after reading persuasive text? *Written Communication, 13,* 291–313.

Chambliss, M. J., & Murphy, P. K. (2002). Fourth and fifth graders representing the argument structure in written text. *Discourse Processes, 34,* 91–115.

Champagne, A. B., Gunstone, R. F., & Klopfer, L. E. (1985). Instructional consequences of students' knowledge about physical phenomena. In L. H. T. West & A. L. Pines (Eds.), *Cognitive structure and conceptual change* (pp. 61–90). Orlando, FL: Academic.

Champagne, A. B., Klopfer, L. E., & Gunstone, R. F. (1982). Cognitive research and the design of science instruction. *Educational Psychologist, 17,* 31–53.

Checkley, K. (1997). The first seven . . . and the eighth: A conversation with Howard Gardner. *Educational Leadership, 55*(1), 8–13.

Chi, M. T. H., Glaser, R., & Farr, M. (1988). *The nature of expertise.* Hillsdale, NJ: Lawrence Erlbaum.

Chi, M. T. H., & Roscoe, R. D. (2002). The processes and challenges of conceptual change. In M. Limón & L. Mason (Eds.), *Reconsidering conceptual change: Issues in theory and practice* (pp. 3–27). Dordrecht, Netherlands: Kluwer.

Chinn, C. A. (1998). A critique of social constructivist explanations of knowledge change. In B. Guzzetti & C. Hynd (Eds.), *Theoretical perspectives on conceptual change: Multiple ways to understand knowing and learning in a complex world* (pp. 77–115). Mahwah, NJ: Lawrence Erlbaum.

Chinn, C. A. (Discussant). (1999, April). *Seeking common ground: Exploring the bonds between conceptual change and persuasion theory and research.* Symposium presented at the annual meeting of the American Educational Research Association.

Chinn, C. A., & Brewer, W. F. (1993). The role of anomalous data in knowledge acquisition: A theoretical framework and implications for science instruction. *Review of Educational Research, 63,* 1–49.

Chipman, S. F. (1993). Gazing once more into the silicon chip: Who's revolutionary now? In S. P. Lajoie & S. J. Derry (Eds.), *Computers as cognitive tools* (pp. 341–367). Mahwah, NJ: Lawrence Erlbaum.

Chissom, B., & Iran-Nejad, A. (1992). Development of an instrument to assess learning strategies. *Psychological Reports, 71,* 1001–1002.

Chiu, S., & Alexander, P. A. (2000). The motivational function of preschoolers' private speech. *Discourse Processes, 30,* 133–152.

Cizek, G. J. (1991). Innovation or enervation: Performance assessment in perspective. *Phi Delta Kappan, 72*(9), 695–699.

Clancey, W. J. (1993). Situated action: A neuropsychological interpretation response to Vera and Simon. *Cognitive Science, 17,* 87–116.

Clark, J. E. (1994). Motor development. In V. S. Ramachandran (Ed.), *Encyclopedia of human behavior* (Vol. 3, pp. 245–255). New York: Academic Press.

Clark, J. E., & Metcalfe, J. S. (2002). The mountain of motor development: A metaphor. In J. E. Clark & J. H. Humphrey (Eds.), *Motor development: Research and reviews* (Vol. 2., pp. 163–190). Reston, VA: National Association for Sport and Physical Education.

Clark, J. E., & Whitall, J. (1989). What is motor development?: The lessons of history. *Quest, 41,* 183–202.

Cobb, P., Wood, T., & Yackel, E. (1990). Classroom as learning environments for teachers and researchers. In R. B. Davis, C. A. Maher, & N. Noddings (Eds.), *Constructivist views on teaching and learning mathematics* (*Journal for Research in Mathematics Education* Monograph No. 4, pp. 125–146). Reston, VA: National Council of Teachers of Mathematics.

Cobb, P., Wood, T., & Yackel, E. (1991). Analogies from the philosophy and sociology of science for understanding classroom life. *Science Education, 75*(1), 23–44.

Cognition and Technology Group at Vanderbilt. (1990). Anchored instruction and its relationship to situated cognition. *Educational Researcher, 19*(6), 2–10.

Cognition and Technology Group at Vanderbilt. (1996). Looking at technology in context: A framework for understanding technology and education research. In D. C. Berliner & R. C. Calfee (Eds.), *Handbook of educational psychology* (pp. 807–840). New York: Macmillan.

Cognition and Technology Group at Vanderbilt. (1997). *The Jasper Project: Lessons in curriculum, instruction, assessment, and professional development.* Mahwah, NJ: Lawrence Erlbaum.

Cohen, A. S. (2000). High-stakes testing in grades K–12: Comments on Paris et al. *Issues in Education, 6*(1/2), 133–138.

Cohen, E. G. (1986). *Designing group work: Strategies for the heterogeneous classroom.* New York: Teachers College Press.

Cohen, E. G. (1994). Restructuring the classroom: Conditions for productive small groups. *Review of Educational Research, 64,* 1–36.

Cohen, E. G., Lotan, R. A., Whitcomb, J. A., Balderrama, M. V., Cossey, R., & Swanson, P. E. (1994). Complex instruction: Higher-order thinking in hetergeneous classrooms. In S. Sharan (Ed.), *Handbook of cooperative learning methods* (pp. 82–96). Westport, CT: Praeger.

Cole, K. C. (1998). *The universe and the teacup.* New York: Harcourt Brace.

Cole, M. (1996). *Cultural psychology: A once and future discipline.* Cambridge, MA: Belknap Press.

Cole, M., & Cole, S. R. (2001). *The development of children* (4th ed.). New York: Worth.

Cole, M., & Engeström, Y. (1993). A cultural-historical approach to distributed cognition. In G. Salomon (Ed.), *Distributed cognition: Psychological and educational considerations* (pp. 1–46). Cambridge, England: Cambridge University Press.

Cole, M., Gay, J., Glick, J. A., & Sharp, D. W. (1971). *The cultural context of learning and thinking.* New York: Basic Books.

College Board. (2005). 2005–2006 course description for AP economics. Retrieved from *www.collegeboard.com*

Conel, J. L. (1939–1963). *Postnatal development of the human cerebral cortex* (Vols. 1–7). Cambridge, MA: Harvard University Press.

Connolly, K. J. & Forssberg, H. (1997). *The neurophysiology and neuropsychology of motor development.* Cambridge, England: Cambridge University Press.

Cooper, L. (1932). *The rhetoric of Aristotle.* New York: Appleton-Century.

Coté, N., & Goldman, S. R. (1999). Building representations of informational text: Evidence from children's think-aloud protocols. In H. van Oostendorp & S. R. Goldman (Eds.), *The construction of mental representations during reading.* Mahwah, NJ: Lawrence Erlbaum.

Court, J. H., & Raven, J. (1995). *Manual for Raven's Progressive Matrices and Vocabulary Scales; Section 7. Research and references: Summaries of normative, reliability, and validity studies and references to all sections.* San Antonio, TX: Psychological.

Covey, S. R. (1990). *The 7 habits of highly effective people: Powerful lessons in personal change.* New York: Fireside.

Covington, M. V. (1984). The self-worth theory of achievement motivation: Findings and implications. *The Elementary School Journal, 85,* 5–20.

Covington, M. V. (1992). *Making the grade: A self-worth perspective on motivation and school reform.* New York: Cambridge University Press.

Cowan, N. (1995). *Attention and memory.* New York: Oxford University Press.

Crocker, J., & Mayor, B. (1989). Social stigma and self-esteem: The self-protective properties of stigma. *Psychological Review, 96,* 608–630.

Cronbach, L. J. (1990). *Essentials of psychological testing* (5th ed.). New York: Harper & Row.

Cronbach, L. J., & Meehl, P. E. (1955). Construct validity in psychological tests. *Psychological Bulletin, 52,* 281–302.

Cronbach, L. J., & Snow, R. E. (1977). *Aptitudes and instructional methods: A handbook for research on interactions.* New York: Irvington.

Crouse, J., & Trusheim, D. (1998). *The case against the SAT.* Chicago: University of Chicago Press.

Csikszentmihalyi, M. (1982). Toward a psychology of optimal experience. In L. Wheeler (Ed.), *Review of personality and social psychology* (Vol. 3, pp. 13–36). Beverly Hills, CA: Sage.

Csikszentmihalyi, M. (1985). Emergent motivation and the evolution of the self. In D. A. Kleiber & M. L. Maehr (Eds.), *Advances in motivation and achievement* (Vol. 4, pp. 93–119). Greenwich, CT: JAI Press.

Csikszentmihalyi, M. (1990). *FLOW: The psychology of optimal experience.* New York: HarperCollins.

Cuban, L. (1986). *Teachers and machines: The classroom use of technology since 1920.* New York: Teachers College Press.

Cuban, L. (1993). *How teachers taught: Constancy and change in American classrooms, 1890–1980.* New York: Teachers College Press.

Cuban, L. (2001). *Oversold and underused: Computers in classrooms.* Cambridge, MA: Harvard University Press.

Cuffaro, H. (1991). A view of materials as the texts of the early childhood curriculum. In B. Spodek & O. Saracho (Eds.), *Issues in early childhood curriculum* (pp. 64–85). New York: Teachers College Press.

Culler, R. E., & Holahan, C. J. (1980). Test anxiety and academic performance: The effects of study-related behaviors. *Journal of Educational Psychology, 72,* 16–20.

Damon, W. (1983). *Social and personality development: Infancy through adolescence.* New York: Norton.

Damon, W., & Hart, D. (1988). *Self-understanding in childhood and adolescence.* New York: Cambridge University Press.

Dansereau, D. E. (1988). Cooperative learning strategies. In C. E. Weinstein, E. T. Goetz, & P. A. Alexander (Eds.), *Learning and study strategies: Issues in assessment, instruction, and evaluation* (pp. 103–120). San Diego, CA: Academic Press.

Dansereau, D. F., Brooks, L. W., Holley, C. D., & Collins, K. W. (1983). Learning strategy training: Effects of sequencing. *Journal of Experimental Education, 51*(3), 102–108.

Darling-Hammond, L., & Sykes, G. (1999). *Teaching as the learning profession: Handbook of policy and practice.* San Francisco: Jossey-Bass.

Davis, P. J., Hersh, R., & Marchisotto, E. A. (1995). *The mathematical experience.* Boston: Birkaüser.

deBono, E. (1990). *Lateral thinking: Creativity step-by-step.* New York: HarperCollins.

Deci, E. L. (1971). Effects of externally mediated rewards on intrinsic motivation. *Journal of Personal and Social Psychology, 18,* 105–115.

Deci, E. L., & Ryan, R. M. (1991). A motivational approach to self: Integration in personality. In R. A. Dienstbier (Ed.), *Nebraska Symposium on Motivation: Vol. 38. Perspectives on motivation* (pp. 237–288). Lincoln: University of Nebraska Press.

Deci, E. L., Vallerand, R. J., Pelletier, L. G., & Ryan, R. M. (1991). Motivation and education: The self-determination perspective. *Educational Psychologist, 26,* 325–346.

De Corte, E. (1999). On the road to transfer: An introduction [Special issue]. *International Journal of Educational Research, 31*(7).

de Jong, T., & van Joolingen, W. R. (1998). Scientific discovery learning with computer simulations of conceptual domains. *Review of Educational Research, 68,* 179–201.

Derry, S. J., & Lajoie, S. P. (1993). A middle camp for (un)intelligent instructional computing: An introduction. In S. P. Lajoie & S. J. Derry (Eds.), *Computers as cognitive tools* (pp. 1–11). Mahwah, NJ: Lawrence Erlbaum.

Detterman, D. K. (1993). The case for the prosecution: Transfer as an epiphenomenon. In D. K. Detterman & R. J. Sternberg (Eds.), *Transfer on trial: Intelligence, cognition, and instruction* (pp. 1–24). Norwood, NJ: Ablex.

Detterman, D. K., & Sternberg, R. J. (1982). *How and how much can intelligence be increased?* Norwood, NJ: Ablex.

Deutsch, M. (1949). The effects of cooperation and competition upon group processes. *Human Relations, 2,* 199–231.

Deutsch, M. (1993). Educating for a peaceful world. *American Psychologist, 48,* 510–517.

Deutsch, W., & Pechmann, T. (1982). Social interaction and the development of definite descriptions. *Cognition, 11,* 159–184.

Devlin, K. (1994). *Mathematics: The science of pattern.* New York: W. H. Freeman.

DeVries, D., & Edwards, K. (1974). Student teams and learning games: Their effects on cross-race and cross-sex interaction. *Journal of Educational Psychology, 66,* 741–749.

Dewey, J. (1897/1972). The psychological aspect of the school curriculum. In J. A. Boydston & F. Bowers (Eds.), *The early works of John Dewey 1882–1903: Vol. 5. 1895–1898.* Carbondale: Southern Illinois University Press.

Dewey, J. (1902/1956). *The child and the curriculum.* In J. A. Boydston (Ed.), *John Dewey: The middle works 1899–1924: Vol. 2. 1902–1903.* Carbondale: Southern Illinois University Press.

Dewey, J. (1913). *Interest and effort in education.* Boston: Riverdale.

Dewey, J. (1944). *Democracy and education.* New York: Macmillian. (Original published in 1916)

Dewey, J. (1991). *How we think.* Buffalo, NY: Prometheus Books. (Original published in 1910)

Diekhoff, G. (1992). *Statistics for the social and behavioral sciences: Univariate, bivariate, and multivariate.* Dubuque, IA: William C. Brown.

Diener, C., & Dweck, C. (1978). An analysis of learned helplessness: Continuous changes in performance, strategy, and achievement cognitions following failure. *Journal of Personality and Social Psychology, 36,* 451–462.

Dienes, Z., & Barry, D. (1997). Implicit learning: Below the subjective threshold. *Psychonomic Bulletin & Review, 4,* 3–23.

diSessa, A. A. (1989). What will it mean to be "educated" in 2020? In R. S. Nickerson & P. P. Zodhiates (Eds.), *Technology in education: Looking toward 2020* (pp. 43–66). Hillsdale, NJ: Lawrence Erlbaum.

diSessa, A. A. (1993). Toward an epistemology of physics. *Cognition and Instruction, 10*(2–3), 105–225.

diSessa, A. A. (2002). Why "conceptual ecology" is a good idea. In M. Limon & L. Mason (Eds.), *Reconsidering conceptual change: Issues in theory and practice* (pp. 29–60). Dordrecht, Netherlands: Kluwer.

Dishon, D., & O'Leary, P. (1984). *Guidebook for cooperative learning.* Holmes Beach, FL: Learning Publications.

Dixon-Kraus, L. (1996). *Vygotsky in the classroom: Mediated literacy instruction and assessment.* White Plains, NY: Longman.

Dole, J. A., & Sinatra, G. M. (1998). Reconceptualizing change in the cognitive construction of knowledge. *Educational Psychologist, 33,* 109–128.

Dominowski, R. L., & Dallob, P. (1995). Insight and problem solving. In R. J. Sternberg & J. E. Davidson (Eds.), *The nature of insight* (pp. 33–62). Cambridge, MA: MIT Press.

Drake, S. (1978). *Galileo at work.* Chicago: University of Chicago Press.

Dreyfus, T., & Eisenberg, T. (1996). On different facets of mathematical thinking. In R. J. Sternberg & T. Ben-Zeev (Ed.), *The nature of mathematical thinking* (pp. 253–284). Mahwah, NJ: Lawrence Erlbaum.

Dunbar, K. (1993). Concept discovery in a scientific domain. *Cognitive Science, 17,* 397–434.

Dunbar, K. (1996). How scientists really reason: Scientific reasoning in real-world laboratories. In R. J. Sternberg & J. E. Davidson (Eds.), *The nature of insight* (pp. 365–395). Cambridge, MA: MIT Press.

Dunbar, S. B., Koretz, D. M., & Hoover, H. D. (1991). Quality control in the development and use of performance assessments. *Applied Measurement in Education, 4,* 298–304.

Duncker, K. (1945). On problem solving. *Psychological Monographs, 58*(5, Whole No. 270).

Durant, W. (1954). *Story of civilization: Part I Our Oriental heritage.* New York: Simon & Schuster.

Durant, W. (1954–1975). *Story of civilization: Parts I–XI.* New York: Simon & Schuster.

Durkin, D. (1978–1979). What classroom observations reveal about reading comprehension instruction. *Reading Research Quarterly, 14,* 481–533.

Dweck, C. (1986). Motivational processes affecting learning. *American Psychologist, 41,* 1040–1048.

Dweck, C., & Leggett, E. (1988). A social-cognitive approach to motivation and personality. *Psychological Review, 95*(2), 56–273.

Dweck, C., & Reppucci, N. (1973). Learned helplessness and reinforcement responsibility in children. *Journal of Personality and Social Psychology, 25,* 109–116.

Dyer, K. F. (1977). The trend of the male-female performance differential in athletics, swimming, and cycling, 1948–1976. *Journal of Biosocial Science, 9,* 325–338.

Ebel, R. L. (1979). *Essentials of educational measurement* (3rd ed.). Englewood Cliffs, NJ: Prentice Hall.

Ebel, R. L., & Frisbie, D. A. (1991). *Essentials of educational measurement* (5th ed.). Upper Saddle River, NJ: Prentice Hall.

Eccles, J. S., Adler, T., & Meece, J. (1984). Sex differences in achievement: A test of alternative theories. *Journal of Personality and Social Psychology, 46,* 26–43.

Eccles, J. S., & Midgley, C. (1989). Stage-environment fit: Developmentally appropriate classrooms for young adolescents. In C. Ames & R. Ames (Eds.), *Research on motivation in education* (Vol. 3, pp. 139–186). New York: Academic Press.

Eccles, J. S., & Midgley, C. (1990). Changes in academic motivation and self-perceptions during early adolescence. In R. Montemayor, G. R. Adams, & T. P. Gullotta (Eds.), *Advances in adolescent development: From childhood to adolescence* (Vol. 2, pp. 134–155). Newbury Park, CA: Sage.

Eccles, J. S., Midgley, C., & Adler, T. (1984). Grade-related changes in the school environment: Effects on achievement motivation. In J. Nicholls (Ed.), *Advances in motivation and achievement* (Vol. 3, pp. 283–331). Greenwich, CT: JAI Press.

Eccles, J. S., Wigfield, A., Flanagan, C., Miller, C., Reuman, D., & Yee, D. (1989). Self-concepts, domain values, and self-esteem: Relations and changes at early adolescence. *Journal of Personality, 57,* 283–310.

Eccles, J. S., Wigfield, A., & Schiefele, U. (1998). Motivation to succeed. In W. Damon (Series Ed.) & N. Eisenberg (Vol. Ed.), *Handbook of child psychology* (Vol. 3, pp. 1017–1095). New York: Wiley.

Educational Testing Service. (1998). *Computers and classrooms: The status of technology in U.S. schools.* Princeton, NJ: Author.

Eggen, P., & Kauchak, D. (1999). *Educational psychology: Windows on classrooms* (4th ed.). Columbus, OH: Merrill.

Eisner, E. W. (1999). The uses and limits of performance assessment. *Phi Delta Kappan, 80*(1), 83–95.

Elawar, M. C., & Corno, L. (1985). A factorial experiment in teachers' written feedback on student homework: Changing teacher behavior a little rather than a lot. *Journal of Educational Psychology, 77,* 162–173.

Elbow, P. (1981). *Writing with power.* New York: Oxford University Press.

Eliot, L. (1999). *What's going on in there? How the brain and mind develop in the first five years of life.* New York: Bantam Books.

Eliot, T. S. (1934). *The rock.* London: Faber & Faber.

Elkind, D. (1961). The development of quantitative thinking: A systematic replication of Piaget's studies. *Journal of Genetic Psychology, 98,* 37–46.

Elliot, A., & Harackiewicz, J. (1996). Approach and avoidance achievement goals and intrinsic motivation: A mediational analysis. *Journal of Personality and Social Psychology, 70,* 968–980.

Elliott, E., & Dweck, C. (1988). Goals: An approach to motivation and achievement. *Journal of Personality and Social Psychology, 54,* 5–12.

Elliott, R. (1987). *Litigating intelligence: IQ tests, special education, and social science in the courtroom.* Dover, MA: Auburn House.

Ellis, H. C., & Hunt, R. R. (1983). *Fundamentals of human memory and cognition* (3rd ed.). Dubuque, IA: W. C. Brown.

Englert, C. S., Raphael, T. E., Anderson, L. M., Anthony, H. M., & Stevens, D. D. (1991). Making strategies and self-talk visible: Writing instruction in regular and special education classrooms. *American Educational Research Journal, 28,* 337–372.

Englert, C. S., Raphael, T. E., & Mariage, T. V. (1994). Developing a school-based discourse for literacy learning: A principled search for understanding. *Learning Disabilities Quarterly, 17,* 2–32.

English, L. D. (1997). *Mathematical reasoning: Analogies, metaphors, and images.* Mahwah, NJ: Lawrence Erlbaum.

English, L. D., & Alexander, P. A. (1997). *A longitudinal and cross-cultural study of the analogical and mathematical reasoning patterns of young children.* Grant funded by the Australian Research Council.

English, L. D., & Halford, G. S. (1995). *Mathematics education: Models and processes.* Hillsdale, NJ: Lawrence Erlbaum.

Ennis, R. H. (1987). A taxonomy of critical thinking dispositions and abilities. In J. B. Baron & R. J. Sternberg (Eds.), *Teaching for thinking* (pp. 9–26). New York: Freeman.

Entwisle, D. R., & Baker, D. P. (1983). Gender and young children's expectations for performance in arithmetic. *Developmental Psychology, 19,* 200–209.

Epstein, H. T. (2001). An outline of the role of brain in human cognitive development. *Brain and Cognition, 45,* 44–51.

Epstein, J. L. (1989). Family structures and student motivation: A developmental perspective. In C. Ames & R. Ames (Eds.), *Research on motivation in education* (Vol. 3, pp. 259–295). San Diego, CA: Academic Press.

Ericsson, K. A., & Simon, H. A. (1980). Verbal reports as data. *Psychological Review, 87,* 215–251.

Erikson, E. H. (1963). *Childhood and society* (2nd ed.). New York: Norton.

Erikson, E. H. (1968). *Psychosocial identity.* In *International encyclopedia of social sciences* (pp. 61–65). New York: Crowell-Collier.

Erikson, E. H. (1980). *Identity, youth, and crisis* (2nd ed.). New York: Norton.

Evans, R. B., Sexton, V. S., & Cadwallader, T. C. (1992). *The American Psychological Association: A historical perspective.* Washington, DC: American Psychological Association.

Eysenck, S. B., Pearson, P. R., Easting, G., & Allsopp, J. F. (1985). Age norms for impulsiveness, venturesomeness and empathy in adults. *Personality and Individual Differences, 6*(5), 613–619.

Farr, R., & Tone, B. (1994). *Portfolio and performance assessment.* San Antonio, TX: Harcourt Brace.

Feldt, L. S., & Brennan, R. L. (1989). Reliability. In R. L. Linn (Ed.), *Educational measurement* (3rd ed.). Upper Saddle River, NJ: Merrill.

Ferrari, M., & Elik, N. (2003). Influences on intentional conceptual change. In G. M. Sinatra & P. R. Pintrich (Eds.), *Intentional conceptual change* (pp. 21–54). Mahwah, NJ: Lawrence Erlbaum.

Finke, R., Ward, T. B., & Smith, S. M. (1992). *Creative cognition.* Cambridge, MA: MIT Press.

Finn, J. D. (1998). *Class size and students at risk: What is known? What is next?* Washington, DC: U. S. Department of Education, OERI, National Institute on the Education of At-Risk Students.

Fischer, K. W. (1980). A theory of cognitive development: The control and construction of hierarchies of skills. *Psychological Review, 87,* 477–531.

Fischer, K. W., & Farrar, M. J. (1988). Generalizations about generalization: How a theory of skill development explains both generality and specificity. In A. Demetriou (Ed.), *The neo-Piagetian theories of cognitive development: Toward an integration.* Amsterdam: North-Holland (Elsevier).

Fischer, K. W., & Grannott, N. (1995). Beyond one-dimensional change: Parallel, concurrent, socially distributed processes in learning and development. *Human Development, 38,* 302–314.

Fiske, E. B. (1988, April 10). America's test mania. *New York Times,* p. C1.

Fiske, S., & Taylor, S. (1991). *Social cognition.* New York: McGraw-Hill.

Fives, H. (2003). *Exploring the relationship of teachers' efficacy, knowledge, and pedagogical beliefs: A multimethod study.* Unpublished doctoral dissertation, University of Maryland, College Park, MD.

Fives, H., & Alexander, P. A. (2001). Teaching as persuasion: A case in point. *Theory into Practice, 40,* 242–248.

Fives, H. L., Alexander, P. A., & Buehl, M. M. (2001). Teaching as persuasion: Approaching classroom discourse as refutational text. In J. V. Hoffman, D. L. Schallert, C. M. Fairbanks, J. Worthy, & B. Maloch (Eds.), *Fiftieth yearbook of the National Reading Conference* (pp. 200–212). Chicago: National Reading Conference.

Flavell, J. H. (1985). *Cognitive development* (2nd ed.). Englewood Cliffs, NJ: Prentice Hall.

Flavell, J. H., Miller, P. H., & Miller, S. A. (1993). *Cognitive development* (3rd ed.). Englewood Cliffs, NJ: Prentice Hall.

Flesch, R. P. (1955). *Why Johnny can't read.* New York: Harper.

Flippo, R. F., & Caverly, D. C. (2000). *Handbook of college reading and study strategy research.* Mahwah, NJ: Lawrence Erlbaum.

Flower, L., & Hayes, J. R. (1981). A cognitive process theory of writing. *College Composition and Communication, 32,* 365–387.

Fogarty, R., Perkins, D. N., & Barell, J. (1992). *How to teach for transfer.* Palatine, IL: Skylight.

Ford, M. E. (1982). Social cognition and social competence in adolescence. *Developmental Psychology, 18,* 323–340.

Ford, M. E. (1992). *Motivating humans: Goals, emotions, and personal agency.* Newbury Park, CA: Sage.

Frederiksen, N. (1984). Implication of cognitive theory for instruction in problem solving. *Review of Educational Research, 54,* 363–407.

Freud, S. (1925). *Collected papers* (Vol. 4). London: Institutes for Psychoanalysis & Hogarth Press.

Freud, S. (1953). Three essays on the theory of sexuality. In J. Strachey (Ed.), *The standard edition of the complete psychological works of Sigmund Freud* (Vol. 7). London: Hogarth. (Original published in 1905)

Freud, S. (1973). *An outline of psychoanalysis.* London: Hogarth. (Original published in 1938)

Frey, K., & Ruble, D. N. (1987). What children say about classroom performance: Sex and grade differences in perceived competence. *Child Development, 58,* 1066–1078.

Friedman, W. (1990). *About time: Inventing the fourth dimension.* Cambridge, MA: MIT Press.

Friend, M., & Bursuck, W. (1996). *Including students with special needs: A practical guide for classroom teachers.* Boston: Allyn & Bacon.

Frisbie, D. A., (1988). Reliability of scores from teacher-made tests. *Educational Measurement: Issues and Practice, 7*(1), 25–35.

Frisby, C. L. (1998). Contextual factors influencing the classroom application of learner-centered principles. In N. M. Lambert & B. L. McCombs (Eds.), *Issues in school reform: A sampler of psychological perspectives on learner-centered school* (pp. 61–79). Washington, DC: American Psychological Association.

Frisch, R. E. (1991). Puberty and body fat. In R. M. Lerner, A. C. Peterson, J. Brooks-Gunn (Eds.), *Encyclopedia of adolescence* (Vol. 2, pp. 884–892). New York: Garland.

Frisch, R. E., Wyshak, G., & Vincent, L. (1980). Delayed menarche and amenorrhea of ballet dancers. *New England Journal of Medicine, 303,* 17–19.

Fuchs, D., & Fuchs, L. S. (1989). Exploring effective and efficient prereferral interventions: A component analysis of behavioral consultation. *School Psychology Review, 18,* 258–281.

Fuchs, D., Fuchs, L. S., Hamlett, C. L. & Stecker, P. M. (1991). Effects of curriculum-based measurement and consultation on teacher planning and student achievement in mathematics operations. *American Educational Research Journal, 28,* 617–641.

Fuchs, D., Fuchs, L. S., Mathes, P. G., & Simmons, D. C. (1997). Peer-assisted learning strategies: Making classrooms more responsive to diversity. *American Educational Research Journal, 34,* 174–206.

Gabbard, C. (2004). *Lifelong motor development* (4th ed.). San Francisco: Benjamin Cummings.

Gage, N. L., & Berliner, D. C. (1998). *Educational psychology* (6th ed.). Boston: Houghton Mifflin.

Gagné, E. D., Yechovich, C. W., & Yechovich, F. R. (1993). *The cognitive psychology of school learning* (2nd ed.). New York: HarperCollins.

Gagné, R. M. (1974). *Essentials of learning for instruction.* Hinsdale, NJ: Dryden Press.

Gagné, R. M. (1977). *The conditions of learning* (3rd ed.). New York: Holt, Rinehart & Winston.

Gallahue, D. L., & Donnelly, F. C. (2003). *Developmental physical education for all children* (4th ed.). Champaign, IL: Human Kinetics.

Gallahue, D. L. & Ozmun, J. C. (1998). *Understanding motor development* (2nd ed.). New York: McGraw-Hill.

Gallego, M., & Cole, M. (2000). Success is not enough: Challenges to sustaining new forms of educational activity. *Computers in Human Behavior, 16,* 271–286.

Galton, F. (1883). *Inquiries into human faculty and its development.* London: Dent.

Galton, F. (1888). Co-relations and their measurement, chiefly from anthropological data. *Proceedings of the Royal Society of London, 45,* 135–145.

Galton, F. (1970). *English men of science.* London: Frank Cass. (Original work published in 1874)

Galton, F. (1979). *Hereditary genius: An inquiry into its laws and consequences.* London: Julian Friedman. (Original work published in 1869)

Garcia, T., & Pintrich, P. R. (1994). Regulating motivation and cognition in the classroom: The role of self-schemas and self-regulation strategies. In D. H. Schunk & B. J. Zimmerman (Eds.), *Self-regulation of learning and performance issues and educational applications* (pp. 127–153). Hillsdale, NJ: Lawrence Erlbaum.

Gardner, H. (1983). *Frames of mind: The theory of multiple intelligences.* New York: Basic Books.

Gardner, H. (1991). *The unschooled mind.* New York: Basic Books.

Gardner, H. (1993). *Multiple intelligences: The theory in practice.* New York: Basic Books.

Gardner, H. (1999). *Intelligence reframed: Multiple intelligences for the 21st century.* New York: Basic Books.

Gardner, H. (2000). *The disciplined mind.* New York: Basic Books.

Gardner, M. (1978). *Aha! Insight.* New York: Scientific American Books.

Garner, R. (1987). *Metacognition and reading comprehension.* Norwood, NJ: Ablex.

Garner, R. (1990). When children and adults do not use learning strategies: Toward a theory of setting. *Review of Educational Research, 60,* 517–529.

Garner, R., & Alexander, P. A. (1991, April). Skill, will, and thrill: The role of interest in text comprehension. In M. C. Smith & S. E. Peterson (Chairs), *What do we know about adults' reading skills: The state of our knowledge and directions for new research.* Symposium presented at the annual meeting of the American Educational Research Association, Chicago.

Garner, R., & Alexander, P. A. (Eds.) (1999). *Beliefs about text and instruction with text.* Hillsdale, NJ: Lawrence Erlbaum.

Garner, R., & Gillingham, M. G. (1996). *Internet communication in six classrooms: Conversations across time, space, and culture.* Mahwah, NJ: Lawrence Erlbaum.

Garner, R., & Gillingham, M. G. (1998). The Internet in the classroom: Is it the end of transmission-oriented pedagogy? In D. Reinking,

M. C. McKenna, L. D. Labbo, & R. D. Kieffer (Eds.), *Handbook of literacy and technology* (pp. 221–231). Mahwah, NJ: Lawrence Erlbaum.

Garner, R., & Zhao, Y. (2000). Afterschool centers in four rural communities in Michigan. *Computers in Human Behavior, 16,* 301–311.

Garner, R., Zhao, Y., & Gillingham, M. (2000). After 3 p.m. *Computers in Human Behavior, 16*(3), 223–226.

Gearhart, M., Herman, J. L., Baker, E. L., & Whittaker, A. K. (1992). *Writing portfolios at the elementary level: A study of methods of writing assessment* (CSE Technical Report 337). Los Angeles: University of California, Center for Research on Evaluation, Standards, and Student Testing. Also retrieved from *http://www.cse.ucla.edu*

Geary, D. C. (1994). *Children's mathematical development.* Washington, DC: American Psychological Association.

Geary, D. C. (1995). Reflections on evolution and culture in children's cognition. *American Psychologist, 50,* 24–37.

Gellman, E. S. (1995). *School testing: What parents and educators need to know.* Westport, CT: Praeger.

Gelman, R. (1969). Conservation acquisition: A problem of learning to attend to relevant attributes. *Journal of Experimental Child Psychology, 7,* 167–187.

Gelman, R. (1972). Logical capacity of very young children: Number invariance rules. *Child Development, 43,* 75–90.

Gelman, R. (1979). Preschool thought. *American Psychologist, 34,* 900–905.

Gelman, R., & Baillargeon, R. (1983). A review of some Piagetian concepts. In P. Mussen (Ed.), *Carmichael's manual of child psychology: Vol. 3 Cognitive development* (E. Markman & J. Flavell, Vol. Eds., pp. 167–221). New York: Wiley.

Gelman, R., & Gallistel, C. R. (1978). *The child's understanding of number.* Cambridge, MA: Harvard University Press.

Gelman, R., & Greeno, J. G. (1989). On the nature of competence: Principles for understanding in a domain. In L. B. Resnick (Ed.), *Knowing, learning, and instruction: Essays in honor of Robert Glaser* (pp. 125–186). Hillsdale, NJ: Erlbaum.

Gelman, S. A., Meck, E., & Merkin, S. (1986). Young children's mathematical competence. *Cognitive Development, 1,* 1–29.

Gentner, D., & Markman, A. B. (1997). Structure mapping in analogy and similarity. *American Psychologist, 52,* 45–56.

Gesell, A. (1940). *The first five years of life* (9th ed.). New York: Harper & Row.

Gesell, A., & Ilg, F. L. (1946). *Child development.* New York: Harper & Row.

Gibbs, J. C. (1979). Kohlberg's moral stage theory: A Piagetian revision. *Human Development, 22,* 89–112.

Gibbs, J. C., & Schnell, S. V. (1985). Moral development "versus" socialization: A critique. *American Psychologist, 40,* 1071–1080.

Gibson, J. J. (1966). *The senses considered as perceptual systems.* Boston: Houghton-Mifflin.

Gick, M. L., & Holyoak, K. J. (1980). Analogical problem solving. *Cognitive Psychology, 12,* 306–355.

Gilligan, C. (1977). In a different voice: Women's conceptions of self and morality. *Harvard Educational Review, 47,* 481–517.

Gilligan, C. (1982). *In a different voice: Psychological theory and women's development.* Cambridge, MA: Harvard University Press.

Gilligan, C. (1993). Adolescent development reconsidered. In A. Garrod (Ed.), *Approaches to moral development: New research and emerging themes.* New York: Teachers College Press.

Gillingham, M. G., Young, M. F., & Kulikowich, J. M. (1994). Do teachers consider nonlinear text to be text? In R. Garner & P. A. Alexander (Eds.), *Beliefs about text and instruction with text* (pp. 201–219). Hillsdale, NJ: Lawrence Erlbaum.

Gillingham, M. G., & Youniss, E. (2000). Making a computer club, making a community. *Computers in Human Behavior, 16,* 257–269.

Ginott, H. (1972). *Teacher and child.* New York: Macmillan.

Ginsburg, H. P., & Opper, S. (1988). *Piaget's theory of intellectual development* (3rd ed.). Englewood Cliffs, NJ: Prentice Hall.

Ginzberg, E. (1972). Toward a theory of occupational choice: A restatement. *Vocational Guidance Quarterly, 20,* 169–176.

Giroux, H. A., & McLaren, P. (1986). Teacher education and the politics of engagement: The case for democratic schooling. *Harvard Educational Review, 56*(3), 232–233.

Gjesme, T. (1975). Slope of gradients for performance as a function of achievement motive, goal distance in time, and future time orientation. *Journal of Research in Personality, 8,* 161–171.

Glaser, R. (1963). Instructional technology and the measurement of learning outcomes: Some questions. *American Psychologist, 18,* 519–521.

Glaser, R. (1984). Education and thinking: The role of knowledge. *American Psychologist, 39,* 93–104.

Glass, G. V. (1978). Standards and criteria. *Journal of Educational Measurement, 15,* 237–261.

Glynn, S. M., Duit, R., & Thiele, R. B. (1995). Teaching science with analogies: A strategy for constructing knowledge. In S. M. Glynn & R. Duit (Eds.), *Learning science in the schools: Research reforming practice* (pp. 247–273). Mahwah, NJ: Erlbaum.

Glynn, S. M., Yeany, R. H., & Britton, B. K. (1991). *The psychology of learning science.* Hillsdale, NJ: Lawrence Erlbaum.

Goetz, E. T., Alexander, P. A., & Ash, M. (1992). *Educational psychology: A classroom perspective.* Columbus, OH: Merrill.

Goldin, G. A. (1992). Toward an assessment framework for school mathematics. In R. Lesh & S. J. Lamon (Eds.), *Assessments of authentic performance in elementary mathematics* (pp. 63–88). Washington, DC: American Association for the Advancement of Science.

Goldman, S. R. (1996). Reading, writing, and learning in hypermedia environments. In H. Van Oostendorp & S. de Mui (Eds.), *Cognitive aspects of electronic text processing* (pp. 7–42). Norwood, NJ: Ablex.

Goldman, S. R. (1997). Learning from text: Reflections on the past and suggestions for the future. *Discourse Processes, 23,* 357–397.

Goleman, D. (1995). *Emotional intelligence.* New York: Bantam Books.

Goodman, K. S., & Burke, C. (1972). *Reading miscue inventory manual.* New York: Macmillan.

Gorodetsky, M., & Keiny, S. (2002). Participative learning and conceptual change. In M. Limon & L. Mason (Eds.), *Reconsidering conceptual change* (pp. 149–163). Dordrecht, Netherlands: Kluwer.

Goswami, U. (1992). *Analogical reasoning in children.* Hillsdale, NJ: Lawrence Erlbaum.

Goswami, U. (2000). Phonological and lexical processes. In M. L. Kamil, P. B. Mosenthal, P. D. Pearson, & R. Barr (Eds.), *Handbook of reading research* (Vol. 3, pp. 251–267). Mahwah, NJ: Lawrence Erlbaum.

Gottfried, E. (1981, August). *Grade, sex, and race differences in academic motivation.* Paper presented at the annual meeting of the American Educational Research Association, Los Angeles.

Graesser, A. C., Golding, J. M., & Long, D. L. (1991). Narrative representation and comprehension. In R. Barr, M. L. Kamil, P. B. Mosenthal, & P. D. Pearson (Eds.), *Handbook of reading research* (Vol. 2, pp. 171–205). White Plains, NY: Longman.

Graham, S. (1984). Communicating sympathy and anger to Black and White children: The cognitive (attributional) consequences of affective cues. *Journal of Personality and Social Psychology, 47,* 14–28.

Graham, S. (1994). Motivation in African Americans. *Review of Educational Research, 64,* 55–118.

Graham, S., & Harris, K. R. (1993). Self-regulated strategy development: Helping students with learning problems develop as writers. *Elementary School Journal, 94,* 169–181.

Graham, S., & Long, A. (1986). Race, class, and the attributional process. *Journal of Educational Psychology, 78,* 4–13.

Graham, S., Taylor, A. Z., & Hudley, C. (1998). Exploring achievement values among ethnic minority early adolescents. *Journal of Educational Psychology, 90,* 606–620.

Graham, S., & Weiner, B. (1996). Theories and principles of motivation. In D. C. Berliner & R. C. Calfee (Eds.), *Handbook of educational psychology* (pp. 63–84). New York: Macmillan.

Granovetter, M. (1973). The strength of weak ties. *American Journal of Sociology, 73,* 1361–1380.

Graves, M. F. (1997, March). *What sort of comprehension strategy instruction should schools provide?* Symposium presented at the annual meeting of the American Educational Research Association, Chicago.

Greene, S. (1994). The problems of learning to think like a historian: Writing history in the culture of the classroom. *Educational Psychologist, 29*(2), 89–96.

Greeno, J. G., Collins, A. M., & Resnick, L. B. (1996). Cognition and learning. In D. C. Berliner & R. C. Calfee (Eds.), *Handbook of educational psychology* (pp. 15–46). New York: Macmillan.

Greeno, J. G., & the Middle School Mathematics Through Application Project Group. (1998). The situativity of knowing, learning, and research. *American Psychologist, 53*(1), 5–26.

Greeno, J. G., Smith, D. R., & Moore, J. L. (1996). Transfer of situated learning. In D. K. Detterman & R. J. Sternberg (Eds.), *Transfer on trial: Intelligence, cognition, and instruction* (pp. 99–167). Norwood, NJ: Ablex.

Gresham, F. (1981). Social skills training with handicapped children. *Review of Educational Research, 51,* 139–176.

Griffin, S., Case, R., & Capodilupo, A. (1995). Teaching for understanding: The importance of the central conceptual structures in the elementary mathematics curriculum. In A. McKeough, J. Lupart, & A. Marini (Eds.), *Teaching for transfer: Fostering generalization in learning* (pp. 123–152). Mahwah, NJ: Lawrence Erlbaum.

Gronlund, N. E. (1993). *How to make achievement tests and assessments* (5th ed.). Boston: Allyn & Bacon.

Grosshandler, D. J., & Grosshandler, E. N. (2000). Constructing fun: Self-determination and learning at an afterschool design lab. *Computers in Human Behavior, 16,* 227–240.

Grotevant, H. D., Cooper, C. R., & Kramer, K. (1986). Exploration as a predictor of congruence in adolescents' career choices. *Journal of Vocational Behavior, 29,* 201–215.

Guilford, J. P. (1959). Three faces of human intelligence. *American Psychologist, 14,* 469–479.

Guilford, J. P. (1967). *The nature of human intelligence.* New York: McGraw-Hill.

Gustafsson, J.-E., & Undheim, J. O. (1996). Individual differences in cognitive functions. In D. C. Berliner & R. C. Calfee (Eds.), *Handbook of educational psychology* (pp. 186–242). New York: Macmillan.

Guthrie, J. T. (1988). Locating information in documents: Examination of a cognitive model. *Reading Research Quarterly, 23,* 178–199.

Guthrie, J. T., McGough, K., Bennett, L., & Rice, M. E. (1996). Concept-oriented reading instruction: An integrated curriculum to develop motivations and strategies for reading. In L. Baker, P. Afflerbach, & D. Reinking (Eds.), *Developing engaged readers in school and home community* (pp. 165–190). Mahwah, NJ: Lawrence Erlbaum.

Guthrie, J. T., Van Meter, P., Hancock, G. R., Alao, S., Anderson, E., & McCann, A. (1998). Does concept-oriented reading instruction increase strategy use and conceptual learning from text? *Journal of Educational Psychology, 90,* 261–278.

Guthrie, J. T., Van Meter, P., McCann, A., Wigfield, A., Bennett, L., Poundstone, C., Rice, M. E., Faibisch, F., Hunt, B., & Mitchell, A. (1996). Growth of literacy engagement: Changes in motivations and strategies during concept-oriented reading instruction. *Reading Research Quarterly, 31,* 306–332.

Guzzetti, B., & Hynd, C. (1998). *Theoretical perspectives on conceptual change.* Mahwah, NJ: Lawrence Erlbaum.

Hadwin, A. F., & Winne, P. H. (1996). Study strategies have meager support. *Journal of Higher Education, 67,* 692–715.

Hakim, J. (1993). *Making thirteen colonies.* New York: Oxford University Press.

Hakuta, K., & McLaughlin, B. (1996). Bilingualism and second language learning: Seven tensions that define the research. In D. C. Berliner & R. C. Calfee (Eds.), *Handbook of educational psychology* (pp. 602–621). New York: Macmillan.

Haladyna, T. H. (1999). *Developing and validating multiple-choice test items* (2nd ed.). Mahwah, NJ: Lawrence Erlbaum.

Haladyna, T. H., Nolan, S. B., & Haas, N. S. (1991). Raising standardized achievement test scores and the origins of test score pollution. *Educational Researcher, 20*(5), 2–7.

Hall, G. S. (1904). *Adolescence.* New York: Appleton-Century-Crofts.

Hallahan, D. P., & Kauffman, J. M. (2000). *Exceptional learners: Introduction of special education* (8th ed.). Boston: Allyn & Bacon.

Hallahan, D. P., Kauffman, J. M., & Lloyd, J. W. (2000). *Introduction to learning disabilities* (4th ed.). Boston: Allyn & Bacon.

Halpern, D. F. (1992). *Sex differences in cognitive abilities* (2nd ed.). Hillsdale, NJ: Lawrence Erlbaum.

Hambleton, R. K. (1996). Advances in assessment models, methods, and practices. In D. C. Berliner & R. C. Calfee (Eds.), *Handbook of educational psychology* (pp. 899–925). New York: Macmillan.

Harper, B., Hedberg, J., Corderoy, B., & Wright, R. (2000). Employing cognitive tools within interactive multimedia applications. In S. P. Lajoie (Ed.), *Computers as cognitive tools: No more walls* (pp. 227–245). Mahwah, NJ: Lawrence Erlbaum.

Harris, K. R., & Alexander, P. A. (Eds.). (1998). Integration, constructivist education [Special issue]. *Educational Psychology Review, 10*(2).

Harris, K. R., & Graham, S. (1996). *Making the writing process work: Strategies for composition and self-regulation.* Cambridge, MA: Brookline.

Harris, K. R., & Pressley, M. J. (1991). The nature of cognitive strategy instruction: Interactive strategy construction. *Exceptional Children, 57,* 392–405.

Harter, S. (1981). A new self-report scale of intrinsic versus extrinsic orientation in the classroom: Motivational and informational components. *Developmental Psychology, 17,* 300–312.

Harter, S. (1985). *Manual for the self-perception profile for children.* Denver, CO: University of Denver.

Harter, S. (1986). *Manual for the self-perception profile for adolescents.* Denver, CO: University of Denver.

Harter, S. (1990). Processes underlying adolescent self-concept formation. In R. Montemayor, G. R. Adams, & T. P. Guilliton (Eds.), *From childhood to adolescence: A transitional period?* (pp. 205–239). Newbury Park, CA: Sage.

Harter, S. (1992). The relationship between perceived competence, affect, and motivational orientation within the classroom: Process and patterns of change. In A. Boggiano & T. Pittman (Eds.), *Achievement and motivation: A socio-developmental perspective* (pp. 77–114). Cambridge, England: Cambridge University Press.

Harter, S. (1996). Teacher and classmate influences on scholastic motivation, self-esteem, and level of voice in adolescents. In J. Juvonen & K. Wentzel (Eds.), *Social motivation: Understanding children's school adjustment* (pp. 11–42). New York: Cambridge University Press.

Harter, S., & Jackson, B. J. (1992). Trait vs. nontrait conceptualizations of intrinsic/extrinsic motivational orientation. *Motivation and Emotion, 16,* 209–230.

Hasselbring, T. S., Going, L., & Bransford, J. D. (1988). Developing math automaticity in learning handicapped children: The role of computerized drill and practice. *Focus on Exceptional Children, 20,* 1–7.

Hastie, R., & Pennington, N. (1991). Cognitive and social processes in decision making. In L. B. Resnick, J. M. Levine, & S. D. Teasley (Eds.), *Perspectives on socially shared cognition* (pp. 308–327). Washington, DC: American Psychological Association.

Hatano, G., & Inagaki, K. (1996). Cognitive and cultural factors in the acquisition of intuitive biology. In D. R. Olson & N. Torrance (Eds.), *Handbook of education and human development* (pp. 683–708). Oxford, England: Blackwell.

Hatano, G., & Inagaki, K. (2003). When is conceptual change intended?: A cognitive sociocultural view. In G. M. Sinatra & P. R. Pintrich (Eds.), *International conceptual change* (pp. 407–427). Mahwah, NJ: Lawrence Erlbaum.

Hawkins, J. (1996). Dilemmas. In C. Fisher, D. C. Dwyer, & R. Yocam (Eds.), *Education and technology: Reflections on computing in classrooms* (pp. 35–50). San Francisco: Jossey-Bass.

Hawley, W. D., & Jackson, A. W. (Eds.). (1995). *Toward a common destiny: Improving race relations in America.* San Francisco: Jossey-Bass.

Hayes, J. R. (1996). A new framework for understanding cognition and affect in writing. In C. M. Levy & S. Ransdell (Eds.), *The science of writing: Theories, methods, individual differences, and applications* (pp. 1–27). Mahwah, NJ: Lawrence Erlbaum.

Hayes, J. R., & Flower, L. S. (1986). Writing research and the writer. *American Psychologist, 41,* 1106–1113.

Haywood, K. M. (1993). *Life span motor development* (2nd ed.). Champaign, IL: Human Kinetics.

Heath, S. B. (1991). "It's about winning!" The language of knowledge in baseball. In L. B. Resnick, J. M. Levine, & S. D. Teasley (Eds.), *Perspectives on socially shared cognition* (pp. 101–124). Washington, DC: American Psychological Association.

Hegarty, M., Mayer, R. E., & Monk, C. A. (1995). Comprehension of arithmetic word problems: A comparison of successful and unsuccessful problem solvers. *Journal of Educational Psychology, 87,* 18–32.

Heider, F. (1958). *The psychology of interpersonal relations.* New York: Wiley.

Heim, M. (1992). The erotic ontology of cyberspace. In M. Benedikt (Ed.), *Cyberspace: First steps* (pp. 59–80). Cambridge, MA: MIT Press.

Hennessey, M. G. (2003). Metacognitive aspects of students' reflective discourse: Implications for intentional conceptual change teaching and learning. In G. M. Sinatra & P. R. Pintrich (Eds.), *Intentional conceptual change* (pp. 103–132). Mahwah, NJ: Lawrence Erlbaum.

Herman, J. L., Aschbacher, P. R., & Winters, L. (1992). *A practical guide to alternative assessment.* Alexandria, VA: Association for Supervision and Curriculum Development.

Herrnstein, R. J., & Murray, C. (1994). *The bell curve: Intelligence and class structure in American life.* New York: Free Press.

Hertz-Lazarowitz, R., & Calderon, M. (1994). Facilitating teachers' power through collaboration: Implementing cooperative learning in elementary schools. In S. Sharan (Ed.), *Handbook of cooperative learning methods* (pp. 300–317). Westport, CT: Praeger.

Heubert, J. P., & Hauser, R. M. (1999). *High stakes testing for tracking, promotion, and graduation.* Washington, DC: National Academy Press.

Hidi, S. (1990). Interest and its contribution as a mental resource for learning. *Review of Educational Research, 60,* 549–571.

Hiebert, E. H., & Raphael, T. E. (1996). Psychological perspectives on literacy and extension to educational practice. In D. C. Berliner & R. C. Calfee (Eds.), *Handbook of educational psychology* (pp. 550–602). New York: Macmillan.

Hiebert, E. H., & Taylor, B. M. (1994). *Getting reading right from the start: Effective early literacy interventions.* Boston: Allyn & Bacon.

Hiebert, E. H., & Taylor, B. M. (2000). Beginning reading instruction: Research on early interventions. In M. L. Kamil, P. B. Mosenthal, P. D. Pearson, & R. Barr (Eds.), *Handbook of reading research* (Vol. 3, pp. 455–482). Mahwah, NJ: Lawrence Erlbaum.

Hillocks, G. (1984). What works in teaching composition: A meta-analysis of experimental treatment studies. *American Educational Research Journal, 93,* 133–170.

Hirsch, E. D., Jr. (1996). *The schools we need and why we don't have them.* New York: Doubleday.

Hofer, B. K. (2000). Dimensionality and disciplinary differences in personal epistemology. *Contemporary Educational Psychology, 25,* 378–405.

Hofstadter, D. R. (1995). *Fluid concepts and creative analogies.* New York: Basic Books.

Holley, C. D., & Dansereau, D. F. (1984). *Spatial learning strategies: Techniques, applications, and related issues.* San Diego, CA: Academic Press.

Holyoak, K. J., & Thagard, P. (1995). *Mental leaps: Analogy in creative thinking.* Cambridge, MA: MIT Press.

Holyoak, K. J., & Thagard, P. (1997). The analogical mind. *American Psychologist, 52,* 35–44.

Hooper, S., & Hannafin, M. J. (1991). Psychological perspectives on emerging instructional technologies: A critical analysis. *Educational Psychologist, 26,* 69–95.

Hopkins, K. D., Stanley, J. C., & Hopkins, B. R. (1990). *Educational and psychological measurement and evaluation* (7th ed.). Englewood Cliffs, NJ: Prentice Hall.

Horn, J. L. (1968). Organization of abilities and the development of intelligence. *Psychological Review, 75,* 242–259.

Horn, J. L. (1985). Remodeling old models of intelligence. In B. B. Wolman (Ed.), *Handbook of intelligence: Theories, measurements, and applications* (pp. 267–300). New York: Wiley.

Hornbeck, D. W. (1990). *Technology and learners at risk of school failure.* Elmhurst, IL: North Central Regional Educational Laboratory.

Horney, M. A., & Anderson-Inman, L. (1995). Hypermedia for readers with hearing impairments: Promoting literacy with electronic text enhancements. In C. Kinzer, K. Hinchman, & D. Leu (Eds.), *Forty-third yearbook of the National Reading Conference* (pp. 448–458). Chicago: National Reading Conference.

Hull, C. L. (1952). *A behavior system: An introduction to behavior theory concerning the individual organism.* New Haven, CT: Yale University Press.

Hunt, E. (1999). Intelligence and human resources: Past, present, and future. In P. L. Ackerman, P. C. Kyllonen, & R. D. Roberts (Eds.), *Learning and individual differences: Process, trait, and content determinants* (pp. 3–28). Washington, DC: American Psychological Association.

Hunt, M. (1982). *The universe within: A new science explores the human mind.* New York: Simon & Schuster.

Hunt, M. (1993). *The story of psychology.* New York: Doubleday.

Husman, J. (1998). *The effect of perceptions of the future on intrinsic motivation.* Unpublished doctoral dissertation, University of Texas at Austin.

Husman, J., & Lens, W. (1999). The role of the future in student motivation. *Educational Psychologist, 34,* 113–125.

Husman, J., Shell, D. F., Just, H. (1996, August). *The inherent time perspective in goal orientation and strategy use.* Paper presented at the annual meeting of the American Psychological Association, Toronto, Canada.

Hyde, J. S., Fennema, E., & Lamon, S. F. (1990). Gender differences in mathematical performance: A meta-analysis. *Psychological Bulletin, 107,* 139–155.

Hyde, J. S., & Linn, M. C. (1988). Gender differences in verbal ability: A meta-analysis. *Psychological Bulletin, 104,* 53–69.

Hynd, C. (2001a). Persuasion and its role in meeting educational goals. *Theory into Practice, 40,* 270–277.

Hynd, C. (2001b). Refutational texts and the change process. *International Journal of Educational Research, 35,* 699–714.

Hynd, C., Alvermann, D., & Qian, G. (1997). Preservice elementary school teachers' conceptual change about projectile motion: Refutation text, demonstration, affective factors, and relevance. *Science Education, 81,* 1–27.

Idol, L. (1997). Key questions related to building collaborative and inclusive schools. *Journal of Learning Disabilities, 30,* 384–394.

Idol, L., Nevin, A., & Paolucci-Whitcomb, P. (1994). *Collaborative consultation.* Austin, TX: PRO-ED.

Inhelder, B., & Piaget, J. (1958). *The growth of logical thinking from childhood to adolescence.* New York: Basic Books.

Inhelder, B., & Piaget, J. (1964). *The early growth of logic in the child.* New York: Harper & Row.

International Society for Technology Education. (1998). *National educational technology standards for students.* Retrieved from *http://cnets.iste.org/index*

International Society for Technology Education and National Council for Accreditation of Teacher Education. (1997). *National educational technology standards for teachers.* Retrieved from *http://cnets.iste.org/index*

Iran-Nejad, A. (1990). Active and dynamic self-regulation of learning processes. *Review of Educational Research, 60,* 573–602.

Jackson, R. M. (1992). The untapped power of student note writing. *Educational Leadership, 49,* 54–58.

Jamentz, K. (1994). Making sure that assessment improves performance. *Educational Leadership, 51,* 55–57.

James, W. (1980). *Principles of psychology* (Vols. 1 & 2). New York: Holt.

James, W. (1979). Talks to teachers on psychology. In G. E. Myers (Ed.), *William James: Writings 1878–1899.* New York: Library of America. (Original published 1899)

James, W. (1992). *Writings: 1878–1899* (Talks with Teachers). New York: Literacy Classics of the United States.

Jenkins, J. J. (1974). Remember that old theory of memory? Well, forget it! *American Psychologist, 25,* 785–795.

Jensen, A. R. (1998). *The g factor: The science of mental ability.* Westport, CT: Prager/Greenwood.

Jetton, T. L. (1994). *Teachers' and students' understanding of scientific exposition: How importance and interest influence what is accessed and what is discussed.* Unpublished doctoral dissertation, Texas A & M University, College Station.

Jetton, T. L., & Alexander, P. A. (1997). Instructional importance: What teachers value and what students learn. *Reading Research Quarterly, 32,* 290–308.

Jetton, T. L., & Alexander, P. A. (1998, April). *Teachers' views of discussion: Issues of control, time, and ability.* Paper presented at the annual meeting of the American Educational Research Association, San Diego, CA.

Jetton, T. L., & Alexander, P. A. (2000, January). *The nature of student involvement: Discussion genres that occur in science classrooms.* Manuscript submitted for publication.

Johnson, D. W., & Johnson, R. T. (1974). Instructional goal structure: Cooperative, competition, or individualistic. *Review of Educational Research, 44,* 213–240.

Johnson, D. W., & Johnson, R. T. (1994). *Learning together and alone* (2nd ed.). Englewood, NJ: Prentice Hall.

Johnson, D. W., & Johnson, R. T. (1999). *Learning together and alone: Cooperative, competitive, and individualistic learning.* Boston: Allyn & Bacon.

Johnson, D. W., Johnson, R. T., & Stanne, M. B. (2000). *Cooperative learning methods: A meta-analysis.* Retrieved from *http://www.clcrc.com*

Jones, B. F., & Idol, L. (Eds.) (1990). *How metacognition can promote academic learning and instruction.* Hillsdale, NJ: Lawrence Erlbaum.

Joyce, B., Weil, M., & Showers, B. (1992). *Models of teaching.* Boston: Allyn & Bacon.

Judd, C. H. (1915). *The psychology of high school subjects.* Boston: Ginn.

Judy, J. E., Alexander, P. A., Kulikowich, J. M., & Willson, V. L. (1988). Effects of two instructional approaches and peer tutoring on gifted and nongifted sixth graders' analogy performance. *Reading Research Quarterly, 23,* 236–256.

Juel, C. (1988). Learning to read and write: A longitudinal study of 54 children from first through fourth grades. *Journal of Educational Psychology, 80,* 417–447.

Kafai, Y., & Resnick, M. (1996). *Constructionism in practice: Designing, thinking, and learning in a digital world.* Mahwah, NJ: Lawrence Erlbaum.

Kagan, S. (1992). *Cooperative learning.* San Juan Capistrano, CA: Resources for Teachers.

Kagan, S., & Kagan, M. (1994). The structural approach: Six keys to cooperative learning. In S. Sharan (Ed.), *Handbook of cooperative learning methods* (pp. 115–133). Westport, CT: Praeger.

Kamil, M. L., Intrator, S. M., & Kim, H. S. (2000). The effects of other technologies on literacy and literacy learning. In M. L. Kamil, P. B. Mosenthal, P. D. Pearson, & R. Barr (Eds.), *Handbook of reading research* (Vol. 3, pp. 771–788). Mahwah, NJ: Lawrence Erlbaum.

Kamil, M. L., & Lane, D. M. (1998). Researching the relation between technology and literacy: An agenda for the 21st century. In D. Reinking, M. C. McKenna, L. D. Labbo, & R. D. Kieffer (Eds.), *Handbook of literacy and technology* (pp. 323–341). Mahwah, NJ: Lawrence Erlbaum.

Kampwirth, T. J. (1999). *Collaborative consultation in the schools.* Upper Saddle River, NJ: Merrill.

Kant, I. (1963). *Critique of pure reason* (N. Kemp Smith, Trans.). London: Macmillan. (Original published 1787)

Kantor, R., Green, J., Bradley, M., & Lin, L. (1992). The construction of schooled discourse repertoires: An interactional sociolinguistic perspective on learning to talk in preschool. *Linguistics in Education, 4,* 131–172.

Kapinus, B., & Haynes, J. A. (1983). *Effects of prior knowledge, text-order, and underlining on recall of information from text.* (ERIC Document Reproduction Service No. ED 237 968)

Kardash, C. M., & Scholes, R. J. (1995). Effects of preexisting beliefs and repeated readings on belief change, comprehension, and recall of persuasive text. *Contemporary Educational Psychology, 20,* 201–221.

Karplus, R., Karplus, E., Formisano, M., & Paulsen, A. (1979). Proportional reasoning and control of variables in seven countries. In J. Lochhead & J. Clement (Eds.), *Cognitive process instruction: Research on teaching thinking skills.* Philadelphia: Franklin Institute Press.

Katz, H., & Beilin, H. (1976). A test of Bryant's claims concerning the young child's understanding of quantitative invariance. *Child Development, 47,* 877–880.

Kaufman, J. J., Gotleib, J., Agard, J. A., & Kukie, M. (1975). Mainstreaming: Toward an explication of the concept. In E. L. Meyen, G. A. Vergason, & R. J. Whelan (Eds.), *Alternatives for teaching exceptional children* (pp. 40–54). Denver: Love.

Kaye, K., & Marcus, J. (1981). Infant imitation: The sensory-motor agenda. *Developmental Psychology, 17,* 258–265.

Kellogg, R. T. (1994). *The psychology of writing.* New York: Oxford University Press.

Keogh, J., & Sugden, D. (1985). *Movement skill development.* New York: Macmillan.

Kerr, S. T. (1996). Visions of sugarplums: The future of technology, education, and the schools. In S. T. Kerr (Ed.), *Technology and the future of schooling: Ninety-fifth yearbook of the National Society for the Study of Education* (pp. 1–27). Chicago: National Society for the Study of Education.

Kiewra, K. A. (1989). A review of note taking: The encoding-storage paradigm and beyond. *Educational Psychology Review, 1,* 147–172.

Kiewra, K. A., Kauffman, D. F., Robinson, D., DuBois, N., & Staley, R. K. (1999). Supplementing floundering text with adjunct displays. *Journal of Instructional Science, 27,* 373–401.

Kindvatter, R., Wilen, W., & Ishler, M. (1996). *Dynamics of effective teaching* (3rd ed.). White Plains, NY: Longman.

Kintsch, W., & van Dijk, T. A. (1978). Toward a model of text comprehension and production. *Psychological Review, 85,* 363–394.

Kinzer, C. K., & Risko, V. J. (1998). Multimedia and enhanced learning: Transforming preservice education. In D. Reinking, M. C. McKenna, L. D.Labbo, & R. D. Kieffer (Eds.), *Handbook of literacy and technology* (pp. 185–202). Mahwah, NJ: Lawrence Erlbaum.

KLICK! (1998). *Handbook.* East Lansing, MI: Kids Learning in Computer Klubhouses.

Koedinger, K. R., Anderson, J. R., Hadley, W. H., & Mark, M. A. (1997). Intelligent tutoring goes to school in the big city. *International Journal of Artificial Intelligence in Education, 8,* 30–43.

Kohlberg, L. (1969). Stage and sequence: The cognitive-developmental approach to socialization. In D. A. Goslin (Ed.), *Handbook of socialization theory and research.* Chicago: Rand McNally.

Kohlberg, L. (1975). The cognitive-developmental approach to moral education. *Phi Delta Kappan, 56,* 670–677.

Kohlberg, L. (1976). Moral stages and moralization: The cognitive-developmental approach to socialization. In J. Lickona (Ed.), *Moral development behavior: Theory, research and social issues.* New York: Holt, Rinehart & Winston.

Kohlberg, L. (1981). *The philosophy of moral development: Moral stages and the idea of justice.* San Francisco: Harper & Row.

Kohlberg, L. (1984). *Essays on moral development: Vol. 2. The psychology of moral development: The nature and validity of moral stages.* San Francisco: Harper & Row.

Kohn, A. (1993). *Punished by rewards: The trouble with gold stars, incentive plans, A's, praise, and other bribes.* Boston: Houghton Mifflin.

Kolodner, J. L. (1997). Educational implications of analogy: A view from case-based reasoning. *American Psychologist, 52*, 57–66.

Koretz, D., McCaffrey, D., Klein, S., Bell, R., & Strecher, B. (1993). *The reliability of scores from the 1992 Vermont portfolio assessment program* (CSE Technical Report 355). Los Angeles: University of California, Center for Research on Evaluation, Standards, and Student Testing.

Korthagen, F. A. J., & Kessels, J. P. A. M. (1999). Linking theory and practice: Changing the pedagogy of teacher education. *Educational Psychologist, 28*(4), 4–17.

Koschmann, T. D., Myers, A. C., Feltovich, P. J., & Barrows, H. W. (1994). Technology to assist in realizing effective learning and instruction: A principled approach to the use of computers in collaborative learning. *Journal of the Learning Sciences, 3*, 227–264.

Kostelnik, M. (1992). Myths associated with developmentally appropriate practice. *Young Children, 47*(4), 17–25.

Kounin, J. S. (1970). *Discipline and group management in the classrooms.* New York: Holt, Rinehart & Winston.

Kozulin, A. (1999). *Vygotsky's psychology: A biography of ideas.* Cambridge, MA: Harvard University Press.

Kraut, R., Patterson, M., Lundmark, V., Kiesler, S., Mukopadhyay, & Scherlis, W. (1998). Internet paradox: A social technology that reduces social involvement and psychological well-being. *American Psychologist, 53*, 1017–1031.

Kreitler, S., Zigler, E., Kagan, S., Olsen, D., Weissler, K., & Kreitler, H. (1995). Cognitive and motivational determinants of academic achievement and behavior in third and fourth grade disadvantaged children. *British Journal of Educational Psychology, 65*, 297–316.

Kubiszyn, T., & Borich, G. (1996). *Educational testing and measurement: Classroom application and practice* (5th ed.). New York: HarperCollins.

Kuhn, D. (1992). Cognitive development. In M. H. Bornstein & M. E. Lamb (Eds.), *Developmental psychology: An advanced textbook.* Hillsdale, NJ: Lawrence Erlbaum.

Kuhn, D., Amsel, E., & O'Loughlin, M. (1988). *The development of scientific thinking skills.* San Diego, CA: Academic Press.

Kulik, J. A., Kulik, C., & Cohen, P. (1980). Effectiveness of computer-based college teaching: A meta-analysis of findings. *Review of Educational Research, 50*, 525–544.

Kulikowich, J. M., & Alexander, P. A. (1994). Error patterns on cognitive tasks: Applications of polytomous item response theory and loglinear modeling. In C. Reynolds (Ed.), *Cognitive assessment: An interdisciplinary dialogue* (pp. 137–154). New York: Plenum.

Kulikowich, J. M., & Alexander, P. A. (in press). Cognitive assessment. In R. Ananda (Ed.), *Encyclopedia of cognitive science.* London: Nature.

Kulikowich, J. M., O'Connell, A. A., Rezendes, G., & Archambault, F. X. (2000, April). Many theories, many methodologies: Blending quantitative and qualitative procedures in the study of classroom dynamics involving technology. In K. Squire (Chair), *The merits of multiple theories of learning in the study of technology use in classroom settings.* Symposium presented at the annual meeting of the American Educational Research Association, New Orleans, LA.

Kulikowich, J. M., & Young, M. F. (2001). Locating an ecological psychology methodology for situated action. *Journal of Learning Science, 10*, 165–202.

Labouvie-Vief, G. (1992). A neo-Piagetian perspective on adult cognitive development. In R. J. Sternberg & C. A. Berg (Eds.), *Intellectual development.* New York: Cambridge University Press.

Labov, W. (1973). Boundaries of words and their meanings. In J. B. Bailey & R. W. Shuy (Eds.), *New ways of analyzing variation in English.* Washington, DC: Georgetown University Press.

Lajoie, S. P. (1993). Computer environments as cognitive tools for enhancing learning. In S. P. Lajoie & S. J. Derry (Eds.), *Computers as cognitive tools* (pp. 261–288). Mahwah, NJ: Lawrence Erlbaum.

Lajoie, S. P. (2000). Introduction: Breaking camp to find new summits. In S. P. Lajoie (Ed.), *Computers as cognitive tools: No more walls* (pp. xv–xxxii). Mahwah, NJ: Lawrence Erlbaum.

Lajoie, S. P., & Azevedo, R. (2000). Cognitive tools for medical informatics. In S. P. Lajoie (Ed.), *Computers as cognitive tools: No more walls* (pp. 247–271). Mahwah, NJ: Lawrence Erlbaum.

Lajoie, S. P., & Derry, S. J. (1993). *Computers as cognitive tools.* Mahwah, NJ: Lawrence Erlbaum.

Lambert, N. M., & McCombs, B. L. (1998). *Issues in school reform: A sampler of psychological perspectives on learner-centered school.* Washington, DC: American Psychological Association.

Lampert, M. (1990). When the problem is not the question and the solution is not the answer. *American Educational Research Journal, 27*, 29–63.

Lampert, M. (1998). Introduction. In M. Lampert & M. L. Blunk (Eds.), *Talking mathematics in school* (pp. 1–14). Cambridge, England: Cambridge University Press.

Lampert, M., & Blunk, M. L. (1998). *Talking mathematics in school.* Cambridge, England: Cambridge University Press.

Landow, G. P. (1992). *Hypertext: The convergence of contemporary critical theory and technology.* Baltimore: Johns Hopkins University.

Lanehart, S. L., & Schutz, P. A. (2001). Facilitating self-regulation in linguistics classrooms. *Academic Exchange Quarterly, 5*(3), 83–87.

Lave, J. (1988). *Cognition and practice.* Cambridge, England: Cambridge University Press.

Lave, J., & Wenger, E. (1991). *Situated learning: Legitimate peripheral participation.* Cambridge, England: Cambridge University Press.

Lawless, K. A., & Kulikowich, J. M. (1996). Understanding hypertext navigation through cluster analysis. *Journal of Educational Computing Research, 14*, 385–399.

Learner-Centered Principles Work Group of the APA Board of Educational Affairs. (1997, November). *Learner-Centered Psychological Principles: A Framework for School Reform and Redesign.* Washington, DC: American Psychological Association.

Lehrer, R. (1993). Authors of knowledge: Patterns of hypermedia design. In S. P. Lajoie & S. J. Derry (Eds.), *Computers as cognitive tools* (pp. 193–227). Mahwah, NJ: Lawrence Erlbaum.

Leinhardt, G. (1989). Math lessons: A contrast of novice and expert competence. *Journal for Research in Mathematics Education, 20*, 52–75.

Leinhardt, G., Stainton, C., & Virji, S. M. (1994). A sense of history. *Educational Psychologist, 29*(2), 79–88.

Lemke, J. L. (1990). *Talking science: Language, learning and values.* Norwood, NJ: Ablex.

Lemke, J. L. (1998). Metamedia literacy: Transforming meanings and media. In D. Reinking, M. C. McKenna, L. D. Labbo, & R. D. Kieffer (Eds.), *Handbook of literacy and technology: Transformations in a posttypographical world* (pp. 283–301). Mahwah, NJ: Lawrence Erlbaum.

Lens, W. (1986). Future time perspective: A cognitive-motivational concept. In D. R. Brown & J. Veroff (Eds.), *Frontiers of motivational psychology* (pp. 173–190). New York: Springer-Verlag.

Lens, W., & Decruyenaere, M. (1991). Motivation and demotivation in secondary education: Student characteristics. *Learning and Instruction, 1*, 145–159.

Lesgold, A. (1993). Information technology and the future of education. In S. P. Lajoie & S. J. Derry (Eds.), *Computers as cognitive tools* (pp. 369–383). Mahwah, NJ: Lawrence Erlbaum.

Lesgold, A. (2000). What are the tools for? Revolutionary change does not follow the usual norms. In S. P. Lajoie (Ed.), *Computers as cognitive tools: No more walls* (pp. 399–408). Mahwah, NJ: Lawrence Erlbaum.

Lesgold, A. M., Lajoie, S. P., Bunzo, M., & Eggan, G. (1992). Sherlock: A coached practice environment for an electronics troubleshooting job. In J. Larkin, R. Chabay, & C. Sheftic (Eds.), *Computer assisted instruction and intelligent tutoring systems: Shared issues and complementary approaches* (pp. 201–238). Hillsdale, NJ: Lawrence Erlbaum.

Leu, D. J., Hillinger, M., Loseby, P. H., Balcom, M. L., Dinkin, J., Eckels, M. L., Johnson, J., Mathews, K., & Raegler, R. (1998) In D. Reinking, M. C. McKenna, L. D. Labbo, & R. D. Kieffer (Eds.), *Handbook of literacy and technology: Transformations in a posttypographical world* (pp. 203–220). Mahwah, NJ: Lawrence Erlbaum.

Leu, D. J., & Reinking, D. (1996). Bringing insights from reading research to research on electronic learning environments. In H. van Oostendorp (Ed.), *Cognitive aspects of electronic text processing* (pp. 43–75). Norwood, NJ: Ablex.

Levin, J. R. (1981). The mnemonic '80s: Keywords in the classroom. *Educational Psychologist, 16*, 65–82.

Levin, J. R. (1993). Mnemonic strategies and classroom learning: A twenty-year report card. *Elementary School Journal, 94,* 235–244.

Levstik, L. S., & Barton, K. (1996). "They still use some of their past": Historical salience in elementary children's chronological thinking. *Journal of Curriculum Studies, 28,* 531–576.

Lewin, K. (1938). *Conceptual representation and measurement of psychological forces.* Durham, NC: Duke University Press.

Lewin, K. (1951). *Field theory in social sciences.* New York: Harper.

Lewis, A. B. (1989). Training students to represent arithmetic word problems. *Journal of Educational Psychology, 81,* 521–531.

Lieberman, A. (1988). *Building a professional climate in schools.* New York: Teachers College Press.

Limón, M. (2002). Conceptual change in history. In M. Limón & L. Mason (Eds.), *Reconsidering conceptual change: Issues in theory and practice* (pp. 259–289). Dordrecht, Netherlands: Kluwer.

Limón, M., & Mason, L. (2002). *Reconsidering conceptual change: Issues in theory and practice.* Dordrecht, Netherlands: Kluwer.

Limón Luque, M. (2003). The role of domain-specific knowledge in intentional conceptual change. In G. M. Sinatra & P. R. Pintrich (Eds.), *Intentional conceptual change* (pp. 133–170). Mahwah, NJ: Lawrence Erlbaum.

Linn, M. C. (1992). The computer as learning partner: Can computer tools teach science? In K. Sheingold, L. G. Roberts, & S. M. Malcolm (Eds.), *This year in school science 1991: Technology for teaching and learning.* Washington, DC: American Association for the Advancement of Science.

Linn, M. C., Songer, N. B., & Eylon, B-S. (1996). Shifts and convergences in science learning and instruction. In D. C. Berliner & R. C. Calfee (Eds.), *Handbook of educational psychology* (pp. 438–490). New York: Macmillan.

Linn, R. L. (1995). *Assessment-based reform: Challenges in educational measurement.* Princeton, NJ: Educational Testing Service, Policy Information Center.

Linn, R. L., & Gronlund, N. E. (2000). *Measurement and assessment in teaching* (8th ed.). Upper Saddle River, NJ: Merrill/Prentice Hall.

Linnebrink, E. A., & Pintrich, P. R. (2002). The role of motivational beliefs in conceptual change. In M. Limón & L. Mason (Eds.), *Reconsidering conceptual change: Issues in theory and practice* (pp. 115–135). Dordrecht, Netherlands: Kluwer.

Lipman, M. (1991). *Thinking in education.* Cambridge, MA: Cambridge University Press.

Lipman, M. (2003). *Thinking in education* (2nd ed.). Cambridge, MA: Cambridge University Press.

Lipson, M. (1995). The effect of semantic mapping instruction on prose comprehension of below-level college readers. *Reading Research and Instruction, 34,* 367–378.

Locke, J. (1938). *Some thoughts concerning education.* London: Churchill. (Originally published 1699)

Lockheed, M. E., Harris, A. M., & Nemceff, W. P. (1983). Sex and social influence: Does sex function as a status characteristic in mixed-sex groups of children. *Journal of Educational Psychology, 75*(6), 877–888.

Loehlin, J. C. (1992). *Genes and environment in personality development* (Vol. 2.). Newbury Park, CA: Sage.

Loent'ev, A. N. (1981). *Problems in the development of mind.* Moscow: Progress.

Luft, J. (1970). *Group processes: An introduction to group dynamics* (2nd ed.). Palo Alto, CA: National Press Books.

Lupart, J. L. (1995). Exceptional learners and teaching for transfer. In A. McKeough, J. Lupart, & A. Marini (Eds.), *Teaching for transfer: Fostering generalization in learning* (pp. 215–228). Mahwah, NJ: Lawrence Erlbaum.

Luria, A. R. (1976). *Cognitive development.* Cambridge, MA: Harvard University Press.

Luria, A. R. (1980). *Higher cortical functions in man* (2nd ed.). New York: Basic Books.

Luria, A. R. (1981). *Language and cognition.* New York: Wiley.

Lyman, H. B. (1991). *Test scores and what they mean.* Upper Saddle River, NJ: Prentice Hall.

MacArthur, C. A., & Haynes, J. B. (1995). Student assistant for learning from text (SALT): A hypermedia reading aid. *Journal of Learning Disabilities, 28*(3), 150–159.

Madaus, G. F., & Kellaghan, T. (1993). Testing as a mechanism of public policy: A brief history. *Measurement and Evaluation in Counseling and Development, 26,* 6–10.

Maehr, M. (1982). *Motivational factors in school achievement.* Paper commissioned by the National Commission on Excellence in Education (NIE 400-81-0004, Task 10).

Maehr, M. L., & Anderman, E. M. (1993). Reinventing schools for early adolescents: Emphasizing task goals. *Elementary School Journal, 93,* 593–610.

Maier, S. F., & Seligman, M. E. P. (1976). Learned helplessness: Theory and evidence. *Journal of Experimental Psychology, 105,* 3–46.

Mandinach, E. B., & Cline, H. F. (1994). *Classroom dynamics: Implementing a technology-based learning environment.* Hillsdale, NJ: Lawrence Erlbaum.

Mandinach, E. B., & Cline, H. F. (2000). It won't happen soon: Practical, curricular, and methodological problems in implementing technology-based constructivist approaches in classrooms. In S. P. Lajoie (Ed.), *Computers as cognitive tools: No more walls* (pp. 377–395). Mahwah, NJ: Lawrence Erlbaum.

Mandler, G., & Sarason, S. B. (1952). A study of anxiety of learning. *Journal of Abnormal and Social Psychology, 47,* 166–173.

Manning, B. H., White, C. S., & Daugherty, M. (1994). Young children's private speech as a precursor to metacognitive strategy use during task execution. *Discourse Processes, 17,* 191–211.

Mansoor, I. (1993). *The use of technology in adult ESL program: Current practice—future promise.* Washington, DC: Southport Institute for Policy Analysis.

Marini, A., & Genereux, R. (1995). The challenge of teaching for transfer. In A. Mc-Keough, J. Lupart, & A. Marini (Eds.), *Teaching for transfer: Fostering generalization in learning* (pp. 1–20). Mahwah, NJ: Lawrence Erlbaum.

Markus, H., & Narius, P. (1986). Possible selves. *American Psychologist, 41,* 954–969.

Markus, H., & Wurf, E. (1987). The dynamic self-concept: A social psychological perspective. *Annual Review of Psychology, 38,* 299–337.

Marsh, H. W. (1990). A multidimensional, hierarchical self-concept and academic achievement: A multiwave, longitudinal path analysis. *Journal of Educational Psychology, 82,* 646–656.

Marsh, H. W. (1992). The content specificity of relations between academic achievement and academic self-concept. *Journal of Educational Psychology, 84,* 43–50.

Marsh, H. W., & Yeung, A. S. (1997a). Causal effects of academic self-concept on academic achievement: Structural equation models of longitudinal data. *Journal of Educational Psychology, 89,* 41–54.

Marsh, H. W., & Yeung, A. S. (1997b). Coursework selection: Relations to academic self-concept and achievement. *American Educational Research Journal, 34,* 691–720.

Martindale, C. (1991). *Cognitive psychology: A neural-network approach.* Pacific Grove, CA: Brooks/Cole.

Maslow, A. H. (1954). *Motivation and personality.* New York: Harper & Row.

Maslow, A. H. (1971). *The farther reaches of human nature.* New York: Viking.

Mason, L. (2002). Developing epistemological thinking to foster conceptual change in different domains. In M. Limón & L. Mason (Eds.), *Reconsidering conceptual change: Issues in theory and practice* (pp. 301–335). Dordrecht, Netherlands: Kluwer.

Matthews, G., Schwean, V. L., Campbell, S. E., Sklofske, D. H., & Mohamed, A. A. R. (2001). Personality, self-regulation, and adaptation: A cognitive-social framework. In M. Boekaerts, P. R. Pintrich, & M. Zeidner (Eds.), *Handbook of self-regulation* (pp. 171–207). San Diego, CA: Academic Press.

Matthews, M. R. (1994). *Science teaching: The role of history and philosophy of science.* New York: Routledge.

May, F. (1990). *Reading as communication: An interactive approach* (3rd ed.). Columbus, OH: Merrill.

Mayer, J. D., & Salovey, P. (1993). The intelligence of emotional intelligence. *Intelligence, 17,* 433–442.

Mayer, R. E. (1982). Different problem solving strategies for algebra word and equation problems. *Journal of Experimental Psychology: Learning, Memory and Cognition, 8,* 448–462.

Mayer, R. E. (1983). *Thinking, problem solving, cognition.* New York: W. H. Freeman.

Mayer, R. E. (1998). *The promise of educational psychology: Learning in the content areas.* Columbus, OH: Merrill.

Mayer, R. E. (2002). Understanding conceptual change: A commentary. In M. Limón & L. Mason (Eds.), *Reconsidering conceptual change: Issues in theory and practice* (pp. 101–111). Dordrecht, Netherlands: Kluwer.

Mayer, R. E., & Hegarty, M. (1996). The process of understanding mathematical problems. In R. J. Sternberg & T. Ben-Zeev (Eds.), *The nature of mathematical thinking* (pp. 29–53). Mahwah, NJ: Lawrence Erlbaum.

McCaslin, M., & Good, T. L. (1996). The informal curriculum. In D. C. Berliner & R. C. Calfee (Eds.), *Handbook of educational psychology* (pp. 622–670). New York: Macmillan.

McGonagill, B. K. (1995). *Defining, developing, and modeling interdisciplinary curriculum.* Unpublished record of study, Texas A&M University, College of Education, College Station, TX.

McInerney, D. M., Roche, L. A., McInerney, V., & Marsh, H. W. (1997). Cultural perspectives on school motivation: The relevance and application of goal theory. *American Educational Research Journal, 34*(1), 207–236.

McKeachie, W. J. (1996, April). *The state of strategy research: Is this old territory or are there new frontiers?* Symposium presented at the annual meeting of the American Educational Research Association.

McKeachie, W. J., Pintrich, P. R., Lin, Y.-G., & Smith, D. A. F. (1990). *Teaching and learning in the college classroom: A review of the literature.* Ann Arbor, MI: National Center for Research to Improve Postsecondary Teaching and Learning.

McKeough, A., Lupart, J., & Marini, A. (1995). *Teaching for transfer: Fostering generalization in learning.* Mahwah, NJ: Lawrence Erlbaum.

McKeown, M. G., & Beck, I. L. (1990). The assessment and characterization of young learners' knowledge of a topic in history. *American Educational Research Journal, 27,* 688–726.

McKeown, M. G., Beck, I. L., Sinatra, G. M., & Loxterman, J. A. (1992). The contribution of prior knowledge and coherent text to comprehension. *Reading Research Quarterly, 27,* 79–93.

McKeown, M. G., & Curtis, M. E. (1987). *The nature of vocabulary acquisition.* Hillsdale, NJ: Lawrence Erlbaum.

McLaren, P. (1998). *Life in schools* (3rd ed.). New York: Longman.

McMillan, J. H. (2001). *Classroom assessment: Principles and practice for effective instruction* (2nd ed.). Boston: Allyn & Bacon.

Mead, M. (1988). *Coming of age in Samoa: A psychological study of primitive youth for Western civilization.* New York: William Morrow.

Means, B., Blando, J., Olson, K., Middleton, T., Morocco, C. C., Remz, A. R., & Zorfass, J. (1993). Washington, DC: U. S. Department of Education, Office of Educational Research and Improvement.

Meece, J. L. (2002). *Child and adolescent development for educators.* Boston: McGraw-Hill.

Meece, J. L., Blumenfeld, P. C., & Hoyle, R. (1988). Students' goal orientations and cognitive engagement in classroom activities. *Journal of Educational Psychology, 80,* 514–523.

Meece, J. L., & Holt, K. (1993). A pattern analysis of students' achievement goals. *Journal of Educational Psychology, 85*(4), 582–590.

Meeker, M., & Meeker, R. (1976). *Structure of the intellect—learning abilities test.* E1 Segundo, CA: SOI Institute.

Mehan, H. (1979). *Learning lessons: Social organization in the classroom.* Cambridge MA: Harvard University Press.

Mehrens, W. A., & Lehman, I. J. (1987). *Using standardized tests in education* (4th ed.). New York: Longman.

Mei, Z., Scanlon, K. S., Grummer-Strawn, L. M., Freedman, D. S., Yip, R., Trowbridge, F. L. (1998). Increasing prevalence of overweight among U.S. low-income preschool children: Centers for Disease Control and Prevention Pediatric Nutrition Surveillance, 1983 to 1995. *Pediatrics, 101*(1). Also retrieved from *http://www.pediatrics.org/cgi/content/full/101/1/e12*

Messick, S. (1980). Test validity and the ethics of assessment. *American Psychologist, 35,* 1012–1027.

Messick, S. (1994). The interplay of evidence and consequences in the validation of performance assessments. *Educational Researcher, 23,* 13–23.

Metsala, J. L. (1997). Spoken word recognition in reading disabled children. *Journal of Educational Psychology, 89,* 159–169.

Metsala, J. L. (1999). Young children's phonological awareness and nonword repetition as a function of vocabulary development. *Journal of Educational Psychology, 91,* 3–19.

Metsala, J. L., & Ehri, L. C. (1998). *Word recognition in beginning literacy.* Mahwah, NJ: Lawrence Erlbaum.

Meyer, B. J. F. (1975). *The organization of prose and its effects on memory.* Amsterdam: North-Holland.

Meyrowitz, J. (1996). Taking McLuhan and "medium theory" seriously: Technological change and the evolution of education. In S. T. Kerr (Ed.). *Technology and the future of schooling: Ninety-fifth yearbook of the National Society for the Study of Education* (pp. 73–110). Chicago: National Society for the Study of Education.

Michener, J. A. (1985). *Texas.* New York: Random House.

Miller, G. A. (1956). The magical number seven, plus or minus two: Some limits on our capacity for processing information. *Psychological Review, 63,* 81–97.

Miller, I. W., & Norman, W. H. (1981). Effects of attributions for success on the alleviation of learned helplessness and depression. *Journal of Abnormal Psychology, 90,* 113–124.

Miller, N. E. (1948). Studies of fear as an acquirable drive: I. Fear as motivation and fear-reduction as reinforcement in the learning of new responses. *Journal of Experimental Psychology, 38,* 89–101.

Miller, R. B., Behrens, J. T., Greene, B. A., & Newman, D. (1993). Goals and perceived ability: Impact on students' valuing, self-regulation, and persistence. *Contemporary Educational Psychology, 18,* 2–14.

Miller, R. B., Greene, B. A., Montalvo, G. P., Ravindran, B., & Nichols, J. D. (1996). Engagement in academic work: The role of learning goals, future consequences, pleasing others, and perceived ability. *Contemporary Educational Psychology, 21,* 388–422.

Minsky, M. (1975). A framework for representing. In P. H. Winston (Ed.), *The psychology of computer vision* (pp. 211–277). New York: McGraw-Hill.

Miserandino, M. (1996). Children who do well in school: Individual differences in perceived competence and autonomy in above-average children. *Journal of Educational Psychology, 88,* 203–214.

Mishler, E. G. (1978). Studies in dialogue and discourse. III. Utterance structure and utterance function in interrogative sequences. *Journal of Psycholinguistic Research, 7,* 279–305.

Mitchell, M. (1993). Situational interest: Its multifaceted structure in the secondary school mathematics classroom. *Journal of Educational Psychology, 85,* 424–436.

Montessori, M. (1964). *The Montessori method.* New York: Schocken Books.

Moore, M. G. (1989, May). *Effects of distance learning: A summary of the literature.* No. PB90-125238/XAB, University Park: Pennsylvania State University. NTIS.

Morrow, L. M. (1997). *Literacy development in the early years: Helping children to read and write* (3rd ed.). Boston: Allyn & Bacon.

Moss, P. A. (1992). Shifting conceptions of validity in educational measurement: Implications for performance assessment. *Review of Educational Research, 62,* 229–289.

Munuchin, P. P., & Shapiro, E. K. (1983). The school as a context of social development. In P. H. Mussen (Ed.), *Handbook of child psychology* (Vol. 4, 4th ed.). New York: Wiley.

Murphy, P. K. (1998). *Toward a multifaceted model of persuasion: Exploring textual and learner interactions.* Unpublished doctoral dissertation, University of Maryland, College Park, MD.

Murphy, P. K. (2001a, April). *Strategic processing of informational texts in the information age.* Symposium presented at the annual meeting of the American Educational Research Association, Seattle, WA.

Murphy, P. K. (2001b). What makes a text persuasive? Comparing students' and experts' conceptions of persuasiveness [Special issue]. *International Journal of Educational Research, 35,* 675–698.

Murphy, P. K. (2003). Rediscovering the philosophical roots of educational psychology [Special issue]. *Educational Psychologist, 38.*

Murphy, P. K., & Alexander, P. A. (2000). A motivated look at motivational terminology [Special issue]. *Contemporary Educational Psychology, 25,* 3–53.

Murphy, P. K., & Alexander, P. A. (2002a). The learner-centered principles: Their value for teacher and teaching. In W. Hawley (Ed.), *The KEYS to effective schools: Educational reform as continuous improvement* (pp. 10–27). Washington, DC: National Education Association and Corwin Press.

Murphy, P. K., & Alexander, P. A. (2002b). What counts: The predictive power of subject-matter knowledge, strategic processing, and interest in domain-specific performance. *Journal of Experimental Education, 70,* 197–214.

Murphy, P. K., & Alexander, P. A. (2004). Persuasion as a dynamic, multidimensional process: A viewfinder for individual and intraindividual differences. *American Educational Research Journal, 41,* 337–363.

Murphy, P. K., Long, J., Holleran, T., & Esterly, E. (2000, August). Persuasion online or on paper: A new take on an old issue. In C. T. Sperl (Chair), *Changing knowledge and changing beliefs: An examination of academic development, epistemology, and persuasion.* Symposium presented at the annual meeting of the American Psychological Association, Washington, DC.

Nafpaktitis, M., Mayer, G., & Butterworth, T. (1985). Natural rates of teacher approval and disapproval and their relation to student behavior in intermediate school classrooms. *Journal of Educational Psychology, 77,* 362–367.

Nagy, W. E., & Scott, J. A. (2000). Vocabulary processes. In M. L. Kamil, P. B. Mosenthal, P. D. Pearson, & R. Barr (Eds.), *Handbook of reading research* (Vol. 3, pp. 269–284). Mahwah, NJ: Lawrence Erlbaum.

National Association of State Boards of Education. (1992). *Winners all: A call for inclusive schools.* Alexandria, VA: Author.

National Cancer Institute. (2003). *Cigarette smoking and cancer: Questions and answers.* Washington, DC: Author. Also retrieved from *http://cis.nci.nih.gov/fact/3_14.htm*

National Center for Chronic Disease Prevention and Health Promotion. (2003). Healthy schools, healthy people: It's a SNAP. *Adolescent and School Health.* Also retrieved from *http://www.cdc.gov/publications.htm*

National Council of Teachers of Mathematics. (1989). *Curriculum standards for teaching mathematics.* Reston, VA: Author.

National Geographic Society. (1991). *Rain forest.* Washington, DC: Author.

Natriello, G., & Dornbusch, S. (1985). *Teacher evaluative standards and student effort.* New York: Longman.

NEA Today Online. (1999, March). *An interview with Howard Gardner.* Washington, DC: National Educational Association. Also retrieved from *http://www.nea.org/neatoday/9903/gardner.html*

Neimark, E. D. (1975). Longitudinal development of formal operations thought. *Genetic Psychology Monography, 91,* 171–225.

Neisser, U. (1967). *Cognitive psychology.* New York Appleton-Century-Crofts.

Nelson-Le Gall, S., & Jones, E. (1990). Cognitive-motivational influences on children's help-seeking. *Child Development, 61,* 581–589.

Newell, A., & Simon, H. A. (1972). *Human problem solving.* Englewood Cliffs, NJ: Prentice Hall.

Newman, R., & Goldin, L. (1990). Children's reluctance to seek help with school work. *Journal of Educational Psychology, 82,* 92–100.

Newsom, J. (1996). Integrating technology with instruction: One district's experience. In S. T. Kerr (Ed.), *Technology and the future of schooling: Ninety-fifth yearbook of the National Society for the Study of Education* (pp. 200–221). Chicago: National Society for the Study of Education.

Nicholls, J. G. (1989). *The competitive ethos and democratic education.* Cambridge, MA: Harvard University Press.

Nicholls, J. G., & Miller, R. B. (1994). Cooperative learning and student motivation. *Contemporary Educational Psychology, 19,* 167–178.

Nicholls, J. G., Patashnick, M., & Nolen, S. B. (1985). Adolescents' theories of education. *Journal of Educational Psychology, 77,* 683–692.

Nichols, J. D. (1996). The effects of cooperative learning on student achievement and motivation in a high school geometry class. *Contemporary Educational Psychology, 21,* 467–476.

Nisbett, R., & Ross, L. (1980). *Human inference: Strategies and shortcomings of social judgment.* Englewood Cliffs, NJ: Prentice Hall.

Nist, S. L., & Holschuh, J. L. (2000). Comprehension strategies at the college level. In R. F. Flippo & D. C. Caverly (Eds.), *Handbook of college reading and study strategy research* (pp. 75–104. Mahwah, NJ: Lawrence Erlbaum.

Nitko, A. J. (1984). Defining "criterion-referenced test." In R. A. Berk (Ed.), *A guide to criterion-referenced test construction.* Baltimore: Johns Hopkins University Press.

Nitko, A. J. (2001). *Educational assessment of students* (3rd ed.). Upper Saddle River, NJ: Merrill/Prentice Hall.

Nix. D. (1990). Introduction. In D. Nix & R. Spiro (Eds.), *Cognition, education, multimedia,* (pp. ix–xiii). Hillsdale, NJ: Lawrence Erlbaum.

Noddings, N. (1992). *The challenge to care in schools.* New York: Teachers College Press.

Nolen, S. B., Haladyna, T. M., & Haas, N. S. (1992). Uses and abuses of achievement test scores. *Educational Measurement: Issues and Practice, 11*(2), 9–15.

Novak, J. D. (1998). *Learning, creating, and using knowledge.* Mahwah, NJ: Lawrence Erlbaum.

Nuttin, J., & Lens, W. (1985). *Future time perspective and motivation: Theory and research method.* Hillsdale, NJ: Lawrence Erlbaum.

Oakes, J. (1990). *Multiplying inequalities: The effects of race, social class, and tracking on opportunities to learn mathematics and science* (Report No. R-3928-NSF). Santa Monica, CA: Rand.

O'Donnell, A. M., & Kelly, J. (1994). Learning from peers: Beyond the rhetoric of positive results. *Educational Psychology Review, 6,* 321–350.

Ogden, C. L., Flegal, K. M., Carroll, M. D., Johnson, C. L. (2002). Prevalence and trends in overweight among U.S. children and adolescents, 1999–2000. *JAMA, 288,* 1728–1732.

Ogden, C. L., Troiano, R. P., Breifel, R. R., Kuczmarski, R. J., Flegal, K. M., Johnson, C. L. (1997). Prevalence of overweight among preschool children in the United States, 1971 through 1994. *Pediatrics, 99*(4). Also retrieved from *http://www.pediatrics.org/cgi/content/ful/99/4/el*

Ogle, C. (1986). K-W-L: A teaching model that develops active reading of expository text. *Reading Teacher, 39,* 563–570.

Orbach, I., & Hadas, Z. (1982). The elimination of learned helplessness deficits as a function of induced self-esteem. *Journal of Research in Personality, 16,* 511–523.

Ormrod, J. E. (1998). *Educationl psychology: Developing learners* (2nd ed.). Columbus, OH: Merrill.

O'Shea, D. J., & O'Shea, L. J. (1997). What have we learned and where are we headed? Issues in collaboration and school reform. *Journal of Learning Disabilities, 30,* 376–377.

Oxford, R. L. (1989). *Language learning strategies around the world: Cross-cultural perspectives.* Honolulu: University of Hawaii Press.

Oxford, R., & Crookall, D. (1989). Research on language learning strategies. *Modern Language Journal, 73,* 404–419.

Paivio, A. (1971). *Imagery and verbal processes.* New York: Holt, Rinehart, & Winston.

Pajares, M. F. (1992). Teachers' beliefs and educational research: Cleaning up a messy construct. *Review of Educational Research, 62,* 307–332.

Pajares, M. F. (1996). Self-efficacy beliefs and mathematical problem solving of gifted students. *Contemporary Educational Psychology, 21,* 325–344.

Pajares, M. F., Miller, M. D., & Johnson, M. J. (1999). Gender differences in writing self-beliefs of elementary school students. *Journal of Educational Psychology, 91,* 50–61.

Palincsar, A. S., Anderson, C., & David, Y. M. (1993). Pursuing scientific literacy in the middle grades through collaborative problem solving. *Elementary School Journal, 93*(5), 643–658.

Palincsar, A. S., & Brown, A. L. (1984). Reciprocal teaching of comprehension-fostering and monitoring activities. *Cognition and Instruction, 1,* 117–175.

Palmer, D. J., & Goetz, E. T. (1988). Selection and use of study strategies: The role of the studier's beliefs about self and strategies. In C. Weinstein, E. T. Goetz, & P. A. Alexander (Eds.), *Learning and study strategies: Issues in assessment, instruction, and evaluation* (pp. 77–100). San Diego, CA: Academic Press.

Papert, S. (1980). *Mindstorms: Children, computers, and powerful ideas.* New York: Basic Books.

Paris, S. G. (2000a) Harmful and enduring effects of high-stakes testing. *Issues in Education, 6*(1/2), 145–159.

Paris, S. G. (2000b). Trojan horse in the schoolyard: The hidden threats in high-stakes testing. *Issues in Education, 6*(1/2), 1–16.

Paris, S. G., & Cunningham, A. E. (1996). Children becoming students. In D. C. Berliner & R. C. Calfee (Eds.), *Handbook of educational psychology* (pp. 117–147). New York: Macmillan.

Paris, S. G., Lipson, M. Y., & Wixson, K. K. (1983). Becoming a strategic reader. *Contemporary Educational Psychology, 8,* 293–316.

Paris, S. G., Wasik, B. A., & Turner, J. C. (1991). The development of strategic readers. In R. Barr, M. L. Kamil, P. Mosenthal, & P. D. Pearson (Eds.), *Handbook of reading research* (Vol. 2, pp. 609–640). Mahwah, NJ: Lawrence Erlbaum.

Paris, S. G., & Winograd, P. (1990). Dimension of thinking and cognitive instruction. In B. F. Jones & L. Idol (Eds.), *How metacognition can promote academic learning and instruction* (pp. 15–51). Hillsdale, NJ: Lawrence Erlbaum.

Paulos, J. A. (1988). *Innumeracy: Mathematical illiteracy and its consequences.* New York: Vantage.

Paulos, J. A. (1998). *Once upon a number: The hidden mathematical logic of stories.* New York: Basic Books.

Pearson, P. D., & Fielding, L. (1991). Comprehension instruction. In R. Barr, M. L. Kamil, P. Mosenthal, & P. D. Pearson (Eds.), *Handbook of reading research* (Vol. 2, pp. 815–860). Mahwah, NJ: Lawrence Erlbaum.

Pellegrini, A. D. (1988). Elementary-school children's rough-and-tumble play and social competence. *Developmental Psychology, 24,* 802–806.

Perkins, D. N. (1991). Technology meets constructivism: Do they make a marriage? *Educational Researcher, 31*(5), 18–23.

Perkins, D. N. (1992). *Smart schools: Better thinking and learning for every child.* New York: Free Press.

Perkins, D. N. (1993). Person plus: A distributed view of thinking and learning. In G. Salomon (Ed.), *Distributed cognition: Psychological and educational considerations.* Cambridge, England: Cambridge University Press.

Perkins, D. N., & Simmons, R. (1988). Patterns of misunderstanding: An integrative model for science, math, and programming. *Review of Educational Research, 58,* 303–326.

Perret-Clermont, A-N., Perret, J-F., & Bell, N. (1991). The social construction of meaning and cognitive activity in elementary school children. In L. B. Resnick, J. M. Levine, & S. D. Teasley (Eds.), *Perspectives on socially shared cognition* (pp. 41–62). Washington, DC: American Psychological Association.

Pesa, J. (1999). Psychosocial factors associated with dieting behaviors among female adolescents. *Journal of School Health, 69*(5), 196–200.

Petersen, N. S., Kolen, M. J., & Hoover, H. D. (1989). Scaling, norming and equating. In R. L. Linn (Ed.), *Educational measurement* (3rd ed.). Upper Saddle River, NJ: Merrill/Prentice Hall.

Peterson, C., Maier, S., & Seligman, M. (1993). *Learned helplessness: A theory for the age of personal control.* New York: Oxford University.

Peterson, P., Dickson, P., & Clark, C. (1990). Educational psychology as a foundation in teacher education: Reforming an old notion. *Teachers College Record, 91,* 322–346.

Petty, R. E., & Cacioppo, J. T. (1986). *Communication and persuasion: Central and peripheral routes to attitude change.* New York: Springer-Verlag.

Phenix, P. H. (1964). *Realms of meaning: A philosophy of the curriculum for general education.* New York: McGraw-Hill.

Phillips, D. C. (1995). The good, the bad, and the ugly: The many faces of constructivism. *Educational Researcher, 24*(7), 5–12.

Phillips, D., & Zimmerman, M. (1990). The developmental course of perceived competence and incompetence among competent children. In R. J. Sternberg & J. Kolligian (Eds.), *Competence considered* (pp. 41–66). New Haven, CT: Yale University Press.

Phillips, G. M. (1973). *Communication and the small group* (2nd ed.). New York: Bobbs-Merrill.

Phye, G. D. (1996). *Handbook of classroom assessment: Learning, adjustment, and achievement.* San Diego, CA: Academic Press.

Piaget, J. (1926). *The language and thought of the child.* New York: Kegan Paul.

Piaget, J. (1930a). *The child's conception of physical causality.* New York: Harcourt, Brace.

Piaget, J. (1930b). *The child's conception of the world.* New York: Harcourt, Brace & World. (Original published in 1926)

Piaget, J. (1932). *The moral judgment of the child.* New York: Free Press.

Piaget, J. (1952). *The origins of intelligence in children* (M. Cook, Trans.). New York: W. W. Norton.

Piaget, J. (1955). *The language and thought of the child* (M. Gabain, Trans.). New York: Noonday Press.

Piaget, J., Montangero, J., & Billeter, J. (1977). Les correlats. In J. Piaget (Ed.), *L'Abstraction Reflechissante.* Paris: Presses Universitaires de France.

Pines, A. L., & West, L. (1983). A framework for conceptual change with special reference to misconceptions. In H. Helm & J. D. Novak (Eds.) *Proceedings of the international seminar on misconceptions in science and methematics* (pp. 47–52). Ithaca, NY: Cornel University Press.

Pinker, S. (1997). *How the mind works.* New York: W. W. Norton.

Pinker, S. (2002). *The blank slate: The modern denial of human nature.* New York: Viking.

Pintrich, P. R. (1994). Continuities and discontinuities: Future directions for research in educational psychology. *Educational Psychologist, 29,* 137–148.

Pintrich, P. R. (2000a). An achievement goal theory perspective on issues in motivation terminology, theory, and research. *Contemporary Educational Psychology, 25,* 92–104.

Pintrich, P. R. (2000b). The role of goal orientation in self-regulated learning. In M. Boekaerts, P. R. Pintrich, & M. Zeidner (Eds.), *Handbook of self-regulation: Theory, research, and applications* (pp. 451–502). San Diego, CA: Academic Press.

Pintrich, P. R., & deGroot, E. (1990). Motivational and self-regulated learning components of classroom academic performance. *Journal of Educational Psychology, 82,* 33–40.

Pintrich, P. R., Marx, R. W., & Boyle, R. A. (1993). Beyond cold conceptual change: The role of motivational beliefs and classroom contextual factors in the process of conceptual change. *Review of Educational Research, 63,* 167–199.

Pintrich, P. R., & Schrauben, B. (1992). Students' motivational beliefs and their cognitive engagement in classroom tasks. In D. Schunk & J. Meece (Eds.), *Student perceptions in the classroom: Causes and consequences* (pp. 149–183). Hillsdale, NJ: Lawrence Erlbaum.

Pintrich, P. R., & Schunk, D. H. (1996). *Motivation in education: Theory, research, and applications.* Englewood Cliffs, NJ: Merrill/Prentice Hall.

Pintrich, P. R., & Schunk, D. H. (2001). *Motivation in education: Theory, research, and applications* (2nd ed). Englewood Cliffs, NJ: Prentice Hall.

Plomin, R. (1986). *Development, genetics, and psychology.* Hillsdale, NJ: Lawrence Erlbaum.

Plomin, R. (1990). *Nature and nurture: An introduction to human behavioral genetics.* Pacific Grove, CA: Brooks/Cole.

Polya, G. (1945). *How to solve it.* Princeton, NJ: Princeton University Press.

Popham, W. J. (1993). *Educational evaluation* (3rd ed.). Boston: Allyn & Bacon.

Popham, W. J. (1998). *Classroom assessment: What teachers need to know* (2nd ed.). Needham Heights, MA: Allyn & Bacon.

Popham, W. J. (2000). *Modern educational measurement: Practical guidelines for educational leaders* (3rd ed.). Boston: Allyn & Bacon.

Popham, W. J. (2002). *Classroom assessment: What teachers need to know* (3rd ed.). Boston: Allyn & Bacon.

Popper, K. K. (1972). *Objective knowledge: An evolutionary approach.* Oxford, England, Clarendon.

Postman, N. (1993). *Technopoly: The surrender of culture to technology.* New York: Vintage Books.

Pratt, M. W., Golding, G., Hunter, W. J., & Norris, J. (1988). From inquiry to judgment: Age and sex differences in patterns of adult moral thinking and information-seeking. *International Journal of Aging and Human Development, 27,* 109–124.

Prawat, R. S. (1989). Promoting access to knowledge, strategy, and disposition in students: A research synthesis. *Review of Educational Research, 59,* 1–41.

Pressley, M. (1995). *Advanced educational psychology for educators, researchers, and policymakers.* New York: HarperCollins.

Pressley, M., & Afflerbach, P. A. (1995). *Verbal protocols of reading: The nature of constructively responsive reading.* Hillsdale, NJ: Lawrence Erlbaum.

Pressley, M., Goodchild, F., Fleet, J., Zajchowski, R., & Evans, E. D. (1989). The challenges of classroom strategy instruction. *Elementary School Journal, 89,* 301–342.

Pressley, M., Levin, J. R., & Delaney, H. D. (1982). The mnemonic keyword method. *Review of Educational Research, 52,* 61–92.

Pressley, M., & McCormick, C. B. (1995). *Cognition, teaching, and assessment.* New York: HarperCollins.

Prinz, P. M. (1991). Literacy and language development within microcomputer-videodisc-assisted contexts. *Journal of Childhood Communication Disorders, 14,* 67–80.

Private Universe [Videotape]. Columbus, OH: Merrill.

Pugach, M. C., & Johnson, L. J. (1995). *Collaborative practitioners, collaborative schools.* Denver: Love.

Pugh, S. L., Pawan, F., & Antommarchi, C. (2000). Academic literacy and the new college learner. In R. F. Flippo & D. C. Caverly (Eds.), *Handbook of college reading and study strategy research* (pp. 25–42). Mahwah, NJ: Lawrence Erlbaum.

Purves, A. (1998). Flies in the web of hypertext. In D. Reinking, M. C. NcKenna, L. D. Labbo, & R. D Kieffer (Eds.), *Handbook of literacy and technology: Transformations in a post-typographic world* (pp. 235–251). Mahwah, NJ: Lawrence Erlbaum.

Quellmalz, E. S., & Hoskyn, J. (1997). Classroom assessment of reasoning strategies. In G. D. Phye (Ed.), *Handbook of classroom assessment: Learning, adjustment, and achievement.* San Diego, CA: Academic Press.

Rafoth, B. A. (1988). Discourse community: Where writers, readers, and texts come together. In B. A. Rafoth & D. L. Rubin (Eds.), *The social construction of written communication* (pp. 131–146). New York: Oxford University Press.

Randhawa, B. S., Beamer, J. E., & Lundberg, I. (1993). Role of mathematics self-efficacy in the structural model of mathematics achievement. *Journal of Educational Psychology, 85*(1), 41–48.

Randi, J., & Corno, L. (2001). Teacher innovations in self-regulated learning. In M. Boekaerts, P. R. Pintrich, & M. Zeidner (Eds.), *Handbook of self-regulation* (pp. 651–686). San Diego, CA: Academic Press.

Raven, J. C. (1940). *Progressive matrices.* London: H. K. Lewis.

Raynor, J. O. (1981). Future orientation and achievement motivation: Toward a theory of personality functioning and change. In G. d'Ydewalle & W. Lens (Eds.), *Cognition in human motivation and learning* (pp. 199–231). Hillsdale, NJ: Lawrence Erlbaum.

Reese, H. W., & Overton, W. F. (1970). Models of development and theories of development. In L. R. Goulet & P. B Baltes (Eds.), *Life-span development psychology: Research and theory.* New York: Academic Press.

Reeve, J. (1996). *Motivating others: Nurturing inner motivational resources.* Boston: Allyn & Bacon.

Reeves, L. M., Weisberg, R. W. (1994). The role of content and abstract information in analogical transfer. *Psychological Bulletin, 115*(3), 381–400.

Rehder, B.(1999). Detecting unsolvable algebra word problems. Journal of Educational Psychology, *91,* 669–683.

Reimann, P., & Schult, T. J. (1996). Turning examples into cases: Acquiring knowledge structure for analogical problem solving. *Educational Psychologist,31*(2), 123–132.

Reinking, D. (1998). Introduction: Synthesizing technological transformations of literacy in a post-typographic world. In D. Reinking, M. C. McKenna, L. D. Labbo, & R. D. Kieffer (Eds.), *Handbook of literacy and technology: Transformations in a post-typographic world* (pp. xi–xxx). Mahwah, NJ: Lawrence Erlbaum.

Reinking, D., Labbo, L. L., & McKenna, M. (1997). Navigating the changing landscape of literacy: Current theory and research in computer-based reading and writing. In J. Flood, S. B. Heath, & D. Lapp (Eds.), *Handbook of research on teaching literacy through the communicative and visual arts* (pp. 77–92). New York: Macmillan.

Reinking, D., McKenna, M. C., Labbo, L. D., & Kieffer, R. D. (1998). *Handbook of literacy and technology: Transformations in a post-typographic world.* Mahwah, NJ: Lawrence Erlbaum.

Reio, T. G., Jr., & Wiswell, A. (2000). Field investigation of the relationship between adult curiosity, workplace learning and job performance. *Human Resource Development Quarterly, 11*(1), 1–36.

Renzulli, J. S. (1986). *Systems and models for developing programs for the gifted and talented.* Mansfield, CT: Creative Learning Press.

Resnick, L. B. (1991). Shared cognition: Thinking as social practice. In L. B. Resnick, J. M. Levine, & S. D. Teasley (Eds.), *Perspectives on socially shared cognition* (pp. 1–20). Washington, DC: American Psychological Association.

Resnick, L. B., Levine, J. M., & Teasley, S. D. (1991). *Perspectives on socially shared cognition.* Washington, DC: American Psychological Association.

Resnick, L. B., & Resnick, D. P. (1990). Tests as standards of achievement in school. In *The uses of standardized tests in American education* (pp. 63–80). Princeton, NJ: Educational Testing Service.

Resnick, L. B., & Resnick, D. P. (1991). Assessing the thinking curriculum: New tools for education reform. In B. R. Gifford & M. C. O'Connor (Eds.), *Changing assessment: Alternative views of aptitude, achievement, and instruction* (pp. 37–75). Boston: Kluwer.

Resnick, M., & Rusk, N. (1996). The Computer Clubhouse: Preparing for life in a digital world. *IBM Systems Journal, 35,* 431–440.

Reusser, K. (1993). Tutoring systems and pedagogical theory: Representational tools for understanding, planning, and reflection in problem solving. In S. P. Lajoie & S. J.Derry (Eds.), *Computers as cognitive tools* (pp. 143–177). Mahwah, NJ: Lawrence Erlbaum.

Reynolds, A. J., & Walberg, H. J. (1991). A structural model of science achievement and attitude: An extension to high school. *Journal of Educational psychology, 84,* 371–382.

Reynolds, C. R. (1982). The fallacy of two years below grade level for age as a diagnostic criterion for reading disorders. *Journal of School Psychology, 19,* 350–358.

Reynolds, C. R. (1994). *Cognitive assessment: An interdisciplinary dialogue.* New York: Plenum.

Reynolds, R. E. (1992). Selective attention and prose learning: Theoretical and empirical research. *Educational Psychology Review, 4,* 345–391.

Reynolds, R. E., & Shirey, L. L. (1988). The role of attention in studying and learning. In C. E. Weinstein, E. T. Goetz, & P. A. Alexander (Eds.), *Learning and study strategies: Issues in assessment, instruction, and evaluation* (pp. 77–100). San Diego, CA: Academic Press.

Reynolds, R. E., Sinatra, G. M., & Jetton, T. L. (1996). Views of knowledge acquisition and representation: A continuum from experience centered to mind centered. *Educational Psychologist, 31,* 93–104.

Rich, F. (1996, February 10). The idiot chip. *New York Times,* Op.ed., p. 23.

Rieber, L. P. (1992). Computer-based microworlds: A bridge between constructivism and direct instruction. *Educational Technology Research and Development, 40,* 93–106.

Rieber, L. P. (1993). A pragmatic view of instructional technology. In K. Tobin (Ed.), *The practice of constructivism in science education* (pp. 193–212). Washington, DC: AAAS Press.

Rigby, C. S., Deci, E. L., Patrick, B. C., & Ryan, R. M. (1992). Beyond the intrinsic-extrinsic dichotomy: Self-determination in motivation and learning. *Motivation and Emotion, 16*(3), 165–185.

Riley, M. S., & Greeno, J. G. (1988). Developmental analysis of understanding language about quantities and of solving problems. *Cognition and Instruction, 5,* 49–101.

Riley, M. S., Greeno, J. G., & Heller, J. I. (1983). Development of children's problem solving ability in arithmetic. In H. P. Ginsberg (Ed.), *The development of mathematical thinking* (pp. 153–196). San Diego, CA: Academic Press.

Risko, V. J., Alvarez, M. C., & Fairbanks, M. M. (1991). External factors that influence study. In R. F. Flippo & D. C. Caverly (Eds.), *Teaching reading and study strategies at the college level* (pp. 195–236). Newark, DE: International Reading Association.

Risko, V. J., Fairbanks, M. M., & Alvarez, M. C. (1991). Internal factors that influence study. In R. F. Flippo & D. C. Caverly (Eds.), *Teaching reading and study strategies at the college level* (pp. 237–293). Newark, DE: International Reading Association.

Roberton, M. A. (1984). Changing motor patterns during childhood. In J. R. Thomas (Ed.), *Motor development during childhood and adolescence* (pp. 48–90). Minneapolis, MN: Burgess.

Robinson, D., & Kiewra, K. A. (1995). Visual argument: Graphic organizers are superior to outlines in improving learning from text. *Journal of Educational Psychology, 87,* 455–467

Roblyer, M. D. (2001). *Ten first steps on the Internet: A learning journey for teachers.* Upper Saddle River, NJ: Merrill/Prentice Hall.

Rock, D. A., Owings, J. A., & Lee, R. (1994). *Changes in math proficiency between eighth and tenth grades.* Washington, DC: National Center for Educational Statistics.

Rogoff, B. (1990). *Apprenticeship in thinking: Cognitive development in social context.* New York: Oxford University Press.

Rogoff, B. (2000). *Culture and development.* New York: Oxford University Press.

Rogoff, B., & Gauvain, M. (1986). A method for the analysis of patterns illustrated with data on mother-child instructional interaction. In J. Valsiner (Ed.), *The role of the individual subject on scientific psychology* (pp. 261–290). New York: Plenum.

Romance, N. R., & Vitale, M. R. (1992). A curriculum strategy that expands time for in-depth elementary science instruction by using science-based reading strategies: Effects of a year-long study in grade four. *Journal of Research in Science Teaching, 29,* 545–554.

Roschelle, J. (1992). Learning by collaborating: Convergent conceptual change. *Journal of Learning Sciences, 2,* 235–276.

Rosenberg, M., & Simmons, R. (1971). *Black and white self-esteem: The urban school child.* Washington, DC: American Sociological Association.

Rosenshine, B. (1997, March). The case for explicit, teacher-led, cognitive strategy instruction. In M. F. Graves (Chair), *What sort of comprehension strategy instruction should schools provide?* Symposium presented at the annual meeting of the American Educational Research Association, Chicago.

Rosenshine, B., & Meister, C. (1994). Reciprocal teaching: A review of the research. *Review of Educational Research, 64,* 479–530.

Ross, S. M., McCormick, D., & Krisak, N. (1986). Adapting the thematic content of mathematical problems to student interests: Individualized versus group-based strategies. *Journal of Educational Research, 79,* 245–252.

Roth, K. J. (1990). Developing meaningful conceptual understanding in science. In B. F. Jones & L. Idol (Eds.), *How metacognition can promote academic learning and instruction* (pp. 139–175). Hillsdale, NJ: Lawrence Erlbaum.

Rotter, J. B. (1954). *Social learning and clinical psychology.* New York: Prentice Hall.

Rousseau, J. J. (1911). *Emile: Or on education.* London: Dent. (Original published 1762)

Rubin, D. C., & Kozin, M. (1984). Vivid memories. *Cognition, 16,* 81–95.

Rubin, K. H., Fein, G. G., & Vandenberg, B. (1983). Play. In E. M. Hetherington (Ed.), *Handbook of child psychology: Vol. 4. Socialization, personality, and social development* (4th ed., pp. 693–744). New York: Wiley.

Rubinstein, J. S., Meyer, D. E., Evans, J. E. (2001). Executive control of cognitive processes in task switching. *Journal of Experimental Psychology: Human Perception and Performance, 27,* 763–797.

Ruble, D. N., Boggiano, A. K., Feldman, N. S., & Loebl, J. H. (1980). Developmental analysis of the role of social comparison in self-evaluation. *Developmental Psychology, 16,* 105–115.

Rubtsov, V. V., & Margolis, A. A. (1996). Activity-oriented models of information-based instructional environments. In S. T. Kerr (Ed.), *Technology and the future of schooling: Ninety-fifth yearbook of the National Society for the Study of Education* (pp. 176–199). Chicago: National Society for the Study of Education.

Rumelhart, D. E. (1980). Schemata: The building blocks of cognition. In R. J. Spiro, B. C. Bruce, & W. F. Brewer (Eds.), *Theoretical issues in reading comprehension* (pp. 33–58). Hillsdale, NJ: Lawrence Erlbaum.

Rumelhart, D. E., & Norman, D. A. (1981). Accretion, tuning, and restructuring: Three modes of learning. In J. W. Cotton & R. Klatzy (Eds.), *Semantic factors in cognition* (pp. 37–60). Hillsdale, NJ: Lawrence Erlbaum.

Rutherford, F. J., & Ahlgren, A. (1990). *Science for all Americans.* New York: Oxford University Press.

Ryan, R. M., & Deci, E. L. (2000a). Intrinsic and extrinsic motivations: Classic definitions and new directions. *Contemporary Educational Psychology, 25,* 54–67.

Ryan, R. M., & Deci, E. L. (2000b). Self-determination theory and the facilitation of intrinsic motivation, social development, and well-being. *American Psychologist, 55,* 68–78.

Ryle, G. (1949). *The concept of mind.* London: Hutchinson.

S. W. C., West, R. F., & Stanovich, K. E. (1999). The domain specificity and generality of belief bias: Searching for a generalizable critical thinking skill. *Journal of Educational Psychology, 91,* 497–510.

Sacks, P. (1999). *Standardized minds: The high price of America's testing culture and what we can do to change it.* Cambridge, MA: Perseus Books.

Sacks, P. (2000). *Standardized minds: The high price of America's testing culture and what we can do to change it.* Cambridge, MA: Perseus.

Sadker, M., & Sadker, D. (1994). *Failing at fairness: How America's schools cheat girls.* New York: Scribner.

Sadker, M., Sadker, D., & Klein, S. (1991). The issue of gender in elementary and secondary education. *Review of Research in Education, 17,* 269–334.

Sadoski, M., Kealy, W. A., Goetz, E. T., & Paivio, A. (1997). Concreteness and imagery effects in the written composition of definitions. *Journal of Educational Psychology, 89,* 518–526.

Sailor, W. (1991). Special education in the restructured school. *Remedial and Special Education, 12*(6), 8–22.

Salisbury, D. J. (1995). Does Cincinnati need another bridge? *Learning and Leading with Technology, 23,* 17–19.

Salomon, G. (1993a). *Distributed cognition: Psychological and educational considerations.* Cambridge, England: Cambridge University Press.

Salomon, G. (1993b). On the nature of pedagogic computer tools: The case of the writing partner. In S. P. Lajoie & S. J. Derry (Eds.), *Computers as cognitive tools* (pp. 179–196). Mahwah, NJ: Lawrence Erlbaum.

Salomon, G. (1995). Reflections on the field of educational psychology by the outgoing journal editor. *Educational Psychology, 30*(3), 105–108.

Salomon, G., Globerson, T., & Guterman, E. (1989). The computer as a zone of proximal development: Internalizing reading-related metacognitions from a reading partner. *Journal of Educational Psychology, 81,* 620–627.

Salomon, G., & Perkins, D. N. (1989). Rocky roads to transfer: Rethinking mechanisms of a neglected phenomenon. *Educational Psychologist, 24,* 113–142.

Salomon, G., & Perkins, D. N. (1996). Learning in wonderland: What do computers really offer education? In S. T. Kerr (Ed.), *Technology and the future of schooling: Ninety-fifth yearbook of the National Society for the Study of Education* (pp. 111–130). Chicago: National Society for the Study of Education.

Salomon, G., Perkins, D. N., & Globerson, T. (1991). Partners in cognition: Extending human intelligence with intelligent technologies. *Educational Researcher, 20*(1), 2–9.

Salovey, P., & Mayer, J. D. (1990). Emotional intelligence. *Imagination, Cognition, and Personality, 9*(1990), 185–211.

Santrock, J. W. (2001). *Educational psychology.* Boston: McGraw Hill.

Sarnacki, R. E. (1979). An examination of test-wiseness in the cognitive domain. *Review of Educational Research, 49,* 252–279.

Satinover, J. (2001). *The quantum brain: The search for freedom and the next generation of man.* New York: John Wiley.

Sattler, J. (1992). *Assessment of children* (3rd ed.). San Diego, CA: Jerome M. Sattler.

Scardamalia, M., Bereiter, C., McLearn, R. S., Swallow, J., & Woodruff, E. (1989). Computer-supported intentional learning environments. *Journal of Educational Computing Research, 5,* 51–68.

Scar, S., Weinberg, R. A., & Waldman, I. D. (1993). IQ correlations in transracial adoptive families. *Intelligence, 17,* 541–555.

Schallert, D. L., Benton, R., Dodson, M., Lissi, M., Amador, N., & Reed, J. (1996, December). *Conversational indicators of social construction of knowledge in oral and written classroom discussion of reading assignments.* Paper presented at the annual meeting of the National Reading Conference, Charleston, SC.

Schank, R. C. (1984). *The cognitive computer.* Reading, MA: Addison-Wesley.

Schank, R. C., & Abelson, R. (1977). *Scripts, plans, goals, and understanding.* Hillsdale, NJ: Lawrence Erlbaum.

Schauble, L. (1990). Belief revision in children: The role of prior knowledge and strategies for generating evidence. *Journal of Experimental Child Psychology, 49,* 31–57.

Schellings, G. L. M., & van Hout-Wolters, B. H. A. M. (1995). Main points in an instructional text, as identified by students and their teachers. *Reading Research Quarterly, 30,* 742–756.

Schellings, G. L. M., van Hout-Wolters, B. H. A. M., & Vermunt, J. D. (1996). Selection of main points in instructional texts: Influences of task demands. *Journal of Literacy Research, 28,* 355–378.

Schickedanz, J. A., Schickedanz, D. I, Forsyth, P. D., & Forsyth, G. A. (2001). *Understanding children and adolescents* (4th ed.). Boston: Allyn & Bacon.

Schoenfeld, A. H. (1985). *Mathematical problem solving.* San Diego, CA: Academic Press.

Schoenfeld, A. H. (1988). When good teaching leads to bad results: The disasters of "well-taught" mathematics courses. *Educational Psychologist, 23,* 145–166.

Schommer, M. (1990). Effects of beliefs about the nature of knowledge on comprehension. *Journal of Educational Psychology, 82,* 498–504.

Schommer, M. (1993). Epistemological development and academic performance among secondary students. *Journal of Educational Psychology, 85,* 406–411.

Schommer, M., Crouse, A., & Rhodes, N. (1992). Epistemological beliefs and mathematical text comprehension: Believing it is simple does not make it so. *Journal of Educational Psychology, 84,* 435–443.

Schön, D. (1983). *The reflective practitioner: How professionals think in action.* New York: Basic Books.

Schön, D. A. (1988). Designing: Rules, types, and words. *Design Studies, 9,* 181–190.

Schraw, G., Bruning, R., & Svoboda, C. (1995). Sources of situational interest. *Journal of Reading Behavior, 27,* 1–17.

Schunk, D. H. (1991). Self-efficacy and academic motivation. *Educational Psychologist, 26,* 207–231.

Schunk, D. H. (2000a). Coming to terms with motivation constructs. *Contemporary Educational Psychology, 25,* 116–119.

Schunk, D. H. (2000b). *Learning theories: An educational perspective* (3rd ed.). Upper Saddle River, NJ: Merrill/Prentice Hall.

Schunn, C. D., & Dunbar, K. (1996). Priming, analogy, and awareness in complex reasoning. *Memory & Cognition, 24,* 271–284.

Schutz, P. A., & Lanchart, S. L. (2002). Introduction: Emotions in education. *Educational Psychologist, 37*(2), 67–69.

Schwab, J. J. (1964). Structure of the disciplines: Meanings and significances. In G. W. Ford & L. Pugno (Eds.), *The structure of knowledge and the curriculum* (pp. 6–30). Chicage: Rand McNally.

Segal, H. P. (1996). The American ideology of technological progress: Historical perspectives. In S. T. Kerr (Ed.), *Technology and the future of schooling: Ninety-fifth yearbook of the National Society for the Study of Education* (pp. 28–48). Chicago: National Society for the Study of Education.

Seifert, K. L., Hoffnung, R. J., & Hoffnung, M. (1997). *Lifespan development.* Boston: Houghton Mifflin.

Seixas, P. (1996). Conceptualizing the growth of historical understanding. In D. Olson & N. Torrence (Eds.), *The handbook of education and human development* (pp. 765–783). Oxford: Blackwell.

Seldin, S. (1999). *Inheriting shame: The story of eugenics and racism in America.* New York: Teachers College Press.

Seligman, M. E. P. (1975). *Helplessness: On depression, development, and death.* San Francisco: Freeman.

Seligman, M. E. P., & Csikszentmihalyi, M. (2000). Positive psychology: An introduction. *American Psychologist, 55,* 5–14.

Semmel, M. I., Gerber, M. M., & MacMillan, D. L. (1994). Twenty-five years after Dunn's article: A legacy of policy analysis research in special education. *Journal of Special Education, 27,* 481–495.

Senge, P. A. (1990). *The fifth discipline: The art and practice of the learning organization.* New York: Currency/Doubleday.

Sfard, A. (1998). On two metaphors for learning and the dangers of choosing just one. *Educational Researcher, 27*(2), 4–13.

Shah, P., Mayer, R. E., & Hegarty, M. (1999). Graphs as aids to knowledge construction: Signaling techniques for guiding the process of graph comprehension. *Journal of Educational Psychology, 91,* 690–702.

Sharan, S. (1994a). Cooperative learning and the teacher. In S. Sharan (Ed.), *Handbook of cooperative learning methods* (pp. 136–348). Westport, CT: Praeger.

Sharan, S. (1994b). *Handbook of cooperative learning methods.* Westport, CT: Praeger.

Sharan, Y., & Sharan, S. (1992). *Expanding cooperative learning through group investigation.* New York: Teachers' College Press.

Shell, D. F., Colvin, C., & Bruning, R. (1995). Self-efficacy, attribution, and outcome expectancy mechanisms in reading and writing achievement: Grade-level and achievement-level differences. *Journal of Educational Psychology, 87*(3), 386–398.

Shepard, L. A. (1989). Why we need better assessments. *Educational Leadership, 46*(7), 4–6.

Shepard, L. A. (1993). Evaluating test validity. *Review of Research in Education, 19,* 405–450.

Shepard, L. A. (1995). Using assessment to improve learning. *Educational Leadership, 54*(5), 38–43.

Shulman, L. S., & Quinlan, K. M. (1996). The comparative psychology of school subjects. In D. C. Berliner & R. C. Calfee (Eds.), *Handbook of educational psychology* (pp. 399–422). New York: Simon & Schuster Macmillan.

Shweder, R. A., Mahapatra, M., & Miller, J. G. (1990). Culture and moral development. In J. W. Stigler, R. A. Shweder, & G. Herdt (Eds.), *Cultural psychology: Essays on comparative human development.* Cambridge, England: Cambridge University Press.

Siegler, R. S. (1991). *Children's thinking* (2nd ed.). Englewood Cliffs, NJ: Prentice Hall.

Siegler, R. S. (1998). *Children's thinking* (3rd ed.). Upper Saddle River, NJ: Prentice Hall.

Sigelman, C. K., & Shaffer, D. R. (1995). *Lifespan human development* (2nd ed.). Pacific Grove, CA: Brooks/Cole.

Silva, T., & Nicholls, J. G. (1993). College students as writing theorists: Goals and beliefs about the causes of success. *Contemporary Educational Psychology, 18,* 281–293.

Silver, E. A., Shapiro, L. J., & Deutsch, A. (1993). Sense making and the solution of division problems involving remainders: An examination of middle school students' solution of processes and their interpretations of solutions. *Journal of Research in Mathematics Education, 24*(2), 117–135.

Simon, H. A. (1978). Information-processing theory of human problem solving. In W. K. Estes (Ed.), *Handbook of learning and cognitive processes* (pp. 271–295). Hillsdale, NJ: Lawrence Erlbaum.

Simon, H. A. (1989). *Models of thought* (Vol. 2). New Haven, CT: Yale University Press.

Simon, T. J., Hespos, S., & Rochat, P. (1995). Do infants understand simple arithmetic? A replication of Wynn (1992). *Cognitive Development, 20,* 253–269.

Simpson, M. L., & Randall, S. N. (2000). Vocabulary development. In R. F. Flippo & D. C. Caverly (Eds.), *Teaching reading and study strategies at the college level* (pp. 43–73). Newark, DE: International Reading Association.

Sinatra, G. M. (2002). Motivational, social, and contextual aspects of conceptual change: A commentary. In M. Limón & L. Mason (Eds.), *Reconsidering conceptual change: Issues in theory and practice* (pp. 187–197). Dordrecht, Netherlands: Kluwer.

Sinatra, G. M., & Pintrich, P. R. (2003). *Intentional conceptual change.* Mahwah, NJ: Lawrence Erlbaum.

Singley, M. K., & Anderson, J. R. (1989). *The transfer of cognitive skill.* Cambridge, MA: Harvard University Press.

Skinner, B. F. (1953). *Science and human behavior.* New York: Macmillan.

Skinner, B. F. (1958). *The technology of teaching.* New York: Appleton-Century-Croft.

Skinner, B. F. (1968). *The technology of teaching.* New York: Appleton-Century-Crofts.

Skinner, B. F. (1984). The shame of American education. *American Psychologist, 39,* 947–954.

Skinner, E. A., & Belmont, M. J. (1993). Motivation in the classroom: Reciprocal effects of teacher behavior and student engagement across the school year. *Journal of Educational Psychology, 85*(4), 571–581.

Slavin, R. E. (1978). Student teams and comparison among equals: Effects on academic performance and student attitudes. *Journal of Educational Psychology, 70,* 532–538.

Slavin, R. E. (1990). Ability grouping and student achievement in secondary schools: A best-evidence synthesis. *Review of Educational Research, 60,* 471–499.

Slavin, R. E. (1994). *Using student team learning* (4th ed.). Baltimore: Johns Hopkins University, Center for Research on Elementary and Middle Schools.

Slavin, R. E. (1995). *Cooperative learning: Theory, research, and practice* (2nd ed.). Boston: Allyn & Bacon.

Slavin, R. E., Karweit, N. L., & Madden, N. A. (1989). *Effective programs for students at risk.* Needham Heights, MA: Allyn & Bacon.

Slavin, R. E., Leavey, M. B., & Madden, N. A. (1985). *Team assisted individualization: Mathematics.* Watertown, MA: Charlesbridge.

Slavin, R. E., & Oickle, E. (1981). Effects of cooperative learning teams on student achievement and race relations: Treatment by race interactions. *Sociology of Education, 54,* 174–180.

Slusher, M. P., & Anderson, C. A. (1996). Using causal persuasive arguments to change beliefs and teach new information: The mediating role of explanation availability and evaluation bias in the acceptance of knowledge. *Journal of Educational Psychology, 88*(1), 110–122.

Smith, M. L., & Rottenberg, C. (1991). Unintended consequences of external testing in elementary schools. *Educational Measurement: Issues and Practice, 10*(4), 7–11.

Snow, R. E. (1981). Toward a theory of aptitude for learning: Fluid and crystallized abilities and their correlates. In M. P. Friedman, J. P. Das, & N. O'Connor (Eds.), *Intelligence and learning* (pp. 345–362). Hilldale, NJ: Lawrence Erlbaum.

Snow, R. E. (1989). Aptitude-treatment interaction as a framework for research on individual differences in learning. In P. L. Ackerman, R. J. Sternberg, & R. Glaser (Eds.), *Learning and individual differences: Advances in theory and research* (pp. 13–59). New York: Freeman.

Snow, R. E., Corno, L., & Jackson, D. (1996). Individual differences in affective and conative functions. In D. C. Berliner & R. C. Calfee (Eds.), *Handbook of educational psychology* (pp. 242–310). New York: Macmillan.

Southerland, S. A., & Sinatra, G. M. (2003). Learning about biological evolution: A special case of intentional conceptual change. In G. M. Sinatra & P. R. Pintrich (Eds.), *Intentional conceptual change* (pp. 317–345). Mahwah, NJ: Lawrence Erlbaum.

Spearman, C. (1904). "General intelligence," objectively determined and measured. *American Journal of Psychology, 15,* 201–209.

Spearman, C. (1923). *The nature of "intelligence" and the principles of cognition.* London: Macmillan.

Spielberger, C. D. (1998). Foreword. In N. M. Lambert & B. L. McCombs (Eds.), *How students learn: Reforming schools through learner-centered education* (pp. ix–xi). Washington, DC: American Psychological Association.

Spiro, R. J., Feltovich, P. J., Jacobson, M. J., & Coulson, R. L. (1992). Cognitive flexibility, constructivism, and hypertext: Random access instruction for advanced knowledge acquisition in ill-structured domains. In T. M. Duffy & D. H. Jonassen (Eds.), *Constructivism and the technology of instruction: A conversation* (pp. 57–75). Cambridge, England: Cambridge University Press.

Spiro, R. J., & Jehng, J. C. (1990). Cognitive flexibility and hypertext: Theory and technology for the nonlinear and multidimensional traversal of complex subject matter. In D. Nix & R. J. Spiro (Eds.), *Cognition, education, and multimedia* (pp. 163–205). Hillsdale, NJ: Lawrence Erlbaum.

Spoehr, K. T., & Spoehr, L. W. (1994). Learning to think historically. *Educational Psychologist, 29*(2), 71–77.

Springer, S., & Deutsch, G. (1985). *Left brain. Right brain.* New York: W. H. Freeman.

Sprinthall, R. C. (1997). *Basic statistical analysis* (5th ed.). Boston: Allyn & Bacon.

Spurlin, J. E., Dansereau, D. F., Larson, C. O., & Brooks, L. W. (1984). Cooperative learning strategies in processing descriptive text: Effects of role and activity level of the learner. *Cognition and Instruction, 1,* 451–463.

Stainback, S., & Stainback, W. (1992). Schools as inclusive communities. In W. Stainback & S. Stainback (Eds.), *Controversial issues confronting special education: Divergent perspectives* (pp. 29–43). Boston: Allyn & Bacon.

Stanovich, K. E. (1986). Matthew effects in reading: Some consequences of individual differences in the acquisition of literacy. *Reading Research Quarterly, 21,* 360–407.

Stanovich, K. E. (1990). Concepts in developmental theories of reading skill: Cognitive resources, automaticity, and modularity. *Developmental Review, 10,* 72–100.

Staton, J., Shuy, R., Peyton, J., & Reed, L. (1988). *Dialogue journal communication: Classroom, linguistic, social and cognitive views.* Norwood, NJ: Ablex.

Steele, C. M. (1988). The psychology of self-affirmation: Sustaining the integrity of the self. In L. Berkowitz (Ed.), *Advances in experimental social psychology* (Vol. 21, pp. 261–302). New York: Academic Press.

Steele, C. M. (1997). A threat in the air: How stereotypes shape intellectual identity and performance. *American Psychologist, 52,* 613–629.

Steffe, L. P., & D'Ambrosio, B. S. (1995). Toward a working model of constructivist teaching: A reaction to Simon. *Journal of Research in Mathematics Education, 26,* 146–159.

Stenmark, J. K. (1991). *Mathematics assessment: Myth, models, good questions, and practical suggestions.* Reston, VA: National Council of Teachers of Mathematics.

Sternberg, R. J. (1977). *Intelligence, information processing, and analogical reasoning: The componential analysis of human abilities.* Hillsdale, NJ: Lawrence Erlbaum.

Sternberg, R. J. (1985a). *Beyond IQ: A triarchic theory of human intelligence.* New York: Cambridge University Press.

Sternberg, R. J. (1985b). But it's a sad tale that begins at the end: A reply to Glaser. *American Psychologist, 40,* 571–573.

Sternberg, R. J. (1993). *Sternberg Triarchic Abilities Test.* Unpublished test.

Sternberg, R. J. (2000). Thinking. In A. E. Kazdin (Ed.), *Encyclopedia of psychology* (Vol. 8, pp. 68–71). New York: Oxford University Press.

Sternberg, R. J. (2003). Who is an expert student? *Educational Researcher, 32*(8), 5–9.

Sternberg, R. J., & Davidson, J. E. (1995). *The nature of insight.* Cambridge, MA: MIT Press.

Sternberg, R. J., & Frensch, P. A. (1996). Mechanisms of transfer. In D. K. Detterman & R. J. Sternberg (Eds.), *Transfer on trial: Intelligence, cognition, and instruction* (pp. 25–38). Norwood, NJ: Ablex.

Sternberg, R. J., & Wagner, R. K. (1986). *Practical intelligence.* Cambridge, England: Cambridge University Press.

Sternberg, R. J., & Williams, W. M. (2002). *Educational psychology.* Boston, Allyn & Bacon.

Stevens, R., & Hall, R. (1998). Disciplined perception: Learning to see in technoscience. In M. Lampert & M. L. Blunk (Eds.), *Talking mathematics in school: Studies of teaching and learning* (pp. 107–149). Cambridge, England: Cambridge University Press.

Stevens, R., Madden, N., Slavin, R., & Farnish, A. (1987). Cooperative integrated reading and composition: Two field experiments. *Reading Research Quarterly, 22,* 433–454.

Stevens, R. J., & Slavin, R. E. (1995). The cooperative elementary school: Effects of student's achievement, attitudes, and social relations. *American Educational Research Journal, 32,* 321–351.

Stewart, I. (1987). *The problem of mathematics.* Oxford, England: Oxford University Press.

Stiggins, R. J. (1991). Relevant classroom assessment training for teachers. *Educational Measurement: Issues and Practice, 10*(1), 7–12.

Stiggins, R. J. (1993). Teacher training in assessment: Overcoming the neglect. In S. Wise (Ed.), *Teacher training in assessment and measurement skills.* Lincoln, NE: Burso Institute.

Stiggins, R. J. (2001). *Student-involved classroom assessment* (3rd ed.). Upper Saddle River, NJ: Merrill/Prentice Hall.

Stipek, D. J. (1988). *Motivation to learn: From theory to practice.* Englewood Cliffs, NJ: Prentice Hall.

Stipek, D. J. (1993). *Motivation to learn: From theory to practice* (2nd ed.). Boston, MA: Allyn & Bacon.

Stipek, D. J. (1996). Motivation and instruction. In D. C. Berliner & R. C. Calfee (Eds.), *Handbook in educational psychology* (pp. 85–113). New York: Macmillan.

Stipek, D. J., & Gralinski, J. H. (1996). Children's beliefs about intelligence and school performance. *Journal of Educational Psychology, 88*(3), 397–407.

Stipek, D. J., & MacIver, D. (1989). Developmental change in children's assessment of intellectual competence. *Child Development, 60,* 521–538.

Storandt, M., & VandenBos, G. R. (1989). *The adult years: Continuity and change.* Washington, DC: American Psychological Association.

Streibel, M. (1986). A critical analysis of the use of computers in education. *Educational Communication and Technology Journal, 34*(3), 137–161.

Stuessy, C., Alexander, P. A., Kulm, G., & McBride, R. (1992). *Teachers as research partners: Teaching a problem-solving curriculum model that integrates mathematics and science.* Arlington, VA: National Science Foundation.

Suchman, L. A. (1987). *Plans and situated actions: The problem of human-machine communication.* Cambridge, England: Cambridge University Press.

Sutton, R. E. (1991). Equity and computers in the schools: A decade of research. *Review of Educational Research, 61,* 475–503.

Swaak, J., & de Jong, T. (1996). The assessment of intuitive knowledge acquired in simulation-based discovery environments. In P. Brna, A. Paiva, & J. Self (Eds.), *Euroaied: European Conference on Artificial Intelligence in Education* (pp. 31–37). Lisbon: Edicoes Colibri.

Tadlock, D. F. (1978). SQ3R: Why it works, based on an information processing theory of learning. *Journal of Reading, 22,* 110–112.

Talamini, J. T., & Page, C. H. (1973). *Sport and Society: An anthology.* Boston: Little Brown.

Tanner, D. E. (2001). *Assessing academic achievement.* Boston: Allyn & Bacon.

Tanner, J. M. (1990). *Foetus into man: Physical growth from conception to maturity* (2nd ed.). Cambridge, MA: Harvard University Press.

Tanner, J. M. (1991). *Adolescent growth spurt.* In R. M. Lerner, A. C. Peterson, & J. Brooks-Gunn (Eds.), *Encyclopedia of adolescence* (Vol. 1, pp. 419–424). New York: Garland.

Terry, P. W. (1933). How students review for objective and essay tests. *Elementary School Journal, 33,* 592–603.

Terwilliger, J. S. (1971). *Assigning grades to students.* Glenview, IL: Scott, Foresman.

Terwilliger, J. S. (1989). Classroom standard setting and grading practices. *Educational Measurement Issues and Practice, 8,* 15–19.

Thagard, P. (1991). Concepts and conceptual change. In J. H. Fetzer (Ed.), *Epistemology and cognition* (pp. 101–120). Dordrecht, Netherlands: Kluwer.

Thorndike, E. L. (1920). Intelligence and its uses. *Harper's Magazine, 140,* 227–235.

Thorndike, E. L. (1924). Mental discipline in high school studies. *Journal of Educational Psychology, 15,* 1–22.

Thorndike, E. L., & Woodworth, R. S. (1901). The influence of improvement in one mental function upon the efficiency of other functions. *Psychological Review, 8,* 247–261.

Thousand, J. S., Villa, R. A., & Nevin, A. I. (1994). *Creativity and collaborative learning: A practical guide for empowering students and teachers.* Baltimore: Paul H. Brookes.

Thurstone, L. L. (1938). Primary mental abilities. *Psychometric Monographs,* No. 1.

Tierney, R., & Damarin, S. (1998). Technology as enfranchisement and cultural development: Crisscrossing symbol systems, paradigm shifts, and social-cultural considerations. In D. Reinking, M. C. McKenna, L. D. Labbo, & R. D. Keiffer (Eds.), *Handbook of literacy and technology: Transformations in a post-typographic world* (pp. 253-268). Mahwah, NJ: Lawrence Erlbaum.

Torrance, E. P., & Safter, H. T. (1999). *Making the creative leap beyond. . . .* Buffalo, NY: Creative Education Foundation.

Toulmin, S. E. (1958). *The uses of argument.* Cambridge, England: Cambridge University Press.

Townsend, E. A., & Burke, P. J. (1975). *Using statistics in classroom instruction.* New York: Macmillan.

Traub, R. E. (1994). *Reliability for the social sciences: Theory and applications.* Thousand Oaks, CA: Sage.

Tschannen-Moran, M., & Woolfolk-Hoy, A. (2001). Teacher efficacy: Capturing an elusive construct. *Teaching and Teacher Education, 17,* 783–805.

Tschannen-Moran, M., Woolfolk-Hoy, A., & Hoy, W. K. (1998). Teacher efficacy: Its meaning and measure. *Review of Educational Research, 68,* 202–248.

Turnbull, A., Turnbull, R., Shank, M., & Leal, D. (1999a). *Creativity and collaborative learning: A practical guide for empowering students and teachers.* Baltimore: Paul H. Brookes.

Turnbull, A., Turnbull, R., Shank, M., & Leal, D. (1999b). *Exceptional lives: Special education in today's schools* (2nd ed.). Upper Saddle River, NJ: Merrill.

Turner, J. C., & Meyer, D. K. (2000). Studying and understanding the instructional contexts of classrooms: Using our past to forge our future. *Educational Psychologist, 35,* 69–85.

Turner, J. C., Midgley, C., Meyer, D. K., Gheen, M., Anderman, E. M., Kang, Y., & Patrick, H. (2002). The classroom environment and students' reports of avoidance strategies in mathematics: A multimethod study. *Journal of Educational Psychology, 94,* 88–106.

Urdan, T. C., & Maehr, M. L. (1995). Beyond a two-goal theory of motivation and achievement: A case for social goals. *Review of Educational Research, 65,* 213–243.

U.S. Congress, Office of Technology Assessment. (1988). *Power on! New tools for teaching and learning* (OTA_SET-379). Washington, DC: Author.

U.S. Congress, Office of Technology Assessment. (1993). *Adult literacy and new technologies: Tools for a lifetime* (OTA SET-550). Washington DC: Author.

U.S. Department of Commerce. (1995, July). *Falling through the net: A survey of the "have nots" in rural and urban America.* Washington, DC: Author.

U.S. Department of Commerce. (1999, July). *Falling through the net: Defining the digital divide.* Washington, DC: Author.

U.S. Department of Commerce. (2000, October). *Falling through the net: Toward digital inclusion.* Washington, DC: Author.

U.S. Department of Health and Human Services. (1994). *Creating a 21st century Head Start: Final report of the advisory committee on Head Start quality and expansion.* Washington, DC: U.S. Government Printing Office.

Valencia, S. W., & Calfee, R. (1991). The development and use of literacy portfolios for students, classes, and teachers. *Applied Measurement in Education. 4,* 333–345.

Valencia, S. W., Hiebert, E. H., & Afflerbach, P. P. (1994). *Authentic reading assessment: Practices and possibilities.* Newark, DE: International Reading Association.

VanSledright, B. (1996). Closing the gap between school and disciplinary history? *Advances in Research on Teaching* (Vol. 6, pp. 257–289). Greenwich, CT: JAI Press.

VanSledright, B. (1998). On the importance of historical positionality to thinking about and teaching history. *International Journal of Social Education, 12,* 1–18.

VanSledright, B. (2002). *In search of America's past: Learning to read history in elementary school.* New York: Teachers College Press.

VanSledright, B., & Alexander, P. A. (2002). *Historical knowledge, thinking, and beliefs: Evaluation component of the Corps of Historical Discovery Project* (#S215X010242). Washington, DC: U.S. Department of Education.

VanSledright, B., & Frankes, L. (1998). Literature's place in learning history and science. In C. Hynd (Ed.), *Learning from text across conceptual domains* (pp. 177–138). Mahwah, NJ: Lawrence Erlbaum.

Vasquez, J. A. (1993). Teaching to the distinctive traits of minority students. In K. M. Cauley, F. Linder, & J. H. McMillan (Eds.), *Annual editions: Educational psychology 93/94.* Guilford, CT: Dushkin.

von Glasersfeld, E. (1991). *Radical constructivism in mathematics education.* Dordrecht, Netherlands: Kluwer.

Vosniadou, S. E. (1994). Capturing and modeling the process of conceptual change. *Learning and Instruction, 4,* 45–69.

Vosniadou, S. E. (2002). On the nature of naive physics. In M. Limón & L. Mason (Eds.), *Reconsidering conceptual change: Issues in theory and practice* (pp. 61–76). Dordrecht, Netherlands: Kluwer.

Vosniadou, S. E. (2003). Exploring the relationships between conceptual change and intentional learning. In G. M. Sinatra & P. R. Pintrich (Eds.), *Intentional conceptual change* (pp. 377–406). Mahwah, NJ: Lawrence Erlbaum.

Vosniadou, S. E., & Brewer, W. F. (1987). Theories of knowledge restructuring in development. *Review of Educational Research, 57,* 51–67.

Vosniadou, S. E., & Brewer, W. F. (1992). Mental models of the earth: A study of conceptual change in childhood. *Cognitive Psychology, 24,* 535–585.

Vygotsky, L. S. (1962). *Thought and language.* Cambridge, MA: MIT Press.

Vygotsky, L. S. (1978). *Mind in society.* Cambridge, MA: Harvard University Press.

Vygotsky, L. S. (1986). *Thought and language* (A. Kozulin, Trans.). Cambridge, MA: MIT Press. (Original work published in 1934)

Vygotsky, L. S. (1987). Thinking and speech. (N. Minick, Trans.). In R. W. Rieber, A. S. Carton (Eds.), *The collected works of L. S. Vygotsky: Vol. 1. Problems of general psychology* (pp. 37–285). New York: Plenum. (Original work published in 1934).

Wade, S. E. (1992). How interest affects learning from text. In K. A. Renninger, S. Hidi, & A. Krapp (Eds.), *The role of interest in learning and development* (pp. 255–277). Hillsdale, NJ: Lawrence Erlbaum.

Wade, S. E., Buxton, W. M., & Kelly, M. (1999). Using think-alouds to examine reader-text interest. *Reading Research Quarterly, 34,* 194-216.

Wade, S. E., Thompson, A., & Watkins, W. (1994). The role of belief systems in authors' and readers' constructions of texts. In R. Garner & P. A. Alexander (Eds.), *Beliefs about text and instruction with text* (pp. 265–293). Hillsdale, NJ: Lawrence Erlbaum.

Walker, L. J. (1989). A longitudinal study of moral reasoning. *Child Development, 60,* 157–166.

Walker, S. N., Sechrist, K. R., & Pender, N. J. (1987). The health-promoting lifestyle profile: Development and psychometric characteristics. *Nursing Journal, 36,* 76–81.

Walsh, P. (1999, Sept. 5). Out teachers' ed: Another week of hot air. *Washington Post.*

Walther, J., & Tidwell, L. (1996). When is mediated communication not interpersonal? In K. Galvin & P. Cooper (Eds.), *Making connections: Readings in relational communication* (pp. 300–307). Los Angeles: Roxbury.

Wason, P. (1966). Reasoning. In B. M. Foss (Ed.), *New horizons in psychology.* London: Penguin.

Watson, J. B. (1913). Psychology as the behaviorist views it. *Psychological Review, 20,* 158–177.

Watson, J. B. (1924). *Behaviorism.* Chicago: University of Chicago Press.

Watson, J. B. (1926). What the nursery has to say about instincts. In C. Murchinson (Ed.), *Psychologies of 1925.* Worchester, MA: Clark University Press.

Watson, J. B. (1930). *Behaviorism* (2nd ed.). Chicago: University of Chicago Press.

Webb, N. M. (1989). Peer interaction and learning in small groups. *International Journal of Educational Research, 13,* 21–40.

Webb, N. M. (1991). Task-related verbal interaction and mathematics learning in small groups. *Journal for Research in Mathematics Education, 22,* 366–389.

Webb, N. M., & Palincsar, A. S. (1996). Group processes in the classroom. In D. C. Berliner & R. C. Calfee (Eds.), *Handbook of educational psychology* (pp. 841–873). New York: Macmillan.

Weiner, B. (1972). *Theories of motivation: From mechanism to cognition.* Chicago: Markham.

Weiner, B. (1980). Cognitive (attributional)-emotion-action model of motivated behavior: An analysis of judgment of help-giving. *Journal of Personality and Social Psychology, 39,* 186–200.

Weiner, B. (1986). *An attributional theory of motivation and emotion.* New York: Springer-Verlag.

Weiner, B. (1991). On perceiving the other person as responsible. In R. A. Dienstbier (Ed.), *Nebraska symposium on motivation* (Vol. 38, pp. 165–198). Lincoln: University of Nebraska Press.

Weiner, B. (1994). Ability versus effort revisited: The moral determinants of achievement evaluation and achievement as a moral system. *Educational Psychologist, 29,* 163–172.

Weiner, B., Frieze, I., Kukla, A., Reed, L., Rest, S., & Rosenbaum, R. (1971). *Perceiving the causes of success and failure.* Morristown, NJ: General Learning Press.

Weiner, B., Graham, S., & Chandler, C. (1982). Pity, anger, and guilt: An attributional analysis. *Personality and Social Psychology Bulletin, 8,* 226–232.

Weinstein, C. E., Goetz, E. T., & Alexander, P. A. (Eds.). (1988). *Learning and study strategies: Issues in assessment, instruction, and evaluation.* San Diego, CA: Academic Press.

Weinstein, C. E., Husman, J., & Dierking, D. R. (2001). Self-regulation interventions with a focus on learning strategies. In M. Boekaerts, P. R. Pintrich, & M. Zeidner (Eds.), *Handbook of self-regulation* (pp. 728–749). San Diego, CA: Academic Press.

Weinstein, C. E., & Mayer, R. E. (1986). The teaching of learning strategies. In M. C. Wittrock (Ed.), *Handbook of research on teaching* (3rd ed., pp. 315–327). New York: Macmillan.

Welch, W. W. (1979). Twenty years of science curriculum development: A look back. In D. C. Berliner (Ed.), *Review of research in education* (pp. 282–308). Washington, DC: American Educational Research Association.

Wellman, H. M., & Gelman, S. A. (1998). Knowledge acquisition in foundational domains. In D. Kuhn & R. S. Siegler (Eds.), *Handbook of child psychology* (5th ed.): Vol. 2. *Cognition, perception, and language* (pp. 523–573). New York: Wiley.

Wentzel, K. R. (1989). Adolescent classroom goals, standards for performance, and academic achievement: An interactionist perspective. *Journal of Educational Psychology, 81,* 131–142.

Wentzel, K. R. (1991a). Relations between social competence and academic achievement in early adolescence. *Child Development, 62,* 1066–1078.

Wentzel, K. R. (1991b). Social and academic goals at school: Achievement motivation in context. In M. L. Maehr & P. R. Pintrich (Eds.), *Advances in motivation and achievement* (Vol. 7, pp. 185–212). Greenwich, CT: JAI Press.

Wentzel, K. R. (1996). Social and academic motivation in middle school: Concurrent and longterm relations in academic effort. *Journal of Early Adolescence, 16,* 390–406.

Wentzel, K. R. (1999). Social-motivational processes and interpersonal relationship: Implications for understanding motivation at school. *Journal of Educational Psychology, 91,* 76–97.

Wentzel, K. R. (2000). What is it that I'm trying to achieve? Classroom goals from a content perspective. *Contemporary Educational Psychology, 25,* 105–115.

Wentzel, K. R., & Berndt, T. J. (1999). Social influences and school adjustment: Overview. *Educational Psychologist, 34,* 1–2.

Wertheimer, M. (1959). *Productive thinking.* New York: Harper & Row. (Original published 1945)

Wertheimer, R. (1990). The geometry proof tutor: An "intelligent" computer-based tutor in the classroom. *Mathematics Teacher, 83,* 308–317.

Wertsch, J. V. (1985). *Vygotsky and the social formation of mind.* Cambridge MA: Harvard University Press.

Westbrook, K. C., & Kerr, S. T. (1996). Funding educational technology: Patterns, plans, and models. In S. T. Kerr (Ed.), *Technology and the future of schooling: Ninety-fifth yearbook of the National Society for the Study of Education* (pp. 49–72). Chicago: National Society for the Study of Education.

White, C. S., & Alexander, P. A. (1986). Effects of training on four-year-olds' ability to solve geometric analogy problems. *Cognition and Instruction, 3,* 261–268.

White, C. S., & Coleman, M. (2000). *Early childhood education: Building a philosophy for teachers.* Columbus, OH: Merrill/Prentice Hall.

White, J. E. (1996, April 29). "Why we need to raise hell," *Time Magazine,* p. 46.

Whitehead, A. N. (1967). *The aims of education and other essays.* New York: Macmillan. (Original published in 1929)

Whitehurst, G. J. & Lonigan, C. (1998). Child development and emergent literacy. *Child Development, 69,* 848–872.

Wigfield, A. (1993). Why should I learn this? Adolescents' achievement values for different activities. In M. L. Maehr & P. R. Pintrich (Eds.), *Advances in motivation and achievement* (Vol. 8, pp. 99–138). Greenwich, CT: JAI Press.

Wigfield, A., & Eccles, J. S. (1989). Test anxiety in elementary and secondary school students. *Educational Psychologist, 24,* 159–183.

Wigfield, A., & Eccles, J. S. (1992). The development of achievement task values: A theoretical analysis. *Developmental Review, 12,* 265–310.

Wigfield, A., & Eccles, J. S. (2000). Expectancy-value theory of achievement motivation. *Contemporary Educational Psychology, 25,* 68–81.

Wigfield, A., Eccles, J., MacIver, D., Reuman, D., & Midgley, C. (1991). Transitions during early adolescence: Changes in children's domain-specific self-perceptions and general self-esteem across the transition to junior high school. *Developmental Psychology, 27,* 552–565.

Wigfield, A., Eccles, J. S., & Pintrich, P. R. (1996). Development between the ages of 11 and 25. In D. Berliner & R. Calfee (Eds.), *Handbook of educational psychology* (pp. 148–185). New York: Macmillan.

Wigfield, A., & Guthrie, J. T. (1997). Motivation for reading: Individual, home, textual, and classroom perspectives [Special issue]. *Educational Psychologist, 32*(2).

Wigfield, A., & Karpathian, M. (1991). Who am I and what can I do? Children's self-concepts and motivation in achievement situations. *Educational Psychologist, 26*(3&4), 233–261.

Wiggins, G. (1991). Standards, not standardization: Evoking quality student work. *Educational Leadership, 48*(5), 18–25.

Wiggins, G. (1998). *Educative assessment: Designing assessments to inform and improve student performance.* San Francisco: Jossey-Bass.

Williams, C., & Bybee, J. (1994). What do children feel guilty about? Developmental and gender differences. *Developmental Psychology, 30,* 617–623.

Willingham, W. W., & Cole, N. S. (1997). *Gender and fair assessment.* Mahwah, NJ: Lawrence Erlbaum.

Wineburg, S. S. (1991a). Historical problem solving: A study of the cognitive processes used in the evaluation of documentary and pictorial evidence. *Journal of Educational Psychology, 83,* 73–87.

Wineburg, S. S. (1991b). On the reading of historical texts: Notes on the breach between school and academy. *American Educational Research Journal, 28,* 495–519.

Wineburg, S. S. (1996). The psychology of learning and teaching history. In D. C. Berliner & R. C. Calfee (Eds.), *Handbook of educational psychology* (pp. 423–437). New York: Macmillan.

Winne, P. H. (1985). Cognitive processing in the classroom. In T. Husen & T. N. Postlethwaite (Eds.), *The international encyclopedia of education* (pp. 795–808). Oxford, England: Pergamon.

Winne, P. H. (1995). Inherent details in self-regulated learning. *Educational Psychologist, 30,* 173–187.

Winne, P. H., & Perry, N. E. (2001). Measuring self-regulated learning. In M. Boekaerts, P. R. Pintrich, & M. Zeidner (Eds.), *Handbook of self-regulation* (pp. 253–269). San Diego, CA: Academic Press.

Wittrock, M. C., & Baker, E. L. (1991). *Testing and cognition.* Englewood Cliffs, NJ: Prentice Hall.

Wlodkowski, R. (1985). *Enhancing adult motivation to learn.* San Francisco: Jossey-Bass.

Wolf, D., Bixby, J., Glenn, J., & Gardner, H. (1991). To use their minds well: New forms of student assessment. *Review of Research in Education, 17,* 31–74.

Wollman, W., & Lawson, A. (1977). Teaching the procedure for controlled experimentation: A Piagetian approach. *Science Education, 61,* 57–70.

Wollman, W., & Lawson, A. (1978). The influence of instruction on proportional reasoning in seventh graders. *Journal of Research in Science Teaching, 15,* 227–232.

Woods, B. S., & Murphy, P. K. (2002). Thickening the discussion: What can William James tell us about constructivism? *Educational Theory, 52,* 43–49.

Woodworth, R. S. (1918). *Dynamic psychology.* New York: Columbia University Press.

Woolfolk, A. E. (1998). *Educational psychology* (7th ed.). Boston: Allyn & Bacon.

Woolfolk, A. E. (2001). *Educational psychology* (8th ed.). Boston: Allyn & Bacon.

Wright, B. J., & Isenstein, V. R. (1977). *Psychological tests and minorities* (DHEW Publication No. ADM 78-482). Rockville, MD: National Institute of Mental Health.

Wulf, F. (1938). Tendencies in figural variation. In W. D. Ellis (Trans.), *A source of Gestalt psychology* (pp. 136–148). New York: Routledge & Kegan Paul. (Original published in 1922)

Wynn, K. (1992). Addition and subtraction by human infants. *Nature, 358,* 749–751.

Yerkes, R. M., & Dodson, J. D. (1908). The relation of strength of stimulus to rapidity of habit-formation. *Journal of Comparative Neurological Psychology, 18,* 459–482.

Yore, L. D. (1991). Secondary science teachers' attitudes toward and beliefs about science reading and science textbooks. *Journal of Research in Science Teaching, 28,* 55–72.

Young, M. F., & Barab, S. A. (1999). Perception of the raison d'être in anchored instruction: An ecological psychology perspective. *Journal of Educational Computing Research, 20*(2), 119–141.

Youniss, J., & Smollar, J. (1989). Adolescents' interpersonal relationships in social context. In T. J. Berndt & G. Ladd (Eds.), *Peer relationships in child development* (pp. 300–316). New York: Wiley.

Zhao, Y. (1998). Design for adoption: Development of an integrated Web-based education environment. *Journal of Research on Computing in Education, 30,* 307–328.

Zhao, Y., & Conway, P. (2001). What's in and what's out?: An analysis of state technology plans. *Teachers College Record. http://www.tcrecord.org/Content.asp?ContentID* Retrieved from=10717.

Zhao, Y., Mishra, P., & Girod, M. (2000). A clubhouse is a clubhouse is a clubhouse. *Computers in Human Behavior, 16,* 287–300.

Zimmerman, B. J. (1989). Models of self-regulated and academic achievement. In B. J. Zimmerman & D. H. Schunk (Eds.), *Self-regulated learning and academic achievement: Theory, research, and practice* (pp. 1–25). New York: Springer.

Zimmerman, B. J. (1990). Self-regulated learning and academic achievement: An overview. *Educational Psychologist, 21,* 3–18.

Zimmerman, B. J. (1995). Self-regulation involves more than metacognition: A social cognitive perspective. *Educational Psychologist, 30,* 217–221.

Zimmerman, B. J. (2001). Attaining self-regulation: A social-cognitive perspective. In M. Boekaerts, P. R. Pintrich, & M. Zeidner (Eds.), *Handbook of self-regulation* (pp. 13–39). San Diego, CA: Academic Press.

Zimmerman, B. J., & Martinez-Pons, M. (1992). Perceptions of efficacy and strategy use in the self-regulation of learning. In D. H. Schunk & J. L. Meece (Eds.), *Student perceptions in the classroom* (pp. 185–207). Hillsdale, NJ: Lawrence Erlbaum.

Zuckerman, D. (1999). Research watch: Girls just aren't having fun. *Youth Today, 8*(4), 10–12.

Name Index

Subject Index